# Introduction to Physical Education, Fitness, and Sport

# Introduction to Physical Education, Fitness, and Sport

## EIGHTH EDITION

## Daryl Siedentop
The Ohio State University

## Hans van der Mars
Arizona State University-Polytechnic Campus

McGraw Hill

*Connect*
*Learn*
*Succeed*™

The McGraw·Hill Companies

Connect
Learn
Succeed™

INTRODUCTION TO PHYSICAL EDUCATION, FITNESS & SPORT, EIGHTH EDITION

1 2 3 4 5 6 7 8 9 0 DOC/DOC 1 0 9 8 7 6 5 4 3 2 1

ISBN 978-0-07-809577-1
MHID 0-07-809577-8

Vice President & Editor-in-Chief: *Michael Ryan*
Vice President & Director of Specialized Publishing: *Janice M. Roerig-Blong*
Publisher: *David Patterson*
Senior Sponsoring Editor: *Debra B. Hash*
Marketing Coordinator: *Angela R. FitzPatrick*
Project Manager: *Erin Melloy*
Design Coordinator: *Margarite Reynolds*
Cover Designer: *Studio Montage, St. Louis, Missouri*
Cover Image: *From upper left clockwise: Digital Vision/Getty Images; Ingram Publishing; image 100/Masterfile*
Buyer: *Laura Fuller*
Media Project Manager: *Sridevi Palani*
Compositor: *MPS Limited, a Macmillan Company*
Typeface: *10/12 New Caledonia*
Printer: *RR Donnelley*

**Library of Congress Cataloging-in-Publication Data**

Siedentop, Daryl.
  Introduction to physical education, fitness, and sport / Daryl Siedentop,
Hans van der Mars.—8th ed.
    p. cm.
  Includes bibliographical references and index.
  ISBN 978-0-07-809577-1 (hardback)
  1. Physical education and training. 2. Physical fitness. 3. Sports. 4. Sports sciences.
I. Van der Mars, Hans, 1955- II. Title.
  GV341.S479 2011
  613.7'1—dc23                                           2011043860

www.mhhe.com

Again, to B.J.—the best thing that ever happened to me.

—D. Siedentop

To Joanne and Katelyn who keep me grounded

—H. van der Mars

# Brief Contents

# Contents

---

**PART FIVE**

**The Subdisciplines of Kinesiology That Support the Physical Education, Fitness, and Sport Professions     297**

# Preface

Concerns about the levels of overweight and obesity among the population has elevated the need for increased physical activity for children, youth, young adults, adults, and the elderly. Addressing these concerns is a primary responsibility for the professionals of physical education, fitness, and sport. Most students who use this text share an important kind of knowledge about physical education, fitness, and sport—you have experienced them! Experiencing physical activity as a participant is important, but it is just the beginning of eventually becoming a professional who provides high-quality physical activity programs.

The eighth edition of *Introduction to Physical Education, Fitness, and Sport* will help you better understand the issues that you must address as a professional and is intended to help you to make decisions about what kind of professional service most appeals to you. The text is meant to emphasize quality services provided by physical activity professionals: physical education teachers, fitness trainers, athletic trainers, coaches, and athletic administrators. The primary emphasis for each type of service is professionalism in developing and sustaining high-quality programs and by becoming active to ensure that programs become more widely available to those who need them.

We have made every effort to inform you of the programs in physical education, fitness, and sport that can achieve these goals, the educational path to service in those professions, and the significant problems that are current in the professional practice of these various areas. We want you to understand the problems, to recognize and confront the problems, and to respect divergent points of view.

The quality and availability of physical education, fitness, and sport has the capacity to affect the nature of our common cultural life and the health of the nation. If physical education, fitness, and sport are to become positive forces in the near future, it will be because a new generation of professionals will provide positive solutions to the many problems that exist in those fields.

The text is divided into five parts, starting with a thorough understanding of the health issues related to physical inactivity described in Part One. Parts Two, Three, and Four describe what is being done in physical education, fitness, and sport to provide better programs that not only focus on effective approaches to physical activity but also influence boys and girls, women and men to become and stay physically active because they have come to enjoy it for its own sake and to understand how important it is for their health and well-being. Part Five describes the foundational subdisciplines in Kinesiology that provide the up-to-date knowledge of how to provide high-quality physical activity programs that are specifically developed to service a particular group; e.g., young children, physical education, fitness programs that are age-specific, and sport programs geared to young children all the way up to senior citizens.

## FEATURES OF THE EIGHTH EDITION

The eighth edition includes updated information about and expanded coverage of the major developments in physical education, fitness, and sport. Special emphasis is given to issues, problems, and programmatic solutions that are of major importance in achieving national goals for healthy lifestyles and lifetime physical activity (PA). Here are some examples of the new material and updates discussed:

- The first three chapters are devoted to describing the importance of physical activity for healthy lifestyles.
  - The first chapter describes the current movement toward healthy lifestyles with particular focus on lifespan PA, the overall goals for the National Plan for PA, the new settings for PA, and the importance of the early years.
  - The second chapter describes the evolution of PA throughout history with special focus on why PA was important (e.g., war, work, etc.). The chapter describes the historical development of PA in physical education, fitness, and sport, including the important influences that led to more or less focus on the importance of PA.
  - The third chapter describes the infrastructure that is developing to support lifetime PA, including the specific goals for the 2010 National Plan for Physical Activity, the goals of the education sector of the national plan, national and state-level organizations and programs to develop and sustain PA and the crucial themes that define our present and future efforts to develop and sustain PA throughout the lifespan.
- Another change is to rearrange the three-chapter groupings with Physical Education first, then fitness, and finally sport. This was done because most students who use the book are in Physical Education programs; many students, however, are also interested in working in the fitness industries; and sport was placed third because many Physical Education teachers also coach sport programs in schools and in the community. We believe this revised structure puts the focus where it needs to be—on why PA is so important, what PA for health and well-being means, and the many different ways that children, youth, and adults can become and stay committed to having PA as a significant part of their daily lives.
- The fitness and sport chapters were mostly upgraded in terms of the current directions in fitness both in the kinds of fitness programs provided and the professional opportunities within the fitness professions. The sport chapters were primarily upgraded with more current information on sport at all levels.
- New information related to the incidence of obesity and overweight.
- New information on, and examples of, lifetime involvement in physical activity.
- New and revised discussions of trends and issues in physical education, fitness, and sport.
- New information on the role of school physical education within the recently unveiled National Plan for Physical Activity.
- Thoroughly revised physical education chapters adding new discussions of philosophical roots of Physical Education curricula.

- New information on an expanded mission of school physical education programs, and updated information regarding the position responsibilities of a school's Physical Activity Director.
- Latest national physical activity guidelines and recommendations, and national health objectives.
- New information on the status of physical education and what constitutes quality physical education.
- Inclusion of new exemplary physical education programs.
- Changes in physical education programs to meet public health goals.
- Updated information on the latest trends in federal and state policy initiatives to develop and sustain infrastructures to support healthy lifestyles and physical activity.
- New examples of programs at the national, state, and local levels to achieve those policy initiatives.
- New information on the public support for school physical education.
- New information differentiating physical education from physical activity behavior.
- Updated information on how technology can be infused in physical education.
- Updated information on National Board Certification for Physical Education professionals.
- Updated information on preparation for careers in a number of physical education, fitness, and sport professions.
- Updated information on the various barriers to delivering quality physical education.
- Changing views on what constitutes fitness and how it is related to healthy lifestyles.

As fields progress, the problems that arise change, sometimes subtly and sometimes quite markedly. The text deals with problems in the ways that reflect the latest information from the various fields. We often state our views but not to the exclusion of other views and always in a way that encourages young professionals to develop their own views on the basis of sound evidence and information.

Finally, the *Introduction to Physical Education, Fitness, and Sport* Online Learning Center (www.mhhe.com/siedentop8e) includes a wide range of tools for instructors. Instructors will be able to download chapter-specific PowerPoint presentations and an Instructor's Manual.

## ACKNOWLEDGMENTS
### Daryl Siedentop:

My professional life and work have been influenced by a number of bright and caring people who took the time to share their insights and experiences with me and who respected me enough to offer their honest and sincere criticisms. My brother, Larry Siedentop, D.Phil., CBE, a Fellow of Keble College, Oxford University, is a world-class scholar in political theory; his commitment to quality scholarship has influenced me greatly. Ken Weller, past president of Central College, was my first mentor. Russ DeVette and Gord Brewer helped me understand and care about sport. Larry Locke, Charles Mand, Don Hellison, and George Graham have been close professional colleagues from whom I have learned in many different ways. The many years I worked on a day-to-day basis with Mary O'Sullivan, Deborah Tannehill, and Sandy Stroot were the best and happiest of my professional life.

The 80 doctoral students whom I have advised to completion have been a constant source of inspiration. That most of them have gone on to important professional careers of their own is a major source of pride in my professional career. My collaborative work with physical education teachers in central Ohio has been a continuing source of information and inspiration—and a constant reality check for me. My thanks go particularly to Chris, Gary, Bobbie, Molly, Jane, Bob, and Carol.

### Hans van der Mars:

The opportunities and successes I have had over the years are all a consequence of the privilege I have had to be surrounded by outstanding mentors, colleagues, and friends within the profession. Most notable is my co-author, Daryl Siedentop, who has provided more professional support than anyone could ever hope for. Victor Mancini, professor at Ithaca College, who was my first mentor in the United States, also believed in me. There are too many colleagues to mention all of them. However, being surrounded by wonderful role models such as Deborah Tannehill, Thom McKenzie, Mary O'Sullivan, Chuck Corbin, Barbara Cusimano, Larry Locke, Judy Rink, Mike Metzler, Patt Dodds, and many others continues to be a source of energy, inspiration, and pride. My co-workers Pam and Connie continue to make coming to work something to which I look forward.

Back in 1983, I never envisioned getting into the business of working with doctoral students. However, it has become an integral and invigorating aspect of my day-to-day work. Finally, I have had the good fortune to work with many outstanding K–12 colleagues such as Lynn Barry, Meg Greiner, Dave Gable, Leslie Hicks, Dani Blackwell, Jon Lambros, and Rand Runco. They continue to show bottomless energy, dedication, and professionalism. They are the consummate physical educators! Thank you!

We both wish to thank the following individuals for their helpful reviews of the eighth edition: Carmine J Cortazzo, Indiana University of Pennsylvania; Craig Leverette, Collin College; Richard Shelton, Northeastern State University; and Patricia Zodda, Rockland Community College.

Thanks to all the folks at McGraw-Hill who have helped with the successful preparation of this new edition. Our development editor, Gary O'Brien, the best we have ever worked with, navigated this edition from the revision process to completion with thoughtful caring and prodigious skill.

# PART ONE

# The Current Context and Evolution of Physical Activity

Nations throughout the world have recognized the need to support healthy lifestyles through physical activity. The increased prevalence of overweight and obesity and the extraordinary costs associated with this epidemic are being addressed with a number of initiatives that focus on healthier diets and increased physical activity. Part 1 of this text is designed to help you understand the dimensions of this crisis and the fundamental strategies that are being employed to address these issues.

Part 1 describes the basic conditions that have influenced the degree of physical activity throughout history from primitive cultures to contemporary societies. You will be made aware of the various philosophies that supported efforts to improve physical activity and how our understanding of physical activity and health evolved over time. For persons of all ages to become and stay engaged with regular physical activity requires that an infrastructure be developed that provides opportunities, starting with those for young children and continuing throughout the lifespan with opportunities for senior citizens.

## CHAPTER 1

# The Dilemma of Our Times: Lifespan Physical Activity and the Obesity Health Crisis

*The NCPPA mission is to unite the strengths of public, private, and industry efforts into collaborative partnerships that inspire and empower all Americans to lead more physically active lifestyles. The reality is that there is an unprecedented synergy building around the issue of physical activity as it pertains to lifestyle behavior patterns and accessible environments that promote physically active lifestyles.*

National Coalition for Promoting Physical Activity (2002)

In 2001 David Satcher, surgeon general of the United States, reported that levels of obesity among Americans had reached epidemic proportions (U.S. Department of Health and Human Services, 2001). Over the next decade, the overweight/obesity numbers have increased. More than two-thirds of all adults and one-third of all children in the United States are now overweight, with nearly 30 percent of adults and 16 percent of children obese (Trust for America's Health, 2010). Approximately 80 percent of overweight adolescents will become overweight adults (Herman, Craig et al., 2009).

The most common method of estimating overweight and obesity is the use of body mass index (BMI) measurement (see Focus On Box 1.1 for BMI measurement details). While all developed nations have experienced increases in overweight and obesity across the last decade, none has had the amount of increase as in the United States. The Organization for Economic Co-Operation and Development (OECD) estimates that by 2020, the percentage of overweight in the United States could reach 72 percent (OECD, 2010).

Approximately 300,000 adult deaths in the United States each year are attributable to unhealthy dietary habits and physical inactivity or sedentary behavior (www.overweightteen.com). Overweight and obesity stem from the imbalance created when energy intake exceeds energy expenditure (Levi, Segal, & Juliano, 2006). This imbalance develops over time when caloric intake

---

**FOCUS ON** — Body Mass Index                                    1.1

Body mass index (BMI) is a way to *estimate* the degree of underweight or overweight among children, youth, and adults. For children and youth, BMI is estimated by having measures of height and weight related to age, which allows for BMI percentiles to be calculated for each age group. Children and youth that have BMIs above the 85th percentile are considered to be overweight. Children and youth with BMIs above the 95th percentile are considered to be obese.

For adults, the formula for computing BMI is weight in pounds divided by height in inches squared and multiplied by 703. For adults, an optimal range for BMI is 18.5–25. A BMI lower than 18.5 is considered to be underweight, a BMI over 25 is considered to be overweight, and a BMI over 30 is considered to be obese.

BMI is used because of the availability of height and weight measures and is an *estimate* of actual levels of body fat. Its accuracy, especially among older youth and adults, can be distorted by factors such as fitness level, muscle mass, and bone structure.

---

through eating and drinking exceeds energy expenditure through physical activity. Children and youth consume more energy-dense foods and are less physically active than they were 25 years ago. In food consumption, the primary factors are higher caloric intake, more dietary fat, higher caloric density of foods, and larger portions. These factors are related to less in-home cooking, greater reliance on take-out food, more fast-food meals, and overreliance on soft drinks, sport drinks, and fruit drinks that are high in calories and sugars.

Reductions in energy expenditure through physical activity are the result of multiple factors, one of which is typically referred to as the *built environment.* Factors such as commuting time, communities designed to foster driving rather than walking or cycling, and lack of public transport reduce physical activity. Children and youth spend increased amounts of time engaged in the electronic culture, playing video games, watching TV, and connecting to the Internet. Lack of indoor and outdoor neighborhood play spaces and programs limit physical activity and in urban communities it is often unsafe for children and youth to be active outdoors in after-school and weekend hours.

The prevalence of overweight and obesity is not distributed evenly across the U.S. population. Higher obesity rates have been linked to regional, economic, and social factors (Trust for America's Health, 2010). Among families living below the federal poverty level, 44.8 percent of children are overweight or obese, while 22.8 percent of children of families with incomes above 400 percent of the federal poverty level are overweight or obese. Except for Michigan, 10 of the highest adult obesity rates are in southern states while 9 of the 10 states with the highest childhood obesity rates are in the South. It should also be noted that 9 of the 10 states in the South also have the highest rates of poverty in the United States. Adult obesity rates among African Americans are at 30 percent or above in 43 states, compared with 19 states for Latinos and only 1 state for Whites, reflecting the disparities among minorities that exist in income, education, and access to health care. The CDC's 2009 Behavioral Risk Factor Surveillance report showed that Blacks were 51 percent more likely and Hispanics 21 percent more likely than Whites to be obese. Children and youths from families living in poverty are more likely to be overweight or obese, and children and youths with disabilities are at greater risk for becoming overweight than nondisabled peers (Meich et al., 2006).

Overweight and obesity are factors related to a large number of health problems, including coronary heart disease, Type 2 diabetes, cancer, high blood pressure, high total cholesterol, stroke, liver and gall bladder disease, sleep apnea, respiratory problems, osteoarthritis, and reproductive health

---

**FOCUS ON** — Health Impact of Overweight and Obesity                    1.2

Research has shown that overweight and obesity are related to a significant number of health problems.

*Type II Diabetes*

- More than 80% of people with type II diabetes are overweight.
- More than 20 million adult Americans have diabetes.
- Another 54 million are "prediabetic."
- Diabetes is the sixth leading cause of death in the United States and accounts for 11% of all U.S. health costs.

*Heart Disease and Stroke*

- People who are overweight are more likely to suffer from high blood pressure, high levels of blood fat, and high LDL cholesterol—all risk factors for heart disease and stroke.
- Heart disease is the leading cause of death in the United States, and stroke is the third leading cause.

- One in four Americans has some form of cardiovascular disease.

*Cancer*

- Persons who are overweight have increased risk for several types of cancer.
- Approximately 20% of cancer in women and 15% of cancer in men is attributable to obesity.
- Cancer is the second leading cause of death in the United States.

*Health Risks Earlier in Life*

- Younger adults who are obese face greater health risks earlier in life. Women who are obese at age 30 are more likely to die at a younger age and significantly more likely to develop cancer.
- Some research suggests obesity in middle age may create higher risk for developing dementia later in life.

SOURCE: Levi et al. (2006).

---

complications (see Focus On Box 1.2, Health Impact of Overweight and Obesity). It is also clear that overweight and obesity can influence psychological and social issues for children, youth, and adults.

## THE COSTS OF OVERWEIGHT AND OBESITY

Children and youths are typically included in their parents' health insurance. Overweight and obese children/youths have more medical problems and miss more school days than children/youth who are normal weight (Sepulveda, Tait et al., 2010), and this often results in parents missing workdays and making more insurance claims related to the health of their children.

Medical spending for obese persons is 42 percent higher than for normal-weight persons (Finkelstein et al., 2009). Obesity costs American businesses more than $13 billion annually in health insurance claims, paid sick leave, and disability and life insurance (Thompson, Edelsberg et al., 1998). Obesity costs a 1,000-employee company approximately $285,000 per year (Finkelstein et al., 2009). The obesity crisis has also led to interesting changes in several industries. For example, the automobile industry consumes as many as 1 billion additional gallons of gasoline yearly due to population overweight and this additional consumption of gasoline produces nearly 10 billion tons of carbon dioxide emissions (Jacobson & King, 2009). The airline industry is estimated to use 350 million more gallons of fuel yearly because of higher total weights of passengers at an extra cost of $275 million per year. This additional consumption releases an extra 3.8 million tons of carbon dioxide into the air.

If these problems continue, the future economic burdens attributable to the high current rates of overweight among adolescents are substantial. Lightwood et al. (2009) constructed models to estimate the costs of excess obesity and associated diabetes and coronary heart diseases among adults who will be ages 35 to 64 in 2020 to 2050. Current adolescent overweight is projected to result in 161 million life years that will be complicated by obesity, diabetes, or coronary heart disease and 1.5 million life years lost. The costs are estimated to be $208 billion from early death or morbidity and $46 billion from direct medical costs.

## FAST FOODS AND THE OVERWEIGHT/OBESITY EPIDEMIC

Lack of sufficient physical activity of the right kind and duration is not the only contributor to the overweight/obesity epidemic. Over the last quarter century the consumption of fast foods has increased dramatically. Children and youths in the United States eat five times the amount of fast food than their counterparts did in the 1980s. Fast food is less expensive than healthy food and is typically more accessible. In most places a healthy salad costs more than a hamburger and fries.

Fast food, as a percentage of discretionary food expenditure, doubled from 20 percent in the 1970s to 40 percent by 1995. Children and youths have also markedly increased their consumption of snacks, averaging three snacks per day in addition to their three regular meals (Piernas & Popkin, 2010). The consumption of sugared beverages has also increased markedly over the past 30 years (Isganaitis & Lustig, 2005), with a corresponding decrease in the consumption of milk. Soft drinks are now a leading source of carbohydrates for 2–18-year-olds, second only to bread.

Fast food is high in fat, saturated fat, energy density, fructose, and glycemic index, yet poor in fiber, vitamins A and C, and calcium. A fast-food meal typically contains 85 percent of recommended daily fat intake, 73 percent of saturated fat, but only 40 percent of the recommended amount of fiber and 30 percent of the recommended amount of calcium. Research has repeatedly linked the consumption of fast food to obesity and to insulin resistance (Bowman et al., 2004).

Growing concern about child/youth overweight and obesity and their associated predicted costs is evident throughout the health and medical communities, and it has become clear that interventions at the federal and state levels would be needed to stem the epidemic. In 2004, the U.S. Congress passed Section 204 of Public Law 108-25, the Child Nutrition and WIC Reauthorization Act of 2004, the initial federal effort to address the overweight/obesity crisis among American children and youths. Section 204 required that "each local educational agency participating in a program authorized by the Richard B. Russell National School Lunch Act or the Child Nutrition Act of 1966 shall establish a local school wellness policy by the school year 2006–2007."

The legislation defined the minimum requirements that local school wellness policies should address in order to continue to get federal financial support for school breakfasts and lunches. These requirements were defined in five requirements that local school wellness policies must address.

1. Includes goals for nutrition education, physical activity, and other school-based activities that are designed to promote student wellness in a manner that the local educational agency determines is appropriate.

2. Includes nutritional guidelines selected by the local education agency for all foods available on each school campus under the local educational agency during the school day with the objectives of promoting student health and reducing childhood obesity.

3. Provides an assurance that guidelines for reimbursable school meals shall not be less restrictive than regulations and guidance issues by the U.S. Department of Agriculture Secretary.

4. Establishes a plan for measuring implementation of the local wellness policy, including designation of one or more persons within the local educational agency or at each school, as appropriate, charged with operational responsibility for ensuring that the school meets the local wellness policy.

5. Involves parents, students, and representatives of the school food authority, the school board, school administrators, and the public in the development of local school wellness policy.

In 2004, only four states had legislation that set nutritional standards for school lunches, breakfasts, and snacks that were stricter than USDA requirements. By 2010, 20 states plus the District of Columbia had set nutritional standards for school lunches, breakfasts, and snacks that are stricter than USDA requirements. A similar improvement in 28 states and the District of Columbia has been made in what are called "competitive foods," that is, foods that are sold in school vending machines, school stores, or through school bake sales (Trust for America's Health, 2010). That still leaves 30 states who have yet to set standards for breakfast and lunches, as well as for competitive foods.

The legislation also established Wellness Councils, which should set goals for physical activity, but did not include a specific reference to physical education. Several states, however, used this opportunity to strengthen requirements for physical education (Siedentop, 2005). The Washington State legislature required that school wellness policies include the establishment of a comprehensive health and fitness curriculum with a minimum time commitment of 100 minutes per week from grades 1 to 8. The Texas legislature required 30 minutes daily or 135 minutes weekly in physical education in elementary and middle schools. South Carolina passed new legislation that would be phased in over several years, requiring 150 minutes per week in physical education (PE) and physical activity (PA) in grades K–5 and requiring high-school students to complete two credits in health and fitness. The North Carolina State Board of Education responded by supporting legislation that requires elementary schools to move toward 150 minutes per week with a certified PE teacher and middle schools to move toward 225 minutes per week in physical education, with districts required to report annually the number of minutes of PE and PA for each school within the district.

California responded with a broadly based plan (California Department of Health Services, 2006) that was enacted and funded by the state legislature. The legislation included very specific requirements for the kinds of foods and drinks made available in schools and required a minimum of 200 minutes for every 10 school days in grades 1 to 6 and a minimum of 400 minutes of PE for every 10 school days in grades 7 to 12. The legislation also included additions to the state budget that would provide $40 million to hire more credentialed physical education teachers and $500 million for the purchase of PE, art, and music supplies to improve the infrastructure of school programs. Many states, however, "suggested" improvements in physical education and school nutrition and even provided guidelines for the improvements but failed to provide funding or an accountability measure to ensure that progress was made. Without such funding, local school districts, already under a heavy burden for funding, were unlikely to implement the suggested improvements.

## NATIONAL GOALS FOR HEALTHY FOODS AND PHYSICAL ACTIVITY IN SCHOOLS

In 1991, in its landmark publication *Healthy People 2000*, the U.S. Public Health Service created a new strategy to deal with the broad issues related to public health. A series of goals were adopted and regular progress related to those goals was reported. In 2000 *Healthy People 2010* (HP 2010) was published with reports on the progress made for the 2000 goals and the establishment of revised goals for the next decade. The first goal of HP 2010 was to help individuals of all ages increase their life expectancy and improve their quality of life. The second goal was to eliminate health disparities among different segments of the population. These two goals focus on two main issues that will be addressed throughout this text: (1) physical education, fitness, and sports need to establish programs that contribute to healthier lifestyles through physical activity, and (2) certain segments of the population need special, coordinated attention for them to achieve the goal of a healthy lifestyle.

*Healthy People 2020* provided reports on progress for the 2010 goals and revised goals for 2020. Of particular interest to the issues of childhood/youth overweight and obesity were goals designed to:

- Increase the percentage of schools that offer nutritious foods and beverages outside of school meals.
- Increase the percentage of schools with a school breakfast program.
- Increase the proportion of the nation's public and private schools that require daily physical education for all students.
- Increase the proportion of adolescents who participate in daily school physical education in school.
- Increase the proportion of adolescents who meet the objectives for aerobic physical activity and for muscle-strengthening activity.

While the federal government has taken the overweight/obesity crisis seriously and has initiated several programs to reduce the prevalence of overweight/obesity throughout the population, it has yet to provide sufficient funding to initiate these programs among the states. The federal legislation for education that has been well funded in the last decade is the No Child Left Behind (NCLB) program that provides school districts with funds to increase the elementary-school performance in reading and mathematics. As school administrators made decisions to strengthen their reading and mathematics programs in elementary schools to meet the requirements of NCLB, an unintended consequence has been a 40-minutes per week time reduction in physical education and a 50-minute per week reduction for recess time (Center on Education Policy, 2008). This likely unintended consequence is particularly disappointing because it is abundantly clear that appropriate levels of physical activity, including

sufficient time in moderate to vigorous physical activity (MVPA), are positively related to increased on-task classroom behavior, cognitive development, and academic performance (Active Education, 2007). Physical and aerobic fitness decline as youth transition from elementary to middle to high school, and this appears to be especially true for females (Basch, 2010). Physical activity affects metabolism and all major body systems and exerts powerful positive influences on the brain and spinal cord, which affects emotional stability, physical health, and ability to learn.

## THE NATIONAL PLAN FOR PHYSICAL ACTIVITY

On May 3, 2010, America's first National Physical Activity Plan (NPAP) was released. The primary vision of the NPAP is that, "One day, all Americans will be physically active and they will live, work, and play in environments that facilitate regular physical activity" (www.physicalactivityplan.org). The NPAP aims to "create a national culture that supports physically active lifestyles. Its ultimate purpose is to improve health, prevent disease and disability, and enhance the quality of life."

The NPAP is organized into eight societal sectors:

- Business and Industry
- Education
- Health Care
- Mass Media
- Parks, Recreation, Fitness, and Sports
- Public Health
- Transportation, Land Use, and Community Design
- Volunteer and Nonprofit

The overarching strategies of the sectors of the National Plan Physical Activity are as follows:

- Launch a grassroots advocacy effort to mobilize support for strategies and tactics included in the NPAP.
- Mount a national physical activity education program to educate Americans about effective

behavioral strategies for increasing physical activity and integrate the program's design with other national health promotion and disease prevention education campaigns.

- Disseminate best practice physical activity models, programs, and policies to the widest extent possible to ensure Americans can access strategies that will enable them to meet federal physical activity guidelines.

- Create a national resource center to disseminate effective tools for promoting physical activity.

- Establish a center for physical activity policy development and research across all sectors of the NPAP.

The two sectors that will be highlighted in this text are the Education sector and the Parks, Recreation, Fitness, and Sports sector. This is not to suggest that the other sectors are less important. For example, the Transportation, Land Use, and Community Design sector has as its primary goal to make the "built environment" safer and more accessible and attractive for walking, running, and cycling. Parents cite five primary barriers to their children's participation in physical activity: transportation problems, lack of opportunities for physical activity in the immediate area, expense, parental lack of time, and concerns about neighborhood safety (*MMWR Weekly*, 2003). The specific strategies for the Education sector and the Parks, Recreation, Fitness, and Sports sector are described in Chapter 3.

## LIFESPAN PHYSICAL ACTIVITY: A REVOLUTION NOT LIMITED BY AGE OR GENDER

Someday, historians will describe the current era as a watershed period characterized by the emergence of the possibility and desirability of lifespan physical activity through physical education, fitness, and sport. While far too many Americans of all ages have yet to invest in and achieve that possibility, it is now clear that it is both possible and desirable. What has

to be done now is to create the opportunities to achieve it.

When we consider participation in physical education, fitness, and sports, what age and gender groups come to mind? If we observe our cultural traditions, our thoughts may go to children at play, youths involved in sports, and young adults participating in recreational activities, with involvement slowly diminishing as they grow older. Very young children are seldom included in this scenario, and we have traditionally thought more about the participation of boys than girls. In addition, although we may think of men as continuing their involvement in moderately active recreation as they age, we are less likely to think of them engaged in strenuous activities. Until quite recently, we would have been unlikely to include women engaged in lifespan physical activity and even more unlikely to think of them as engaged in strenuous physical activity. Our tradition has been to think of elderly persons as largely inactive except, perhaps, for a quiet walk the afternoon.

Historically, we think of physical education, fitness, and sports programs as limited primarily to older children, youths, and young adults. Furthermore, far too many of us have viewed appropriate participation for girls and women to be less rigorous than for males, and some have considered female participation to be out of bounds altogether. Thankfully, these stereotypes have been mostly dismantled. Our former ideas are being replaced with a vision of lifespan involvement in physical activity beginning at a very young age and continuing through the lifespan, not only for boys and men but also for girls and women. These changes in perception, and the changes in opportunities that accompany them, lie at the heart of the revolution we are now experiencing, a revolution that is not limited by age or gender.

This vision of lifespan involvement in physical activity does not mean that every person must be a committed athlete from childhood through old age. Indeed, from a public health perspective, regular moderate physical activity is more important than vigorous physical activity (Morrow & Gill, 1995). It also means that people are increasingly likely to view involvement in some regular physical activity—walking, joining a fitness club, recreational sport, dance, or cycling—as fundamental to their sense of a good life, regardless of age or gender. The lifespan involvement goal for physical activity is unlikely to be achieved unless children, youths, and adults truly enjoy their activities. We now understand that engagement in physical activity is more likely to occur when it is enjoyable, and enjoyment is much more likely when persons have a strong sense of self-efficacy for the particular activity. Self-efficacy (Bandura, 1994) is defined as people's beliefs about their capabilities to produce designated levels of performance in activities. Self-efficacy for physical activity develops through successful, enjoyable experiences.

The concept of play is also important to our understanding of how to develop and sustain physical activity from early childhood through adulthood. While we fully understand the strong impulse among children to want to "play," we are less likely to recognize the play of adults whether it be a game of golf, a long cycling trip with friends, a regular visit to a fitness center, the weekly softball games, or learning new dance forms. If we want children, youths, and adults to become and stay physically active we have to ensure that their activity experiences are enjoyable and that they grow in the mastery of their favorite activities, thus developing the self-efficacy for

those activities that will sustain their involvement throughout the lifespan.

## The Early Years

Physical movement is the basic language of early childhood, from birth to ages 6 or 7 (Boucher, 1988). Early childhood is a crucial period for promoting the development of motor skills and physical activity. Child development experts have long recognized the fundamental importance of providing children with opportunities for physical movement and motor play. Traditionally, the physical activity of young children has been informally arranged and monitored at home with no specific purpose other than to keep children involved in some activity with the responsibility for their activity exclusively monitored by parents.

Many families now have access to programs for young children that focus on physical activity and the development of motor skills. Most of these programs are in the private sector; that is, they are franchises that provide fee-for-service early childhood physical activity programs. Because they are fee-for-service operations, they tend to be more frequently found in suburbs and in more affluent neighborhoods in cities. The Focus On Box 1.3, Early Childhood

---

**FOCUS ON**    Early Childhood Physical Activity Program Websites          **1.3**

*Baby Power Forever-Kids* (www.babypower.com): Gymnastic and musical parent–child play programs for ages 6 months to 3 years

*Pee Wee Workout* (www.peeweeworkout.com): Health and fitness program for preschool and elementary-school children

*Gymboree* (www.gymboree.com): Children's play, fitness, music, and art programs

*Fitwize 4 kids* (www.Fitwize4kids.com): Innovative circuit-training program with specially designed resistance-training equipment

*Kinderdance* (www.kinderdance.com): Motor development, gymnastics, and fitness program for ages 2–8 years old

*The Little Gym* (www.thelittlegym.com): Movement skills, gymnastics, sports, and games for infants and toddlers

*Jumpbunch* (www.jumpbunch.com): Home-based physical-activity program to promote fun, fitness, and self-esteem

*Kid-Fit* (www.kid-fit.com) Preschool physical education program designed to install healthy lifestyle habits in children 2–5

Physical Activity Program Websites (with Internet addresses), shows several program providers that give you an idea of the kinds of available programs.

Some programs have been developed in the private sector and marketed to preschools. The Spark Early Childhood curriculum grew from the SPARK (Sport and Physical Activity for Kids) elementary-school curriculum. This early childhood program was developed specifically for preschool teachers. The program is organized with 12 activity units with daily lesson plans for each unit. Each lesson plan is scripted. Children who live in less affluent neighborhoods are most likely to have access to early childhood programs such as Head Start, a government-funded early childhood program that focus on early education, support for healthy foods, and physical activity. Children's playgrounds are increasingly being designed with apparatus that accommodate activities that are developmentally appropriate for young children and encourage children to explore new movement experiences.

Sport opportunities are now available to children at an earlier age than in the past. It is no longer unusual to see 5-year-olds enrolled in soccer, baseball, swimming, or gymnastics programs. As we will show in Chapters 10 to 12, there is growing concern in America about the downside of young children increasingly involved in competitive sports programs at a very young age. Most experts in child development agree that sport experiences for boys and girls up to the age 11 should focus on learning game rules, playing different positions, using modified equipment, rules, and playing fields, limiting uniforms, and encouraging boys and girls to participate together.

Sports programs for young children are sponsored by a variety of local organizations. Community recreation programs often offer a variety of sport experiences for children and do so with modest fees. Volunteer organizations, such as local Kiwanis or Lions clubs, often sponsor sports programs for young children. These organizations raise funds, create rules for participation, decide what sports to offer, and determine what levels of competition will exist for various age groups.

Preschool children also have opportunities to be physically active and to learn motor skills in private preschool programs and in government programs such as Head Start. Their education in motor-skill development, sports, and dance continues as they begin their formal education in schools from kindergarten through elementary grades. The time spent in elementary-school physical education differs markedly from state to state, depending on the policies that state government has adopted and the school funding formula within the state. Since most states rely on local property taxes as their major source of revenue for schools it is not unusual for suburban schools to have much stronger physical education programs than for city or rural schools.

## Youth: The Transition Years

Boys and girls who are in the upper-middle-school grades and into high school tend either to become more active or more sedentary than in elementary or early middle school. Time in physical education at middle- and high-school levels has been reduced dramatically over the past several decades. In many states, students who participate on school sports teams or in the marching band or ROTC programs are exempt from having to take physical education courses (NASPE, 2006). The major point to be made here is that during this age span, adolescent boys and girls move toward making physical activity a central part of their lifestyle or move toward a lifestyle that is increasingly devoid of physical activity.

In 2009–2010, for the twenty-first consecutive year, participation in high school sports teams increased. Nearly 4.5 million boys and 3.1 million girls competed in school teams (National Federation of State High School Associations, 2010). Programs differ markedly in the manner in which school sports participation is funded, depending primarily on the financial resources of the local district, the size of the schools, and the state regulations under which the school operates. Facilities and staffing for interscholastic sports have increased markedly, including weight-training facilities and the employment of full-time athletic trainers. As we will show in Chapters 10 to 12, there are a number of issues that have developed in interscholastic sports over the past several decades, including sport specialization, pay-to-play programs, and hiring coaches who are not teachers.

Some high-school students do not participate in the interscholastic sports program, but still have a very active involvement in physical activity and sport. Two examples are Andrea and William. Andrea owns her own horse and has trained and competed in equestrian sports. She boards her horse at a nearby stable and goes there nearly every day after school to train and care for her horse. She hopes someday to compete in an equestrian three-day event competition, so she trains regularly in dressage (precise replicating of figures and moves) and in jumping. William has taken karate lessons for 6 years. He has slowly advanced in local karate competitions and is beginning to make a name for himself. He trains at a small karate studio, which occupies a storefront in one of the area shopping malls. He has grown very strong and is able to make the very quick movements that define karate. His room at home is filled with trophies he has won in local competitions. Neither Andrea nor William has played on a school team.

While the increasing numbers of boys and girls competing in interscholastic sports programs has increased each year, there are also large numbers of girls and boys who try out for high-school sports teams but do not make the final cut that determines the team members for any given season. While some high schools support intramural sports programs, many do not, and there are far fewer community sports programs for teenagers than for students at elementary and middle-school ages.

## Young Adulthood

We define young adults as women and men who have finished high school and gone on either to further education or the workforce. They are in a time of separation from youth and are establishing patterns of work and play that will shape their future. What follows is a sample of the many ways that young adults participate in physical activity.

Over the past several decades, private and public colleges and universities have developed sport, recreation, and fitness facilities and programs for enrolled students, faculty, and staff. Indeed, the quality of those facilities and the programs they offer are now one of the strongest determining factors of where potential students choose to pursue their undergraduate degrees.

The Ohio State University (OSU), like most colleges and universities, has invested enormously in providing ample opportunities for students to stay physically active and to learn new activities. While there are no "requirements" demanding that students take physical activity classes, the OSU Sport, Fitness, and Health program offers more than 60 elective sport and fitness courses each quarter of the academic year, which attract more than 15,000 students each year. More than 20 different types of fitness classes are available to students (see Focus On Box 1.4, University Elective Fitness Classes).

Students also have the opportunity to join one or more of the 79 sport clubs sponsored by the Intramural and Recreational Sport Department. Each club has a faculty advisor. Some of the clubs, such as the equestrian club, women's rugby club, and water-ski club teams compete in regional and national championships. Other clubs, such as the alpine-ski club, the cycling club, and the scuba club take trips during quarter breaks.

The university also has built an Outdoor Adventure Center that includes a climbing center with two state-of-the-art climbing walls, offering students more than 50 routes for climbing. Classes and workshops are offered so that students can prepare for backcountry trips during weekends and semester breaks.

A wide range of intramural competitions is offered for men's, women's, and coed teams. The program also offers training for student officials and managers to ensure that intramural competitions run smoothly. The intramural program is managed

---

**FOCUS ON**   **University Elective Fitness Classes**   **1.4**

*Making Fitness Fun and Attractive for University Students*

- **20/Cycle/20:** 20 minutes of strength training, then 40 minutes of cycling, and then 20 minutes of core strength and flexibility work

- **Body Sculpt:** Focus on muscular strength and endurance with resistance tubing, free weights, and resistance balls

- **Boot Camp:** For students who want maximum exertion exercise focusing on running, jumping, squatting, and sprinting

- **Cardio Funk:** Mixed-level aerobics with funky dance steps

- **Cardio Kickbox:** Cardio-based class utilizing kickboxing choreography

- **Cardio Sculpt:** Equal balance of cardio and strength work

- **Express Abs:** A 25-minute express class of abdominal workouts

- **Get on the Ball:** A 1-hour class using resistance balls to add instability and greater challenge

- **H$_2$O Challenge:** Mixed-intensity water workouts with a cardio focus

- **Hatha Yoga:** Focus on mindful practice, breath work, tension release, and relaxation

- **Indoor Cycle:** 40–45 minutes of strength cycling followed by 15 minutes of strength and flexibility training

- **Mixed Aerobics:** A warm-up, then 40 minutes of mixed-impact aerobics

- **Personalized Training:** Individualized training aimed at developing your own pace and level of workout

- **Pilates:** Introduction to Pilates training, working toward improved posture, lung capacity, increased flexibility, and core strength

- **Power Yoga:** A 90-minute class teaching ujjayi breathing and bandha engagement for poses and floor work

- **Step Kickbox:** Step combos, kickboxing choreography and style, for strength and endurance training

- **Step/Sculpt:** 30-minute step combinations for cardiovascular work and 30 minutes of strength training

- **Sunrise S&S:** Early-morning strength and stretching using resistance tubing

- **Super Step:** 45 minutes of step combos for cardio work, finishing with 5 minutes of strength training and 5 minutes of flexibility work

- **Total Body:** Focus on muscular strength and endurance as well as cardio improvement

SOURCE: Ohio State University (2008).

---

by a professional staff of more than 35 full-time persons with the assistance of more than 400 student assistants, many of whom are fulfilling internship requirements for recreation, sport and exercise education, exercise science, and sport management academic programs.

Young adults who move into the workforce rather than pursue higher education degrees typically have a harder time finding the type and quality of physical activity programs that attract them to regular involvement. Some corporations and businesses offer support for employees who become and stay involved with fitness or recreation programs. Indeed,

many corporations have realized that the investment they make in developing facilities and programs for employees greatly reduces the costs of their employee health programs.

Most often, however, young adults entering the workforce have to find and join fitness centers, YMCA programs, or community recreation and sports programs in order to stay engaged with the kind of physical activity they most enjoy. The community programs are most often the responsibility of parks and recreations departments and typically require participation fees in the form of daily, monthly, or yearly memberships. Community programs often involve the development of a variety of recreational sites such as parks, softball fields, and walking/biking trails. Softball, for example, is still one of the most popular recreational sports in America, with nearly five million participants each year. The Parks and Recreation Department of Columbus, Ohio, organizes and administers 114 softball leagues competed on 126 city-owned softball fields, involving 878 local teams in organized league play and nearly 100 tournaments for 4,000 local and regional softball teams. Each year more than 13,000 games are played with an estimated 35,000 players. Leagues are typically formed for men's, women's, coed, and age-group players.

## The Older Adult

Prior to the 1960s, it was common to believe that older adults should not engage in moderate to vigorous physical activity, which is one reason why golf and bowling were the most popular activities. Fortunately, this particular myth has been blown apart in recent years. Older women and men now walk, jog, and cycle, not only because it is good for their health but also because it has become part of their chosen lifestyle.

Exercise across the lifespan is an essential component of health.

Older persons also compete. In the late 1960s, a group of American and Canadian men and women, who had competed in track and field through youth and young adulthood, were trying to find ways to continue participating in their preferred sport. They started by beginning to take part in age-group track and field in Europe, where an age-group track and field movement had already begun. The experiences were so successful that age-group clubs and competitions began to develop in North America.

In 1985 the first World Masters Games attracted 8,000 athletes to Toronto, Canada. During those games, a steering committee was elected to plan for an international governing body for master's track and field. Thus, the World Association of Veteran Athletes (later changed to World Masters Athletics) was formed and sponsored the second World Masters Athletics Championships in Sweden. In 2002, the fifth World Masters Games attracted more than 20,000 athletes to Melbourne, Australia. The organization now sponsors three regular events: outdoor track and field, cross-country, and indoor track and field.

Another important venue for older athletes is the U.S. Masters Swimming organization that oversees 500 affiliated masters swim clubs for adults aged 18 or older with a total membership of more than 42,000 age-group swimmers. It is now common for city recreation departments to organize age-group competitions for older adults, such as over-50 and over-60 basketball leagues. If you attend a local fitness center, whether a community recreation fitness center or a private fitness center, you are likely to see a wide range of age groups, including persons in the 50–80 age groups. The involvement of older persons is not just about concerns to remain healthy but also because of the pleasure they find in working out. Many seniors prefer low-impact activities such as walking, jogging, swimming, or water aerobics, activities that are designed to minimize the stressful impact of exercise on aging joints.

The National Senior Games Association is a nonprofit member of the U.S. Olympic Committee dedicated to motivating senior women and men to lead a healthy lifestyle by participating in the senior games movement (www.nsga.com). The 2011 Summer Games in Houston, Texas, attracted 15,000 women and men to compete in 17 different sports. Twenty-four states now hold state-level summer games competitions.

People in the developed world now have greater life expectancy than ever before. The number of adults in the 65–84 age group increased to 12 percent of the total population in 2010 and is expected to increase to 17 percent of the population by 2025. It is increasingly clear that regular physical activity is important in helping elderly people maintain the quality and length of their lives. A sedentary lifestyle, on the other hand, is estimated to account for 50 percent of the decline in strength, flexibility, and aerobic fitness.

## THE NEW SETTINGS FOR PHYSICAL ACTIVITY

The research that has shown the importance of physical activity in sustaining healthy lifestyles has led both the public sector and private sector to provide facilities and programs that attract and retain persons who increasingly want to make physical activity a key element in their lifestyles. Home fitness has also been on the rise for at least the last decade. It is increasingly common to find homeowners who have either designed a fitness room in a new home plan or converted a room in their home to include a treadmill or elliptical trainer, a stationary bicycle, and free weights as the most likely means of engaging in health physical activity without having to travel to a fitness center.

The number of sport clubs and fitness centers has also increased markedly over the past decade. The numbers of tennis and golf clubs have increased substantially, as have clubs that include indoor and outdoor swimming pools. Sport and fitness clubs often have attractive lounges and often have child-care services available. These clubs are fee-for-service oriented and are typically more expensive than community centers and YM or YWCA centers.

One of the most robust and successful developments in opportunities for physical activity has been the widespread development of worksite fitness programs. The Wellness Councils of America (www.welcoa.org) reported that 81 percent of businesses with 50 or more employees have some form of wellness promotion, with typical components of exercise, smoking cessation classes, back care programs, and stress management. While developing and sustaining these programs cost the businesses substantial amounts of money, the return is well worth the investment. Businesses that invest in worksite health-promotion programs realize a return of $3 to $6 for every dollar invested over a 2- to 5-year period (Engbers L. H., van Poppel, M. N., Chin A Paw, M. J., & van Mechelen, W. (2005). This is mostly attributable to a 26 percent reduction in health care benefits and a 20 percent reduction in workers' compensation claims. After reviewing 120 research studies, the National Company Group on Health reported that within five years of initial implementation, a typical result was a $3.48 reduction in care costs per dollar invested and a $5.82 reduction in costs per dollar invested owing to lower absenteeism. It is now clear that businesses and corporations that spend money to build and sustain worker-wellness programs create a more stable workforce and reduce health costs substantially. It should be noted that this movement has produced an increasing need for trained wellness and fitness professionals.

## The Emerging Characteristics of Lifespan Physical Activity

Physical activity across the lifespan is an emerging phenomenon. While we cannot predict how it will continue to evolve and mature, we can predict with some certainty what several of the emerging characteristics of the movement must achieve to be successful.

First, we must recognize the importance of an early start. Habits of participation in physical activity begin early in childhood. Motor-skill development and the enjoyment of physical activity must develop with very young children. It is clear that unfit children tend to become unfit adolescents and unfit adults. This should become a major goal of day care and preschool programs, as well as an important issue in the home.

We have made substantial success in reducing the gender stereotypes that have historically made it difficult for girls and women to become and stay engaged with physical activity. Hopefully, we are approaching the time when girls and women will have full opportunities for lifespan physical activity in ways similar to those that men have enjoyed for some time. Being fit is not gender specific! Physical education, fitness, and sport can no longer afford to organize or categorize activities or roles on the basis of gender rather than skill or interest. An important goal for all physical education, fitness, and sport professionals should be to eliminate gender bias from how children and youth are socialized into physical activity and from the opportunities available to them throughout their lifespan.

Because the median age of our population increases with each passing decade, we are experiencing a shift in emphasis from youth to adults. The median age reached to 35 in 2010 and is expected to be above 40 by 2020. While we cannot afford to ignore the crucial importance of appropriate starts for very young children, it is clear that physical activity programs and facilities that cater to older persons are also a necessity. This is yet another issue where increased health in old age that is partially due to commitment to regular physical activity will help enormously in containing national health costs.

Over the past several decades, we have witnessed the emergence of an enormous private-sector industry that provides physical activity opportunities to children, youths, and adults. With health and fitness becoming a major national agenda, the private sector quickly began to provide facilities and fee-for-service programs to meet the challenges of that agenda. The emergence of this new industry, while bringing attractive new opportunities for participation, has also revealed the increasingly strong relationship between wealth and opportunity in physical education, fitness, and sport. Physical education

programs in suburban school districts tend to be more robust with better facilities than urban school districts, particularly the parts of urban districts that serve the poorest segment of the population. Private-sector sport and fitness programs are abundant in the suburbs but much less available in the inner city and rural areas.

The effort to further develop the public and private-sector efforts to push forward the physical activity agenda has been greatly supported by the increasing amounts of quality information available from research focused on physical activity and physical activity programs. We have a much stronger scientific base of understanding about the appropriate kinds and amounts of physical activity that lead to healthy lifestyles and the kinds and amounts of physical activity that too often produce injuries. This scientific base has also shown clearly the enormous financial impact a healthy citizenry can have on federal, state, and local budgets. Colleges and universities have responded to new professional roles that are necessary to provide highly trained women and men to fill the many positions in the expanding wellness and fitness industry, including those that exist as stand-alone private programs and those that are embedded in schools, community facilities, and corporations.

Technology has transformed our lives in so many ways, including both *knowledge about* physical education, fitness, and sport and how *we do* physical education, fitness, and sport. The World Wide Web is an extraordinary source of information, as the number of websites cited in this text will attest. High-tech exercise equipment allows you to carefully control the amount and time of components in any piece of equipment. Nearly every sport has been influenced by the use of technology to improve equipment that allows for better performance—golf clubs, vaulting poles, and running shoes, to name just a few. The professional work of physical education teachers, sport coaches, and fitness professionals has been changed significantly by the availability and use of technology. We should expect that this trend toward technology improvements will continue to change how we play and exercise, and how we learn.

## THE MAJOR ISSUES WE FACE AND WHAT WE NEED TO DO TO CONFRONT THEM

The bad news is that America, like the rest of the world, is experiencing an epidemic of overweight and obesity. The good news is that we now know that physical activity throughout the lifespan is both possible and achievable—and at a modest cost, compared to the extraordinary health costs we will face if the epidemic continues or worsens. More bad news is that opportunities for access to healthier foods and access to quality programs of physical activity are not distributed evenly across our population. Race, place, and socio-economic status severely affect the opportunity to be active and healthy. If you are poor, black, or Hispanic, and live in an inner city, you have few places that cater to your activity needs and interest, the food you can afford to buy does not support a healthy diet, your local environment is unsafe for children and youths, and you have few support services.

Historically, educational and policy efforts to improve physical activity opportunities for persons of all ages have focused primarily on individuals. Although individual responsibility is important, there is increasing recognition that we must deal with the structural and environmental issues that are associated with poor health, obesity, and inactivity.

Reductions in physical activity are caused by a number of factors related to what is now commonly referred to as the *built environment*. Communities are designed to foster driving rather than walking or biking. Very few children or youths walk to school. They either get on a school bus or a parent drops them off at school. Children and youth spend more time with video games, watching TV, and using the computer. Parents cite five primary barriers to their children's participation in physical activity: transportation problems, lack of opportunities for physical activity in the immediate area, expense, parental lack of time, and concerns about neighborhood safety (*MMWR Weekly*, 2003). In Chapter 3 the concept of a *physical activity infrastructure* will be explained.

The infrastructure to support physical activity is weak throughout the nation and weakest in those places where it is most needed. It is unwise to think that the nation can confront and solve health problems that are due largely or partially to physical inactivity without developing a more supportive infrastructure.

This book is intended to provide you with knowledge of physical education, fitness, and sport and especially the kinds of career opportunities that are available within those three sectors. While there are many specialized professional roles in each of the three sectors, we must also understand how we can be better boundary-crossers, because it is clear that our overweight and obesity health crisis will not be solved by persons working solely within their own sector. Physical education, fitness, and sport professionals must work together to develop and sustain programs that address the health and physical activity issues that confront the nation. Each must be aware of the opportunities in the other sectors and be advocates for healthy lifestyles through better nutrition and appropriate levels of physical activity. They all must also be aware of and supportive of recreation and health programs within their communities and work to develop relationships with those programs. Developing comprehensive programs that bring the several professions together to work collaboratively to solve problems at the local and state levels are necessary if we are to achieve the healthy lifestyle goals that result in a healthier citizenry.

## SUMMARY

1. The United States has an epidemic of overweight and obesity that has enormous implications for health costs, human productivity, and longevity.

2. Overweight and obesity is caused by poor nutrition and lack of physical activity.

3. Overweight and obesity are related to a number of serious medical problems and represent an increasing share of the nation's medical costs.

4. National goals for physical activity and healthy foods in schools are designed to reduce the

percentage of children and youths that are over-weight or obese.

5. The National Plan for Physical Activity provides strategies for improving physical activity across eight sectors with the Education Sector and the Parks, Recreation, Fitness and Sport sectors especially relevant to this text.

6. We now know that physical activity across the lifespan is not only possible but is necessary to combat the overweight/obesity epidemic.

7. There is no reason why physical activity should be limited by age or gender.

8. Physical activity in the early years is especially important and represents a new field for physical activity professionals.

9. Sports programs for young children are increasingly available but are not without problems.

10. Teenage boys and girls find physical activity opportunities through school sport, community programs, and specialized activities in the private sector.

11. Young adults increasingly find activity programs available at their worksite, through private-sector fitness programs, and in community recreation/fitness programs.

12. The emerging characteristics of lifespan involvement in physical activity include the recognition of an early start, the breakdown of gender and age stereotypes, the shift from emphasis on youths to adults, the shift from the public to the private sector, an increasingly strong scientific base, the creation of new professional roles, the increased availability of information, and the use of technology.

## DISCUSSION QUESTIONS

1. What physical activity opportunities have you had growing up? What were the characteristics of those opportunities that you liked best?

2. How would you describe the degree to which physical activity was an important issue in your K–12 physical education classes?

3. What were the physical activity habits of your parents? Did they change as you grew older?

4. What were the school lunches like in your middle- and high-school days? What types of foods and drinks were available in school stores and vending machines?

5. Were physical activity opportunities for girls the same as for boys in your school PA programs and outside of school PA programs?

6. Are you convinced that the potential national costs associated with overweight and obesity are sufficiently serious that more attention to PA opportunities at all ages are worth the financial support to develop and sustain them?

7. To what extent were you aware of the issues described in Chapter 1?

## CHAPTER 2

# The Evolution of Physical Activity Philosophies and Programs

*Running, then, is my discipline, my specialty, my secret, and these golden days of perfection on the road are the wholeness that results.... In those moments my philosophy becomes, "I run, therefore I am." And from that point I view all creation.*

Dr. George Sheehan, physician, age-group runner and foremost philosopher of the running movement

Physical activity has been important throughout history, but for very different reasons. The purpose of this chapter is to explain how physical activity has evolved for physical education, fitness, and sport.

## THE GYMNASTIC PHILOSOPHIES AND SYSTEMS: THE BEGINNING OF PHYSICAL EDUCATION IN AMERICA

As Europe developed in the 1800s, the emerging countries were highly nationalistic, leading to a major emphasis on developing a strong military, with substantial efforts devoted to developing and sustaining physical strength and endurance. A significant aspect of the education of children and youths (especially boys) were the gymnastics systems. In Germany, the major proponent of their developing system was Friedrich Ludwig Jahn. The Jahn system included jumping, running, throwing, climbing, vaulting, and simple games of running and dodging. The apparatus needed included horizontal bars, vertical ropes, ladders, vaulting horses, parallel bars, running tracks, and jumping pits. The training took place in Turnvereins, which were clubs for exercise and sport. The Jahn system was brought to the United States by three of Jahn's students—Charles Beck, Charles Follen, and Francis Leiber—all of whom became prominent figures in early American physical education. The first American application was at the Round Hill School in Northhampton, Massachusetts. By 1890, with massive immigration of Germans to the United States, there were 300 Turnvereins with more than 40,000 members, primarily in the Midwest of the United States.

The goal of the Swedish gymnastics system, developed by Per Henrik Ling, was to develop the

An early twentieth-century physical-education class for college men.

Swedish vigor and national pride and renew the spirit of the Norse history of the nation through participation in a scientific system of gymnastics. Activities included swinging, climbing, vaulting, resistance exercises, and passive therapeutic manipulation. The apparatus included swinging ladders, rings, vaulting bars, and stall bars. The Ling system was brought to the United States by Hartwig Nissen, a Swedish diplomat who later developed a manufacturing company producing gymnastics equipment, eventually doing business worldwide. Boston philanthropist Mary Hemenway gave funds to build the Hemenway Gymnasium at Harvard College and invited Baron Nils Posse, a graduate of Ling's Royal Institute of Gymnastics, to introduce the Ling system to America. Posse founded the Posse Normal School of Gymnastics that provided a two-year teacher-training program in the Posse system. The system was incorporated into the Boston school system in 1890 with Edward Hartwell, an important leader in American physical education, as first director of physical training for the school system.

American leaders were quick to recognize the need for the development of American systems of what then was still commonly referred to as *gymnastics*. Catherine Beecher, director of the Hartford Seminary for Girls and founder of the Western Female Institute, developed a system of "appropriate female activities," which included archery, swimming, horseback riding, calisthenics done to music, and calisthenics using light weights and wands. Beecher created a system of 26 lessons in physiology and 2 in calisthenics with light exercise, all designed to correspond with the assumption prevalent at that time – that programs for men were too vigorous and required too much strength for women.

Dioclesian Lewis developed the first American system based on the "grace" of the Beecher system and the scientific nature of the Ling system. Activities included exercise routines vigorous enough to raise the heart rate but not as vigorous as prescribed in the German system. The routines were accompanied by music and also included social games and

An early twentieth-century rhythmic gymnastics class for college women.

Even in competition, activity costumes for women reflected nineteenth-century views of women.

dance routines. Progressive schools were the first to adopt the Lewis system. In 1860 Lewis founded the Boston Normal Institute for Physical Education and in 1861 published the *Gymnastics Monthly and Journal of Physical Culture*, which can be considered the first American physical education journal (Weston, 1962).

In 1861 Edward Hitchcock was appointed director of Hygiene and Physical Culture at Amherst College. His program focused on physical development with measurement of bodily development from the baseline start of the program to progress over time. Activities included marching, unison calisthenics, exercises, and some sports and games. Apparatus included horizontal bars, rack bars, ladders, weights, rings, Indian clubs, ropes, and vaulting horses. Hitchcock is widely recognized as creating the first truly American physical education program with an emphasis on a scientific base and consistent measurement of progress, a model that would be emulated in the twentieth century.

In 1879 Dudley Sargent was appointed to the faculty of physical training and named director of the Hemenway Gymnasium at Harvard University. Sargent moved the physical activity effort forward by amalgamating existing systems into a scientifically defensible, comprehensive program of physical education. Activities included calisthenics, German and Swedish exercises, and specialized machine exercises. Apparatus included bars, rings, vaulting horses, ropes, ladders, parallel bars, and specialized exercise machines. Sargent is considered to be one of the most influential leaders in the history of American physical education.

## THE EMERGENCE OF PHYSICAL ACTIVITY IN AMERICAN PHYSICAL EDUCATION

In 1885 William G. Anderson was deeply concerned about his own lack of training and preparation to be a physical educator (Lee & Bennett, 1985a). Twenty-five-year-old Anderson had graduated from medical school and was employed at the Adelphi Academy as an instructor of physical training, even though his only experience in the field had been as a young participant in the German Turnverein club in Quincy, Illinois. In 1885 there were no institutions that prepared people to be what was then called a gymnastics teacher.

Anderson wanted to create a forum within which people interested in physical training, physical education, and the various gymnastic systems could discuss with and learn from one another. He invited a group of interested people to meet at Adelphi Academy on November 27, 1885. Sixty interested persons gathered for that historic meeting. The participants decided to form an organization, the Association for the Advancement of Physical Education. Dr. Edward Hitchcock, who had founded the first college department of physical education at Amherst College 24 years earlier, was elected to be the first president. Dr. Dudley Sargent was elected as vice president. This meeting marked the birth of the physical education profession.

Delphine Hanna, who had graduated from the Brockport Normal School in New York in 1874, went on to earn a B.A. from Cornell University and an M.D. from the University of Michigan. After teaching in public schools she became concerned about the health and physical status of children, leading her to complete a course at the Sargent School of Physical Training. She then accepted a position at Oberlin College in Ohio, where she developed the nation's first teacher preparation program in physical education. Among her students at Oberlin were Thomas Wood, Luther Halsey Gulick, and Fred Leonard, all of whom went on to important leadership positions in physical education.

In 1893 an International Congress on Education was held in Chicago in conjunction with the Chicago World's Fair (Lee & Bennett, 1985a). Because the National Education Association had, two years earlier, recognized physical education as a curricular field, a physical education section of the congress was organized, enabling physical educators from North America to meet to discuss issues related to what had become a fully recognized school subject. From that time on, the physical education profession began to view education rather than medicine as its parent field.

At that symbolically meaningful conference, a 28-year-old physical educator from Stanford University, Thomas Wood, presented a view for the *new physical education*:

> Physical education must have as an aim as broad as education itself and as noble and inspiring as human life. The great thought in physical education is not the education of the physical nature, but the relationship of physical training to complete education, and then the effort to make the physical contribute its full share to the life of the individual, in environment, training, and culture (Lee & Bennett, 1985a).

That conference marked the end of the era in which gymnastics dominated the physical education curriculum, and also marked the beginning of the modern era of physical education. Wood's best students at Stanford were Clark Hetherington, who was to become a major force in the new American physical education, and Luther Halsey Gulick, who became director of the YMCA training school at Springfield, Massachusetts. In 1927 Wood and Rosiland Cassidy, another great pioneer of American physical education, published a landmark textbook entitled *The New Physical Education*.

These four—Wood, Hetherington, Gulick, and Cassidy—became the primary exponents of the new, more comprehensive approach to physical education in America. In the years between the turn of the century and the end of World War II, the character of American physical education took shape, creating an umbrella profession embracing a number of growing movements, including dance, YMCA/YWCA, playgrounds, recreation, outdoor education, sport, fitness, health education, and intramurals. It was during this period, as the umbrella profession formed, that much of the early organizational work in those separate yet related fields took place (see Focus On Box 2.1) leading eventually to what today we know as the American Alliance for Health, Physical Education, Recreation and Dance.

Physical education was to have its ups and downs in the twentieth century. Two world wars and the Great Depression exerted substantial pressures on the field of physical education. Many of those who

**FOCUS ON**   CHRONOLOGY AT A GLANCE—The Emergence of a Profession   2.1

| | | |
|---|---|---|
| Western frontier expansion | 1825 | Charles Beck hired as first teacher of physical education in United States |
| | 1827 | First competitive football game played |
| | 1827 | First public swimming pool opened, in Boston |
| | 1834 | First rules of baseball published |
| Era of muscular Christianity | 1837 | Western Female Institute founded by Catherine Beecher |
| | 1848 | First Turnverein formed, in Cincinnati |
| | 1851 | First YMCA formed, in Boston |
| | 1861 | Hitchcock appointed director of hygiene and physical culture at Amherst |
| American Civil War | 1861 | Boston Normal Institute for Physical Education founded by Dio Lewis |
| | 1866 | First state legislation requiring physical education passed, in California |
| | 1874 | Tennis introduced in United States |
| Expansion of Industrial Revolution | 1879 | Sargent appointed assistant professor of physical training at Harvard |
| | 1883 | YMCA Training School started at Springfield, Massachusetts |
| | 1883 | Swedish gymnastics introduced to United States by Nissen |
| | 1885 | Adelphi Conference held; Association for Advancement of Physical Education formed |
| Free, universal education | 1885 | Professional physical education program at Oberlin started by Delphine Hanna |
| | 1887 | Softball invented in Chicago |
| | 1889 | Boston Physical Training Conference held |
| | 1890 | Hartwell named supervisor of physical education for Boston |
| Urbanization | 1891 | Physical education recognized as curricular field by National Education Association |
| | 1893 | Department of physical education and hygiene formed in NEA |
| Substantial immigration | 1895 | First public golf course built |
| | 1896 | Olympic Games revived in Athens, Greece |
| | 1896 | Volleyball invented in Holyoke, Massachusetts |
| | 1897 | Society of College Gymnasium Directors formed |
| Expansion of public schooling | 1901 | First master's-degree program in physical education started at Teachers College |

*(continued)*

**FOCUS ON**   **CHRONOLOGY AT A GLANCE—The Emergence of a Profession (*continued*)**   **2.1**

| | 1903 | Gulick appointed director of physical education for New York schools |
| | 1903 | Delphine Hanna appointed first female full professor of physical education |
| | 1905 | National College Athletic Association formed |
| | 1906 | Playground Association of America formed |
| | 1908 | First high-school swimming pool built, in Detroit |
| | 1909 | National Association of Physical Education for College Women initiated |
| | 1910 | Four objectives of physical education identified by Hetherington |
| | 1911 | National Park Service formed |
| | 1913 | Intramural programs established by Michigan State and Ohio State |
| World War I | 1916 | First state supervisor of physical education named, in New York |
| Roaring Twenties | 1924 | Doctoral programs in physical education first offered by Teachers College and New York University |
| | 1926 | First dance major formed at University of Wisconsin |
| | 1927 | *The New Physical Education* published by Wood and Cassidy |
| Stock market crash | 1930 | *Research Quarterly* first published by Education Association |
| | 1930 | National Recreation Association formed |

were either drafted or volunteered for military service in the two wars were rejected because of inadequate levels of fitness, leading to concerns about the effectiveness of school physical education programs. School physical education programs were forced to emphasize fitness and to move away from the more broadly based programs that had developed.

In December 1954, just when physical education programs had begun to expand beyond a primary focus on fitness an article entitled "Minimum Muscular Fitness Tests in School Children" was published in the Journal of Health, Physical Education and Recreation (Kraus & Hirschland, 1954). The article reported the results of a study comparing the performance of American and European children on tests of minimum muscular fitness. The shocking results showed that 60 percent of the American children failed the test, compared to only 9 percent of the European children. This led President Eisenhower to pass an executive order to form the President's Council on Youth Fitness. In 1958 the nation celebrated its first Presidential Fitness Week. In 1960 President John Kennedy published an article in *Sports Illustrated* entitled "The Soft American," leading to another flurry of activities and pressures to force school physical education programs to focus more on fitness.

In the 1970s and 1980s physical education gradually began to move away from the traditional activities of fitness programs (e.g., push-ups, pull-ups, squat thrust, mile run, etc.) and toward a *lifestyle physical activity* model, a broader approach that focused on students gaining skills in activities and enjoying the activities so much that they would pursue them outside of the physical education classes.

## THE EMERGENCE OF FITNESS

What we now call *physical fitness* has been important since the beginning of human life on our planet, but the reasons that fitness has been important differs dramatically as human societies developed. What follows is designed to explain the various precipitating factors that have influenced fitness throughout history.

The lifestyle of primitive women and men (pre-10,000 B.C.) was based on the continual tasks of hunting and gathering food in order to survive (Dalleck & Kravitz, 2002). This required extensive physical activity, both in the hunting and gathering tasks and in their daily lives. Successful hunting episodes were typically followed by celebration trips to neighboring tribes to visit family and friends. These trips were often of 6 to 20 miles, contributing to their physical activity. The celebrations also included dancing and cultural games. This pattern of subsistence demanded a high level of physical activity and fitness.

The Neolithic agricultural revolution (10,000–8,000 B.C.) ended the primitive lifestyles described above and marks the beginning of what we know as civilized life. This period was characterized by agricultural developments, especially animal and plant domestication and the invention of the plow. The long hunting trips of their ancestors were now unnecessary. This era marks the beginning of a more sedentary lifestyle, with a marked decrease in physical activity.

The ancient civilizations (2500–250 B.C.) of China and India took markedly different approaches to physical activity. The Chinese recognized that lack of physical activity was related to many health problems, including problems that we now recognize as heart disease and diabetes. The Cong Fu gymnastics system was developed to maintain a healthy body. The practice of Cong Fu included various stances and movements, characterized by different foot positions and movements derived from the fighting styles of various animals. The early Chinese also took part in archery, badminton, dancing, fencing, and wrestling. China, therefore, was likely the first civilization to understand the importance of physical activity to health and longevity.

The earliest cultures that included physical activity as a primary aspect of the development and quality of their culture were the early Greek and Roman Empires. Greek culture had a major focus on physical development and sport. What the Greeks called "gymnastics" included a wide range of physical fitness activities and sports; however, the gymnastics education of young Greeks was limited to boys. Physical activity education took place in temples and in the gymnasium, which was typically an outdoor facility for physical training and sport, and in the Palaestra, a center for boxing and wrestling. Physical prowess and beautiful physical form for males were much admired in early Greek culture. The focus on physical activity was also related to the importance in Greece to have a strong military force.

Greek boys were encouraged to become athletes and to compete in the large number of "games" that made up the Greek sporting calendar. The series of what were called the Panhellenic Games consisted of the Olympic Games, honoring the god Zeus; the Pythian Games, held at Delphi, the sacred site of the god Apollo; the Isthmian Games held in Corinth to honor Poseidon, the sea god; and the Nemean Games held to honor Zeus (Mechikoff & Estes, 2006). Contrary to belief, Greek athletes were not amateurs, with substantial monetary prizes at each of the games.

The Roman Empire was built through wars whereby emerging civilizations were conquered and put under the control of Rome, leading to what was called the Roman Empire. Military training was a key element of the education of boys, with primary goals of developing the obedience, discipline and physical prowess to be a soldier. Skills such as running, jumping, swimming, wrestling, horsemanship, boxing, fencing, and archery were all taught both as appropriately healthy exercise and for military preparation.

Like the Greeks, the Romans dedicated their many sporting events to the gods that were then worshiped by the Romans. Running events, wrestling, ball games, and equestrian competitions were common. Some sporting events, such as chariot races and gladiatorial contests, were often held in large facilities, with women and men attending and a great deal of betting taking place. Women were not as marginalized in the Roman Empire as they were in the Greek city-states. Participation in swimming, dancing, and light exercise was common among the women of the privileged classes.

During the Dark (A.D. 476–1000) and Middle Ages (900–1400) physical activity became crucial to survival. As a result, the art, music, and sport cultures that had developed in Greece and Rome were substantially reduced, while physical activity, comprised typically of life-sustaining gathering foods, was revived and became fundamental to survival.

The Renaissance (1400–1600) saw a widespread revival in the development of a culture that valued learning, art, and physical activity. Most of the leaders of the Renaissance supported physical activity and created the notion that higher levels of physical activity were important to intellectual learning.

What is known as the National Period in Europe (1700–1850) was an extraordinarily robust period for the development of physical activity and fitness. As described in this chapter, this period marked the development of "gymnastic systems" in Germany, Denmark, Sweden, Great Britain, and Germany. Of particular interest was the system developed in Sweden by Per Henrik Ling, who had a strong medical background. The Ling system consisted of three areas, each of which had somewhat different purposes: educational gymnastics, military gymnastics, and medical gymnastics (Matthews, 1969). Ling was the first to recognize that physical activity programs should be based on the individual needs of persons.

As cited earlier, the influence of European gymnastic systems greatly influenced the beginning of American fitness and physical education programs. Physical activity and fitness continued to develop in America and was influenced by a number of persons and events. Early in the twentieth century, President Theodore Roosevelt, who became devoted to physical fitness due to his childhood asthma, was a major proponent for physical activity, fitness, and physical education. In 1917 the United States entered World War I and found a major problem in finding military recruits with adequate levels of fitness. One-third of those drafted for military duty were unfit for combat and many more were found to be highly unfit for military training (Wuest & Bucher, 1995).

The Great Depression that followed the stock market crash of 1929 severely affected physical activity programs which had developed in school physical education and in clubs and recreation facilities. The physical activity and fitness movement was to move forward slowly but was again set back when nearly half of all draftees for World War II were rejected or given noncombat positions owing to low fitness levels (Rice, Hutchinson, & Lee, 1958).

In 1939 Germany began a major war initiative in Europe. In 1941 the Japanese attacked Pearl Harbor with a massive air attack. More than 15 million Americans served in the armed forces during World War II, including 216,000 women in newly created branches of the Army, Navy, and Coast Guard. All of the women and men inducted into the armed forces had to undergo tests of physical fitness before they could begin basic training. When a substantially large number failed the tests, the reaction was widespread criticism of American physical education in schools, leading to a new emphasis on research on fitness and fitness testing and the development of new physical activity programs for school physical education (Weston, 1962).

In the early 1950s, it was reported that nearly 60 percent of American children had failed the Minimum Muscular Fitness Tests in Children (Kraus & Hirschland, 1954), while only 9 percent of children from European countries had failed the test. This and other issues led to a White House conference in 1956. The outcome of the conference was the creation of the President's Council on Youth Fitness and the President's Citizens Advisory Committee on the Fitness of American Youth (Neiman, 1990). In the 1960s an issue of *Sports Illustrated* included an article by President J. F. Kennedy entitled "The Soft American," which led to a national effort to develop youth fitness programs.

The events during World War II also led to the beginning of what we now know as the academic field of kinesiology. With the widespread focus on physical fitness, it became necessary to investigate the outcomes of various approaches to fitness, thus leading to the development of the research fields of exercise science and motor learning.

In 1968 Dr. Kenneth Cooper published a small paperback book entitled *Aerobics* that would yield enormous influence over the physical activity and fitness movements for a generation. The book introduced the term *aerobics,* which would not only become commonplace in our language system but would also reveal the extraordinary importance of cardiovascular fitness. By 1973 the book had gone through its twentieth printing. Cooper is credited with being one of the key figures in revolutionizing the field of medicine away from disease treatment to disease prevention through aerobic exercise. He went on to establish the Cooper Aerobics Institute in Texas, an organization that has continued to be vitally important to the movement for physical activity for healthy lifestyles.

Over the past quarter century, fitness for healthy lifestyles has become the overwhelmingly favored approach, leading to a substantial growth of fitness centers that include apparatus for developing strength in all the muscle groups of the body, swimming pools, and indoor jogging spaces. As you will see in Chapters 7 to 9, this period in our history also resulted in a considerably larger demand for women and men to staff the many positions in fitness centers, which, in turn, has led to more opportunities for students in colleges and universities to obtain a major or minor in health-related fitness programs.

## THE EMERGENCE OF ORGANIZED SPORT IN AMERICA

If the late nineteenth century is interesting for its development of gymnastic-oriented physical education programs, it is even more remarkable as a period of development in sport. During the post–Civil War period, sport grew up: It changed from loosely organized games with many local variations to organized networks with widely recognized rules and national bodies to oversee the further development of the sport. The standardization of sport in America grew because the nation was becoming an increasingly industrialized, urbanized culture with increasing wealth, transportation and communication primarily due to the size of the emerging middle class.

When a sport becomes institutionalized, rules governing its conduct become standardized, bodies are formed to enforce those rules, standards for competition are set, championships are formed, records are kept, and traditions and rituals are developed and shared by people who participate in or watch the sport. Sports that can be described as having "come of age" during this period are the following (Lucas & Smith, 1978):

| | |
|---|---|
| Archery | Pedestrianism |
| Baseball | Polo |
| Bicycling | Roller-skating |
| Billiards | Rowing |
| Boxing | Rugby |
| Canoeing | Sailing |
| Cricket | Shooting |
| Croquet | Skiing |
| Cross-country running | Soccer |
| Curling | Swimming |
| Fencing | Tennis |
| Football | Track and field |
| Gymnastics | Trapshooting |
| Handball | Volleyball |
| Ice hockey | Water Polo |
| Lacrosse | Wrestling |

Many of these developing sports had their roots in other countries. Some, like golf and tennis, were played in the United States as much as they were played in Europe. Other American sports, such as baseball and football, had origins in European games but had been substantially modified to become unique sports rather than variations of sports played elsewhere. Some of these European-influenced American variations eventually produced further variations of their own. For example, softball was invented in Chicago in 1887 as a variation of baseball. Basketball, on the other hand, invented in 1891 at the YMCA school in Holyoke, Massachusetts, by James Naismith, was strictly American and was created to meet the need for an indoor sport of skill and activity in the winter months. Likewise, volleyball, invented by William Morgan at the YMCA in Holyoke, Massachusetts, is a particularly American sport that has since spread throughout the world.

Women were involved in this American sport expansion from the beginning. In the same winter than Naismith invented basketball, Senda Berenson adapted the game for her students at Smith College, a nearby institution. By 1899, a committee had formalized a set of women's basketball rules with the result that the game was played widely by girls and women (Spears & Swanson, 1978).

The era between World War I and the beginning of the Great Depression in the 1930s was a particularly important time for the expansion of sport in America. The giant American industrial economy had moved into high gear. A large middle class was emerging. Radios and automobiles were within the financial means of more persons, leading to an important period of growth for sport at all levels. This was the era of Bobby Jones in golf, Babe Ruth and Lou Gehrig in baseball, Jack Dempsey in boxing, Man O'War in horse racing, Johnny Weissmuller in swimming, Bill Tilden and Wills Moody in tennis, and Charlie Paddock and Mildred "Babe" Zaharias in track and field. It was an era of heroes and heroines, of huge crowds (there were 120,000 spectators at a high school championship in Chicago), and of unparalleled media interest.

Smith College women's basketball in 1904. Senda Berenson tosses up the ball.

## SPORT ON THE COLLEGE CAMPUS

Perhaps the most unique feature of the development of sport in America is the phenomenal way in which sport grew on the college and university campuses. In 1850 there was very little sport participation of any kind on American college/university campuses, and nowhere did intercollegiate sport exist. Yet, by the turn of the century, sport had assumed a critical social function on most campuses and intercollegiate competition had begun to move toward the central position it was to occupy in the twentieth century sports scene (Lucas & Smith, 1978).

What is perhaps most remarkable about the rapid development of sport on college/university campuses is that it occurred largely through the effort of students and, at the outset at least, despite the often serious opposition of the administration and faculty. Still, as schedules grew more ambitious,

| FOCUS ON | Chronology of Sports' Early Growth Period | 2.2 |
|---|---|---|

| | |
|---|---|
| 1852 | First collegiate competition—a crew race between Harvard and Yale |
| 1859 | First intercollegiate baseball game—Amherst versus Williams |
| 1869 | First intercollegiate football game—Rutgers versus Harvard |
| 1873 | First track and field competition—part of Saratoga regatta |
| 1875 | Intercollegiate Association of Amateur Athletes of America formed |
| 1883 | Intercollegiate Lawn Tennis Association formed |
| 1890 | First intercollegiate cross-country meet—Cornell versus Penn |
| 1890 | First women's tennis club at University of California |
| 1891 | Basketball invented at Springfield College |
| 1892 | University of California forms women's basketball team |
| 1895 | First intercollegiate hockey competition at Johns Hopkins |
| 1895 | Intercollegiate Conference of Faculty Representatives formed (later became the Big Ten Conference) |
| 1896 | First intercollegiate swim meet (Columbia, Penn, Yale) |

Intercollegiate football was a big spectator sport in the 1920s.

travel became more costly, training tables became popular, and equipment became indispensable, it was clear that financial support was necessary. Although student-organized athletic associations could handle those problems at the beginning, the problems soon became complex. Faculty and administrative intervention was not only necessary but became the only way to solidify intercollegiate sports programs and ensure their future success.

The emergence of faculty and administrative control marked the beginning of what was to become a robust national intercollegiate system. Major abuses in the early years threatened the survival possibilities of the intercollegiate sport movement. The major abuses had to do with eligibility (there were no rules about it) and with how athletes were treated by their universities. The extremes to which early intercollegiate sports stars were treated is revealed in the following quotation.

One outstanding example was the captain of Yale's football team, James Hogan, who was twenty-seven years old at the turn of the century when he began his intercollegiate career. He occupied a suite of rooms at Yale's most luxurious dormitory and was given his means at the University Club. His tuition was paid and he was given a $100 a year scholarship. He and two others were additionally given the privilege of selling game programs from which they received the entire profit. Furthermore, Hogan was an appointed agent for the American Tobacco Company and received a commission on every package of cigarettes

An early twentieth-century gymnastics class at a school for Black girls.

sold in New Haven. If that wasn't enough, Hogan was given a ten-day vacation trip to Cuba during the school term after the football season was successfully completed. (Lucas & Smith, 1978, pp. 212–13)

Athletes often competed for different colleges or universities in the same season. Many were paid and many were "for hire," often being enrolled as "special" students for a short time while they competed. The beginning of faculty/administration control was a critically important step in helping intercollegiate athletics became accepted as an appropriate and useful aspect of university life and as a contributor to the overall goals of a university education.

The first faculty athletic committee was formed at Harvard in 1882, a pattern soon adopted by most colleges and universities. The next important step was the formation of an association of universities, which we now know as *athletic conferences*. In 1895 the Intercollegiate Conference of Faculty Representatives

was formed, which immediately established eligibility requirements for entering students, for continued participation, and for transfer students. It also placed limitations on athletic aid and how coaches were hired and retained. That conference, later to be known as the Big Ten, became the model through which other institutions throughout the country joined together to exert institutional control over intercollegiate athletics, and in so doing, ensured a continued role for sport in university life.

Intercollegiate sport for women was under better control from its beginning, with many campuses creating women's athletic associations. In 1917 Blanche Trilling of the University of Wisconsin organized a meeting through which the Athletic Conference of American College Women was formed (Spears & Swanson, 1978).

## SPORT DURING THE DEPRESSION, WORLD WAR II, AND BEYOND

The Great Depression of the 1930s to 1940s saw dramatic downturns in all of these developments in sport. Spectator sport faired poorly, leading to a major shift to participatory sport. Youth sport, family sport, and informal kinds of participation increased substantially. Softball exemplified this shift from spectator to participant. Invented in Chicago in 1877, softball required less space and less equipment than baseball. In the 1930s softball became America's most popular recreational sport. By 1940, at the end of the Depression, more than 300,000 organized softball clubs and the Amateur Softball Association had more than 3 million affiliated players (Gerber, et. al., 1974).

World War II took its toll on both professional and amateur sport, but not quite as seriously as during World War I. Sport in high schools, colleges, and universities continued, albeit at a somewhat reduced level. Professional sport also suffered but not to the extent that competitions in the major sports were severely affected.

The growth in sport in the immediate postwar era was merely a prelude to the startling expansion

A women's tennis class, 1932.

that was to follow. In 1954 the Supreme Court upheld the decision in *Brown v. Board of Education* that eliminated the separate but equal ethic that had created segregated schools in America, leading to a prolonged era in which civil rights were expanded to all Americans. In 1972 Title IX of the Education Amendments passed the U.S. Congress, creating the framework within which girls and women could finally achieve access to sport opportunities. In 1975, Congress passed Public Law 94-142, a far-reaching piece of legislation designed to ensure the rights of Americans with disabilities, which eventually led to creation of the Special Olympics and other programs in which persons with disabilities could participate in sport programs.

In 1962 Rachel Carson's book *The Silent Spring* was published, warning Americans of the environmental dangers of pesticides and chemicals and setting off a major environmental movement that provided the framework for engaging in sport outdoors, especially in wilderness areas. Sports such as cross-country skiing and backpacking grew enormously popular during this time. The "aerobic era" that started primarily as a fitness breakthrough also created distance running as a new participant sport.

Local, regional, and national races, from 5 kilometers to 26.2-mile marathons, became popular. In 2010 45,000 runners competed in the New York Marathon in men's, women's, wheelchair, and hand cycle divisions.

The other major dynamic to have developed during this period was the increasing expansion of youth sport opportunities. Youth sport programs are offered in many different sports, with youth soccer being the largest program for girls and boys. Children started to train earlier in their lives, and for many children the training has become more specialized for one sport.

School sport and intercollegiate sport also grew enormously during this period, with a clear trend toward specialization in one sport. School sport has become increasingly expensive and many school districts now rely on a "pay to play" approach. In these cases, the parents pay a fee directly to the school district, while in others the fee is paid to a booster club, which in turn uses the funds to support the school sports program. It should also be noted that this growth in school sport programs has led to a substantial increase in the need for athletic trainers in schools. Many colleges and universities now offer degrees in athletic training.

## PHILOSOPHICAL INFLUENCES IN AMERICAN PHYSICAL EDUCATION, FITNESS, AND SPORT

The legacy of the European gymnastic systems described earlier derived from a strong sense of patriotism for the emerging nations. These systems were created to unify the nation's citizens and to develop a strong sense of nationalism. Friedrich Jahn devoted his life to developing German patriotism. The motto he adopted for his gymnastic society (The Turners) was *"Frisch, froh, stark, ist die Turnerei,"* which means "Gymnasts are vigorous, happy, strong, and free" (Gerber, et. al., 1974). Although nationalism was never the primary philosophical goal of emerging American gymnastic systems, a strong sense of nationalism nonetheless accompanied the effort to respond to the large number of persons who failed their fitness tests during World Wars I and II.

The most compelling influence on early American life was Puritanism—a set of beliefs derived from the stricter forms of religion that grew out of the European Reformation. This was a stern view of human life that left little room for physical activity that was unrelated to work and took a harsh view of anything that was playful. By the mid-1890s, however, the eastern half of America was well developed and the strong hand of the Puritan philosophy was gradually losing its grip on the social life of our young nation. It is within this context that religion and sport reached an understanding through the philosophy that came to be known as *muscular Christianity,* the label given to the philosophy that physical fitness and sporting prowess are important avenues through which mental, moral, and religious purposes are developed.

A major influence on this development came from the American philosopher Ralph Waldo Emerson, whose writings and teaching included a central role for fitness and sport. Emerson reckoned that moral and physical courage were partly dependent on body fitness. "For performance of good mark," he said, "it (the body) needs extraordinary health." In his *The Conduct of Life,* Emerson noted that "the

first wealth is health." He admired the great men of the past and urged young people to read their exploits. Yet sometimes youth does not take readily to books, he noted. *"Well, the boy is right, and you are not fit to direct his bringing up, if your theory leaves out gymnastic training, archery, cricket, gun and fishing rod, horse and boat, all are* educators, liberalizers" (Lucas & Smith, 1978, p. 88).

## THE EMERGENCE OF PHYSICAL ACTIVITY FOR GIRLS AND WOMEN

No examination of the philosophies that influenced the development of physical education, fitness, and sport would be complete without an understanding of the evolution of masculinity-femininity ideals. While the muscular Christianity movement provided strong philosophical support for physical education, fitness, and sport, it did so much more for boys and men than for girls and women.

The nineteenth-century views of masculinity and femininity were highly stereotyped, drawing particularly from the Victorian period in England, when girls and women were raised to occupy narrow and circumscribed roles. In America, girls of that period were socialized to the "feminine virtues" of piety, purity, submissiveness, and domesticity (Spears & Swanson, 1978). Although mild forms of exercise were thought to be useful for females, vigorous exercise and competitive sports were considered to be inappropriate, both because girls and women were then thought to be genetically unfit for vigorous exercise (such activity would harm them) and because vigorous and competitive activities were thought to be unladylike. In one of his popular novels, the famous American writer Henry James had one of his characters express the then prevailing belief that Americans were suffering from "the most damnable feminism . . . the whole generation is womanized . . . the masculine character is passing out of the world" (Lucas & Smith, 1978, p. 288).

Gradually, however, this prejudice against female participation in sport and fitness activities began to slowly erode. Physical activity programs for girls began to develop, albeit with activities that were less strenuous than those for boys. Sport programs for girls and women began to develop, but the early programs were focused on activities that were less strenuous than those for boys and men and sporting activities were watched closely so as to not promote "unladylike behavior." While progress against these prohibiting points of view slowly began to develop so that girls and women had access to more fitness and sport activities, it was not until 1972, when Title IX of the Education Amendments passed in the U.S. Congress, creating the framework within which girls and women might finally have equal access to physical education, fitness, and sport, leading fairly quickly to an explosion in women's sport, from youth sport all the way to elite levels.

## RECENT PHILOSOPHICAL INFLUENCES FOR PHYSICAL ACTIVITY

Three other philosophical movements had an impact on physical education, fitness, and sport in the post-1950 era. The *environmental movement* provided the framework for engaging in physical activity outdoors, especially in wilderness areas, with activities such as cycling, cross-country skiing, and backpacking seeing substantial growth. The environmental movement also led to the growth of adventure education in school physical education programs.

The *civil rights* movement provided the framework for the further collapse of racial barriers in sport, fitness, and physical education. African American children and youth typically were placed in segregated schools that had substantially fewer possibilities for physical activity, through physical education or interscholastic sport. Between 1955 and 1965 forms of protest and and/or civil disobedience, such as the Montgomery, Alabama, bus boycott, the "sit-ins" across the southern states, and the march from Selma to Montgomery (1965) attracted national

attention. These events led to both federal and state legislation that dismantled segregation in schools and opened access to community facilities. Most important of this legislation was the Federal Civil Rights Act of 1964 that banned discrimination in employment practices and public accommodations.

After passage of the Civil Rights Act schools and their sport teams became integrated and Black athletes became highly recruited in large universities. The integration of professional sports, that began when Jackie Robinson joined the Brooklyn Dodgers major league baseball team, spread rapidly. Community recreation facilities were integrated and, gradually, neighborhoods also began to become integrated.

The era we are now in has been greatly influenced by what we might call the *fitness and wellness movement*. The overweight/obesity crisis, described in Chapter 1, has broadened our understanding of the importance of healthy lifestyles, not only for personal reasons but also for the reduction of enormous health costs to the nation. Our concept of the relationship of physical fitness to healthy lifestyles has evolved considerably. The aerobics era put into place an entirely new approach to healthy lifestyles, now ranging from daily fitness walks, to jogging, to competitive running in age groups, and to an enormous increase in cycling. Bicycle travel is now one of America's strongest growth markets in recreational vacations, leading to substantial interest in the development of a national bicycle route system, building on more than 40,000 miles that now exist in North America (www.adventurecycling.org).

We also have a better understanding of the differences between fitness for healthy lifestyles and fitness for specific performance in sports. As the fitness/wellness movement gained strength over the past 10 years, we have seen a substantial increase in facilities for fitness and wellness. The fitness/wellness industry now includes about 22,000 companies and nonprofit organizations that operate about 30,000 fitness and recreation centers (www.firstresearch.com) and have combined annual revenues of more than $23 billion. As you will see in Chapters 8 and 9, this has led to a substantial increase in jobs in the fitness industry and to the emergence of university and private programs that train women and men for positions within the fitness/wellness industry.

Another major influence on the direction of physical education, sport, and fitness has been the development of the academic discipline of kinesiology. Exercise physiology was the first research discipline to develop, having already produced a history of successful research and having productive relationships with other scientific disciplines. The period of the 1960s–1980s saw the further development of a series of specialized research fields that joined together under the kinesiology umbrella, biomechanics, motor control, motor learning, sport psychology, sport sociology, sport history, sport philosophy, and sport pedagogy. Eventually, each of the subdisciplines would develop their own research journals, thus increasing substantially our knowledge of various aspects of physical education, fitness, and sport.

## SUMMARY

1. Early primitive cultures promoted physical activity because their capacity to survive required daily activity to hunt and gather foods.

2. Early Greek culture promoted physical activity for males because sporting-type activities and preparation for war were vital to their culture.

3. Early Roman culture promoted physical activity, primarily for males, to sustain a military force to defeat and occupy other cultures and also for sport.

4. The European gymnastic systems were developed for purposes of nationalism, training for military purposes, and for health.

5. Early American physical activity systems were initially developed by using variants of the European systems but gradually changed to accommodate outcomes that were focused on physical fitness and sport.

6. The Puritanism influence from early America led Americans to believe that physical activity was useful only for work and that play was not appropriate. This thinking gradually gave way to what became known as Muscular Christianity.

7. Toward the end of the nineteenth century and the beginning of the twentieth century, American physical education programs, initially influenced by European gymnastic systems, grew and began to promote an American physical activity curriculum that included dance, sport, recreation, and fitness.

8. Physical activity for girls and women evolved slowly during the late nineteenth and early twentieth centuries and continued to expand slowly until the passage of Title IX of the Education Act resulted in a boom period of growth for girls and women in physical education, fitness, and sport.

9. The Civil Rights Act of 1964 finally allowed for equal participation for African Americans in physical education, fitness, and sport through integrated schools and access to public and private facilities.

10. In twentieth-century America, fitness movements developed after WWI and WWII recruits were deemed unfit for service and after short-lived polio epidemics.

11. The current physical activity and wellness movement related to the overweight/obesity epidemic has led to a massive expansion of the physical activity and fitness industries and created many new career opportunities for women and men interested in physical activity.

12. The discipline of kinesiology developed to provide significant research for physical education, fitness, and sport.

## DISCUSSION QUESTIONS

1. What were the key ways in which physical education changed throughout history?

2. What were the primary influences for the development of physical education in America?

3. In what ways did physical education in America change from its earliest forms to its current forms?

4. What are the precipitating cultural issues that seem to influence the degree of attention to fitness?

5. At what point did fitness evolve from its relationship to work and survival to becoming part of the developmental process?

6. At what point did fitness for girls and women begin to develop and what different forms did it take?

7. What were your reactions to the early development of sport on college and university campuses?

8. How did Americans modify sports developed in Europe, and which sports were created in America?

9. How and when did concerns about physical activity begin to develop physical activity as a new cultural dimension that combines physical education, fitness, and sport?

10. How does the new emphasis on physical activity differ from the major historic emphases in physical education, fitness, and sport?

## CHAPTER 3

# Developing an Infrastructure to Support Physical Activity and Healthy Lifestyles

*Our nation's young people are, in large measure, inactive, unfit, and increasingly overweight. In the long run, this physical inactivity threatens to reverse the decades-long progress we have made in reducing death from cardiovascular diseases and to devastate our national health care budget. Full implementation of the strategies recommended in this report will require the commitment of resources, hard work, and creative thinking from many partners in federal, state, and local governments; nongovernmental organizations; and the private sector. Only through extensive collaboration and coordination can the resources be maximized, strategies integrated, and messages reinforced.*

A Report to the President, 2000

A physical activity infrastructure includes facilities, spaces, and programs enabling children, youths, and adults to become and stay physically active. The "enabling" provision requires that the infrastructure be attractive, accessible, and safe. In a study of discretionary use of time among youths, the Carnegie Council on Adolescent Development (1992) suggested that "in a youth-centered America, every community would have a network of affordable, accessible, safe, and challenging opportunities that appeal to the diverse interests of young adolescents" (p. 77). Currently, however, the environments in which young people grow from childhood through adolescence tend to make it easy to be sedentary and difficult to be active.

The physical aspects of the activity infrastructure focus on the accessibility of bicycle paths, hiking trails, exercise facilities, playing fields (e.g., softball, soccer, etc.), gymnasiums, swimming pools, and the like. The programmatic aspects of the activity infrastructure include various public, community, and private-sector organizations, staffed by well-prepared physical education, fitness, and sport personnel, who cooperate to develop and sustain

Exercise facilities are found in many private and public venues.

attractive physical activity programs, that enable children, youths, and adults to become and stay physically active.

To achieve this, we must have policies, programs, and leadership at federal, state, and local levels. The 2010 National Plan for Physical Activity outlines the primary strategies that need to be developed in order to achieve the vision that "one day, all Americans will be physically active and they will live, work, and play in environments that facilitate regular physical activity" (www.physicalactivityplan.org).

Because children and youths spend a substantial part of their time in schools, it is clear that the Education sector of the National Plan for Physical Activity is vitally important (see Focus On Box 3.1, Education Sector Strategies). The importance of the Education sector is even more compelling owing to the fact that over the past several decades, schools in America have come under increasing pressures to improve the academic performance of students with the result that time spent in recess, classroom activity breaks, and physical education has been reduced.

## FOCUS ON    Education Sector Strategies    3.1

**Strategy 1**    Provide access to and opportunities for high-quality, comprehensive physical activity programs, anchored by physical education, in pre-kindergarten through grade 12 educational settings. Ensure that the programs are physically active, inclusive, safe, and developmentally and culturally appropriate.

**Strategy 2**    Develop and implement state and school-district policies requiring school accountability for the quality and quantity of physical education and physical activity programs.

**Strategy 3**    Develop partnerships with other sectors for the purpose of linking youth with physical activity opportunities in schools and communities.

**Strategy 4**    Ensure that early childhood settings for children 0 to 5 years promote and facilitate physical activity.

**Strategy 5**    Provide access to and opportunities for physical activity before and after school.

**Strategy 6**    Encourage post-secondary institutions to provide access to physical activity opportunities, including physical activity courses, robust club and intramural programs, and adequate physical activity and recreational facilities.

**Strategy 7**    Encourage post-secondary institutions to incorporate population-focused physical activity promotion training in a range of disciplinary degree and other certificate programs.

## FOCUS ON — Parks, Recreation, Fitness, and Sports Sector Strategies     3.2

**Strategy 1**   Promote programs and facilities where people work, learn, live, play, and worship to provide easy access to safe and affordable physical activity opportunities.

**Strategy 2**   Enhance existing parks, recreation, fitness, and sports infrastructure to build capacity to disseminate policy and environmental interventions that promote physical activity.

**Strategy 3**   Use existing professional, amateur, and college athletics and sports infrastructures and programs to enhance physical activity opportunities in communities.

**Strategy 4**   Increase funding and resources for parks, recreation, fitness, and sports programs and facilities in high need areas.

**Strategy 5**   Improve physical activity monitoring and surveillance capacity to gauge program effectiveness in parks, recreation, fitness, and sports settings based on geographic population representation and physical activity levels, not merely numbers served.

**Strategy 6**   Increase social marketing efforts to maximize use of recreation programs and facilities and promote co-benefits with environmental and other related approaches.

---

The Parks, Recreation, Fitness, and Sports sector is also crucially important to the overall achievement of the National Plan for Physical Activity. While in recent years the time available for leisure has increased, that time has, unfortunately, been used primarily in sedentary activities. This sector aims to create changes that provide access, education, and resources that encourage people of all ages to incorporate fun and meaningful physical activity into their daily lives (see Focus On Box 3.2, Parks, Recreation, Fitness, and Sports Sector Strategies).

To create and sustain a successful infrastructure for physical activity requires cooperation among a large number of organizations whose goals are to improve physical activity and health among the population. At a 1995 meeting of the American Heart Association representatives of more than 30 health organizations agreed to create a physical activity coalition. Thus, the National Coalition for Promoting Physical Activity (NCPPA) was formed (www.ncppa.org). An initial task of the NCPPA was to develop strategic objectives to guide its work. The initial strategic objectives were (1) to champion public policies that reduce barriers to physical activity, (2)

to increase the adoption of activity-friendly community models, (3) to promote incentives that result in greater adherence to recommended physical activity behaviors through community, schools, and worksite environments, and (4) to influence policy and environmental changes for populations with low rates of physical activity.

The NCPPA now has 15 leadership level organizations (see Focus On Box 3.3, NCPPA Member Organizations), seven national strategic partner organizations (see Focus On Box 3.4, NCPPA Lead Organizations), and a Federal Advisory Panel consisting of the Centers for Disease Control and Prevention, the President's Council on Physical Fitness and Sports, and the National Institutes of Health.

In 2001 the federal Physical Education for Progress (PEP) act was passed, providing funds to initiate, expand, and improve K–12 physical education programs. Between 2001 and 2009 PEP funding provided $333,294,637 to 1,155 agencies in all US states, the District of Columbia, and Puerto Rico. In 2010, the PEP program was consolidated, along with a number of other federal programs, into a new federal authority called Successful, Safe, and Healthy Students.

**FOCUS ON    NCPPA Member Organizations    3.3**

American Alliance for Health, Physical Education, Recreation, and Dance (www.aahperd.org)

American Cancer Society (www.cancer.org)

American College of Sports Medicine (www.acsm.org)

American Council on Exercise (www.acefitness.org)

American Heart Association (www.americanheart.org)

International Health, Racquet, and Sports Club Association (www.ihrsa.org)

McNeil Nutritionals (www.viactiv.com)

MEND Foundation (www.mendfoundation.org)

National Academy of Sports Medicine (www.nasm.org)

National Athletic Trainers Association (www.nata.org)

National Recreation and Parks Association (www.nrpa.org)

The Pharmaceutical Research and Manufacturers of America (www.phrma.org)

Snow Sports Industries America (www.snowsports.org)

United States Tennis Association (www.usta.org)

YMCA of the USA (www.ymca.org)

**FOCUS ON    NCPPA Lead Organizations    3.4**

American Alliance for Health, Physical Education, Recreation, and Dance

American Cancer Society

American College of Sports Medicine

American Council on Exercise

American Heart Association

Athletic Republic

International Health, Racquet, & Sports Club Association

McNeil Nutritionals

National Athletic Trainers Association

National Recreation and Park Association

Snowsports Industries America

Sporting Good Manufacturing Association

United States Tennis Association

YMCA of the USA

The National Association for Health and Fitness (NAHF) was founded in 1977 with the primary vision of improving the quality of life for individuals through the promotion of physical fitness, sports, and healthy lifestyles by fostering and supporting the work of Governor's and State Councils on physical fitness and sports in all U.S. states and territories (www.physicalfitness.org). The primary focus of NAHF is to encourage active living, increase community involvement, support quality physical education in schools, support worksite health and active-aging programs.

The Shaping America's Youth (SAY) network is primarily a clearinghouse for information on state and local efforts to support physical activity and healthy lifestyles for America's children and youths (www.shapingamericasyouth.org). SAY not only provides a source for information on physical activity initiatives and programs throughout the United States, but also convenes a series of 21st Century Town Meetings, each one engaging between 1,000 and 1,500 people. The primary purpose of this organization is to discover and share information about programs that are successful in achieving goals for healthy lifestyles among children and youths.

## STATE-LEVEL EFFORTS TO SUPPORT PHYSICAL ACTIVITY INFRASTRUCTURES

National organizations, such as those cited on the previous page, fulfill important leadership roles in establishing and sustaining physical activity infrastructures. But state policies, state funding, and state accountability systems have a crucial role in creating and sustaining polices that require physical activity programs and physical activity facilities in schools and communities. The U.S. Department of Health and Human Services Centers for Disease Control and Prevention 2010 State Indicator Report on Physical Activity provides information on state-level progress on key indicators related to the development of state physical activity infrastructures (www.cdc.gov/physicalactivity/). Of all middle and high schools, 89.1 percent allow community-sponsored use of PA facilities by youth outside of normal schools hours, Fifty percent of youth have parks or playgrounds, community centers, and sidewalks or walking paths available in their neighborhoods. Twenty states require or recommend regular elementary school recess. Thirty-seven states require elementary, middle, and high schools to teach physical education. Forty-six percent of middle and high schools support or promote walking/biking to and from school. Eight states require moderate to vigorous intensity physical activity in licensed childcare facilities.

These data reveal the uneven strength in physical activity policy among the states. Some states have been quite active in developing physical activity policies, while others have done very little. The Robert Woods Johnson Foundation Center to Prevent Childhood Obesity has proposed that states enact the following policies to develop a more robust infrastructure (www.rwjf.org):

- Adopt state standards for physical activity in schools that include minimum requirements for recess, physical education, and activity throughout the school day and adopt similar standards for pre-school, after-school, and childcare programs.

- Adopt a quality physical education curriculum to engage all students in moderate to vigorous activity during classes.

- Incorporate a physical fitness outcome indicator in state school-performance ratings to better balance academic and health goals.

- Support the development of bike paths, sidewalks, and other infrastructure needed to enable children to walk or bike to school.

- Connect roadways to complementary systems of trails and bike paths that provide safe places to walk and bike.

- Through the Safe Routes to School program support the development of paths, sidewalks, and other infrastructure needed to enable children to walk or bike to school and to encourage families to walk and bike.

Commitment to environmental conservation and aerobic training come together in some outdoor recreational pursuits.

When states enact policies that address the issues described above, they must also provide the funding to support the enactment of the policies and create a monitoring system to ensure that the policies are being enacted appropriately and a reporting system to allow the state to assess the degrees of progress toward healthy lifestyles outcomes.

## LOCAL EFFORTS TO SUPPORT PHYSICAL ACTIVITY

While federal and state policies and funding are fundamentally important to achieving state and national goals for physical activity, it is at the local level that the activity actually takes place. Whether in large metropolitan cities, medium-sized towns, or rural small towns, the local governments and local school districts must work together to provide the programs and facilities that promote and sustain physical activity among children, youth, and adults. The most effective approach to improving physical activity in all these situations is what is most commonly referred to as *joint use.* The most typical partnership in joint-use ventures is that between the local school district and the town/city parks and recreation department. The two most common forms of joint use are *co-location,* which refers to planning to construct facilities on adjacent properties and *community schools,* where the facility is designed to be the center of the community and is open to all members of the community, all day, every day, evenings, and weekends.

Joint use projects typically develop with specific goals that define the joint utilization of school facilities. Some joint-use approaches are specifically designed to support the school mission. For example, agencies or other nonprofit organizations may provide school services that support the advancement of student performance and well-being and offer social services to families of students. These services enable the families to provide better home environments to support their children (Filardo et al.,

2010). Another common approach is to focus the joint use on the goal of enhancing community well-being by providing facilities and programs that support community health, physical activity, and continuing education.

Joint-use strategies developed by schools and their local partners can play a very important role in combating the overweight/obesity epidemic among children, youth, and adults not only through the development of shared facilities but also through the development of specific programmatic features that create and sustain attractive physical activity opportunities for children, youths, and adults. For example, in California, the city of Pleasanton and the Pleasanton Unified School District jointly funded the construction of three middle-school gymnasiums. The city operates programs in the gymnasiums during nonschool hours and weekends. Another example is in the community of Perry, Ohio, which built a new high school that includes a comprehensive community sport and recreation center, open for joint use to students, faculty, staff, and community residents. The physical education program and school sport teams use the facility, and it is also open to students and residents 30 hours per week for drop-in activity.

In Centerburg, Ohio, the high school partnered with the local YMCA to create and share an extensive fitness facility used by students and members of the community. The fitness facility is used by physical education classes, sport teams, and by members of the community. The city of Merced, California, experienced a major population growth spurt in the early 1990s, leaving the residents without adequate parks and recreation facilities. The city and the school district entered into a joint-use partnership to resolve the problem. The partnership has continued to grow, with the city and school district partnering on grant opportunities, revitalizing blighted facilities, and developing new recreational spaces.

Community schools are developed as partnerships between the local school district and other community resources to develop and sustain an integrated focus on academics, health, and social services (www.communityschools.org). The primary goals are improved student learning, stronger families, and healthier communities. Schools are the center of the community and are open to everyone, all day, every day, evenings, and weekends. In the last decade, initiatives to develop community schools have spread to 44 states and the District of Columbia. Community schools work purposefully to integrate academic, health, and social services to improve both student and adult learning, and to strengthen families and promote healthier communities.

The American Alliance for Health, Physical Education, Recreation, and Dance (AAHPERD) has a School-Community Recognition program to honor exemplary programs of collaboration within communities to support healthy lifestyles. One recipient was the Bay Shore Middle School in New York where the focus was on changing the physical activity behaviors of middle school students. The school formed a Wellness Alliance with local physicians and hospital workers who helped to develop the middle school wellness program with new equipment donated by the community. A wellness environmental walking course was also developed and is used both by students and the community.

## THE ROLE OF ALLIED FIELDS IN THE PHYSICAL ACTIVITY INFRASTRUCTURE

While this text focuses primarily on physical education, fitness, and sport and the professional opportunities in those fields, it is important to recognize the roles of the professional fields of recreation, health, and dance in supporting the physical activity infrastructure (see Focus On Box 3.5, Allied-Field Websites 3.5). While these three fields provide different contributions to the physical activity infrastructure, they each have important roles to play in developing and sustaining a lifetime commitment to physical activity.

What is now increasingly referred to as the recreation and leisure-services industry is a large national industry providing varied career opportunities for women and men. This industry includes recreational, sport, travel, and tourism programs provided by private-sector companies and corporations, as well as traditional recreation providers such as the YMCA, the YWCA, community recreation programs, state recreation departments, and federal parks and recreation.

The U.S. National Park Service was founded in 1916 (www.nps.gov). Today, the National Park Service controls and supervises programs in 400 national park sites throughout the United States. Last year, more than 225 million persons visited national park sites. The National Recreation and Parks Association (NRPA) (www.nrpa.org) was founded in 1965 through the merger of six national organizations, each of which was dedicated to the provision of educational and leisure activities through programs in recreation centers and parks. NRPA is funded through membership dues, conference and event sales, and charitable contributions. These funds are used primarily to conduct research, education, and policy initiatives that serve to extend and strengthen the availability of activity through parks and recreation centers.

Over the past several decades the *health professions* have gradually shifted from a primarily remedial or medical approach to a primarily preventive or wellness approach. Whereas remediating sickness and disease was a main agenda for the health professions early in the twentieth century, the focus on developing and sustaining healthy lifestyles gradually became the primary agenda as we moved toward the twenty-first century. The development and expansion of the health-enhancement industry and the explosion of interest in health-related issues pertinent to people of all ages has increasingly focused on the healthy lifestyles issues with the concept of *wellness* defining the desire to develop and sustain healthy lifestyles with a major focus on appropriate levels of physical activity.

The services of the health-enhancement industry are delivered to people through five major components: school health education, government and community health programs, nonprofit health

## FOCUS ON — Allied-Field Websites 3.5

### Recreation

| | |
|---|---|
| American Association for Leisure and Recreation | www.aahperd.org/aalr |
| American Trails | www.americantrails.org |
| American Hiking Society | www.americanhiking.org |
| American Recreation Coalition | www.funoutdoors.com |
| American Therapeutic Recreation Association | www.atra-online.com |
| National Recreation and Park Association | www.nrpa.org |
| Therapeutic Recreation | www.recreationtherapy.com |
| Wilderness Education Association | www.weainfo.org |
| League of American Bicyclists | www.bikeleague.org |

### Health

| | |
|---|---|
| American Association for Health Education | www.aahperd.org/aahe |
| American College Health Association | www.acha.org |
| American Public Health Association | www.apha.org |
| American School Health Association | www.ashaweb.org |
| Department of Health and Human Services | www.os.dhhs.gov |
| National Institutes of Health | www.nih.gov |
| Society for Public Health Education | www.sophe.org |
| National Education Association—Health Information Network | www.neahin.org |
| Action for Healthy Kids | www.actionforhealthykids.org |

### Dance

| | |
|---|---|
| National Dance Association | www.aahperd.org/nda |
| Folk Dance Association | www.folkdancing.org |
| American Dance Therapy Association | www.adta.org |
| Dance Vision | www.dancevision.com |
| DanceDanceDance | www.dancedancedance.com |

organizations, worksite health programs, and private-sector fee-for-service programs. The demand for health services related to physical activity has increased substantially with the result that professional preparation for persons to work within the health-enhancement industry has increased over the past few decades.

Providers in the health-enhancement industry fall into two categories: the for-profit health-enhancement industry in the private sector and the nonprofit health organizations in the public sector. Health enhancement has become big business over the past decade. The private sector of the health-enhancement industry is largely unregulated.

Although many health professionals working in the private sector do have appropriate certifications and licenses, many do not. School health educators are certified and licensed to teach in the same way as all teachers, typically with a K–12 Health Education license. A graduate degree, the Masters of Public Health (MPH), is a widely sought and highly valued degree in the health professions.

Nonprofit organizations, such as the American Heart Association (www.americanheart.org) and the American Lung Association (www.lungusa.org), have become increasingly active in the health-enhancement industry. The main purposes of nonprofit health associations are to generate financial support for research and program development in the particular health area they service, to educate the public about the central issues surrounding their focus, and to influence people to lead healthier lifestyles. The AHA sponsors competitive road races, fun runs, and walkathons, while the ALA sponsors the Great American Smoke-Out each year. Perhaps most importantly, these organizations fund substantial research projects to increase our knowledge about healthy lifestyles.

Dance is a significant human activity in virtually every known culture and throughout history. The field of dance takes many forms. Dance can be a cultural art form such as modern dance and ballet. Dance is often pursued in schools in the forms of folk dance, creative dance, and the movement-education curriculum in the early elementary grades.

Step aerobics is one of the many popular forms of aerobics.

Dance has also become an important fitness activity as seen in the aerobic dance movement.

Dance is an important part of many cultures, ranging from folk dance to ballroom dancing, to the jitterbug and swing dancing popular in the 1950s and 1960s, and to the rock-and-roll dancing in more recent years. The late 1980s, with the publication of Dr. K. Cooper's book "s", started aerobic dancing, which became one of the most popular forms of fitness training for that generation. Many elementary schools include a form of creative dancing in their physical education curriculum. In the educational reform climate of the 1980s and 1990s, arts education became a focus of curriculum reform in schools with the result that dance education became a part of the integrated-arts approach in many elementary and middle schools. The National Dance Association is a member of AAHPERD with primary goals of developing curricular and pedagogical materials to foster the growth of dance education in schools.

## THE CRUCIAL THEMES DEFINING OUR PRESENT AND FUTURE

### Theme 1: Distributing Opportunity for Physical Activity More Equitably

For many years we have known that the health status of a particular socioeconomic class is typically better than that of the classes below them and worse than that of classes above them (Hertzman, 1994). There is increasing evidence that in nations where socioeconomic distances among classes have been reduced relevant health markers have improved. One of the two overarching goals of *Healthy People 2010* is to eliminate health disparities based on race, gender, and socioeconomic status.

### Theme 2: Focusing on Younger Populations

Physical education, fitness, and sport programs have tended to focus primarily on children, youths, and young adults. Our current efforts have to extend

Activity infrastructure for young children.

that focus in both directions, that is, focus more on infant and early childhood programs as well as programs for older adults. It is increasingly clear that physical activity skills and motivation to engage in physical activity are developed in early childhood. Educating parents of young children about the importance of early physical activity and providing better physical activity programming in day care and early childhood learning centers are crucially important to achieving our national goals.

## Theme 3: Gender Equity in Physical Education, Fitness, and Sport

In Chapter 2 we described the differences in how girls and women were introduced to physical activity through physical education, fitness, and sport programs. The primary theme throughout that time was the belief that women could not participate in the same way boys and men did because it was not thought that they were as physically capable and could not tolerate the rigor and intensity that boys and men could. It was also believed that, for some reason, maintaining their femininity required them to participate differently than men. While we have made great progress in providing more equal treatment for girls and women, we still have a long way to go. Girls and women now run marathons and participate in physical fitness competitions, as well as in organized sports. In many cases, however, they still suffer discrimination in terms of access to facilities, equipment, and programs. Physical education, fitness, and sport professionals need to be advocates for girls and women and they need to band together to develop and sustain advocacy programs that provide greater opportunity and support for girls and women.

## Theme 4: Toward an Expanded Physical Education

Schools are typically the hub of the developmental triangle—home, community, school—in which children and youths learn and grow. In far too many schools physical education has become so restricted in terms of time, facilities, and equipment that it cannot possibly play the key role of educating students toward healthy lifestyles that include regular physical activity. Physical educators not only need more time with students in their classes but also in developing recess, lunch-time, and after-school physical activity programs. Physical educators also need to link closely to parents of their students, providing them with information about the progress of their daughters and sons, but also to urge parents to enable their children to be involved in community physical activity, fitness, and sport programs.

## Theme 5: Toward an Inclusive Rather than Exclusive Sport Culture

Sport plays an enormously important role in American culture. The explosion of child and youth sports over the past several decades has been extraordinary, but it also has its downside. The number of sport programs for young children has increased markedly in the last few decades, but there is increasing evidence that programs for children have become too intense. This has resulted in far too many injuries and has caused an increasing number of girls and boys to drop out of the programs. There is also an increasing tendency for young children to specialize in one sport rather than exploring several sports in different seasons. Interscholastic sport has become "big time" in America, but for those students who are not good enough to make the varsity team there is very little opportunity for them to be involved in their sport. We must begin to create community programs that allow youths to continue to pursue their interest in a sport even though they are not selected to be on the school varsity team.

Early specialization.

## SUMMARY

1. A physical activity infrastructure includes facilities, spaces, and programs enabling children, youths, and adults to become and stay physically active.

2. The enabling provision requires that the infrastructure be attractive, accessible, and safe.

3. A physical activity infrastructure also requires accessible facilities with community and private-sector programs staffed by well-prepared physical activity professionals.

4. The Education Sector and the Parks, Recreation, Fitness, and Sport sector of the National Plan for Physical Activity are particularly important to improving the physical activity of children, youths, and adults.

5. Improving and sustaining physical activity throughout the infrastructure requires the cooperation of a large number of organizations from the private and public sectors.

6. Federal and state policies and funding are fundamentally important to develop the infrastructure and support physical activity programs.

7. Local community efforts to develop and sustain physical activity opportunities, particularly those that involve joint-use facilities, are crucial to increasing physical activity throughout the lifespan.

8. The allied fields of recreation, health, and dance have much to contribute to developing high-quality and attractive programs for people throughout their lifespan.

9. Physical activity throughout the lifespan will be greatly enhanced by paying more attention to creating programmatic responses to the five "crucial themes" that have tended to limit accessibility to good and safe physical activity and sport programs.

## DISCUSSION QUESTIONS

1. Describe the primary components of the physical activity infrastructure in your local area.

2. What physical activity programs exist for young children, youths, and adults in your local community?

3. How would you see your professional future fitting into the notion of a physical activity infrastructure?

4. What recreation, health, and dance programs for young persons and adults can be identified in your local community?

5. Does your college or university provide certification/licensure major programs in recreation, health, and dance?

6. What is your take on the strategies suggested for the Education sector?

7. What is your take on the strategies suggested for the Parks, Recreation, Fitness, and Sports sector?

# Physical Education

Physical education has been an accepted part of the curriculum of American schools for about a century. Even in the midst of current educational reform, physical education is still described as a necessary subject that has the potential to contribute a great deal to the education of children and youths. Yet there is also a substantial amount of "fizz-ed bashing," both in the serious literature of education and in the popular media. Think for a moment about how the television and movie industries typically stereotype physical education teachers!

School is still one institution that touches us all—and that touches us at crucial periods of our development as individuals. It is vitally important that physical education thrive as a well-taught, credible, and well-accepted subject in our schools. What is physical education? What activities are acceptable and necessary? What kinds of programs seem to work? How can physical education programs become a more integral part of the total school curriculum? To what extent can school physical education programs aid in reversing the rising levels of overweight and obese youth? What are some of the key issues that physical education programs face today? How can school physical education lift itself from being a marginalized subject to a true core subject? What does a quality physical education program look like if it is to address the current public health problems? The three chapters in Part 2 are designed to help you examine these questions and related issues, reach conclusions that are informed by evidence and thoughtful argument, and develop your vision of what you want quality physical education to be like.

## CHAPTER 4

# Basic Concepts of Physical Education

*Modern Physical Education with its emphasis upon education through the physical is based upon the biologic unity of mind and body. This view sees life as a totality. Correct in their appraisement that the cult of muscle is ludicrous, those who worship at the altar of mental development too frequently neglect the implications of unity. "Socrates with a headache" is always preferable to a brainless Hercules, but the modern spirit in Physical Education seeks the education of man through physical activities as one aspect of the social effort for human enlightenment.*

Jesse Feiring Williams, 1930

Physical education has been a school subject in America for more than 100 years. For most of that time, it was a minor subject, seldom attracting attention of educators or the public. The times when physical education did attract national attention were always times when the lack of fitness among American youths became an issue. This was especially evident on three occasions. First, during a polio epidemic in the early part of the twentieth-century. Second, during World War II when countless draftees were rejected for poor fitness levels. And third, during the mid-fifties when a research study showed that 60 percent of American children/youth failed a test of minimum muscular fitness compared to only 9 percent of European children. This the number of fitness reasons in World War II, and during the mid-1950s when a research study showed that 60 percent of American children/youths failed a test of minimum muscular

fitness compared to only 9 percent of European children. This led President Eisenhower to form the President's Council on Youth Fitness.

The recent epidemic of child/youth overweight and obesity has once again brought physical education into the national spotlight. Curiously, this national focus on increasing the physical activity of children and youths developed during the same period when time for physical education in America's schools had diminished due to the federal No Child Left Behind legislation, which caused schools, especially at the elementary level, to devote more time to reading and mathematics (e.g., Center for Education Policy, 2007; Trost & van der Mars, 2009). As you will see in this chapter and Chapter 5, many physical education programs have changed to better respond to this current health crisis.

A physical education program is defined both by the content to be learned and the manner in which

> **FOCUS ON**    Key Historical Influences on the Development of Physical Education    **4.1**
>
> 1. Concerns about health and fitness and character development were at the heart of the early formal gymnastic systems. Concerns about fitness have occurred periodically as reactions to rejection of draftees for military service and to epidemics such as polio.
> 2. Progressive-education theory focused on the development of the whole child and led to the
>
> developmental perspective known historically as "education-through-the-physical," which is still the most widely accepted approach to articulating goals for physical education.
> 3. The continuing development of sport in the twentieth century merged with the developmental approach to make physical education largely a sport-based curriculum.

it is taught. That is, programs are defined both by their curricular choices and the pedagogy used to deliver those curricular choices. The programmatic approaches to physical education described in this chapter will show different choices of activities and different approaches to teaching those activities. The various programmatic approaches are described with as little bias as possible so that you can (a) decide which approach seems most suitable to help children and youths in today's schools become physically educated people, (b) better articulate your own philosophy about the role and importance of school physical education, and (c) justify your underlying decisions when developing or revising a school physical education curriculum.

## A PRIMER ON THE TWENTIETH CENTURY PHILOSOPHICAL INFLUENCES IN PHYSICAL EDUCATION

Why do children in most K–2 physical education classes get to try different combinations of movements? Why do students in many programs get asked to reflect on their "level of responsibility?" Why do certain teachers seem more concerned with students learning to get along with each other than with learning how to throw and catch? And what has prompted infusion of team-building activities, high-ropes courses, and multiday outdoor excursions in contemporary physical education? To answer these

questions effectively, it is important that you develop an understanding and appreciation for the primary roots of today's programs in physical education, fitness, and sport. Hence, we offer a short overview of the main trends and philosophies that have their roots in the mid-twentieth century, but are very much reflected in today's programs.

The most important influence on physical education in the twentieth century was the developmental model, often referred to as "education through the physical" or the "new physical education." This model was wholly consistent with progressive-education theory, which so dominated ideas about schooling and learning in the first half of the twentieth century (Focus On Box 4.1).

## Twentieth Century Influences on Modern Physical Education: 1900–1950

In 1910, Clark Hetherington earned the title of "father of modern physical education" with his landmark paper "Fundamental Education." Hetherington described both the scope and the categories of the *new* physical education.

> This paper aims to describe the function and place of general neuromuscular activities, primarily play activities, in the educational process . . . To present the thesis, four phases of the education process will be considered: Organic education, psychomotor education, character education, and intellectual education. (Weston, 1962, p. 160)

Hetherington's four phases became the four primary objectives of the new physical education. For the better part of the twentieth century, these objectives were used to explain and justify the presence of physical education in the school curriculum. Although different leaders and organizations explained the objectives somewhat differently, the differences were minimal. Charles Bucher, a leading mid-twentieth century American physical educator, suggested the following goals a half-century after the Hetherington goals were formulated. Notice the similarity to the Hetherington goals.

1. *Physical development objective:* The objective of physical development deals with the program of activities that builds physical power in an individual through the development of the various organic systems of the body.

2. *Motor development objective:* The motor development objective is concerned with making physical movement useful and with as little expenditure of energy as possible and being proficient, graceful, and aesthetic in this movement.

3. *Mental development objective:* The mental development objective deals with the accumulation of a body of knowledge and the ability to think and to interpret this knowledge.

4. *Social development objective:* The social development objective is concerned with helping an individual in making personal adjustments, group adjustments, and adjustments as a member of society. (Bucher, 1964, p. 155)

A typical physical education lesson included fitness, skill development, knowledge, and social development. Lesson plans organized around the four objectives quickly became the standard in the physical education curriculum in schools.

A corollary feature of this developmental model for physical education was the establishment of the **multi-activity curriculum** approach to program design. For *full* development to be ensured, proponents believed, each child had to experience a *variety* of activities. Because physical education sought a diversity of physical, mental, and social goals and

Using modified equipment is essential for developing skillfulness.

because each child was unique in her or his own development, a wide variety of activities was needed to fulfill the promise of this developmental model: team sports, individual sports, adventure activities, fitness activities, and dance all found acceptance within the multi-activity framework.

In 1927 a national committee officially sanctioned the multi-activity model. The idea and guidelines to use this model were published as a monograph, "The Physical Education Curriculum," in 1938 and eventually were revised through seven editions. This was as close as we would get to a *national* curriculum for physical education in the United States. The primary feature of this curriculum model was a *block* or *unit* plan. Across a school year, students would experience a fairly large number of activity units, some sports, some fitness, some dance, and some outdoor adventure. This unit model with the multi-activity approach became the main programmatic feature of American physical education, and it mostly remains in place today. In today's programs, a unit of instruction may range in length from 5 to 12 lessons, interspersed with an occasional one-day unit. In the last two decades, teachers have started to recognize the value of longer units (18 to 20 lessons) which offer greater opportunity for students to actually improve at a particular activity. As we will show, teachers using sport education (Siedentop, Hastie, van der Mars, 2011) would take this "less is more" philosophy, by teaching perhaps only two sports per grading period, but going into greater depth (i.e., teaching more content) as opposed to a select few rudimentary techniques, followed by minimally structured game-play.

Later on, in 1971 the American Alliance for Health, Physical Education, Recreation, and Dance (AAHPERD) would launch the Physical Education Public Information (PEPI) project, designed to inform the public about the goals of physical education (Biles, 1971). PEPI's five primary concepts showed that Hetherington's four objectives were alive and well in physical education:

1. A physically educated person is one who has knowledge and skill concerning her or his body and how it works.

2. Physical education is health insurance.

3. Physical education can contribute to academic achievement.

4. A sound physical education program contributes to development of a positive self-concept.

5. A sound physical education program helps an individual to attain social skills.

Notice Hetherington's influence. The language was different, but the emphasis on fitness, skill, knowledge, and social development remained and can still be seen in many of today's programs.

## Twentieth-Century Influences on Modern Physical Education: 1950–2000

The period from 1950 to the present was one of diversity and ferment. The "education-through-the-physical" philosophy, which was the dominant underlying belief system for the profession in the early twentieth century, was not seriously challenged until the 1950s. Then a series of societal and professional developments provided the context for diversification, specialization, and accompanying philosophical ferment within physical education, fitness, and sport. In brief, cultural factors such as the post-1950 reformist movement in education, the civil rights movement, the fitness renaissance, and the era of specialization in universities all came together in a fairly short time span which produced serious questioning of basic philosophical assumptions underlying the physical education field at that time. This gave rise to four distinct philosophical orientations. They include: human movement, humanistic sport and physical education, play and sport education, and experiential and adventure education.

**Human Movement**    The first serious challenge to a half-century of unified philosophical belief in physical education came during the 1950s with the development of the *human movement philosophy*. First developed in England during the late 1930s by the German immigrant Rudolph Laban, the notion that a human movement philosophy could underlie physical education took hold in England in the 1940s. After World War II, American physical educators began to learn about this philosophy and saw in it a more satisfying intellectual and emotional approach to their subject matter.

Laban's philosophies (published in *Modern Educational Dance*) are clearly reflected in the work by American physical education leaders Rosalind Cassidy and Eleanor Metheny. For example, Eleanor Metheny, a leading advocate for one of the early and most important movements provided a basic definition of the human movement approach, a definition that still finds widespread acceptance today:

> If we may define the *totally educated person* as one who has fully developed his ability to utilize constructively all of his potential capacities as a person in relation to the world in which he lives, then we may define the *physically educated person* as one who has fully developed the ability to utilize constructively all of his potential capacities for movement as a way of expressing, exploring, developing, and interpreting himself and his relationship to the world he lives in. (Metheny, 1954, p. 27; emphasis in original)

The philosophy of human movement provided a strong and appealing framework for changing school physical education programs to what became known as movement education. It also formed the basis for revamping professional physical education teacher education programs in universities. The movement education curriculum was typically divided into educational gymnastics, educational dance, and educational games. It advocated a more open, exploratory approach to teaching through guided discovery, with a strong focus on student success. The class climate was largely noncompetitive.

In movement education a program is organized on the basis of three concepts and underlying principles: body awareness, space, and qualities of movement. Within that framework, teachers select and present material based on how it can help students develop a greater understanding of human movement. Notice how this is fundamentally different from contemporary physical education, in which programs are organized around activities such as volleyball, soccer, dance, or track and field, where learning content organized from the simple to the complex and presented to children in accordance with their physical maturity and general readiness.

In movement education, teachers employ movement exploration and guided discovery. The climate is typically noncompetitive and success oriented. Most of the elementary texts in physical education methods used in universities today still reflect the rather substantial changes that occurred in physical education from 1955 to 1975. And as you will see

later in this chapter, the philosophy underlying human movement continues to be an influential force in American physical education.

## Humanistic Sport and Physical Education

Philosophies in physical education, fitness, and sport often reflect ideas and ideals that are popular in the intellectual and social climate of the surrounding society. Nowhere is this more clearly seen than in the **humanistic philosophies** in sport and physical education of the 1960s and 1970s. One of the important factors in American culture in this period was *third-force psychology* or *humanistic psychology*. These ideas reached maturity as a popular movement in America during the social turmoil of the 1960s and 1970s. Humanistic psychology focuses on the full development of individual potential through personal growth and self-development.

Two major educational movements of the post-1950 era were the renewed emphasis on science and mathematics and the humanistic-education movement. Humanistic education promoted open education, affective education, values clarification, and less emphasis on competition for grades and academic outcomes. Children's personal and social development was thought to be as important—if not more important—as their academic development.

At the same time, fueled by the same societal factors, a companion movement developed within the world of intercollegiate and professional sport that led to the humanistic sport and physical education movement. This movement is represented in a series of popular books condemning abuses in sport at the time, criticizing how athletes were treated, and advocating reforms that would allow sport to be devoted more to the personal development of the athletes. Examples include Jack Scott's *Athletics for Athletes,* Olympic medalist Don Schollander's *Deep Water*, Leonard Shector's *The Jocks*, Glenn Dickey's *The Jock Empire, and* Dave Meggyesy's *Out of Their League*, a strident criticism of Meggyesy's experience in football.

Humanistic sport and physical education proponents were critical of then-current practices and were advocates of new forms of participation:

In fact, the counterculture ethic reverses every value of the Lombardian ethic. Cooperation replaces competition, an emphasis on process replaces an emphasis on the product, sport as a co-educational activity replaces sport as a stag party, a concern for enjoyment replaces a concern for excellence, and an opportunity for spontaneity and self-expression replaces authoritarianism. (Scott, 1974, p. 159)

Though no longer described in the terms used during its developmental period, this movement has clear ties to several current philosophies in physical education. For example, Donald Hellison's influential 1973 book *Humanistic Physical Education* sets forth the conceptual and theoretical basis for the emerging humanistic movement in physical education. Hellison stressed personal development, self-expression, and improved interpersonal relationships as primary goals for physical education. His work developed into a major curricular and pedagogical force in physical education, known now as the Personal and Social Responsibility model (Hellison, 1984, 1995, 1996). Although it has been applied widely, especially in elementary-school physical education, it has manifested its strong social commitment most clearly in programs for at-risk urban youths.

## Play Education and Sport Education

The traditional philosophy of physical education had emphasized *using* activities to reach valuable educational goals—physical, mental, social, and moral goals. In the 1970s, based partly on Eleanor Metheny's (1954, 1970) influential work, some began to argue that the activities of physical education were valuable *in and of themselves*. Siedentop (1972, 1976, 1980) expressed this point of view in a philosophy known as **play education**. Play education's goal was to help students acquire skills and develop an affection for the activities themselves. Play educators were to be transmitters and transformers of valuable cultural activities:

Play is the proper classification for physical education, both from a logical and psychological perspective. Classifying physical education as a form of play puts it clearly in perspective alongside other primary institutionalized forms of play—art, music, and drama . . . This classification allows us to recognize that the activities of the weekend golfer or skier, the after-dinner tennis player, and the noon-time handball player are analogous to those of the painter, the member of the community theater, or the musician. Each is at play, at an institutionalized form of play, and it is only the play form that distinguished one from the other. (Siedentop, 1980, p. 247)

From the point of view of play education, physical education did not need to be justified by reference to outcomes beyond involvement in the activities:

We must have the good sense and courage to stand up and defend our field on the basis of the personal and cultural meaning in our subject matter. . . . We do not have to *use* our activities. There is no doubt that they can be used, and often for quite legitimate and noble purposes. But those other purposes are of a different order than play education. In play education we can let our subject matter be just what it is—institutionalized forms of play that are of fundamental importance to the culture in which we live and grow. (Siedentop, 1980, p. 259; emphasis in original)

The philosophy of play education did not directly influence curriculum development in schools. Nonetheless, many physical educators began to argue more boldly that their subject matter (however defined) was valuable in and of itself and did not need to be justified by reference to external objectives or outcomes.

Play education never became a reality because it was more a philosophy than a prescription for developing a physical education program. However, in 1986 a similar philosophical point of view was expressed as **Sport Education** (Siedentop, Mand, & Taggart, 1986). The intent of Sport Education was to educate students in the skills, values, and attitudes of good sport so that they might enjoy and participate themselves and so that they would be active contributors to a healthier sport culture:

The rationale for sport education rests on a few very basic and important assumptions. The first is that sport derives from play; that is, sport represents an institutionalized form of competitive motor play. The second is that sport is an important part of our culture and that sport occupies an important role in determining the health and vitality of the entire culture; that is, if more people participate in good sport, then the culture is stronger. The third assumption follows from the first two. If sport is a higher form of play and if good sport is important to the health and vitality of the culture, then sport should be the subject matter of physical education. The development of good sportspersons and the development of a better sports culture should be central to the mission of physical education. (Siedentop et al. 1986, pp. 188–189)

If play education lacked a clear program prescription, Sport Education did not. Within the structure of the physical education lessons students become members of teams for the duration of a season (unit), they practice skills and strategies, participate in scheduled competition among teams, keep season records, and determine season champions (Siedentop, 1994; Siedentop et al., 2011).

Traditionally in the United States, sport is typically defined in terms of the traditional sports (e.g., tennis, soccer, basketball, etc.). Sport Education advocates define sport that is decidedly European in nature using a "sport for all" orientation. That is, sport would include a host of activities that clearly involve physical activity which in the United States would not be considered a sport. "Sportive" people who would go for a 15-mile walk, a 30-mile bike ride, or a cross-country trek would be considered as engaging in sport. By defining sport more broadly, the Sport Education user can design activities around all the seasons (e.g., rope jumping, etc.) for physical fitness and strength.

### Experiential and Adventure Education

The emergence of character-education models in England in the 1800s was a prelude to the current focus on experiential and adventure education. Much of what is done in experiential and adventure education grew from the Outward Bound movement, as defined by its five core values (www.outwardbound.com):

1. Adventure and challenge
2. Compassion and service

3. Learning through experience
4. Personal development
5. Social and environmental responsibility

The climbing walls and challenge courses on many school sites today reflect the popularity of adventure activities. Moreover, it is not uncommon to see students meeting off campus outside of regular school hours as they cycle, climb, hike, and/or canoe over the course of multiple days. Project Adventure (www.pa.org) is a nonprofit organization devoted to supporting adventure programs in schools and communities. It provides curriculum materials for developing programs at all school levels and workshops to prepare physical educators to deliver adventure programs.

## NASPE'S MOVE TOWARD NATIONAL GOALS AND STANDARDS

In the 1990s the National Association for Sport and Physical Education (NASPE), an association within the AAHPERD, began to develop a set of national goals and standards for physical education. The first part of this initiative was called the Outcomes Project, which sought to answer the question, What should students know and be able to do as a result of physical education? In 1992 NASPE published its first outcomes statement, which established a set of national content standards for physical education. In 2004 NASPE (NASPE, 2004b) revised the content standards to those shown in Focus On Box 4.2. The outcomes project and the resulting standards provided, for the first time, a national consensus that defined the physically educated person. Each of the 2004 standards is further delineated by *student expectations* that are defined for grades K–2, 3–5, 6–8, and 9–12. What is expected of the student is then still further delineated by examples of performance outcomes for that standard at each of the grouped grade levels. Some of the performance expectations are shown in Focus On Box 4.3.

---

**FOCUS ON**   NASPE Content Standards in Physical Education   **4.2**

A physically educated person:

1. Demonstrates competency in motor skills and movement patterns needed to perform a variety of activities.

2. Demonstrates understanding of movement concepts, principles, strategies, and tactics as they apply to the learning and performance of physical activities.

3. Participates regularly in physical activity.

4. Achieves and maintains a health-enhancing level of physical fitness.

5. Exhibits responsible personal and social behavior that respects self and others in physical-activity settings.

6. Values physical activity for health, enjoyment, challenge, self-expression, and/or social interaction.

SOURCE: National Association for Sport and Physical Education, 2004b.

---

**FOCUS ON**   Samples from NASPE Performance Outcomes   **4.3**

*Competency in motor skill and movement patterns*

Grades K–2

Skips, hops, gallops, slides using mature form

Demonstrates a smooth transition between locomotor skills in time to music

Grades 3–5

Performs a tinikling step to 3/4 time

Dribbles then passes a basketball to a moving receiver

Grades 6–8

Places the ball away from an opponent during a tennis rally

Designs and performs gymnastics or dance sequences

Grades 9–12

Uses a variety of ground stroke placements to keep opponent moving during a tennis match

Dribbles a soccer ball at moderate to fast speeds, while maintaining control of the ball, evading opponents, and shielding the ball

*Understanding of movement concepts, principles, strategies, and tactics*

Grades K–2

Corrects movement errors in response to feedback

Identifies body planes correctly

Grades 3–5

Describes how heart rate is used to monitor exercise intensity

Accurately recognizes the critical elements of a catch made by a fellow student and provides feedback to that student

Grades 6–8

Describes basic principles of training and how they improve fitness

States the biomechanical reason to extend elbow in striking skills

Grades 9–12

Develops realistic short-term and long-term personal fitness goals

Explains appropriate tactical decisions in a game of softball

*Participates regularly in physical activity*

Grades K–2

Engages in moderate to vigorous activity on an intermittent basis

Participates in chasing and fleeing activities outside of school

Grades 3–5

Participates in organized sport activities in local community

*(continued)*

Monitors his or her physical activity by using a pedometer

Grades 6–8
Sets realistic physical-activity goals and strives to attain them

Participates in health-enhancing activity during and outside of school

Grades 9–12
Accumulates a recommended number of minutes of MVPA outside of PE class five or more days per week

Demonstrates effective time management skills to allow opportunity for PA to be created or found during the day

### Achieves and maintains a health-enhancing level of physical fitness

Grades K–2
Engages in a series of locomotor activities

Increases arm and shoulder strength by traveling hand-over-hand along a horizontal ladder

Grades 3–5
Runs the equivalent of two laps around a regulation track without stopping

Meets the age- and gender-specific health-related fitness standards defined by FITNESSGRAM

Grades 6–8
Self-assesses heart rate before, during, and after vigorous PA

Maintains heart rate in target zone for a minimum of 20 minutes

Grades 9–12
Develops a personal fitness profile based on fitness assessment results

Maintains appropriate levels of cardio-respiratory endurance, muscular strength and endurance, flexibility, and body composition

### Exhibits responsible personal and social behavior that respects self and others in PA settings

Grades K–2
Shows compassion for others by helping them

Accepts all playmates without regard to personal differences

Grades 3–5
Cooperates with class members by taking turns and sharing equipment

Assesses and takes responsibility for his or her own behavior without blaming others

Grades 6–8
Shows self-control by accepting a controversial decision by a referee

Seeks out, participates with, and shows respect for a peer with lesser skill ability

Grades 9–12
Invites less-skilled students to participate in a warm-up activity prior to class

Shows leadership by diffusing conflict during competition

### Values physical activity for health, enjoyment, challenge, self-expression, and/or social interaction

Grades K–2
Willingly tries new movements and skills

Exhibits both verbal and nonverbal indicators of enjoyment

Grades 3–5
Selects and practices a skill on which improvement is needed

Chooses to participate in group physical activities

Grades 6–8
Sees learning new activities and skills as challenging

Invites all students, regardless of ability, to participate in activities

Grades 9–12
Enjoys working with others in a sport activity to achieve a common goal

Identifies reasons to participate in PA

SOURCE: NASPE (2004b).

The NASPE standards and performance outcome suggestions represented the first national effort (1) to define what physical education programs in schools should attempt to achieve and (2) to provide examples that define outcomes. It should be noted, however, that this initiative did not specify the actual activities that should be taught at each grade level that would lead to reaching the desired outcomes. That is, it does not prescribe an activity curriculum. Outcomes at each grade level could be achieved using very different activities. Physical education teachers, even in school districts that have adopted the NASPE standards, are essentially free to choose the activities that compose their yearly curriculum at each grade level. One can even imagine that a physical education teacher could choose to use dodgeball as a regular activity in the physical education yearly schedule and argue that it met NASPE standards, even though that activity is widely viewed as highly inappropriate for physical education.

## CONTEMPORARY CURRICULUM AND INSTRUCTION MODELS

Views of what physical education *should be* often involve a philosophical point of view within which there is a strong value orientation (Jewett & Bain, 1985). The education-through-the-physical model started with optimal individual development within a democratic social framework as its primary value orientation. From that value orientation, Physical Educators set goals and chose activity experiences to meet those goals, thereby creating a physical education curriculum that is taught to students using an instructional process that reflects those values. A *curriculum* is not just a group of activities. Rather, it is a sequence of activities based on an explicit programs mission, taught from a particular *instructional* perspective, that lead to outcomes that reflect a value orientation.

The purpose of this section is to introduce you to important curriculum and instruction models that are prominent within American physical education. Some are more appropriate for elementary school grades, while others are more prevalent in secondary school programs. Still others can be employed across the full K–12 spectrum.

## The Skill Themes Model

As noted earlier, American physical educators such as Eleanor Metheny and Rosalind Cassidy were influenced by the work of Rudolph Laban, whose influence in the movement arts, especially dance, was widespread in Europe. The movement education curriculum was organized around three areas: educational dance, educational gymnastics, and educational games. Movement education was innovative in both teaching method and curriculum design. Teaching methods emphasized problem solving, guided discovery, and exploration. The curriculum is defined by movement concepts, such as absorbing force or striking, rather than games or sports. The aesthetic dimension of performance was highly valued. Competition was kept to a minimum.

The movement-education approach gradually evolved into the skill themes model, mainly through the influence of the Canadian physical education and dance educator Sheila Stanley and American physical educator Kate Barrett. Today, the most prominent advocates of the skill themes model are George Graham, Shirley Holt-Hale, and Melissa Parker, who suggest that "skill themes are fundamental movements that form the foundation for success in sports and physical activities in later years.... Initially we focus on one skill at a time, and then in later grades they are combined with other skills and used in more complex settings, such as those found in dance, games, and gymnastics" (p. 17; Graham, Holt-Hale, & Parker, 2010). (See Focus On Box 4.4 for examples of skill themes.)

Teachers who use the skill themes model focus on helping young children learn to perform a variety of locomotor, nonmanipulative, and manipulative motor skills such as throwing, catching, volleying, dribbling, balancing, striking with implements, and dodging. They also learn movement concepts such

| FOCUS ON | Skill Themes* | 4.4 |
|---|---|---|
| Locomotor Skills | Nonmanipulative Skills | Manipulative Skills |
| Walking | Turning | Throwing |
| Running | Twisting | Catching/collecting |
| Hopping | Rolling | Kicking |
| Skipping | Balancing | Punting |
| Galloping | Transferring weight | Dribbling |
| Sliding | Jumping and landing | Volleying |
| Chasing, fleeing, dodging | Stretching | Striking with racquets |

*Examples of skills taught in skill theme elementary-school physical education programs. The list is not all-inclusive but provides examples of skill themes.

SOURCE: Adapted from Graham et al., 2010

as location (self-space and general space), directions (such as up/down, forward/backward, and right/left), levels (such as low and high), pathways (such as straight, curved, and zig-zag), and extensions (such as large/small and far/near) (Graham et al., 2010).

The skill themes model typically has all children involved in activity all of the time during class sessions, also ensuring that a fair portion of that time is devoted to moderate-to-vigorous activity (MVPA), thus meeting a key national physical activity recommendation (U.S.D.H.H.S., 2008), and the physical education–related health objectives in Healthy People 2020 (U.S.D.H.H.S., 2011). Teachers constantly observe students and provide feedback and encouragement. As a result, children learn how to assess their own progress and how to provide assistance to classmates by observing their efforts and providing feedback. Students progress through four generic levels of skill proficiency (Graham et al., 2010). Most students begin at the precontrol level where responses are often awkward, and repeated movements in succession cannot be done. They advance to the control level where correct skill movements appear more frequently. Students then can move to the level where the skill is used in combination with other skills in less predictable situations.

Finally, they achieve the proficiency level where they can focus outward, on the goal or larger dimensions of the activity, while performing the skill without having to pay attention to the critical elements of the skill. This final stage is important because achieving proficiency allows children to participate successfully in a number of game, sport, dance, and gymnastic activities.

The progress that students make is of course determined to a large degree by the amount of time that they have to learn. If K–5 physical education occurs only once per week, then teachers can achieve only limited outcomes. If, however, children in the K–5 grades have daily physical education, they can develop a thorough repertoire of skills that are useful in a large number of games, sports, dances, outdoor, and gymnastic activities. If children reach middle school without reasonable proficiency in a number of skills, they are unlikely to be able to participate successfully in the activities typically included in middle-school physical education programs. Many physical education advocates have become convinced that the greatest investment schools can make in physical education is to provide sufficient time in the K–5 grades.

## The Health-Optimizing Physical Education Model

Fifty years ago, physical education programs that emphasized fitness development would have students doing jumping jacks, push-ups, sit-ups, sprints, and distance running, using approaches not unlike those typically seen in the military, typically with the whole class participating in unison following commands from the teacher. In hindsight, this approach had two serious flaws. First, an assumption was made that each person would respond in the same way to a particular fitness regimen. Research on how heredity genetic endowment affects people's response to exercise (Bouchard & Rankinen, 2001) has clearly shown this assumption to be false. Some people improve a lot, others improve somewhat less, while others may improve very little. Moreover, just because you improve in one area of health-related fitness (e.g., cardio-vascular performance) does not guarantee that you improve to the same extent in terms of muscular strength. Just as one's hair color and height have a genetic link, so does response to exercise.

Second, in the 1970s, partly as a consequence of the physical fitness boom, physical educators were trained to use a performance-oriented fitness development model when teaching children and youth (Corbin, Pangrazi, & Welk, 1994). This model was based on research done with adults which was shown to work. It is fair to say, however, that for the majority of students this was not exciting or fun. It is also fair to say that this model for fitness probably turned many students away from adopting a physically active lifestyle. The required amounts and sustained intensities of exercise needed simply did not match the natural activity pattern of children and youth, and consequently were aversive.

Over the past decade, data on the increasing rates of overweight and obesity among American children and youths have led to a flurry of reports and recommendations to increase the amount of time that children and youths participate in physical activity, particularly physical activity that is of a moderate-to-vigorous nature. Thom McKenzie, in his 2007 Dudley A. Sargent Commemorative Lecture, described the problem in clear terms:

> Sedentary living is a serious global public health problem that is associated with numerous preventable diseases. Schools are in a position to be the most cost-effective public resource to combat inactivity. In schools Physical Educators are positioned to be the strongest advocates for a healthy, active lifestyle. To effectively promote physical activity on school campuses and to encourage it in communities beyond the school day, Physical Educators will need to develop skills that are not typically stressed in undergraduate physical education teacher education programs.

Health-Optimizing Physical Education (HOPE) has as its primary goal that children and youths develop and value a physically active lifestyle. The HOPE approach also seeks to ensure that schools provide adequate daily physical activity for students, including an appropriate amount of MVPA. In HOPE models, physical educators typically have an expanded role that goes beyond their responsibilities to plan and teach the physical education classes. HOPE models typically aim to engage students in physical activity not only in physical education classes, but also at recess, during classroom breaks, at the start of the school day, and through programs that involve students in physical activity outside of school hours (Brewer, Luebbers, & Shane, 2009). HOPE models also help students learn ways of managing their physical-activity behavior through planning, goal setting, self-monitoring, self-reinforcement, and resisting negative influences that prevent engagement in physical activity.

Many advocates of HOPE support an ecological approach that emphasizes the multiple levels of influence and the role of various environments that affect the physical activity levels of children and youths (e.g., Sallis & Glanz, 2006; Ward, Saunders, & Pate, 2007). The ecological model suggests that

- Physical education instruction be designed to increase the enjoyment of physical activity.
- Physical education activities allow students to interact socially while being physically active.

- Physical activity beyond the physical education class and beyond the school setting is promoted.

- Students learn behavioral skills such as goal setting, overcoming barriers, and seeking support.

- Physical activity homework incorporates family members in physical activity.

- Schools engage with community agencies to provide after-school physical-activity opportunities.

- Schools support physical-activity breaks in classrooms and physical-activity sessions to start the school day.

Physical educators and school leaders who are interested in developing a HOPE program in their school or district can gain access to a number of programmatic approaches that have been used throughout the United States. Some of these are described briefly:

- SPARK (Sports, Play, and Active Recreation for Kids) is a nationally tested program that includes instructional and content resources for pre-K, K–2, 3–6, middle school, and high school. It also includes strategies and guidelines for creating after-school physical activity opportunities. SPARK has a full-fledged professional staff development program available as well as a full menu of individual workshops (www.sparkpe.org).

- M-SPAN (Middle School Physical Activity and Nutrition) was the first HOPE program to focus especially on middle-school students (www.sparkpe.org/programMiddlePE.jsp). It also includes a strong emphasis on maximizing the use of an entire school's physical activity venues before school hours, at lunchtime, and after school hours.

- PEforLife is a national nonprofit organization promoting middle- and secondary-school physical education programs that focus on developing lifetime physical-activity habits (www.PE4life.org).

- Take10! is a classroom-based physical-activity program for elementary schools that integrates grade-specific academic materials with MVPA in 10-minute segments in the classroom (www.take10.net).

- The Active and Healthy Schools program provides resources for teachers to facilitate physical activity throughout the school day beyond the regular physical education lessons (including the before school, recess, and lunch recess periods), to encourage better eating, and teach sun safety (www.activeandhealthyschools.com/).

HOPE-like models have become somewhat popular at the high-school level. In some high schools, the primary space for physical education looks very much like a community fitness center—and, in many cases, it is exactly that! Schools join forces with community agencies and organizations such as boys and girls clubs, parks and recreation, and community education to develop and sustain fitness centers at high schools that are used by students during the school day and then are also accessible for community members during after-school and weekend hours. Most of these HOPE models include information about nutrition and healthy lifestyles, along with the physical-activity portions of the program.

Nonetheless many secondary-school physical education programs today still have a separate physical fitness unit that operates about three weeks in the fall and then sometimes one in the spring. For the remainder of the year, the program remains focused on sport-oriented units. Concerns about overweight and obesity problems along with associated illnesses and health care costs have brought the importance of moderate to vigorous physical activity (MVPA) into the spotlight for physical educators at all levels. With all we now know about the health benefits of physical activity, it is important that each physical education lesson afford students the opportunity to accumulate substantial amounts of physical activity. Although this can be accomplished through many types of content, it is now more common that each lesson include time and content that has a distinct health-related fitness focus.

The HOPE goals can be achieved by any program that (1) contributes adequately to the amount of MVPA that students get in their physical education classes and (2) influences them to lead a more physically active lifestyle beyond the physical education program. What HOPE has done is to make those the primary goals and to focus on them consistently throughout the entire physical education program.

## The Concepts-based Physical Education Model

Over the last five decades, concept-based physical education has emerged as a prominent curriculum model. With its roots in the basic instruction programs of colleges and universities (Corbin & Cardinal, 2008), concepts-based physical education courses first emerged during the 1960s as an alternative to the traditionally required skills courses on college campuses. Since then, Fitness for Life has emerged as a widely used and well-known concepts-based curriculum model in high schools. Developed by Charles Corbin, its primary goal is the promotion of lifelong physical activity and healthy lifestyles that will contribute to a person's lifelong fitness, wellness, and health. Fitness for Life trains students to become well-informed fitness consumers who are fit and engaged in physical activity, and who understand the principles and strategies to develop and maintain fitness, know how to self-assess their fitness, and develop realistic fitness and activity goals, manage their physical activity, and make informed decisions about all matters related to fitness, wellness, and health. As students move through the curriculum, they learn about fitness-, health-, and wellness-related concepts and strategies such as fitness planning, managing stress, understanding the differences between skill- and health-related fitness, and making informed choices as a fitness consumer (e.g., discriminating between quality fitness-related products and quackery).

The Fitness for Life model now has been expanded to include curricular resources for use in high schools (Corbin & Lindsey, 2007), middle schools (Corbin, Le Masurier, & Lambdin, 2007) and elementary schools (Corbin, Le Masurier, Lambdin, & Greiner, 2010). All include extensive ancillary resources for teachers to deliver the program. The elementary-level Fitness for Life program increases the role of the classroom teachers by encouraging them to allocate time throughout the school week for classroom-based physical activity breaks and instruction about fitness concepts.

When employing Fitness for Life, teachers alternate classroom-based sessions with activity sessions. During the classroom sessions teachers introduce students to the key concepts and principles that underlie fitness development. The activity sessions are linked with the content from the classroom sessions. For example, if the topic is on developing flexibility, the classroom session will provide the context, during which students learn to define flexibility, under what type of fitness it falls (i.e., skill- vs. health-related fitness), and why maintaining flexibility is important. In the related activity sessions, students learn how to assess their flexibility and engage in safe exercises that directly target flexibility.

There is some evidence that students (especially boys) who were instructed using the Fitness for Life curriculum in high school are less likely to be sedentary beyond the completion of the course compared to those students who participated in a more traditional physical education course (Dale, Corbin, & Cuddihy, 1998). Moreover, the differences in physical activity levels were sustained for at least 1 1/2 years after completion of the Fitness for Life course (Dale & Corbin, 2000).

## The Academic Integration Model

In the 1960s and 1970s, the academic discipline of kinesiology emerged, extending and deepening the knowledge base in what were increasingly referred to as the subdisciplines of kinesiology: motor behavior, biomechanics, exercise physiology, sport sociology, sport psychology, sport humanities, and sport pedagogy (see also Chapter 13). In the 1980s, some high-school physical education programs moved to a concepts curriculum (Siedentop et al., 1986) in which knowledge of the kinesiology subdisciplines was blended with activity programs that split time between the classroom and the gymnasium. Lawson and Placek (1981) defined this model as "a unique blend of performance skills and experience in sport, exercise, dance, and contests with that knowledge about performance which is derived from the disciplinary foundations of our field" (p. 6).

In the 1980s, AAHPERD published a series of booklets entitled *Basic Stuff*, which focused on important concepts in exercise physiology, kinesiology, motor learning, motor development, sport humanities, and the psychosocial aspects of sport. This series sought to provide physical education teachers with information and strategies to incorporate disciplinary knowledge into their physical education classes.

The academic discipline model gradually gave way to an emphasis on *integration*. The integration model suggests that knowledge and skills traditionally taught in gymnasiums and those traditionally taught in classrooms can be integrated. A Russian folk dance might be taught during a fifth-grade social studies unit, the early Olympic Games could be taught in a ninth-grade history class, or the concept of force in a ninth-grade science class might be illustrated by how force is generated when performing a shot put or high jump. Likewise, physical educators could easily teach environmental knowledge and skills in outdoor education units and incorporate many scientific principles in a middle-school track-and-field unit.

Integration seems to be most popular in elementary and middle schools where subjects such as language arts can be integrated easily with physical education or outdoor adventure skills can be easily integrated with a classroom focus on environmental education. Integration has been a major goal of schools that are often referred to as *magnet* or *alternative schools*. An excellent example is an alternative elementary school where adventure education is the integrating force for the entire school curriculum (Stroot, Carpenter, & Eisnaugle, 1991).

The academic integration model, however, has seen reduced use in elementary and middle schools in recent years as education reform in the wake of the No Child Left Behind Act caused schools to focus on increasing the time devoted to subjects included on yearly state tests. These tests typically focus on basic knowledge in reading, mathematics, and science, that is, the application of how that knowledge is integrated into more practical settings is less often tested.

It should be noted that the academic integration model has become very popular in elective physical education programs in the eleventh and twelfth grades of high school in Australia, New Zealand, and England (Macdonald & Leitch, 1994). Often these programs offer beginning preparation for careers in athletic training, physical therapy, and sport management.

## The Personal and Social Responsibility Model

An important educational influence of the 1960s to 1970s was the humanistic education movement that focused on treating students as individuals and focusing primarily on personal growth and social responsibility rather than solely on academic achievement. In physical education, this approach has been developed and articulated consistently by Donald Hellison (1973, 1978, 1983, 2003).

The personal and social responsibility model (PSRM) is designed to help young people cope better with a complex social world, to achieve a higher degree of control over their own lives, and to contribute more positively to the small social worlds of which they are a part. The primary medium through which these goals are sought is physical education: the gymnasium, the weight room, and the playing field. The PSRM is well tested and has been used successfully in a variety of settings. In the 1990s, problems associated with youths became a major issue in American life (Carnegie Council on Adolescent Development, 1992): vandalism, dropout rates, teen pregnancy, violence, and drug use drew national attention. Many physical education teachers in urban schools, particularly middle and high schools, feel that cooperation, social development, and responsibility are as important outcomes as skill and fitness (Ennis, Ross, & Chen, 1992). For these teachers and for many others, PSRM continues to be a useful curricular and pedagogical approach, either in its full form or as a supporting pedagogical strategy in the physical education curriculum.

Many physical education teachers, especially elementary specialists, have used aspects of the PSRM to assist with maintaining appropriate behavior in class and to help children learn to be more responsible. For example, many elementary-school physical education teachers create a simple system for students to gauge their own behavior during physical education class. These students can use a four- to five-level chart to assess their own behavior in cooperating, helping, and avoiding harm to other students during class. As students leave the gymnasium, they indicate the level on the chart that represents their social and behavioral performance during the class. If the teacher disagrees with the choice made by a student, the teacher and student discuss their differences in perceptions of behavior for that day.

The PSRM does not specify particular activities, but it does create a particular pedagogical approach. Hellison (1995) developed a five-level progression of personal and social development (see Focus On Box 4.5). Level 1 focuses on respect for others; level 2, on demonstrating effort within class; level 3, on

---

## FOCUS ON    Hellison's Responsibility-in-the-Gym Model                    4.5

**Major focus:** Put kids first! Teachers have to care about students as whole persons. The teacher–student relationship is fundamentally important. Teachers have to respect students' struggles, individuality, and capacity for growth.

**Purpose:** To help students take responsibility for their own well-being and learn to be sensitive and responsive to the well-being of others.

| Responsibility Levels | Instructor Values |
|---|---|
| 1. Respect for others' rights and feelings | Respect for students, equity, and empowerment |
| • Control temper and words. Offer empowerment. <br> • Acknowledge right to be included. <br> • Foster peaceful conflict resolution. | |
| 2. Effort | Self-paced task mastery, task variation, competitive choices |
| • Explore effort and new tasks variation. Competitive choices. <br> • Self-motivation. <br> • Learn persistence. | |
| 3. Self-direction | Empowerment |
| • Independence <br> • Goal-setting progressions <br> • Resisting peer pressure | |
| 4. Helping | Well-being of others |
| • Sensitivity and responsiveness <br> • Leadership <br> • Group welfare | |
| 5. Outside the gym | Values transfer |
| • Trying levels in other settings <br> • Being a role model | |

Source: Adapted from Hellison, 1995.

self-direction as a learner and class member; level 4, on helping others; and level 5, on demonstrating those qualities outside the physical education setting. The levels are viewed as a progression, that is, students have to learn to control themselves and show respect for the rights and feelings of their classmates before they can focus on self-motivation and persistence in the learning setting.

## The Sport Education Model

A more recent entry into the physical education curriculum and instruction literature is Sport Education (Siedentop, 1994; Siedentop et al., 2011). Although Sport Education was created as a way to help students learn and enjoy various sports, it has also been used for a large number of activities such as dance, cycling, outdoor adventure activities, and various other fitness activities.

Within this model, sport, dance, and fitness activities are organized as *playful competitions*, thus deriving its main conceptual focus from what Siedentop (1980) describes as "play education." Sport Education has five defining characteristics that distinguish it from more traditional forms of physical education:

1. Sport Education is divided into *seasons* that are longer than typical physical education units in a multi-activity program. Elementary-school seasons last 10 to 12 class sessions; middle-school seasons, 12 to 15 class sessions; and high-school seasons, 15 to 22 class sessions.

2. Students are organized immediately into teams, and they retain that *affiliation* throughout the season.

3. Seasons are built around a series of *competitions* that grow increasingly complex as students master the techniques and tactics involved in the activity for that season. Accommodations are made as well for students with varying skill and experiences by employing graded competition, where contests pit teams of similar skill level against each other so that the outcome of the contest is more likely to be uncertain.

4. The season ends with a *culminating event* that not only determines the seasonal champion but also provides a festive way to conclude the experience. Across all levels, sport always has a distinctly festive nature, yet this is what is largely absent when students engage in sport during physical education.

5. Records are kept throughout the season so that students and teams can mark their progress.

In Sport Education, teams are organized so that each team has a mixture of more and less-skilled students. A great deal of the responsibility for ensuring a successful season falls on the team members. Each team member has a role to play in ensuring that the team performs well and that the season is a success. The roles are determined partially by the nature of the activity; that is, in a sport activity, each team would have a coach, manager, statistician, trainer, and the like, or in a dance activity, each team would have a coach, manager, choreographer, costume designer, music manager, and the like. Each student on each team would also have a role ensuring that the competitions are run smoothly and appropriately; that is, each team member would act as a referee and/or scorekeeper for competitions during the season. Most Sport Education seasons use a three-team model so that the competition is between team 1 and team 3 with team 2 acting as the *duty team*, providing the referees and scorekeepers and managing the transition between competitions.

Being successful at play increases enjoyment.

As students gain experience in Sport Education, their roles can be expanded. Each team might have a *publicist*, and the three students acting in that role for their teams would together decide how to publicize the season and the performances of teams and individuals. In one middle-school model, the team publicists together created a weekly column in the school newspaper that featured the standings and highlights of the Sport Education seasons. In a national trial of Sport Education in New Zealand, one high school added the role of athletic trainer to the model. The trainer had to be knowledgeable about the kind of injuries likely to occur in the activity for the season, have a training kit ready to assist if a student was injured, and provide assistance to the teacher in such a case.

The Sport Education model is based on the assumption that *good* competition is both fun and educationally useful. The model developed from the views that students should be able to compete against other students of reasonably equal abilities and that the games, sports, and activities should always be *small-sided* so that all players are in the action continuously. Thus, in a volleyball season, a 3 v 3 competition would be preferable to the standard 6 v 6. In an elementary-school soccer season, a series of competitions might begin with a 2 v 2 competition, then move to 3 v 3, and culminate with a 5 v 5 competition. In addition to employing smaller team sizes, the model also encourages teachers to modify the conditions of play to help students acquire techniques and tactics. That is, teachers may lower the baskets in basketball or a lower the net and provide friendlier balls in volleyball.

The Sport Education model has been used at all levels from third grade through high school (Bell, 1998; Jones & Ward, 1998; Siedentop et al., 2011). It has also made inroads in the delivery of Basic Instruction programs universities (e.g., Bennett & Hastie, 1997). For example, the Physical Education Teacher Education program at West Virginia University employs Sport Education in its Basic Instruction program (Meeteer, Housner, Bulger, Hawkins, & Wiegand, in press). Moreover, it can help raise disability awareness (e.g., Foley, Tindall, Lieberman,

& Kim, 2007). Teachers have found the model to be an excellent vehicle for helping students to assume more responsibility for their own sport involvement. The team-membership feature produces situations that require students to work together to achieve team goals. The various roles of Sport Education (coach, referee, scorer, trainer, statistician) require responsible performance from every team member for the season to move forward. Teachers also report that Sport Education produces excitement among students and encourages them to seek other sport opportunities outside the school (Grant, 1992; Kinchen, 2006).

The Sport Education model can accommodate a wide variety of activities other than traditional team and individual sports. For example, it has been used for a weight-lifting and strength-training season for high-school girls (Sweeney, Tannehill, & Teeters, 1992) in which students were judged both on the weight lifted and on the lifting technique. It has also been used for a dance season (Graves & Townsend, 2000; Richardson & Oslin, 2003) in which students learned and performed dances from the 1960s to 1990s (see Focus On Box 4.6). It has also been used for an elementary-school level bicycle safety season in which students learned cycling skills and safety skills, a season that culminated with a synchronized team bicycle ride (Sinelnikov, Hastie, Cole, & Schneulle, 2005).

Sport Education is now used widely in New Zealand, Australia, England, Korea, and Japan where reports from teachers are promising and enthusiastic. Sport Education has also been investigated more thoroughly than most curriculum and instruction models. Two national reviews in Australia indicated that students preferred the Sport Education model to their previous experiences in physical education. Recently, Wallhead and O'Sullivan (2005) and Kinchin (2006) conducted comprehensive reviews of all the completed research on Sport Education. The evidence shows that:

1. Students prefer Sport Education compared to their prior physical education experiences.

---

**FOCUS ON** — Sport Education Dance Fever Season     **4.6**

| | |
|---|---|
| Day 1 | Introduce dance skills, explain dance fever competition, assign students to dance troupes. |
| Days 2–7 | Introduce dances of various eras; practice dance techniques; dance troupes assign members to various roles; introduce dance-judging techniques. |
| Days 8–12 | Dance troupes learn dances from the 1950s to 1990s. |
| Days 13–15 | Dance troupes choose and practice dances for competitions. |
| Day 16 | Dance fever competition, 1950s to 1960s. |

| | |
|---|---|
| Day 17 | Dance fever competition, 1970s. |
| Day 18 | Dance fever competition, 1980s. |
| Day 19 | Dance fever competition, 1980s. |
| Day 20 | Dance fever competition, 1990s. |
| Day 21 | Culminating event and awards. |

*Student roles*: Choreographer, fitness trainer, disc jockey, master of ceremonies, dance judge

*Possible dances*: Twist, Mashed Potato, Funky Chicken, Swim, Disco Duck, Hustle, YMCA, Saturday Night Fever, Break Dancing, Moonwalk, Robotics, Cabbage Patch, Macarena, Electric Slide, Line, Men in Black

SOURCE: Adapted from Graves & Townsend (2000).

---

2. Students who experience Sport Education for the first time report that they hope their teacher continues to use the model.

3. Students show enthusiasm for Sport Education across a diversity of sport education settings.

4. Both boys and girls work harder in the Sport Education context.

5. Students demonstrate better attendance, are more appropriately dressed for activity, and are less likely to avoid participation.

6. Students like the longer Sport Education seasons because there is more time to learn the activity, more time to play it, and more time to be with teammates.

7. Students demonstrate loyalty to their teams.

8. Lower-skilled students appreciate teammates who encourage and support their development.

9. Lower-skilled students particularly seem to benefit from their Sport Education experiences.

10. Girls tend to gain confidence and are more willing to participate.

11. Most students report they had improved in terms of developing better techniques and applying tactics.

12. The model's emphasis on persistent team membership promotes students' personal and social development through improving student responsibility, cooperation, and trust skills.

13. Sport Education provides typically nonparticipating and lower-skilled students a more equitable learning environment.

14. Learning opportunities for all students are higher in both quality and quantity.

Furthermore, there is now a sizable number of professional articles showing teachers how to use the model at various grade levels and across various activities (e.g., Alexander, Taggart, & Luckman, 1998; Bell, 1998; Jones & Ward, 1998; Sluder, Buchanan, & Sinelnikov, 2009).

## The Adventure Education Approach

Two major trends together have led to the development of **adventure education** in physical education. First, the idea that adventure activities—particularly risk activities in the natural environment—have the potential for education and character development has grown consistently in educational philosophy throughout the twentieth century and into the twenty-first. Second, public interest in outdoor recreation has increased substantially for the past several decades. Taken together, these two trends have made it possible for physical educators to conceptualize and implement an adventure education curriculum within physical education.

Adventure education often includes wilderness sports and outdoor pursuits. Activities such as backpacking, kayaking, scuba diving, and caving take place in natural environments and often involve some risk. Adventure education includes not only these *natural* activities but also those created for specific educational purposes. Thus, a high-ropes course or an initiatives course is designed and built so that students can experience the challenge inherent in the design. A high-ropes course is a series of obstacles that the student must overcome from 20 to 40 feet in the air, on ropes strung between trees in a wooded area. Although a harness secures the students, there is no net underneath them as they climb, crawl, and jump through the ropes course. Such higher risk activities provide excellent means to having students learn about their own limits, build their confidence, and develop cooperation skills. In initiatives, 8 to 20 participants work together to solve an unusual task, such as how to get all members of a group over a 12-foot-high wall.

There are two sets of goals within adventure education programs. The first set of goals is to gain to develop skills, to participate safely, and to gain utmost satisfaction from participation—for example, to ski well enough to do it safely and to be excited about doing it again. These kinds of goals are traditional and are not unlike those of other physical education curriculum models (Siedentop et al., 1986).

A second set of goals, however, has more to do with problem solving, self-concept, and personal growth. These goals are typically emphasized in the *adventure* portion of the program, in activities where obstacles are designed to produce some risk, and with the assumption that the risk produces anxiety and stress for the participants. When participants learn to deal with the stress and to overcome the anxiety to solve the problem created by the obstacle, then personal growth is assumed to occur. Because

this is often done within the context of a *group*, the interactions among members of the group also become an important educational focus.

Adventure education can also be taught successfully in gym classes, on the grounds around the school, and at outdoor camps. Climbing walls and bouldering walls are increasingly being used in schools at all levels. Some schools develop spaces in the immediate school area that accommodate learning outdoor skills. Beginning skills in orienteering, for example, can be taught using maps of school grounds. Many adventure activities can be modified to teach in regular school facilities. Indeed, some of the best adventure units in schools are taught within regular school facilities. Some schools develop outdoor adventure education units at school to introduce students to skills and activities, following it with an adventure education trip to an outdoor facility. In this model, students may spend extended periods of time together, sharing meals and staying overnight. The group experience fosters a sense of involvement and intimacy that is difficult to recreate in regular physical education classes at the school site.

The purposes of adventure education show both similarities to and differences from more traditional physical education goals (Siedentop et al., 1986, p. 215):

1. To learn outdoor sports skills and enjoy the satisfaction of competence.

2. To live within the limits of personal ability related to an activity and the environment.

3. To find pleasure in accepting the challenge and risk of stressful physical activity.

4. To learn mutual dependency of self and the natural world.

5. To share this experience and learning with classmates and authority figures.

Teaching within this model is obviously different from meeting in classes at an appointed hour in a gymnasium. More time is needed. Instruction often takes place in small groups. Risk is involved, so safety becomes a paramount concern. Because travel

Adventure education, such as a high-ropes course, provides exciting challenges.

involves longer time together, more quality time is spent with students. Teachers must have skills for interacting with and guiding students in such situations. Also, particularly with wilderness sports, teachers must have some substantial experience and skills in the activity being taught.

Physical educators can gain the needed skills and knowledge to build adventure education into their program. For example, *Project Adventure* is a nonprofit organization with excellent resources. They have published helpful curriculum materials to assist teachers in implementing adventure education at elementary-, middle-, and high-school levels (www.pa.org). Project Adventure also is a source for much of the equipment needed to do adventure activities and provides workshops specific to different kinds of adventure activities. Many physical education teachers have become Project Adventure–certified and have implemented semesterlong courses in high schools, and have integrated adventure education into elementary- and middle-school physical education curricula.

Another example of a program where teachers can broaden their skills and knowledge is the National Outdoor Leadership School (NOLS—www.NOLS.edu). The increasing interest in integrating different school subjects and the green movement has also given rise to programs where traditional adventure education is combined with environmental education. For example, through the *Green Edventures* program where traditional adventure education content is integrated with classroom subjects such as environmental education and marine biology (www.greenedventures.com).

## The Games-based Teaching of Sport Games Model

In 1986 British physical educators Rod Thorpe, David Bunker, and Len Almond published a book entitled *Rethinking Games Teaching*. The book called into question the traditional approach to teaching games. That is, begin by teaching skills, and after students develop skills to a certain level, educators teach how to use the skills in games. Proponents call their approach "teaching games for understanding" (TGFU), and argue that students first have to understand the tactical problems posed by games in order to see how the skills should be used. TGFU (sometimes also referred to as the "games sense approach") has now become a prominent international movement among physical educators who subscribe to this point of view and want to learn more about how to implement it in elementary-, middle-, and high-school physical education. Many physical education teachers have suffered through the frustration of teaching a sport unit by beginning with isolated skill drills with some modicum of success shown by students, only to see them unable to use the skill appropriately in even a modified-game environment.

Advocates of the games-based approach to teaching games note that games are in essence a set of problems that needs to be solved. That is, in a game of hockey, the offense has to determine ways to maintain possession of the puck and create scoring opportunities, whereas the defense's problem is to prevent the opposing team from scoring, and to regain possession of the puck. When viewed from this perspective, you can see how players must learn both to execute technical and tactical moves, and understand when to use both.

This movement is as much about pedagogy as it is about curriculum, but it has given a strong boost to those physical educators who still see games and sports as fundamental parts of the physical education curriculum. In America it is common to hear this approach described as a tactical games approach to teaching sport skills (Mitchell, Oslin & Griffin, 2006). Another valuable addition to this movement toward better teaching of sports and games came in 2001 with the publication of Australian Alan Launder's book *Play Practice: The Games Approach to Teaching and Coaching*. In this book, Launder uses the term *technique* as a substitute for what traditionally had been called a *skill*. That is, passing in volleyball, jump shooting in basketball, and fielding ground balls in softball are all techniques. They are all actions to control an object such as a ball or shuttlecock. Launder argues that techniques + tactics = skill. He offers a number of examples of how teachers could develop techniques and tactics together using small-sided and tactically simplified mini-games, then gradually increasing the complexity of the game as students improve in their execution and understanding of needed techniques and tactical moves—what he calls the development of "game sense."

What the teaching games movement has achieved is a much stronger sense of how to organize games units for a physical education curriculum. Small-sided games with simple rules in smaller spaces with modified rules are used to teach techniques and tactics simultaneously so that students learn to understand how the nature of the tactical situation determines what techniques are needed to be successful.

It should be noted that in many parts of the world, the teaching games movement, originally brought forward in physical education, has begun to be adopted by national sport organizations as the preferred approach to use in developmental programs in junior sport. The Australian Sports Commission, for example, has developed a series of game sense–coaching resources for junior sport.

## The Eclectic Curriculum

Historically, most school districts require that a curriculum be developed for each subject matter taught in the district. For physical education, it is most common for the district curriculum to begin with either the NASPE standards or the state-level standards and then list all the activities that can be taught in the district. In many, if not most districts, the list of activities taught in physical education is very large. This is because of the possible liability issues if a physical education teacher sponsors an activity not on the approved list and a student gets injured during class, leaving the teacher, as well as school and district administrators liable. Likewise, the instructional strategies used by physical education teachers within a school district might vary widely, because specific requirements for instructional strategies are typically not included in district curriculum documents. Thus, traditionally, American physical educators have been free to choose both the specific content and the instructional strategies that they use in their classes. However, over the past decade or so, this tradition has begun to change somewhat as concerns over the low reading scores of young children have led to the development of K–3 reading curriculum and instruction models that are typically adopted at the district level. That is, all K–3 teachers in a district are trained to teach reading through a particular approach to the reading curriculum and use particular instructional strategies suggested by the curriculum developers.

School districts (and states) are now also starting to make similar decisions about what is to be taught in physical education. For example, recent Texas legislation required all school districts to adopt one of four state-approved health and physical education curriculum models for elementary schools, each of which includes suggestions for instructional practices. In another example, in Florida a one-semester course on health and fitness is required, typically in the ninth grade. These courses typically involve both classroom instruction and fitness activities in the gymnasium or fitness center. It should also be noted that it is common for students who are involved in school sport, band, Junior ROTC, cheerleading, or drill teams to be exempted from the fitness-course requirement.

Still, in most school districts the choice of activities and the instructional strategies used to teach those activities are left to the individual physical education teachers. And because of this, most programs still reflect the multi-activity model that has been historically prominent in America—that is, short activity units with modest amounts of instruction.

The differences between the models described in this chapter and this approach are substantial. Teachers cannot do skill themes, Sport Education, health-related physical education, adventure education, or the personal and social responsibility model without devoting substantial time to the content of the model and without using the pedagogical approach recommended by the model. Offering a large variety of activities in a program does not, in and of itself, ensure a good program; indeed, the multi-activity approach typically ensures that students will be unlikely to develop sufficient skill in the activity to pursue it outside of the class.

## The Subject Matter of Physical Education?

This chapter began with the assertion that it is more difficult to define *physical education* than to define either *sport* or *fitness*. The review of curricular options shows how valid that assertion is in contemporary physical education. Within these various curricula, one might see small children moving creatively to a poem, ninth-graders rappelling down the outside wall of their gymnasium, fifth-graders working hard as members of a soccer team engaged in a championship match, tenth-graders working out personal-fitness programs as part of a self-control exercise, and third-graders using different implements to hit different kinds of objects as part of a movement-education lesson on striking.

A stranger, viewing all such scenes and asking what is going on, might be told, "This is physical education!" If this stranger is middle-aged and has experienced a traditional form of physical education, it is easy to understand why (s)he might ask, "What's going on?" It is also easy to see why the answer—"This is physical education!"—might be surprising: The activities look so different from the traditional stereotype of "fizz-ed."

Each curriculum model has a different view of the subject matter of physical education. What *is* physical education? Is it education in sport? Is it fitness education? Is it social development? Is it development through risk and adventure? Is it movement? Is it just about getting students to be physically active? Instead, is it all these things—and maybe more? A subject matter so loosely defined that it excludes very little is inevitably going to include activities that are hardly useful or very difficult to defend by any criteria.

The question then becomes, "If physical education encompasses everything, can it ever stand for something specific and important?" Before answering that question, we turn to a key issue for physical education: The distinction between physical education and physical activity.

## Physical Education and Physical Activity—The Same or Different?

Despite its presence in U.S. schools for almost a century, physical education is oftentimes marginalized. Yet, over the course of its history it has been targeted as a possible solution to the ills of the nation, such as poor military readiness, or the apparent lack of youth fitness. The rising levels of overweight and obese children and youth over the last three decades are currently a major driving force behind the support for school physical education. The current support is unprecedented in terms of its scope. Parents are in strong support (see Focus On Box 4.7) as are many scientific and professional organizations (e.g., AAHPERD, American Heart Association, American Academy of Pediatrics), as well as several government agencies (e.g., Centers for Disease Control and Prevention, and the United States Department of Health & Human Services).

From the national health objectives in Healthy People 2020 (U.S.D.H.H.S., 2011) to the national physical activity recommendations for children, youth (NASPE, 2004a) and adults (U.S.D.H.H.S., 2008), to NASPE's new "Let's Move in Schools" initiative (www.aahperd.org/letsmoveinschool/), the focus on both physical education and physical activity has

never been greater. One problem is that the lines between the two have blurred. That is, the terms are used interchangeably, and, consequently, they have come to be regarded as the same thing. Although they are very much related, they are not the same!

**Physical Activity Defined**    *Physical activity* is defined as any kind of bodily movement that results in caloric expenditure. In its *2008 Physical Activity Guidelines for Americans*, the Department of Health and Human Services describes physical activity as bodily movement that enhances health. (U.S.D.H.H.S., 2008).

To derive health benefits a person needs to engage in an activity for at least a moderate level of intensity, but also include some activities that are more vigorous. Appropriate activities include jogging, rope jumping, swimming, dance, fitness activities, and playing games such as soccer and racquetball. Activities used for active transportation (e.g., to and from school or work) would also make important contributions.

The school day and environment includes several opportunities for structured and unstructured physical activity including physical education lessons, recess, lunch recess, before-, and after-school periods. The key is for physical educators to view their program as one that promotes and facilitates physical activity for all students throughout the full school day, not just the formal physical education class.

---

**FOCUS ON**    Public Support for School Physical Education      **4.7**

1. Ninety-five percent of parents said that physical education should be included in the school curriculum for all students in kindergarten through grade 12.

2. Eight-five percent of parents and 81% of teachers believe that students should be required to take physical education every day at every grade level,

and 92% of teens said that they should receive daily physical education.

3. More than 75% of parents and teachers believe that school boards should not eliminate physical education for budgetary reasons or because of the need to meet stricter academic standards.

SOURCE: http://www.aahperd.org/naspe/advocacy/events/mayWeek/keypoints.cfm

---

*FOCUS ON* — Healthy People 2020's Physical Activity in Schools                          4.8

**PA–4:** Increase the proportion of the nation's public and private schools that require daily physical education for all students.

**PA–5:** Increase the proportion of adolescents who participate in daily school physical education.

**PA–6.1:** Increase the number of states that require regularly scheduled elementary-school recess.

**PA–6.2:** Increase the proportion of school districts that require regularly scheduled elementary-school recess.

**PA–7:** Increase the proportion of school districts that require or recommend elementary-school recess for an appropriate period of time.

**PA–10:** Increase the proportion of the nation's public and private schools that provide access to their physical activity spaces and facilities for all persons outside of normal school hours (that is, before and after the school day, on weekends, and during summer and other vacations).

SOURCE: www.healthypeople.gov/hp2020/

---

The national physical activity recommendations for children and youth (U.S.D.H.H.S., 2008) are as follows:

1. Children and adolescents should do 60 minutes (1 hour) or more of physical activity daily.

   **Aerobic:** Most of the 60 or more minutes a day should be either moderate- or vigorous-intensity aerobic physical activity, and should include vigorous-intensity physical activity at least 3 days a week.

   **Muscle-strengthening:** As part of their 60 or more minutes of daily physical activity, children and adolescents should include muscle-strengthening physical activity on at least 3 days of the week.

   **Bone-strengthening:** As part of their 60 or more minutes of daily physical activity, children and adolescents should include bone-strengthening physical activity on at least 3 days of the week.

2. It is important to encourage young people to participate in physical activities that are appropriate for their age, that are enjoyable, and that offer variety.

The strong emphasis on increasing physical activity levels among children and youth is also reflected in the physical activity-related national health objectives recently proposed in Healthy People 2020 (www.healthypeople.gov/hp2020/). Those that directly target school settings are shown in Focus On Box 4.8.

The body of research on the relationship between physical activity and chronic disease risk reduction is now quite clear: Regularly engaging in moderate to vigorous physical activity throughout one's lifespan has enormous benefits. For example, physical activity can help reduce the risk of cardiovascular disease, reduce blood pressure, reduce cholesterol, reduce the risk of certain types of cancer (e.g., colon cancer), as well as reduce the risk of Type II diabetes. In addition, it can help improve mental health and reduce stress in that it can reduce anxiety and feelings of depression; it can improve one's mood and self-esteem (e.g., Landers, 1997). And the positive relationship between physical activity and academic achievement is especially pertinent for physical education professionals (Active Living Research, 2009; Centers for Disease Control and Prevention, 2010a; Trost & van der Mars, 2009; Trudeau & Shephard, 2010).

At the same time, however, physical activity has been systematically squeezed out of daily life in many developed countries. Thus, the fundamental question is: How do we educate and help prepare children and youth to come to value and enjoy physical activity to the point where they deliberately choose it over the countless competing sedentary activities, to make it a daily habit? This is where school physical education programs can make important contributions.

## Physical Education Defined

As a former K–12 student you have seen countless physical educators at work. Some you likely judged to be good, some to be mediocre, and some not so good. As a consequence you have formed your own ideas of what constitutes good physical education. The profession also has explicit expectations of what makes for "good quality" physical education, as well as standard for professional practice. As would be the case for physicians and attorneys, if you choose to be a physical educator, it is critical that you come to respect and accept the standards of professional practice set forth by your own profession.

The primary mission of every school physical education program is to equip all students with the skills, knowledge, and dispositions needed to make physical activity an integral part of daily life. NASPE defines quality physical education programs as those that (a) provide opportunities to learn, (b) deliver appropriate instruction, (c) deliver meaningful content, and (d) include ongoing student and program assessment (http://www.aahperd.org/naspe/publications/teachingTools/QualityPE.cfm).

Focus On Box 4.9 provides a brief overview of these four key program quality characteristics. Moreover, NASPE recommends that (a) schools provide 150 minutes of instructional physical education for elementary-school children, and 225 minutes for middle- and high-school students per week for the entire school year; and (b) teachers who deliver such programs are certified professionals.

In addition, the Centers for Disease Control and Prevention recently highlighted two key evidence-based strategies for improving the quality of school physical education programs (Centers for Disease Control and Prevention, 2010b). They include the implementation of a well-designed curriculum and provide physical education teachers with appropriate training and supervision.

## Well-designed Curriculum

The Centers for Disease Control (CDC) described a well-designed program as one that: (a) is founded on national, state or district-level content standards that outline what students should know and be able to do as a result of completing that program; (b) provides lessons during which students can reach moderate to vigorous physical activity (MVPA) at least 50% of the lesson time, and (c) include regular assessments to determine whether students are accumulating enough MVPA and achieving the desired learning objectives.

Improving the curriculum can be achieved by carefully selecting activities that inherently provide more opportunities for MVPA. Activities like aerobics, dance, and games such as soccer and team handball by their nature simply provide more opportunities for students to accumulate desirable levels of physical activity levels. On the other hand, MVPA levels during softball, kickball or gymnastics will likely be less (Centers for Disease Control and Prevention, 2010b).

## Appropriate Training and Supervision for Teachers of Physical Education

There is good evidence that teachers are central to improving the quality of physical education programs. Their skills include effective classroom management, activity design and selection, getting support and feedback on their instructional performance, and having peer-based mentoring support from master teachers. Moreover, proper training and support in developing sound class management skills, implementing specific curriculum programs, and having access to ongoing professional development are all critical to ensuring that students reach the desirable physical activity levels (Centers for Disease Control and Prevention, 2010b).

Recess, lunch recess, and before- and after-school programs offer significant physical activity opportunities. They have a more recreational character, though they also offer tremendous opportunities for learning. On the other hand physical education

**FOCUS ON** — NASPE's Definition of "Quality" School Physical Education — **4.9**

**1. Opportunity to Learn:**

- All students are required to take physical education
- Instructional periods totaling 150 minutes per week (elementary) and 225 minutes per week (middle and secondary school)
- Physical education class size consistent with that of other subject areas
- Qualified physical education specialist provides a developmentally appropriate program
- Adequate equipment and facilities

**2. Meaningful Content:**

- Written, sequential curriculum for grades P–12, based on state and/or national standards for physical education
- Instruction in a variety of motor skills designed to enhance the physical, mental, and social/emotional development of every child
- Fitness education and assessment to help children understand, improve, and/or maintain physical well-being
- Development of cognitive concepts about motor skill and fitness
- Opportunities to improve emerging social and co-operative skills and gain a multicultural perspective
- Promotion of regular amounts of appropriate physical activity now and throughout life?

**3. Appropriate Instruction:**

- Full inclusion of all students
- Maximum practice opportunities for class activities
- Well-designed lessons that facilitate student learning
- Out-of-school assignments that support learning and practice
- Physical activity not assigned as or withheld as punishment
- Regular assessment to monitor and reinforce student learning

**4. Student and Program Assessment:**

- Assessment is an ongoing, vital part of the physical education program
- Formative and summative assessment of student progress
- Student assessments aligned with state/national physical education standards and the written physical education curriculum
- Assessment of program elements that support quality physical education
- Stakeholders periodically evaluate the total physical education program effectiveness

SOURCE: Adapted from: http://www.aahperd.org/naspe/publications/teachingTools/QualityPE.cfm

lessons should first and foremost be educational in nature. This does not mean that students cannot have fun or enjoy themselves during the lessons. Given this distinction how do you see the relationship between physical education and physical activity? Reflecting on your own physical education experience as a student, how close did your K–12 physical education programs come to meeting these indicators of program quality? How well would you be able to explain this relationship? Once employed as a teacher, how will you help school administrators,

parents, and other constituents really understand the educative value of your physical education program?

Historically, one of the primary problems of physical education in schools is that teachers are largely free to decide how to deliver their program without any appreciable oversight or accountability by building and district administration, or by the state. Imagine if your physician were allowed to practice medicine in this way! Would you really want your medical care to be left to someone who still employs medical practices from the 1960s?

Thus, the perspective of "I can decide what I teach and how I teach" is not a defensible position. Like physicians, physical educators have a responsibility to provide the best possible care to their students.

## Physical Education for Students with Disabilities

The roots of what we now refer to as Adapted Physical Education go back to the 1920s when the parents of children who had been paralyzed in the 1915–1917 polio epidemic were ready to begin the children's public schooling (Sherrill, 2004). These children suffered from structural defects of the spine and lower extremities that were treated with corrective exercises: thus, *corrective physical education* was born. The main foci of this new field were strength, balance, and flexibility exercises to correct postural and structural defects and medical/remedial exercises to relieve health problems.

The next stage of development began during and shortly after World War II when thousands of service personnel needed both rehabilitation from injuries and special activity programming through which they could enjoy leisure. The field grew slowly and began to use the term *Adapted Physical Education* to describe the work done primarily in schools. In the early 1960s, the work of the Kennedy and Shriver families provided new impetus to expand the field to include sports and recreation, which eventually led to the creation of the Special Olympics and the field took on a broader agenda as *Adapted Physical Activity* (Stein, 2004). The information in Chapter 9 shows clearly the enormous growth of sports and physical activity for persons with disabilities.

The field continued to grow and captured the increasing attention of federal legislators, culminating in an extraordinary series of federal laws (DePauw, 1996):

- 1968 PL 90-170, Elimination of Architectural Barriers Act
- 1973 PL 93-112, Rehabilitation Act, prohibiting discrimination on the basis of disability

- 1975 PL 94-142, Education of All Handicapped Children Act, which requires a free and appropriate education for all children and youths with disabilities, including specifically physical education
- 1978 PL 95-606, Amateur Sports Act, which recognizes athletes with disabilities as part of the U.S. Olympic movement
- 1990 PL 101-476, Individuals with Disabilities Education Act (IDEA), extending provisions to young children and incorporating provisions of previous laws
- 1990 Americans with Disabilities Act, which extended the broad protection of the Civil Rights Act of 1964 to people with disabilities

The key legislation that catapulted Adapted Physical Education into a new era was **Public Law 94-142.** It singled out physical education and intramurals as important school activities and required that they be made available to students with special needs. A key provision of PL 94-142 was the goal of placing students in the *least restrictive environment* (LRE) to meet their needs and making every effort to ensure that they eventually become *mainstreamed* into regular classrooms that "qualify" as the LRE. This led to the movement most frequently referred to as **inclusion** with its emphasis on Adapted Physical Education not being strictly a placement but a system of services with sufficient supports to enable most students to receive their education as part of the regular classroom population (Sherrill, 2004). Inclusion represents an alternative philosophy to LRE, with the goal that all students with disabilities should be in regular classrooms. It needs to be pointed out, though, that LRE is the law. Although there are many arguments, pro and con, about inclusion, proponents tend to rest their case on the ethical position that any segregation of students with disabilities is inherently unequal. The key provisions of PL 94-142 were incorporated into the IDEA legislation, which was reauthorized in 2004.

The field of Adapted Physical Education encompasses three main types of programs: adapted, corrective, and developmental (Jansma & French, 1994).

Elite athletes come in all forms.

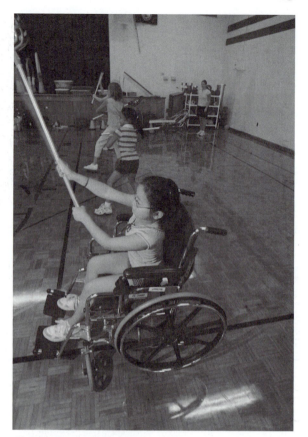

Children with disabilities can take full part in physical education classes.

An *adapted program* focuses on the modification of regular activities to enable individuals with disabilities to participate safely and successfully. A *corrective program* focuses on the rehabilitation of functional postural and body-mechanics deficiencies. A *developmental program* focuses on basic fitness and motor-skill training to raise students' skills and abilities to the point where they can participate with peers.

*Adapted physical activity* is the broad label used to describe a profession, a scholarly, interdisciplinary field of study, and the delivery of services to persons with disabilities to facilitate their lifelong active and healthy living (Sherrill, 2004). The importance of creating opportunities is especially pertinent for children and youth with disabilities.

Within that field, adapted physical education (APE) has become a robust area of teacher preparation, research, and scholarship, and the delivery of services. For example, Rimmer, Yamaki, Davis, Wang, and Vogel (2011) found that compared to typically developing peers, obesity was more prevalent in adolescents with physical and cognitive disabilities, especially among boys, 18-year-olds, and youths with cognitive disabilities. And the promotion of physical activity among people with disabilities is now also fertile ground for research. Rimmer, Chen, McCubbin, Drum, and Peterson (2010) reviewed the research on exercise interventions targeting people with a variety of disabilities. They noted that even though numerous studies have been

An accessible environment
is important.

conducted to determine the impact of exercise interventions, the body of literature was not sufficiently robust to make broad recommendations about the most effective ways of using exercise/physical activity interventions.

The Adapted Physical Activity Council is part of the new American Association for Physical Activity and Recreation (AAPAR) within AAHPERD. The *Adapted Physical Activity Quarterly* is the primary research journal for the field, publishing articles that continue to advance our understanding of the issues faced by those who deliver services to persons with disabilities and enabling APA practitioners to improve those services. Many universities now have master's degree and/or doctoral degree programs to prepare future APA specialists.

## DOES PHYSICAL EDUCATION HAVE A CENTRAL MEANING?

What does physical education mean? How should the field's content be defined? Is it physical activity? Is it fitness? Is it sport? Is it skill? Is it social development? Is it risk and adventure? Is it all of those things together? What follows are scenes that can be found in physical education today:

- Young children move to the sounds of a drum, each carrying a scarf. They change directions and change the level of their bodies as they move. The teacher, holding the drum, encourages them from time to time or gives them new directions in the form of a problem question, but does not tell them what to do.

- A coed group of ninth-graders works in a well-equipped Nautilus training room. They work in pairs, each carrying a chart on a clipboard. The teacher moves about, interacting with each pair, but provides no group cues or directions. Students move from machine to machine periodically.

- A group of 55 seventh-graders is receiving instruction from a teacher. The students are scattered in groups of four or five around a large gymnasium. Each group has a ball. The teacher gives instructions to the group and then signals for the group to begin practice. During practice, the teacher moves about, mostly watching to see that things are going smoothly. After several minutes, the teacher signals for attention, gives some feedback on what she has seen, and then gives new instructions for a slightly different task.

- Fifth-graders enter the gym and move into one of six areas to begin a group practice on soccer warm-up activities. At a signal, the groups form into teams. One member of each group leaves to pick up materials while two other members put on referee shirts. Shortly after, three small-sided soccer games begin, with students acting as referees and coaches. On the gym wall, there is a soccer season schedule and the standings for this soccer league. After 5 minutes, the game ends; within 3 minutes, a new game has begun, involving similar teams, but made up of different children.

- Twenty-four helmet-wearing seventh-graders have harnesses around their waists. They stand beneath a clearing in a wooded area and look up to see a ropes course 40 feet above their heads, with different configurations of wood and rope at different places on the course. Their teacher is giving them instructions on belaying techniques, safety, and appropriate procedures for moving through the ropes course.

- A teacher sits with a group of ninth- and tenth-graders at the start of a lesson, describing what will be done that day. The teacher solicits comments on the students' feelings about their progress, talking about individual growth and responsibility. There is talk about levels, and students learn that today is a fitness day when they will work on their individually developed programs.

- A group of eleventh-graders have toured community health and fitness facilities as part of their assignment in physical education. They also have monitored their own activity and nutritional intake for 6 weeks. Based on their own data and what is available in the community, they each plan a comprehensive health-fitness plan for themselves, which they can easily do within their own community. They include their plans in a portfolio that they are building for evaluating their eleventh-grade physical education experience.

- Twenty-four ninth-graders enter the gym. The teacher quickly organizes them into coed teams, and two basketball games start immediately. Each team has one substitute. The games begin and it is clear that there is little offensive or defensive strategy. Girls seldom touch the ball as boys dominate the action. The teacher sits in a chair working on some plans and occasionally monitors the class action. Skilled players dominate and most girls and a few boys move up and down the floor but seldom pass or shoot.

All of these scenes are part of today's physical education. You will recognize in these scenes the various models reviewed in this chapter, except for one that is! Does the last scene remind you of your physical education? As you look at the other scenes, can you recognize a common theme among them? Is there a common meaning that can be attributed to each of the scenes? Is it easy to see that the pedagogy of the first seven themes is different from the eighth scene?

Recently, James Sallis, a prominent health psychologist who is heavily involved in research on studying the effectiveness of the various health-optimizing physical education programs, proposed the physical education "Teaching Practices Hall of Shame." Examples of such teaching practices include teachers (a) making students stand in line waiting for a turn, (b) using physical activity for punishment, (c) focusing mostly on star athletes, and (d) big people throwing balls at little people (Sallis, 2011).

When you think about what it takes to deliver a quality physical education program, you must think about both content and pedagogy. Whatever you choose as the key outcomes for students, you will not accomplish them without blending content and pedagogy in ways that help you achieve your outcomes. A key to developing that capacity is to always think: What is it that *these* students need in terms of content, and how can I best deliver it to *them* (pedagogy) so that they will not only improve, but also enjoy what they are learning? Teaching is always specific to the students being taught, what their needs are, and the context in which you teach them.

## SUMMARY

1. Over the last century, school physical education has periodically received national attention as part of the various efforts to improve physical fitness, improve military readiness, and most recently address public health concerns related to consequences of preventable chronic disease health risks such as cardiovascular disease, high blood pressure and cholesterol levels, Type-2 diabetes, and so on.

2. No single definition of physical education has gained widespread acceptance in contemporary professional circles, but it is generally described in terms of what content is taught, and the instructional approaches used to deliver this content.

3. Education-through-the-physical was the dominant curricular philosophy for the first half of the twentieth century, while sport-based programs became the norm in the second half of the century.

4. The fourfold objectives of physical education (i.e., physical development, motor development, mental development, and social development) dominated thinking in physical education starting early on in the twentieth century. It formed the basis for the emergence of the multi-activity curriculum, which became the standard organizing theme for lesson and program planning in physical education. It still permeates many of today's curriculum models and school programs.

5. Four philosophical perspectives form the roots of today's curriculum models and school programs. They include: Human Movement; Humanistic Sport and Physical Education; Play Education and Sport Education; and Experiential and Adventure Education.

6. NASPE has developed national content standards along with grade-level specific performance outcomes indicating what students should know and be able to do upon completion of the various grade levels.

7. The skill themes model is the most appropriate curriculum and instruction model for children in grades K–3.

8. Health-optimizing physical education (H.O.P.E.) has developed as a response to recent public health concerns.

9. The concept-based physical education model has as its primary goal to have students become informed consumers of knowledge related to fitness, physical activity, and wellness, so they are more likely to make physical activity a part of daily life.

10. The academic integration model focuses on the emerging knowledge base in the subdisciplines of physical education. It has gained strength recently because of the emphasis on academic excellence in schools.

11. The personal and social responsibility model has emerged as a distinctive curricular option with a focused purpose. Social problems especially in urban environments gave rise to the notion that developing traits such as cooperation, social development, and responsibility are as important outcomes as developing skill and fitness.

12. The Sport Education model is an inclusive and more authentic approach to students learning about sport. It emphasizes appropriate competition and learning about multiple roles within sport.

13. Adventure education uses risk and challenge to develop personal and social skills through a variety of natural and contrived activities.

14. Games-based approaches to teaching sport games seek to develop students' "Game Sense," which reflects understanding of and skillful use of the techniques and tactical dimensions of the game. Successful game play is viewed as solving the tactical problems of creating scoring opportunities and preventing the opponent from scoring.

15. Most physical education programs today are still conceptualized as an eclectic model that combines the various curricular approaches described in this chapter. Consequently, K–12 programs are organized around the philosophy of students needing only brief introductory exposure to a large variety of activities using short units.

16. Debates are ongoing on what constitutes the central subject matter of physical education.

17. Increasing physical activity levels of students has become a central outcome measure of physical education programs and is part of the national health objectives set forth in Healthy People 2020. It is essential to not equate physical education and physical activity.

18. The quality of school physical education programs is defined by (a) students' opportunity to learn, (b) inclusion of meaningful content, (c) use of appropriate instructional strategies, (d) regular use of assessment of student learning and program delivery, (e) having a well-designed yearly program, and (f) appropriate training and supervision of physical education teachers.

19. State requirements for physical education differ markedly and heavily influence physical education programs in schools.

20. Adapted Physical Education has developed into a specialized area, which now focuses on inclusion.

21. It is still not clear what the central focus of physical education is.

## DISCUSSION QUESTIONS

1. To what extent was your school program rooted in the education-through-the-physical philosophy? What were its main features?

2. Is the multi-activity approach useful? If yes, explain how any real objectives can be accomplished with short-term units. Is the variety engendered by this approach appropriate? If not, why does it continue to be the dominant approach to delivering physical education?

3. In this day of national concerns of increased levels of overweight and obesity, why is the time for physical education and recess in schools being reduced in many school districts?

4. To what extent do the problems exposed by the humanistic sport and physical education advocates still exist today?

5. In what way was play education a radical departure from the education-through-the-physical approach?

6. Which of the newer curriculum models most appeals to you? Explain. Which least appeals to you? Explain.

7. The dominance of team sports in most physical education programs is being called into question as part of the shift to a more public health-oriented approach to physical education. Given that, how would you justify using sport education as a central model for your physical education program?

8. What was physical education like in your high school? Were the classes coed? Did boys and girls like or dislike it equally?

9. In your own words, describe what you see as a truly quality physical education program. How does it compare to NASPE's description of a quality program?

10. How would you explain the relationship between physical activity and physical education? Are they the same or different? How are they different?

11. Relative to students with special needs, inclusion is a philosophy in which they are to be placed in regular classrooms with the needed support services regardless of the type and/or severity of the disability. Do you believe that is an appropriate standpoint? Explain and support your position.

12. What kind of physical education experience would adolescents have to have in order to influence their lifestyle choices about physical activity and health?

13. What do you believe should be the central focus of physical education at elementary-school, middle-school, and high-school levels? Can you develop a definition of physical education that accurately reflects that perspective?

14. Historically, education has been under local control (i.e., districts have broad control over how schools are structured and managed). Do you believe that the state and/or federal governments should have at least some level of influence over the delivery of physical education (or any other subject matter)? Explain your reasons.

# CHAPTER 5

# Physical Education Programs and Professions

*Whereas a high quality daily physical education for all children in kindergarten through grade 12 is an essential part of a comprehensive education: Now, therefore, be it resolved by the House of Representatives (the Senate concurring), that the Congress encourages State and local governments and local education agencies to provide high quality daily physical education programs for all children in kindergarten through grade 12.*

House Concurrent Resolution 97, 100th Congress

Physical education is best known as a subject offered in schools. Most people who prepare to become physical education teachers complete a curriculum that culminates with not only a degree but also a teaching certificate. Does physical education take place *only* in schools? Here again, as we indicated at the beginning of Chapter 4, a problem of definition arises. If physical education is limited, *by definition*, to activities that occur in schools, then how do we describe programs that look similar to physical education in schools but are conducted in other places? All the curriculum models described in Chapter 4 could easily be implemented in places other than schools. Moreover, if school physical education programs define themselves only by the promotion of physical activity, then other professionals and programs look even more similar. Consequently, physical educators will have a more difficult time explaining the unique contribution of their school-based physical education programs.

Then there is the changing role of physical educators within the school campus. Physical educators have a key role to play in maximizing physical activity opportunities throughout the entire school day. Planning and implementing a program that focuses only on the delivery of the regular physical education classes is now seen as too narrow a delineation of the physical educator's job responsibilities. New generations of physical educators will need to embrace a role in which they are campus leaders in creating physical activity opportunities for students before-school, during recess, lunch recess and/or during after-school hours.

We want to make one thing very clear: Although this chapter (as well as the next the next two) focus on school physical education programs, it should be obvious that physical education in its broader sense can take place as well in other settings where physical activity is a primary focus. There are countless examples of programs whose focus is similar to that of the goals and objectives espoused by school physical education programs. Adventure education is often done in summer camps and by private agencies such as Outward Bound. Fitness programs are conducted in commercial health centers, spas, and family centers such as the YMCA and the YWCA. Children and youths learn and participate in sport (that is, they become *educated* in sport) in community programs. Movement skills are learned in countless settings including preschools, gymnastic academies, and dance studios. Sport and fitness programs with strong social-development goals can be found in church camps, Police Athletic League programs, and family centers such as a Jewish Community Center. Are these all physical education?

How you answer that question will reflect how narrow or broad your concept of physical education is and how it affects the lives of children and youths. Most professionals in other fields tend to take the broader rather than the narrower perspective. Certainly, if you are serious about the notion of a *lifespan* physical education—as advocated in Chapter 1—then the broader perspective is necessary.

Obviously, school physical education is important. School is still the one institution in our culture that touches the lives of virtually all children and youth, since they spend many of the days during their formative years there. It is the institution to which we have delegated a primary responsibility for passing on the best of our culture and for trying constantly to improve the culture. You do not have to be rich to go to school, nor do you have to have special talents to take part in the school curriculum. If the goal of physical education for all—another position advocated in Chapter 1—is ever realized, then the school will have played the most important role in achieving it.

The U.S. Congress declared its support for high-quality, daily physical education in the 1987 Concurrent Resolution, a summary of which is on the first page of this chapter. Can you imagine the impact of such an idea? If every boy and girl, from kindergarten through grade 12, received a high-quality 30-minute daily physical education lesson, they would all accumulate nearly 1,000 hours of quality physical education during their school years. Many good outcomes could be accomplished if that were a common commitment by local school districts. Is it really too much to ask? Not if you consider that a boy or girl who participates for 4 years on a high-school basketball team would accumulate more than 1,000 hours of practice, with a lower student–teacher (coach) ratio, better equipment, and much greater access to facilities. As we will highlight further in Chapter 6, one of the key challenges for the physical education professions will be to help develop this greater commitment by policy makers toward school physical education.

On January 18, 2005, a headline for an Associated Press story read, "Health Experts Say Schools Failing Phys Ed." The article was critical of how physical education was taught (condemning the "throw out the ball" approach) and also was critical of states and school districts for not requiring more physical education and not supporting better teaching. Indeed, in 2005, physical education was frequently addressed in all media outlets, simply because of the startling data about childhood and youth overweight and obesity (see Chapter 1). The major solution to the "obesity epidemic" is to provide more and better physical activity for children and youths. All federal guidelines specifically support more and better physical education, as well as after-school and community physical-activity programs. Both the federal government and our professional organizations have provided specific guidelines and recommendations about the duration, frequency, and intensity of activity needed to secure the health benefit (e.g., U.S.D.H.H.S., 2008). Moreover, school physical education was identified as one of only five effective intervention strategies with sufficient empirical support to increase the physical activity level of children and youth (Centers for Disease Control and Prevention, 2001). Yet, daily physical education or its equivalent for the entire school year for all students occurs only in 3.8, 7.9, and 2.1 percent of all elementary, middle, and high schools, respectively (Lee, Burgeson, Fulton, & Spain, 2007).

As you learn about the exemplary programs described in this chapter, keep in mind that physical education can be good even in schools where facilities are modest and time is less than adequate. But if school physical education is to live up to its potential, the *state* and *school districts* must strengthen requirements for physical education and hold districts and schools accountable for meeting those requirements. The next section includes several examples of physical education programs that have made concerted efforts in (a) delivering quality physical education lessons, (b) creating physical activity opportunities throughout the school day and beyond, and (c) showing students how physical activity engagement can be integrated with activities typically viewed as pertaining to other school subjects (e.g., social studies).

## EXEMPLARY PHYSICAL EDUCATION PROGRAMS

As you will see in the next chapter, there are substantial problems in contemporary physical education. However, in this chapter, we focus on programs that do accomplish their goals. The programs described are real, and each typically represents one or several of the physical education models described in Chapter 4. You will see that in many of the examples programs that have gone well beyond just ensuring that students partake in quality physical education lessons.

## A Comprehensive Health-Related Elementary School Model

Health-related physical education has developed in the wake of evidence strongly supportive of the health benefits of a physically active lifestyle at a time when health care costs to the nation have become a major political issue. Virgilio (1996) describes a comprehensive healthy lifestyles elementary-school program that grew from his work in developing the national Heart Smart fitness program (Virgilio & Berenson, 1988). This comprehensive model recognizes that children are unlikely to get sufficient physical activity in the time allotted to physical education in the elementary-school curriculum. The emphasis in this model is placed "on learning motor skills and participating in sport to stay physically active and develop lifelong movement skills" (Virgilio, 1996, p. 4). The program emphasizes learning lifelong skills and participating in high amounts of regular physical activity, utilizing many of the materials and programs from the Heart Smart program. According to this model, children develop their own personalized fitness portfolio, which they carry with them through their elementary-school years.

In addition, the model stresses a strong parent education component, using newsletters, parent seminars, progress reports, parent–teacher conferences, PTA demonstrations, and a parent resource room. The progress reports include summaries of the child's fitness progress, physical-activity levels, and recommended areas for improvement. The parent resource room contains videos, computer software, cookbooks, cassettes, and educational games that parents could check out and use at home with their children. The model also involves parents in extending and improving participation in physical activity at school in nonattached time. Parents serve as aides in classes, monitor playground activity, help build or repair equipment, and participate in a committee that serves as an advocacy group for the goals of the program.

The model also includes a home-based activity program. Families are encouraged to commit to a family contract to exercise together, using a specific, family-developed schedule. Parents assist children in their fitness homework; for example, they can develop a fitness trail through their neighborhood and use it regularly. Parents are also encouraged to develop summer activity packets, which would include activity plans, reading lists, games, and opportunities in the community. The nutrition component of the program is also extended to the home through

Classes that are well organized and well managed result in more activity.

the parent newsletter and through family activities designed to improve the nutritional content of family meals.

Classroom teachers include health, nutrition, and cardiovascular fitness in the classroom curricula. They are also asked to ensure that the children get at least 30 minutes per week of physical activity within their classroom (i.e., in addition to their physical education and recess time). The school cafeteria also plays a central role in the program. The parent committee meets with the school-lunch staff to ensure that school meals reduce sodium, fat, and sugar levels. Cafeterias are decorated to promote healthy choices in food selection. If the school uses a snack service, the service is encouraged to stock relatively healthy snack foods.

The physical education teacher, in conjunction with the parent committee, seeks to develop links with community agencies that offer physical-activity programs for children. Efforts are made as well to get children into after-school activity programs or, if none exist in the community, to develop such a program at the school site. Special projects such as youth sport fairs and community health fairs are developed. The entire effort is designed to affect lifestyle choices, and the total environment of the child—school, home, and community—is enlisted in that effort.

## The Active and Healthy School Program

In the Mesa Public School district, several schools have implemented the Active and Healthy Schools program. Beyond the regular physical education lessons, teachers using this program set up designated activity areas throughout the school's various physical activity venues and provide the needed equipment. Each of these "zoned recess" areas is clearly marked off with signs that explain the designated activity for that area.

An important feature of this program is to provide students at the school with multiple activity choices to accommodate the multiple-activity preferences and multiple-skill levels. For example, there is a specific area for jump rope activities, soccer, football, and so on. In an effort to encourage students of all skill levels and interests, students can also choose from activities such as bowling, beach ball volleyball, hula hoops, scoops and balls, Frisbees, and so on. These, too, have their own designated areas. Moreover, the physical education teacher regularly alters the menu of activity choices to ensure that the activities taught during the physical education lessons are also available during recess and lunch recess periods. Visual point-of-decision prompts are displayed throughout the school building and outdoors directing students to the various activity venues.

The Active and Healthy Schools program is an excellent example of how the physical education program can be linked closely with multiple other program areas in the school. For example, during staff meetings, time is allocated for the physical education teachers to introduce and demonstrate new classroom-based activities. The physical education teacher then provides ongoing support to classroom teachers by introducing the use of age-appropriate classroom-based physical activity breaks. These activity breaks typically last no more than 3–5 minutes in duration, and generally occur during the transition between subjects (i.e., going from language arts to math). Many of the classroom-based physical activity breaks can be designed so that they provide not only physical activity, but also integrate student learning into academic core content areas such as mathematics, technology, science, or language arts.

In addition, the physical education program is linked closely with the school's food service program to help students learn to make healthier food choices. Here, too, students are presented with various visual reminders to aid them in making their choices. Then when students have made selections and are seated for breakfast or lunch, the food service personnel and/or the physical education teacher walks around and offers social reinforcement for the food choices made.

And finally, the Active and Healthy Schools program also includes a Sun Safety component. Especially pertinent in the Arizona climate, students learn how they can protect themselves against the dangers of extended sun exposure through frequent hydration, the use of sunscreen, seeking shaded areas for activity, and wearing appropriate clothing, UV sunglasses, and wide-brimmed hats.

The importance of building such close connections between the physical education program and other program areas within the school cannot not be

Children have an inherent drive to play.

underestimated. Physical education teachers can give their program greater presence and be a much more prominent force within the broader mission of the school.

## A High-School Healthy Lifestyles Program

The Lake Park High School physical education program—winner of the 2006 Blue Ribbon Award from the Illinois Association for Health, Physical Education, Recreation, and Dance—aims to "aid students in achieving their fullest potential through the acquisition of knowledge and skills necessary to attain healthy levels of well-being and to maintain active lifestyles throughout the lifespan" (http://w3.lphs.org/academics/dept/pe/philosophy.htm). Students in the ninth and tenth grades take physical education one semester and health education for one semester. The ninth-grade physical education program focuses on the knowledge and skills necessary for the maintenance and/or improvement of health-related fitness. All students learn about their own levels of fitness and, with the help of their teachers, plan for improvement or maintenance programs. They are also taught to use technology to learn about and monitor different components of fitness. Facilities for the East Campus and West Campus include a life laboratory, weight room, cardio-fitness center, dance room, and strength-training center as well as gymnasiums. Other ninth-grade units are fitness basics, jump rope, volleyball, weight training, net games, and aerobic games.

The tenth-grade program starts with an introduction to fitness unit that includes an orientation to the Life Lab, health-related fitness components, skill-related fitness components, warm-up and cool-down procedures, and heart-rate targeting using heart-rate monitors. The tenth-grade program starts with a fitness evaluation and review of healthy lifestyles concepts, followed by units in tennis, badminton, weight training, aerobics, and volleyball.

In the eleventh and twelfth grades, students choose semester-long activities that include team activities, cross-training and aerobic wellness, strength and conditioning, introduction to dance arts, strength training, and personal wellness, including nutrition and exercise. The program also offers a Leadership Training Fitness certification course and a Leadership Training Coaching certification course.

This program model is highly consistent with the current emphasis in physical education on preparing students to take active control of their health and physical activity as they move into adulthood. It is also exemplary in combining a basic program for all students in the ninth and tenth grades, but allowing students a choice of activities in the eleventh and twelfth grades. If we want high-school students to take responsibility for their own healthy lifestyles, we should provide programs that allow them some choice in what they pursue. This is typically achieved through providing students elective choices of courses within the requirement that they take physical education each of the 4 years in high school.

## A Rural School's Effort to Maximize Physical Activity During the School Day

A number of years ago at Independence Elementary School in Oregon, Meg Greiner (NASPE's 2005 Elementary Physical Education Teacher of the Year) celebrated National Physical Education and Sport week by bringing her school's entire student population and full staff into her gymnasium and leading them in 15–20 minutes of dance. All students (just under 400) already were participating in regular physical education three times per week for 35 minutes, which is more than most of the nation's elementary schools were doing. The classroom teachers and principal asked the teacher to make this activity session part of every school day after noticing improved readiness to learn among the school's diverse students (over 40 percent Latino) immediately following these activity sessions. This became known as TEAM-Time (**T**ogether **E**veryone **A**chieves **M**ore).

TEAM-Time a good example of how a physical education program can increase physical activity for the entire school population (including the staff).

The program is recognized and valued by classroom teachers and has the full support of the school's administration.

All students have an assigned spot in the gym, and to ensure safety and understanding among the younger students, fourth-graders are assigned to assist with a kindergarten schoolmate. The 20-minute period includes a warm-up phase, followed by a more aerobic phase requiring more jumping and other dynamic moves, followed by a choreographed dance or rhythmic activity. The cool–down, which consists of slower movements, focusing techniques, and stretching, includes slower music to prepare students for transitioning to the classroom. This is followed up with the flag salute and daily affirmations. The original intent of TEAM-Time was to address students' general classroom behavior early in the day, but research found that TEAM-Time did much more than that: it has fostered a positive school community connection, instilled a culture of movement, and improved their academic performance significantly as well.

## An Upper-Elementary School Sport Education Program

The upper-grades curriculum at Olde Sawmill Elementary School in Dublin, Ohio, was based on the Sport Education model described in Chapter 4 (Darnell, 1994). In grades 4–6, the curriculum was sport oriented. Students were placed on teams at the start of the school year and remained with their teams throughout the year as they worked for points toward an all-sport award. Students selected a name for the team and team colors. Captains and assistants were assigned and selected for each new sport season. A schedule of competition was arranged for each season.

Each day that the students had physical education, they did everything as members of their team. When they entered the gym, they had an assigned space where team members did their warm-ups together, led by their team captain. A period of skill practice followed, with captains again leading their teams through the assigned drills. As the season

Team fitness conditioning during a Sport Education season.

progressed, less time was allocated for team skill practice and more time was allocated for games.

In each sport season, students had multiple roles beyond that of player, including coach, referee, or scorekeeper. Simple performance records were kept during each game. Short-duration, small-sided games were used for team sport competition. Teams earned points toward an overall season championship in a number of ways, including winning games, practicing as a team at recess, behaving as good sportspersons, passing the knowledge tests, and exhibiting leadership.

In the soccer season, each class typically had three or four teams. Captains led teams during the class and administered schedules and assignments between class sessions. The soccer season began with a 2 against 2 (two players versus two players) round-robin competition in which games lasted 4 minutes. Captains assigned players from their team for each of the 2 against 2 games. Students not playing at any given time were involved as either referees or scorekeepers. Captains were instructed to have all of these assignments completed and written out before the class began.

After the 2 against 2 round-robin competition was completed, a 4 against 4 round-robin competition began. Here the game became more complex, requiring more teamwork and careful execution of skills. Again, captains made all assignments, and all students participated in some capacity during each game. At the end of the soccer season, an overall soccer champion was named for each class, based on points accumulated during game and practice time, as well as by good sportspersonship. At the end of the season, intramural time was used for interclass matches at the same grade level.

The gymnastic season was done differently, but still taught gymnastics primarily as a competitive sport. The first part of the season focused on compulsory competition, in which each team member had to learn and perform a group of gymnastic skills. Students warmed up and practiced each day as a team, with captains not only leading during class but also handling administrative duties between classes. As part of learning the skills, students also learned how to judge the performance of those skills. The compulsory competition was a routine involving the activities being practiced. Students chose routines at three levels of difficulty. They then made up their own routine, following the guidelines for their level of difficulty.

Compulsory competition took place over a number of class sessions, with students acting as judges. Students earned points, based on performance within their own level of difficulty. The team championship was determined by total points won in competition and for practicing.

An optional competition followed the compulsory part of the season. There students chose one event in which to practice and compete. Each day there was an opportunity to practice and take part in at least one optional competition. Coaches again administered the assignment of students to events and determined when each would compete. All individual performances counted toward a team total. Students served as judges for the optional performances as well. At the end of the gymnastic season, interclass competitions were arranged during intramural time. At the end of the season, an overall champion was determined, individual awards were presented for each event, and awards for sportspersonship and coaching were also presented.

By the end of a school year, all students would have learned to be a coach, a referee, a judge, a scorekeeper, and a record keeper. Each would likely have been on some teams that lost, on some that won, and on some that finished toward the middle. They would have learned and experienced what makes any sport a sport, and how the sport can be enjoyed from various perspectives. Moreover, they would have had to learn to deal with setbacks, enjoy the success of a team, and more.

## A High-School Program Blending Health and Wellness, Outdoor Pursuits and Sport

The physical education staff at Tahoma High School in Covington, Washington, developed a curriculum around the state's "Essential Academic Learning Requirements" for health and fitness. Across the four semesters, the physical education program seeks to have students move from Quality Producers in semester 1, to Effective Communicators in semester 2, to Complex Thinkers in semester 3, and finally to Community Contributors in semester 4. For example, in the first semester, students develop a Wellness Plan that includes a fitness, stress management, and nutrition plan. In the second semester, students implement, evaluate, and revise their plan, where necessary. This revised plan is implemented in the third semester with the expectation that they expand their wellness goals and objectives and link it with their life and career goals. In the fourth and final semester, students plan and implement an event that is directly linked to wellness in the community. In the past few years, Tahoma high-school's seniors have organized events around the removal of invasive plant species, planting of native species, and trail building and maintenance in surrounding community park and nature preserves, all geared toward ensuring safety and enjoyment for those visiting the parks. In addition, they can apply for a Health and Fitness Leadership position. In that position, they would assist or mentor their peers in semesters 2 and 3.

Bouldering offers exciting challenges.

Students complete four semesters and meet on an A-B schedule, with class periods of 103 minutes in length. Students can choose courses from the Club Fitness, Outdoor Academy, and Sports/Dance program areas. The Club Fitness includes both beginning and advanced strength and conditioning; the courses in the Team Sports/Dance area are delivered using the sport education model, and the Outdoor Academy offers courses in which students are introduced to integrated subject-matter instruction in physical education along with language arts and environmental science. For example, in the fly-fishing course students not only learn to fly fish, they also learn to conduct water-quality tests in the streams where they fly fish, and they read classics such as *A River Runs Though It* by Norman Maclean and *Testament of a Fisherman* by Robert Traver.

Teachers from the various subject matters accompany the students to the various nature preserves around the greater Seattle-Tacoma area. According to physical education department chair Tracy Krause (a National Board-certified physical educator and NASPE's 2008 High School Teacher of the Year), students develop a deeper understanding of and appreciation for the ways in which they can engage in physical activity and the environment in which that takes place. This program offers an excellent example of how physical education need not be focused exclusively on team sports, physical fitness, or outdoor pursuits. Clearly the expertise of the physical education faculty allows for the blending of the multiple areas of our subject matter. Moreover, it is a good example of how physical educators can make their program highly visible within the surrounding communities.

## A Districtwide Healthy Lifestyles Curriculum

The 18,000 students in the Spokane School District experience a K–10 physical education program that is more like being a member of a health club than being in a traditional physical education class. Students both study a healthy lifestyles curriculum and live it in their classes. Students take part in age-appropriate noncompetitive games and activities that have specific endurance and strength features. They rotate through these games and activities, through fitness and activity stations, and through lessons on fitness and health. As in many current approaches, technology in the form of heart monitors, pedometers, and computer tracking of progress contributes to student interest and serves as a form of accountability. Students quickly learn what activities are appropriate for developing and sustaining muscular strength and endurance, cardiovascular capacity, flexibility, and body composition. Pop music is played in many classes, contributing to an atmosphere quite different from the "drills and skills" approach to physical education.

## A Middle School Combining the Personal and Social Responsibility Model with Activities

The Marston Middle School in San Diego was selected as a California Middle School Demonstration Program in physical education in 2006. Marston's physical education program developed a variation of the personal and social responsibility model (PSRM) (See Chapter 4; pp. 62–64) that is used in conjunction with an activity program that builds across the sixth- to eighth-grade years. Each year, the first 6 weeks emphasize responsibility; the second 6 weeks emphasize accepting personal differences; the third 6 weeks teach respect; the fourth 6 weeks develop a sense of caring; the fifth 6 weeks build trust; and the sixth 6 weeks emphasize showing appreciation.

The theme for sixth-grade activities is "working cooperatively to achieve a common goal" and include orienteering, pretesting in the five components of fitness, games from around the world, tumbling, dance and rhythms, an introduction to track and field, and fitness post-testing. The theme for the seventh grade is "meeting challenges and making decisions." The activity schedule includes cooperative activities, fitness pretesting, lacrosse, combatives, volley tennis, fitness lab orientation, fitness training, fitness concepts, fitness testing, track and field, dance, and swimming. The instructional theme for the eighth grade is "working as a team to solve problems." Activities include cooperative games, fitness pretesting, dance, track and field, strength and conditioning, soccer, leisure activities, flag football, lacrosse, and fitness post-testing.

Several activities, such as track and field, are repeated in each of the 3 years, thereby allowing students to gradually build their skills and understanding of an activity. Fitness pre- and post-testing occurs each year with fitness activities of various kinds included in each year's activity program. The students are continuously confronted with situations where the yearly theme (for example, working cooperatively to achieve a common goal in the sixth grade) is incorporated with the PSRM goals for each of the 6-week sections of the year. Thus, in the fourth 6-week period of the sixth grade, students work cooperatively to achieve the common goal of caring.

The three female and three male physical education teachers at Marston Middle School work to build a shared commitment to these curricular and instructional approaches. Their work has been rewarded with California's Physical Education and Health Education Exemplary School Award.

# An Elementary-School Adventure Program

A portion of the physical education curriculum at the Worthington Hills Elementary School in Worthington, Ohio focused on adventure activities (Moore, 1986). Students learn sports and engage in fitness activities, just as many other children in elementary-school physical education programs do. But what makes this program special is the manner in which risk, adventure, and cooperation were woven into the curriculum throughout the school year.

The regular activity program includes elements of adventure and cooperation throughout the year. For example, team sports were always introduced initially through cooperative games such as volleyball, where two teams work together to keep the ball in play. Skill instruction and practice for activities such as archery and orienteering were also done as part of the regular school curriculum.

For several weeks during the school year, special adventure activities become the focus of the curriculum. Climbing and rappelling are two skills taught to all students. The gymnasium contains three indoor climbing walls: A horizontal climbing course that traverses 60 feet along one wall and two vertical climbing courses of differing levels of difficulty. There are also several rappelling stations throughout the gymnasium. Each course is attractively decorated, with the help of the art teacher, to look like a mountainous challenge. Climbing and rappelling are technical skills that have a strong element of perceived risk and challenge but are, in fact, very low in actual risk when done properly. Students are encouraged to extend themselves, improve their skills, and take new risks. Students who reach the top of one vertical course—where a snowy peak had been painted—can sign their name. At the top of another course, they honk a horn while touching the golden egg depicted at the top of the beanstalk course.

Students have more opportunity to practice those and other adventure skills in the intramurals program. A final component of the adventure curriculum is a series of field trips. Sixth-graders go on a 3-day camping trip in which the adventure curriculum learned indoors is extended to natural settings. In addition, on several 1-day trips to a nearby adventure center, students participate in a high-ropes course, group-initiatives courses, field archery, and orienteering, thus extending the skills learned originally at the school to a wooded, natural setting.

The goals and objectives of the adventure program described here have much in common with those of the social-development program described previously. Both are concerned primarily with personal growth, cooperation, sharing, and responsibility. They differ primarily in the means through which those goals are achieved.

# A High-School Program with a Fitness Emphasis

At Needham High School in Needham, Massachusetts, students are required to complete 16 quarters of physical education across their 4-year program (Westcott, 1992). The program's emphasis on physical fitness is from a personal perspective involving individual goals and lifestyle outcomes. The core of the program is a six-quarter series of wellness courses, ranging from fundamentals of fitness to nutrition to stress management. These courses involve extensive classroom work as well as activity involvement.

Needham students are also required to choose three fitness courses from a range of activity options, including aerobics, cross training, fitness games, stretching, and weight training. The third set of requirements are in the lifetime sport category, where students again choose from a variety of offerings including archery, badminton, golf, jazz dance, tennis, and volleyball. In the final four quarters of required physical education, students can then choose from any of the three main areas: wellness, fitness, and lifetime sports.

All students at Needham High School receive an individual fitness evaluation each year, focusing on the health-fitness factors of cardiovascular endurance, muscular endurance, muscular strength, flexibility, and body composition. It includes a cumulative computer printout of their evaluation with specific information related to strengths and weaknesses.

The physical education staff at Needham worked diligently over a period of almost 10 years to write the grants necessary to obtain activity equipment, testing equipment, and educational materials needed to run this exemplary program. Students graduating from Needham High School left the program knowing a great deal about fitness and their own strengths and weaknesses related to fitness. They also have had an excellent opportunity to develop lifestyle skills and commitments that will lead to a long-term commitment to personal health fitness.

## A High-School Program with an Outdoor Pursuits Option

Physical education at Sisters High School in central Oregon is in some ways typical of physical education in other high schools. Students can take a semester in which they participate in traditional sport activities. The program's department head, Rand Runco, coaches the girls' basketball team. However, together with colleagues from other subjects, Runco has also developed the Interdisciplinary Environmental Expeditions (IEE) program which combines physical education with social studies, science, and English. This program combines content from these three subjects with a focus on providing service to others in one's community. The unique aspect of the service component is that the concept of community is broadened to include the world at large. Specifically, students who are accepted into the IEE program provide service to citizens in Nepal. Runco learned about the living conditions of many Nepalese when he first traveled to Nepal. He used his experiences as the springboard for extending his physical education program by building in a centerpiece service-learning component.

In the prerequisite course in physical education students learn to employ the needed skills to make weeklong treks on foot across challenging terrain. Basic outdoor skills such as pitching tents, cooking in the outdoors, choosing appropriate clothing, reading topographical maps, using compasses, and canoeing are learned on campus and in the outdoors around the school's community. For example, rolling a canoe is first practiced in the indoor pool of a local hotel. Students then progress to canoeing on the nearby Deschutes River. Completion of this course is required as part of the students' application to the advanced course. In the advanced course, students prepare for and travel to Nepal to take essential supplies and necessities to local Nepalese citizens who live in highly remote regions of the country. Through this interdisciplinary coursework students learn the skills and knowledge needed to make what have become annual trips.

A recent example of a specific project is the installation of water filters vital to orphanages and teaching programs for young Nepalese women. The interdisciplinary experiences for students who make these trips are powerful in that they not only learn to successfully navigate mountainous terrain and extreme climates, they also learn to recognize and value the enormous economic and cultural differences between the environment in which they grew up and that of the Nepalese people. Students have reported that the whole experience has been life changing in that they have come to view their own environment in a fundamentally different way, and upon graduation from high school, many have chosen majors in their university education other than what they had originally planned.

## A Research-Based National Elementary School Program

Project SPARK (Sports, Play, and Active Recreation for Kids) originated as a 5-year national research study funded by the National Institutes of Health. While it began as a research-based elementary physical education program, it currently also incorporates resources for middle-school and high-school physical education programs. Moreover, it includes resources for implementing after-school physical activity programs, and a coordinated school health component (McKenzie, Sallis, & Rosengard, 2009). Following the research phase, the program focused on dissemination through a nonprofit organization originally housed at San Diego State University. However, because dissemination efforts far exceeded the capacity, the university licensed the rights to disseminate SPARK programs to SPORTIME (http://www.sportime.com/), one of the largest physical education equipment distributors, thereby commercializing the highly successful program.

SPARK offers elementary-school physical education curricula, staff development, and follow-up support to school districts, elementary-school physical education specialist teachers, and classroom teachers nationwide. The national diffusion network of the U.S. Department of Education validated SPARK as an exemplary program.

The program has several major goals. The first is to prepare children to be physically active through an emphasis on skills and play, along with learning how to manage their own behavior. SPARK also organizes lessons so that students are physically active for a large percentage of class time, by deliberately including activities that inherently provide greater opportunity for physical activity. Like the aforementioned Active and Healthy School program, SPARK also works with the school food service and classroom teachers to provide support for students to be active and make healthy choices in nutrition.

Project SPARK is unique among physical education programs in that it is based on extensive research that shows improvement in physical activity, fitness, academic achievement, motor-skill development, student enjoyment, improvement in body composition, and teacher acceptance of the program.

## An Early-Elementary Skill Themes Program

A class of first-graders at Maryland Avenue School in Bexley, Ohio, is spread out across the gymnasium space. Each student has a small racquet and a foam ball. The teacher periodically asks the students to try a new way to strike the ball with the racquet, most often in the form of a question: "Can you keep the ball up in front of you by hitting it softly?" A student occasionally loses control of his or her ball but retrieves it without interfering with the activity of

Basic skills are important early learning experiences.

classmates. It gradually becomes clear that the progression of activities is leading toward the development of striking skills that will be useful later in sports such as tennis, badminton, softball, hockey, and lacrosse. With each series of questions asked by the teacher, the children are carefully guided toward forehand, backhand, overhand, and underhand striking patterns. The children do not know—or care, for that matter—that eventually this will all lead somewhere. They are obviously enjoying the activity for what it is at the moment. There is no competition among the children. The learning is success oriented. The children often have to make decisions about what they will do in response to the prompts and questions from the teacher.

Skill Themes use movement skills, rather than traditional sport skills, as organizing principles for activity. The children in this program will have units in striking, throwing/tossing, catching, and dodging. Later, in upper-elementary-school grades, they will use these skills in the more conventional games that dominate the curriculum.

Skill Themes curricula are most often divided into the areas of educational games, educational gymnastics, and educational dance. The themes from which curricular units are developed are movement themes rather than sport themes. In the educational gymnastics portion of the curriculum, children have lessons that focus on balance, transferring weight, hanging and swinging, bearing weight on different body parts, and locomotion—both on the feet and on different body parts. Small apparatuses—such as boxes, benches, balance beams, bars, ropes, rings, and inclined planks—are used as aids in exploring movement possibilities. This approach to physical education stresses the cognitive involvement of children, the development of positive self-concepts, and the establishment of a broad repertoire of movement skills (Siedentop, Herkowitz, & Rink, 1984; Graham, Holt-Hale, & Parker, 2010).

## New Physical Education at a Middle School

Madison Junior High School in Naperville, Illinois, is recognized nationally as a leader in developing a new approach to physical education that emphasizes preparing students for lifetime health and physical activity. Featured nationally on CNN and in *USA Today*, the program has influenced the direction of physical education in many parts of the nation. The Madison program (http://schools.naperville203.org/madison/academics/PhysicalEducation20071211.asp) was built on a limited set of clear goals (e.g., lifetime activity, understanding and being able to monitor and direct one's own efforts), an innovative change in physical education facilities, and a dramatic increase in the use of technology to support program goals.

Students at Madison have physical education 5 days a week. One day is spent in the "health club" working on cardiovascular and strength machines. (The health club looks much more like a community health and fitness center than a sport training facility, which is a real clue to what the goals are all about). A second day is spent doing the weekly cardio run/walk. The other 3 days are spent in activities such as in-line skating, using the climbing wall, or participating in individual or team sports.

Technology is ever present. Students wear heart rate monitors when working in the health club or doing their weekly cardio run/walk. In the autumn and again in the spring, they test and record their progress at a series of computer-aided fitness test stations. These stations measure flexibility, blood pressure, body composition, upper-body strength, and cardiovascular performance.

In 2001, the school district entered into a partnership with PE4life, a national nonprofit organization dedicated to promoting quality physical education programs nationally. The partnership created the PE4life Institute so that teachers, administrators, and community representatives can attend programs where they learn how to develop and sustain "New PE" approaches (www.PE4life.org).

PE4life launched its Center for the Advancement of Physical Education (CAPE) on National PE Day, May 5, 2004 (www.pe4life.org/cape.php). CAPE's mission is to build evidence on healthy lifestyles approaches and delivery systems. A PE4life program is designed to

- Provide quality, daily physical education that meets the needs of all students.

- Provide a wide variety of health and fitness activities to promote a healthy lifestyle.

- Provide authentic, individualized assessment as a meaningful part of the learning process.

- Incorporate technology into physical education on a regular and continuing basis.

- Emphasize and provide support for the physical education staff's continuing education.

- Continually communicate with parents, administrators, and other stakeholders.

- Meet or exceed the National Association for Sport and Physical Education (NASPE) standards for physical education.

CAPE used the FITNESSGRAM test (a health-related fitness test) to compare the ninth-grade students at Madison Junior High with non-PEforlife students in California. In all six categories, the PEforlife students far outpaced their California peers. Of the 1,500 ninth-graders at Madison, only 3 percent were found to be overweight or obese, compared to 32 percent of their California counterparts.

## A High-School Program Emphasizing Community Linkages

Seattle's 25 high schools have embarked on a curriculum-development initiative to add interesting, challenging activities to their curricula and to do so by partnering with community, professional, and private-sector sport organizations (Turner, 1995). Each of the high schools was challenged to add a new alternative activity to its traditional list of offerings. Most of those alternative activities required partnering with a local agency or a national organization. For example, they have taken advantage of the U.S. Tennis Association's program of equipment, assemblies, and instruction as well as the First Swing golf program sponsored by the Professional Golfers Association. Locally, the Seattle Fire Department paramedics have taught CPR classes, and the Seattle Parks and Recreation Department, in cooperation with U.S. Rowing, has provided free rowing instruction. An added benefit of these efforts is the knowledge students gain about where activities are done in the community, along with the skills to take part in them. The partnering allows for the use of equipment and expertise that no single school could afford.

## A State Wellness Curriculum for High Schools

Kansas created the Physical Dimensions/Focus curriculum for physical education in high schools (http://www.srph.tamhsc.edu/centers/rhp2010/html /nutrition/physicaldimensions.htm). Through the use of surveys, the program staff identified several problems in the state's physical education programs. Some of these programs included a low enrollment in elective physical education classes, a one-year physical education requirement for Kansas schools, high rates of students reporting that physical education was neither enjoyable nor beneficial to them, and physical education was no longer required in elementary and middle schools.

The program encompassed three areas:

1. *Healthy Heart*. This area focuses on developing the skills and knowledge necessary for reaching health-enhancing levels of fitness and regular habits of physical activity.
2. *Team Power*. This area develops the students' ability to compete and cooperate together to achieve a common goal.
3. *Life Adventures*. This area focuses on developing the lifelong goals of recreational and leisure skills.

Students received 3 weeks of instruction in each of the three dimensions every 9 weeks. Students who successfully complete the curriculum receive a certificate of achievement (the High School Ph.D.).

## A Virtual High-School Physical Education Program

Some students in Florida high schools can now fulfill their physical education requirements online (Brooks, 2003). This fitness-focused program requires students to work out three to four times per week and report their workouts on the Web. Students also have reading assignments in fitness and nutrition and complete regular writing assignments. Students have choices about the form of exercise they pursue to fulfill their course requirements. Some jog and run, but others swim, dance, surf, cycle, or do yoga. Students are required to keep online logs of their workouts, including heart-rate numbers at various points during the workout. Physical education instructors in Florida's Virtual School speak monthly with parents of students enrolled to make sure that students are actually doing their workouts. Some students select this approach to make their regular school schedule less crowded, whereas others seem to prefer it because it enables them to work out alone or with close friends.

## A High-School Program with Sport Education as the Central Focus

At New Albany High School (NAHS) in Indiana, teacher Jason Orr revived the physical education program over the past 7 years, by infusing sport education as the main focus. After being introduced to sport education at a conference, Orr gradually infused this curriculum and instruction model into NAHS's program, building in new dimensions and improvements with each new season.

When students at NAHS take physical education, they now experience sport in a full and authentic manner. Beyond serving as player, students learn to coach, be an official, scout, and so on. Teams are formed using a draft system, where the teacher, together with students from the class, form teams. Teams practice and compete over the course of a 30-lesson season that includes a pre-season, with team practices, the regular competition, and a post-season. Standings are kept and posted.

Because of the length of the regular competition, a season is oftentimes interrupted for the purpose of having an all-star game in which players voted on by peers and officials are picked by the coaches. Classwide practice clinics are another example of how the regular competition schedule may be put on hold for a day. And while the main competition occurs within individual classes, the post-season has teams from different periods compete against each other. The season concludes with a culminating event of between-class games that are broadcast over NAHS's radio-TV system. These post-season matches are attended by as many as 600 students. Winners have their team photo added to a wall of champions, and they receive Sport Education Champion t-shirts. In addition, their name is engraved on a 6-foot-tall Sport Education Victory trophy.

In the last few years, two important developments have occurred in Orr's program. First, the excitement of his program has spilled into other classrooms. Colleagues in chemistry and history have infused the central features and themes of Sport Education ideas into their classes and have coined the curriculum "Chem. Ed." and "History Ed." Second, in addition to the enthusiasm from other teachers, numerous students who have completed their physical education requirements have expressed an interest in pursuing their education at the post-secondary level in physical education, sports business (administration/management), and sport sciences. This has prompted the formation of

the Sport Education Leadership Club. Through this club, interested students are introduced to the various different, exciting aspects of the realm of sport and physical education. They are expected to complete 10 community service hours that aid the physical education and/or athletic department. Most participants put in well over these hours. Then on Senior Class Day, a senior who has exemplified leadership and who has expressed a genuine interest in the field of physical education, sport, or fitness receives the Sport Education Leadership Award, which also includes a monetary award.

## A STATE APPROACH TO REVITALIZING HIGH-SCHOOL PHYSICAL EDUCATION

While much of the education community over the past several decades has focused on "reform," carrying with it the connotation that things have gone wrong and need to be corrected, North Carolina has chosen a different path (Veal, Campbell, Johnson, & McKethan, 2002). Key leaders from state professional organizations and state education departments came together to plan for the revitalization effort. A steering committee made up of high-school physical educators, higher-education faculty, and a representative from the Department of Instruction was formed to create a long-range plan and to suggest ways to fund the effort. Their effort led to high-school physical education teachers and university teacher educators joining together to create and implement the Physical Education Partnership for Sport Education (PEPSE). This project aimed to help selected high-school physical education programs to re-create their physical education learning environments with a focus on curricular revision and assessment. The project enabled physical education teachers within high schools to build a shared vision, purpose, and sense of values. The idea was to allow teachers to come together to effect change from the "inside-out" rather than have change imposed from the outside.

The sport education curriculum and instruction model was chosen because it had a strong assessment component, had been successfully implemented in research projects, and was compatible with NASPE standards. Eventually, all North Carolina public high-school physical educators were invited to participate in PEPSE. Ten schools from different regions within the state were selected to participate in the initial trial of the project. The teachers in these schools were paired with physical education teacher educators from nearby colleges and universities. All participants met for a 3-day workshop to discuss strategies for implementation. Model units using the sport-education approach were prepared in advance so that participants could discuss their implementation. Participants observed sample classes demonstrating how the model could be used.

All PEPSE-participating teachers then piloted the model in classes during the autumn of 2000. The teachers and their university partners collected data during these classes, using a variety of research instruments. The partnership reconvened in November 2000 to review the data and discuss the pilot experiences. Teachers rated the model as successful or very successful. Some teachers indicated that students in the nonpilot classes asked if they could have the model in their classes.

An excellent example of collaboration in North Carolina is the work by East Carolina University's Activity Promotion Laboratory, the North Carolina Healthy Schools organization (www.nchealthyschools .org), North Carolina's Department of Public Instruction, and the Be Active North Carolina organization. With support from the other organizations the people at East Carolina University developed physical activity "energizers" that could be used for infusing classroom physical activity breaks (www .beactivenc.org/getactive/schools/energizers/). They are free for use by any physical education program.

The North Carolina effort is a model for how other states might attempt to reinvigorate high-school physical education. The North Carolina effort could be replicated using different models, but having in common the strategy to engage high-school physical education teachers in the opportunity to rethink the manner that they provide content to students and the kind of instructional model that they use with students.

## PHYSICAL EDUCATION TEACHERS AS PHYSICAL ACTIVITY DIRECTORS

In 2004 the U.S. Congress reauthorized the Child Nutrition Act that provides funds to support school breakfast and lunch programs. A provision of the reauthorization was that local school districts that receive funding under the program must create School Wellness Councils and establish school wellness policies that include "goals for nutrition education, physical activity, and other school-based activities that are designed to promote student wellness" (U.S. Congress, 2004). This legislation has not only encouraged many states to increase the time requirements for physical education but also has brought in the possibility for physical-activity programs that are in addition to time requirements for physical education. Some states—Kentucky, for example—have created legislation for total time requirements in physical education and physical activity and given schools some leeway in deciding how to allocate time to meet those requirements. Even in states where time requirements for physical education are strong, there is a movement toward including additional physical activity during the school day and after school. In many states, the person on the local Wellness Council who is responsible for physical education and physical activity is called the physical activity director.

In elementary schools, classroom teachers are being encouraged to provide short "activity breaks" during the school day. The nationally available Take 10! program is a classroom-based physical activity program for grades K–5 students (www.take10.net). The Take 10! materials provide safe and age-appropriate 10-minute physical activities that integrate academic learning objectives with activity. Students do these activities within their classrooms.

Many teachers are now more aware of the increasing evidence that supports the idea that increased physical activity during the school day results in more attentive and more on-task student behavior. There is also a movement to ensure that time for recess is not reduced and that efforts are made to provide recess activities that keep children active throughout the 15-minute periods.

Based in part on the emerging research on the relationship between physical activity and brain development (Ratey, 2008), Leslie Hicks, the physical education professional at Basha Elementary School in Chandler, Arizona, has formed the Fit Kids Club. In the last few years she has expanded her physical education program by adding several new dimensions. After laying the groundwork with her principal and classroom colleagues, she infused the use of physical activity breaks in classrooms. She streamlined the inclusion of such activity breaks by developing DVDs in which Fit Kids Club members do various fitness-type moves to music. Each session is approximately 4 minutes in length. Classroom teachers employ these DVD clips during the natural transitions between lesson topics (e.g., switching between reading and math). Leslie assisted the classroom teachers by helping them develop specific management routines for the starting and ending of the activity breaks. While the students engage in the activity break, the classroom teacher can prepare the next lesson segment.

In addition to the classroom breaks, students at Basha Elementary School can also join a running/walking club that meets weekly after school and participate in a multitude of games and other activities in designated activity zones during recess and lunch recess. The reactions from the staff and the school's administration have been so positive that the district administration has committed to provide the needed resources to make this a districtwide effort at all its elementary schools.

In Wake County, North Carolina, the school district has developed Wellness Academies and You (WAY)—a research-based obesity-prevention program focused on nutrition, wellness, and physical activity—implemented in elementary schools. In addition to the regular physical education program, the district has also expanded the number of high-school fitness centers and introduced "Hopsports," a multimedia fitness program for middle and high schools.

The Madison Middle School Youth Development Program of Madison, Wisconsin, is supported by the school district in partnership with the community recreation department. Youth resource centers have been developed at seven middle schools, offering a variety of after-school, evening, and weekend programs. After-school clubs include riding, drama, music, bowling, dance, skiing, and canoeing. They also offer after-school sports for seventh- and eighth-graders and intramural sports for sixth-graders. Each middle school has a recreation counselor and a youth resource director.

The Coyote Ridge School District of Broomfield, Colorado, offers "Play It Again Gym" for 1 1/2 hours each Monday for students in grades 1–5. Students play a variety of games and activities that have been introduced in the physical education program. The program, which is free of charge, focuses on being active, having fun, and making new friends.

None of the above efforts has reduced the emphasis on physical education in the school district. Indeed, it appears that many physical activity programs being developed in response to the national imperative to increase physical activity for children and youths have attempted to reinforce and expand the opportunities for physical activity provided in the physical education program.

Several of the aforementioned examples reflect a move to what is referred to as a comprehensive school physical activity program. While the need for good quality and quantity of regular physical education classes remains, for future physical education programs to flourish, they have to commit to a more comprehensive approach to ensuring that school campuses are the place where students engage in health-enhancing physical activity throughout the day. Nationally, this movement is gradually gaining steam. Using First Lady Michelle Obama's Let's Move campaign (http://www.letsmove.gov/) as a springboard, NASPE recently unveiled the "Let's Move in

Schools" campaign. In addition to delivering quality physical education lessons, Let's Move in Schools aims to maximize all K–12 students' opportunities for health-enhancing physical activity through the delivery of quality physical education programs, along with access to physical activity during before- and after-school times, recess and lunch recess, as well as the use of physical activity breaks during classroom instruction of academic subjects. Moreover, it includes wellness and fitness programming for the school staff and opportunities on the school's campus for family and community involvement in physical activity.

A consequence of the broader mission of a physical education program with the comprehensive school physical activity focus is a fundamentally different job description of the physical education teacher with fundamentally different day-to-day responsibilities. Physical activity directors would, of course, continue to teach regular physical education

classes. Examples of additional activities include assisting classroom teachers with infusing classroom physical activity breaks; developing linkages with the school's food-service personnel to promote healthier eating behavior; overseeing the training of playground supervisors who would assist in facilitating physical activity during recess and lunch recess; connecting with outside agencies to ensure that an after-school program includes opportunities for physical activity.

## What Makes These Programs Work?

The physical education programs described in this chapter are not the only ones that are unique and exemplary. There are many good programs conducted in many different places. Those described here represent different approaches to physical education, approaches that reflect the various models described in Chapter 4. What properties do they share? Are there features or characteristics common to all of these programs?

Our own experience with reviewing and/or seeing these programs and many others in action is that they do share several characteristics. First, in each program, a physical educator or a group of physical educators exerted substantial leadership to get the program started and to maintain it until it was sufficiently established.

Second, although each of these programs is obviously different, each stands for something *specific*. In each program, there is a main theme or focus—fitness, sport education, adventure, movement, personal growth, and so on. Good comprehensive programs tend to be either of two types. Either they have a main theme, which runs through the program, or they join two or three main themes. The key is that the central mission of the program is clearly communicated in everything that the teachers do within the school environment. Instead of hiding in their offices, teachers in such programs are visible throughout the entire school campus, actively promoting the importance of physical activity, and constantly seeking ways to make their program be a positive and ever-present force on campus.

Recess offers ample physical activity opportunities.

Third, the programs not only look exciting but also, by all reports, tend to *be* exciting for the students who participate in them. Clearly, the teachers who have created and maintained them are excited about what they do. This excitement reflects a sense of purpose and a set of expectations that are no doubt communicated in many ways to students, fellow teachers, administrators, and parents.

Fourth, very few of the teachers who were responsible for these programs had major commitments in coaching interscholastic teams. The problem of the role conflict that is suggested by this fact is reviewed in Chapter 6.

Fifth, and perhaps most important, is the support received from the school's administrators. Such support needs to be cultivated over time. Without this support, efforts to improve programs are less likely to succeed. In most cases, physical educators cannot assume that their principal is up to date on the recent developments in the field. Principals may know what the district policies are specific to physical education but have little if any knowledge about national recommendations for physical education and the current trends within the field. Teachers of the programs we have highlighted here have invested significant time and energy on educating and persuading their building principals that the planned renewal is vital to the students, and thus makes important contributions to the school as a whole. Thus, the basic message is: Don't wait for the administration to come to you with help and assistance—physical educators must initiate it and follow through. Only then will you have a better chance to get administrators to really support your program.

## TECHNOLOGY IN PHYSICAL EDUCATION

Technology has made strong contributions to improving physical education in schools. Although too many schools cannot afford the kinds of technology described in this section, it is nonetheless important to note how it is being used to improve the learning experience for students. Examples of technology in physical education are everywhere:

- Heart monitors enable students to track exercise patterns. The data can be downloaded into computers, where they can be displayed graphically and used by students and teachers (Hinson, 1994).

- The Internet enables students and teachers to take part in newsgroups that address needs and interests related to physical activity and teaching (LaMaster, 1996).

- Countless websites support teachers in lesson planning, assessment, promoting their program, and other issues. (See Focus On Getting Connected to Physical Education and Physical Activity Websites on page 102.)

- An online technology newsletter for K–12 physical education keeps students and teachers up to date with the latest developments in the use of technology in physical education. See www.pesoftware.com/news.

- Increasingly, departments of kinesiology or physical education are offering a master's degree program in an online format (e.g., Jacksonville State University and Central Washington University). The Kinesiology Department at California State University at Northridge offers an online master's specialization program in technology and physical education.

- Students at public middle and high schools in Fargo, North Dakota, conduct personal fitness assessments using Polar heart rate monitors and the TriFIT 700 System, a portable fitness-evaluation system (www.fargo.k12.nd.us/education/components/scrapbook/default.php?sectiondetailid=2403).

- Pedometers are widely used to count steps per day in fitness evaluation. Students wear the pedometers throughout the day and compare their activity with national standards.

- Videotapes enable teacher educators and staff-development leaders to help prospective and practicing teachers improve their practice by analyzing tapes (Everhart & Turner, 1995).

- Teachers who are looking to increase the focus on health-related fitness in delivering their program, can make use of equipment that incorporates computer technology such as the GameBike, which is a plug-and-play video game controller in which movements on the screen can be controlled with body movement. It works with a large number of racing games now available (www.gamebike.com). Similar products include Dance-Dance-Revolution, and Wii Fitness.

- Teachers and student-teacher supervisors use camcorders to help students and student teachers evaluate their performances.

A number of software programs are available for use in physical education and by physical education teachers. Teachers have access to software programs that can be used for such diverse teaching purposes as grading, banner and sign making, awards, and yearly calendars (Wilkinson, Hillier, & Harrison, 1998). Teachers can also use software programs to plan and analyze student-learning activities such as workout programs, cardiovascular evaluation, health-risk appraisal, and diet analysis. For several years, Bonnie Mohnson has offered

physical educators extensive support through her website (www.pesoftware.com) by keeping teachers up to date on the latest trends and developments in hardware, software, and technology.

One text on the sport education model (Siedentop, Hastie, & van der Mars, 2011) provides Web-based resources that teachers can use to plan and implement that model. The materials include tournament forms, banners, fair-play posters, seasonal planning forms, and posters for student roles (coach, referee, scorekeeper, manager, statistician, etc.). Teachers can download the forms, modify them, and use them in their classes, thus substantially reducing the planning time needed to implement the model.

Tutorials for fitness, interactive software for sport instruction, educational games, simulations for fitness and sport, and laboratory exercises for health and fitness are available directly for student use. Through these software programs, students can play a virtual racquetball game, discover how the heart works, or learn rules of and strategies for a variety of sports.

Telecommunications can also be used to enhance instruction and expand the student experience in physical education. Physical education listservs can be created for each class or for a school physical education program. This allows for e-mail messages to be sent and received. Bulletin boards are electronic-message systems by which individuals can post and read messages. Chat rooms can be created for students to discuss issues related to their class work. Web pages can be created for physical education programs to communicate to students, parents, and the community. Links from Web pages can allow direct access to resources needed by students and their parents.

Technology can also be used to extend physical education in interesting ways. During the Winter and Summer Olympics, many physical education classes in the United States link up with classes in the host countries to discuss issues involving the games. A junior high school in Nebraska used e-mail to organize a track meet involving 17 schools around the world; the schools conducted similar meets and compared times, distances, and heights for each event. Overall results and standings were distributed to each school (Mills, 1997).

**FIGURE 5.1**    PE Central website frontpage.

Using the Web has become second nature to most students and teachers. Key websites are listed throughout this text. A primary example of the success of websites in physical education is PE Central, developed under the leadership of George Graham and Mark Manross at Virginia Tech (See Figure 5.1). This comprehensive website includes pages for students, teachers, parents, administrators, and other professionals. Physical educators can obtain useful information and numerous resources across a wide range of topics, including class management, lesson ideas, assessment, use of various media, and the like. The most popular sections of this website are lesson ideas, assessment ideas, health, the job center, adapted physical education, and the "Log it" link.

This last feature allows students to keep track of their own physical activity levels. It also includes links to other important sites, which is typical of how the Web works. In a recent 6-month period, PE Central averaged 150,000 unique visitors, and an average of about 2.7 million pages of the site were accessed per week.

Another important site for physical educators at all levels is the free monthly newsletter at PELINKS4U (www.pelinks4u.org). The free monthly newsletter includes sections on adapted physical education, coaching, elementary-school physical education, secondary-school physical education, and health, fitness, and nutrition. As the name of the site suggests, you can also find links to many other sites that are of interest to physical educators (See Focus On Box 5.1).

| FOCUS ON | Getting Connected to Physical Education and Physical Activity Websites | 5.1 |

### Teaching and Curriculum Sites

| | |
|---|---|
| Elementary Physical Education Curriculum | www.awesomelibrary.org/health.html |
| EPEC | www.michiganfitness.org/EPEC/default.htm |
| Expert Village | www.expertvillage.com |
| Fuzzy Yellow Balls | www.fuzzyyellowballs.com |
| Health and PE | www.awesomelibrary.org/health.html |
| Healthy Kids Challenge | www.healthykidschallenge.com/ |
| Healthy People | www.healthypeople.gov/2020/ |
| How to | www.howcast.com |
| Into Sports | www.intosports.com |
| Let's Move | www.letsmove.gov/ |
| Move for Life | www.beactivenys.org/mfl/ |
| PE Central | www.pecentral.org/ |
| PE4Life | www.pe4life.org |
| Physical Education Software | www.pesoftware.com/news |
| Play Sports | www.playsportstv.com/ |
| Teach PE | www.teachpe.com/ |
| Tennis Essentials | www.essentialtennis.com |
| Tennis Instruction | www.tennis.com/instruction/ |
| The Physical Educator | www.thephysicaleducator.com/ |
| TV Turn off Network | www.tvturnoff.org/ |
| Take 10—Classroom-based Phys. Act | www.take10.net/ |
| Small Steps (U.S. Dept of Health and Human Resources) | www.smallstep.gov/ |

| **FOCUS ON** | Getting Connected to Physical Education and Physical Activity Websites *(continued)* | **5.1** |

SPARK | www.sparkpe.org/

**Supplementary Information Sites**

| AAP: Overweight and Obesity | www.aap.org/obesity/index.html |
| American Assoc. for Child's Right to Play | www.ipausa.org |
| CASPER—Center for Adv. of Standards-based Physical Education Reform | www.supportrealteachers.org/ |
| Centers for Disease Control and Prevention | www.cdc.gov/HealthyYouth/PhysicalActivity/ |
| The Citizenship through Sports Alliance | www.sportsmanship.org/ |
| Coordinated School Health Initiative | www.cdc.gov/healthyyouth/cshp/ |
| National Board for Professional Teaching Standards | www.nbpts.org/ |
| National Institute for Fitness and Sport | www.nifs.org/Club/Scripts/Home/home.asp |
| National Institute of Child Health and Human Development | www.nichd.nih.gov/ |
| PELinks4U | www.pelinks4u.org/ |
| Physical Education Update | www.physicaleducationupdate.com/ |
| School Health Policies and Program Studies | www.cdc.gov/HealthyYouth/shpps/index.html |
| Sports Media | www.sports-media.org/ |
| School Health Policy Guide | www.nasbe.org/healthy_schools/hs/ |
| VERB (A national advertising campaign for PA) | www.cdc.gov/youthcampaign/ |

**Adapted Physical Education**

| American Association of Adapted Sports Programs | www.aaasp.org |
| Motor Opportunities Via Education (Move) | www.move-international.org |
| Nat'l. Center on Physical Activity & Disability | www.ncpad.org |
| Nat'l. Consortium for Physical Education and Recreation for Individuals with Disabilities | www.ncperid.org |
| Palaestra | www.Palaestra.com |
| Special Olympics | www.specialolympics.org |

**Related Health and Fitness/Sport Sites**

| Alliance for a Healthier Generation | www.healthiergeneration.org/ |
| American Obesity Association | www.obesity.org/ |
| ExRx.net | www.exrx.net/ |
| Facts on Kids Health | www.fitnessforyouth.umich.edu |
| Human Kinetics | www.humankinetics.com/ |
| National Alliance of Youth Sports (NAYS) | www.nays.org/ |
| National Center for Chronic Disease Prevention and Health Promotion—Nutrition and Phys. Act. | www.cdc.gov/nccdphp/dnpao/ |
| National Coalition for Promoting Physical Activity (NCPPA) | www.ncppa.org |

*(continued)*

| National Strength and Conditioning Association | www.nsca-lift.org/ |
| Sporting Goods Manufacturer's Association | www.sgma.com/ |
| The Nemours Foundation | www.kidshealth.org/ |
| United States Olympic Committee | www.teamusa.org/ |

### Advocacy and Policy Target Sites

| The Council of State Governments | www.csg.org/ |
| FirstGov.gov | www.usa.gov/ |
| HealthierUS.Gov | www.healthfinder.gov/ |
| National Association of State Board of Education | www.nasbe.org/healthy_schools/hs/ |
| National Conference of State Legislatures | www.ncsl.org/ |
| National Governor's Association | www.nga.org/ |
| National School Boards Association | www.nsba.org/ |
| Society of State Directors of H.P.E.R. | www.thesociety.org |
| U.S. Conference of Mayors | www.usmayors.org/ |
| U.S. House of Representatives | www.house.gov/ |
| U.S. State Senate | www.senate.gov/ |
| The White House | www.whitehouse.gov/ |

### Professional Societies and Related Organizations

| A.A.H.P.E.R.D. | www.aahperd.org |
| Action for Healthy Kids | www.actionforhealthykids.org |
| American College of Sports Medicine | www.acsm.org/ |
| American Council on Exercise | www.acefitness.org./ |
| Assoc. for Supervision and Curr. Dev. | www.ascd.org |
| Institute of Medicine | www.iom.edu/ |
| Int'l. Council for Health, Phys. Educ., Rec., Sport, and Dance | www.ichpersd.org |
| NASPE | www.aahperd.org/Naspe/ |
| National Academy of Kinesiology | www.nationalacademyofkinesiology.org |
| The President's Council on Fitness, Sports and Nutrition | www.fitness.gov/ |

### Brain-Based Research Resources Sites

| Brain Gym | www.braingym.org/ |
| Dr. John Ratey | www.johnratey.com/newsite/index.html |
| Energizing Brain Breaks | www.brainbreaks.blogspot.com/ |

### Nutrition-Related Information Sites

| CDC—Fruits and Veggies Matter | www.fruitsandveggiesmatter.gov/benefits/index.html |
| USDA Team Nutrition | www.healthymeals.nal.usda.gov/ |

The advent of websites such as YouTube has given rise to an endless array of video clips on activities of all kinds that can be used for instructional purposes. For example, a teacher who is teaching a rock-climbing, track-and-field or tennis unit can now easily direct students to specific YouTube links that highlight key information about the technical execution of the techniques at hand.

Another recent development would the use of various types of hardware that teachers can use while teaching. Products like tablet computers, iPads, and now even advanced phones allow teachers to collect data during classes on student performance. No doubt the explosion of "Apps" will soon include those that are useful and pertinent for all physical education professionals.

A final example of how technology can be used for instructional purposes would be the use of podcasts. Teachers can provide an overview of key information that students could access via the school's or program's website as part of a course project.

## THE PHYSICAL EDUCATION TEACHER

Trained professionals who hold certificates indicating that they have passed the requirements to be licensed as teachers in their states teach physical education in schools. Many certified physical education teachers also gain employment teaching in YMCAs/YWCAs, health spas, community or recreation centers, and private sport clubs. You do not *have* to be certified to teach physical education in those settings, but a teacher certificate is often an advantage in competing for those jobs because many of the essential skills needed for effective program planning, instruction, and management in physical education transfer to these programs.

Schools are required to hire people who are certified in the subject matter that they will teach. Each state has a Department of Education that includes an office that sets and oversees the teacher certification requirements and related processes. Each state has its own rules regarding the certification requirements

for beginning teachers, as well as requirements for maintaining certification. For example, in some states, teachers who obtain their initial teaching certificate have a set number of years to obtain a "continuing" certificate. In order to obtain this, teachers may need a master's degree from an accredited university program. Although school districts in some states have some limited discretion to hire noncertified personnel on a short-term basis, in the long run, the only way to teach in schools is to be a certified teacher. States also vary in their certification requirements for those who already have a teaching certificate in one subject (e.g., math or elementary education), but who wish to also get a state endorsement to teach physical education. In most cases, the state departments of education from the 50 states have reciprocal agreement, so that a teaching certificate obtained in Kansas is recognized in virtually all other U.S. states. How you acquire certification is described in the next section.

## What Do Professional Physical Education Teachers Do?

The most obvious duty of physical education teachers is to teach their physical education lessons. But that is not all they do! Professional teachers occupy a number of important roles that require skilled performance to fulfill their professional obligations (Siedentop, 1991; Siedentop, Herkowitz, & Rink, 1984; Siedentop & Tannehill, 2000):

- Teachers *plan* lessons, units, and whole curricula. They also plan for equipment replacement, facility use, field trips, and special events.
- Teachers *manage* not only groups of students, but also the use of parent volunteers, teaching aides, student helpers, equipment inventories, and the like.
- Teachers *collaborate* with other teachers, school administrators, parents, activity professionals in the community, and university faculty members.
- Teachers continue their *professional development* through the reading of professional

journals, regularly attending conferences, participating in staff-development programs, and professional contacts at other schools and in the community.

- Teachers *counsel* students in regard to not only the goals of physical education but also in family issues and personal matters.

- Teachers *represent* their schools, the physical education profession, and the teaching profession in general. They are expected to be knowledgeable and to behave in ways consistent with a professional role.

Together, these roles constitute professional life. If teachers aspire to achieve more respect for their professional status, then they have to be willing to accept the extra obligations that professionals typically carry. That means not only doing the primary job of instruction as well as possible but also attending to and performing well in these other important roles.

## A Day in the Life of Two Teachers

Jay is a specialist in elementary-school physical education. He leaves his house at 7:20 each morning for the half-hour drive to the neighboring suburb where he teaches. When he arrives, he posts a list of things for his gym helpers to do when they come in; then he heads for his three-times-per-week 8:00 a.m. conference to work on individual education plans (IEPs) for students with disabilities. Following the meeting, he grabs a quick cup of coffee in the teachers' lounge before heading to the gym to make sure that the equipment has been set up properly. He does a last-minute check of his lesson plans for the day and chats with the gym helpers, who are just finishing their tasks.

His first class will arrive at 9:10, and he will have four consecutive 35-minute classes this morning. When one class leaves the gym, the next is waiting at the door with their teacher. At 11:30, he ends his morning classes but moves directly to early lunch duty where he monitors students in the school cafeteria. At the second lunch period, he eats his own

lunch in the teachers' lounge, usually more quickly than he should because the noon hour is when he has squeezed in some intramural time for his students.

After intramural time, he has a planning period of 35 minutes—his only one during the week. Then he has three more classes before the gym helpers arrive at 3:30 to put away equipment and to prepare for the next day. Jay does some paperwork related to the day's lessons, checks in the office for any school messages or mail, stops to talk with the first-grade teacher, and then heads home at 4:15 p.m., where he does more school planning before he has dinner.

Joan leaves her home at 7:00 each morning for the short drive to the high school where she teaches and coaches. The school enrollment has grown, so classes now begin at 7:30. She has a planning period during the first period, but she is expected to be in her office when school officially begins at 7:30. She will teach six classes, supervising the locker room before and after each class. Two of her classes will have a fitness orientation, three will be on soccer, and one is a special elective class she started on weight training for females. She has some lunch-supervision duties but manages to spend a pleasant 45 minutes in the teachers' lounge having lunch and chatting with her colleagues. Her last 50-minute class is over at 3:00, and she has a half-hour to prepare for her basketball practice.

The season has just started, so when practice is over at 5:30, she grabs a quick dinner on her way to scout the team that her school will play against the next weekend. She returns home at 9:30 p.m., works on her practice plans for the next day, and organizes the scouting information she gathered at the opponents' game. She will need to be up at 6:15 the next morning to be at school by 7:30, to go through the routine again.

Only those who have taught or have observed a teacher for a full day can appreciate the intensity of these schedules. The coaching added to the full day of teaching extends the intensity longer in the day. When you teach and coach, you are *responsible* for the students in your care. If you try hard to do a good job of teaching and coaching, you are busy interacting with your students/players most of the time you are with them. All in all, the job of physical education teacher is a demanding one that is often seriously underappreciated.

## Teaching as Part of a Team Effort

Physical education teachers at any individual school and within a district are part of a teaching team. This is especially true for large elementary schools and for nearly all middle schools and high schools. In these situations, there will be physical education faculty members who have to work together to make the school program successful. South Carolina is the first state to have not only physical education standards for its K–12 schools, but also state assessment of the degree to which schools are meeting those standards (Rink & Williams, 2003). With state assessment of student performance in physical education, it becomes possible to begin to make comparisons among schools in terms of their success (or lack thereof) in meeting those standards.

Castelli and Rink (2003) used data in South Carolina to compare high- and low-performing secondary school physical education programs. Their results show clearly that having an effective school physical education program requires that physical education teachers work as a team and that the team be supported by the school administration. The physical education faculty in the high-performing schools in this study had regular and effective communication, clear teacher roles, high expectations, and enthusiasm among the faculty, a department leader who served as liaison with school administrators, and (as we noted earlier) an active school administration that was supportive of the team's effort. On the other hand, in the low-performing schools, the teachers tended to act as individuals, communicated only informally and mostly about procedures, lacked effective department leadership, and had a passive school administration.

As mentioned in Chapter 4, teaching physical education in schools, therefore, is not a "do your own thing" task. To be successful in accomplishing important goals, teachers have to work together, help each other, and be committed as a group to the school's goals for physical education—and they have to have the support of the school and district administrators.

## PREPARING TO BECOME A PHYSICAL EDUCATION TEACHER

As we noted earlier in this chapter, the primary way to become a physical education teacher is to attend a college or university and to enter a teacher-preparation program. Some states have experimented with *alternative* routes to certification for teaching, but these all involve college graduation and, eventually at least, some specific teacher preparation. The purpose of this section is to describe the different ways in which teachers are prepared.

Because the U.S. Constitution leaves the responsibility for education to the states, the *rules* for teacher certification are made by state legislatures. Teacher education in the United States takes place almost exclusively at colleges and universities. Programs of teacher education in colleges and universities must adhere to *standards* that are devised by state legislatures or state departments of education.

## Differences Among States

Because states differ markedly in their approach to teacher certification, what a student has to do to become certified as a physical education teacher differs dramatically from state to state. Here are some of the ways in which states differ:

1. *Level of certification.* The three main kinds of certification in physical education are K–12, which allows you to teach at any grade level; K–6, which specializes training and restricts teaching to the elementary school; and 7–12, which specializes training and restricts teaching to the middle and secondary schools. Relatively few states have K–6 certification, whereas K–12 is the certification most commonly received by graduating physical education majors.

2. *Number of teaching specialties.* States with many small, rural schools tend to require more than one teaching major or a teaching major with one or two teaching minors. Thus, the newly graduated teacher is certified in more than one teaching area (physical education and history, say, or physical education, general science, and health). This enables principals in small schools to use staff more effectively. In states with more consolidation and larger school districts, the trend has been toward certification in only one subject area.

3. *Amount of field experience.* There has been a strong trend in teacher education over the past several decades to increase the amount of contact that teacher candidates have with schools and students. This is typically done through what is called a **field** or *school-based* **practicum experience**. These experiences range from observation through full-scale teaching. Some states require extensive amounts of field experience before candidates start their official student teaching. Other states require none. Thus, first-year teachers may differ dramatically in the amount of teaching experience they have received in their preparation programs.

The actual curriculum that teacher candidates receive differs, depending on how the state in which they prepare creates standards reflecting the differences we have described. A student in a state that emphasizes K–12 certification and that requires two teaching majors, but no field experience before student teaching, receives a preparation very different from that of a student in another state who is working toward a K–6 certificate, where only physical education as a teaching area is required and where there is a strong emphasis on field experience. What does your state require or allow? How do its requirements differ from those of neighboring states? What do you think would be the best approach to preparing teachers in your state? These are all interesting questions, discussion of which will quickly get you deeply involved in opinions about teacher education.

## National Standards for Beginning Physical Education Teachers

NASPE published the first-ever standards for initial teacher education in physical education in 1995. The second revision occurred in 2008 (NASPE, 2009a), and now also includes standards for teachers who have been teaching for at least 3 years. The teacher education standards are meant to prepare students to deliver a physical education program that is consistent with the NASPE content standards described in Chapter 4. Thus, the outcomes that define a physically educated person are aligned with the standards for preparing beginning teachers of physical education. NASPE's current standards for beginning teachers are listed in Focus On Box 5.2. Each standard is accompanied by a series of outcomes that more specifically define what the beginning teacher should know and be able to do upon completion of the program. Standards such as these will eventually influence the curriculum that students who want to be physical education teachers take in their physical education Teacher Education program.

In the United States, teachers are licensed at the state level, and each state differs somewhat in how it reviews teacher education programs to grant them the right to prepare teachers. When national standards are adopted by a parent professional organization such as NASPE, they are quickly adopted at the state level also and used as the template through which accreditation teams periodically review each public and private institution approved to prepare teachers in that field. That is, to continue to be approved, the institution must successfully pass the state review. In this way, the standards quickly become the guidelines that individual institutions use to plan their Physical Education Teacher Education programs.

The highest credential an American teacher can achieve is to earn recognition from the National Board for Professional Teaching Standards (www.nbpts.org). To become a National Board Certified Teacher (NBCT) is to be recognized as having achieved the highest benchmark for teacher quality. NBPTS certification takes between 1 and 3 years to complete and measures what accomplished teachers

| FOCUS ON | NASPE Standards for Beginning Physical Education Teachers | 5.2 |

### Standard 1: Scientific and Theoretical Knowledge

*Physical education teacher candidates know and apply discipline-specific scientific and theoretical concepts critical to the development of physically educated individuals.*

Elements—Teacher candidates will:

1.1  Describe and apply physiological and biomechanical concepts related to skillful movement, physical activity, and fitness.

1.2  Describe and apply motor learning and psychological/behavioral theory related to skillful movement, physical activity, and fitness.

1.3  Describe and apply motor development theory and principles related to skillful movement, physical activity, and fitness.

1.4  Identify historical, philosophical, and social perspectives of physical education issues and legislation.

1.5  Analyze and correct critical elements of motor skills and performance concepts.

### Standard 2: Skill and Fitness Based Competence°

*Physical education teacher candidates are physically educated individuals with the knowledge and skills necessary to demonstrate competent movement performance and health enhancing fitness as delineated in the NASPE K–12 Standards.*

Elements—Teacher candidates will:

2.1  Demonstrate personal competence in motor skill performance for a variety of physical activities and movement patterns.

2.2  Achieve and maintain a health-enhancing level of fitness throughout the program.

2.3  Demonstrate performance concepts related to skillful movement in a variety of physical activities.

### Standard 3: Planning and Implementation

*Physical education teacher candidates plan and implement developmentally appropriate learning experiences aligned with local, state, and national standards to address the diverse needs of all students.*

Elements—Teacher candidates will:

3.1  Design and implement short and long term plans that are linked to program and instructional goals as well as a variety of student needs.

3.2  Develop and implement appropriate (e.g., measurable, developmentally appropriate, performance based) goals and objectives aligned with local, state, and /or national standards.

3.3  Design and implement content that is aligned with lesson objectives.

3.4  Plan for and manage resources to provide active, fair, and equitable learning experiences.

3.5  Plan and adapt instruction for diverse student needs, adding specific accommodations and/or modifications for student exceptionalities.

3.6  Plan and implement progressive and sequential instruction that addresses the diverse needs of all students.

3.7  Demonstrate knowledge of current technology by planning and implementing learning experiences that require students to appropriately use technology to meet lesson objectives.

### Standard 4: Instructional Delivery and Management

*Physical education teacher candidates use effective communication and pedagogical skills and strategies to enhance student engagement and learning.*

Elements – Teacher candidates will:

4.1  Demonstrate effective verbal and non-verbal communication skills across a variety of instructional formats.

4.2  Implement effective demonstrations, explanations, and instructional cues and prompts to link physical activity concepts to appropriate learning experiences.

4.3  Provide effective instructional feedback for skill acquisition, student learning, and motivation.

*(continued)*

**FOCUS ON** — NASPE Standards for Beginning Physical Education Teachers *(continued)* — 5.2

4.4 Recognize the changing dynamics of the environment and adjust instructional tasks based on student responses.

4.5 Utilize managerial rules, routines, and transitions to create and maintain a safe and effective learning environment.

4.6 Implement strategies to help students demonstrate responsible personal and social behaviors in a productive learning environment.

**Standard 5: Impact on Student Learning**

*Physical education teacher candidates utilize assessments and reflection to foster student learning and inform instructional decisions.*

Elements—Teacher candidates will:

5.1 Select or create appropriate assessments that will measure student achievement of goals and objectives.

5.2 Use appropriate assessments to evaluate student learning before, during, and after instruction.

5.3 Utilize the reflective cycle to implement change in teacher performance, student learning, and/or instructional goals and decisions.

**Standard 6: Professionalism**

*Physical education teacher candidates demonstrate dispositions essential to becoming effective professionals.*

Elements—Teacher candidates will:

6.1 Demonstrate behaviors that are consistent with the belief that all students can become physically educated individuals.

6.2 Participate in activities that enhance collaboration and lead to professional growth and development.

6.3 Demonstrate behaviors that are consistent with the professional ethics of highly qualified teachers.

6.4 Communicate in ways that convey respect and sensitivity.

Source: NASPE, 2009.

should know and be able to do. Teachers complete a rigorous portfolio and submit it to NBPTS to be evaluated. As of May 2011, 1,669 physical education teachers have received this prestigious recognition (www.nbpts.org). In certain states and school districts teachers who wish to become Board certified can get financial support to offset the cost associated with the certification process. Importantly, there is evidence that Board-certified teachers have effects on student achievement beyond that produced by teachers who are not Board certified (Bond, Smith, Baker, Hattie, 2000; Goldhaber & Anthony, 2004; Vandevoort, Amrein-Beardsley, & Berliner, 2004).

## Certification for Teaching Adapted Physical Education

The Individuals with Disabilities Education Act (IDEA) mandates that children and youths with disabilities receive physical education services and specially designed services (adapted physical educa-

tion) from qualified personnel. However, the law does not specify what is meant by "qualified." Some states have interpreted the law to mean that teachers are certified in physical education, whereas others are more lenient and interpret the law to mean that personnel have teaching certificates in any field. Those states that have developed special requirements for adapted-physical education teachers typically do so as an add-on validation or endorsement to a previously earned teaching certificate.

About one-third of the states now offer a validation/endorsement in adapted Physical Education. In 1995 the National Consortium for physical education and Recreation for Individuals with Disabilities (NCPERID) developed Adapted physical education National Standards (APENS) and a national certification examination to measure knowledge of those standards. The project to develop the standards and APENS examination was federally funded under the leadership of Luke Kelly at the University of Virginia (NCPERID, 1995). The APENS exam is for all teachers who consider themselves qualified and competent adapted-physical educators. The minimum qualifications to take the exam are a bachelor's degree in physical education (or an equivalent in kinesiology, exercise science), a valid teaching certificate, 200 hours of experience providing adapted-physical education services, and 12 semester credit hours of coursework that specifically addresses the needs of students with disabilities. This usually includes an introductory survey course in adapted physical education. It is hoped that the APENS examination process will serve as a motivation and a resource for those states that have not yet developed a validation or endorsement program.

The programs described in this chapter show that physical education can be done well and can contribute significantly to the education of all children and youth. Nonetheless, physical education in schools is beset by problems and by controversial, unresolved issues. Those problems and issues are explored in Chapter 6.

## Building a Vision for the Future

The programs described in this chapter, while different in certain respects, all seem to be focused primarily on helping students adopt and value physically active lifestyles. Some programs do it with a fitness/health-club approach whereas others do it with a recreational-activity focus. What does seem consistent across approaches is the manner in the pedagogical strategies they develop. If you want girls and boys to *adopt* and *value* a physically active lifestyle, you have to develop an instructional process, an instructional climate, and a school environment that is inviting, fun, and success-oriented. Students need to know that you really care about their futures, are there to help them, and have the knowledge and commitment to help them achieve program goals. Many teachers also develop a pedagogical climate where students learn to respect and support each other, despite the differences in their native abilities or their different work ethics.

Obviously, it becomes difficult to accomplish lifestyle goals without sufficient time with students. What is clear in many of the programs cited here is

Regularly engaging in physical activity beyond physical education should be a central goal.

the ways that they find to engage students outside of class time, with drop-in activities, after-school opportunities, physical education homework, and the like. Moreover, positive steps are being taken in many states to improve the state of physical education. Focus On Box 5.3 includes examples of progress. We will address the role of policy changes and development in more detail in Chapter 6. Physical education will prosper if more physical educators, working together in school districts, take the *Field of Dreams* approach; that is, "If you build it, they will come." The "it," of course, is an exciting program taught by teachers who care about and provide excellent instruction to their students.

It is also clear that a physical education program in a school district needs to be conceptualized as a K–12 program. Teachers at elementary-, middle-, and high-school levels have to come together so that the goals and process of the program are consistent through the students' school years. When middle-school physical education builds on an excellent elementary-school program and high-school physical education builds still further on the middle-school program, then the likelihood of achieving a total programmatic impact on students is greatly increased.

What is your vision for the future? Which of the programs presented earlier most appeals to you? When you go to look for a job as a newly certified physical education teacher, what kind of program would you most like to join? This time that you are spending as an undergraduate should be used

---

**FOCUS ON**    **Recent State Legislation to Strengthen Physical Education**     **5.3**

In the wake of the federal legislation requiring local school districts to address school wellness issues, several states have passed legislation to strengthen physical education. Here are a few examples:

### Arkansas

- Created a statewide Child Health Advisory Council.
- In 2007–08, K–12 students must receive 150 minutes per week of physical education.
- Established a maximum student-to-teacher ratio of 30 to 1.

### Kentucky

HB 52 was introduced requiring that:

- School council wellness policies provide for a minimum of 30 minutes of structured moderate to vigorous physical activity per day; 150 minutes per week, or the equivalent per month.
- School councils report progress data.
- Structured physical activity be considered part of the instructional day.

### Washington

- Created a comprehensive health fitness curriculum with a minimum of 100 minutes per week in grades 1–8.
- PE assessment strategies must be in place by 2008–2009.
- Developing a statewide assessment of physical education outcomes using a variety of assessment tools.

### North Carolina

Passed HB 1373, in which the state adopts and phases in the following between now and 2015:

- Required physical education taught by certified teachers at every grade level.
- Class sizes can be no bigger than those in core academic subjects.
- Assessments must be implemented measuring knowledge, skill, and fitness.

Source: Adapted from NASPE (2010).

- Mandates 150 minutes of physical education every week.

### Texas

- All districts must adopt the Coordinated School Health model.
- Requires 30 minutes daily or 135 minutes weekly of daily physical education/physical activity in grades 1–8.
- Requires each elementary school to adopt one of four approved school health models.

### California

- Requires a minimum of 200 minutes every 10 schools days in grades 1–6.
- Requires a minimum of 400 minutes of physical education for every 10 school days in grades 7–12.
- Physical education must be delivered by a credentialed physical education teacher.
- Budgeted $40 million to support hiring of more physical education teachers.

### Georgia

The recently passed (and funded) "State Health and Physical Education Act" (HB 229) mandates that beginning in 2011–2012:

- Georgia school systems conduct annual fitness assessments and comply with state physical education instruction requirements.
- The governor is provided with an annual report about the results.
- A recognition program is developed.

### Michigan

SB 365 was introduced aimed at:

- Eliminating the use of exemption from the physical education course for students who are capable of taking it and not physically fit.
- Prohibiting public school districts from crediting students' participation in extracurricular activities involving physical activity as a means of meeting district physical education requirements.

wisely to help you gain the skills that will enable you to compete successfully for a position in a program that emphasizes the programmatic elements that you think are necessary to achieve your vision.

Can you envision a K–12 school campus where all students (a) have access to physical activity venues and take advantage of these opportunities throughout the school day? (b) make healthy food choices when going through the lunch lines? and (c) feel safe psychologically, regardless of who they are? Can you see how physical education programs have a central role in accomplishing this vision? The recently unveiled National Physical Activity Plan (www.physicalactivityplan.org) demonstrates the central role of the education sector in efforts to increase physical activity levels of all children and youth. Virtually all of them spend a large amount of time on most days of their formative years in schools. Most schools (especially secondary schools) have expansive facilities specifically designed for physical activity (McKenzie & Lounsbery, 2009). In addition, there is now clear evidence that time spent in physical education and physical activity is related to academic achievement and cognitive functioning (Centers for Disease Control and Prevention, 2010a; Sattelmair & Ratey, 2009; Trost & van der Mars, 2009). Pate, Davis, Robinson, Stone, McKenzie, and Young (2006) argued persuasively that this then places the responsibility of providing maximum opportunities for daily physical activity of all students squarely on schools.

The National Physical Activity Plan reflects the physical activity potential of school campuses and how physical education programs are central to bringing this potential to fruition (see Focus On Box 5.4). As you review these strategies and tactics, ask yourself the following questions:

1. What roles and responsibilities do school physical education programs (and their full staff) have relative to implementing these various strategies and tactics?

2. Who is best positioned to help create increased opportunities for physical activity during the before-school, lunch-time, recess, and after-school time periods?

---

**FOCUS ON**   **Education Sector Strategies and Tactics in the National Physical Activity Plan**   **5.4**

**STRATEGY 1: Provide access to and opportunities for high-quality, comprehensive physical activity programs, anchored by physical education, in pre-kindergarten through grade 12 educational settings. Ensure that the programs are physically active, inclusive, safe, and developmentally and culturally appropriate.**

*TACTICS*

- Advocate for increased federal funding of programs such as the Carol White Physical Education for Progress (PEP) grant program.

- Include in funding criteria the development of state-of-the-art, comprehensive physical activity demonstration programs and pilot projects, and effective evaluation of those programs.

- Include a preference for adoption of physical education (PE) and physical activity (PA) programs demonstrated to provide high amounts of physical activity. Widely disseminate successful demonstration and pilot programs and those with practice-based evidence. Work with states to identify areas of great need, prioritizing funding efforts toward lower-resourced communities.

- Provide adequate funding for research that advances this strategy and all other education sector strategies.

- Require preservice and continuing education for physical education and elementary classroom teachers to deliver high-quality physical education and physical activity programs.

- Provide continuing education classes and seminars for all teachers on state-of-the-art physical activities
  *(continued)*

for children that provide information on adapting activities for children with disabilities, in classrooms and physical education settings.

- Encourage higher education institutions to train future teachers and school personnel on the importance of physical activity to academic achievement and success for students from pre-kindergarten through grade 12.

**STRATEGY 2: Develop and implement state and school-district policies requiring school accountability for the quality and quantity of physical education and physical activity programs.**

*TACTICS*

- Advocate for binding requirements for Pre-K–12 standards-based physical education that address state standards, curriculum time, class size, and employment of certified, highly qualified physical education teachers in accordance with national standards and guidelines, such as those published by the National Association for Sport and Physical Education (NASPE).

- Advocate for local, state, and national standards that emphasize provision of high levels of physical activity in physical education (e.g., 50 percent of class time in moderate-to-vigorous activity).

- Enact federal legislation, such as the FIT Kids Act, to require school accountability for the quality and quantity of physical education and physical activity programs.

- Provide local, state, and national funding to ensure that schools have the resources (e.g., facilities, equipment, appropriately trained staff) to provide high-quality physical education and activity programming.

- Designate the largest portion of funding for schools that are underresourced. Work with states to identify areas of greatest need.

- Develop and implement state-level policies that require school districts to report on the quality and quantity of physical education and physical activity programs. Develop and implement a measure-

ment and reporting system to determine the progress of states toward meeting this strategy. Include in this measurement and reporting system data to monitor the benefits and adaptations made or needed for children with disabilities.

- Require school districts to annually collect, monitor, and track students' health-related fitness data, including body mass index.

**STRATEGY 3: Develop partnerships with other sectors for the purpose of linking youth with physical activity opportunities in schools and communities.**

*TACTICS*

- Develop plans at local levels for leadership and collaboration across sectors, such as education, youth-serving organizations, and parks and recreation.

- Develop and institute local policies and joint use agreements that facilitate shared use of physical activity facilities, such as school gyms and community recreation centers and programming.

- Prioritize efforts to target communities and schools by working with states to identify areas of greatest need.

- Develop partnerships with organizations that encourage citizen involvement, community mobilization, and volunteerism to link to and sustain community opportunities for physical activity.

**STRATEGY 5: Provide access to and opportunities for physical activity before and after school.**

*TACTICS*

- Support Safe Routes to School efforts to increase active transportation to and from school and support accommodations for children with disabilities. Encourage states to adopt standards for the inclusion of physical activity in after-school programs.

- Require a physical activity component in all state and federally funded after-school programs, including 21st Century Community Learning Centers.

| FOCUS ON | Education Sector Strategies and Tactics in the National Physical Activity Plan *(continued)* | 5.4 |

- Work with community college systems to include physical activity training as part of early childhood and school-age child-care preparation programs.
- Subsidize the transportation and program costs of after-school programs through local, state, and federal sources.

- Provide resources for innovative pilot projects in the after-school setting.
- Encourage states to abide by national after-school accreditation standards on physical activity as applicable, and advance state licensure requirements in alignment with those standards.

SOURCE: Adapted from: www.nationalphysicalactivityplan.org

3. Who would be the key person to assist classroom teachers with building physical activity breaks into the classroom subjects (especially on days when students do not have a physical education lesson)?

4. Who could/should be the prime person to train adult supervisors of recess periods to help promote physical activity on elementary-school campuses?

5. Who should be aware of and be able to connect with the various outside agencies and programs that have physical activity as a primary focus?

Notice how (a) the physical education program and its staff is the "anchor program" to create the increased access and opportunities for physical activity, and (b) the considerable overlap between the national health objectives set forth in Healthy People 2020 (See Chapter 4, Focus On Box 4.8) and the education strategies and tactics in the National Physical Activity Plan. The willingness and ability of school physical education programs to actively contribute to this national, multifaceted physical activity promotion effort will in large part determine its future place in schools.

## SUMMARY

1. Although a broad view of physical education takes into account all the settings in which people learn, practice, and enjoy sport and fitness activities, the school is still the setting where physical education can best serve the majority of children and youth.

2. School physical education programs have a central goal: Promotion of physical activity. However, that cannot be the only goal.

3. There is considerable support for school physical education at the federal government level. It has developed national physical activity guidelines and recommendations for children, youth, adults, and older adults.

4. High-quality daily physical education for all students is a hope for the future. It is necessary if we are to achieve fully the goals of physical education.

5. High-quality programs can and do exist with a broad range of curricular approaches including fitness, comprehensive-skill-grouped, sport education, personal growth, adventure education, movement education, and comprehensive elective programs. Many of them include program components that support physical activity opportunities on campus beyond the physical education lessons.

6. Increasingly, physical educators' role is described in terms of being a "physical activity director." In addition to teaching regular lessons, current and future physical activity directors will be responsible for planning and coordinating opportunities for physical activity on the entire campus throughout the day.

7. Characteristics of exemplary programs include leadership by a qualified physical educator, a

specific programmatic theme, a sense of excitement, (a) teacher(s) whose main interest is this program (as opposed to coaching), and strong support from school administrators.

8. Technology has advanced significantly in the last two decades, and it can make important contributions to how teachers plan, teach, assess, and organize their program, and support student learning.

9. Physical education teachers earn certificates in the state in which they graduate from an approved teacher education program.

10. The physical education teacher plays a number of diverse roles including planner, manager, colleague, member of a profession, counselor, and representative of the school and school district.

11. Teachers lead intense daily lives in schools, teaching, and supervising students. After-school coaching responsibilities can increase the length of the school day.

12. States provide different levels of certification, and while variations do exist, the most common being K–12, K–6, and 7–12.

13. NASPE's national standards for beginning teachers provide a mechanism for improving the quality of teacher preparation in physical education. Teachers can remain current through professional development in the form of seeking an advanced degree, attending professional conferences and workshops, and National Board Certification.

14. National certification is available in the area of adapted physical education through the APENS exam.

15. In 2010, the National Physical Activity Plan was unveiled, bringing together eight different sectors in society, including education. The central goal of the plan is to increase the physical activity levels of all people, including children and youth. Schools figure prominently in the national plan. Relative to physical education, the plan emphasizes increasing physical activity opportunities on school campuses for all students throughout the school day. It also targets the development of policies that would support promotion of physical activity opportunities.

## DISCUSSION QUESTIONS

1. What staff and facilities would an elementary school with 400 students require to implement a daily physical education program? What would a high school with 1,000 students require?

2. Should all students have access to all of the school's physical activity venues? If not, why? What access did you have to physical activity at high school beyond taking the regular physical education classes?

3. If you had 5 minutes to make your case for quality physical education to school district- or state-level policy makers, what would you ask for and how would you support and justify it?

4. Which exemplary program did you like most? Why? Which did you like least? Why?

5. Are there programs in your region that you think are exemplary? Which of the characteristics described in the chapter, if any, do they manifest?

6. Do you know people who are now teacher-coaches? Are their professional lives like those of the teachers described in this chapter? What roles do they occupy? Which role are you drawn to more right now? Why?

7. What certification is available in your state? If you are certified in your state, where else does that certification allow you to teach?

8. How does your teacher preparation program compare with the current NASPE standards for beginning teachers?

9. Given the strategies and tactics outlined in the National Physical Activity Plan, how well do you think your high-school physical education program was doing in implementing them? How do you see yourself contributing to implementing these various strategies and tactics?

## CHAPTER 6

# Problems, Issues, and the Future of Physical Education

*In the United States, Physical Education in schools continues, along with art and music, to be disposable: Embraced when budgets are full and public outcries loud, restricted when money is scarce. Currently, finances are strained in most states, but the recognition of the value and importance of physical activity has never been higher. It is an interesting period in school Physical Education K–12 in the United States.*

George Graham, 1990

Chapters 4 and 5 described both the curriculum and instruction models that are currently used in physical education and provided examples of exemplary physical education programs at elementary-, middle-, and high-school levels. This chapter focuses on problems and issues in physical education, some of which are issues across the K–12 spectrum and some of which are specific to elementary-, middle-, or high-school physical education. As you will see, some problems cannot be solved without stronger legislation at the state level whereas others are more specific to individual schools or districts and can be solved with stronger leadership from administrators and stronger support from parents.

## GENERAL PROBLEMS IN PHYSICAL EDUCATION

Some significant problems cut across the K–12 spectrum. Although they may not manifest themselves in exactly the same ways for the elementary-school program as they do for the middle- or high-school program, they are nonetheless endemic problems that seriously diminish the quality of instruction and seriously jeopardize the likelihood of achieving significant programmatic outcomes.

### Time Available for Physical Education

Lack of sufficient time may be the most serious problem that cuts across K–12 physical education. When an elementary-school physical education specialist has a class that meets one day each week, it is equally difficult to imagine that significant outcomes will be achieved. The recent national concern about child/youth overweight and obesity has resulted in many states increasing the time requirements for physical education. That is a positive step forward! However, as we will note later in this chapter, it is also clear that few states have accountability mechanisms to ensure that time requirements are met by individual school districts.

Many school districts face financial problems and use reduced physical education to save resources that can be used to improve the core academic subjects, particularly reading and math. Moreover, the No Child Left Behind (NCLB) federal legislation was passed in 2001. Physical education's exclusion as a core subject within NCLB made it an easy target for state and local school-district policy makers, and resulted in significant loss of allocated time for the noncore subjects (see Table 6.1). What is most unnerving about these decisions is that there is now a sizable body of evidence to support the claim that more physical activity during the day improves student attention and engagement in the classroom, and thus may make a positive contribution to academic achievement (e.g., Active Living Research, 2009; Centers for Disease Control and Prevention, 2010a;

Trost & van der Mars, 2009). For example, Trost and van der Mars (2009) concluded that there is enough support to draw the following conclusions:

1. Decreasing (or eliminating) the time allotted for physical education in favor of traditional academic subjects does not necessarily improve academic performance.

2. Increases in the time spent per week in physical education will not impede students' academic achievement.

3. Increased time in physical education may make small positive contributions to academic achievement, particularly for girls.

4. Physical activity is beneficial to general cognitive functioning.

This makes it very difficult for a program to accomplish its many purported objectives. In terms of accumulating sufficient daily physical activity (an accepted core program outcome), physical education lessons alone simply provide insufficient time for students to reach even the minimum recommended daily amount of physical activity (U.S.D.H.H.S., 2008). In fact, Tudor-Locke, Lee, Morgan, Beighle, and Pangrazi (2004) reported that when at school, sixth-grade students accumulate only about 8 to

**TABLE 6.1** Changes in Instructional Time in Elementary Schools Since No Child Left Behind Was Enacted.

| Subject | % of districts Increasing Time | % of districts Decreasing Time | Average Increase (Min. per wk.) | Average Decrease (Min. per wk.) |
|---|---|---|---|---|
| Language Arts | 58 | | 141 | |
| Math | 45 | | 89 | |
| Social Studies | | 36 | | 76 |
| Science | | 28 | | 75 |
| Art and Music | | 16 | | 57 |
| Physical Education | | 9 | | 40 |
| Lunch recess | | | 5 | |
| Recess | | 20 | | 50 |

SOURCE: Adapted from Center for Educational Policy, 2007.

11 percent on average of the recommended daily total physical activity during physical education lessons. They accumulate the largest amount of school-based physical activity during lunch recess (approximately 15 percent).

As can be seen in Table 6.1, time for physical activity beyond physical education in elementary schools has decreased as well. While the multiple benefits of recess are well documented (e.g., Pellegrini & Bohn, 2005), policy makers in many school districts have opted to reduce time for recess, or in some cases eliminate it altogether. Hence, creating increased access and opportunities for physical activity throughout the school day for all students beyond physical education lessons is of utmost importance.

In some states, such as Kentucky, new legislation increases the total school time that has to be allotted for physical education and physical activity, but many districts choose to increase the time using physical activity breaks with large numbers of students participating, with no increased time for physical education. This is not to suggest that physical activity breaks are not useful. However, what it does suggest is that if 90 minutes per week in physical education/physical activity are required and 60 of those 90 minutes are in physical activity, then physical education is left with essentially one class period per week. Worse yet, in cases where schools are required to report how much physical activity time is provided, some large high schools may actually count the passing time between class periods as physical activity time.

## Class Size

Class size is an equally difficult issue, and one over which teachers unfortunately have little to no say. The National Association for Sport and Physical Education (NASPE) suggests that class size for physical education be similar to that of other subject areas with a maximum ratio of 1:25 for elementary school, 1:30 for middle school, and 1:35 for high school. Currently, 30 states have no state mandate in place that puts limits on class sizes. The remaining

states include mandates where the student to teacher ratio must be comparable to those in effect for other subjects (NASPE, 2010a).

Large-sized classes create significant problems for physical education teachers. Management issues become more difficult and cut into instructional and practice time. The space and amount of equipment is often geared to the lower ratios, forcing students into sharing equipment and space, thus reducing their opportunities to practice and be active. Large classes make it very difficult for teachers to individualize instruction, increase the risk of injury, and increase the amount of "off-task" behavior among students.

Skilled physical education teachers find ways to deal with large class sizes by using strategies such as small-group work, cooperative learning, peer teaching, station work, and small-sided games. However, teachers oftentimes spend more time monitoring group activity and maintaining on-task behavior and less time providing individual attention and feedback for the purpose of helping students improve.

## Exemptions/Waivers

Over the past two decades, states and school districts increasingly have resorted to various forms of exemptions. Students can obtain an exemption from physical education for: (a) religious reasons; (b) demonstrating high levels of competency; (c) involvement in other school-based activities such as band, cheerleading, ROTC, or interscholastic activities; (d) a long-term physical or medical disability, and (e) involvement in physical activity in programs or settings not affiliated with the school.

Little is known about what initially prompted the use of exemptions/waivers from physical education. Perhaps policy makers perceive participation in physical education as less important or relevant. Another possible reason is that they believe that what is accomplished in physical education can also be accomplished on a football team, in a marching band, or in ROTC. This has become a particularly difficult argument to make in an era when the primary goal for physical education is to help students adopt and value a physically active lifestyle.

Given your knowledge and understanding of school districts' practices in allowing exemptions from physical education, consider the following questions:

- Should exemptions be allowed? Why or why not?
- What circumstances would warrant exemption from physical education (i.e., one would not have to take the course)?

- What are the consequences of allowing students to be exempt from physical education?
- As a teacher, if your school district were considering a proposal that would allow students to seek exemptions for involvement in ROTC, band, or interscholastic sport, what would you use as a counterargument against such proposals?

NASPE (2006c) published a position statement strongly opposing the use of exemptions/waivers from required physical education. An added concern is that states and school districts may use exemptions as a means to avoid providing adapted physical education to students with disabilities (Thomas, 2004). Perhaps the recent concern about child/youth overweight and obesity and the manner in which school physical education programs are responding to the concern will lead to the elimination of exemptions/waivers.

In recent years, legislation has been introduced in certain states to reduce or eliminate exemptions/waivers from physical education. NASPE (2010a) reported that 32 states allow districts to use exemptions/waivers. According to Lee, Burgeson, Fulton, and Spain (2007), exemptions for religious reasons decreased by almost 50 percent in elementary and middle schools. Yet, exemptions for high physical competency increased from 0.5 to 4.9 percent in elementary schools, and from 2 to 10.5 percent in middle schools. Moreover, the percentage of districts allowing exemptions for participation in community sports activities increased from 2.1 percent to 8.9 percent. More than 20 percent of the high schools that required physical education allowed exemptions for other school-based activities (e.g., band, ROTC, chorus) and school-based sports. Finally, exemptions allowed because of a cognitive disability increased from 31.4 to 44.1 percent, while exemptions because of a long-term physical or medical disability increased from 66.3 to 85.7 percent.

The use of exemptions/waivers is typically a state or district decision. Depending on where you were a K–12 student, you yourself may have been exempted from physical education. Regardless, it is essential that as a teacher you understand that such exemptions/waivers are essentially a loophole that diminishes the likelihood that your program can positively impact all students. Moreover, together with your colleagues, you will want to develop persuasive arguments that you can use when the opportunity arises to eliminate the policy that is in effect (see Focus On Box 6.1).

## Physical Activity as a Form of Punishment

Especially in light of the strong focus on promoting physical activity behavior, it is hard to imagine that physical educators still subject their students to punishment in the form of physical activity. No doubt the culture of "drop and gimme 50" within interscholastic and intercollegiate sport programs continues to spill over into physical education, especially in secondary schools. However, NASPE (2009d) is unequivocal in its position: "administering or withdrawing physical activity as punishment is inappropriate and constitutes an unsound education practice" (p. 2). In numerous states (e.g., California, Hawaii, and Massachusetts), physical activity used for punishment is considered a form of corporal punishment.

The absence of a state- or district-level policy that aims to ban this practice essentially implies tacit approval of the practice. Moreover, the actual prevalence of this form of punishment is difficult to track. According to Lee et al. (2007), between 2000 and 2006, the percentage of states that prohibit schools from using physical activity as punishment for bad behavior among students in physical education increased from 2.1 to 16 percent, and the percentage of states that actively discouraged schools from this practice also increased, from 25.5 to 56 percent. That is the good news.

However, in almost a third of the nation's schools (32.3 percent) school staff members are allowed to use physical activity (e.g., running laps or pushups) to punish students for inappropriate conduct in physical education. In only 8.9 percent of schools, school staff was actively discouraged from using this practice (Lee et al., 2007). Needless to say further progress is needed in this area.

Another form of punishment involves the withholding of access to physical education or other physical activity such as recess for inappropriate behavior in other classrooms or for not completing assignments in academic subjects is seen more in elementary schools. Lee et al. (2007) reported that this practice occurs in just over one-fifth (22.6 percent) of schools in the United States. School staff was actively discouraged from employing this practice in only 11.4 percent of schools.

We believe that resorting to this approach to behavior control says more about the quality of the overall behavior management system that teachers employ in their classes. If you are truly committed to guiding your students toward enjoying physical activity and leading physically active lives, you cannot turn around and use the same behavior as a means of punishment. While it might have the desired effect in the short term, it certainly sends conflicting messages, and students may question your credibility.

## Facilities

Traditionally, school physical education facilities have been built as gymnasiums with the basketball court(s) as the main feature of the facility. In elementary schools, the gym is smaller than in middle or high school. In temperate climates, it is not unusual that 80 percent of elementary-school physical education is taught outside on school playgrounds. Even in colder climates, many children receive physical education in a multipurpose room or auditorium rather than in a gymnasium.

We have seen evidence in this text that many high schools have refurbished facilities to create a health and fitness center and that others have developed new facilities built on the health club model with strength- and cardio-training facilities as the main features. Inadequate facilities make good physical education difficult but not impossible. Great facilities make good physical education easier to achieve, but the facilities in and of themselves are not sufficient to guarantee a quality program.

A key issue for physical education programs (especially in secondary schools) is actually how they can increase the use of the available facilities, especially before school times and lunch periods. Little is known about what school districts spend annually on maintaining the many physical activity venue. But Farrey (2008) reported that the annual cost of maintaining a football field alone could go as high as 250,000 dollars. There are ways in which schools could make field- and gym-spaces available for recreational play.

**Skill Equity**　It is clear that peers value competence in physical activity and sport. That is, one way in which children and youth can achieve better status among their peers is to be perceived as physically competent (Evans & Roberts, 1987). However, a problem that persists in physical education is the inability to provide equitable learning experiences for less-skilled children and youth. Less-skilled students typically get fewer opportunities to practice and have less success than do their more-skilled peers (Siedentop, 1991). When games are played, the less-skilled students sometimes get few real opportunities to take part in meaningful play. Moreover, in many cases, teachers tend to pay more attention to the higher-skilled students. You can see how the "rich get richer and the poor remain poor."

Lesser-skilled students often don't try. They tend to have negative expectations for themselves, because of their previous lack of success in physical education (Portman, 1995) and the lack of assistance from the teacher or their classmates. They also are often the object of ridicule from classmates and criticism from teachers. It is no wonder that such students try to find excuses to avoid participation or to be absent from physical education. The only fair description of what has happened to them is physical *mis*education.

Physical educators have the responsibility to provide equitable learning experiences for all children, regardless of skill level. Indeed, it is obvious that helping a less-skilled student to improve in ways that are recognized by peers not only is important in the physical domain but also produces benefits in the social and emotional domains.

Procedures for modifying activities to make them developmentally appropriate are available in our professional literature (NASPE, 1992; Siedentop, 1991). Physical educators must renew their commitment to helping less-skilled students experience success and improve in ways that contribute to the development of lifespan activity habits.

## Liability

We live in an era where citizens have become increasingly assertive about prosecuting in courts of law to maintain their rights and to redress grievances. Physicians, for example, spend enormous amounts of money on malpractice insurance because of the number of lawsuits brought against them—suits in which patients try to hold them *liable* for alleged inappropriate or negligent practice of medical skills.

This era of liability has reached physical education. In the 1970s, it would have been fairly common to find trampolines used in physical education. Today, it is almost impossible to find one in schools because there are simply too many safety issues that might lead to liability litigation for the teacher and school. The same is true for apparatus on elementary-school playgrounds. The newer approaches to outdoor play apparatus for elementary schools takes into full account the safety of the children.

Virtually every school district has a risk management office. People in this office are charged with assessing the risk of being held liable when developing a new program or any school-based activity. Despite being certified and well-trained in teaching activities such as rock climbing and other higher-risk activities typical of outdoor pursuits, teachers may not be allowed to infuse such content into their curriculum; school (district) administrators may view this content as too high risk.

Teachers also are more aware of liability issues. Adventure activities such as climbing and rappelling and the apparatus needed to pursue such activities are commonly found in schools today, but teachers are more aware of the safety issues, the safety equipment, and the level of instruction that needs to be provided for students to use the apparatus. They also carefully monitor student activity and are quick to remediate unsafe behavior. Issues of liability won't go away, but teachers today are much more aware of how to organize, teach, and manage students to create safe learning and practice environments.

The importance of being vigilant in supervising your students cannot be overstated. If a student is injured at a time when no teacher was present, this teacher (and perhaps even the school's principal and district) is at risk of being sued for negligence. Another example would be a situation where a student gets injured and either the type or design of an activity is questioned.

## Gender Equity

The issues of Title IX in sport are discussed in Chapters 11 and 12. Many physical educators today do not realize the profound influence that Title IX had on physical education starting in the 1970s. Title IX, which was enacted in 1972, states, "No person in the United States shall, on the basis of sex, be excluded from participation in, be denied the benefits of, or be subjected to discrimination under any education program or activity receiving federal financial assistance" (Title IX, 2005). Because every public school in America receives some form of federal funding, all physical education programs come under the aegis of the provisions of Title IX. In physical education, the most important specific influences of Title IX were on (1) coeducational classes, (2) assignment of teachers according to skill rather than gender, (3) grouping based on ability rather than gender, and (4) equal access for girls and boys to the entire physical education curriculum.

Sadly, physical education does not have a particularly admirable history with respect to gender equity. Girls have been denied access to learning and participating in certain sports. Female teachers have not always been able to teach those activities for which they are best prepared. In many secondary schools, dysfunctional working relationships between male and female physical educators are partly the cause of such situations. In certain cases contact between the male and female may be nonexistent even if their respective offices are less than 90 feet apart! The consequence of working in such dysfunctional programs is that planning and scheduling is very difficult, and facilities and equipment do not get shared equally. Each side may end up hoarding and hiding equipment from the other side.

Today, the effects of Title IX for physical education are mixed. In many programs, girls have access to the full range of activities offered. On the other hand, research has indicated that there has been a reduction in the number of female physical education teachers in high schools (Hulstrand, 1990). Coed classes are more common, but many programs still have sex-segregated classes. In our own research (Siedentop & O'Sullivan, 1992), we have found that female high-school teachers oftentimes are marginalized in their own departments, and girls are getting fewer opportunities in physical education classes and liking it less than boys do. In another study, Olafson (2002) found that adolescent girls disliked their physical education classes intensely and tried to find ways to avoid them. This finding is particularly salient in an era when adolescent girls are among the most at-risk population for overweight and obesity. We should all work toward the situation where girls and boys have the same access to all activities, learn together, and get equal opportunities to practice and improve and where teaching assignments are made on the basis of competence and experience rather than gender.

## Good and Bad Competition

A continuing concern within physical education is the proper role and level of competition. Many of the abuses associated with organized sport (see Chapter 12) are assumed to be the result of an overemphasis on competition, of a win-at-all-costs perspective. It is not uncommon for physical educators to advocate reducing competition, to replace competitive activities with cooperative activities, and to modify competitive activities in ways that reduce competitiveness. In its most extreme form, this kind of criticism within the physical education profession suggests that competitive activities are inherently harmful for children.

The issue can be viewed from another perspective (Siedentop, Mand, & Taggart, 1986). The issue is not whether competition is all good or all bad, but rather, how we can eliminate *bad* competition and emphasize *good* competition. Good competition creates a *festival* atmosphere, with all the attendant traditions, rituals, and celebrations. Good competition creates a *forum* within which children and youths can test themselves against accepted standards of excellence. Good competition involves *rivalry* but never the kind of rivalry in which one side can win only to the extent that the other side loses. Good competition also means *striving* within the rules and traditions to make the best effort possible—and then, when the competition is over, understanding that the winning or losing has little meaning outside the competition itself.

Bad competition, on the other hand, should be eliminated. Using the rules to gain an advantage, assuming that the only way to win is to have the best score, disregarding the traditions and rituals of the activity, and letting the outcomes affect the participants after the competition is over are all indications of inappropriate competition. Students in physical education should learn the differences between good and bad competition. The only way that they can do this is to have these things pointed out to them as they experience good competition.

Good competition is more easily attainable when individuals or teams are evenly matched. No one enjoys a competition that is terribly one-sided. The sport education model (see Chapter 4) creates mixed-ability teams. For example, a class of 30 middle-school students would be divided into three teams, each of which would have 10 players. Teams would be chosen or assigned to ensure that each team had a similar mix of less- to more-skilled players. When the first competition would take place—in 3 against 3 volleyball, for example—each team would have an A, B, and C team in the competition so that less-skilled teams and more-skilled teams would compete against each other, with each victory counting the same toward the seasonal championship. Small-sided teams of reasonably equal abilities can easily be created in a number of physical education curriculum and instruction models. In tennis a teacher could have girls' singles, boys' singles, and coed doubles. In each competition, there would be A, B, and C level matches, again each match counting the same toward the final outcome.

A related central aspect of sport is that of Fair Play. The level and quality of Fair Play also affects the quality of the competition. Teachers cannot assume that students have a clear understanding of what all encompasses Fair Play. Fair Play goes well beyond a post-game handshake. Siedentop, Hastie, and van der Mars (2011) described Fair Play as follows:

- *Full and responsible participation.* This means being on time and prepared to actively and enthusiastically participate in all class activities.

- *Giving your best effort.* Teams perform better when each teammate gives full effort as a player and in other possible nonplaying roles (e.g., coach, official, scorekeeper).

- *Being a good sport.* Maintaining self-control, showing respect for teammates and opponents at all times; and if conflicts do arise, respecting and valuing ways to resolve those conflicts peacefully and swiftly.

- *Respect the rights and feelings of teammates, opponents, and officials.* This is reflected in playing hard and by the rules; respecting those who enforce the rules; and being graceful in victory while dignified in defeat.

- *Being helpful and not harmful.* This includes looking for ways to help teammates, recognizing and expressing appreciation for good play by others, and at all cost avoiding putdowns and bullying.

## ISSUES IN ELEMENTARY-SCHOOL PHYSICAL EDUCATION

One of the most important findings in education over the past decade has been evidence showing that boys and girls who reach the end of third-grade reading well below their grade level will likely have great difficulty being successful throughout grades 4–12. Reading well is essential to success in almost all school subjects. Similarly, there is solid evidence that children who reach the end of third grade and are overweight/obese will quite likely remain overweight/obese throughout their school years and into adulthood (e.g., Serdula, Ivery, Coates, Freedman, Williamson, & Byers, 1993; Singh, Mulder, Twisk, van Mechelen, & Chinapaw, 2008; Wang & Lobstein, 2006). For example, as early 1993, Serdula and her colleagues reported that approximately half of school-aged children were obese once they reached adulthood. And the risk of becoming obese as adults is twice as high for obese children as it is for nonobese children.

In the past two decades, the prevalence of overweight and obesity among children in the United States has doubled and the prevalence among adolescents has tripled (American Academy of Pediatrics, 2003). Currently, nearly 16.7 percent of children and adolescents are overweight, and 17.1 percent are obese (Koplan, Liverman, Kraak, & Wisham, 2006). Overweight and obesity are not distributed normally across the population. Low-income children and African American children have higher obesity rates. Twenty-three percent of teens from families living in poverty were overweight, compared to 14 percent of those not living in poverty (Meich, Kumanyika, Stettler, Link, Phelan, & Chang, 2006). In Ohio, recent data showed that 37.6 percent of third-graders were overweight/obese (Ohio Department of Health, 2006).

It has been abundantly clear that elementary schools in conjunction with community organizations and parents are primary battlegrounds to combat this epidemic of overweight and obesity. Why use schools? Because they exist in all communities, are attended by nearly all children, provide safe environments, and have facilities, equipment, and trained personnel (McKenzie & Kahan, 2008). As noted previously, overweight and obese children who move beyond the third grade are likely to remain that way through adolescence and into adulthood. As we will show in more detail later in this chapter, the most likely solution to this problem is for elementary schools to offer daily physical education, have active recess periods and activity breaks in classrooms, and work with community agencies and parents to provide physical activity in after-school and weekend programs.

As we noted earlier, for many schools the effects of the NCLB Act have resulted in less time in physical education, a reduction in recess time, and more interest in providing extra academic time than in extra physical activity time—this despite the fact that there is substantial national agreement that children ages 5–12 should receive 60 minutes of moderate-to-vigorous physical activity daily (Strong et al., 2005; U.S.D.H.H.S., 2008). We know that the early elementary-school years are especially important for children to develop fundamental motor skills, to become comfortable when moving, and to enjoy moving in various activities. Children who reach third grade with only modest motor-skill development are less likely to enjoy and be successful in physical education throughout the remainder of their school years.

## Elementary-School Specialist Teachers

The traditional elementary school is organized around the *self-contained classroom,* in which one teacher provides instruction in all the subjects. Over the years, specialist teachers have begun to relieve the classroom teacher of some of the instructional responsibilities in areas such as physical education, art, and music. Most states now certify specialist teachers in those areas.

States that have laws requiring physical education instruction in the elementary school seldom specify that the instruction has to be done by a specialist teacher. However, the National Children and Youth Fitness Study II found that 83 percent of the children in grades 1–4 who were tested in the study had physical education at least once per week from a specialist teacher. That finding is higher than most estimates. Regardless of what the actual percentage might be, it is clear that many school districts hire elementary-school physical education specialists even though they are not required by law to do so.

The issue here is clear. Most classroom teachers have had only one course in physical education methods as part of their teacher preparation. They are not well prepared to teach physical education. The demands on their curricular time and pressures for improvements in academic achievement have increased year by year. They cannot possibly do all the things expected of them—and physical education is too often the subject that gets left out. The physical education specialist has extensive training to do the job and has that job as his or her sole teaching interest. Children clearly benefit more from specialist teaching than from physical education instruction given by the classroom teacher.

In many school districts, elementary-school physical education specialists travel from school to school, often serving three or four schools each week. The specialist teacher teaches one lesson per week, and the classroom teacher follows up with a second and perhaps a third lesson that week. The specialist teacher is often responsible for providing lesson plans for the classroom teacher that build on what was taught during the specialist's one lesson with the children. Being a traveling specialist is a difficult job. Continuity is hard to achieve. The specialist sometimes does not feel that he or she is a member of any single-school faculty. It is clear that elementary-school physical education will take a major step forward when *each* school has at least one specialist physical educator.

School districts that want children to have a daily period of physical education have one to three full-time specialist physical educators in each elementary school. The benefits of such an arrangement are clear. The school district obviously values physical education. Groups of specialist teachers can work together, each teaching in those activities for which he or she is best prepared. That this situation might someday become the norm for elementary schools everywhere is the hope behind the movement for high-quality, daily physical education.

## Elementary-School Facilities

Have you seen a well-designed, fully equipped elementary-school gymnasium? What a bright, joyful, interesting place it is! How clearly it contributes to the potential of a program to accomplish program goals. Yet many children do not have the benefit of instruction within such a facility.

The facilities for physical education obviously affect what can be taught (choice of activities) and how it will be taught (teaching method). For example, in many schools, the gymnasium also serves as the lunchroom. In those cases, the physical educator has to collaborate with the lunch personnel to ensure that loss of lesson time is minimized, without shortchanging the lunch periods. This is just one example of how high-quality physical education can still occur in an elementary school without a real physical education facility. The issue here is providing appropriate facilities and equipment so that teachers can help children achieve the full range of benefits within a subject such as physical education.

Beyond having the elementary-school gymnasium, physical educators can make important contributions

to ensuring that students use the outdoor facilities to the greatest extent possible as well. There is good evidence that in elementary schools, strategies such as providing appropriate equipment, adding permanent markings (e.g., hopscotch, foursquare), and providing encouragement and prompting by adults results in higher physical activity levels in students (e.g., Jago & Baranowski, 2004; Lopes, Vasques, Pereira, Maia, & Malina, 2006; McKenzie, Sallis, Elder, Berry, Hoy, Nader, Zive, & Broyles, 1997; Stratton & Mullan, 2005; Verstraete, Cardon, De Clercq, & De Bourdeaudhuij, 2006).

## Developmentally Appropriate Practices

Those who have studied effective elementary-school physical education specialists have come away in awe of the manner in which they provide interesting, innovative, and **developmentally appropriate** experiences for a variety of children—some more skilled than others, some more fit than others, some more interested than others (Rauschenbach, 1992; Siedentop, 1989). In its continuing efforts to promote high-quality physical education for children, NASPE published a position statement titled: *Appropriate Instructional Practice Guidelines for Elementary School Physical Education* (NASPE, 2009b). The document contrasts 35 specific practices across five areas, including: (a) establishing a learning environment; (b) instructional strategies; (c) curriculum; (d) assessment; and (e) professionalism. Teachers' attention to such aspects as maximizing successful student engagement, safety, equity, use of technology, competition, physical activity for punishment, fitness testing, and advocacy are contrasted with multiple examples of appropriate and inappropriate teacher practices. NASPE has published similar position statements for both middle and high schools (NASPE, 2009c, 2009d). Professional physical educators are those who consistently strive to employ such teaching practices. In addition, teachers can inform parents, school principals, and policymakers about what constitute appropriate professional teaching practices.

## Curricular Issues

Another area of disagreement among physical education professionals is the question of what constitutes the best curriculum model for elementary-school physical education. Of the various models described in Chapter 4, is it the skill-theme model? A health-related fitness model like SPARK? Is it the games-based model? Should it be an age-appropriate version of a health-fitness model? Nearly every professional agrees that physical education for young children (grades K–3) should not include highly specific-skill practice and competitive games that mirror the parent versions of sport games.

There seems to be increasing agreement that the K–3 years should focus primarily on issues of fundamental motor-skill development with the skill-theme model as the most appropriate and well-defined approach. There is also agreement that these early years in physical education should *always* be fun, what physical education philosopher Scott Kretchmar described as allowing children to "find their playgrounds" in a "joy-oriented" physical education (Kretchmar, 2008). He argued persuasively that joy-oriented physical education is grounded in meaning, what young children come to value and what it means to their lives.

On the other hand, health-related physical education is grounded, at least partly, in such mandates of efficiency as time on task and good heart rates. Moreover, the latter is more utilitarian in nature, in that we use physical activity toward making a healthier body for a better quality of life in later years. Kretchmar (2008) argued that this utilitarian focus makes physical activity appear more like a duty or an obligation in which the inherent joy in movement is largely ignored. While that in itself is an appropriate foundation, when teaching 5 to 8-year-olds, physical educators can and should deliver health-related fitness content in ways that are developmentally appropriate, more playful in nature, and mirrors their natural activity patterns (i.e., relatively short bouts of high intensity). Unfortunately, we have witnessed third-graders being made to run the mile by their teacher, reflecting an approach to fitness development where teachers treat children as if they were adults (Corbin, 2002). We should not be surprised many children regard this as a very negative experience and come to view physical activity of any type as something to avoid.

Thus, for students to *adopt and value a physically active lifestyle*, the overarching goal must pay attention to the meaning that young children derive from their motor experiences, because we are all more likely to adopt and value behavior patterns that provide us with joyful experiences. Joy-oriented physical education requires a very specific pedagogical approach. It seems, however, reasonable to argue that joy in movement activities is more likely when one is reasonably skillful. Thus, both these positions have merit, and finding ways to bring them together, especially in the K–3 years, would prove useful.

What does seem clear is that physical education in the K–3 years should not be watered-down versions of what we present to adolescent students. In the Sport Education model (Siedentop et al., 2011), we have always argued that fourth grade is probably the best starting age to begin students in a curriculum and instruction model that involves working together, teamwork, specific activity–related technique and tactical-learning tasks, and age-appropriate competition formats. In grades 4–5, elementary-school students can begin to learn more institutionalized forms of motor activity, such as sports; adventure-education skills; and activities related to health-fitness such as strength-training, cardiovascular-training, and stretching techniques.

This kind of professional debate is very healthy but is not "won" in the sense of settling the issues. Elementary-school physical education teachers are free to develop their own programs. Currently, district physical education syllabi typically are defined so broadly that nearly any approach would be "in-bounds."

## ISSUES IN SECONDARY-SCHOOL PHYSICAL EDUCATION

Concern about the quality and viability of physical education in many high schools has been expressed consistently in the professional literature and at conferences for over 20 years. One article described high-school physical education as an "endangered species" that will probably fail if it continues on its present course (Siedentop, 1987). Hoffman (1987) wrote about the "decline and fall of physical education." Although many remain optimistic about elementary-school physical education, we should all be concerned about why high-school physical education appears to be so devalued by students, parents, and policy makers. Possible explanations are explored in this section.

## The "Busy, Happy, and Good" Syndrome

In 1983 Judith Placek investigated how teachers conceptualized successful teaching in secondary-school physical education. In the article reporting her findings, Placek coined a phrase that has become famous in the profession: Most teachers think that keeping students "busy, happy, and good" (Placek, 1983) is the main gauge of their own success. If students are well behaved, fairly active in class, and reasonably happy, then teachers believe they have been successful. But what about significant learning? Do physical educators believe that student learning is a primary expectation and responsibility? What about students getting excited about performing better or becoming more fit? As Griffey (1987) argued, "The sense of mastering something important is denied most students in secondary physical education programs in this country" (p. 21). Perhaps more worrisome, when students are busy, happy, and good, school administrators are usually quite satisfied. One of the keys to solving this problem is for school administrators to show more interest in a physical education program focused on important learning outcomes. Instead, too many high-school classes end up without that instructional and learning focus. Earlier we differentiated the need for a clear educational focus in physical education lessons from the more recreational orientation that characterizes before-school and lunchtime drop-in programs in schools. To be sure, both are an essential part of a comprehensive program, but too often it is difficult to tell the difference between the two.

## Multi-Activity Curriculum

Many people who have assessed the problems of secondary-school physical education agree that the multi-activity (or eclectic) curriculum contributes to the general lack of outcomes. Many high-school programs comprise a series of short-term units covering a wide variety of activities. (See Chapter 4 for the history of the multi-activity approach.) However, can 3- to 7-day units provide sufficient in-depth learning to produce lasting outcomes? Taylor and Chiogioji (1987) gave an answer that most experts would agree with:

> The generally accepted goals of physical education are to promote physical fitness, self-esteem, and cognitive and social development. However, the practice—the proliferation of and emphasis on teaching too many activities in too short a time—has made these goals more difficult to attain. The smorgasbord approach of requiring team sports, individual sports, dance, physical fitness activities, all within the space of one school year lessens those students' opportunities to master any one activity through which they can meet the stated goals. (p. 22)

Improvement, achievement, and mastery are themes that are neither readily apparent in multi-activity programs nor likely in programs that focus on keeping students busy, happy, and good.

There clearly *are* excellent high-school physical education programs. It is interesting to note that some people believe that a dominant characteristic of such programs is that they have a main curricular theme:

> The (good) programs stood for something specific. We learned about good fitness programs, good social development programs, and good adventure programs. Each of the programs had a main focus that defined and identified the program. While many of these programs were multidimensional, each had a main theme that dominated the curriculum. (Siedentop, 1987, p. 25)

Main-theme curricula allow students to focus for longer periods of time on mastering content (Siedentop & Tannehill, 2000). Whatever the activity, it takes time for students to develop basic techniques, to understand the manner in which the activity is pursued or competed, to master tactics involved with the activity, and to engage in the activity for a long-enough time to gain confidence and develop sufficient skill to enjoy the activity. When they enjoy the activity, students are more likely to continue to pursue it outside of school time. The curriculum-instruction models described in Chapter 4 and the examples shown in Chapter 5 all depend on allowing sufficient time for students to become skilled and confident in the activity, thus allowing them to experience the enjoyment of performing the activity.

Examples of main-theme curricula for developmental physical education, adventure education, sport education, fitness and wellness, and integrated physical education can be found in Siedentop and Tannehill (2000). There is evidence from high-school reform models that a more focused curriculum improves student interest and achievement. Thus, it may provide one way that high-school physical education can rescue itself from its current troubles.

## Difficult Teaching Situations

If high-school physical education is in trouble, certainly part of the reason is the difficult situation that many of its teachers face. The difficulties involve combinations of class size and heterogeneity of skill levels, coed participation (addressed in the next section), and poor urban play environments (also see next section). In some schools, it is not uncommon to find 50 to 70 students in a physical education class although classes in, say, English or algebra are considerably smaller. With that many students, there are always problems of classroom management, equipment, and space. Good teaching can be done in such situations, but it is difficult. However, what is worse is when two teachers choose to combine two classes and claim they are "team teaching," while other parts of the campus facilities sit idle. In many such cases, the class periods have no real instructional focus.

A second factor is the marked heterogeneity of the skill levels of a typical secondary-school physical education class. Varsity-level athletes are scheduled in the same class as inexperienced, unskilled students (unless they are exempted from physical education). Whereas algebra teachers and chemistry teachers can expect their students to have a basic level of skill and understanding, physical educators have no such luxury. Physical educators must often accommodate enormously diverse levels of skills and interests in any given class, which makes effective teaching difficult. In programs where students *elect* classes and in programs where classes are based on progressions in skill (for example, Tennis I, Tennis II), this major problem is reduced substantially. The high-school program described in Chapter 5 uses a fitness-skill testing procedure to place students in classes that are developmentally appropriate for them. Practices such as these enhance the quality of experience for the student and enable teachers to teach more effectively.

## Coed Participation

Traditionally, boys and girls have been taught in separate classes in secondary-school physical education. Before Title IX, it was generally known that the girls' physical education classes were better taught and more interesting than the boys' classes. Title IX made coeducational classes mandatory, except in rare instances. It is true that in many places girls had less access to instruction, time, and equipment in physical education than did boys. It is not entirely clear that in the 31 years since Title IX, this particular provision of the law has "worked" as well as many had hoped it would.

The assumption of Title IX was that sex-integrated classes would lead to more sex-equitable classes. Some coed classes meet that assumption while others do not. Some studies have also shown that lower-skilled girls are often marginalized in coed physical education classes (Scraton, 1990; Siedentop & O'Sullivan, 1992). Olafson (2002) interviewed adolescent girls in physical education and found that many of them disliked their physical education classes intensely and tried to find ways to avoid them. Coed teaching is often difficult for teachers because of the wide range of abilities that they encounter, especially when invasion games are the focus of the curriculum, reflecting, no doubt, a history of girls having less opportunity to learn to excel in invasion games (e.g., basketball, soccer, and touch football).

The issue of coed or sex-segregated physical education has also been addressed in other parts of the world. In England, as a result of extensive study of girls' participation in high-school physical education, Scraton (1990) recommended that a girls-centered physical education be developed that emphasized physicality, consciousness raising, and confidence building in physical activity settings. Scraton believes in the ultimate value of coed physical education but believes also that, in most current situations, a girls-centered approach will increase the likelihood that young women will benefit from subsequent coed participation.

The Australian Sports Commission (1994) developed a national policy for junior sport that speaks specifically to coed participation:

> Physical differences between girls and boys under the age of 12 are generally considered irrelevant to sporting ability. However, socialization may—and often does—prevent girls from developing sporting competencies equal to those of boys. Current evidence suggests that skill development in mixed groups is generally appropriate, but that competition should remain single-sex until it can be shown that girls will not be disadvantaged in mixed-sex contests. (p. 11)

The Australian policy provides a middle ground—that is, coed participation in skill development but separation for competition.

Many physical education teachers have found that coed classes are fine for sports such as archery, bowling, and skiing. Most problems develop during invasion games such as touch football, basketball, and soccer. In many cases, some team and contact sports have been dropped from the curriculum to accommodate coed teaching (Geadelmann, 1981). Remember, this debate is not about the goal, which is a gender-equitable physical education. Rather, it is about the means to achieve that goal.

Treanor and her colleagues (1998) studied perceptions of coed physical education among middle-school students. Forty percent of boys and 33 percent of girls preferred same-sex classes, and 27 percent of boys and 30 percent of girls preferred a coed class structure. Both boys and girls reported that they performed skills better, played team sports better, and received more learning opportunities in same-sex classes. Boys tended to like physical education more than girls, and that difference increased from the sixth to the eighth grade. The study was possible because teachers had become frustrated by the challenges of teaching coed classes and wanted to experiment to see what differences occurred.

From the perspective of whether the opportunities to practice are similar for boys and girls, Hannon and Ratliffe (2007) found that high-school girls get more opportunities to practice in single-sex classes compared to coed classes when activities such as soccer, flag football, and soccer are taught. In addition, teachers in the same single-sex classes tended to be more actively engaged in their teaching given the higher rates of instructional interactions.

Globally, more than 20 years of research on boys' and girls' physical activity levels across various contexts (e.g., physical education classes, total day) is quite conclusive: Boys consistently reach higher levels of activity. But does the class composition (i.e., single sex versus coeducational) affect boys' and girls' physical activity levels? Using pedometers, Hannon and Ratliffe (2007) reported that male and female high-school students accumulated similar or higher steps per minute in coed settings than in single-gender settings. Meanwhile, McKenzie, Prochaska, Sallis, and Lamaster (2004) found that girls tended to be more active in coeducational classes compared to girls-only classes.

There are several approaches to solving the problems discussed in this section, problems that are most significant for students in middle- and high-school physical education. In middle schools, physical education is typically scheduled by class. That is, students go to physical education with the students who are in their other classes. With some activities, providing different groupings is quite easy. In a tennis unit, for example, students can learn and practice together, but competitions could be boys' singles, girls' singles, and coed doubles. Even in invasion games, where girls tend to be marginalized in coed competitions, this solution works especially well for large classes. Importantly, these kinds of solutions do not violate the provisions of the Title IX legislation (Gabbei, 2004).

As described in the previous section, a quality coed physical education is much more easily achieved if students can elect the courses they take. In some cases, girls and boys might want to learn and participate together in a flag-football course or a fencing course. In other cases, girls might be more comfortable learning in a girls' flag-football course and boys in a boys' flag-football course. There is some evidence (Prusak, Treasure, Darst, & Pangrazi, 2004) that adolescent girls are more motivated and enjoy their physical education experiences more if they have chosen the course.

## Role Conflict

It is clear that many women and men become physical education teachers partially, if not mostly, because they want to coach (Stroot, Collier, O'Sullivan, & England, 1994; Templin, Sparkes, Grant, & Schemmp, 1994). Thus, the potential for role conflict exists from the outset of their careers. Not surprisingly, therefore, some evidence shows that some women and men who teach and coach suffer from role conflict (Chu, 1981; Locke & Massengale, 1978). Teaching is one role; coaching is another role. Performing in both roles can produce role conflict and role strain. *Role conflict* exists when there are incompatible expectations for the different roles— for example, high expectations for coaching and low expectations for teaching. *Role strain* exists when total role demands require more time and energy than a person has to give. The daily schedule, in and of itself, is sufficient to produce role strain over time. Role conflict also builds gradually, especially for head coaches, because the coaching role receives more attention than the teaching role, the expectations are higher, and the immediate rewards are greater. Coaching performance is very public and under the regular scrutiny of parents, administrators,

and the community. Teaching is very private in comparison.

When role strain occurs, something eventually has to give. In some cases, the most likely casualty is quality teaching. That, however, is not inevitable. O'Connor and Macdonald (2002) found that some teacher-coaches manage the issues quite well, actually enjoy the dual responsibilities, and particularly like the differences in the student–teacher relationships in the two settings. There is also some evidence that some high-school physical education teachers seek out responsibilities in school sport because it provides more challenge and satisfaction than they find in their teaching (O'Sullivan, Siedentop, & Tannehill, 1994).

The issue of role conflict among those who both teach and coach has been exacerbated during the last decades as high-school sports has taken on added importance. Many high-school athletes now specialize in one sport and train year-round to get better at it. A boys' football coach or a girls' volleyball coach not only works many hours during the preseason and competition season but also often spends extensive time and energy working with players during the off-season. Most high schools now have a strength-and-conditioning facility, and coaches often spend time with their athletes in that facility throughout the school year. The increased attention to and popularity of high-school sports has provided both a higher status for coaches within the community and greater demands that their teams perform well, all of which increases the chances of role conflict. Role conflict tends to increase when the role of coaching is supported more strongly than the role of teaching. As one coach put it, "I did not have any support for my teaching. They supported me as a coach, but as a teacher I could do anything or nothing at all. To sit on the bleachers and roll out the ball would have been fine" (Stroot, Faucette, & Schwager, 1993).

It is fair to point out that the recent national attention on child/youth overweight and obesity has made school boards and school administrators pay more attention to the nature and quality of physical education in their school districts. Many physical education programs (see Chapter 5) have answered this call and implemented unique and innovative models that require planning and a renewed sense of good teaching for the district physical education staff. Most of these efforts are *programmatic* in the sense that all teachers are meant to take part and do their fair share in implementing the new models. One might suspect that in districts that have renewed their effort in physical education programming will pay more attention to the quality of new hires among the physical education staff in the district. This will make it more difficult for a principal to hire a new physical education teacher who might be a great defensive coordinator for the varsity football team but whose credentials and commitment to physical education might be less robust. What is very clear is that strong and sustained support from the school's administration is vital for any reform effort aimed at improving the physical education program.

There is no simple solution to this problem. Some people have suggested that coaching become part of the teaching assignment, thus allowing coaches to have a much lighter teaching load during their seasons. Some school administrators prefer to hire coaches who are classroom teachers, as opposed to physical education teachers, thus avoiding this problem or, perhaps, shifting it to another group of people. Still others have suggested that the responsibilities for both teaching and coaching be separated altogether, especially given the added responsibilities for teachers to integrate health and fitness concepts (Konukman, Agbuga, Erdogan, Zorba, Demirhan & Yilmaz, 2010).

Those who would teach would begin their work in the mid-afternoon and would continue through the evening hours, staffing recreational and community programs in schools. If secondary-school physical education is to thrive, this problem must be solved.

## Rethinking Secondary-School Physical Education

There has been widespread discussion and debate about the possibility of rethinking how secondary-school physical education is conceptualized and de-livered to youths (Locke, 1992; Siedentop, 1992; Vickers, 1992). These discussions have proceeded on the assumption that, in many places, high-school physical education is so sufficiently dysfunctional that it needs to be replaced rather than repaired—completely reinvented rather than improved.

Fortunately, there is evidence that such change can take place—and some interesting models have emerged. In New Zealand, more than 150 high schools have replaced a traditional multi-activity approach with the sport education model in a drastically revised tenth-grade program (Grant, 1992). In Florida, a required fitness semester is followed by semester-long courses in a variety of activities (Graham, 1990). In many places, there have been experiments with health and fitness clubs in high schools, using an adult model of participation rather than the more compliance-oriented, regularly scheduled model common to most schools (Cohen, 1991). In other schools, physical educators have adopted a total-fitness perspective similar to the Needham High School program described in Chapter 5 (Westcott, 1992).

What is most needed at the moment is a better understanding of how such innovative programs get started and how they are sustained. They are exciting. They give us all hope for the future. Unfortunately, they too often have a way of not outliving the creative people who developed them.

## Physical Education in Urban High Schools

Urban high schools often present difficult teaching situations. physical education facilities are typically old and inadequate, and class sizes are large. Moreover, many urban youths grow up in relative poverty and fail to develop healthy behaviors with regard to physical activity and good nutrition.

Urban play environments are inadequate, and those that do exist are typically unsupervised (Knop, Tannehill, & O'Sullivan, 2001). They are also typically dominated by skilled adolescent boys to the exclusion of others. Violence and the fear of violence too often pervade the lives of these adolescent boys and girls. For physical education to be successful in such settings, it must create trust through both sensitive curricular choices and appropriate teaching tactics, must build and sustain a sense of community so that students know they are cared for and feel some responsibility for the group, and must find multiple ways for students to be successful (Knop, 1998).

Two successful models for urban high-school youths are worth noting. The first is the social-development model created by Don Hellison (1995, 1996), which is described in Chapter 4. This model has been applied successfully in a number of urban high schools, using very different curricular approaches but maintaining the focus on the development of personal responsibility. A second model is the "sport for peace" curriculum (Ennis, Satina, & Solomon, 1999). This is a variation of the sport education model described in Chapter 4, but includes a strong focus on conflict resolution and good decision making during the sport season.

Physical education has much to offer in the form of positive youth development and physical fitness, both of which are important to the future of urban youth. Unfortunately, most urban schools are under extreme pressure to raise test scores in math, reading, and science, so most of their energies go to those parts of the curriculum.

## The Intramural Program

*Intramural activity* is typically defined as activity beyond the regular instructional program but confined within the school. The traditional model for portraying the relationships among instructional physical education, intramurals, and interscholastic sport is a pyramid (see Figure 6.1). The base of the pyramid is the instructional physical education program, which reaches all the students. The second tier in the pyramid is the intramural program, which provides activity opportunities for students who are interested in extending their skills and engaging in more competitive situations. The top of the pyramid reaches fewer students but is intended for those who are especially talented, providing them with more practice and competitive opportunities. In the

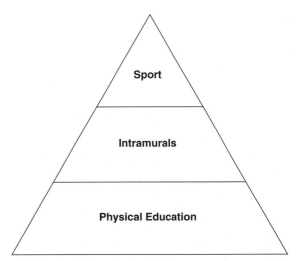

**FIGURE 6.1** Traditional pyramid model for physical education programs.

best of all worlds, **intramurals** would occupy a place of major importance in the school day. Many students would participate. A wide variety of activities would be available. Students could extend and refine the skills learned in the instructional program. Students could have an important competitive experience without making the daily commitment necessary to be on an interscholastic team. That ideal is seldom achieved. In fact, in many schools, the intramural program is virtually nonexistent, thus eliminating a major component in any complete physical education program.

Intramurals suffer from a number of problems. Schools often do not have the resources to hire personnel to administer and conduct these programs. Teachers, with full class loads, are often not enthusiastic about the extra burden imposed by such an assignment. Furthermore, several parts of the facilities used in the instructional program are often taken over immediately after school by the sport teams. Students find it difficult to go home and then return to school for intramurals. And as the pressure on the sport coaches at the schools continues to increase coaches become more aggressive in controlling facilities. An example of this occurred when one of the authors was witness to a basketball coach taking over the gymnasium for team practices during lunch periods.

A major problem in sustaining intramural programs in middle and high schools is the fact that a great majority of students are bussed to and from school. Buses typically await students immediately after the last class period. As school districts have consolidated over the past 50 years, schools have tended to become larger with more students living farther from school facilities. Thus, students, especially the freshmen and sophomores, find it very difficult to stay at school for intramurals or to return to school for intramurals later in the day. High schools typically start earlier in the day, often with 7:30 a.m. classes, so students finish the school day earlier. Intramurals would help fill the middle and later afternoon with useful and fun activities if problems of transportation and facilities could be mitigated. It is this very time in the afternoon that youth specialists throughout the nation have labeled as the most at-risk time for adolescents, time that should be filled with programs that appeal to their interests and make it less likely they will engage in problem behaviors. Such programs might be especially attractive for juniors and seniors who drive to school themselves and are thus less dependent on buses or on parents transporting them.

The immense popularity of intramurals in colleges and universities and the equally notable success of community recreation programs suggest strongly that boys and girls will take advantage of recreational sport and fitness opportunities that are available in reasonable facilities at reasonable times and with reasonably competent staff. Intramurals have much to offer the secondary-school physical education program and deserve to be done well.

## CONCLUDING ISSUE: STANDARDS, ASSESSMENT, AND ACCOUNTABILITY

A final issue that cuts across K–12 physical education deserves our attention. It seems difficult to imagine that physical education can improve markedly without some forms of assessment and accountability at the school, district and state level. This issue is directly related to the presence or absence of policies or mandates at each of the levels that impact physical education.

In a 2000 report to the president of the United States, the secretary of Health and Human Services and the secretary of Education (A Report to the President, 2000) urged that a standardized assessment of student performance in physical education be developed to provide a means of holding physical education programs accountable (www.cdc.gov/nccdphp/dash/presphsactrpt). The report urged that physical education be included among the subjects on which students are tested as part of state education assessment systems. If states were to enact legislation that put these recommendations into practice, one could expect that dramatic changes would occur in school programs.

In October 2002, a national Healthy Schools Summit was held in Washington, D.C. (www.actionforhealthykids.org). Designed to bring together the nation's leading education and children's health and nutrition organizations, the summit was convened in an effort to improve children's health and educational performance through better nutrition and physical activity in schools.

The assumption of this summit was that the *responsibility* for developing healthy lifestyles in children belongs not only to physical education teachers, but also to the entire school and to families and the community as they connect with the school. The summit focused on the obesity epidemic, on making nutrition and physical activity a priority for the whole school community, on marketing better nutrition and physical activity to children, on how to fund change, on coalition building, and on family and community involvement. This is exactly the kind of total effort that is needed to achieve real gains in the health and well-being of children and youth.

Thus, support for quality physical education programs and physical activity from many different quarters of society is reflected in the increased attention given and the many national recommendations and guidelines. But recommendations and guidelines are just that. By themselves they do not have the power to change current practices. Policies with strong accountability and oversight do have this potential.

A current example of proposed legislation at the federal level is what has become known as the Fit Kids Act. In early 2011, during the 112th Congress, H.R. 1057 and S. 576 were introduced (www .govtrack.us). While similar bills were unsuccessful in the 110th and 111th Congress, passage of these bills would amend the Elementary and Secondary Education Act (ESEA) and target quality physical education and physical activity for all public school children. A summary of H.R. 1057 reflects the main features of the bill:

> Amends the Elementary and Secondary Education Act of 1965 (ESEA) to require annual state and local educational agency report cards to include specified information on school health and physical education programs. Includes the promotion of healthy, active lifestyles by students within ESEA grant programs that support school counseling, smaller learning communities, community learning centers, and parental involvement in their children's education. Revises the professional development program for teachers and principals to include training for physical and health education teachers, and training on improving students' health habits and participation in physical activities. Directs the Secretary of Education to contract with the National Academy of Sciences (NAS) for a study that: (1) assesses the effect health and physical education have on students' ability to learn; and (2) makes recommendations for improving, and measuring improvements to, their health and physical education in schools. (www.govtrack.us/congress/bill.xpd? bill=h112-1057&tab=summary)

The support for physical education is evident again given the endorsement given to the bills by national organizations outside of physical education. Some of these organizations include American Heart Association, American Stroke Association, Afterschool Alliance, National Association for County and City Health Officials, National Recreation and Park Association, Obesity Action Coalition, Researchers Against Inactivity-related Disorders, Shaping America's Health, and the Trust for America's Health.

## Assessment and Accountability: A Multilayered Problem

Assessment refers to "tasks and settings where students are given opportunities to demonstrate their knowledge, skill, understanding, and application of content" (Siedentop & Tannehill, 2000, pp. 178–179). Assessment has multiple purposes: teachers assess to support and encourage learning and growth and also use it as the basis for grades.

Physical education teachers who use assessment do so primarily to motivate students and to help them learn more. They use skill tests, rating scales, checklists, portfolios, journals, written tests, and observations of game play to develop assessment profiles of their students. Some assessments are *formative*. That is, they are intended to provide feedback on developing skills, knowledge, and tactics. This type of assessment typically occurs throughout a unit, is aimed at helping students progress, and is thus process oriented. Other assessments are *summative*, which means they provide a final judgment on outcomes achieved at the end of a unit. Such assessments are product oriented.

Physical educators have to regularly report grades. In some school districts, a grading format must be followed and gives guidance to the physical educator. In other districts, physical education teachers devise their own grading schemes and are required only to turn in grades at the end of each grading period. The "busy, happy, and good" approach described earlier in many cases has teachers assign grades on the basis of attendance, dress, and participation. That is, to earn the top grade, students have to attend class, be on time, be dressed for class, and participate in activities with no serious behavior problems. Whether they actually know more or get better at an activity does not factor into the grade. Some teachers may add "effort" to their grading scheme to differentiate between students who participate minimally and those who participate enthusiastically. In some districts, physical education may still be graded pass/fail, which only strengthens the tendency to use attendance, dress, and participation as grading criteria. What maintains this approach to assessment of students?

Improving physical education is embedded in three related concepts: standards, assessment, and accountability. At the national level, NASPE has developed physical education as a set of national content *standards* (see Chapter 4) with benchmarks that are specific to grade-level outcomes. It has also placed great importance on *assessing* student progress toward meeting content standards. To that end, it produced a set of field-tested and validated assessment protocols for elementary and secondary-school programs that are linked directly with its national content standards, called PE-Metrics (NASPE, 2010b, 2011).

However, the real issue yet to be addressed remains: In the absence of real accountability and oversight, what use are standards and assessments if there is no real accountability beyond that which the individual physical educator does for himself or herself? Progress will occur only when policies or mandates with built-in accountability and oversight are put in place (Siedentop, 2009).

## The Role of Policy in Physical Education

One approach that is gaining increased attention is the role of how policy development or change (or lack thereof) directly affects the quantity and quality of physical education. As we showed in Chapter 1, similar efforts are underway that target other health behaviors such as food and beverage consumption in schools (e.g., Johnston, O'Malley, Bachman, & Schulenberg, 2010; Trust for America's Health, 2010).

Policies reflect rules of conduct and requirements for people and organizations that are established at various levels (e.g., federal, state, school district, and school level). But as we will show, not all policies are created equal. State legislation that includes policies (or mandates) that are poorly written and/or have no real accountability mechanism (i.e., oversight) or funding support built into them have little, if any, influence on the actions of people within organizations.

Many states have increased their physical education requirements, in part as a consequence over the national child/youth overweight and obesity concerns. Two states, California and South Carolina, deserve a closer look. California was the first state to receive an A in the University of Baltimore's yearly review of state legislation to stem the childhood obesity epidemic (Siedentop, 2007). California law now requires a minimum of 200 minutes of physical education for every 10 school days in grades 1–6 and a minimum of 400 minutes of physical education for every 10 school days in grades 7–12. The new legislation also required that a credentialed physical education teacher teach physical education. Each school district must administer a physical-fitness test annually to all students in grades 5, 7, and 9 during the months of February to May. Student involvement in sports, band, ROTC, drill teams, and the like cannot be substituted for meeting the physical education requirement. And in 2006, the state budget included $40 million to hire more physical education teachers.

Now, here is the rub! California, like most states, has little oversight and accountability for school districts to enforce the physical education requirements. A recent study sponsored by the California Endowment (2008) showed that 48 percent of elementary schools and 24 percent of middle and high schools were noncompliant with the physical education time requirements. Class sizes, especially in urban schools, are so large (for example, 70 students per class) that no real outcomes can be expected. Many districts have chosen to allow for substitutions for the high-school physical education requirement. Pass rates for the FITNESSGRAM fitness tests are low. Fewer than 30 percent of students meet all six health-related fitness standards in grades 5, 7, and 9. The pass rate for African American and Latino students is well below that of white students. None of this is intended to demean the state of California where state legislators have successfully passed important legislation. What is true for California is true for most states: There is very little oversight and accountability at the state level for districts to comply with whatever physical education requirements are demanded by state law.

South Carolina has established itself as a national leader in physical education by adopting state standards and putting into practice the nation's first state assessment system for outcomes in physical education (Rink & Mitchell, 2003). Recent school wellness legislation in South Carolina requires that students in grades K–5 complete an average of 150 minutes per week in physical education and physical activity (60 minutes in physical education and 90 minutes in physical activity) with a student-to-teacher ratio of no more than 28:1 (Siedentop, 2007). All high-school students are required to complete 2 credits of health and fitness courses. The legislation also requires the phase-in of student-to-certified physical education teacher ratios so that in 2008 the ratio for elementary schools is 500:1, which means that elementary schools with more than 500 students will have to employ more than one physical education teacher. Schools in South Carolina are required to report yearly the number of minutes in physical education and the minutes of additional physical activity weekly. These measures created a modest amount of accountability in that state. Unfortunately, the severe economic recession has forced the state to put the annual statewide assessments on hold, at least until the state's financial picture improves.

## Current Trends in State-Level Physical Education Requirements

Historically, education has been considered an enterprise that should be under local control. Currently, there is no federal law that requires physical education to be taught in schools. Consequently, states vary widely in the mandates that are in effect for physical education as part of the state education system (NASPE, 2010a). Local school districts can set their own policies regarding the number of weekly minutes of physical education, the number of physical education credits required for high-school graduation, the use of exemptions (i.e., substituting other activities for physical education), class size, assessment of student performance, and so on. Focus On Box 6.2 offers a sample of current trends in state-level physical education requirements that show substantial variation across states (NASPE, 2010a). And these actually reflect an improvement since 2006!

Unfortunately, compared to 2006, not all trends show improvement. For example, more than half of all states (32) permit waivers and/or exemptions for students from taking physical education, a 77 percent increase! And fewer states (27 percent) require physical education grades to be included in students'

---

**FOCUS ON**    State Requirements for Physical Education                6.2

- Only five states require physical education in every grade K–12 (Illinois, Iowa, Massachusetts, New Mexico, and Vermont).

- Forty-three states (84 percent) mandate elementary-school physical education, 40 states (78 percent) mandate middle-school physical education, and 46 states (90 percent) mandate high-school physical education.

- Only one state aligns with the nationally recommended 150 minutes per week of physical education in elementary school and 225 minutes per week in middle and high school.

- Forty-eight states (94 percent) have their own state standards for physical education, but only 34 states (67 percent) require local districts to comply or align with these standards.

- Only 19 states (37 percent) require some form of student assessment in physical education.

- Fewer states (14 versus 22 in 2006) require physical education grades to be included in students' grade point averages.

- Only 13 states (25 percent) require schools to measure body mass index (BMI) and/or height and weight for each student.

SOURCE: From NASPE (2010a).

grade point average (GPA). Finally, most states (80 percent) have instituted the use of school report cards. However, only five states include physical education as one of the academic areas on the report card.

There is now ample evidence to show that students who engage in regular physical activity of appropriate intensity and duration are better students academically (Centers for Disease Control and Prevention, 2010a). Physically active students are also more attentive and have enhanced concentration (California Endowment, 2008). Aerobic activity increases blood flow to the brain and speeds recall and reasoning skills. Furthermore, elementary school students who engage in physical activity sessions prior to school as well as physical activity breaks during the school day have increased attention and perform better academically. As we noted earlier, No Child Left Behind has reduced the amount of time spent in physical education. It is important that the physical education leadership at state and district levels work to develop state rules that hold districts accountable for issues such as minimum number of minutes in physical education, class sizes, and the use of exemptions.

Two considerations point to the complexity of using policy development in improving school physical education. First, well-intended legislative proposals that are poorly written likely will not have the desired effect. A recent analysis of state-level policies show that most were drafted with such ambiguity that they allow districts and schools to interpret them in ways that essentially get around the intent of the legislation (Isaac, Baker, McCullick, Lux, & Tomporowski, 2011).

Second, increasing time in physical education on the basis of state mandates alone is not enough; improving health indicators are very complex. Evidence of this can be found in a recent analysis of the impact of state physical education requirements on physical activity levels and weight of high-school students. Cawley, Meyerhoefer, and Newhouse (2007) found that students in states with specified time requirements for physical education did increase the time they spent physically active in their

physical education classes spent by an average of 31 additional minutes per week. The additional time in physical education increased the number of days per week that girls exercised vigorously and participated in engaged in strength-building activity. But the added time in physical education did not produce lower BMI levels or the probability that a student was not overweight. A reminder that it is not the sheer time spent in physical education, but rather the amount of time spent physically active during physical education. This, of course, goes back to the quality of instruction provided by teachers in the programs.

There have been recent suggestions from within and outside the physical education profession to provide greater accountability for outcomes in school physical education. One newspaper article addressed the issue by posing this question: "What if your children brought home a report card that said they were flunking fitness?" (Wier, 2004). There are two important ways to look at that quote. The first is that it recognizes that without stronger accountability, physical education will continue to be done poorly in many schools. On that point, the same article included a quote by Dr. Judy Rink, a leader in the South Carolina state assessment project, who noted, "We had a lot of administrators who called teachers in and said, 'What's going on here?' We recognized that we have to be a player. You've got to get people's attention. Right now there is no accountability, and without that we're just blowing in the wind."

A second way to consider the quote is to suggest that the major—and perhaps the only—outcome in physical education is physical fitness. This is no doubt owing to the strong national concern about the epidemic of overweight and obesity among children and youth in America. Robert Pangrazi, a leading spokesman for physical education's contribution to healthy lifestyles, has argued that physical education should strive to be held accountable not for improving students' fitness level, but rather for increasing the amount and quality of physical activity for children and youth (Pangrazi, 2010). He argues that through the use of pedometers and other measuring methods it is fairly easy to collect reliable data on students' physical activity levels, both in and outside of physical education classes. Student logs can be kept and used as data for assessment and accountability purposes. The weekly cardio run/walk and computer-based records from the fitness-center work done 2 days per week by students in PE4life programs (see Chapter 5) could provide similar kinds of data. These arguments, made by some of the strongest leaders in our profession, deserve to be considered seriously.

The debate about accountability is likely to continue and grow more heated in the near future. Many physical educators who provide extraordinarily good experiences for their students may be reluctant to jump on an accountability bandwagon for fear it will require them to attend to things they do not believe to be central to a good physical education. Many physical educators who practice a "throw out the ball" or "busy, happy, and good" model of physical education are likely to resist any form of accountability because it would jar them from their comfortable positions. There also is another threat—namely, that a sole focus on fitness or physical activity outcomes and accountability might backfire. Gard (2004) commented,

> There is a distinct possibility that a future funding body, say a national government, might decide that comprehensive physical education, complete with specialist teachers, syllabus documents, a varied curriculum and occupying a significant place in school timetables, is an appalling extravagance when all we are trying to do is to reduce body weight.

It should be clear that without state-level accountability, school districts can largely ignore state regulations. Consequently, individual schools are more likely to ignore such regulations as well. It is this scenario that allows formal assessment in physical education to continue to focus primarily on attendance, dress, general conduct, and participation or effort. Changing this situation will be physical education's next battleground. Therefore, it is important that as a physical education professional you come to know your state's physical education policy profile, and understand the role and influence of policy (i.e., state-, district-, and school-level requirements). Perhaps most importantly, physical educators are important players in helping shape and/or change those policies that affect their programs.

## THE FUTURE OF PHYSICAL EDUCATION IN A SPORT/FITNESS CULTURE

Physical education faces a conundrum. While parents of school-aged youth strongly support school physical education (see Focus On Box 6.3), one of the most intriguing and disturbing issues facing the profession is the apparent lack of interest in and support for physical education as a school subject among school district and state-level policy makers. This marks exactly that point in our history when fitness and sport seem to be more popular than ever! Expenditures for fitness and sport in the private

---

**FOCUS ON — Parent Support for Healthier Schools                    6.3**

- Parents nearly unanimously agree (98 percent) that their child's school should offer opportunities for physical activity throughout the day, whether through physical education, activity breaks, recess, and/or after-school programs.

- Most all parents (96 percent) agree that physical education has a positive impact on their child's academic performance.

- Most all parents (96 percent) support limiting students' access to unhealthy snacks and sugar-sweetened beverages.

- Almost two-thirds of parents (63 percent) believe schools play a major role in instilling healthy habits in students.

Source: http://www.healthiergeneration.org/uploadedFiles/For_Media/HSP%20Parent%20Survey%20Overview.pdf

sector have increased steadily since the mid-1960s. The sport and fitness industries are booming, to say the least. Moreover, parents spend substantial amounts of money on lessons, clubs, and camps for their children—and a great deal of time and energy supporting community groups that sponsor sport and fitness activities for children and youths. Farrey (2008) reported that parents will spend enormous amounts of time and money on private instruction for their sons and daughters in the hopes of landing athletic scholarships in college. Participation has increased, spending is up, and interest is higher than ever before.

How can school physical education be in decline in this era when fitness and sport are so popular? How can school physical education suffer from lack of support when the support is so willingly provided in the private sector? These serious and disturbing questions deserve to be carefully considered. There are no easy answers, but the fact remains that school is the one institution that touches the lives of *all* children and youths. The same cannot be said for the community sport program and most certainly not for the elite, private sport/fitness club.

Is school physical education an endangered species? Will it survive in this era of popular support for fitness and sport? If it is to survive and even to grow, what do we need to do to change how it is conceptualized and taught? How physical education professionals answer the third question may indeed determine the answer to the first and second questions. If lifespan sport, fitness, and quality physical education are to become more of a reality in the future, then school physical education must begin to achieve its goals more completely.

As we showed in Chapter 5 (Focus On Box 5.4), the National Physical Activity Plan targets the development and implementation of state and school-district policies that require school accountability for the quality and quantity of physical education and related physical activity opportunities.

Historically, school physical education programs have focused on the delivery of physical education lessons. If asked what the overall mission of their physical education program is, most teachers would

likely respond with statements such as: To teach students to value physical activity and be physically active for a lifetime. However, there is evidence that physical educators rarely ever encourage middle-school students to be physically active beyond the regular lessons (McKenzie, Catellier, Conway, Lytle, Grieser, Webber, Pratt, & Elder, 2006). Moreover, students tend not to compensate (i.e., seek out more) physical activity after school on days they do not attend physical education classes (e.g., Dale, Corbin, & Dale, 2000; Morgan, Beighle, & Pangrazi, 2007), or on weekends (Brusseau, Kulinna, Tudor-Locke, van der Mars, & Darst, 2011).

Given the increased percentage of overweight and obese children, youth and adults (Ogden & Carroll, 2010) (see Figure 6.2), as well as the plethora of national recommendations, guidelines and mandates specific to physical activity, it should be obvious that the role and delivery of school physical education is in need of fundamental change.

While ensuring that physical education lessons provide the optimal opportunities for physical activity and other learning outcomes is essential, it can no longer be the sole focus. That is, a school physical education program should be the centerpiece program in which the physical educator coordinates and promotes physical activity throughout the school day. The periods before school, recess, lunch periods, and after-school times all are potential periods for students to be physically active. In addition, the infusion of physical activity breaks in classrooms during the instruction of academic subjects is gaining ground. Consequently, this broadens the scope of the physical educator's daily work as well. This has given rise to the notion of physical education teachers being physical activity directors (e.g., Brewer, Luebbers, & Shane, 2009; Castelli & Beighle, 2007).

We noted this in Chapter 4 as well, but it bears repeating here: Be sure you understand the following key distinction: physical education lessons should have a strong **educational** focus, while physical activity opportunities during before-school, lunch, recess, and after-school time may be more **recreational** in nature, although these settings offer excellent informal opportunities for learning. It should be clear

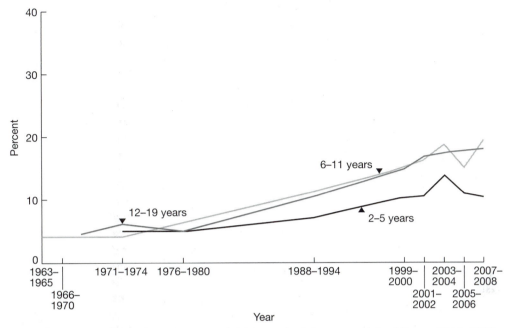

**FIGURE 6.2**  Trends in obesity among children and adolescents: United States 1963–2008.

Obesity is defined as body mass index (BMI) greater than or equal to sex- and age-specific 95th percentile from the 2000 CDC Growth Charts.

*CDC/NCHS, National Health Examination Surveys II (ages 6–11), III (ages 12–17), and National Health and Nutrition Examination Surveys (NHANES) I–III, and NHANES 1999–2000, 2001–2002, 2003–2004, 2005–2006, and 2007–2008.*

that physical education teachers can link their objectives and content for the physical education lesson with the out-of-class time activities. There is no reason why students who are learning about floor hockey or basketball cannot be afforded the chance to hone their skills and game play during recess times, intramurals, or during a recreational after-school program.

Any effort to build physical activity opportunities throughout the entire school day for all students requires a coordinated effort among multiple people to create such conditions. Individual physical education teachers cannot be expected to accomplish this task by themselves. Other (school) individuals such as health education teachers, classroom teachers, building administrators, parents, students, and perhaps other community members all have a role to play. Two examples of how this can be accomplished

include NASPE's Comprehensive School Physical Activity Program, and the Coordinated School Health Program, developed by the Centers for Disease Control and Prevention (www.cdc.gov/Healthy Youth/CSHP/). NASPE's Comprehensive School Physical Activity Program (CSPAP) constitutes the centerpiece program within the new Let's Move in Schools campaign. It includes the following target areas:

1. A quality physical education program
2. Physical activity during school (e.g., classroom physical activity breaks, lunch recess, and recess)
3. Before- and after-school physical activity
4. Wellness programming for school staff
5. Involvement by families and the community

The CDC's Coordinated School Health Program also includes the physical education program as one of the eight central programs' components. However, it takes a broader focus in that it targets students' physical, mental, and emotional health, as is reflected in the various program components:

1. Health education
2. Physical education
3. Health services (e.g., those provided by physicians, nurses, dentists, etc.)
4. Nutrition services (i.e., services that directly affect the quality of and access to food and beverages)
5. Counseling and psychological services (e.g., school counselors, psychologists, and social workers)
6. Healthy school environment (i.e., the physical and aesthetic surroundings as well as psychological climate)
7. Health promotion for the school staff
8. Family and community involvement

In these comprehensive models, physical education professionals are part of a larger team whose primary goal is to create the healthiest possible school environment for all students. Undoubtedly, this vision of physical education programs is radically different from the program that you likely experienced as a K–12 student. Until now, most staff members (i.e., physical educators, health educators, classroom teachers, administrators, food service personnel, etc.) have worked largely in isolation. Within a truly comprehensive school physical activity program, a typical day for a physical educators will look different and will include activities that traditionally have not been regarded as "part of my job" (see Focus On Box 6.4).

Physical educators must still ensure delivery of quality physical education lessons, and aggressively promote physical activity throughout the day; the food service staff members will still be primarily responsible for the type and quality of food provided in schools; and classroom teachers still have achievement in academic subjects as their primary task. Yet, working together they can shape a school environment that more likely contributes the health and wellness of children and youth.

---

**FOCUS ON**    A Day in a Life of a Physical Activity Director    6.4

Jesse arrives at school at 7:30 a.m. He has been the school's physical activity director now for 2 months and is slowly settling into the role. He has started a campuswide campaign to have his school campus become the most active and healthiest campus in the district. He gathers the materials he prepared yesterday to use during a 7:45 a.m. meeting with six classroom teachers who each have volunteered to infuse physical activity (PA) breaks in their classrooms. Immediately following the meeting, Jesse meets with two of the teachers and schedules time to visit their classrooms to see the classroom teachers' first attempt at using PA breaks later that morning and the next day during his planning period. After that, he returns to the office to get ready for his first-, second-, and third-period seventh-grade physical education periods that start at 9:05 a.m.

9:00 a.m.: Before he heads to the gym where his first-hour class is in the middle of Pickle ball Sport Education season, he confirms with one of his girls' physical education colleagues to make sure that the four activity equipment carts are ready in time for the first lunch period drop-in activity session. He reminds her to tell the PA facilitators (students from the neighboring high school who are completing a service learning project) that the auxiliary gym is available today for the drop-in PA session, because the eighth-grade physical education class is scheduled for a mountain biking trip in the nearby park.

9:55 a.m.: Jesse has an uneventful first period, and quickly checks his email to confirm the time and place to meet with a representative from a local outdoor equipment store at 4:00 p.m. that day. Jesse is hoping to set up a partnership with the store's manager where he would be able to rent 50 pairs of rollerblades (with protective gear) for an upcoming 4-week unit. The manager would visit the school and offer a workshop during both lunch periods where interested students could come and try out rollerblading.

11:50 a.m.: Other than a student spraining an ankle while playing a fierce Pickle ball match during the second period, and the gym's sound system malfunctioning briefly during third period, both periods have good matches and students report excitement for the next few days of matches. Jesse returns to the office and prepares to meet briefly with the principal and the district's food service director to discuss ways to reduce the amount of food wasted during lunch periods. During the last half of his planning period, Jesse prints new signs that offer directions and rules for playing different modified games for the lunchtime PA drop-in sessions. During the printing, he continues drafting a short survey to determine interest and preferences among his school's faculty and staff colleagues in starting an after-school staff fitness program on Tuesdays and Thursdays after school hours. He has already received commitment from a local health club (where he is a member) to provide instructors on a trial basis for a 6-month period. With permission from his principal and the district's risk management office, Jesse has agreed to let the health club promote the availability of such classes to health club members, allowing them to work out alongside the school's faculty and staff.

12:00 Noon: As fourth-period students return to the locker room, the PA facilitators arrive to prepare for the day's lunchtime drop-in PA sessions. Jesse directs them to the girls' PE office where the carts are located. He escorts them to ensure that they are headed to the right outdoor PA venues. As the middle-school students arrive and start their recreational play, Jesse offers an overview of PA facilitators' duties and responsibilities to four high-school students who have applied to become PA facilitators in the next semester. After he finishes this, he checks in with

his colleague who will oversee the PA facilitators for the first lunch period, and ask him to make sure that the PA facilitators encourage those students who stand on the perimeter of the activity venues to join in the activity, and also leave enough time for students to return equipment at the end of the first lunch period. Jesse returns to his office.

1:15 p.m.: At the end of the second lunch period, the PA facilitators return the equipment carts, reporting that all equipment is accounted for, but that two soccer balls have lost air. Jesse thanks them and high-fives them, reminding them that they are key players in having his school become the district's most active school.

1:20 p.m.: Jesse checks the attendance files on his tablet PC for the last two class periods of the day to ensure they are updated, and pulls out a box of pedometers. Ten students in both periods will be asked to wear the pedometer for the duration of the class period. The last two Pickle ball periods go smoothly. The students who wore pedometers enter their step counts on his tablet PC during the lesson closure, and students return to the locker room.

3:15 p.m.: The students have left, and Jesse checks in with his colleague to see how the PA facilitators did during the lunch PA sessions. Based on the feedback, Jesse sends a quick email to the high-school teacher who oversees the service learning program to thank him for sending such quality students. Afterward he gathers his materials for his 4:00 p.m. meeting. As he heads out, he swings by the classroom of a colleague in math education. This colleague is the school's site council chair. Jesse requests some time at next week's site council meeting to discuss possible fundraisers and to seek assistance with writing a small grant proposal from a local hospital.

4:00 p.m.: Jesse meets with the manager of the Outdoor Store and discusses logistical and liability issues related to the planned workshop, among other issues.

4:45 p.m.: As Jesse leaves the store, he spots the district's superintendent. He invites her to

---

**FOCUS ON**    A Day in a Life of a Physical Activity Director *(continued)*    **6.4**

come visit his school in the next couple of weeks to witness the progress in efforts to make better use of his school's facilities. The superintendent agrees to the visit. In return, the superintendent asks Jesse to prepare a short 5-minute presentation for the next school board meeting on his efforts, because she wants all the district's principals to see and hear about how Jesse's physical education program is being reshaped.

5:08 p.m.: Jesse arrives at his health club for a quick 30-minute swim workout. After he completes his swim, he swings by the group exercise director's office and asks when the club is planning to replace the spinning bikes, and if the club

would consider donating a number of them to his school when that time arrives. The director makes note of the request and promises an answer later that week.

6:15 p.m.: Jesse arrives at his 12-year-old daughter's soccer practice session and offers to help the coach. After the practice ends, Jesse and his daughter head home.

9:10 p.m.: Jesse reviews the grant proposal guidelines from the local hospital. He emails his school's physical education colleagues and urges them to provide him with requests for new equipment with a rationale as to how it will impact the largest number of students.

---

## BECOMING ARCHITECTS OF A THRIVING PHYSICAL EDUCATION PROFESSION

The second strategy and accompanying tactics for the Education sector in the National Physical Activity Plan (see Focus On Box 5.4) targets the development and implementation of state and school-district policies that require school accountability for the quality and quantity of physical education and physical activity programs. It is difficult to accurately predict what school physical education will look like in 2030. What is certain is that moving school physical education toward credibility can only happen through delivery of quality programs with accountability at school, district, and state levels. As a future professional physical educator you will be the architect of programs that can shape the school environment to guarantee maximum access and opportunity for positive physical activity experiences for all students.

What is certain is that continuing in ways that characterize many programs is not a viable option. Programs that lack a real mission, that reintroduce the same basketball chest pass and bounce pass over and over again in each grade level, that cater largely to already highly skilled students, that focus only on traditional team sports, that have few, if any, expectations beyond attendance, dress, and general conduct

will continue to be a heavy drag on moving the profession forward. Continued delivery of such programs reflects what Kretchmar (2006) described as teachers employing "Easy Street" techniques:

> [A] brief review of rules, a quick survey of basic skills, very little practice and feedback, and perhaps a little play in only a simplified game form (perhaps, a larger ball, fewer players) so that a lack of skill does not get in the way of having some fun. But skills are not practiced diligently; old habits are never relinquished; new habits are not developed; attitudes are not changed; nobody is inducted into any one of the many movement subcultures that are asking for new members; learning plateaus are never encountered because they are never reached; and advanced challenges are never met. Much of the good stuff of movement remains hidden. (p. 349)

It should be obvious as well that accumulation of physical activity is becoming a centerpiece outcome measure for physical education programs. As a profession, we need to learn to collaborate with the many other programs and agencies that are also in the business of promoting physical activity in children and youth. Recently, Bulger and Housner (2009) argued persuasively that "Physical educators must be willing to demonstrate the entrepreneurial spirit and self-initiative that will lead to the development of strong relationships with these alternative providers and potential collaborators . . . " (p. 447).

With the steady increase in the percentage of overweight and obese children and youth, so has the call for the public health perspective within physical education as a foundation for justifying our place in schools in recent years. Moreover, there is increasing pressure in education and physical education for programs to employ evidence-based curriculum models and teaching practices (e.g., McKenzie, Sallis, & Rosengard, 2009). And, as we showed earlier, (a) the public is willing to invest and support school physical education programs that provide the kinds of comprehensive programs that we have presented here, and (b) numerous states have passed legislation mandating increased minutes of physical education and physical activity. These are all steps in the right direction to be sure. But, as the movement toward evidence-based programs gains steam, future physical educators will need to demonstrate that such investments are indeed justified. Claiming that your program seeks to teach students about the importance of a physically active lifestyle by providing positive and fun activities alone will likely not impress policy makers nor add credibility to your program. Physical education's place and status within the larger education institution will improve only the programs that can demonstrate that their students are indeed informed about healthy lifestyles, fitness and wellness; are skilled movers; have strong self-efficacy toward being physically active; and actually seek it out on their own beyond their physical education lessons.

## SUMMARY

1. There are several general problems faced by most programs in K–12 physical education. They include insufficient time allocated for physical education, class size, use of exemptions/substitutions, use of physical activity as punishment, liability, the adequacy of the facilities, and the difficulty of teaching groups of students with a wide variety of skill levels. In addition, gender equity has been an ongoing problem despite Title IX.

2. Many teachers view competition as something to be avoided within physical education. Competition is an inherent dimension of many types of activities. However, depending on how teachers design the activities and teach students about Fair Play, competition can be appropriately included in programs.

3. Problems more specific to K–5 physical education include that of too few schools requiring that physical education specialists be hired, and classroom teachers often not actively teaching physical education.

4. Facilities for elementary-school physical education are often inadequate, which can hamper program development, especially in terms of maximizing physical activity opportunities beyond regular physical education lessons.

5. Within the profession, there is general agreement over the need to focus on developing fundamental motor skills in grades K–3, but disagreement about the nature of elementary school physical education in the upper grades.

6. Too many secondary-school physical educators are content to keep their students busy, happy, and good, instead of focusing on learning and achievement.

7. The multi-activity program does not allow enough time in any one activity to realize important goals.

8. Large class size, heterogeneity of skill levels within a class, and the demands for coed teaching have all made it more difficult to teach secondary-school physical education.

9. The dual demands of teaching and coaching often produce role strain and role conflict, with the result that teaching is sometimes relegated to a lesser status.

10. Intramurals should occupy a central place in the activity opportunities for high-school youth. However, time, facilities, and staffing problems often cause them to be minimally important if not eliminated altogether.

11. Credibility can be earned only when real outcomes are achieved in physical education programs and are then communicated effectively to the public.

12. Liability concerns have prompted teachers to pay more attention to instruction, curriculum, and supervision and have also resulted in some activities being deleted from the curriculum.

13. physical education has a poor history regarding equity for girls; Title IX has begun to remedy that history of discrimination.

14. Skill equity requires that less-skilled students get equal opportunity and experience success.

15. The development of content standards and assessment tools represents progress.

16. The role of policy development and change is now widely recognized as a key process in improving the quality and quantity of physical education. But such efforts will lack broad impact if legislation and policies lack district or state-level accountability and oversight. Without that, physical education will continue to suffer despite being in an era where sport and fitness have assumed major cultural importance.

17. School physical education should provide the foundation for lifespan involvement in sport, fitness, and physical education, but to do that (and shed its marginalized status), it must begin to achieve its goals more completely.

18. The Comprehensive School Physical Activity Program and Coordinated School Health Program represent important efforts in helping school physical education become a more central part of the school's mission.

## DISCUSSION QUESTIONS

1. Were you taught by an elementary-school physical education specialist? What was your elementary-school physical education program like?

2. What was your high-school physical education program like? Were you kept busy, happy, and good? Did you have fun? If not, why not?

3. What would an ideal elementary- or secondary-school program be like? What facilities would be needed? What teacher-to-student ratio would be adequate?

4. What are the requirements for physical education in your state? Did your school's program exceed them?

5. Did your high school have intramurals? If so, what were they like? What role should intramurals play, relative to the instructional and interscholastic sport programs?

6. What credibility did the physical education program have in the schools that you attended, among students and among teachers?

7. How were equity issues handled in schools that you attended? Did girls have equal access to facilities? Did they receive equal funding?

8. Why do you think that physical education is suffering during a time when fitness and sport are booming? How can that be changed?

9. Why might teachers be reluctant to take on the broader role of physical activity director?

10. What do you believe to be most important policies or mandates that should be considered at the state level?

11. What would be your argument to the school district for limiting class sizes in physical education? What about eliminating the use of exemptions or substitutions for being in band, ROTC, interscholastic athletics, and the like?

12. Should there be a statewide assessment of students' physical fitness? Defend your position.

# Fitness

Fitness has periodically been a concern in America since early in the twentieth century, when World War I draft rejects produced a national fitness crisis. Fitness then was defined as strength, flexibility, and speed, tested by push-ups, sit-ups and sprints, and was focused on children through young adults.

In mid-century, fitness again became a national concern as new evidence showed the importance of fitness for health throughout the lifespan. In the late 1960s, the concept of cardiovascular fitness first swept the nation, fueled by Kenneth Cooper's book *Aerobics*. Fitness became important throughout the lifecycle and many adults began to strive to achieve the "fit" look.

In recent years, the obesity crisis among children, youths, and adults produced a national concern about health costs related to treating diseases associated with obesity. In this part of the text, we examine the various ways in which fitness is now defined, the components of fitness, the variety of fitness programs available at all ages, the breadth of the fitness professions, and the current issues related to fitness.

## CHAPTER 7

# Basic Concepts of Fitness

*Scientists and doctors have known for years that substantial benefits can be gained from regular physical activity. The expanding and strengthening evidence on the relationship between physical activity and health necessitates the focus this report brings to this important public health challenge. Although the science of physical activity is a complex and still-developing field, we have today strong evidence to indicate that regular physical activity will provide clear and substantial health gains. In this sense, the report is more than a summary of the science—it is a national call to action.*

Audrey Manley, surgeon general of the United States 1996

In 1996 the U.S. surgeon general issued a landmark report titled *Physical Activity and Health* (U.S. Department of Health and Human Services, 1996). That report, as the quotation at the start of this chapter indicates, not only presented the most convincing case ever for the relationship between physical activity (PA) and health but also served as a national call to action to increase physical activity among children, youths, and adults of all ages, especially among the many Americans who live essentially sedentary lives.

In Chapter 1 we provided a thorough description of the current concern in America for the health costs associated with overweight and obesity among children, youth, and adults. Three hundred thousand adult deaths are attributed to medical problems that are the results of over-

weight and obesity. Health insurance claims have skyrocketed. Work days lost due to complications that are the result of overweight/obesity result in substantial productivity losses and increased health insurance costs. The incidence of overweight and obesity is not distributed normally across the population. Families living below the federal poverty level have nearly twice the incidence of overweight and obesity. Adult obesity rates for African Americans are substantially higher. Children and youths with disabilities are more likely to be overweight or obese.

Obesity rates among children and youth are of particular concern to professionals in physical education, fitness, and sport. Childhood obesity has more than tripled in the past 30 years. Obese children and youths typically have high cholesterol

---

## FOCUS ON — Determining Overweight and Obesity Rates                    7.1

The prevalence of overweight and obesity in the population is most often estimated by use of body mass index (BMI), which is calculated by the individual's body weight divided by the square of his or her height multiplied by 703. This calculation is used because an individual's height and weight are easy to measure and are always parts of medical records and school records, thus inexpensive compared to other methods. For children and teens, the BMI figure is plotted on the CDC BMI-for-age growth charts for girls or boys to obtain a percentile ranking, indicating the relative position of the child's BMI among children of the same gender and age.

*Weight Status*

| *Category* | *Percentile Range* |
| --- | --- |
| Underweight | Less than the 5th percentile |
| Healthy weight | 5th percentile to less than 85th percentile |

*Weight Status*

| *Category* | *Percentile Range* |
| --- | --- |
| Overweight | 85th to less than 95th percentile |
| Obese | Equal to or greater than the 95th percentile |

For adults, overweight and obesity ranges are determined by dividing body weight (in kilograms) by the square of your height (expressed in meters).

| *BMI* | *Classification* |
| --- | --- |
| <18.5 | Underweight |
| 18.5–24.9 | Normal |
| 25.0–29.9 | Overweight |
| 30.0–39.9 | Obese |

BMI is used to broadly categorize population groups. Its accuracy can be distorted by factors such as muscle mass, bone structure, and fitness level.

SOURCE: Centers for Disease Control, *Defining Overweight and Obesity*, 2008.

---

and high blood pressure, both risk factors for cardiovascular disease. These children and youths are also at greater risk for bone and joint problems, sleep apnea, and social or psychological problems. They are also more likely to remain overweight in adulthood, thus increasing their risk for heart disease, type 2 diabetes, stroke, and several types of cancer (www.cd.gov/HealthyYouth/obesity). Focus On Box 7.1 describes how overweight and obesity categories are determined.

Many still use the term *fitness* in a global sense, encompassing physical, social, moral, mental, and spiritual fitness. Although that use of the term might be sufficient in everyday language, it is not specific enough to guide policy or programs. Others have said that fitness is an adequate amount of strength and endurance to meet the needs of everyday life, but that too is very misleading. What are the needs of daily life? Whose life? Some women and men sit at a desk all day and watch TV in their leisure. They have enough strength and endurance to do that, but they are very unlikely to be fit.

## A CONTEMPORARY UNDERSTANDING OF FITNESS

Research in exercise science, medical sciences, and health has led to a changing concept of physical fitness—one that is not only more meaningful but also more useful in providing directions for physical education, fitness, and sport professionals as they implement programs designed to help children, youths, and adults of all ages improve their fitness. The first step in this contemporary understanding was to recognize that the umbrella concept of fitness had to be understood in relation to a large number of related concepts (see Focus On Box 7.2). Fitness is currently viewed as a series of components, each of which is specific in its development and maintenance. Typically, fitness components are divided into two basic categories: those essentially related to health and those related to motor-skill performance. An additional category, cosmetic fitness, will also be considered because of its importance in the culture.

- *Aerobic* The process of metabolizing body fuels through exercise in the presence of oxygen
- *Anaerobic* The process of metabolizing body fuels through exercise without oxygen
- *Body Composition* The relative amounts of muscle, fat, bone, and other vital body parts
- *Cardiovascular Endurance* The ability of the circulatory and respiratory systems to supply fuel during sustained exercise
- *Exercise* Leisure-time physical activity conducted with the intention of developing physical fitness
- *Health* A state of being associated with freedom from disease and illness, including the positive component of wellness

- *Healthy Lifestyles* Presence of appropriate physical activity, nutrition, and stress-management behavior patterns
- *Hypokinetic Diseases* Conditions related to physical inactivity or low levels of habitual activity
- *Leisure Activity* Physical activity undertaken during discretionary time
- *Physical Activity* Bodily movement that is produced by skeletal muscle and substantially increases energy expenditure
- *Wellness* A state of positive biological and psychological health in the individual, exemplified by quality of life and a sense of well-being

Sources: Corbin, Pangrazi, & Franks, 2000; Costill, 1986.

The distinction between these two basic fitness categories is quite important. **Health fitness** is important for the prevention and remediation of disease and illness leading to a better quality of life. **Motor-performance fitness** is essential to performing well in sports and work that requires physical skill, strength, and/or endurance. The components of health fitness are general in the sense that they apply to everybody; that is, each person should strive to develop and sustain a reasonable level of health fitness to enjoy a better quality of life (see Focus On Box 7.3). Motor-performance fitness is more functional and specific to the task or activity that enables the performer to do well. A football tackle, a sprinter, a tennis player, and a swimmer need different amounts of each of the motor-performance components; that is, the training for motor-performance fitness is functionally related to the goals of each activity. Health fitness, on the other hand, is not related to shooting baskets more accurately or to jumping farther. It is related to living better, being more resistant to diseases, and increasing the likelihood of living longer.

Health fitness is an important component of **wellness,** which is often referred to as the overall goal for healthy individuals. Historically, health has been thought of primarily as the absence of disease and illness, but wellness not only relies on a positive emphasis of factors but also includes aspects of living well beyond physical health. Wellness is considered to be a dynamic process of change and growth rather than a static state (Fahey, Insel, & Roth, 2007). The components of wellness are physical wellness, emotional wellness, intellectual wellness, spiritual wellness, interpersonal and social wellness, and environmental wellness. These dimensions are not separate but interact to develop and sustain the state of being described as wellness. For example, the self-esteem that comes with emotional wellness is likely associated with better eating habits and a more regular physical activity program, all working to produce a better quality of life (Fahey et al., 2007).

## Health Fitness

Health fitness is important for the prevention and remediation of **hypokinetic diseases,** the most serious of which have been those related to the heart and vascular systems and, more recently, to

## FOCUS ON    Components of Health Fitness    7.3

*Body Composition*: The body's relative amount of fat and fat-free mass (muscle, bone, and water).

**Assessment**

Underwater weighing: Person is weighed out of water and underwater, with correction made for amount of air in lungs when underwater.

Skinfold measures: Half of the body's fat is located just under the skin. Calipers are used to measure skinfolds (two thicknesses of skin and the fat just under the skin) at various places around the body.

Body mass index: BMI is calculated by dividing body weight (in kilograms) by the square of the individual's height (in meters).

Body circumference measures: Use of various height, weight, waist, thigh, and hip measurements to estimate body fatness.

Bioelectric impedence analysis: Electrodes placed on body with low doses of current passed through the skin. Muscle has less resistance to current, making possible an estimate of body composition.

*Cardiovascular Endurance*: The ability of the body to perform prolonged, large-muscle, dynamic exercise at moderate to high levels of intensity.

**Assessment**

Laboratory test of maximal oxygen consumption: Person runs on a treadmill, and the air inhaled and exhaled is analyzed while the person exercises to exhaustion.

1-mile walk test: For person who meets criteria for safe exercise but have low levels of fitness. Calculate (1) time it takes to complete a brisk 1-mile walk and (2) exercise heart rate at end of the walk.

3-minute step test: The individual steps continuously at a steady rate for 3 minutes; then heart rate during recovery is calculated.

1.5-mile run–walk test: A time test; faster times indicate a greater capacity to consume oxygen.

*Flexibility:* The ability to move a joint through its full range of motion.

**Assessment**

Because flexibility is specific to each joint, there are no general assessments of flexibility. No evidence exists to establish norms for flexibility. Too much flexibility may be as problematic as too little.

Sit and reach test: Most common flexibility test. Person is seated with knees fully extended and feet flat against a measuring device. Keeping knees extended, person reaches as far forward as possible.

Range-of-motion assessments: Flexibility in any joint can be measured by a goniometer, which provides the degrees of motion capable at that joint.

*Muscular Endurance*: The ability of a muscle or muscle group to remain contracted or to contract repeatedly for a long period of time.

**Assessment**

Dynamic curl-up: Sit on mat with legs bent more than 90 degrees so that feet remain flat on floor and arms extended at sides with palms down and fingers extended. Two tape marks 4.5 inches apart are placed on floor so that fingers touch the first tape mark. Curl head and shoulders forward so that fingers touch second tape mark. Repeat curl every 3 seconds until exhaustion.

Dynamic push-up: Support body in push-up position from the toes with hands just outside the shoulders and back and legs straight with toes tucked under. Lower body until upper arm is parallel to floor or until elbow is bent at 90 degrees. Do one push-up every 3 seconds until exhaustion.

*Strength:* The amount of force a muscle can produce with a single maximum effort.

**Assessment**

Muscular strength can be assessed by taking one-repetition-maximum (1RM) tests for various muscle groups. Upper-body strength is best tested by 1RM effort on a seated press machine or a bench press machine. Lower body is best tested by a 1RM effort on a leg press machine.

SOURCES: Fahey, Insel, & Roth, 2008; Corbin, Welk, Corbin, & Welk, 2008.

Although historically an important competitive sport, running is often pursued now for its cardiovascular benefits.

The major difference in athletic performance today is increased levels of sport-specific fitness.

the several conditions specifically related to obesity, particularly type II diabetes. We have lived through 35 years of emphasis on aerobic exercise—road racing, marathons, triathlons, aerobics of all kinds (low-impact, water, and so on), cycling, and power walking. In that time, people have learned that regular aerobic exercise of the right intensity and duration can help control weight, reduce the percentage of fat in body composition, improve circulatory function, control blood-glucose levels, increase insulin sensitivity, and reduce stress and depression (Blair, Kohl, & Powell, 1987; Fahey, Insel, & Roth, 2008).

Aerobic work contributes primarily to cardiovascular fitness, which consists of a fit heart muscle, a fit vascular system, a fit respiratory system, and fit muscle tissue capable of using oxygen efficiently (Corbin, Welk, Corbin, & Welk, 2008). Cardiovascular

activities increase heart health by increasing the blood and oxygen supply and decreasing the work and oxygen demand on the heart, thus increasing its efficiency (Fahey et al., 2007). This does not mean that to develop and sustain a healthy cardiovascular system you need to become a daily distance runner! What it does mean is that you need to engage in an aerobic activity three to five times per week at a sufficient intensity to develop and sustain an appropriate level of cardiovascular fitness. This can be accomplished through walking, jogging, cycling, swimming, and using fitness machines such as treadmills and elliptical trainers. If you want to improve your cardiovascular fitness, then you need to gradually increase the intensity of the exercise in ways that raise the heart rate sufficiently to produce a training effect.

In recent years, it has become clear that core strength and flexibility is an important ingredient in health fitness. Many youths and adults suffer from health problems that originate with lack of strength, stability, and flexibility in the core musculature of the back. Core stability is achieved through strengthening the muscles that stabilize the spine. Core strength is achieved through strengthening the muscles that bend, extend, and rotate the spine (Corbin et al., 2008). The most well-known "system" for achieving core strength and flexibility is Pilates, developed early in the twentieth century by German gymnast and boxer George Pilates (Fahey et al., 2007). Pilates focuses on strengthening and stretching the core muscles of the back. Exercises are done on mats, with bands, and with training balls (www.pilatesmethodalliance.com).

Physical activity in the form of resistance training has many benefits (Fahey et al., 2008; Pollock & Vincent, 1996; Westcott, 1993). These include positive effects on bone-mineral density, body composition, muscular strength, glucose metabolism, serum lipids, maximal oxygen consumption, and basal metabolism. We have just begun to understand that resistance training, especially when done with lighter weights and increased repetitions, can improve aerobic capacity. Not only is metabolic rate increased during a strength workout, but also, as a result, it is increased slightly throughout the day. Although our cultural perception of strength training is typically muscular young men in weight rooms, it is clear that regular resistance work is important for women and men, both young and old. Indeed, some regular resistance work is especially important as people get older.

It is important to note that not all exercise programs require high levels of exertion to achieve health benefits. There are moderate forms of exercise that provide important health benefits. Exercise programs such as yoga, Pilates, tai chi, and Sittercise improve posture, balance, flexibility, muscle strength, and mood. These programs are especially useful for persons recovering from injuries, older adults, and those who have physical disabilities.

The recent national attention focused on the problems of obesity in the population, especially the increase in obesity among children, has given new urgency to our awareness of the need for physical activity among children and youths. Obesity is typically defined as an excessive amount of body fat relative to fat-free body mass (Fahey et al., 2008). Individuals with a BMI of 25–29.9 are considered overweight, and those with a BMI of 30 or more are considered obese. Estimates suggest that 65 percent of American adults are currently overweight or obese. The relationship between obesity and diabetes

has produced a new term, *diabesity* (Kaufman, 2005). The concerns about the increase in obesity are due partially to the estimated $117 billion a year spent on health costs related to that condition (www.healthyamericans.org).

Gains in health fitness are not permanent. The body systems adjust to lower levels of physical activity in the same way they adjust to higher levels (Fahey et al., 2008). When you stop exercising, you are likely to lose up to 50 percent of fitness improvements in just 2 months. Not all fitness gains reverse at the same rate, however. Cardiovascular gains are quick to reverse; strength gains are slower. Strength gains can also be sustained with less frequent workouts, whereas maintaining cardiovascular gains typically requires regular workouts. The lesson here is straightforward: To maintain health fitness you have to "keep on keeping on"!

## Motor-Performance Fitness

When people today talk about physical fitness, they are likely to mean health fitness. When someone asks "Are you physically fit?" the question probably relates to health fitness. Fitness classes in schools and fitness centers are most likely to have a health-fitness focus. This does not mean that motor-performance fitness is not important—it simply means that it is different.

The goal of motor-performance fitness is to perform a motor skill better, typically a sport skill. Focus On Box 7.4 defines the six components of motor-performance fitness. Every sport, and even different roles or positions in sports, requires a different combination of these components. Obviously, the training for tennis would be dramatically different than the training for being a lineman in football, but each of those training programs would include some focus on each component. Even within a sport, the training would be different depending on the role or position played within the sport; that is, the speed that a defensive lineman needs in football is different from the speed needed by a wide receiver or running back, and their training for increasing and maintaining their speed would be different.

| FOCUS ON | Components of Motor-Performance Fitness | | 7.4 |
|---|---|---|---|
| *Agility* | The ability to move the body accurately and rapidly in different directions. Shown in activities such as skiing, wrestling, and soccer. | *Power* | The ability to transfer energy into force at a fast rate. Shown in activities such as shot put and blocking in football. |
| *Balance* | The maintenance of equilibrium while moving or stationary. Shown in activities such as balance beam and skating. | *Reaction Time* | The time elapsed between stimulation and the onset of movement in response to that stimulation. Shown in sprint starting or change of possession in invasion games. |
| *Coordination* | The ability to use body parts to perform motor skills smoothly and accurately. Shown in activities such as kicking, batting, dribbling, or shooting a ball. | *Speed* | The ability to perform a skill in a short period of time. Shown in sprinters, wide receivers, and base stealers. |

SOURCE: Corbin et al., 2008.

If walking, jogging, and aerobics are the most visible methods of developing and sustaining aerobic fitness, then activity in the weight room or in a fitness center with strength machines has become the most visible sign of motor-performance fitness. There is no doubt that power plays a central role in sport performance at any level and in virtually every sport. Power is functionally related to a specific motor activity, and the training to increase power will be different depending on the activity; that is, the power to put the shot is developed differently than the power needed to increase the speed of the serve in tennis. The same tends to hold true for the other components of motor-performance fitness. Many athletes work to improve their agility, balance, reaction time, speed, and coordination, but the specific training activities that they use are designed to increase each of those components in ways that are specific to their use in the sport. For example, a defensive back in football needs to react quickly to an offensive play and move quickly—either forward, backward, or sideways—to be in the position to defend successfully. The components of reaction time, agility, and speed would likely be combined in training activities to improve play at that position. The increased understanding of motor-performance fitness and the important role that it plays in sport has led to a new profession, most commonly referred to as strength trainer or strength and conditioning coach.

## COSMETIC FITNESS

It would be a mistake not to recognize that for many people, youths and adult, looking good is an important outcome of fitness activities. One of the significant shifts in public perception over the past several decades is the change in what is considered to be an attractive physical appearance. It was not too many years ago that a man with well-defined muscular features was often described as "muscle-bound"— and was not necessarily admired for looking that way. If a girl or a woman had well-defined muscular features, she might have been socially ridiculed. Not so today!

Looking fit is in—and looking strong is an important part of looking fit. This is true for both men and women:

Perhaps the most prevalent and least understood reason people train with weights is to add quality to their lives. Many people engage in strength training simply because they look better and feel better when they do. They find the training process enjoyable, and the training product well worth the effort. For most people, controlled physical exertion is a satisfying experience, and increased muscle strength is a gratifying accomplishment. Something about becoming stronger enhances a person's self-image. (Westcott, 1982, p. 4)

If **cosmetic fitness** is not confused with health fitness, then it can be a positive addition to the overall fitness movement. The more that our culture encourages adoption of an active lifestyle, the better off future generations will be. There is, however, a downside to some aspects of the motivation to "look better." The incidence of eating disorders among youths and young adults is far too high. Television and magazine advertising have made the slim, athletic look the preferred body shape to sell products. This has produced what the Australian physical educator Richard Tinning (1985) called "the cult of slenderness." In some cases, the quest for cosmetic fitness leads to inadequate consumption of nutrients, leading to a diminished appetite that puts the health of the person at substantial risk.

The fact is that people come in all shapes; that is, their genetic endowments play a significant role in determining their body shape. Whatever that body shape may be, it can be enhanced by regularly engaging in health-fitness activities. If people engage in these activities to "look better" and "feel better about themselves," that is appropriate, but if they carry that too far, they put their health at risk.

## THE DOSE–RESPONSE DEBATE

Current investigations and discussions, referred to here as the "**dose–response debate,**" are about what is needed to generate health benefits—that is,

how much of what kind of activity, at what intensity, for how long, and how frequently (Pate, 1995). Put simply, what "dose" of exercise is necessary to achieve the beneficial health "responses"? The dose–response debate developed since the late 1980s as a new, specialized field of scholarship called "exercise epidemiology" began to present evidence on the relationship of physical activity to all causes of mortality (Blair, Kohl, Paffenbarger, Cooper, & Gibbons, 1989). Dividing activity patterns into five groups, from low activity to high activity, researchers found that men in the least-fit category were 3.44 times more likely to die during the follow-up period than those in the most-fit category, and the least-fit women were 4.65 times more likely to die than the most-fit women (Blair, 1992). Figure 7.1 shows these data and indicates clearly that the most impressive improvements in mortality are between groups 1 and 2—that is, between the least-active group and the group that gets some activity regularly. There are some additional modest improvements as people move to the more-active groups, but clearly the major problem is in the sedentary group and the major gain to be achieved is by modest increases in physical activity as part of lifestyle.

In a summary of research related to dose–response issues, Rankinen and Bouchard (2002) concluded that ample evidence supports the assertion that regular physical activity has beneficial effects on all health outcomes. They also asserted that "there is strong suggestion of an inverse and linear relationship between regular physical activity and rates of all-cause mortality, total CVD [cardiovascular disease] and coronary heart incidence and mortality, and incidence of type 2 diabetes mellitus" (p. 6).

Fitness improves when the amount of exercise is gradually increased—a principle often referred to as *progressive overload*. Most fitness professionals use a dose formula based on the frequency, intensity, duration (time), and type of activity (FITT). *Frequency* is related to the need for body systems to recover and rebuild. The FITT recommendations for aerobic activity would of course be different from that for strength training. The examples

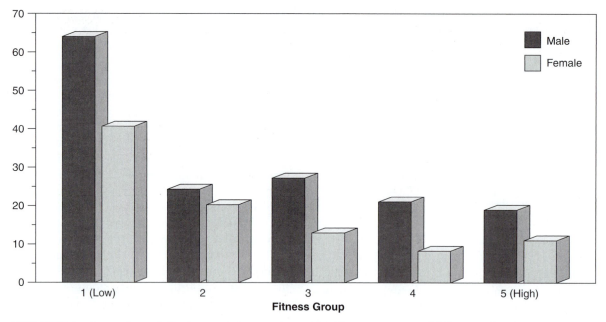

**FIGURE 7.1** Age-adjusted death rates (all causes) per 10,000 person-years of follow-up for men (10,000+) and women (3,000+) in the Aerobics Center Longitudinal Study.

NOTE: *Subjects were apparently healthy at baseline, physical fitness was assessed by maximal exercise testing on a treadmill, and the average length of follow-up was slightly more than 8 years. Rates are based on 240 deaths in men and 43 deaths in women. Data for this figure were taken from Blair et al., (1989).*

shown here are for aerobic activity. Many joggers, cyclists, and swimmers work out most days of the week. If their exercise intensity and duration are within their capacity, their bodies will adapt and recover sufficiently to sustain that level of frequency. The American College of Sports Medicine (ACSM) recommendation is for an energy expenditure of 1,000–3,000 calories per week achieved through three to five workouts per week.

*Intensity* refers to the level of exercise stress that is progressively increased to produce the desired outcome. For aerobic exercise, intensity is typically calculated by subtracting your age from 220 (maximum heart rate for a well-trained young person) and then multiplying that figure by an appropriate percentage related to previous training (Focus On Box 7.5). The ACSM recommendation for intensity is 60–90 percent of maximum heart rate. *Duration* refers to the amount of time that you engage in aerobic activity. The ACSM recommendation is

between 20 and 60 minutes or more. For purposes of improving aerobic fitness, the *types of activities* recommended are jogging, cycling, brisk walking, aerobic dancing, and swimming. Of course, aerobic activity can also be done in fitness centers using elliptical trainers, stationary bicycles, or treadmills.

For strength training, the FITT recommendations would be somewhat different. For frequency, it is often recommended that hard workouts be alternated with easy workouts to allow for recovery and to prevent injury. For intensity, exercise bouts would gradually increase the amount of weight resistance. For strength training, time or duration refers to the number of sets (consisting of 8 to 12 repetitions) that are done for each muscle group as part of the total workout. For each type of activity, the most common approaches use free weights or machines.

An alternative method to using a dose—response approach to training, either for health

| **FOCUS ON** — Calculating Your Target Heart-Rate Zone | 7.5 |
|---|---|

Your target heart-rate zone should be between 65 and 90 percent of your maximum heart rate (MHR).

1. Estimate your MHR by subtracting your age from 220.

2. Multiply your MHR by 0.65 and also by 0.90 to calculate your target heart-rate zone.

For example, a 21-year-old would calculate her target heart-rate zone as follows:

MHR = 220 − 21 = 199 beats per minute (BPM)

Lower range of zone = 199 × 0.65 = 129 BPM

Upper range of zone = 199 × 0.90 = 179 BPM

Fitness benefits are gained when the heart rate stays within the parameters of the zone. Unfit people or people just starting an exercise program should use the lower end of the range for their threshold.

---

purposes or for improvement in a specific activity, is the concept of "training effects." This may be especially important for people, young or old, who are trying to improve their fitness either for health purposes or for specific improvement in performing an activity. One of the biggest problems in our nation's health is the number of people—women and men, young and old—who are badly out of shape. For them, the main issue is to get started in a modest fitness program and to see some immediate results—that is, to see the training effects that can be achieved very early in a fitness program. For example, some very modest aerobic training will lower resting heart rate. Some modest strength training will show a capacity to perform daily tasks better. When people undertake a beginning effort in fitness that results in modest exercise done at least several times per week, they will experience improvement. They will be able to walk for a longer period of time without tiring. They will be able to lift a weight with less effort and can begin to lift a heavier weight. As Figure 7.1 shows, the most important improvement in age-adjusted death rates occurs between the least-fit and the next least-fit groups, showing that modest improvements in health-related fitness can be very important. Having people focus on key training effect indicators can be a major motivational influence to keep them involved in their fitness effort.

The dose formula for exercise prescription for healthy adults under age 65 is to do moderately intense cardio 30 minutes per day, five days per week or vigorously intense cardio 20 minutes per day, 3 days per week and do 8 to 10 strength-training exercises, 8 to 12 repetitions of each exercise twice a week. If weight loss is a key outcome, 60 to 90 minutes of physical activity per week may be necessary (www.acsm.org).

The U.S. Department of Health and Human Services has recently developed physical activity guidelines for children and adolescents in three component categories. For aerobic activity children and adolescents should do 60 minutes or more of PA daily with most of the 60 or more minutes devoted either to moderate- or vigorous-intensity aerobic activity at least 3 days per week. For muscle strengthening, children and adolescents should use part of their 60 minutes or more of daily physical activity engaged in unstructured play (e.g., playground equipment, tug of war, etc.) or structured activity (e.g., lifting weights or working with resistance bands). For bone strengthening, children and adolescents should include, as part of their 60 minutes or more of daily PA, engaged in activities that produce force on the bones.

The developing evidence relating physical activity to health and mortality variables created a new understanding of health-related activity, what many referred to as moderate-to-vigorous physical activity (MVPA) (Simons-Morton, 1994). MVPA takes into account a broader range of physical activities than did health-related aerobic fitness, particularly activities that are near the moderate end of the range, such as brisk walking.

Which of the two dose formulas was correct? One appears to be anchored in the concept of fitness, albeit health-related fitness. The other is clearly anchored in health, particularly related to reductions in all causes of mortality. We have much to learn in both approaches, and it is impossible at this time to determine which is preferable. Blair and Connelly (1996, p. 194), in reviewing studies from both traditions, have suggested a holistic view that makes sense at this time:

> Most of these projects used the standard exercise prescription described by the ACSM as the training stimulus, although others have evaluated various combinations of frequency, intensity, and duration. It is still common, however, for scientists and clinicians to consider two somewhat competing views of the effects of physical activity: one on the role of physical activity in promoting health and the other on physical activity to improve fitness. We disagree with this approach of categorizing physical activity as contributing to health or fitness. We think physical activity works through multiple biological pathways to improve both health and function.

The Physical Activity Pyramid shown in Figure 7.2 reflects this holistic view. Some combination of strength training, flexibility work, aerobic conditioning, and MVPA is the way to achieve a level of physical activity that contributes significantly to health and well-being.

The introduction of MVPA has also greatly influenced how we think about fitness for children and youths. NASPE now suggests that the overarching goal for school physical education is for students to "adopt and value a physically active lifestyle." If this goal is considered seriously, then fitness in physical education will likely mean less about exercises and fitness testing and more about helping students find activities that they enjoy and helping them to get better at those activities so that they will voluntarily participate in those activities outside of school and in the future.

In 2009 the American College of Sports Medicine released specific new exercise recommendations for adults, particularly those interested in weight loss (Donnelly, Blair, Jakicic, Manore, Rankin,

and Smith, 2009). The average adult should get between 150 and 250 minutes per week of moderate intensity exercise. A greater volume of exercise or more intense exercise will lead to greater weight loss, and recognition that there is a dose-response effect for exercise. An average of 200–300 minutes of exercise per week is needed to maintain weight loss. Lifestyle physical activity, such as taking stairs instead of elevators, using pedometers, and completing a minimum number of steps per day will help to achieve weekly goals. Moderate diet restriction will accelerate weight loss, when combined with recommended exercise levels.

## THE SOCIAL GRADIENT IN HEALTH AND FITNESS

This review of basic concepts of fitness related to health would be incomplete without noting how social and economic status within a society affects health and longevity. We know that the proximal causes of degenerative diseases—commonly referred to as "risk factors"—are physical inactivity, smoking, and a high-fat diet. These risk factors, however, are not distributed normally across populations within societies. The fact is that as we move our lens *down* the social-class structure of developed nations, we see that risk factors and health problems increase, resulting in increased mortality (Siedentop, 1996c).

This socioeconomic impact on health and fitness is what health epidemiologists refer to as the **social gradient** in health; that is, the health status of a particular class within a nation is typically better than that of the classes below it and worse than that of the classes above it (Hertzman, 1994). The social-gradient hypothesis argues that relative social and economic deprivation within societies accounts for better or poorer health. Hertzman (1994) suggests that "one's place in the social hierarchy and the experiences which follow from it appear to be powerful determinants of the length and healthfulness of life" (p. 169). Note that the term

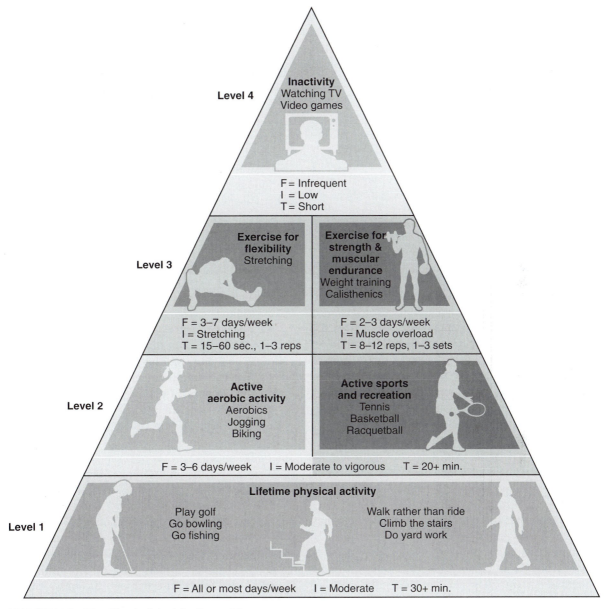

**FIGURE 7.2**  The Physical Activity Pyramid.
Source: *Corbin et al., (2008).*

*determinants* is used purposely because relative deprivation "influences life-style choices and differential access to high quality social environments" (Marmot, 1994, p. 213).

Traditionally, fitness has been viewed nearly totally as an *individual* responsibility (Tinning, 1990). When people are unfit or less fit than might be desirable, the less-than-optimally fit people get the blame for their condition. A **socioecological view,** on the other hand, looks to the social contexts within which people live their lives as partial explanations for their levels of health and fitness:

> Health is increasingly understood to be a social commodity, much like other social commodities such as housing and education. Some get more of it, some get less, and those at the top of the social stratification tend to do better than those at the bottom. Too many are, in current government parlance, underserved. For this reason, new strategies for empowerment, social support, and community-based services are advocated as broad and powerful strategies for health. (Vertinsky, 1991, p. 83)

The socioecological view is supported by evidence showing that in nations where income inequality is less, life expectancy is higher (Wilkinson, 1994). Also, increases in life expectancy have been shown in countries that have reduced income inequality in the current generation. People in lower socioeconomic groups have less access to nutritious food and to information about nutrition—and the foods high in fat are among the least expensive. Urban areas are in decay and are typically unsafe for outside physical activity. Very little infrastructure is available to support and sustain involvement in physical activity for children, youths, or adults. Although individual responsibility remains an important and compelling concept in the effort to improve the health and vitality of our nation, we must also realize that there are structural problems that have profound impact on individual motivation and responsibility.

If society is to become healthier and if a more fit citizenry can help achieve that public health goal, then we have to recognize this approach to understanding the social complexities of fitness and activity across the variety of groups within our society. We must view fitness as both an individual and a social issue—and we must attempt to develop a society in which more people have access to safe, affordable, and inclusive opportunities to pursue a physically active lifestyle.

# FITNESS-TRAINING CONCEPTS AND PRINCIPLES

In the 1970s and 1980s aerobic exercise and cardiovascular health were the main emphasis in health fitness. We have already considered the notion of a cardiovascular heart-rate training zone and the frequency, intensity, and duration recommended for cardiovascular exercise. Muscle strength and flexibility were much less prominent in exercise prescriptions and discussions about the health benefits of regular exercise. Muscles make up more than 40 percent of body mass (Fahey et al., 2008), and they are where a substantial portion of the metabolic-energy reactions in the body take place. This section further considers some of the principles associated with aerobic activity and also emphasizes the principles and benefits associated with resistance training.

When you train properly, the muscles and the energy systems that fuel those muscles become more efficient and stronger. This is true whether the muscles in question are the heart and leg muscles of a marathon runner or the arm and shoulder muscles of a javelin thrower. In that sense, the basic mechanisms underlying fitness training are the same for health fitness, motor-performance fitness, and cosmetic fitness.

When you train appropriately, the muscular system *adapts* to the training stresses; that is, when the training *load* increases, muscles are stressed and they adapt and improve their function (Fahey et al., 2008; Westcott, 1982). For aerobic fitness—or for endurance activities such as distance running, cross-country skiing, and cycling—it is important that individuals be able to use oxygen efficiently. That is why aerobic (with-oxygen) conditioning is so central to health fitness. To use oxygen efficiently, a person must have a fit heart muscle that is capable of pumping large amounts of blood. The blood, too, must be fit in that it must be capable of carrying large quantities of oxygen (which it does through hemoglobin). The arteries must be fit in that they must be free from elements that prevent the flow of blood.

Finally, the muscles that the blood flows to must be fit so that they are capable of using the oxygen brought by the blood to energize them for activity.

## General Training Principles

The human body adapts to meet the demands that are placed on it. Short-term adaptations, when done repeatedly, gradually translate into long-term improvements. The FITT (frequency, intensity, time, type) activity principles described earlier in this chapter form the primary basis for planning an individual fitness program. The FITT formula, however, needs to be applied with great **specificity,** which means that to produce a desired effect, exercises must be related to the bodily component in which improvement is sought. Improvement via aerobic conditioning requires that the FITT formula be used with aerobic activities such as running or cycling or treadmill, and elliptical trainer workouts. If you want to improve your arm and shoulder strength, then you have to apply the FITT formula to the muscles of the arms and shoulders.

Fitness training also should respect the principle of **progressive overload,** which means that the "load" or exercise chosen must be done at a level that produces a conditioning effect. If the load is too small or light, then the effect is not achieved. If the load is too large or too small, then the required amount of exercise will not be able to be accomplished. But if you gradually increase an appropriate beginning load, then small increments of improvement over time will eventually lead to significant improvement.

A final training principle is to allow for appropriate **recovery time.** The muscular system needs time to adapt to training stresses because the physiological and biochemical mechanisms responsible for gains in fitness operate during the rest intervals between exercise bouts. The frequency that one can exercise with safety varies with the fitness component being developed and the level of fitness that the person has in that component. After some beginning work, most people can engage in aerobic work every day as long as all-out efforts are avoided.

Most strength-training guides recommend that at least one day of rest be taken between strength workouts for the same muscle groups.

These principles of training are relevant to health fitness, motor-performance fitness, and cosmetic fitness. Each should be applied somewhat differently, depending on the kind of fitness a person is trying to achieve.

## Health-Fitness Training

People interested in health fitness typically engage in some form of aerobic training. The more faithfully that they adhere to a workout schedule that represents the intensity, duration, and frequency required for cardiovascular improvements, the more likely they are to achieve those improvements. Other people prefer more moderate physical activity and perhaps walk for 30 minutes before or after dinner each night. Still others achieve their health-fitness goals through a form of workouts known as "interval training" in which more intense exercise periods are alternated with rest periods to allow for recovery.

In recent years, it has become clear that a total health-fitness program needs to include regular attention to core strength and flexibility. Twenty-nine muscles attach to the body's core: the abdomen, pelvic floor, sides of the torso, back, buttocks, hip, and pelvis (Fahey et al., 2007). Core muscles not only stabilize the spine but also assist in transferring force between the upper and lower body. Core training typically focuses on holistic movements and exercises that work on groups of muscles rather than isolating muscles, such as isolating the biceps in a biceps curl exercise. Most core training uses whole-body exercises that force the core muscles to stabilize the spine. The most famous approach to core training is Pilates, an exercise program that focuses on strengthening and stretching the core muscles to create a solid base of support for whole-body movement (www.pilatesmethodalliance.com).

The frequency of exercise patterns depends on which of these approaches people choose; that is, the moderate-activity approach typically requires daily exercise, whereas the continuous-aerobic and interval-aerobic approaches can achieve results with three to five workouts per week.

Current evidence for the long-term benefits of health fitness suggests that activity of moderate intensity is appropriate. If infrequent, high-intensity fitness activities are imposed on children and youths, as they often are during infrequent fitness-testing days in physical education, these children and youths less likely to continue involvement in fitness programs.

To ensure that children, youths, and adults engage in appropriate physical activity that improves and sustains their health, we must focus on helping them to develop self-efficacy for the activities in which they engage. Those who enjoy a good run, a long bike ride, or 30 minutes on an elliptical trainer will more likely continue to stay engaged. Those who enjoy strength training with free weights or muscle-group-specific machines will more likely stay engaged. Self-efficacy is achieved through a gradual set of experiences where persons experience success in activities that, for them, have a high fun quotient.

## Continuous and Interval Training

Two kinds of aerobic training are used both for health-fitness purposes and by athletes training for endurance events: continuous and interval exercise. Walkers, joggers, and cyclists typically favor the continuous form of training, engaging in sustained exercise with their heart rate at or above the threshold level. Some runners and many swimmers tend to favor interval training where vigorous exercise bouts are interspersed with rest periods.

There is no doubt that both continuous training and interval training are sufficient to build and maintain high levels of health fitness. Continuous exercise is probably the better form for beginners simply because it is less intense and can be adjusted easily and done almost anyplace. **Interval training** tends to be more intense (that is, intense exercise periods, followed by rest periods) and typically needs a measured distance to

be done appropriately—for example, a 25-meter swimming pool or a 400-meter running track. The great value of interval training is that it allows you to do more work during any given exercise period. The exercise period can be more intense because it is followed by a rest period that allows for some recovery before the next exercise period begins.

The minimum continuous program for achieving and maintaining health fitness would involve exercising to lift the heart rate to the target threshold level and to maintain it there for 30 minutes (15 minutes would be an absolute minimum to achieve any training effect). This should be done three to five times per week. The same outcomes could be achieved through an interval program in which the trainee exercises at 80 percent of the maximum heart rate for a 2- or 3-minute period, then walk or do some mild jogging for the same length of time, and then repeat the work–rest intervals.

## Anaerobic Training

**Anaerobic exercise** is short-duration exercise completed without the aid of oxygen (which distinguishes it from aerobic exercise). Anaerobic exercise builds muscle mass. It has some health-related benefits in that it positively affects resting metabolic rate, enhances bone density, and may contribute to long-term weight control (Gutin, Manos, & Strong, 1992). The main functional outcome of anaerobic exercise, however, is to move quickly and deliver great force, which is why anaerobic training is highly relevant to sprinters, wrestlers, football players, gymnasts, and other athletes who must move explosively or deliver a substantial amount of force in a short time. Common anaerobic training activities are sprinting, weight lifting, plyometrics, and running stairs.

The threshold for building and maintaining anaerobic fitness is much higher than that for aerobic training. Athletes must perform at near-maximum effort for short distances or time periods, then allow a sufficient rest for nearly complete recovery before repeating the effort. Thus, virtually all anaerobic training is of the interval variety with much longer rest intervals than in aerobic training.

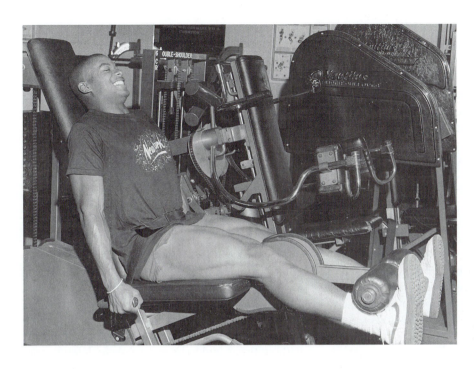

Strength training is often done on sophisticated weight machines.

## Strength Training

**Strength training,** the primary component of motor-performance fitness, is best done through some form of exercise against resistance, typically through weight training. In this form of fitness training, there are four primary variables to be considered (Fahey et al., 2008; Westcott, 1982):

1. Amount of resistance (weight) per lift
2. Number of repetitions of each lift (a set)
3. Number of sets per workout
4. Number of workouts per week

The phrase used most commonly among strength-training enthusiasts is *repetition maximums* (RMs); for example, 5RM means a five-repetition maximum, and 10RM means a 10-repetition maximum. Thus, a 5RM load is the most weight one can lift five times in succession, and a 10RM load is the most weight one can lift 10 times in succession.

In strength training, there is a direct corollary to the aerobic–anaerobic distinction made earlier. To build muscle *endurance,* one would perform numerous repetitions against a fairly low resistance. To build muscle *strength,* one would perform few repetitions against a much higher resistance. As in aerobic–anaerobic training, the results are highly specific to the nature of the exercise stress. The benefits of strength training are substantial.

Weight-training experts generally agree that weight loads at or exceeding 75 percent of one's maximum lifting capacity are most beneficial for developing and maintaining strength. (A 10RM weight load is generally thought to be about 75 percent of maximum for most individuals.) The five general training principles of specificity, progressive overload, recovery time, intensity, and duration apply to strength training just as they do to aerobic and anaerobic training. As the person gets stronger, the weight load gradually is increased even though the basic workout program remains the same.

The rest interval in resistance training is a function of the amount of resistance used. With less resistance—in a program to develop endurance and strength for purposes of wellness—a rest period of

1–3 minutes between sets is appropriate. For higher levels of resistance—to build maximum strength for some specific activity or for cosmetic purposes—a rest period of 3–5 minutes between sets is appropriate.

Strength training is done most often using either free weights or highly specific exercise machines that target specific muscle groups. Any of these approaches offers sufficient variety to exercise what most people consider to be the 10 major targets for a complete program (chest, back, shoulders, triceps, biceps, quadriceps, hamstrings, lower legs, forearms, and neck). The degree to which each of those areas is included in a strength program, however, is highly specific to the desired outcomes of the program. Sprinters will have a strength program very different from that of discus throwers, and each of those will be substantially different from a program for basketball or volleyball players. You can be sure, however, that any athlete who is trying to get better at his or her sport will be involved in a strength-training program of some kind.

## Flexibility

Physical activity is crucially important to maintaining good health. Activity requires movement. Movement is not possible without an adequate level of the fitness component commonly called *flexibility. Static flexibility* refers to the linear or angular measurement of the limits of the range of motion at a joint. *Dynamic flexibility* refers to the rate of increase in tension in a relaxed muscle as it is stretched.

Increased flexibility allows for easier and more efficient performance of exercise activities. As we grow older, our flexibility decreases, and that inhibits our capacity to move efficiently. Regular flexibility work is now a key component of most exercise programs. Like other training modalities, flexibility work is defined by frequency, intensity, and duration.

Flexibility work should be done at least three times per week after moderate or vigorous activity. Four to five stretches for each major muscle group are recommended, typically during the cooling-down period after exercise. Muscles should be slowly elongated and held for 30 seconds with low levels of force. Flexibility work before exercise, when muscles are not yet warmed up, is not recommended.

## THE MEASUREMENT OF FITNESS AND PHYSICAL ACTIVITY

The measurement of fitness and physical activity continues to be a source of considerable debate in the physical education, fitness, and health professions. The debate focuses on the measurement of health fitness and physical activity behavior. Motor-performance fitness has one primary assessment, which is the outcome of the performance itself; that is, fitness to jump higher in track and field is best assessed by the height achieved in competition. Fitness training for basketball involves training to jump higher, to run up and down the floor more quickly without tiring, and to be more agile to defend opponents better. The fact that a basketball player can bench press 200 pounds will not mean much unless it translates directly into better performance in the game.

Likewise, there is no useful way to measure the effects of a strength program that is undertaken for cosmetic purposes. Do you think you look better? Do you feel better about yourself? Do other people think you look better? If so, then the program is a success.

The most complete program for measuring physical fitness and physical activity is the combination of the FITNESSGRAM and ACTIVITYGRAM created by the Cooper Institute. The FITNESSGRAM test measures aerobic capacity using one of three tests: the Progressive Aerobic Cardiovascular Endurance Run (PACER), a 1-mile run, or a walk test (for ages 13 or older). Body composition is measured by skinfold measurements, body mass index, or bioelectric impedance analysis. Abdominal strength and endurance are measured by curl-ups. Upper-body strength and endurance are measured by push-ups, modified pull-ups, or the flexed-arm hang. Trunk extensor strength and flexibility are measured by trunk lifts, back-saver sit and reach, and shoulder stretch. The FITNESSGRAM technology allows users to reliably assess performance and record the results. Detailed reports can be made available to students, parents, and school administrators.

Fitness testing always involves the reporting of results. A measure is obtained from a test, and that measure must be interpreted and reported. The traditional method is to test a large number of subjects and then report *norm-referenced scores*— that is, a score that tells you where you stand relative to the performance of the larger group. If you are in the fiftieth percentile, then you are average for that group. A more recent approach has been to interpret and report scores on the basis of criteria that are thought to produce a health benefit or indicate a reduced risk for a specific health problem, a method of scoring and reporting known as **criterion-referenced health (CRH) standards** (Corbin & Pangrazi, 1992).

CRH standards have two distinct advantages. First, they assess fitness or physical activity against absolute standards that indicate minimum levels necessary to achieve health outcomes (Cureton,

1994). Second, they provide immediate diagnostic feedback about whether performance is adequate to promote health. Cureton (1994) argued that separate CRH standards should be used for physical fitness and physical activity and that children and youths should be encouraged to meet both sets of standards. There is also a strong consensus now that any award system associated with fitness or physical activity programs should be related to CRH standards rather than norm-based performances.

Another possibility is to reduce standards to "zones of interpretation" (Whitehead, 1994). An *interpretation zone* allows people to use fitness-performance or physical activity data to understand whether they are (1) at risk for hypokinetic disease, (2) at a level that will contribute to health, or (3) at a level necessary for some athletic performance. Figure 7.3 shows the differences among norm-referenced standards, CRH standards, and interpretation zones.

Body composition is considered to be one of the most important measures of health fitness. A high percentage of body fat relative to bone and muscle has been shown repeatedly to be a predictor of risk for a wide range of degenerative diseases (Ross &

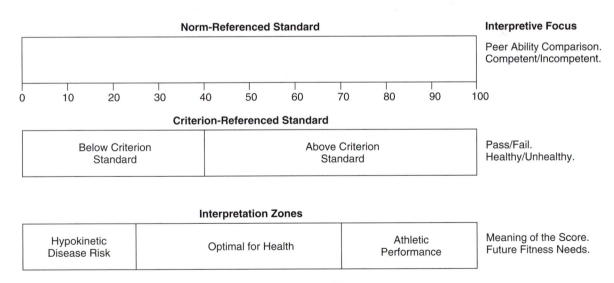

**FIGURE 7.3** Three methods for interpreting the results of fitness assessments.

SOURCE: *Adapted from Whitehead, 1994.*

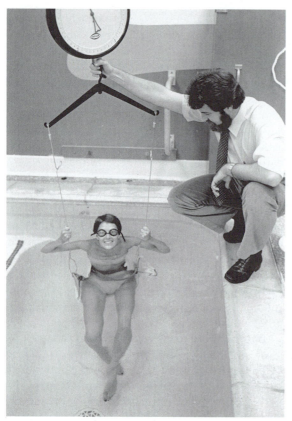

Hydrostatic weighing provides the most accurate estimate of body composition.

Pate, 1987). Body composition is a much better measure of health fitness than is body weight. Many people who begin to take part in health-fitness programs do not lose weight quickly. What happens is that the composition of their body changes as the percentage of fat decreases and the percentage of muscle increases—with weight staying level or declining only slightly.

In fitness tests, technicians estimate body composition by taking skinfold measurements at two or three places (triceps, subscapular, and medial calf, in the National Children and Youth Fitness Study [NCYFS] II), and using the sum of these to estimate body fat. This method is relatively inexpensive and, if done carefully, can provide a sufficiently accurate gross measure of body composition to note changes

that occur with training. Exercise-science laboratories, however, use a more accurate method of estimating body composition: hydrostatic or underwater weighing. Briefly, this method involves weighing the body on land and under water to estimate body density. Fat is lighter per unit volume than water (Costill, 1986) and therefore floats—people with a higher percentage of body fat have a lower density and therefore are good floaters.

## Measuring Moderate-to-Vigorous Physical Activity

There are many problems associated with the measurement of physical activity, particularly moderate-to-vigorous physical activity (MVPA). For example, what activities count as "moderate" or as "vigorous"? One study might consider sustained walking moderate, and another study might label it vigorous. Walking, of course, can range from quite leisurely to intensely active (as in power or race walking). Researchers have had difficulty getting reliable data on the amount of time a person spends in MVPA (Lea & Paffenbarger, 1996).

Heart rate monitors and accelerometers are two kinds of devices that have been used to provide more reliable information on MVPA (Beighle, Pangrazi, & Vincent, 2001). Heart-rate monitors can be calibrated to estimate energy expenditure but tend to be influenced by factors such as age, mode of exercise, and body size. Accelerometers store data that allow for assessment of the frequency, intensity, and duration of physical activity, and they can detect the intermittent activity of young children, which is an important variable in estimating MVPA. A major problem with accelerometers is that they are expensive. It appears now that the most cost-effective and widely accessible devices for measuring MVPA are pedometers, that measure the number of steps taken during activity. Although they are not sensitive to some forms of activity, such as cycling, they do allow for a valid assessment of the amount of daily activity. They are also very useful for teachers and parents who want to help children and youths develop active lifestyles. The goal for adults

A bicycle ergometer test is one good way to measure cardiovascular function.

| FOCUS ON | Pedometer Target Zones | 7.6 |
| --- | --- | --- |

| Category | Steps/Day |
| --- | --- |
| Sedentary | < 5000 |
| Low active | 5,000–7,500 |
| Somewhat active | 7,500–9,999 |
| Active | 10,000–12,500 |
| Very active | > 12,500 |

Source: Based on values from Corbin, Welk, Corbin, & Welk, 2008.

is typically set at 10,000 steps per day (see Focus On Box 7.6). It is also possible to calculate the number of calories expended each day from the step count. Pedometers are not overly expensive and can be used in a number of ways to help people learn more about the amount of activity they need and how they can get it through modest changes in their lifestyles.

The Cooper Institute has also developed an AC-TIVITYGRAM, an assessment tool for recording physical activity data and interpreting those data relative to standards related to healthy lifestyles. In schools, ACTIVITYGRAM assessment is conducted over 2 school days and 1 nonschool day (weekend or holiday). Students record their physical activity for each 30-minute period between the hours of 7:00 a.m. and 10:30 p.m. Entries include the time of day, the number of minutes in activity, the intensity level of the activity, and the type of activity (chosen from an Activity Pyramid). Information for each student is entered into a computer so that a summary analysis can be provided to students and parents. The report summarizes the 3-day activity and provides recommendations on how to increase or maintain physical activity based on guidelines developed by the Council for Physical Education for Children (COPEC), a division of NASPE.

Another promising method of informally measuring fitness is to estimate caloric expenditure of various activities. The unit of measurement used for this purpose is called a metabolic equivalent (MET) (Corbin & Pangrazi, 1996). METs are designed to estimate the metabolic cost of activity. One MET equals the number of calories expended at rest (resting metabolism). Activity that is twice that intensity measures 2 METs. Activities such as slow walking, slow stationary cycling, and bowling are typically 3 METs or less and are considered to be light activities. Activities that reach a level of 6 METs are labeled moderate, such as brisk walking, tennis, or mowing the lawn with a power mower. Activities that are 7 METs or higher are considered to be vigorous, such as jogging, fast cycling, mowing the lawn with a hand mower, and many sports.

Recently, there has been considerable debate about fitness testing in schools. The most compelling argument has been to focus on the pedagogical perspective on youth fitness testing in schools (Silverman, Keating, and Phillips, 2008). This perspective suggests that (1) fitness testing should be implemented as a fundamental part of fitness instruction; (2) fitness testing should be used to assess the quality of fitness instruction and student learning; and (3) all students should be able to meet health-related fitness standards. Far too often fitness testing has been done at the start of a school year and then not related to the physical education curriculum or used as a measurement device to assess the quality of the program in enhancing student fitness.

## Informal Measurement of Fitness

Most adults are not interested in formal tests of fitness although they do often want to monitor their fitness levels informally. This is particularly true for cardiovascular fitness. A simple way to do this is to regularly take your own heart rate during exercise and as you recover from exercise: Check your pulse rate, either at the carotid artery in the neck or at the radial artery in the wrist; count beats for 10, 20, or 30 seconds; multiply that total by 6, 3, or 2 to calculate the rate per minute that your heart is beating.

As we saw earlier in this chapter, the method of calculating your target heart rate for maximum benefit in aerobic activity is to take a maximum heart rate of 220, subtract your age, and multiply by 0.65 and 0.90. Thus, if you are 35 years old, the lower range of your target heart-rate zone would be $220 - 35 = 185 \times 0.65 = 120$. The upper range of your target heart-rate zone would be $185 \times 0.90 = 167$. This is the threshold heart rate you would need to reach during exercise to gain maximum aerobic benefit. It should be noted, however, that you can do aerobic exercise at a heart rate below the target rate and still gain substantial benefit.

Another use of pulse rate as an informal measure is to assess your capacity to recover from exercise in which the pulse rate is elevated. The more-fit person will recover the resting pulse rate more quickly. People have different resting pulse rates. One way to calculate the resting pulse rate is to take it immediately upon awaking in the morning. If you keep a record of your morning resting pulse rate, you will be able to see clear signs of improvement in fitness as that pulse rate lowers. A second way is to take your normal resting pulse rate while standing before you begin to exercise. The time it takes to return to that rate after exercise is a good measure of fitness; that is, the more quickly you recover the preexercise heart rate, the better your fitness level.

Yet another way to monitor aerobic conditioning is to keep track of distance and time for the same kind of exercise. Thus, if you do brisk walking as a main aerobic exercise, you can walk measured distances and simply know the total time it took to complete the distance. Walking further in the same amount of time is a good measure of improved cardiovascular fitness.

If we want children and adolescents to develop physical activity habits that lead to healthy lifestyles we must plan and deliver programs that help them to develop self-efficacy for whatever activities they engage in to achieve and sustain fitness levels.

Self-efficacy is developed when persons develop a strong belief in their capabilities to produce designated levels of performance (Bandura, 1994). The development of self-efficacy is best achieved by several primary sources of influence. Learning to be good at a particular activity builds a strong belief in one's personal efficacy, while failures tend to undermine that development. Thus, building gradual success in any physical activity is fundamentally important to developing self-efficacy. A second approach to creating and strengthening self-efficacy is through observing others who are similar to oneself succeed by sustaining effort, leading to a belief that they too can be successful if they continue to try. A third factor is to strengthen the belief of students that they can succeed at any activity in which they engage. When students begin to believe they can be successful in an activity they try harder and are much more likely to be successful. The importance of self-efficacy will be more fully explained in Chapter 9.

## SUMMARY

1. The health benefits of fitness and physical activity are better known now than ever before.

2. Early definitions of fitness were too broad and failed to distinguish between fitness characteristics related to health and those related to motor performance.

3. Current definitions of fitness distinguish between *health fitness*, with cardiovascular efficiency as the main component, and *motor-performance fitness*, with strength as the main component.

4. The major benefits of health fitness include a stronger heart, better circulatory function, increased oxygen-carrying capacity of the blood, more favorable body composition, and reduced levels of fat in the blood.

5. Motor-performance fitness is directly related to improved performance in physical skills.

6. Moderate and high levels of regular physical activity are associated with decreases in all causes of mortality and morbidity as well as with other health benefits.

7. The dose–response debate contrasts a view that is anchored in health-related fitness and cardiovascular functioning and a view that is anchored in health alone, particularly with regard to reductions in all causes of mortality.

8. Cosmetic fitness can be important to psychological well-being and is part of today's focus on an active, healthy lifestyle.

9. The social gradient in health and fitness reveals that socioeconomic status is strongly related to better or poorer health and fitness.

10. Muscles adapt to training by becoming more efficient and stronger, enabling people to do more intense or longer-duration work or to do the same work with less effort.

11. Five general training principles for fitness are exercise specific to the fitness component where improvement is desired, progressive overload of the exercise stress, adequate recovery time between bouts, appropriate intensity within bouts, and appropriate length of the bout.

12. Health fitness is achieved through aerobic training with exercise bouts of sufficient intensity, duration, and frequency.

13. To improve and maintain aerobic fitness, a person must reach a threshold of training, sustain it for 15 to 20 minutes, and repeat this exercise three to five times per week.

14. Aerobic fitness can be achieved through continuous exercise at or just above the aerobic threshold or through interval training, in which shorter, more intense exercise bouts are interspersed with rest periods.

15. Anaerobic training requires nearly maximum effort for short periods, followed by long recovery periods.

16. Strength-training factors include the amount of resistance per lift, the number of repetitions per set, the number of sets per workout, and the number of workouts per week.

17. *Endurance* strength training uses lower resistances with more repetitions; *power* strength training uses higher resistances with fewer repetitions.

18. A typical power-strength training program involves five or six repetitions with a 5RM or 6RM workload, two to four sets per workout, and three workouts per week.

19. Motor-performance fitness is best measured through improved performance in the activity for which the fitness training is used.

20. Health fitness is typically measured through physical-fitness tests or through direct measures of cardiovascular functioning and body composition.

21. Criterion-referenced fitness standards have distinct advantages over norm-referenced standards, and zones of interpretation allow for people to understand their level of risk for hypokinetic disease.

22. The measurement of physical activity, especially MVPA, can be done informally through a variety of approaches that typically include self-monitoring of frequency, duration, and intensity of activity and attention to heart-rate measures and more formally with programs such as the ACTIVITYGRAM.

23. The development of self-efficacy for physical activity is fundamentally important to achieving success in physical education or fitness classes.

## DISCUSSION QUESTIONS

1. Should health fitness become a major, independent goal of school physical education? Why or why not?

2. To what extent are the differences in kinds of fitness misunderstood by the public? How can the public become better educated?

3. For which population groups might cosmetic fitness be more important than health fitness? How can that emphasis be changed? Should it be changed?

4. Give one example of how each of the training principles is violated. Which principle is violated most often?

5. How can aerobic fitness be developed and maintained in everyday life? How can strength fitness be developed and maintained?

6. How fit are you? Answer in terms of your health and motor performance. What factors in your life have contributed to your fitness or to your lack of fitness?

7. What fitness programs have you enrolled in? Which appealed to you? For what reasons? Which did not appeal to you? For what reasons?

8. To what extent do youths and adults suffer from the societal pressures to look fit?

9. How will the focus on moderate levels of physical activity affect fitness programs?

10. What do physical education teachers or fitness trainers have to do to help the people they serve to develop self-efficacy for fitness to such an extent that they will value it enough to continue to be fit throughout their lifespan?

## CHAPTER 8

# Fitness Programs and Professions

*Promotion of physical activity for children, adolescents, young adults, the middle-aged, and older adults is one of the most effective means of improving health and enhancing function and quality of life. All governments of the world should initiate policies to increase individual participation in physical activity by creating an environment that will encourage an acceptable level of physical activity in the whole population. This will require cooperation of governmental agencies, scientific and professional bodies, the private sector, and other community groups.*

From Consensus Statement of the International Scientific Consensus Conference on Physical Activity, Health, and Well-Being, Québec City, 1995

In Chapter 7, we established the increasingly strong scientific evidence relating physical activity and fitness to positive health, mortality, and quality-of-life outcomes. We also indicated that motor-performance fitness has become increasingly important to success in sports and is important for quality-of-life outcomes among elderly people. It is also clear that many people engage in fitness activities to develop and maintain the kind of appearance that helps them feel good about themselves. In this chapter, we review information about fitness levels in the population, fitness programs, and career opportunities in the various professional fields that support the fitness movement.

From a national policy perspective, it is clear that health fitness is the most important aspect of the entire fitness movement. The U.S. government has brought the issue to the nation's attention through a series of goals and reports that began in 1979 with the publication of *Healthy People: The Surgeon General's Report on Health Promotion and Disease Prevention.* That was followed in 1990 by *Healthy People 2000* (U.S. Public Health Service, 1991), which established more than 300 health objectives in 22 priority areas, the first of which was "physical activity and fitness." Data related to achievement of the objectives are tracked and reported (Spain & Franks, 2001). No one thought that all the target goals could be reached in a single decade. One of the goals—increasing the number of worksite fitness programs—has been met, and we got close to meeting a few of the other goals. For example, the death rate from coronary heart disease declined, nearly achieving the target goal; and 16 percent of people 18 years and older engaged in vigorous physical activity 3 or more days per week for at least 20 minutes per session (the target was 20 percent). For other goals, however, the picture was bleak. Overweight and obesity indicators rose rather than fell. The CDC reported that almost half of all American youths were not engaged in regular physical activity and 14 percent of high-school students reported having no recent physical activity. Enrollment in physical-education classes fell to 25 percent. The proportion of adolescents in grades 9–12 who participate in daily physical education fell precipitously (from 42 percent in 1991 to 27 percent in 1997 (the target was 50 percent).

Early in 2000, *Healthy People 2010* (U.S. Department of Health and Human Services, 2000) was published, starting the second chapter in the nation's effort to become healthier. *Healthy People 2010* had two overarching goals: to increase the years of healthy life for all people and to eliminate health disparities based on race, gender, and income. *Healthy People 2020* has four primary enabling goals: to promote healthy behavior, to protect health, to achieve success in quality health care, and to strengthen community prevention. For our purposes, our main interest is goal 22: Improve health fitness and quality of life through daily physical activity. Table 8.1 describes that goal.

Many states have now developed state-level healthy people plans and programs. The only way to progress toward achievement of those goals is through widely accessible and inclusive programs with competent leadership. While state programs have been created, and in some states, passed as legislation in the state congress, the funding to support the programs has been either inadequate or missing entirely. In the following chapter, we will review problems and issues related to fitness and physical activity.

## FITNESS LEVELS AMONG CHILDREN AND YOUTHS

In the mid-1950s, data from comparative fitness tests (Kraus & Hirschland, 1954) of European and American children showed that American children were far behind European children, setting off the first large-scale, national children's fitness movement. Most tests and surveys of child and youth fitness since then have produced information that is discouraging, to say the least. The popular media have again focused attention on the low levels of fitness among children and youths. *U.S. News and World Report* (Levine, Wells, & Knopf, 1986) and *Time* magazine (Toufexis, 1986) featured stories on child and youth fitness, and the conclusions were gloomy indeed. The *Time* feature suggested that children were "getting an F for flabby."

It is difficult to make historical comparisons of child and youth fitness because fitness tests have historically emphasized motor-performance items rather than health-fitness items. Another complicating factor is the recent emphasis on the accumulation of moderate-to-vigorous physical activity (MVPA), which is even more difficult to monitor and quantify, and still more difficult to compare with more traditional fitness measures such as the 1-mile run. In 1985 the results from the National Children and Youth Fitness Study (NCYFS I) were released. This nationwide study assessed the degree to which fifth- through twelfth-graders were fit and active. Because our understanding of what fitness is and of how it should be measured had improved greatly by the early 1980s, the NCYFS was then the most rigorous study of youth fitness ever conducted in the United States. The investigators tested 8,800 boys and girls and completed surveys regarding the youths' activity habits.

The two results that are most alarming are the measure of **body composition** (skinfold test) and the cardiopulmonary measure (1-mile run–walk). The skinfold test data indicated that the average score for both boys and girls was in the moderately high range, indicating some risk for problems associated with too much body fat. The average scores for the 1-mile run–walk showed that many girls did more walking than running and that many boys and girls could do no better than slowly jogging for that distance.

A similar fitness study (Milverstedt, 1988) in 1985, the National School Population Fitness Survey, examined a large number of elementary and secondary students on six fitness items and

| TABLE 8.1 Healthy People 2020 Goal 22 for Physical Activity |
| --- |

PA-1: Reduce the proportion of adults who engage in no leisure-time activity. Target: 32.6% Baseline: 36.2%

PA-2: Increase the proportion of adults who meet current federal physical activity guidelines for Aerobic PA and for muscle-strengthening activity. Aerobic PA Target: 47.9% Baseline: 43.5% (Moderate Intensity 150 minutes per week or Muscle-strengthening) Target: 24.1%, Baseline 21.9% (muscle-strengthening activities on 2 or more days per week).

PA-3: Increase the proportion of adolescents who meet current Federal PA guidelines for aerobic PA and muscle-strengthening activity. Target: 202%, Baseline 18.4%

PA 4: Increase the proportion of the nation's public and private schools that require daily PE for all students. Elementary-School Target: 4.2% Baseline: 3.8% Middle and Junior High Schools: Target: 8.6%, Baseline 7.9% Senior High Schools: Target: 2.3%, Baseline 2.1%

PA 5: Increase the proportion of adolescents who participate in daily physical education. Target: 36.6%, Baseline: 33.3%

PA 6: Increase the number of states that hold regularly scheduled elementary-school recess. Target: 17 states, Baseline: 7 states

Increase the proportion of school districts that require regularly scheduled elementary-school recess. Target: 62.8%, Baseline 57.1%

PA 7: Increase the proportion of school districts that require or recommend elementary-school recess for an appropriate period of time. Target: 67.7%, Baseline 61.5%

PA 8: Increase the proportion of children and adolescents who do not exceed recommended limits for screen time or recommended limits for use of a computer or computer games outside of school and for non-school work. No television or screen time on an average weekday (children aged 0–2) Target: 44.7%, Baseline: 40.6%

No more than 2 hours per day (TV, videos, video games) (children aged 2–5) Target: 83.2%, Baseline 75.6%

No more than 2 hours per day (TV, videos, video games) (children/adolescents 6–14) Target 86.8%, Baseline 78.9%

Children aged 2–5 Target: to be set in the next decade. Baseline 97.4% no more than 2 hours per day.

Children aged 6–14 years. Target 100%, Baseline 93.3%

Adolescents in grades 9–12 Target 82.6%, Baseline 75.1%

PA 9: Increase the number of states with licensing regulations for physical activity provided in child care. Require activity programs providing large muscle or gross motor activity development. Target 35 states, Baseline 25 states Require children to engage in vigorous or moderate PA Target: 13 states, Baseline 3 states

Require number of minutes of PA per day or by length of time in care Target 11 states, Baseline 1 state

PA 10: Increase the proportion of the nation's public/private schools that provide access to their physical activity spaces/facilities outside of normal school hours. Target: 31.7%, Baseline: 28.8%

PA 11: Increase the proportion of physician office visits that include counseling or education related to physical activity. Target 14.3%, Baseline 13.0

Increase the proportion of physician visits that include counseling about exercise Target 8.7%, Baseline 7.9%

Fun and challenging physical activities are important for children.

compared the results with national norms. Of the 9,678 boys tested, only 11 reached the 85th percentile on all six items! Thus, we should be concerned not only about the *average* scores on fitness tests but also about the low number of high scores.

In 1987 the results of NCYFS II were released. This study examined the fitness levels and activity patterns of 6- to 9-year-old children (4,853 in the sample). The tests were similar to those in NCYFS I.

The low fitness scores were alarming, leading to the concerns voiced in the national media. The body-composition data indicated that the 6- to 9-year-olds in the study carried more body fat than the children tested 20 years earlier (Ross & Pate, 1987). The general picture of these major national tests seems clear. Children carry more body fat than is healthy. Between 1980 and 1994, the percentage of overweight children doubled, and data indicated that this trend was continuing (Koplan, Liverman, Kraak, & Wisham, 2006). The percentage of youths who are overweight has more than tripled since the mid-1970s (Pangrazi, 2003). Children typically do not have well-developed cardiopulmonary capacity.

Children, especially girls, perform poorly in tests of upper-body strength.

The general notion that children are not fit has been argued in both the professional and the popular literature since the 1970s. In the 1990s, the accuracy and fairness of that perception began to be questioned (Corbin & Pangrazi, 1992). Blair (1992) argued that we have been looking at the fitness data through the wrong set of lenses. He argued that physical activity that results in a particular level of energy expenditure per day is associated with important health benefits. (The figure is calculated to an energy expenditure of 3,000 calories per 1,000 grams of body weight per day, or 3 Kcal/kg of body weight.) Blair recalculated the NCYFS II data and concluded that 77 percent of the boys and girls tested had met that standard, a finding that did not support the common perception of a nation of unfit children.

The effort to produce an accurate, reliable picture of the fitness levels of children and youths has also been hindered by the widespread use of norm-referenced scores to gauge fitness levels. A norm-referenced score places any single child or youth in relation to all the other children or youths who took the tests when the norms were established. What do you know if you are a 12-year-old girl and you rank in the 70th percentile on the 1-mile run? You know only that you ran a time that was faster than about 69 percent of those tested and slower than about 30 percent of those tested. This outcome tells you nothing about whether the time that you ran is a good indicator of your fitness level.

In most important tests, norm-referenced reporting has been replaced by criterion-referenced health (CRH) standards. CRH standards compare performances to criteria that indicate *potential risk* where amounts of activity may be inadequate to contribute to health benefits. Thus, a performance score is immediately comparable to a standard related to health risks rather than to the performance of other children or youths.

Scientific evidence supporting the link between health-fitness indicators and adult hypokinetic disease and mortality grows stronger with each passing year. Children who are low on fitness measures in elementary school tend to remain at risk during

The World Health Organization estimates that 30–45 million children worldwide are obese and 155 million are overweight. Although the two key elements in any plan to reduce obesity and overweight involve caloric intake and energy expenditure (physical activity), restricting food intake in young children is generally discouraged because children need nutrients to grow and develop. For the first time in history, a generation of children has the misfortune to live a completely sedentary lifestyle. Many children get transported rather than transporting themselves. Television, video games, and the computer occupy far too much of their discretionary time; their recreation is attending to multimedia rather than being active. Research in Canada has shown that children who live a lifestyle more representative of previous generations are leaner, stronger, and more aerobically fit than children who live a "modern" lifestyle. The differences are mostly attributable to the presence of regular physical activity among children whose lifestyle is more representative of a previous generation.

SOURCE: Trembal, Barnes, Copeland, & Esliger, 2005

adolescence. Young children who are obese tend to become obese adolescents and then obese adults. On the other hand, children who are active and healthy tend to remain so as adolescents and into adulthood. Thus, measures of childhood physical activity and health are predictive of adolescent and adult patterns. This underscores the importance of strong programs of physical education and physical activity for young children. The children who need help can be identified, and there are intervention programs to help them (Bouchard, Shephard, & Stephens, 1993; Corbin, 2002; Sallis & McKenzie, 1993).

Traditionally, concerns about improving physical fitness or achieving healthier lifestyles have been considered to be matters of personal responsibility. Recently, however, it has become clear that child/youth obesity has become a public health epidemic and many have argued that to address the causes of the epidemic and improve the situation we must shift our view of obesity away from the medical model, focusing on individuals, to a public health model, focusing on the population (Schwartz & Brownell, 2007) (see Focus On Box 8.1). While personal responsibility will no doubt remain a significant issue in programs to prevent obesity, an equal effort must be focused on the environmental issues that are considered to be precipitating factors of the epidemic. These would include foods that have a higher caloric value, more dietary fat, and higher caloric density. Consumption of such foods is related to less in-home cooking, greater reliance on take-out food, more fast-food meals, and eating in restaurants. Foods served at school breakfasts and lunches and in-school vending machines have tended to include nonnutritious ingredients (Levi, Segal, & Juliano, 2006).

Reduction in physical activity is caused by a number of factors primarily related to what is now commonly referred to as the "built environment." Factors such as communities designed to foster driving rather than walking/biking, lack of public transit, and an increase in commuting reduce opportunities for physical activity. Children and youths tend to spend more time watching TV, using the computer for games, or connecting with the Internet than they did a generation ago, thus reducing physical activity (Siedentop, 2007). The federal legislation, No Child Left Behind, has caused a 14 percent reduction in time for physical education in schools (Jennings, 2006). The fact that most students are bused to and from school reduces participation in after-school programs that include physical activity opportunities. Parents report five primary barriers to their children's participation in physical activity: transportation problems, lack of opportunities for physical activity in the immediate area, expense, parents' lack of time, and concerns about neighborhood safety (Centers for Disease Control and Prevention, 2003).

These are issues that must be confronted with social policy, legislation, and community efforts as well as with greater personal responsibility. For example, the 2004 federal legislation renewing the National School Lunch Act required all schools that receive federal support for school lunches to establish nutrition guidelines ensuring that only healthy foods will be available in school during the school day (Senate Report 108–345, 2006). The same legislation required schools to develop "wellness councils" to improve nutrition and physical activity within the school day. In 2005 the federal Department of Transportation created the national Safe Routes to School Program with an initial appropriation of $54 million, primarily to improve the infrastructure so that more students could walk or bike to school. Many states have since developed "walk to school programs." In Chapter 7, we addressed this issue with legislative and policy actions to increase physical education and physical activity for children and youths.

In 2005 the U.S. Department of Health and Human Services redefined the recommended levels of physical activity from 20 minutes of vigorous activity at least three days per week to 60 minutes of activity, that includes vigorous exercise some of the time, at least five days a week. Between 1993 and 2003, the percentage of high-school students meeting the former level of recommended PA remained fairly steady, ranging between 63 and 66 percent. In 2005, 2007, and 2009, only about one-third of high-school students met the revised recommended levels of physical activity (36 percent, 35 percent, and 37 percent for those three years), thus increasing concern about developing better activity programs for that age group.

Many states have adopted the Centers for Disease Control's Coordinated School Health Program, a model that consists of eight interactive components including health education; physical education; health services; nutrition services; counseling, psychological, and social services; a healthy school environment; health promotion for staff; and family/community involvement. The model allows for issues such as physical activity promotion to be considered and dealt with throughout the school program and by developing relationships with community agencies.

## ACTIVITY PATTERNS AMONG CHILDREN AND YOUTHS

Participation in physical activity among children and youths is difficult to assess because information is typically obtained from self-reports, diaries, questionnaires, and reports from parents. These reporting mechanisms often are not reliable. The NCYFS II survey found that nearly 85 percent of 6- to 9-year-old children participate in some activity through a community organization, typically public park and recreation programs, community-based sport programs, church programs, YMCA/YWCA programs, scouting groups, and private health clubs (Ross & Pate, 1987). The same survey found that children watch just over 2 hours per day of television during the week and 3.5 hours per day on weekends; these figures are substantially lower than those from many other national surveys.

The following conclusions can be reached regarding evidence of activity patterns among children and youths (American Sports Data, 1999; Rosenbaum & Leibel, 1989; Sallis, 1994; Sallis & McKenzie, 1993; U.S. Department of Health and Human Services, 1996):

1. The self-reports of children indicate that 90 percent or more are active at a level required for health benefits, an outcome that differs markedly from observational studies.

2. Studies monitoring the heart rates of children throughout the day show that most children are sufficiently active to meet the American College of Sports Medicine's (ACSM, 1990) recommendations for adult activity levels.

3. A large proportion of children do not get regular physical education from a specialist teacher.

4. When activity in physical-education classes is monitored, it is not uncommon for children to have as little as 2 minutes of vigorous activity in a 30-minute lesson.

5. More than 34 percent of American children and youths can be classified as overweight or obese. Girls are more likely to be obese than

Children are more likely to be active if activity is supported by their parents.

boys. African American and Hispanic children and youths are obese at nearly twice the rate of non-Hispanic whites.

6. Only about one-half of American young people (ages 12–21) regularly participate in vigorous physical activity. One-fourth report no vigorous physical activity.

7. Only 21.3 percent of all adolescents participate in school physical-education programs 1 or more days per week in their schools.

8. Data assessing *Healthy People 2000* goals show that 41 percent of ninth-graders participate in physical activity on a daily basis, but the figure declines to 13 percent by the twelfth grade.

9. The participation data are all higher for males than for females. Because girls appear to be less active than boys, special programs may be needed to motivate and sustain their participation.

10. In the 1990s, the fastest-growing age group in frequent activity participation were children 6–11 years of age, and the steepest decline of all age groups was found in the 12–17 age bracket, a factor that continued in the 2000s.

As children develop into their adolescent years, two things seem clear. First, too many children reduce their physical activity substantially. Secondly, it appears that highly active children tend to develop habits that persist into adolescence, while those who are less active and less successful in activity tend to do less and less. Lack of regular participation in physical activity among youth is a serious problem simply because the teen years are when adult habits begin to emerge.

Substantial evidence indicates that participation in sport and physical activity among youths reaches a peak at or about age 11 and declines through the teen years (Coakley, 2007, Sallis 1994). In some cases, this decline occurs as a result of reduced opportunities to participate (for example, the relatively low number of students who participate on school teams). In other cases, the decline is a reaction to how the sport is organized and conducted (many youths say it is no longer "fun."). Adolescence is also the stage of life where girls and boys become interested in other pursuits such as work, dating, more serious academic interests, and so on. Some youths do become interested in physical activity more in line with an adult model such as participation in fitness centers, cycling, and informal recreational sports.

In 2005 the U.S. Department of Health redefined the recommended levels of PA from 20 minutes of vigorous activity at least three days per week to 60 minutes of PA per week that includes vigorous activity, some of that time at least five days per week. Between 1993 and 2003, the percentage of high-school students meeting the former level of PA ranged between 63 and 66 percent. From 2005 to 2009, however, only about one-third of high-school students met the new recommended levels.

The relationship between diminishing amounts of physical activity among teens and the prevalence of inactivity among the adult population strongly suggests that more effort needs to be made to increase physical activity among teens and to do so through programs that are widely available and are attractive to teens because of the programs' high fun quotients.

## FITNESS LEVELS AMONG ADULTS

It is difficult to obtain reliable and valid information about adult fitness levels. Whereas fitness testing of children and youths can be done in schools, no such

opportunity exists for adults. Both public- and private-sector agencies have tried to estimate levels of fitness and physical activity among adults, but these estimates come most frequently from surveys and questionnaires and are extremely variable: Some show that as much as 78 percent of the population have an active lifestyle, and others show that as little as 15 percent do (Blair, Kohl, & Powell, 1987). The best estimate we have is from the documentation for *Healthy People 2010* (see Figure 8.1), which shows estimated activity levels for women and men related to the 2010 goals. Those figures seem surprising in an era that has been described as a renaissance of fitness. There is little doubt that the fitness boom, at its outset, was primarily a "yuppie" phenomenon; that is, it was primarily confined to young, middle- and upper-class women and men, particularly those in professions. Television and magazine advertisements catered to that group because they had more disposable income. In 1990 there were 51.5 million frequent fitness participants in the United States, a significant increase since the 1950s (Lauer, 2006). The baby boomers and yuppies are now older, and much of our attention is devoted

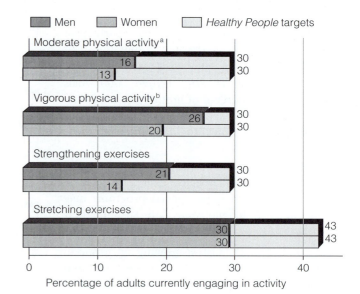

**FIGURE 8.1** Current levels of physical activity among American adults
Sources: *National Center for Health Statistics. 2004;*
DATA2010: The Healthy People 2010 Database, January 2004 Edition (http://wonder.cdc.gov/data2010).

[a]Moderate physical activity for 30 or more minutes on 5 or more days per week
[b]Vigorous physical activity for 20 or more minutes on 3 or more days per week

to the health and activity problems of our younger generation, most often referred to as the "millennial" generation (Generation Y).

Another way to estimate participation in healthy physical activity is to focus on the facilities and programs that have been developed to accommodate health-related physical activity. Health-club membership in 2005 reached 41.3 million, 138 percent higher than the 17.4 million in 1987 (Lauer, 2006). In 2005, 6.2 million Americans used the services of a personal trainer, up 55 percent since 1999. The Curves for Women franchise, initiated in 1995, uses a 30-minute exercise routine that combines strength training and sustained cardiovascular activity using hydraulic resistance. In the first 5 years, Curves had 1,000 locations and over 9,000 in 10 years. Today, Curves for Women operates over 10,000 locations worldwide serving more than 4 million women an-

nually (www.curvesforum.com). The significant growth of college and university health and fitness centers, cited in Chapter 1, shows how important regular physical activity is becoming to that generation. The senior population also has more access to facilities and programs that support physical activity. Home fitness rooms are now big business for builders and those who remodel homes. Fitness rooms typically include both cardiovascular and strength-training equipment, along with a television set. Most retirement communities and senior-citizen centers now have facilities and programs that encourage physical activity among their residents and attendees.

Another way to look at fitness levels among adults is to examine factors that indicate a high degree of risk for cardiovascular disease (CVD). The data in the Focus On Box 8.2 show that inactivity is the

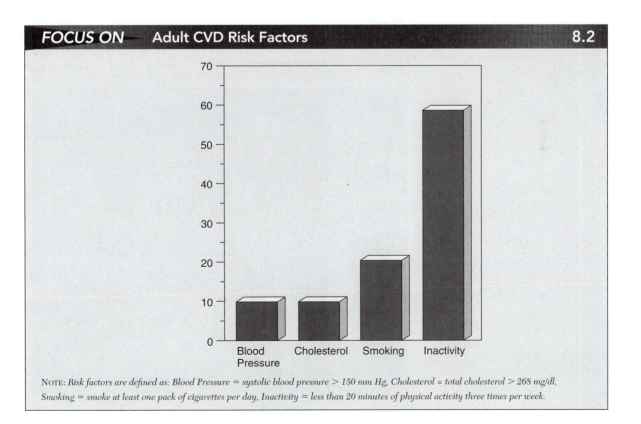

**FOCUS ON**    Adult CVD Risk Factors    **8.2**

NOTE: *Risk factors are defined as: Blood Pressure = systolic blood pressure > 150 mm Hg, Cholesterol = total cholesterol > 268 mg/dl, Smoking = smoke at least one pack of cigarettes per day, Inactivity = less than 20 minutes of physical activity three times per week.*

most prevalent CVD risk factor. Adults over the age of 60 who have higher levels of cardiorespiratory fitness live longer than those with lower levels, regardless of their levels of body fat (Sui, 2007). Previous data had shown that inactive adults are twice as likely to die of CVD as active adults (Sallis & McKenzie, 1993). These data support the notion that activity levels rather than fitness-test data are more important indicators for public health purposes.

A national movement that focuses more on regular activity and less on body composition is Health at Every Size, sponsored by the Wellness Councils of America (www.welcoa.org). The Health at Every Size program has three major components. The component of self-acceptance affirms the worth of human beings irrespective of differences in weight, physical size, and shape. The component of physical activity supports increasing social, pleasure-based movement, and the component of normalized eating disavows externally imposed rules for eating and seeks a more peaceful relationship with food by relearning to eat in response to physiological hunger and fullness cues.

The image of an active lifestyle may be quite different than the reality of an active lifestyle. Initiated in 1987, the American Sports Data in the *Super-Study of Sports Participation* (Lauer, 2006) suggests that the fitness boom reached its apex in 1990 with participation numbers decreasing substantially by 2005. Among children and youths, ages 12–17 years, the drop is 41 percent. Focus On Box 8.3 shows the 1998–2004 changes in various forms of fitness-exercise participation.

What is clear is that more people of all ages are becoming better educated about health fitness and the importance of regular physical activity. Evidence seems clear that more adults and children or youths have been made more aware about the benefits of physical activity and the health risks associated with inactivity. As Chapter 9 will show, however, the access to and the financial resources to support healthy lifestyles are not distributed evenly across our population. The broadening of the fitness movement to include older Americans is an important trend, especially when one considers that the large population segment known as the baby boomers are moving into that age group.

Mass exercise sessions take on the atmosphere of a festival.

| FOCUS ON | Changing Styles of Exercise* | | | 8.3 |
|---|---|---|---|---|
| Exercise Type | 1998 | 2000 | 2004 | Change (%) |
| Pilates | | 173,900 | 1,100,541 | +506.2 |
| Stationary cycling | 1,076,500 | 2,879,500 | 3,143,100 | +2.8 |
| Weight machines | 1,526,100 | 2,518,200 | 3,090,300 | +102.5 |
| Free weights | 2,555,300 | 4,449,400 | 5,205,600 | +130.8 |
| Treadmill exercise | 439,600 | 4,081,600 | 4,746,300 | +979.7 |
| Fitness walking | 2,716,400 | 3,798,100 | 4,029,900 | +48.4 |
| Running/jogging | 3,713,600 | 3,615,200 | 3,731,000 | +0.5 |
| Aerobics | 2,122,500 | 1,732,600 | 1,576,700 | −25.7 |
| Fitness swimming | 1,691,200 | 1,454,200 | 1,563,500 | −7.5 |
| Home gym exercise | 390,500 | 757,700 | 934,700 | −139.4 |

*U.S. population 6 years and older.
SOURCE: Lauer, 2006.

## FITNESS AND ACTIVITY PATTERNS AMONG OLDER ADULTS

No age group incurs greater public health costs than do older citizens. We live in a "graying America." Baby boomers (those born between 1946 and 1964) are entering the senior-citizen age range, and it is clear that they will live longer than previous generations (Mathieu, 1999). Not only has life expectancy increased steadily over the past 100 years, but the fastest-growing age group in America are also those 75 years old and older.

All signs indicate that older citizens are becoming more active. Perhaps this is due to the increased knowledge that the benefits of regular physical activity to health and well-being are nowhere more clear than among older citizens (Mathieu, 1999). One study classified elderly walkers into three groups. The study showed that those in the least-active walking group were more than twice as likely as those in the other groups to suffer a heart attack or some other coronary event, even when differences in risk factors (such as age, hypertension, and cholesterol levels) were taken into account (Physical Activity Today, 1999). Even for older people who have become sedentary and are seriously at risk for hypokinetic diseases of various kinds, the benefits of becoming more active are typically quick to appear and are tremendously important to improving lifestyle.

Thirty years ago, the common perception was that weight lifting was an activity only for young

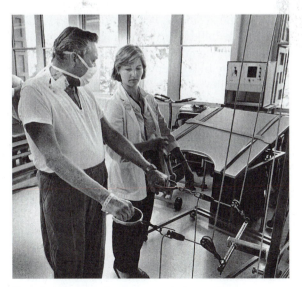

Exercise plays an important role in cardiac rehabilitation.

Adult women and men often participate together in group exercise.

professionals. In 2001 a coalition of 46 national organizations released the *National Blueprint: Increasing Physical Activity Among Adults Age 50 and Older* (www.agingblueprint.org), designed to promote physical activity among America's aging population. We must remember that most women and men who are now seniors grew up in an era when very little was known about the specific health benefits of exercise. Indeed, most norms for that era suggested that older people, especially women, should not be active. To overcome this early socialization and to establish patterns of effective participation require both education and well-planned and accessible programs. We must also recognize that physical inactivity is not distributed evenly across the senior population. Inactivity is more frequent among lower-income groups and among minority populations.

men. No more! Resistance exercise may well be to the next generation what aerobic conditioning was to the previous one. The number of older citizens who regularly use strength equipment nearly doubled in the 1990s (American Sports Data, 1999). For older citizens to maintain their mobility and avoid the risk of broken bones associated with falling and osteoporosis, they must maintain an adequate level of muscular strength. Even terribly frail older adults can quickly realize important lifestyle gains through regular resistance exercise. And the increasing evidence that exercise is a good antidote to depression is especially important for older citizens, who suffer more frequently from this mental illness. All new evidence points to the conclusion that appropriate exercise can reduce and in some cases reverse the adverse effects of biological aging and also have significant psychological benefits (Duda, 1991; U.S. Department of Health and Human Services, 1996).

Fitness and physical activity for seniors will be an important research field for the future and is already an important new direction for fitness

## FITNESS AND PHYSICAL ACTIVITY PROGRAMS FOR CHILDREN AND YOUTHS

Most parents would like their children to learn about fitness at school and develop and maintain an adequate level of fitness through school physical-education programs. The federal government agrees with that view, having two decades ago cited fitness development and maintenance as a fundamental goal for the nation's elementary and secondary schools (Bennett, 1986). The Centers for Disease Control and Prevention (1997) developed the policy guidelines through which this agenda should be pursued. These guidelines for school and community programs to promote lifelong physical activity among young people are shown in Focus On Box 8.4. What will be clear as you review the guidelines is that the concept of "program" extends beyond physical-education classes to the entire school and out to the local community.

In Chapter 7, the minimum guidelines for child and youth engagement in physical activity were

1. Establish *policies* that promote enjoyable, life long PA.
   - Require daily physical education K–12.
   - Require health education K–12.
   - Commit adequate resources for PA instruction and programs.
   - Hire professionally trained people.
   - Require that PA programs meet the needs and interests of children.

2. Provide physical and social *environments* that encourage PA.
   - Provide access to safe spaces/facilities in school and community.
   - Prevent PA-related injuries/illness.
   - Provide time in the schoolday for unstructured PA (to accumulate a significant percentage of weekly PA requirements).
   - Do not use PA as punishment.
   - Provide health promotion for school faculty.

3. Implement planned and sequential *physical education (PE)* curricula that emphasize participation in PA and that encourage students to develop the knowledge, attitudes, motor skills, and confidence needed to adopt physically active lifestyles.
   - Make PE curricula consistent with national standards.
   - Impart knowledge of PA to students.
   - Develop students' positive attitudes toward, motor skills for, and confidence in participating in PA.
   - Promote participation in enjoyable PA in school, community, and home.

4. Implement planned and sequential *health education (HE)* curricula that encourage students to develop the knowledge, attitudes, and behavioral skills needed to adopt physically active lifestyles.
   - Make HE curricula consistent with national standards.

- Promote collaboration among PE, HE, and classroom teachers for PA instruction.
- Develop students' mastery of behavioral skills needed to adopt and maintain positive lifestyle behaviors.

5. Provide *extracurricular PA programs* that meet students' needs and interests.
   - Provide a diversity of developmentally appropriate PA programs for the largest number of students.
   - Link students to community PA programs, and use community resources to support extracurricular PA programs.

6. Include *parents and guardians* in PA instruction and extracurricular PA programs, and encourage them to support their children's participation in enjoyable PA.
   - Encourage parents to advocate for high-quality PA instruction and programs for their children.
   - Encourage parents to support their children's participation in appropriate, enjoyable PA.
   - Motivate parents to be role models for PA and to plan family activities that include PA.

7. Provide PE, HE, recreation, and health-care professionals with *training* that imparts the knowledge and skills needed to effectively promote PA among youths.
   - Through higher education, provide preservice training for education, recreation, and health-care professionals.
   - Teach educators how to deliver PE that provides a significant percentage of each student's weekly PA.
   - Teach active learning strategies needed to develop knowledge about, attitudes toward, skills in, and confidence in PA.
   - Create environments that enable youths to enjoy PA instruction and programs.
   - Qualify volunteers who coach sport and recreation programs for youths.

*(continued)*

---

**FOCUS ON**    **Youth Physical-Activity (PA) Recommendations by the Centers for Disease Control** *(continued)*    **8.4**

8. Provide *health services* that assess PA among youths, reinforce PA among active youths, counsel inactive youths and refer them to PA programs, and advocate for PA instruction and programs for youths.

   - Regularly assess PA, reinforce active youths, and refer inactive youths.

   - Advocate for school and community PA instruction and programs.

9. Provide a range of developmentally appropriate, noncompetitive *community sport and recreation programs* that are attractive to youths.

10. Regularly *evaluate* school and community PA instruction, programs, and facilities.

    - Conduct process evaluations to determine how policies, programs, and training are implemented.

    - Conduct outcome evaluations to measure students' achievement of PA knowledge, behavioral skills, and motor skills.

SOURCE: Adapted from *Guidelines for School and Community Programs to Promote Lifelong Physical Activity Among Young People*, Centers for Disease Control and Prevention, Public Health Service, U.S. Department of Health and Human Services, 1997.

---

presented. The key elements of those suggestions are as follows (NASPE, 2004a: Sallis, 1994):

- Children should accumulate at least 60 minutes, and as much as several hours, in physical activity on most if not all days.

- Most of the 60 or more minutes per week should be either moderate or vigorous-intensity aerobic activity and should include vigorous-intensity aerobic activity at least 3 days per week.

- As part of their 60 minutes or more of daily PA, children and adolescents should include muscle-strengthening PA at least 3 days per week.

- As part of their 60 or more minutes of daily PA, children and adolescents should include bone-strengthening PA on at least 3 days per week.

- Activities for children should be age appropriate.

- Extended periods of inactivity for children are discouraged.

- Adolescents should be physically active daily for at least 30 minutes.

It is not possible for these guidelines to be met solely through physical-education classes. Thus, activity programs for children and youths must be available after school, on weekends, and in the community or at home. Nonetheless, the health imperative for the nation suggests strongly that school physical education should be strengthened not only by allotting more time to it but also by finding creative ways to extend the physical-education program beyond that provided in the regular school schedule.

Some research suggests that parents are not always aware that their children are overweight or obese (He & Evans, 2007). The tendency is for parents to underestimate the degree to which their children are overweight or obese. The factors accounting for these misperceptions are the children's sex and ethnicity, the mothers' weight status, and the level of family education and income. This, of course, creates problems for teachers, health workers, and physicians who attempt to deal with cases of childhood overweight and obesity.

Following are examples of creative and persevering physical educators developing and sustaining fitness and physical activity programs in their schools.

These examples should be considered together with the information on child and youth sport presented in Chapter 11 to form a comprehensive view of activity opportunities and programs.

1. *Schoolwide programs at the elementary level.* Some schools have adopted a schoolwide approach to programming for fitness. At a certain time of the day, for example, all classes might take a 15-minute jog or do various other kinds of aerobic activities.

2. *Fitness clubs.* At the elementary- and middle-school levels, many physical educators have successfully developed fitness clubs that provide incentives for students to engage regularly in fitness activities outside physical-education class time. For example, students might chart the course of a cross-country bicycle trip on a map by carefully keeping track of the miles they ride their bicycles each week.

3. *Fitness-remediation programs.* Some physical educators and health educators have developed programs for students that are particularly at risk in health fitness. After initial diagnosis with a health-fitness test, at-risk students and their families are informed of the problems, and the children are enrolled in a remedial program. A special fitness class is developed for these students, and progress is monitored until the children have improved sufficiently to move out of the at-risk category.

4. *Daily fitness programs.* Daily fitness first appeared on a national scale in Australia (Siedentop & Siedentop, 1985). Daily fitness is a program that separates fitness programming and goals from physical-education instruction. Each day, classroom teachers take 20 minutes to work with their children in aerobic activities. Fitness materials are provided, eliminating the need for extensive planning by the teacher. The children also get physical-education instruction, but the goals and activities of the two programs are kept separate.

5. *Fitness courses.* Many schools, particularly middle and high schools, have instituted a required fitness course, often at the ninth-grade level. The purpose of the course is to educate students about fitness, test them, help them to plan personal fitness programs, and teach them the kinds of activities that will help them maintain an adequate level of health fitness. The assumption is that after completing the course, students will be more able and more likely to develop and maintain a personal fitness program.

6. *Fitness elective courses.* Many high schools have started to offer a variety of fitness elective courses, ranging from aerobics to weight training to body shaping. These courses typically focus on the range of fitness outcomes—aerobic, motor performance, and cosmetic.

7. *Fitness centers.* Some middle and high schools have developed fitness centers that accommodate both classes and drop-in activities. Hoover High School in San Diego, California, operates a 2,800-square-foot fitness center (Samman, 1998) used for physical-education classes, sport teams, staff members, and the community. An after-school fitness club is open to all students.

8. *A complete high-school fitness program.* Westcott (1992) described a high school in which physical education is required all 4 years, and a fitness focus defines the program. Students take a series of wellness courses, all of which have a fitness-related focus. They also choose from a series of activity courses that emphasize different approaches to fitness, including lifetime sports, fitness walking, aerobics, weight training, and the like.

9. *A state-requirement approach.* Florida requires all ninth-grade students to complete a semester of physical-education credit in personal fitness (Johnson & Harageones, 1994). A state syllabus has been prepared and staff development programs are offered to teachers to help them prepare to teach the course, which involves both classroom and gymnasium sections. The course has three objectives: to develop a healthy level of fitness, to

understand fitness concepts, and to understand the significance of lifestyle to health and fitness.

The CDC guidelines make it clear that to fully serve the physical activity needs of children and youths, educators and community leaders must take a comprehensive approach that goes beyond regularly scheduled classes to build a *physical activity infrastructure* that links school, home, and community to help all citizens stay active. Schools and physical education alone cannot achieve the nation's goals for physical activity. These objectives can only be achieved by developing and sustaining the physical activity infrastructure. Chapter 3 described the elements of a healthy lifestyles infrastructure and provided information on how states and communities are moving to build and sustain such an effort.

## FITNESS AND PHYSICAL ACTIVITY FOR PEOPLE WITH DISABILITIES

Historically, programs for physical activity and fitness for people with disabilities have been framed in a medical rationale which strongly focused on rehabilitation. Physical activity was focused on activities of daily living such as dressing, ambulating, or lifting items (*PCPFS Research Digests,* 1999). The new paradigm for active, healthy lifestyles for people with disabilities is one of inclusion and integration. For the most part, people with disabilities gain similar benefits from physical activity as do people without disabilities.

To participate fully in physical activity, children, youths, and adults with disabilities have many barriers to overcome. People with mobility problems confront many architectural barriers that make it difficult to sustain activity. Many people with disabilities deal with health problems caused by living sedentary lifestyles. People with learning disabilities and mental retardation are less likely to have access to recreational and fitness activities. People that have inefficient movement patterns and poor body alignment due to a disability expend more energy doing simple, normal tasks, leaving them too fatigued for leisure-time physical activity. Regardless, people with disabilities can derive health benefits from activity in much the same way as do people without disabilities.

People with disabilities need to develop cardiovascular fitness, muscular strength, and flexibility just as do people without disabilities. With some conditions, heart-rate formulas need to be adjusted to compensate for the disability. For people with conditions that affect capacity to participate in cardiovascular exercise, a rating of perceived exertion may be a better indicator than a heart-rate formula. Most people with disabilities can gain marked benefits from participating in activities to increase muscular strength. The specific nature of some disabilities require special assistance in resistance training, such as a spotter, and the resistance training should be designed specifically for the person's disability. For example, people who use wheelchairs should develop the muscle groups that counterbalance those used for daily ambulation. Flexibility exercises, specifically designed relative to the disability, should be done at the outset of a training session and again at its conclusion. Problems of overweight and obesity are no different for people with disabilities than for those without disabilities. Here, the issue is to increase the levels and duration of activity to reduce the percentage of body fat.

As will be shown in Chapter 5, there is increasing participation in sport for people with disabilities. Public Law 94–142 ensured that children and youths with disabilities would be placed in the least restrictive environment in schools and should have access to a physical-education program that meets their needs and helps them improve their fitness levels.

## AAHPERD EFFORTS TO PROMOTE PHYSICAL ACTIVITY AND FITNESS

The American Alliance for Health, Physical Education, Recreation, and Dance (AAHPERD), the main professional organization for sport, fitness, and physical-education    professionals    (now    most

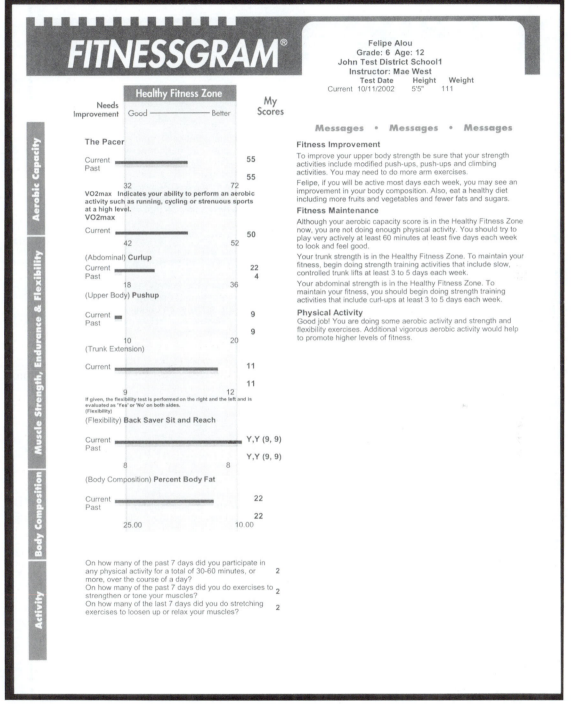

Sample report from a FITNESSGRAM.

# ACTIVITYGRAM®

**Hank Williams**
**AGRAM 123 - 08/01/2002**
**Sandra District School1**

**MINUTES OF ACTIVITY**

Goal

Minutes of Activity

Non-school Day — 280

School Day 1 — 280

School Day 2 — 330

60 MINUTES

**Messages • Messages • Messages**

The chart shows the number of minutes that you reported doing moderate (medium) or vigorous (hard) activity on each day. Congratulations, your log indicates that you are doing at least 60 minutes of activity on most every day. This will help to promote good fitness and wellness. For fun and variety, try some new activities that you have never done before.

**TIME PROFILE**

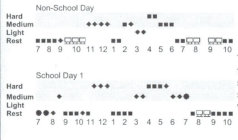

**Non-School Day**

Hard
Medium
Light
Rest

7 8 9 10 11 12 1 2 3 4 5 6 7 8 9 10

Legend ◆ Most of the time(20 minutes)   ■ All of the time (30 minutes)
● Some of the time (10 minutes)  🖵 TV/Computer Time

The time profile shows the activity level you reported for each 30 minute period of the day. Your results show that you were active both during and after school and that you were also active on the weekend. Keep up the good work.

**School Day 1**

Hard
Medium
Light
Rest

7 8 9 10 11 12 1 2 3 4 5 6 7 8 9 10

**School Day 2**

Hard
Medium
Light
Rest

7 8 9 10 11 12 1 2 3 4 5 6 7 8 9 10

**ACTIVITY PROFILE**

Rest

Muscular Activity | Flexibility Activity

Aerobic Sports | Aerobic Activity

Lifestyle Activity

▨ Participated in these types of activities

▨ Did not participate in these types of activities

The activity pyramid reveals the different types of activity that you reported doing over a few days. Your results indicate that you participated in regular lifestyle activity as well as some activity from the other levels. This is great! The variety in your program should help you stay active.

ACTIVITYGRAM provides information about your normal levels of physical activity. The report shows what types of activity you do and how often you do them. It includes information that you reported for two or three days during one week.

ACTIVITYGRAM is a module within FITNESSGRAM 7.0 software. FITNESSGRAM materials are distributed by the American Fitness Alliance, a division of Human Kinetics.
www.americanfitness.net

©The Cooper Institute for Aerobics Research

Sample report from an ACTIVITYGRAM.

commonly referred to as "the alliance"), has a long history of promoting physical fitness and continues to play a central role in national efforts to promote physical activity and fitness. AAHPERD has developed and promoted a series of fitness testing and motivational programs since the 1970s. In 1993 AAHPERD partnered with the Cooper Institute for Aerobic Research (CIAR) to develop educational materials, an assessment program, and an incentive program—which is called the "Physical Best-FITNESSGRAM" program.

In 1999 AAHPERD joined the Cooper Institute and Human Kinetics Publishers to form the American Fitness Alliance (AFA) (www.americanfitness.net). The AFA produces a number of materials that are widely used in schools and elsewhere.

- *Physical Best* provides the educational component of a comprehensive health-related fitness-education program, supplying curriculum materials, activity guides, and teacher certification.

- The FITNESSGRAM test for evaluating K–12 students' physical fitness includes a test-administration manual, software, and related tools. The software includes an ACTIVITY-GRAM option, which allows students to enter up to 3 days of physical activity data and assess their own progress toward goals.

- *The Brockport Physical Fitness Test*, a national test developed especially for youths with disabilities, has features and tools similar to FITNESSGRAM.

- The *FitSmart* test is designed to assess high-school students' knowledge of concepts and principles of fitness. It includes a test manual and software.

- The *You Stay Active* recognition system is a program for setting goals and recognizing achievement of those goals. It includes a manual and incentive awards.

In 1995 AAHPERD joined the ACSM and the American Heart Association (AHA) to form a National Coalition for Promoting Physical Activity (*Update,* 1995). The coalition focuses on communication and education about physical activity and its relation to health and acts as a physical activity advocate to federal and state governments concerning relevant policy and legislation; to corporations such as insurance companies, which might provide incentives for people to become and stay active; and to foundations that fund relevant research and development programs.

The alliance has also initiated, with the AHA, a program called Jump Rope for Heart. This program has both educational and fitness-development objectives. It also serves as a major fund-raiser for both the AHA and the AAHPERD. Children solicit pledges and then engage in continuous rope jumping to demonstrate the value of aerobic fitness activity, as well as to raise money.

*Sport for All* is a collaborative effort of The National Association for Sport and Physical Education (NASPE), Sportime, and Human Kinetics. The program's intent is to increase the quality of physical activity for children. The program includes three modules: SportFun for ages 3–5, SportPlay for ages 5–7, and SportSkill Basic for ages 8–10. Each module includes Activity Card Packets. Individuals can train as *Sport for All* program leaders through the NASPE. *Sport for All* is intended to be used in camps, recreation centers, after-school programs, and day-care centers.

Strength-training stations are increasingly common at worksites, schools, and fitness centers.

## WORKSITE FITNESS AND WELLNESS PROGRAMS

Worksite fitness and wellness programs have become increasingly common over the past 25 years. According to the Wellness Councils of America, 81 percent of businesses with 50 or more employees have some form of health-and-fitness promotion program (www.welcoa.org). Companies develop and sustain worksite fitness and wellness programs because they reduce health-care costs, increase productivity of employees, and reduce absenteeism (http://prevent disease.com). For example, after the first year of implementing a worksite wellness program, Johnson & Johnson Corporation saw a 9 percent decrease in sick leave. Absenteeism among Bonne Bel Corporation employees declined by 50 percent after the second year of implementing an employee wellness and fitness program. The Prudential Insurance Company reduced health-care costs by $1.93 for every $1 they spent to support their employee wellness and fitness program.

Employees who are more fit and healthy work more productively, are absent less often, and cost companies less in insurance claims. The more risk factors that employees have (smoking, high blood pressure, inactivity, and the like), the higher are the medical costs incurred by the company. There is also considerable support for the notion that company-supported wellness and fitness programs increase employee morale, reduce employee turnover, and prove helpful in recruiting new employees. The Wellness Councils of America is a national, nonprofit membership organization dedicated to promoting healthier lifestyles, especially through health-promotion initiatives at worksites. They also act as the national clearinghouse and information center for worksite wellness.

A worksite fitness and wellness program is typically made up of some combination of the following items (www.fitresource.com):

### Fitness

- Personalized fitness programs
- Fitness testing
- Employee fitness facilities
- Organized classes and activities

### Nutrition

- Healthy-heart programs
- Nutritional guidance
- Weight management

### General Health

- Health-risk appraisal
- Healthy back programs
- Blood pressure screening
- Cholesterol testing
- Smoking cessation
- Stress management
- Health-education programs

The Adolph Coors Company has won a number of national awards for helping their employees adopt and value healthy lifestyles. The company operates a large wellness center, gymnasium, clinic, and counseling center for its employees. Participation in the fitness and wellness programs is voluntary, but workers who do take part receive a 5 percent reduction in their insurance payments. The program includes a testing program to determine what aspects of wellness and fitness that employees most need to improve, a range of activity programs that include specific rehabilitation programs such as cardiac rehabilitation, sports, and a wide variety of fitness activities. Many of these activities are offered with a "club" concept so that members who enjoy the same activities can participate together, thus increasing the motivation to continue participation. The entire effort is seen as a "win-win" for both employees and the company.

Shephard (1999) reports that companies support worksite fitness programs to attract employees with good attitudes toward health, reduce absenteeism, increase productivity, and reduce health-care costs. Companies not only provide facilities for exercise but often form company sport teams or provide breaks for calisthenics during the day. Larger companies often provide a health-assessment area near their fitness facility. Some companies charge a fee

This high-tech exercise system allows a person to swim in place against a current.

for using facilities, but the fee is much less than the cost of membership in a community or commercial fitness facility.

Although worksite fitness and wellness programs are becoming more widely available, it is not clear that the majority of employees participate, particularly on a regular basis. As health fitness has become a major issue in public health—and for corporations, too—the research field of exercise adherence has developed to investigate why people stay in fitness programs or leave them (Dishman, 1988). Lack of time, lack of suitable facilities, poor leadership, and inadequate programs are key reasons why employees do not participate (Shephard, 1988). Personal factors such as income, education, perceived vulnerability, positive motivation, and strong sense of self-efficacy are positively related to participation (Landers, 1997).

There are good reasons for worksites to involve themselves more in employee health-promotion and fitness programs. The savings in reduced absenteeism and health-related insurance costs are substantial. Also, a healthy and physically fit workforce is likely to be more productive and happier than a less fit or less healthy workforce. Although such outcomes are less direct and more difficult to

measure, they may prove to be even more important than other benefits in the long run (Baun & Bernacki, 1988).

## NATIONAL EFFORTS TO PROMOTE FITNESS AND PHYSICAL ACTIVITY

Historically, the federal government's concern with fitness has been in response to high rates of military draft rejects during wartime or in response to national health epidemics such as the severe polio epidemic of 1916. In the mid-1950s, a "fitness crisis" occurred in the United States, the result of a series of tests showing that American children were much less fit than European children (see Chapter 2). In 1955 President Dwight Eisenhower, an avid golfer, convened a national conference of experts to examine fitness problems. Soon thereafter, the president suffered a heart attack, after which he spoke out even more vigorously about federal involvement in the nation's fitness. In 1956 an executive order created the President's Council on Youth Fitness, which was eventually to become the President's Council on Physical Fitness and Sport. More recently, its name was changed once more to reflect a more expansive and inclusive focus: President's Council on Fitness, Sport and Nutrition (PCFSN).

President John F. Kennedy continued this emphasis and published a much-discussed article in *Sports Illustrated* (1960) titled "The Soft American." Since then, the number of federal agencies involved in promoting and investigating fitness and physical activity has increased considerably. In 1978, the U.S. Department of Health, Education, and Welfare produced a major report that listed exercise as one of the twelve categories of behavior that are important determinants of health status (Blair et al., 1987). The federal government then established national objectives in the area of healthy lifestyle and fitness, known as the 1990 Objectives because they were articulated as goals to be met by the year 1990. Of the 226 specific objectives defined, 34 were related directly to physical fitness and health.

The President's Council on Fitness Sport and Nutrition (PCFSN) serves to encourage and motivate citizens of all ages to become physically active and to participate in sport. The PCFSN advises the president and the secretary of Health and Human Services on how to encourage more Americans to be physically fit and active. The 16-member Council is appointed by the president and currently co-chaired by Drew Brees, quarterback for the National Football League's New Orleans Saints, and Dominique Dawes, former Olympic Gymnast.

The PCFSN collaborates with public- and private sector sponsors to conduct its programs and to produce public information materials. Among these programs and materials are the following:

- *The President's Challenge Physical Activity and Fitness Awards* program, a recognition program for both school-aged youth and adults. The youth fitness test includes the following test components: Performance on curl-ups, shuttle run, endurance walk/run, pull-ups (or flexed arm-hang), and the V-sit (or the sit and reach). The adult fitness test includes: a 1-mile walk (or 1.5 mile run, sit and reach, push-ups, half sit-ups, and BMI.

- The *Presidential Active Lifestyle Award* + (PALA+) was recently unveiled. This is an expansion of the original Presidential Active Lifestyle Award (PALA) which promoted daily physical activity among youth. PALA+ adds a nutrition component aimed at improving daily eating habits. Youth who commit to increasing physical activity and better eating for at least six out of eight weeks earn the PALA+ Award.
- *Web site* www.fitness.gov, a gateway Web site to access programs, publications and other resources of the PCFSN
- *PCFSN Research Digest,* a quarterly publication, summarizing scientific research about topics related to physical activity, fitness, and since 2011 also nutrition.
- *State Champion School Award,* an annual award program for schools, conducted in collaboration with state departments of education
- *Demonstration Centers,* conducted in coordination with state departments of education to recognize exemplary elementary-, middle-, and high-school physical-education programs

Both the 1996 publication of the U.S. surgeon general's "Report on Physical Activity and Health" and the 1997 recommendations from the CDC, which focused on policies and strategies for increasing physical activity and healthy lifestyles among children and youths, have placed the importance of fitness and physical activity more squarely in the public view than ever before. With increasing evidence of an obesity epidemic widely publicized, the campaign for activity and fitness has grown stronger, and the federal government is increasingly involved. In 2000 the secretary of Health and Human Services released "Promoting Better Health for Young People through Physical Activity and Sport" (U.S. Department of Health and Human Services, 2000). This report included strategies for families, after-school programs, youth sports and recreation programs, and community support. It was followed in 2001 by "Increasing Physical Activity: A Report on Recommendations of the Task Force on Community

Preventive Services" (Centers for Disease Control and Prevention, 2001). This report focused on the crucial roles that communities can play in supporting physical activity, including community campaigns, school physical education, and the creation of infrastructure to support activity.

Will these policies and programs help improve the nation's fitness and physical activity? It is clear that the federal government is playing a proactive role in emphasizing the importance of activity. As we show in the next chapter, programs and infrastructures are needed, especially for those in the population who are most at risk. Now it remains to be seen whether the infrastructure and programs can be developed and sustained at the local level.

## LEGISLATIVE EFFORTS TO IMPROVE CHILD AND YOUTH FITNESS

In the past several years, a number of efforts have been made at the federal level to combat the child and youth obesity epidemic and to improve fitness opportunities for school-aged children. Earlier in this chapter, we cited the reauthorization of the federal School Lunch Act that required school districts that receive federal funding for school lunch programs to create school wellness councils to address nutrition, nutrition education, and physical activity. Most states have now passed legislation to further define, for the respective states, the requirements that local school districts will have to meet in the areas of school lunches, school breakfasts, foods sold in vending machines, foods sold in school stores, and time requirements for physical education, recesses, and physical activity outside of physical education or recess. Also cited was federal legislation to support developing infrastructure to encourage students to walk or bike to school.

The House of Representatives introduced the Fitness Integrated with Teaching Kids Act (FIT Kids Act) as a proposed amendment to the No Child Left Behind legislation. The key elements of this legislation would require schools to report multiple measures of the performance of their physical-education

programs, including progress toward achieving the national goal of 150 minutes per week for elementary physical education and 225 minutes per week for high-school physical education. It would also require school districts to support professional development for their physical-education teachers. This act was approved by the U.S. House of Representatives and sent to the U.S. Senate and is still under consideration but has not been put to a vote.

The Personal Health Investment Today (PHIT) legislation has also been introduced into the House of Representatives. This legislation would change federal tax law to allow for the use of pretax dollars to cover expenses related to sports, fitness, and other physical activities. Citizens could invest up to $1,000 annually to pay for physical activity engagement by investing money in existing pretax Flexible Spending Accounts, Health Saving Accounts, Medical Savings Accounts, and/or medical reimbursement arrangements.

The Carol M. White Physical Education Program (PEP) was passed by Congress in 2001 with a $5 million appropriation. In 2007 the level of support had increased to $73 million. PEP grants are awarded to local school districts to purchase equipment and train teachers in physical-education methods, with particular attention to health- and wellness-based physical-education programs. The National Coalition for Promoting Physical Activity, a consortium of 17 national organizations, is a key organization in supporting legislation to improve opportunities for children and youths (www.ncppa.org).

## PHYSICAL FITNESS INSTRUCTION: BY WHOM?

The evidence in this chapter shows that fitness and physical activity are pursued by children, youths, and adults in many different places—at home, in schools, and in health spas, fitness centers, sport clubs, and weight-training centers. Fitness facilities and equipment are now commonly found not only in fitness centers of various kinds but also in homes, workplaces, public and private schools, colleges and universities, community facilities, and country clubs. While walking for exercise remains the most widely used form of physical activity for adults, it is clear that many families use the fee-for-service health-club industry. In 2006 there were 29,069 health clubs in the United States, serving 41.3 million members and 23.6 million nonmember patrons, that is, those who pay a daily fee or gain access to a health club via a hotel, hospital, or worksite facility (Active Marketing Group, 2007).

The largest of the health-club chains is Curves with 10,000 locations serving 4.2 million members, followed by Gold's Gym, Lady of America, Health Fitness Corp, Bally Total Fitness, and 24-Hour Fitness World Wide. The largest group of members is the 18- to 34-year age group, accounting for 36 percent of the total club membership, with 32 percent membership among the 35–54 age group, and 19 percent among the 55+ age group. Fifty-seven percent of the membership is female, and 50 percent of the membership has a household income of at least $75,000.

The difficulty in answering the question raised in this section—"by whom?"—is that there is no *national* certification for fitness instructors. Many organizations offer certification for various roles in the fitness professions, such as the American College of Sports Medicine, the Institute for Aerobics Research, the National Strength and Conditioning Association, the International Dance Exercise Association, and the Aerobics and Fitness Association of America. Many fitness centers now require certification as a condition of employment, and having certification is now a major factor in securing a job within the fitness industry. Still, there are fitness centers where fitness leaders and advisors have no certification.

Another crucial issue for anyone aspiring to a career as a fitness professional is the value of various certifications. Currently, there are at least 50 organizations nationally offering more than 400 different certifications (Pierce & Herman, 2004). The issue here is straightforward: Not all certifications are alike. Many organizations offer their certification process online. They sell study materials, and then eventually, the student takes a certification exam

online. Other organizations require the student to attend classes and seminars, and then eventually, sit for an exam under the proctoring of the organization. Students interested in entering the fitness professions and physical-education teachers who want to add a fitness certification to their résumé should be very careful to thoroughly investigate the organization from which they will obtain certification. When one moves into the job market, employers will probably know the differences among the various certifying agencies and be more likely to employ women and men who have obtained their certifications from reputable national organizations that require rigorous study and examination to achieve the certification (See Focus On Box 8.5 for information on fitness certification providers).

The National Board of Fitness Examiners (NBFE) was formed in 2003 to begin to move toward a national standard for fitness trainers (http://nbfe.org). The NBFE is in the process of creating a national examination to ensure an approved level of competency for instructors in the health-and-fitness industry. Part 1 will be a written examination, and Part 2 will be a hands-on performance assessment where each candidate will be presented with 8 to 10 "client interactions" to test the candidate's readiness to provide safe and expert instruction for clients. It seems clear that as the fitness industry continues to expand providers will want to employ women and men who have obtained their certification from reputable national organizations.

## SPORT MEDICINE AND THE REHABILITATIVE SCIENCES

The material in this chapter and others makes it clear that sport and physical fitness are pursued by people of all ages and in many different venues—schools, health clubs, weight-training centers, parks, sports venues, and the like. Child and youth sport, interscholastic sport, collegiate sport, professional sport, and recreational sport have all experienced substantial growth in the past quarter-century. That growth has been accompanied by a

---

**FOCUS ON** — **Personal Trainer Certification Organizations**          **8.5**

**ACE** (American Council on Exercise)
Home study available. Exam on location or online.
Prerequisites: 18 years old, CPR/AED certification
Cost: $219–249 for exam

**ACSM** (American College of Sports Medicine)
Home study available. Exam taken on location.
Prerequisites: High-school diploma, 18 years of age, and current adult CPR certification
Cost: $219–279 for exam

**AFAA** (Aerobics and Fitness Association of America)
Home study available. Exam taken on location.
Prerequisites: N/A
Cost: $469 for 3-day workshop that includes certification

**AFPA** (American Fitness Professionals and Associates)
Home study available. Exam taken on location.
Prerequisites: 18 years or older and high-school diploma.
Cost: $370

**IFPA** (International Fitness Professionals Association)
Home study available. Exam taken on location.
Prerequisites: N/A
Cost: $349

**ISSA** (International Sports and Sciences Association)
Home study available. Exam taken on location.
Prerequisites: CPR/AED certification
Cost: $595

**NASM** (National Academy of Sports Medicine)
Home study available. Exam taken on location.
Prerequisites: 18 years or older, CPR/AED certification
Cost: $549

**NCSF** (National Council on Strength and Fitness)
Home study available. Exam taken on location.
Prerequisites: 18 years or older, CPR/AED certification.
Cost: $549

**NFPT** (National Federation of Professional Trainers)
Home study available. Different exam options.
Prerequisites: High-school diploma
Cost: $450

SOURCE: About.com-Exercise.

---

parallel growth in the professions that serve these many participants, both by providing instruction about fitness and safety and by providing professional services in the care and prevention of sport- and fitness-related injuries.

**Sport medicine** is a generic term used to encompass many areas of specialization related to physical performance and injuries related to physical performance.

A sport-medicine team is required to provide health care to athletes and to those who are regularly involved in fitness work and may incur injuries. Key to this team are athletic trainers and physicians. Medical specialists who can often be found in sport-medicine centers include family-practice physicians, orthopedists, neurologists, internists, ophthalmologists, and pediatricians. One is also likely to find dentists, podiatrists, nutritionists, and physical therapists in some way related to the sport-medicine team. Nurses, physician's assistants, and other health-care professionals are also involved.

## Athletic Training

The most highly developed sport vocation is that of athletic trainer. The National Athletic Trainers' Association (NATA) is one of the strongest of all sport, fitness, and physical-education associations. The mission of NATA is "to enhance the quality of health care for athletes and those engaged in physical activity, and to advance the profession of athletic training through education and research in the prevention, evaluation, management, and rehabilitation of injuries" (www.nata.org). Increasingly, where there are well-developed sport programs you will find athletic trainers, with high schools and universities hiring athletic trainers as full-time personnel.

The chief function of NATA is to supervise and control the certification of athletic trainers through its education program and its board of certification (NATABOC). All athletic trainer students complete a rigorous major program at a college or university. The program includes substantial study in basic and applied sciences, along with extensive professional content including risk management and injury prevention. The program also requires a minimum of 2 years of academic clinical education through which students gain clinical experience with a variety of patient populations (www.NATA.org). These clinical experiences are under direct supervision of qualified clinical instructors who are certified athletic trainers or other health-care professionals. NATA also offers certification through a master's-degree program that typically takes a minimum of 2 years of study.

Athletic trainers are certified through a rigorous examination process that is developed and controlled by a board of certification. The examination assesses candidate knowledge in areas of prevention, clinical evaluation and diagnosis, immediate care, treatment, rehabilitation and reconditioning, organization and administration, and professional responsibility. A committee of athletic trainers prepares questions, and a panel of independent judges validates the questions. Exams are scored by an independent, professional testing organization. In addition, the candidates must pass a competency evaluation checklist from a certified athletic trainer and present proof of certification in standard first aid and cardiopulmonary resuscitation. Those who successfully complete the examination process become certified athletic trainers, a certification typically required for employment.

Most high schools are now hiring full-time athletic trainers, partially in response to the problems of liability and to research showing that the injury rate in schools without full-time trainers is much higher than in schools with such services (Rankin, 1989). The employment potential for athletic trainers is good, and the profession they enter is obviously well controlled, perhaps being a model for other sport and fitness vocations to emulate. Specific skills are identified, and specific programs are arranged to help young men and women acquire those skills. Meaningful, supervised experience is required. Then, entrance to the field is controlled by examination and presentation of a skills checklist.

## ACE Certification

The American Council on Exercise (ACE), a nonprofit organization, has certified more than 40,000 fitness professionals in 107 countries (www.acefitness .org). Certification is available for becoming a personal trainer, group fitness instructor, lifestyle and weight management consultant, clinical exercise specialist, and advanced health and fitness specialist. To be eligible for any of these certifications, candidates must be at least 18 years of age and have a current CPR certification. For the clinical exercise specialist certification, candidates must also have completed a 4-year bachelor's degree in an exercise science or related field or have current ACE personal trainer certification. For the Advanced Health [H11001] Fitness Specialist certification, candidates must also have a 4-year bachelor's degree in exercise science or related field, a current ACE personal trainer certification, and at least 300 hours of work experience designing and implementing exercise programs for healthy individuals and/or high-risk individuals.

Students in an ACE certification program begin with self-study materials and then schedule and take an ACE exam review course. They then take an online diagnostic practice test prior to taking the certification exam at an ACE site. The certification exam is followed by ACE practical training programs.

## ACSM Fitness-Instruction Certification

The mission of the American College of Sports Medicine (ACSM) is to promote and integrate scientific research, education, and practical applications of sport medicine and exercise science to maintain and enhance physical performance, fitness, health, and quality of life (www.acsm.org). ACSM is the nation's largest professional organization of exercise scientists, physicians, physiologists, physical educators, and fitness instructors or managers interested in the implementation of fitness programs.

ACSM offers different levels of certification within two specific tracks. The Health and Fitness certification track offers three certification levels for individuals who work in settings where the exercise participants are apparently healthy and exercising for health maintenance. The Clinical track offers three certifications for those who work with low-to moderate-risk individuals or patients with acute or controlled diseases in hospital-based or medically supervised settings.

ACSM is also heavily involved in the continuing education of the professionals it serves. ACSM endorses more than 180 conferences a year in which those professionals can earn continuing medical-education credit. Since most professional organizations now require a certain level of continuing education to maintain certification, these conferences are often heavily subscribed.

## Strength and Conditioning Coach Qualification

The National Strength and Conditioning Association (NSCA) is an international nonprofit association with 30,000 members in 52 countries. NSCA's primary goal is to support and disseminate research-based knowledge to improve athletic performance and fitness. NSCA has created a registry of qualified members who have been certified as strength and conditioning specialists. To qualify, one must have current NSCA membership and current certification as an NSCA certified strength and conditioning specialist. Candidates must have a bachelor's degree in exercise science or a related field, CPR certification, and a minimum of 2 years full-time employment in a collegiate or professional setting or 2 years as a graduate assistant in strength and conditioning at an institution recognized by NSCA as a Graduate Recognition program. Candidates must also maintain an average of two NSCA-approved continuing education credits per year when employed as a strength and conditioning professional.

In 2002 NSCA released new professional standards and guidelines for strength and conditioning specialists. The standards and guidelines document is designed to identify areas of liability exposure, increase safety standards, and decrease the likelihood of injuries that might lead to legal claims. The standards and guidelines concentrate on athletic preparticipation screening, personnel qualifications, program supervision, facility and equipment inspection, emergency planning and response, record keeping, youth participation, and the use of supplements, ergogenic aids, and drugs (NASPE, 2002).

## Master's Degree in Fitness

Master's degree programs are widely available in a number of fitness-related areas: adult fitness, fitness programming, cardiac rehabilitation, strength development, fitness management, corporate fitness, and exercise physiology. The exact requirements for each degree depend on the specific focus for the master's program. Most programs include ACSM certification of one kind or another.

Although these degree programs differ in the specific course required for graduation, they do have much in common (Hall & Wilson, 1984). Because they are *graduate* programs, the entrance criteria are those common to the graduate program at the institution offering the degree. The criteria typically include at least a 2.75 to 3.00 undergraduate grade point average (GPA), a certain level of performance on the Graduate Record Examination (GRE) or a similar test, and a background in the core sciences related to fitness.

Specific prerequisites for entrance most often involve previous coursework in anatomy, physiology, and exercise physiology. Some programs also require coursework in chemistry, mathematics, physics, kinesiology, and measurement. The degree programs themselves combine advanced coursework, acquisition of the technical skills associated with fitness (for example, testing), practical experience within the program, and, often, an internship in an agency dealing with fitness (for example, corporation, hospital, or fitness center).

Most programs take from 12 to 24 months to complete. In some programs, students must complete a thesis to graduate.

These programs require that candidates have a good background in science courses, and they emphasize the underlying scientific basis of fitness. A student who aspires to a career in a fitness-related profession should thus be sure to acquire the appropriate scientific expertise.

## SUMMARY

1. It is clear that inactivity is a risk factor for hypokinetic disease.

2. Youth fitness testing indicates that boys and girls in the fifth through twelfth grades rank poorly in tests of body composition and cardiopulmonary efficiency.

3. Similar testing among children in the 6- to 9-year-old group indicates alarmingly high percentages of body fat and inadequate cardiopulmonary functioning.

4. Some experts believe that when activity is considered rather than fitness testing, children and youths are more fit than reports indicate.

5. Research on activity patterns among children is uneven but indicates that too few get regular physical education and that those who do are less active within physical education than they should be.

6. Participation in sport declines dramatically as children approach adolescence.

7. There is often insufficient time within school physical education classes to develop and maintain health fitness, which has led to a national movement to provide daily physical education that emphasizes health fitness.

8. A number of different effective fitness programs have been developed in school physical education, including schoolwide elementary programs, fitness clubs, remediation programs, daily fitness programs, fitness courses, and a strong fitness focus within the physical-education class.

9. AAHPERD has promoted fitness strongly through testing and incentive programs such as the FITNESSGRAM and Jump Rope for Heart.

10. Although reliable data on fitness levels of adults are difficult to obtain, the best estimates are that 20 percent of adults get sufficient health-fitness exercise, 40 percent get some but not sufficient benefits from exercise, and 40 percent are sedentary.

11. The recent fitness boom is mostly a young-adult, relatively upper-income phenomenon in which the *appearance* of fitness participation seems more pervasive than actual participation.

12. Surveys of activity patterns among adults and seniors indicate that exercise decreases with age and is relatively higher among males, in suburban communities, among professionals, among high-school and college graduates, and among whites.

13. Most fitness professionals expect the fitness movement to continue to expand because of increased media exposure, discretionary income, acceptability among women, influence of elite sport, and emphasis within the health and medical professions.

14. Worksite fitness programs are becoming increasingly available but are strongly influenced by the availability of facilities.

15. The federal government has become heavily involved in promoting health fitness and has developed specific objectives for the nation to achieve in the twenty-first century.

16. Most fitness programs are developed and led by uncertified personnel although several organizations, such as the ACSM, NSCA, and ACE, have well-developed certification programs.

17. Many universities now offer master's degree programs in fitness that combine advanced training in exercise science with training in the skills needed to work professionally within the fitness area. These programs typically require an internship and, sometimes, a thesis.

## DISCUSSION QUESTIONS

1. Why is it that the fitness boom has been primarily a young-adult, upper-income phenomenon?

2. What can be done to promote regular fitness habits among children?

3. How fit are you? What either motivates you to maintain or prevents you from maintaining an adequate level of fitness?

4. What were fitness programs like when you were in elementary and high school? Were they effective?

5. What can communities do to promote fitness? Who should pay for community-based programs?

6. Why is it in the interest of corporations and businesses to promote fitness among their employees?

7. Will specializing in fitness become more of a profession with increasing certification and preparation? Would such a trend be good?

8. In what sense does the manner in which fitness programs are organized and taught influence the degree to which those involved become committed to physical activity as part of their lifestyle?

## CHAPTER 9

# Problems and Issues in Fitness

*For years we have tried the same fitness philosophy; that is, trying to achieve fitness goals by compelling children to exercise. We should realize that it is time to try something different. As professional physical educators we must recognize that "getting children fit" (by itself) is not the answer if children and youth do not develop the lifetime habits of physical activity.*

Charles Corbin, 1987, speaking of perennial
problems in the fitness curriculum

Physical activity and physical fitness are more important to our national health agenda than at any time during our history. All experts realize that physical activity and fitness can be achieved in a number of ways—through child and youth sports, interscholastic sports, recreational sports for adults, participation at fitness and health centers, membership in a worksite wellness program, informal recreational activities, and regular physical activity done within and outside the home. Chapter 7 introduced you to the differences among health-fitness, motor-performance fitness, and cosmetic fitness. Each of these is of different importance to those who participate.

Most clearly, health fitness is important to life itself, both to living well and to living free from degenerative disease. That kind of importance has both personal and social significance. Motor-performance fitness is important, too. For the high-school volleyball player, jumping higher and hitting more strongly is of immediate short-term importance. The strength and endurance of an Olympic athlete are important not only to him or her but also

to each of us who roots for the athlete and takes pride in his or her accomplishments. Cosmetic fitness has a different kind of importance; it enhances self-esteem and builds confidence, qualities that may be important to achievement in school, at work, and in social relationships. Therefore, although we tend to focus more on health fitness, we should not forget the importance of motor-performance and cosmetic fitness in the lives of people for whom those qualities are central to success.

Life expectancy for Americans has tended to increase with each generation. Life expectancy for males is now over 75 years and for females over 80 years. Retirees now represent a larger proportion of our population than ever before. Health costs for an aging population are extraordinary. Senior citizens who maintain an adequate level of health-related fitness not only have a better quality of life but also help reduce national health-care costs. Experts, however, have cautioned that, unless we can deal successfully with the current epidemic of overweight and obesity among children and youths, the current young generation may be the first in

American history to have shorter life expectancy than their parents (Daniels, 2006).

The vast majority of modern occupations are mostly sedentary. The requirements of daily life in a mostly urban society are insufficient to develop and maintain an adequate level of heath fitness. What most experts now describe as the "built environment" tends to discourage rather than encourage physical activity. Generations ago, the hours now spent watching television, working at a computer, or playing electronic games were spent in some sort of physical activity. Healthy foods are now more expensive than unhealthy foods. Eating in fast-food restaurants and taking home carry-out food has dramatically increased over the past quarter-century. Put simply, it is easier and less expensive to eat unhealthy foods than to eat healthy foods. All these factors have contributed to the crisis of overweight and obesity. Americans, for the most part, are increasingly aware of these issues. More than $35 billion is now spent annually on weight-loss-related products and services (Levi, Segal, & Gadola, 2007). It is to the effects of these societal developments that we now turn.

## THE COSTS OF INADEQUATE HEALTH FITNESS

Traditionally, health and fitness were seen nearly exclusively as issues of personal responsibility. Today, although that point of view is still seen as important, it has become clear that the costs of inadequate fitness in the population constitute a major national problem that must be dealt with through programs designed to reach specific segments of the population. The costs associated with inadequate levels of health fitness now represent a substantial proportion of the yearly gross national product (Pritchard & Potter, 1990). The increased prevalence of overweight and obesity among children and youths has convinced many in the health professions that the future costs of health care will be catastrophic if we cannot combat the epidemic in the near future (Barrett, 2007).

The United States spends more than $1.5 billion on health care each year, a figure that has doubled in the past 5 years and is expected to double again within 6 years (Siedentop, 2007). Overweight and obesity are now the second leading cause of death in the United States.

In Chapter 1, we provided the details associated with this epidemic, namely that overweight and obesity are not distributed evenly across the population. African Americans and Hispanics are more prone to overweight and obesity, largely because they do not have the economic means to purchase healthier foods and also because the neighborhoods in which they grow up and live are less likely to make it easier to engage in physical activity.

Inadequate levels of physical activity among various population groups are not simply an individual issue. The problem also has economic and social implications that affect us all. Americans who are most often at risk for health problems due to lack of health-related fitness and healthier diets are those for whom fitness information and opportunities for physical activity are less accessible. Thus, issues of socioeconomic status, race, and gender need to be understood and factored into proposed programmatic solutions.

### Precipitating Factors Related to the Overweight and Obesity Crisis

In Chapter 1, we described the primary precipitating factors that lead to overweight and obesity. The two primary factors are caloric imbalance created when intake of foods and drinks exceeds energy expenditure through physical activity. We are all no doubt familiar with the availability and lower costs for fast foods that have a high caloric density and often come in larger portions. Many families now rely on take-out food rather than on in-home cooking. Foods served in school breakfast and lunch programs, school vending machines, and school stores have included too many nonnutritious ingredients. Schools have increased their revenues through contracts with vendors who sell nonnutritious snacks and drinks and advertise those products on school campuses (Molnar, Garcia, Boninger, & Merrill, 2006).

Another factor associated with these current health issues related to physical activity is what experts now refer to as the *built environment,* which encompasses the range of physical and social elements that make up the structures of communities (Papas, Alberg, Weing, Helzlsouer, Gary, & Klassen, 2007). Factors such as commuting time, communities designed to foster driving rather than walking/biking, and lack of public transit reduce physical activity. Forty years ago, more than half of all children in the United States walked or cycled to school, while today only 10 percent do (ncdot.org). The average American adult takes 42 percent fewer walking trips than a generation ago (Wilkinson, Eddy, MacFadden, & Burgess, 2002). Research has shown that physical activity is substantially higher among people living in high-walkable communities compared to low-walkable communities (Sallis & Kerr, 2006). Access to parks and recreation space has been limited, including the lack of safe, accessible indoor facilities for physical activity during periods of inclement weather. Physical activity among children and youths has decreased while time spent on video games, electronic games, watching TV, and connecting to the Internet has increased. Historically, schools have been embedded within communities and have served as centers for community activity, accessible to most children, youth, and adults by walking or cycling. More recently, larger schools are built in more remote locations that are accessible primarily through driving, an issue particularly prevalent with middle and high schools (Beaumont & Pianca, 2002).

Since the federal No Child Left Behind (NCLB) legislation, schools have increased their focus on language arts, and math, leading to a reduction in time allotted for other subjects. Most notably, for purposes here, is a reported 14 percent reduction in time for physical education (Jennings, 2006). Financial strains on schools have also contributed to reduced time allotted to recess and after-school programming.

Suburban sprawl and urban decay both contribute to decreased physical activity among persons of all ages. Parents cite five primary barriers to their children's participation in physical activity: transportation problems, lack of opportunities for physical activity in the immediate area, expense, parents' lack of time, and concerns about neighborhood safety (Centers for Disease Control and Prevention, 2003).

## FITNESS BEHAVIOR: SHORT TERM AND LONG TERM

There is no doubt that the public is becoming more aware of the importance of health-related fitness. Most current polls show that as many as 90 percent of Americans *believe* that regular exercise is important to health and well-being, but many Americans do not exercise regularly.

A major issue in improving the health fitness of our society is determining how to confront this difference between belief and behavior. Why do people who *know* that regular exercise is important still fail to exercise regularly? Coming to grips with this problem and finding workable solutions to it may be the most important advancements of all.

Another issue preventing many adults (and adolescents) from engaging in health-related fitness activities is the attractiveness of alternative activities, such as watching a game or a movie or playing an electronic game. One approach to these problems is to start with lower-intensity activity such as walking or cycling. Starting a walking program and gradually increasing both the pace of the walk and the distance walked has helped many adults to not only improve their health but also prepare them for participation in physical activities that have a heavier workload. This is referred to as *lifestyle physical activity* and would also include gardening, climbing stairs, doing housework, or engaging in light-to-moderate sports such as table tennis, bowling, and golf (Corbin, Welk, Corbin, & Welk, 2008).

When a person has engaged regularly in lifestyle physical activity for some time, he or she will have a sufficient base to begin to engage in aerobic activities and more active forms of sport and recreation. Using the physical activity dose formula of 30 minutes per day of moderate-to-vigorous physical activity (MVPA) to a total 210 minutes per week is an alternative strategy to reach health-fitness goals. Brisk walking for 30–40 minutes a day, in addition to sound nutrition and absence of risk factors such as smoking, will lead to health benefits that are very similar to those achieved through more vigorous health-related fitness activities. What is crucial to each, however, is the commitment to sustained involvement; that is, activity has to become a part of lifestyle.

In the past few years, it has become clear that the overarching goal for school-based physical education is for children and youth to *adopt and value a physically active lifestyle*. This issue was addressed more completely in Chapters 4, 5, and 6, and it should be abundantly clear that this is a long-term goal. Short-term approaches such as an obligatory 5 minute fitness session at the start of each physical education lesson and using antiquated fitness testing that has little to do with health-related fitness likely works against the achievement of that goal for many girls and boys.

Getting people to exercise in ways that are fun and satisfying is a first step. Helping them to become fit (in the health-fitness sense) is a second step, but it is unfortunately the step at which many fitness programs stop. To achieve a commitment to lifetime fitness, programs must also help their participants establish patterns of exercise that fit their recreational interests, exercise regularly but also teach them self-testing skills, fitness-planning skills, consumer information, and related information, such as sound nutritional planning. Research is beginning to show that fitness programs that have this lifestyle emphasis tend to produce commitment; that is, those who complete such a program tend to think and behave differently in the long term (Rider & Johnson, 1986, Slava, Laurie, & Corbin, 1984).

Motivation is, of course, the key to getting children, adolescents, and adults into activity programs and keeping them involved in those programs. It is clear that programs for children and adolescents must address three major motivations if those programs are to be successful (Weiss, 2000). First, boys

and girls want to develop and demonstrate physical competence through skills, fitness, or appearance. Second, they want to be accepted and supported within a peer social group, including appreciation and support from significant adults. Third, they want to have fun, which means that activity experiences have to be positive and that potentially negative aspects of the experience have to be minimized. Fitness experts, physical educators, recreation personnel, and sport coaches all need to keep those motivations in mind as they implement sport, recreation, and activity programs.

## DEVELOPING SELF-EFFICACY FOR PHYSICAL ACTIVITY

In 1977 the American psychologist Albert Bandura published an article entitled "Self-Efficacy: Toward a Unifying Theory of Behavioral Change." Bandura argued that one's perceived self-efficacy defines their capabilities to produce designated levels of performance. Persons who have high self-efficacy for any particular action approach tasks as challenges to be mastered rather than threats to be avoided. Research has shown that exercise self-efficacy is an important predictor of the adoption and maintenance of exercise behaviors (Fletcher & Banasik, 2001).

When young children first learn to be physically active they crawl before they walk and they walk before they run. Learning is much more likely to be successful if it consists of activities that are perceived by the learners as "fun". The most effective way to begin to create and then develop a strong sense of self-efficacy is through a series of significant mastery experiences (Bandura, 1994). A second way of developing and strengthening self-efficacy is through observing persons similar to oneself succeed by sustained effort, thus increasing one's own sense that success is possible. A third way of developing and strengthening self-efficacy is to persuade persons that they have the capability to succeed.

The most successful strategy for helping children, adolescents, and adults to improve their self-efficacy for physical activity is to provide a series of activities that are fun and gradually become more difficult, allowing learners to experience continual success, a strategy referred to in psychology as successive approximation. As children and youths engage in physical activity that is both fun and "doable" they will gradually come to view themselves not only capable of being successful in physical activity but will be more likely to seek it out in their discretionary time.

Sadly, fitness programs in schools have had a long history of starting with a fitness test that typically ensures that most students will perform poorly and feel embarrassed about their performance. The best strategy to develop PA self-efficacy is to start young children with activities that are doable and have a very high fun quotient and then very gradually make them more complex. Gradually, as students move through their school years, this strategy will help them to have confidence in their capabilities to be physically active, to overcome barriers that hinder their physical activity (barriers efficacy), to seek out friends with whom they can be physically active (asking efficacy), and to find or create environments that support their physical activity (environmental-change efficacy) (Ryan & Dzewaltowski, 2002).

Teachers in schools and those who work with children and youths in fitness centers should take care to evaluate the differences among the children with regards to their level of self-efficacy for physical activity. A convenient way to do so is through using a physical activity self-efficacy scale through which they can modify the activity program to meet the needs of the individuals taking part. An example of a self-efficacy scale that would be useful for use with students in third grade through high school is shown in Focus On Box 9.1 on physical activity self-efficacy.

Self-efficacy is not developed overnight. It develops through a series of physical activity experiences in which participants are successful and fully enjoy what they have done. In schools, this likely means that teachers will have to differentiate activities for students who have different capacities and predispositions for physical activity. Self-efficacy will develop, albeit slowly, when boys and girls take part in fun activities that are modestly differentiated to allow them to be successful. As they grow in self-efficacy for PA, the differences can be reduced, and most students will be able to participate successfully.

| *FOCUS ON* **Physical Activity Self-Efficacy Scale** | | | | | 9.1 |
|---|---|---|---|---|---|
| *I am confident that . . .* | Not at All | Rarely | True | Moderately True | Always True |
| I can overcome barriers with regard to physical activity if I try hard. | | | | | |
| I can find ways to be physically active and to exercise. | | | | | |
| I can accomplish the PA goals I set. | | | | | |
| When I find barriers to PA I can find solutions to overcome the barriers. | | | | | |
| I can be physically active even when I am tired. | | | | | |
| I can be physically active even without the support of my family or friends. | | | | | |
| I can be physically active without the help of a teacher or trainer. | | | | | |
| I can be physically active even if I have no access to a gym or fitness center. | | | | | |

# DEVELOPING A FITNESS-EDUCATED PUBLIC

A major step forward in any national effort to improve the health fitness of citizens will be taken when the general public becomes better educated about fitness issues. This means that the *average* person on the street will know about the different kinds of fitness, what needs to be done to develop and maintain health fitness, and what fitness products and services are appropriate to fitness goals. We are certainly a long way from being able to take that step forward.

Part of the problem associated with educating the public is that the popular media—through advertising and promotion of products—create false impressions that make it even harder for the general public to understand the *real* issues about fitness. Skinner (1988) has identified three general media-related problems:

1. The media image of a fit person is typically someone who has a young, hard, thin, and beautiful body. That kind of body is neither necessary for health fitness nor attainable by most people, no matter what they might do!

2. The impression left by the media is that fitness miracles can occur quickly and often without any real effort on the part of the person undertaking the fitness program. The media goal seems to be to get people started in a program by buying products (a diet book, a workout video, a piece of exercise equipment). Whether you stay in that program is not the main interest of the company.

3. Whose product is being promoted?

4. The media seem to create instant experts who have celebrity status but who may have no training in exercise science and who may actually know very little specific information about fitness.

Making sure that citizens, young and old, have appropriate, accurate knowledge about fitness and fitness activities is fundamentally important to improving the nation's health. Have you recently seen youths or adults doing the hurdler's stretch, the quadriceps stretch, or the standing toe touch? All are contraindicated by research as inappropriate and potentially dangerous. Have you seen children, youths, or adults doing straight-leg sit-ups, deep knee bends, or double leg lifts as strengthening exercises? Again, all are contraindicated by research as potentially dangerous, and for each of those exercises there is a safer, more appropriate exercise. Have you seen youths or adults who decide to start a fitness program and on the first day try to run for 60 minutes at what they think is an appropriately brisk pace? If so, they don't understand the principle of progressive overload and moving gradually in

Many young adults are serious about their fitness workouts.

Fitness instructors focus on appropriate postures for workouts.

small increments in any fitness activity, whether for strength, flexibility, or cardiovascular improvements.

Accurate information about the various aspects of health fitness is widely available in books, in magazine articles, and on the Internet. The best venue through which the public will become better educated about health fitness and motor-performance fitness is school health and physical education—at least it should be! The American Public Health Association has long noted the importance of school programs that are available to all children and youth:

> The school, as a social structure, provides an educational setting in which the total health of the child during the impressionable years is a priority concern. No other community setting even approximates the magnitude of the grades K–12 school education . . . Thus, it seems that the school should be regarded as a . . . focal point to which health planning for all other community settings should relate. (McGinnis, Kanner, & DeGraw, 1991)

If school physical education continues to dwindle and private health clubs continue to grow, then future generations will learn about fitness and have access to fitness programs more and more as a result of the socioeconomic status (SES) of their parents. The fitness gap between rich and poor will grow. Fitness will continue to be seen primarily as an indi-vidual issue, even though the costs to the public of an unfit society will be enormous.

## EQUITY ISSUES IN FITNESS AND ACTIVITY

Gender, race, and SES are key factors in understanding differences in health, fitness, and activity participation in the United States. National data on physical activity participation (National Center for Health Statistics, 2004) shows that in all age groups females were less active than males and blacks, and Hispanics were less active than whites. Black males typically fared as well as white males, but black females fared much worse than white females. It is also clear that young people from lower-income families tend to be less active than those from middle- and upper-income families. This reflects the social gradient in health and activity described in Chapter 7, which means simply that socioeconomic groups are typically healthier than the groups below them and less healthy than the groups above them.

Currently, 66 percent of adults are overweight or obese, and 50 percent of all children and adolescents are overweight or obese (Wang & Beydoun, 2007). Gender, race, and socioeconomic factors all influence the prevalence of overweight and obesity. Obesity rates for high-school males are 15.2 percent for non-Hispanic whites, 15.9 percent for non-Hispanic blacks, and 21.3 percent for Hispanics. For high-school females, the rates are 8.2 percent for non-Hispanic whites, 16.1 percent for non-Hispanic blacks, and 12.1 percent for Hispanics. It is clear that the SES of individuals and families is partially related to the incidence of overweight and obesity (Wang & Beydoun, 2007). Obesity is more prevalent among adults below the poverty line (34.7 percent) than among adults above the poverty line (28.7 percent) (Levi et al., 2007). Urban and rural children are somewhat less likely to be active and more likely to be overweight and obese. There is no reason to suggest that this is based on genetic differences; indeed, the evidence strongly suggests

**FOCUS ON**　Helping Girls Become and Stay Involved in Physical Activity and Sport　　**9.2**

- Girls should be encouraged to become involved in sport and physical activity at an early age.
- Practices that enhance girls' opportunities to be physically active must be developed and supported.
- Recreational activities, physical education, and community sport programs are ideal ways to facilitate health-related fitness and the acquisition of skills.
- Involvement in sport and physical activity has great potential to enhance a girl's sense of competence and control. Leaders should incorporate cooperative as well as competitive opportunities in nonthreatening environments.

- Parents, coaches, and teachers should be aware that girls' motives for participating are not only to be competitive but also to socialize, improve skills, be with friends, and have fun.
- Coaches and physical educators should provide equal access and attention for girls.
- When adults observe girls being treated inequitably, they should intervene.
- Involvement in physical activity and sport promotes psychological well-being and is an anxiety reducer for adolescent girls, thereby acting as a natural, cost-effective mental health program.

SOURCE: President's Council on Physical Fitness and Sport (1997).

that the main determinants are environmental rather than genetic.

Physical activity and obesity are obviously related. Research has shown that minority children and youths are more at risk than whites, that girls are more at risk than boys, and that minority girls are the most at risk (Kimm et al., 2002; Strauss & Pollock, 2001). In the last decade of the twentieth century, overweight increased significantly among all children and youths, but the rate of increase among African American and Hispanic children was nearly twice that for whites. Research has also shown that participation in physical activity declines markedly among girls during adolescence, with the largest declines among black girls. From ages 8–9 to 18–19, the decline was 64 percent for white girls and nearly 100 percent for minority girls. By the ages of 16 to 17, 31 percent of white girls and 56 percent of black girls reported no regular leisure-time physical activity. The long-term health implications of these data for this age cohort of girls are substantial.

Only recently have physical activity and fitness studies begun to focus on girls' and women's issues. Traditionally, most physical activity and fitness

research has been conducted on males (Wells, 1996). Currently, there are three important trends in girls' physical activity participation (Tucker Center for Research on Girls and Women in Sport, 2007). First, girls are participating in sports in record numbers, from youth sport to interscholastic sports, extreme or action sports, and Olympic sports (see Focus On Box 9.2). Second, girls' participation in MVPA outside of organized sports is declining. Third, girls' participation rates in all types of physical activity lags consistently behind those of boys, and the dropout rates from sport are also higher than for boys.

The decline of PA for girls as they grow older has serious health consequences. Exercise has been shown to reduce the risk of breast cancer (Physical Activity Today, 1996), and its benefits for combating problems associated with osteoporosis are well known. It is also clear that participation in physical activity and sport has important psychological and social, as well as physiological, benefits (Bunker, 1998). It becomes increasingly important that programs specifically designed to reach and assist girls and women be developed and implemented (see Focus On Box 9.3).

---

**FOCUS ON** — Helping Young Girls Get and Stay Healthy — 9.3

In 2002 the Department of Health and Human Services' Office on Women's Health launched a new Web site (www.4girls.gov) to encourage adolescent girls to choose healthy behaviors.

Young girls (12–16), especially minority girls, are particularly at risk for physical inactivity and all the problems associated with inactivity.

One section of the Web site deals with being "Fit for Life" and provides girls with the tools to develop exercise plans that are safe, enjoyable, and long-lasting. That section also provides education about strength training, eating outside the home, and maintaining a healthy weight. A fitness questionnaire can be filled out to help girls understand their own needs.

The site also includes a parent/caregiver section that can be used to help address issues that adolescent girls face.

SOURCE: www.fitness.gov/4girlspressrelease.html.

---

Residents of lower socioeconomic neighborhoods in urban areas are particularly at risk for health problems associated with physically inactive lifestyles. In urban areas, there is crime in the streets, high-density housing with few open spaces, working parents with little time for supervision of outdoor activity, relatively few recreation facilities, and little adult leadership (Sallis, 1994). The Carnegie Council on Adolescent Development (1992), in a landmark study of discretionary time among youths, concluded that "young adolescents who live in low-income neighborhoods are most likely to benefit from supportive youth development services; yet they have the least access to such programs and organizations."

Opportunity for physical activity and fitness is not a level playing field in the United States. Those who have had restricted opportunity and support have become the most at risk for a number of health problems related to physical inactivity. Thus, whether one views this problem primarily as a social–moral issue or chiefly as a cost–benefit issue from the standpoint of health costs, the solution is the same—namely, to remove barriers and to target supportive programs at those among us whose opportunities have been most restricted (see Focus On Box 9.4). This is a *structural* problem requiring public policy and programs for its solution. Exhorting people to show more individual responsibility may be an element in this solution, but in and of themselves, such exhortations are unlikely to change anything.

## CERTIFICATION OF FITNESS LEADERS

In Chapter 8, we described some of the programs that provide certification in the fitness industry. When choosing a fitness or physical activity program consumers should make enquiries about the level of fitness certification among workers in the program. Consumers should also become more familiar with the types of certification offered, and with particular concerns about certification programs that are available through the mail with minimum requirements. The American College of Sports Medicine certification program described in Chapter 8 is an example of a quality program with more rigorous requirements.

This problem of certification for exercise leaders is tied to the problem of public education about fitness. The more that the public knows about fitness, the more likely people are to demand appropriate leadership in fitness classes and to be able to discriminate between good and bad practices. In the final analysis, an informed public might create such widespread consumer awareness that inappropriate fitness leadership would be driven from the market. Still, requiring exercise leaders to obtain

**Dealing With the Obesity Epidemic: Complex Relationships**    **9.4**

In 2004 Julie Gerberding, director of the CDC, said, "If you looked at any epidemic—whether it's influenza or plague from the Middle Ages—they are not as serious as the epidemic of obesity in terms of the health impact on our country and our society" (Trust for America's Health, 2004). The statistics are clear. Sixty-five percent of American adults are overweight or obese. One in every seven children is either overweight or obese. Sport, physical-education, and fitness leaders have to provide leadership in dealing with these issues.

When dealing with children or youths, it is particularly important to understand that obesity is a complex social and psychological problem as well as a physical problem (Berger, 2004). Fitness and physical-education professionals who deal with these problems as though they were solely about more activity and better diet will probably fail to

achieve desired goals. Short-term weight loss without a long-term plan for lifestyle change nearly always results in some short-term improvement followed by a rapid return to the lifestyle habits that produced the problems in the first place. The worst scenario is a fitness or physical-education professional trying to move obese children or youths to some "ideal" body composition and form. We know that it is possible to be *reasonably fit* and at the same time to be overweight in terms of body composition (a BMI of 25–29.9).

Physical-activity, exercise, and fitness programs should focus on helping children and youth improve their health rather than primarily on losing weight (AAALF, 2003). This takes patience and understanding as well as activity programs where children and youths can be successful and have fun.

certification by an agency such as the ACSM would represent another major step forward in the fitness movement.

## FITNESS TESTS OR ACTIVITY ESTIMATES?

As epidemiological data on exercise related to mortality have become available, it has become clear that inactivity is a serious risk factor but that moderate activity is nearly as valuable as a preventive measure as is vigorous activity (Blair, 1992). This has led some fitness experts to argue for measures of activity in children and youths as more valid estimates of health fitness than fitness tests themselves (Freedson & Rowland, 1992).

The notion is quite simple. A healthy lifestyle includes activity. Moderate activity is sufficient to serve public health goals, and many of the kinds of activities that people enjoy most are moderate in nature—that is, walking, recreational cycling,

gardening, and the like. Earlier in this chapter, we noted that fitness education must focus on long-term goals and that changes in lifestyle are the main long-term outcomes. If that is so, then one must at least give serious consideration to the argument that measures of daily activity are, from this perspective, valid indicators of fitness.

In contrast to measures of activity, mass fitness testing with students competing against one another is typically counterproductive to fitness and activity goals. This does not mean that fitness testing has no place in school or agency programs. Pate (1994) suggests the following guidelines for fitness testing:

- Testing should be used to identify at-risk children, but their privacy should be respected in both testing and remediation.

- Award systems should be based on criterion-referenced standards, not norm-based tables.

- Accumulated activity, as well as performance on fitness tests, should become part of the evaluation strategy with children and youths.

- Self-testing can reduce some of the unfortunate side effects of mass fitness testing in physical education classes.

- The primary purposes of fitness testing should be diagnosis, providing feedback, setting goals, and charting improvements.

## FITNESS AND AGING: CHANGING VIEWS AND EXPECTATIONS

The American population is graying. Not only are there more older citizens than ever before, but our senior citizens have become one of our largest population groups. Every day, more than 4,000 Americans celebrate their 65th birthday. While this population group has traditionally viewed vigorous physical activity as inappropriate, recent awareness of the importance of the role of physical activity in the later stage of life has begun to change the views of older persons. Increasingly, fitness for older Americans will become a major issue in the sport, fitness, and physical education professions.

The dimensions of the problems associated with an aging population are substantial. The number of Americans age 65 and older will almost double between now and 2030, from 34.8 million in 2000 to 70.3 million in 2030 (Civic Ventures, 2011). The post–65-year-old group will soon be the dominant social and political group in America. The most rapid growth is among the oldest of the old! There are currently 66,000 Americans older than 100, which is 20 times the number of centenarians who were alive in 1960. Federal estimates are that there will be 214,000 centenarians by 2020 and 834,000 by 2050.

The most important issue resulting from all of this is not necessarily how to increase life expectancy further. Rather, it is how to help older citizens maintain their productive living capacity and better enjoy their later years. A pertinent corollary of this issue is reducing national health-care costs.

Golf is an activity enjoyed by people of all ages.

The benefits of activity in later years are beginning to be understood. Along with appropriate diet, exercise appears to be a key factor in controlling the effects of aging. It now seems that many of the so-called signs of aging (hearing loss, hair loss, reduced heart and lung function) are not as much signs of aging as they are signs of inactivity and poor nutrition (Kotulak & Gorner, 1992). Exercise programs do increase physical and physiological function among the elderly, thus having major effects on physiological aging and quality of life (Shephard, 1996). Quite elderly and even bedridden people have dramatically improved their physical status through planned exercise and nutrition interventions.

One of the most common ailments of senior citizens is depression of various kinds and intensities. The fact is that the declines that often accompany aging tend to produce depression and lower self-esteem. Studies, however, have shown that sedentary seniors who participate in regular physical activity programs experience long-term psychological benefits (News, 2001). This is all more proof of the prophylactic and remedial benefits of regular activity.

Contemporary surveys of activity participation among the post–65-year-old age group are encouraging. It is clear that activities such as walking, cycling, aerobics, and calisthenics are popular with and doable by women and men in this age group. It is also clear that SES is strongly related to activity in later years. Women and men who can afford to retire in retirement communities or care centers have access to planned activities and to easily accessible exercise facilities that cater to older adults.

We are just now beginning to investigate and understand the problems associated with motivating older adults to incorporate regular physical activity into their lifestyles (Duda, 1991). Educating older people about the importance of physical activity must emphasize the personal meaning of the activity and the personal investment that the individual makes when entering an activity setting. It will take a great deal to overcome the traditional myth that people slow down because they get older. It appears that the opposite is more nearly true—that is, people get older because they slow down!

## FITNESS ISSUES IN PHYSICAL EDUCATION

Many children first encounter physical fitness in their school physical education program. These children will be in school for their formative years of childhood and the crucial years of adolescence. Therefore, what their physical education classes teach them is likely to be of major importance in the formation of habits and attitudes that might last a lifetime.

The issues and problems associated with fitness programs within physical education are complex and not amenable to simple solutions. Nonetheless, to neglect them would be a serious mistake.

Leaders in the fitness movement have been particularly critical of school physical education programs. In 1986 Kenneth Cooper, the physician who made the nation aware of aerobics, commented that fitness among children was so poor that we may "see all the gains made against heart disease in the past 20 years wiped out in the next 20 years" (*ARAPCS Newsletter*, 1986, p. 4). More recent evidence estimating children's physical activity, rather than their

performance of fitness tests, has reduced that concern but not changed the clear fact that too many children are obese and inactive and that during adolescence, many youths become much less active.

The elementary-school years are particularly crucial in forming habits and predispositions among children. The research on physical activity among young children and the effects it has on later life are quite similar to the research on reading in early elementary years. If children leave the third grade reading below grade level, they are highly likely to be poor-performing students throughout their school years. If children leave the third grade overweight or obese, they are likely to remain so throughout their school years and into adulthood.

To be fair, one should consider the frequency and duration of physical education time as a "dose" and the outcomes with children as a "response." What is clear over the past decade is that many schools have reduced the amount of time allotted to physical education in order to focus more on reading and math. This reduction in "dose" will most certainly have a negative effect on student activity (response). In many states, the classroom teacher is also the physical education teacher and may not be sufficiently prepared to plan and deliver a physical activity or fitness program to children that will not only help them to become more fit but, just as important, help them enjoy physical activity so much that they seek it out in nonattached time.

In 1994 Pate and Hohn suggested that the primary goal of physical education should be to promote lifelong physical activity and fitness. In the same year, Simons-Morton (1994) suggested that this goal would be accomplished through a "health-related physical education." The National Association for Sport and Physical Education recently published the second edition of *Moving Into the Future: National Standards for Physical Education* (NASPE, 2004b). The overall goal is stated as physical activity critical to the development and maintenance of good health. The goal of physical education is to "develop physically educated individuals who have the knowledge, skills, and confidence to enjoy

Extreme sports have become popular among the millennium generation.

a lifetime of healthful physical activity." We should note that the overarching goal is not about fitness but about healthy physical activity. In 2007 the Trust for America's Health conducted a survey among chronic disease directors and state directors of health promotion and education to find out what these experts believed are the most important strategies for obesity prevention and reduction (Levi et al., 2007). The strategy that gained the most support from the experts was "increasing physical education and activity in schools, including before and after school programs" (p. 89).

Fitness in physical education used to mean push-ups, sit-ups, jumping jacks, and running. Many teachers "tested" fitness at least once each year, but students often had little preparation, except for the obligatory 5 minutes of exercises at the start of class.

Most students endured it, but if it taught them anything it was to dislike what they had learned as fitness activities. Today, one is more likely to see a physical education teacher who helps students learn how to use a pedometer, to chart courses to walk/run around their neighborhood, to establish realistic goals, and to record activity to reach those goals. Currently, there are many varied and attractive approaches to health-related fitness and physical activity in physical education.

Many physical educators believe that the major problem in achieving more in fitness and activity is the lack of time. If one looks at time only in terms of scheduled class time, the concern is well founded. Most elementary specialist teachers see children 1 or 2 days a week. Middle-school physical education is often 3 days per week, and the norm for high-school physical education is 5 days per week for 1 year in the ninth grade. Physical educators need to expand their horizons beyond class schedules. Physical education programs should include attractive, inclusive, invitational programs for children and youths in nonattached school time. School physical education should also be the place where children learn about community programs, are encouraged to participate, and are helped to gain access to such programs, especially those that are after-school, weekend, or summer programs.

The guidelines recommended by the CDC (1997) clearly indicate that fitness and physical activity are *schoolwide* responsibilities. For children and youths to build habits that lead to a lifetime commitment to activity, we must develop activity as a *social norm* in the school. This can be done only if the entire school believes in and supports that norm, particularly through the development of attractive programs that include all children and youths. The guidelines also suggest that the school is the hub of a school–family–community connection that supports physical activity for children and youths. In this sense, the physical education of children and youths becomes the responsibility of not only the physical education teacher but also the other classroom teachers, the principal, the parents, and the community leaders.

## ))) ) GET CONNECTED to Fitness Websites

### Fitness for Children and Youths

| | |
|---|---|
| Healthy Schools | www.healthyschools.net |
| President's Council on Physical Fitness and Sports | www.fitness.gov |
| Project Fit America | www.projectfitamerica.org |
| Health and Fitness for Kids | www.howtobefit.com/kid-fitness.htm |
| Shaping America's Youth | www.shapingamericasyouth.com |
| Fitness for Youth | www.fitnessforyouth.umich.edu |
| Physical Activity for Youth with Disabilities | www.hhs.gov/od/physicalfitness.html |
| President's Challenge | www.presidentschallenge.org |

### Fitness for Adults

| | |
|---|---|
| Worksite fitness programs | www.fitwellinc.com |
| Active | www.active.com |
| Project Fit America | www.projectfitamerica.org |
| Senior Fitness Association | www.seniorfitness.net |
| Fifty-Plus Fitness Association | www.50plus.org |

### Fitness-Related Professions and Organizations

| | |
|---|---|
| Healthy People 2010 | www.healthypeople.gov |
| National Athletic Trainers' Association | www.nata.org |
| American Physical Therapy Association | www.apta.org |
| National Strength and Conditioning Association | www.nsca-lift.org |
| American College of Sports Medicine | www.acsm.org |
| American Council on Exercise | www.acefitness.org |
| American Occupational Therapy Association | www.aota.org |
| Fitness Management | www.fitnessworld.com |
| Cooper Institute | www.cooperinst.org |
| President's Council on Physical Fitness and Sport | www.fitness.gov |
| Aerobics and Fitness Association of America | www.afaa.com |
| American Fitness Professionals & Associates | www.afpafitness.com |
| Aquatic Exercise Association | www.aeawave.com |
| National Association for Health and Fitness | www.physicalfitness.org |
| National Coalition for Promoting Physical Activity | www.ncppa.org |
| United States Water Fitness Association | www.uswfa.com |
| Canadian Fitness & Lifestyle Research Institute | www.cflri.ca |
| Get Active America | www.getactiveamerica.com |

## SUMMARY

1. Health, motor-performance, and cosmetic fitness are important both to individuals and to society. However, the demands of everyday modern life are typically insufficient for the development and maintenance of fitness.

2. The costs to society of inadequate health fitness are substantial; they include the costs of expensive health insurance, rehabilitation, reduced productivity, and lost workdays.

3. To maintain health fitness, a person must make appropriate activity a regular part of her or his lifestyle.

4. Fitness programs that affect lifestyles incorporate education, activity, planning skills, and consumer information in a comprehensive effort to produce permanent changes in exercise behavior.

5. Media images of fitness are often misleading. A national fitness-education effort would help curb the amount of fitness misinformation and help the public make wider choices about personal fitness.

6. The social gradient in health and physical activity results in inequitable access to activity programs and facilities.

7. Certification for fitness leaders would help to ensure that appropriate fitness testing and prescriptive programs are available.

8. The size of the senior population is growing, and seniors are living longer. Many seniors have many misconceptions about fitness and do not engage in activity that is as vigorous as it could be. Fitness in old age is important both for maintaining functional capacity and for improving quality of life.

9. Physical education has been strongly criticized for its lack of appropriate fitness programming, but fitness is just one of many objectives that physical educators attempt to reach.

10. The lack of sufficient time for activities that meet minimum health-fitness requirements appears to be the biggest problem for school physical education.

11. Health-related fitness among schoolchildren and youths will not be given appropriate attention until it becomes a schoolwide objective rather than an objective for physical educators alone.

12. Although substantial fitness research has been completed in the past several decades, much remains to be done at both the basic and the applied levels.

13. To achieve national goals in health and physical activity, we must develop a physical activity infrastructure of accessible programs and facilities.

## DISCUSSION QUESTIONS

1. Of what should fitness education consist if the goal is to incorporate regular fitness into the student's lifestyle?

2. Have the media advanced or hindered the goals of fitness education? How could the media be used more effectively to promote those goals?

3. Should fitness be a required school subject? Should students have to meet fitness standards on a regular basis?

4. Should physical education have fitness as its most important goal? Why or why not?

5. How can fitness be made important for *all* segments of the national population? Will it remain a mostly upper-middle-class movement?

6. If the children of today are unfit, will the adults and seniors of tomorrow also be unfit?

7. How can we reduce the amount of fitness misinformation and help the public make wiser choices about personal fitness?

# Sport

Most people who read this text have had a positive experience in sport. For many, like us, sport has been at the center of their lives and has helped form many of the fundamental experiences of their development as individuals. The sport culture in which we live is a dynamic, evolving enterprise. In many cases, the sport culture does well; in other cases, however, it does poorly. How will it evolve in the future? Who is responsible for helping sport to evolve in such a way that it will serve everyone in the future more fully than it serves us now?

These are important questions that we cannot answer without a thorough understanding of what sport is, how and by whom it is practiced, and the major problems and issues that specialists in this field must face and solve. The three chapters in Part 4 will increase your understanding of and critical thinking about sport.

## CHAPTER 10

# Basic Concepts of Sport

*The very elaborations of sport—its internal conventions of all kinds, its cere-
monies, its endless meshes entangling itself—are for the purpose of training
and testing and rewarding the rousing motion within us to find a moment of
freedom. Freedom is that state where energy and order merge and all complexity is purified into a simple coherence, a fitness of parts and purpose and
passions that cannot be surpassed and whose goal could only be to be itself.*

A. Bartlett Giamatti, former commissioner of Major League Baseball
and president of Yale University, 1989

Sport has been a part of civilized societies throughout history. In some cases, as in Greece in the fifth
century BCE, sport was of central importance to
the culture. At other times, as during the repres-
sive asceticism of the Middle Ages, sport was officially frowned upon but still enjoyed by common
people in villages and towns. At the height of the
Roman Empire, athletes formed a strong labor
union, bargaining for higher appearance fees and
prizes and keeping out athletes who would not
support the union. Sport even flourished in varied
forms in early America despite the Puritan sanctions against it. Until recently, however, few people
tried to examine and analyze sport—to understand
what it is, from what human motivations it springs,
and what role it occupies in culture.

Sport has been studied and analyzed by scholars in many disciplines since the 1950s—and increasingly since the mid-1970s when a national
and world sport culture developed beyond what
anybody could have imagined 100 years ago. The
main argument in this chapter is that sport derives
from the play impulse in human behavior, as do

art, music, and drama. Yet few artistic or dramatic
performances draw 80,000 spectators on an autumn afternoon, nor do musical events capture the
national interest in the way the National Collegiate
Athletic Association's annual basketball championship, known simply as "the Final Four," does.
The extraordinary success of recent Olympic
Games throughout the world foreshadows the development of a global sport culture that knows no
boundaries of race, gender, ethnicity, or age. Understanding sport better and forming judgments
about its role in culture are what this chapter is
about.

Most people who read this text have had significant experiences in the world of sport. Many people who aspire to a career in the physical education, fitness, and sport professions had childhood
and youth experiences in sport that were the primary motivating factors in their choice of career.
You probably *know* sport from an experiential
point of view, having participated and been a spectator, perhaps having been a referee or a coach. The
purpose of this chapter is to provide a conceptual

framework from within which you can understand your own experience of sport as well as that of the individual and the society.

By any measure, sport is important. The statistics on the number of people who are spectators and participants are impressive. The amount of money spent on sport is enormous. Sport heroes and heroines are used by corporations to advertise their products. Events such as the World Series, the Super Bowl, and the Final Four have become national celebrations, but these kinds of celebrations are also repeated endlessly in cities and towns everywhere during each of the sport seasons that together compose the sport year. For many people, young and old alike, sport has an almost religious significance.

The intensity of sport involvement is not defined by gender.

## SPORT: THE NATURAL RELIGION

Michael Novak (1976), in *The Joy of Sports*, argued that sport is a natural religion and that we must understand it as such to grasp its fundamental importance. He describes what it is like to be a *believer* among unbelievers:

> Faith in sports, I have discovered, seeks understanding.... Other believers know how hard it is to put into words what they so deeply and obscurely know. They have also argued with their wives and friends, and even in their own heads. All around this land there is a faith without an explanation, a love without a rationale. (Novak, 1976, p. xiii)

Novak's argument is not based on using a simple religious metaphor to explain sport, does not come from a sportswriter talking about the "sacrifice" of an athlete, and is not an athlete saying, "You gotta believe." His argument is based on qualities and characteristics fundamental to the sport experience and to the role that this experience plays in individual and social life:

> I am saying that sports flow outward into action from a deeper natural impulse that is radically religious: an impulse of freedom, respect for ritual limits, a zest for

symbolic meaning, and a longing for perfection. The athlete may of course be pagan, but sports are, as it were, natural religions. (Novak, 1976, p. 19)

How is sport a religion? Sport is organized and dramatized in a religious way. There are rituals (for example, the coin toss and the opening lineups). There are costumes (or "vestments," to use the religious phrase). There is a sense of powers that are outside one's control (the ball bounces to the left, the wind blows at an inopportune moment). There are those who enforce rules and mete out punishments (referees). Sport also can, when done well, teach qualities that are religious in nature, such as perseverance, courage, and sacrifice. In sport, athletes often strive for perfection just as many people do in religious orders. In sport, as in religion, there are heroes and heroines who provide models of perfection to strive for, who are admired for what they did, and who become almost saint-like. Such is the *religious* nature of sport.

Sport, like religion, can be intensely personal, yet in its fullest sense, it is *communal*. What we see and experience in sport takes us out of ourselves and lets us glimpse at something more perfect than we know ordinary life to be. The late A. Bartlett Giamatti, former president of Yale University and former commissioner of Major League Baseball, argued that sport can do this for both participant and spectator, thus further enhancing its communal nature:

> To take acts of physical toil—lifting, throwing, bending, jumping, pushing, grasping, stretching, running, hoisting, the constantly repeated acts that for millennia have meant work—and to bound them in time or by rules or boundaries in a given enclosure surrounded by an amphitheater or at least a gallery is to replicate the arena of humankind's highest aspiration. That aspiration is to be taken out of the self. (Giamatti, 1989, p. 34)

Believers in sport should neither be ashamed of their beliefs nor be reluctant to defend those beliefs. Being better able to explain and defend your commitment to sport can be a source of personal satisfaction as well as a powerful professional tool. In addition, you should not have to tolerate having others make fun of sport.

> Sports are not merely fun and games, not merely diversions, not merely entertainment. A ballpark is not a temple, but it isn't a fun house either. A baseball game is not an entertainment, and a ballplayer is considerably more than a paid performer. No one can explain the passion, commitment, discipline, and dedication involved in sports by evasions like these. (Novak, 1976, p. 23)

It is clear that for many people—perhaps for you, too—sport participation provides a source of deep personal meaning. Eleanor Metheny (1970), one of America's leading physical education scholars of the mid-twentieth century, described how sport creates conditions within which people test themselves and discover a great deal about who they are in moments of self-revelation during competition:

> Or, as the competitors in the early Olympic contests put it, every man who would submit his own excellence to the test of sport competition must "stand naked before his gods" and reveal himself as he is in the fullness of his own human powers. Stripped of all self-justifying excuses by the rules of sport, he must demonstrate his own ability to perform one human action of his own choosing, and naked of all pretense, he must use himself as he is, in all the wholeness of his being as a man. (Metheny, 1970, p. 66)

Sport has the power to teach. As Wilfred Sheed (1995) points out, sport is not necessarily a force for good, but it is indeed a force. It is such a powerful force that it not only tells you much about yourself as an individual but also reveals a great deal about the society within which sport is pursued. There is good reason, then, for us to consider sport seriously.

## LEISURE, PLAY, GAMES, AND SPORT

To understand sport, we have to examine the motivations from which it arises, the forms it takes, and the ways it has developed historically. We also have to understand four related concepts: *leisure, play, games,* and *competition*. We use the terms in our ordinary language when we discuss sport, but we also should understand their specific, technical meanings.

### Leisure

Sport developed historically as a leisure-time activity. Leisure can be distinguished from work by examining the attitude of the person, the nature of the activity, and the time dimension of the activity.

1. **Leisure** can be viewed as an attitude of freedom or release from the demands of ordinary life. This is the subjective component of an understanding of leisure, indicating the great joy and satisfaction derived from leisure activities.

2. The notion of leisure as an activity shifts the focus from the person to the event and those who are responsible for providing the services the event represents—for example, going to a golf course to play a round of golf. Leisure activities are often distinguished from work activities, in that leisure is freely chosen and not obligatory.

3. Viewed as time, leisure has traditionally been the discretionary time left over after work, family, and personal maintenance commitments are handled. The time aspect of leisure shows the leisure–work distinction most readily because the leisure attitude can be found in

work and because leisure and work activities are not always easily distinguishable. Some activities are work for some people but leisure for other people.

Leisure attitude, leisure activities, and leisure time are often thought to be related to play—that is, a playful attitude, play activities, and play time. It is in the linkage to the concept of play that we see the fundamental meaning of sport.

## Play

**Sport as a Form of Play**  Most scholars agree that sport is a manifestation of play and that sports are institutionalized forms of play. Play is also thought to be the motivating impulse underlying the development of drama, art, and music. It was the Dutch historian Johan Huizinga who first conceptualized the role of play as a basic motivation in human activity. Huizinga defined play as follows:

> Summing up the formal characteristics of play we might call it a free activity standing quite consciously outside "ordinary" life as being "not serious," but at the same time absorbing the player intensely and utterly. It is an activity connected with no material interest, and no profit can be gained by it. It proceeds within its own proper boundaries of time and space according to fixed rules and in an orderly manner. It promotes the formation of social groupings which tend to surround themselves with secrecy and to stress their differences from the common world by disguise or other means. (Huizinga, 1962, p. 13)

Play, then, is different from ordinary life, different certainly from what we typically refer to as "work." Play does not produce the products that work does, yet it seems to absorb us at least as completely, and often more so. Play, anthropologists tell us, is something that all people everywhere do, in one form or another.

The French sociologist Roger Caillois (1961) refined Huizinga's definition. His characteristics of play are now most commonly cited when sport and play are discussed and analyzed. Caillois suggested that play is free, separate, uncertain, economically unproductive,

Sport involvement often combines fun and seriousness.

and governed by rules or by make-believe. It is through an analysis of these characteristics of play that we can see how sport derives from play.

1. *Free.* Sport is most playful when people enter into it voluntarily. To the degree that sport is required or that the player cannot choose when to participate, sport becomes less playful.

2. *Separate.* Sport is conducted in places where the time and space limits are fixed in advance. It is often conducted in places designed especially for that activity—for example, the soccer stadium, baseball field, golf course, or tennis court. The playful nature of the activity seems to be enhanced when the space for doing it is separate in this sense.

3. *Uncertain.* Sport is most playful when it is uncertain, when the contestants in a competition are evenly matched. Uneven competition is not fun for participants and is boring for spectators. Much effort is made in organized sport to ensure equal competition. Handicaps are provided as in golf. School competition is often grouped by size of school, wrestling by weight class.

4. *Economically unproductive.* Activity is most playful when it does not result in any new wealth being created (as opposed to work, where creating wealth is the main purpose of the activity). A game itself typically produces no wealth as a *contest* even though participants may be paid and much money may be made from other sources—television, concessions, parking, and so on. To the extent that new wealth is produced, the playfulness of the activity decreases.

5. *Governed by rules.* Play is almost always regulated. Even young children at play typically begin by creating rules. Sport, of course, is governed by rules that standardize the competition and are agreed to by all participants as necessary for the contest to proceed. Rules are typically established to define the activity, to ensure fairness, and to produce a winner. Further, rules in sport are completely arbitrary, which is one way that play differs from work where rules tend to make sense. Why three strikes? Why two serves in tennis but not in badminton? Why 10 yards for a first down? The point is that sport is a social agreement to compete within arbitrary rules—which makes it playful—and violating those rules denies the agreement and tends to destroy the playfulness (Giamatti, 1989).

6. *Governed by make-believe.* Play that is not rule governed is dominated by make-believe. Sport typically relies on the rule-governed characteristic of play whereas drama relies on the make-believe characteristic. Still, we can see in the sport play of young children the union of these two characteristics because the children often assume the identities of their favorite players as they take part in games.

It is in these ways that we can see sport as a form of play. Clearly, *sport does not have to be playful.* We can imagine forms of sport in which each characteristic is barely present—so much so that the sport activity is mostly devoid of the play element. Such sport forms seldom survive long; it appears that for people to want to continue in sport, the play element must be present. How to maintain the play element in sport is a major focus in Chapter 12.

It is in this sense that we need to think when we use *play* as a verb—that is, I *play* basketball, or let us go *play* a game of golf, or did you *play* racquetball last night? The term does not mean merely that you have participated. Instead, it means that you have *played.*

Play is viewed by most scholars as an irreducible form of behavior present in all animal life, finding its fullest expression in human behavior. Play, therefore, represents a fundamental category of behavior that needs no further explanation. People play. Why? Because play not only is fundamental to life but also is the mode of behavior through which some of life's most meaningful moments occur.

Play is not a trivial concept. It is a concept rich with psychological, sociological, and historical meaning. It is also a sufficiently strong and rich concept to provide insight into what sport is, what sport means to people who play and watch it, and what role sport occupies in culture. It is also clear that experiences in physical education and fitness can and should have a strong playful element to sustain pleasurable involvement in those activities.

## Child's Play and Adult Play

Most developmental psychologists believe that play is the most basic form of behavior in young children and that it is through play that children acquire much of their early knowledge about the physical and social world in which they live. Do adults play also? They say, "Let's play," but do they play as children do? Adults in a racquetball court, on a golf course, or in a football game certainly do not look the same as children do when they play. We have to recognize that there are *different ways of playing*.

Caillois (1961) has suggested that ways of playing can be placed on a continuum according to the degree of spontaneity, orderliness, and regulation present in the play form. At one end of the continuum is what we typically see in the play of young children: turbulence, gaiety, spontaneity, and diversion. At the other end of the continuum is what we typically see when adults play their sports: calculation, subordination to rules, contrivance, and ritual.

This is not to suggest that one way of playing is necessarily *better* than the other way of playing. Each is appropriate at different times and for different purposes. Typically, as children grow and develop, they change their play activities toward the adult end of the continuum. It is this end of the continuum that is characterized by practice, training, rituals, costumes, skill, and strategy. That way of playing obviously appeals to the more mature person—it simply has more sustaining motivation. The appreciation for practice, strategy, skillfulness, ritual, and tradition is the main characteristic of mature involvement in play.

As play forms mature and as players mature in those forms (sport), it becomes necessary to create obstacles that must be overcome to achieve the goal of the play. The creation of new obstacles and the overcoming of them to produce a definite result are essential to continued motivation in play. Golfers, as they improve at the sport, continually look for new challenges in the courses they play. A good golf course, in this sense, is one that has obstacles that a player must overcome to shoot a good score. Thus, narrow fairways, sand traps, water hazards, and strategically placed trees all create obstacles that require strategy and skill to overcome. These obstacles make the play of golf more challenging and interesting, and they considerably increase the rewards of shooting a good score.

Sport, then, derives from the play instinct in human behavior and the play element in culture. When sport is most playful, it is most meaningful to the participants. When sport loses its playfulness, the meaning is lessened for the participants (but not necessarily for the spectators).

## Games

Although the terms *game* and *sport* are often used interchangeably, there are important distinctions between them. One way to view sport is as a game occurrence—but sport can be viewed in other ways, too. Therefore, the two concepts are related in some ways but not in others.

A **game** is "any form of playful competition whose outcome is determined by physical skill, strategy or chance employed singly or in a combination" (Loy, 1969, p. 56). There are three important parts to this definition. First, games derive from play. Second, games involve competition. Third, the outcome of the game is determined by use of physical skill, strategy, or chance. Not all games are sport, but sport is always a game. This is true even though we do not typically describe some sport involvement as game involvement; competing in a mile run is not described as "playing a game," but it does fit the definition. Some scholars differentiate games from contests and describe activities such as swimming or marathoning as contests rather than as games, but the activities are so similar that each can be referred to as a "game" in the sense defined here.

Competition is a defining characteristic of games and a fundamental quality of sport. In all team games, players must cooperate in order to play the game well; thus cooperation or "team play" is crucial to success in competitions.

Sports are games that involve combinations of physical skill and strategy. Games that have outcomes determined primarily by chance—dice, for example—are not sports. Even though there clearly are *chance elements* in sport, such as weather changes or the errant bounce of a ball, these are not the primary determinants of outcomes. Games that involve strong elements of strategy but involve no physical skill are also not sports; bridge, chess, and other board games are examples.

Each sport game is different because each game poses a problem to be solved—what Almond (1986) termed the game's **primary rules**. The primary rules of a game identify how the game is to be played and how winning can be achieved. The primary rules of a game are what make basketball different from volleyball, even though both games are played with a ball on a court.

Games also have many **secondary rules**, which typically define the institutionalized form of the game, or what we might call the *parent* game. Secondary rules can be altered or modified to make the game more developmentally appropriate or different in some other way without changing the essential character of the game, which is defined by the primary rules. The 3-second zone rule and the 10-second half-court rule in basketball are examples of secondary rules. They can be changed without changing the essential elements that define the game as

Extreme sports, popular with the millennial generation (Gen Y), often involve high-risk maneuvers.

basketball. The primary rule of volleyball is to strike the ball over a net in a divided court in such a way that it either cannot be returned by opponents or hits the floor within the opponent's side of the court. Secondary rules include the height of the net, the size of the ball, the size of the court, and the number of hits per side.

Sport games can be categorized in several ways, but for our purposes, it will be most useful to examine a category scheme based on the similarities among the primary rules that define the games (Almond, 1983). This game classification has four categories: (1) territory or invasion games, (2) target games, (3) court games, and (4) sector games.

1. *Territory* or *invasion games* are defined by the problem of needing to invade the space of the opponent to score. Two types of territory-invasion games are those in which goals are used (basketball, ice hockey, soccer, team handball, lacrosse, water polo, and so on) and those in which lines are used (American football, Australian rules football, rugby, speed-ball, and so on). Territory-invasion games can be further subdivided according to whether the game involves the use of the hand with a ball (basketball), the foot with a ball (soccer), or a stick with a ball (hockey).

2. *Target games* are defined by the primary rules of propelling objects with great accuracy toward targets. Target games can be subdivided according to whether the opponents are directly opposed (croquet, horseshoes, curling, and so on) or indirectly opposed (golf, bowling). In the former, one plays directly against one's opponent, often hitting the other player's ball, for example. In the latter, one plays against the target (the pins, the par on the golf hole) and then compares scores with an opponent.

3. *Court games* are those in which an object is strategically propelled in such a way that it cannot be returned by an opponent. Court games can be subdivided according to whether the court is divided (badminton, tennis, table tennis, and so on) or shared (handball, squash, jai alai,

and so on). Court-divided games typically use a net. Court-shared games typically rely on rebounds from walls.

4. *Sector games* are defined by primary rules that require one opponent to strike an object such as to elude defenders on the field. The shape of the field might differ somewhat (fan shaped or oval shaped), but the basic natures of the games are similar. Cricket, baseball, softball, and rounders are examples.

A knowledge of games—of their meaning and function—is fundamental to the person interested in understanding sport. New games develop all the time. Sometimes the new games become sports; sometimes they do not. Frisbee is a good example. On any spring afternoon, you can see students throwing Frisbees in open spaces, but there is seldom a *game* going on, and no one would call it a *sport*. Yet Frisbee has developed into a sport/game called "ultimate Frisbee"—one for which there are rules and growing traditions. Frisbee as a sport is in the process of becoming *institutionalized;* that is, it is changing from an informal game to an institutionalized sport. To become institutionalized, a sport must be defined with standardized rules to which all players adhere, must have a governing body, and must encompass a growing sense of tradition that binds people to it.

Not all sports fit these categories of games. Track and field, swimming, wrestling, surfing, ski jumping, and bobsledding are all sports but are seldom referred to as games even though many of these sports are part of the Olympic Games or Pan American Games. An entirely new group of sports have developed over the past quarter-century, created mostly by young people, many of whom were associated with youth subcultures most commonly referred to as Generation X or, more recently, the millennial generation, known also as Gen Y. These sports are most commonly described as "extreme sports" and include skateboarding, in-line skating, snowboarding, skiing, and BMX racing. Many scholars associate the development of these sports as similar to the counterculture sport movement of surfing in the 1960s.

Many of these new sports combine high-level athletic skill along with high-level risk. Extreme sports also tend to encourage individual creativity that creates higher risk. Skateboarding hero Tony Hawk explained the motivation for participation in these new, risk activities: "I liked having my own pace and my own rules … and making up my own challenges" (Finger, 2004, p. 84). Participation in extreme sports was motivated by an individualism that was nearly opposite of the values espoused by youth and school sports—that is, the values of teamwork, cooperation, conformity, and character (Lauer, 2006). Many of these sports are in the process of becoming institutionalized as demonstrated by the creation of the X Games and the ESPN television channel.

## Competition in Sport and Games

Sport and games involve competition. Without competition, there is no game. Yet competition is among the most seriously misunderstood concepts in physical education, fitness, and sport. Almost everybody has strong views about competition. Some people advocate competition at all costs as a positive virtue. Others view competition as inherently bad and want to make sports less competitive. Because competition is a controversial issue, it is necessary to examine the concept closely and to understand its different meanings in relation to the concepts of sport and games. Competition is almost always defined first as a rivalry in which opponents strive to gain something at the expense of each other. This definition tends to emphasize the use of the term in economics and business. Far too often, competition in sport is defined exclusively in this economic sense. One form of competition, stemming from the world of economics, is **zero-sum competition**. In a zero-sum competition, whatever is gained by one competitor must necessarily be lost by the other competitor; that is, to the extent that I win, you must lose. One sometimes hears overzealous coaches state that "winning isn't the most important thing, it's the only thing" or "defeat is worse than death." Those kinds of remarks reflect a zero-sum view of competition.

The concept of competition is far richer than that—especially when used in reference to sport. There are three important and related meanings of the concept of competition (Siedentop, 1981). The first meaning is *to come together,* which denotes the festive aspects of competition. When the term is used as a noun (as in "Let's have a competition"), we can sense the notion of a festival. All the world's great sport competitions are clearly festivals—the Olympic Games, the Super Bowl, the World Cup in soccer. We find similar festivals on a smaller scale at high-school football games, children's soccer games, and adult equestrian competitions. This festive nature of sport is the clearest evidence of its communal importance. Sport involves rituals and traditions. The *festive* nature of competition is where the rituals and traditions are most easily seen, and the festive nature of sport competition is one of its most appealing attributes.

A second meaning of the concept of competition is to strive to achieve an objective; it is what we call the *competence* meaning of the term. The words *compete* and *competence* derive from the Latin word *competere.* Competition provides a forum within which people strive to become competent, to become excellent. When rules and conditions are standardized, performances can be compared fairly, and competitors can learn about their strengths and weaknesses.

Many scholars believe the pursuit of competence—trying to get better—is a fundamental, sustaining motivation for sport involvement (Alderman & Wood, 1976; Coakley, 2007; Eitzen & Sage, 2003). This belief comes from evidence showing that young athletes rank wanting to get better as a primary motivation for their continued participation. They also rate being with friends and being part of a team (affiliation) as a strong motivation. It also should be noted that these motivations are ranked higher than the excitement of competition or beating another person or team.

The third meaning of the concept of competition is the one with which we are most familiar—to be in a state of *rivalry.* The opportunities for rivalry within sport are many and varied: team against team, individual against individual, individual against a record, individual against a previous best performance, individual against a physical barrier. Many of these rivalry motivations coexist in one contest. When 55,000 runners started the New York Marathon last year, it is difficult to describe their competitive motivation as a zero-sum rivalry. If that were true, there would be three winners (men's, women's, and seniors) and 54,997 losers! The fact is that few athletes view their own competition as a zero-sum phenomenon. Occasionally a coach does, or a parent, or a sportswriter.

Within the boundaries of a sport, individuals and groups compete, but seldom, if ever, is that competition a zero-sum arrangement. There are many ways to win and to lose within a competition, and the winning and losing have meaning only within the competition and, even then, only momentarily. If winning or losing has meaning that carries over from the competition to other aspects of life, then it clearly diminishes the play element in the competition.

Sport, therefore, can be understood as a game occurrence in which playful competition is the primary motivational force. The *players* can practice diligently, train seriously, prepare strategically, and compete vigorously yet still manifest the play element in its fullest. Factors such as unevenly matched opponents, required participation, economic consequences, and pressures for winning that carry over to real life outside the sport event seriously diminish the play element in sport.

## THE INSTITUTIONALIZATION OF SPORT

Somewhere, sometime, someone thought of a new game to play. Rules were suggested, the goal of the game was explained, equipment was probably designed, and special space was acquired. The game was played and enjoyed. Perhaps it was enjoyed sufficiently that others who have seen it want to play it. The rules were then written down, a sketch of the space (for example, field or court) was made, and the needed equipment was listed. Each time that the new game was played, it was no doubt changed slightly to meet local needs and interests and to accommodate local problems with equipment and facilities. Eventually, however, some *common form of the game* was needed because many people wanted to try the game. At that point, the game began to become institutionalized (see Focus On Box 10.1).

No doubt, something akin to this process happened for the several games invented in America in the late nineteenth century—basketball, softball, and volleyball. They started as local games for local purposes. Today, they are international games with rules, traditions, rituals, governing bodies, and championships. When volleyball is played in a developing nation, it is essentially the same game as that played here and everywhere else. The game has a common form that is recognized internationally. It has become a fully institutionalized sport.

It is important to understand sport as a social institution. Most people who enter the various professions associated with sport can do so because sport is thoroughly institutionalized in developed societies. Think for a moment of the role that the following professionals occupy relative to sport:

- The orthopedic surgeon who is a sport-medicine specialist
- The sportswriter
- The radio or television sport commentator
- The sport manager

---

**FOCUS ON** — Sport Institutionalization in Progress: The Evolution of Extreme Sports — **10.1**

In the 1980s, when the term *extreme sports* first was used, it referred to adult sports such as skydiving, scuba diving, surfing, rock climbing, waterskiing, mountain biking, and hang gliding. The magazine *Outside,* with its focus on marketing outdoor clothing from The North Face and Patagonia, was a main resource. Competitions were mostly local. Also in the 1980s, young boys were increasingly drawn to activities that represented values (individualism, risk, a flair for creating their own performance clothing) that were nearly the opposite of those espoused in youth and school sport (cooperation, teamwork, subordination to leadership, uniforms).

The label "Extreme Sports" was used by ESPN in 1995 in their planning for the initial Extreme Games (now the X Games). The X Games are now held each year. The 2011 Summer X Games 17 were held in Los Angeles; the 2010 Winter X Games 12 were held in Aspen.

The Summer X Games competitions are Freestyle BMX, MotoX, Skateboarding, Surfing, and Rallying. Within each of these competition categories are subcategory competitions; for example, the competition categories within Freestyle BMX are Vert, Park, and Big Air. The Winter X Games competitions are Skiing, Snowboarding, Snowmobiling, and Snowskating. The competition categories within Snowboarding are Slopestyle, Snowboarder, SuperPipe, and Best Trick. In many categories, there are separate competitions for men and women.

The X Games are shown live on ESPN and ABC with videoclips available on ESPN.com. Nearly 40 million viewers tuned in to X Games coverage with the highest rating ever for young male viewers. Attendance has increased steadily, currently reaching near 150,000. Concurrent with the X Games competitions is the X Fest sports and music festival with live music and interaction with competitors. The increasing difficulty of the "tricks" performed by X Games competitors has been assisted by innovations in technologies—for example, advances in ski design, rubber-soled climbing shoes, artificial climbing walls, and better-designed and lighter knee braces. Extreme sports are now competed throughout the world with the Planet X Games in Australia, the Asian X Games, the Latin X Games, and the Dubai X Games.

- The referee or umpire
- The sport administrator
- The coach
- The trainer
- The equipment specialist
- The sport promoter
- The sport strength coach

Conspicuously absent from that list is the sport performer! The sport performer is the *only* person necessary for sport to take place at a local level, at a level that is casually organized, flexible, and *not yet institutionalized.* (How many of these other sport types are necessary for a pickup softball game?) All roles other than participant develop as sport becomes more highly institutionalized to the point in some sports where all these sport specialists far outnumber the people who actually play the game.

## The Codification of Rules

As a sport becomes institutionalized, it adopts certain characteristics. First, the rules governing the sport are *codified.* The same rules are supposed to govern all contests, and there is typically a system through which the codified rules are enforced and, from time to time, changed. How people are to play the game and what is expected of them within the game are defined primarily by the rules and secondarily by the traditions that develop within the sport as it becomes institutionalized. Why does the crowd get so quiet when a golfer putts, whereas in basketball the crowd makes extra noise when an opponent shoots a free throw? The answer cannot be found in the nature of the two skills or in the official rules of the two sports but only in the traditions of how the two sports have developed over time.

## The Role of the Referee

The codification of rules for a sport typically produces the need for trained officials and referees. The importance of a referee to a sport is misunderstood by the public and often by sportspersons, too.

The referee plays a crucial role in ensuring a fair contest.

The nature of sport is to strive for victory within a set of rules and conditions that are similar for all contestants; that is, sport is meaningful only when it is a *fair* contest. The main role of the referee is to ensure fairness by seeing that all contestants honor the rules and that no contestants get an advantage that is disallowed by the rules. The more highly institutionalized a sport becomes, the greater is the need to train and supervise referees so that the contests are played as much in accordance with the rules as is possible.

## The Genesis of Sport Organizations

As sport becomes more institutionalized, it is natural that those associated with the sport want to see whether they, or their teams, are the best for that particular sport season. It seems to be in the nature of sport competition to want to find out who is best at the moment. For people to find out who is best, certain conditions need to be present. First, of course, all participants and teams have to be playing the same game, using the same rules. After the game becomes standardized, there has to be a schedule of playing that allows individuals and teams to compete against others. Also, an agreement has to be reached for a means through which the best can be selected each season. This all requires organization—and these very motivations led to the formation of sport associations and sport conferences.

A group of local teams might form a league to arrange a predictable schedule and to determine a local champion at the end of a sport season. A city or a state might organize a competition that allows a champion to be determined at that level. A national organization such as the Athletic Congress or the NCAA organizes individual and team championships for its members nationwide. An organization has to be created to arrange these competitions, to schedule facilities, and to secure officials. At most local levels, these organizations can be staffed by volunteers. As the sport becomes more institutionalized, however, the organizations become more formal and require full-time workers. This creates the need for trained people to do these specialized jobs and leads to the development of professions such as sport management, sport promotion, and sport administration.

## The Importance of Records

As soon as a sport begins to become standardized, people begin to keep records. Records are important to sport in many ways. Many have argued that the central motivation in sport is striving for excellence. Records are one important way that excellence is defined and preserved. They provide standards against which participants measure their improvement and set their goals. They also provide items of great interest to those who follow the sport but do not necessarily participate in it.

Without standard rules and good officiating, records could not assume the importance that they

do in sport. When we can be reasonably sure that the competition was fair, then the record produced becomes part of the legend of the sport. The records that are of most general interest are those describing the limits beyond which men, women, or teams have yet been unable to go (Weiss, 1969).

Think of the almost magical importance that new records create in the world of sport. My memories are of Michael Johnson obliterating the 200-meter sprint world record in the 1996 Olympics and Bob Beamon not only breaking the world record in the long jump at the Mexico City Olympics but also moving the record completely through the 28-foot barrier by jumping over 29 feet. I can recall Joe Dimaggio's 56-game hitting streak and the first sub-4-minute mile run by Roger Bannister, Wilt Chamberlin's 100-point NBA game, as well as Wilma Rudolph's four gold medals at the Rome Olympics. You are more likely to remember Michael Phelps's eight medals in swimming at the Beijing Olympics in 2008, Tiger Woods's domination of the PGA Men's Tour, the Boston Patriots undefeated season of 2007–08, or the classic match-up between the Boston Celtics and Los Angelis Lakers in the 2010 NBA finals. These memorable moments not only set new standards for athletes of the future but also give us a momentary glimpse of what is possible in human endeavor.

Records become standards through which young athletes define their improvement. Research has shown that for many young athletes the primary motivation for continued participation is increased *competence,* the desire to get better at some event or skill that has value in the sport culture. *Getting better* is most easily judged in reference to standards within the sport, and standards are typically records of past performances by others in similar age groups and settings. For example, most aspiring age-group swimmers know exactly what a new personal best time means for them. They know what the time means not only with respect to their local swim team and local competition but also compared with regional, state, and national norms for the same event and the same age group. Their progress and their potential will be defined and charted by those kinds of comparisons.

In other sports, the comparison of performance and the establishment of competence cannot be accomplished so neatly through records as it can in swimming or track and field. In sports such as basketball or baseball, the records are important— batting average, points per game, rebounds, strikeouts— but they are all established under slightly different conditions against different kinds of opponents. Thus, in sports such as these, it becomes necessary to test oneself directly against the competition to find out one's own limits.

Records, however, are not just benchmarks that provide goals that define excellence. Performing in record fashion or witnessing a record-setting performance is deeply important to the nature of sport, and it is one reason why people pursue sport, both as athletes and as spectators. Records play a vital role in sport. They provide much of the tradition of a sport. They define sport heroes and heroines. They provide standards for measuring one's improvement. They provide goals for which to strive. For the afficionado who follows the sport, they provide endless hours of pleasure in reading, discussing, even arguing about the relative merits of one performance versus another, one performer versus another, or one team versus another.

## The Public Nature of Institutionalized Sport

As sport becomes institutionalized, it assumes a public role. It becomes part of a culture, locally at first, then perhaps regionally, and, for some sports, nationally and even internationally. The general importance of the sport at any of these cultural levels is proportional to the number of people who are interested in following the sport—the more fan interest there is, the more public attention is devoted to the sport.

It is this facet of institutionalized sport that is responsible for sport journalism, sport broadcasting, and sport literature. The first two, at least, are historically recent phenomena, depending as they do on modern technologies. It is no simple coincidence that the late nineteenth century in the United States was not only the period of the emergence of organized sport as a major cultural phenomenon but also the time at which communications technologies began to emerge in their modern forms.

The invention of the telegraph in the 1840s made it possible to communicate sport results over long distances. By the 1880s, newspapers had begun to devote separate sections to sport in their daily editions. The emergence of radio allowed for immediate vicarious enjoyment of live sport events across great distances. Television, of course, completely revolutionized sport spectating and is probably mainly responsible for the recent, enormous growth in sport. Now cable and satellite capabilities provide immediate worldwide access to endless numbers of different sporting events.

Sport is now big business as information and entertainment. Sport sections in newspapers have grown larger. The number of sport magazines in shops seems endless. Books on the techniques of various sports are widely available. DVDs for sport instruction have also become widely available. All of this sport-related information has created new jobs for persons who want a nonparticipant sport vocation. Sport literature and sport films have come of age. Books such as David Halberstam's *The Breaks of the Game* (basketball) and *The Amateurs* (rowing), Mark Harris's *Bang the Drum Slowly* (baseball), and W. P. Kensella's *Shoeless Joe*, from which the film *Field of Dreams* was made, provide a serious sport literature. When *Chariots of Fire* captured the Academy Award for Best Picture in 1981, it marked the start of an era of sport films that won critical acclaim and were box-office hits—for example, *Bull Durham, Tin Cup, A League of Their Own, The Legend of Bagger Vance, Remember the Titans,* and *Secretariat.* In 2005 *Million Dollar Baby,* a film about a female boxer, won the Academy Award for Best Picture.

All of this public attention has made sport a part of our everyday life in America. It has created a number of new sport professions, and it has contributed to the further institutionalization of sport—more rituals, more traditions, more attention to records. It has moved sport from the periphery of American culture, where it was in the 1850s, to the center—all in the relatively short period of one century.

## SPORT SPECTATING

Sport spectating is among our most frequently mentioned leisure-time activities. Early in the twentieth century, watching sports was considered to be an inappropriate behavior, especially if done too often. The term used by physical education professionals was *spectatoritis,* and its medical connotation was purposely chosen. It was thought to be like a disease.

Most of us enjoy watching sports on occasion. Many of us enjoy watching sports often. Are we wasting our time? Should we be using our time in a more productive way? We cannot completely understand sport without including sport spectating in the analysis.

The sport spectator is not like a fan who responds emotionally but not intellectually to sport. The sport spectator is also often a sophisticated, knowledgeable, and appreciative viewer. Fans watch sport not just to see the contest, not just to see who wins, but also to see athletes perform within a contest in which the standards are clear and rules are enforced so that the playing field is indeed "level." Modern television has created new generations of informed spectators. Instant replay, telestrators, slow-motion replay, and technical analysis by commentators have provided viewers with an in-depth education in the skills and tactics of the sport being viewed. The subtle nuances that show the individual excellence of players or the collective excellence of a team offensive or defensive maneuver are revealed immediately after an exciting moment during a contest so that the viewer not only participates in the excitement of the moment but also gets an immediate education in what produced that excitement.

Often, however, the sport spectator is not just a knowledgeable observer, a detached connoisseur who lacks emotion and passion about sport events. The sport spectator is also often a fan. Some sport events can be watched for the sheer pleasure of seeing grace in action, an excellent contest, or a well-played game, but other sport competitions must be viewed from one side or the other. How often have you sat at a competition next to a seemingly calm, mature viewer who at some point in the game transformed into an exuberant, partisan fan? How often have you experienced the same transformation yourself?

Sport loyalties often run deep. Modern society is extremely mobile. People move often. Sport is one of the few cultural institutions that has provided a sense of enduring meaning and continuity in the midst of mobility and change. A person's allegiance to a local team, to a university team, or to a professional team can form a sense of belonging and permanence. This is one of the important meanings of being a fan. Fans *root* for their team. The choice of terms is important. A *root* is the attached or embedded part of any structure, the part that holds the structure in position, the essential or core part of the structure. To root for a team means to *be rooted* in the fortunes of that team:

> To watch a sports event is not like watching a set of abstract patterns. It is to take a risk, to root and to be rooted. Some people, it is true, remain detached; they seem like mere voyeurs. The mode of observation proper to a sports event is *to participate*—that is, to extend one's own identification to one side, and to absorb with it the blows of fortune, to join that team in testing the favors of the Fates. (Novak, 1976, p. 144; emphasis in original)

The behavior of the sport fan, then, is an important part of the sport; to understand what sport is and how it has become so important to us, we must consider the role of the fan. The term *fan,* short for *fanatic,* is related to the Latin word *fanum,* which translates as "temple" or "feast." The original relationships of these terms take us full circle to the religious nature of sport, where we began this chapter.

One kind of aesthetic beauty is seen in form sports such as diving.

## SPORT AESTHETICS

Have you ever watched a game or a sport performance and seen something done by an individual or a team that made you say, "That's beautiful"? If so, you have reacted to the aesthetic quality of sport, the beauty that sometimes seems so evident in sport performance. In that sense, sport is the people's art!

Sport and athletes have always been subjects for art. In early Greek culture, where sport was so fundamental to social life, artists often used athletes as subjects, creating sculpture and decorating vases with depictions of athletes in action. Throughout history, artists have been intrigued by the physical beauty of the athletic body and the visual beauty of athletic performance. The fact that sport and athletes have been the subjects for artists' portrayals,

however, does not mean that sport itself has aesthetic value.

To understand the aesthetic value of sport, we must find beauty *in sport* rather than in paintings or sculpture. As sport became the object for intellectual analysis and investigation during the twentieth century, aestheticians, as well as historians, psychologists, and sociologists, began to consider it seriously. Their work has helped us understand the artistic dimensions and qualities of sport.

If sport *is* art, then it most certainly is a performing art—like music, dance, and drama. The beauty of the art is found in the performance itself, and it is through understanding the source of that beauty in performance that we can begin to appreciate the aesthetic qualities of sport. When considering **sport aesthetics**, we must divide sport into two categories: (1) form sports and (2) all other sports.

## Aesthetics of Form Sports

In some sports, the physical form of the performance is the determining factor in the competition— diving, gymnastics, and figure skating are prime examples. In these sports, the performer consciously works toward achieving a physical form that is aesthetically pleasing, that is beautiful. These kinds of sport performances are typically decided by a judging system, and the judges look for aesthetic qualities in the performance.

The aesthetic qualities evident in **form sports** are harmony, form, dynamics, flow, gracefulness, rhythm, and poise (Lowe, 1977). *Harmony,* for example, refers to the correct relation of parts to a whole, the way in which a sequence of movements brings about a harmonious whole. The instructions in an international gymnastics handbook describe it this way:

> While in all exercises on the apparatus we are always involved with harmony, this concept and evaluation factor will have to be given even greater attention in the floor exercises, where handsprings, Saltos and kips are combined with pauses and gymnastic elements; where strength and movement have to follow in a harmonious manner, harmony will play an ever greater role. (Lowe, 1977, p. 176)

It is in form sport that the aesthetic qualities of sport are most easily seen and most often remarked on. Commentators, spectators, and sportswriters often use descriptive aesthetic language when talking or writing about gymnastics, ice dancing, synchronized swimming, and diving.

What is important to remember about form sports is that they are *sports*! The goal of a sport performance is to achieve victory, to strive to do the best you can to win. In other artistic performances, this competition element is less obvious. In form sport, the athlete wants her or his performance to look beautiful in order to gain a position as high as possible in the competition. Does this mean that in sports other than form sports the aesthetic quality is lost? I do not think so.

## Aesthetic Quality of Other Sports

The beauty and artistry in figure skating or diving are easily seen, but what beauty can we find in a rugby match, a marathon run, or an ice-hockey game? Of course, games and contests do not have to be beautiful to be enjoyable for spectator and competitor alike. It is common, after a hard-won victory, to hear a coach or player say, "It wasn't pretty, but we got the job done." Nonetheless, both competitors and spectators feel enhanced enjoyment of sport when a good competition also has an aesthetic quality.

In what ways do we experience sport as beautiful? Carlisle (1974) has suggested four types of beauty present in sport:

1. *The beauty of a well-developed body in motion.* The high hurdler, the agile football running back, the field-hockey player winding between defenders, and the slalom skier all show efficient, graceful effort applied to solving a particular performance problem.

2. *The beauty of a brilliant play or a perfectly executed maneuver.* This quality combines the beauty of the physical performance with strong competitive intelligence in which decisions are made quickly and then well executed. This happens especially in team sports where all the players on a team move as if in some intricately choreographed series of maneuvers to achieve a competitive outcome. Bill Bradley (Rhodes Scholar and professional basketball player for

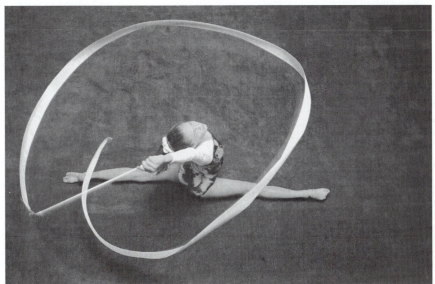

Rhythmic gymnastics have a high aesthetic quality.

the New York Nicks) described that beauty in this way: "In my Knicks days, there was no feeling comparable to the one I got when the teams came together—those nights when five guys moved as one. The moment was one of beautiful isolation, the result of the correct blending of human forces at the proper time and to the exact degree" (Bradley, 1998, p. 21).

3. *The beauty in a dramatic competition.* Sport is most aesthetically appealing when the outcome is uncertain. Competitions that ebb and flow in favor of one team or competitor, then the other, produce a dramatic tension that is among the most attractive of the aesthetic qualities of sport. This quality is experienced more strongly when the spectator is involved, rooting for one team or the other, rather than by the more detached observer.

4. *The beauty in the unity of an entire performance.* No doubt, each of us can remember a game or competition that engendered high-level excellence for all competitors, in which the dramatic tension of competition produced a unified experience that is perhaps the ultimate beauty in sport. In outstanding sport events, such beauty is apparent from the outset through to the dramatic conclusion of the game or event.

Sport in which athletes exhibit some or all of these aesthetic qualities helps explain why sport is so popular and has achieved such a central role in culture.

## SPORT ETHICS

*Ethics* is a branch of the subdiscipline of philosophy termed *axiology,* the study of values. Ethics, or *moral philosophy,* is concerned with how people *ought* to behave, particularly in situations in which there is potential for behaving well or poorly. For many reasons, sport has always been considered an important place in which to learn about ethical or moral behavior. The traditional general term used to discuss and examine ethical behavior in sport is *sportsmanship* although a better, gender-neutral term is *fair play.*

Many people believe deeply that participation in sport builds character and that some of the character traits it develops predispose people toward ethical behavior. Coaches often ascribe this power to sport when they talk at banquets about the developmental experiences that youths get through sport. On the other hand, we do not need to have had much experience in sport, as either a participant or a spectator, to know that players sometimes cheat, that coaches bend rules, that fights occur, and that it is possible for youths to learn unethical behavior through sport experience. How, then, is sport related to ethics, and how is ethics related to sport?

### Fair Play and the British Tradition

The concept of **fair play** encompasses how a sportsperson behaves not only during a contest but also before and after it. The notion of fair play means that one plays by the rules, does not take unfair advantage of an opponent even when the opportunity arises, treats the opponent with respect, and shows modesty and composure in both victory and defeat. Although elements of fair play can be seen historically in many sport cultures, it was the aristocratic British sport of the nineteenth century that elevated fair play to a way of life as well as a way of competing in sport.

The philosophy of fair play in nineteenth-century England was termed *Arnoldism* after the popular headmaster of the Rugby School, an elite secondary school. Thomas Arnold believed that sport should be played fairly and vigorously with opponents always honoring one another, showing both moral character and team spirit.

Because American sport was strongly influenced by British sport, it is not surprising that the philosophy of fair play still permeates sport today, especially sport in schools. This philosophy not only prescribes how one ought to behave within sport but also uses sport as a metaphor for how life should be lived. It is the antithesis of a "win-at-all-costs" approach to

Competitors are often bonded together in their quest for excellence.

sport competition. Within the tradition of fair play, the primary goal of sport is victory within the letter and spirit of the rules, but not victory at any cost.

> Honorable victory is the goal of the athlete, and, as a result, the code of the athlete demands that nothing be done before, during, or after the contest to cheapen or otherwise detract from such a victory. (Keating, 1973, p. 170)

## Rules and the Nature of Games

Those who study the ethical nature of sport often focus on rules and how rules are related to the purposes of games. The argument made is that the game is changed when the rules are bent, broken, or misused, and, therefore, that it is not possible *really* to win unless the rules are kept:

> The end in poker is not to gain money, nor in golf to simply get a ball into a hole, but to do these things in prescribed (or, perhaps more accurately, not to do them in proscribed) ways: that is, to do them only in accordance with rules. Rules in games thus seem to be in some sense inseparable from ends.... If the rules are broken, the original end becomes impossible of attainment, since one cannot (really) win the game unless he plays it, and one cannot (really) play the

game unless he obeys the rules of the game. (Suits, 1976, pp. 149–150)

The rule violations referred to in such an analysis are of course those done intentionally. Rules are often broken in games, and referees are there to notice the infractions and to apply the appropriate penalty so that the game may continue. The purpose of the penalty is typically to restore evenness to the contest, to provide for the offended player or team some measure that makes up for what was lost—a free throw in basketball, a loss of yardage in football, or time off the ice in hockey.

Considerable evidence shows that cheating in organized competitive sports is a growing problem (Morgan, 2007). What might be considered cheating ranges from a baseball catcher quickly making a slight movement of the caught pitch back into the strike zone to influence the umpire to call the pitch a strike or an offensive lineman anticipating the snap count to gain the edge on a blocking assignment to the use of performance-enhancing substances by athletes in a growing number of professional sports. Evidence over the past decade has shown that use of performance-enhancing drugs has moved into high-school sports as young athletes seek to gain athletic scholarships to major universities and the adulation and potential income that is earned by the small percentage that make it all the way to professional sport.

## THE DEVELOPMENTAL POTENTIAL OF SPORT

Parents, educators, and youth-development specialists want children to become involved in sport programs because they believe that sport experiences make positive contributions to the development of children and adolescents. The developmental expectations include a healthier child due to regular involvement in the physical activity provided in sport programs and the social–psychological benefits of self-confidence, resilience, and capacity to work productively within a peer group, all of which contribute to a growing sense of self-efficacy (Policy Studies Associates, 2006).

The venues for sport as child or youth development include out-of-school community and agency programs that include sport and physical activity in their programs, community sport programs that provide age-group instruction and competition, private-sector programs that provide fee-for-service programs (particularly in sports such as gymnastics and ice hockey), and school physical education, intramural, and interscholastic sports programs. Some of these programs are inclusive in the sense that all children or youths that want to participate are included, whereas others are selective.

Most out-of-school programs (such as those administered by the Boys and Girls Clubs of America or local recreation departments) include physical activity and sport as part of their programming. There is substantial evidence that out-of-school programs, either community programs or agency programs, can contribute to child or youth resiliency. Evidence suggests that well-run programs improve school attendance and grades, lower dropout rates, and inspire higher aspirations. Indeed, evidence also shows that many of these programs use sport and physical activity as the "hook" to recruit and retain children and youths in their programs (Policy Studies Associates, 2006).

Does sport build character as so many sport enthusiasts have argued for centuries? Or does sport corrupt character, teaching children and youths how to cheat cleverly and take advantage of rules and opponents? The answer is, Sport teaches! It has the capacity to teach not only positive outcomes but also negative outcomes. Sport, when done well, teaches valuable lessons of perseverance, teamwork, and loyalty. Whether any sport experience is more likely to build character than to corrupt depends on those who plan, administer, and teach in the program.

## SUMMARY

1. Sport has been a part of every civilized culture but has been taken seriously by scholars only in recent times—a fact that is surprising, given the amount of money and attention devoted to sport by people of all ages.

2. *Sport* has rituals, costumes, symbolic meaning, a striving for perfection, a system of rules, and a means for enforcing the rules—all the elements of a natural religion. These elements underscore the seriousness with which we should view sport.

3. Sport derives from play—activity that is free, separate, uncertain, economically unproductive, and governed by rules or make-believe. Although sport does not have to be playful, participants enjoy it most when it is.

4. *Play* is an irreducible form of human behavior that provides meaning in life and is thought to be a creative element in culture.

5. Child's play is characterized by spontaneity, exuberance, and gaiety; adult play is typically characterized by practice, training, ritual, skill, and strategy.

6. A *game* is a playful competition where outcomes are determined by combinations of physical skill, strategy, and chance. Games derive from play, and sports can be thought of as games or contests in which skill and strategy predominate.

7. Games are, by definition, competitive; a "non-competitive game" would be a contradiction in terms.

8. Sport games have *primary rules*, which define the problem to be solved, and *secondary rules*, which give form to the game but can be altered without changing the essence of the game.

9. Sport games can be categorized as invasion games, target games, court games, and sector games.

10. *Competition* has three related meanings. First, it is a festival that provides a forum for contests and carries with it traditions and rituals. Second, it is a striving for competence within the rules of the forum. Third, it is a rivalry for victory.

11. Competition in sport is seldom a zero-sum arrangement in which losers must lose to the extent that winners win.

12. As sport becomes more institutionalized, an increasing number of professional roles develop. The process of institutionalization ranges from local to international.

13. Sport becomes more institutionalized as rules are codified, referees are specially trained, organizations form to manage and administer activities, records are kept formally, and public communication develops through radio, television, newspapers, magazines, books, and videocassettes.

14. Spectating is an important part of institutionalized sport. Sport spectators are among the most knowledgeable and sophisticated spectators for any cultural pastime.

15. Spectators are also often fans who have deep loyalties to teams and who contribute to the total meaning of the sport experience.

16. Sport has aesthetic value and can be viewed as an art form. Form sports, in particular, have high aesthetic value, in that performances are judged by the degree to which they achieve beautiful physical form and motion.

17. There are four types of aesthetic value in sport: the beauty of trained bodies in motion, the beauty of a brilliant play or performance, the dramatic tension produced by competition that is uncertain, and the unity of a well-played game or match.

18. *Sport ethics* is the study of values in sport. It focuses primarily on sportsmanship.

19. The fair-play tradition of British sport involves both how to compete and how to behave before, during, and after the competition.

20. Most of sport ethics focuses on rules and their violation because rules give the sport its form, and violations of them break the contract between opponents to compete fairly.

## DISCUSSION QUESTIONS

1. How do important local sport events, such as a high-school football game, show the characteristics of sport as a natural religion?

2. Can scholarship and professional athletes still be engaged in play when they are playing their sport? Explain your answer.

3. To what extent does the game-classification system depend on similarities and differences in primary rules?

4. How do views of competition among the general public differ from views among athletes themselves?

5. What kinds of rules and practices should be adopted in school sports to ensure that competition is as good as it can be?

6. What kinds of sport events or performances have you found to be aesthetically pleasing? What about them has caused you to react this way?

7. What personal experiences have you had that highlight controversial issues in sport ethics? How did you and other people involved react?

8. What have been your experiences in sport regarding the concept of "fair play?"

9. How would you define cheating in the sports that you play?

## CHAPTER 11

# Sport Programs and Professions

*Sports are the highest products of civilization and the most accessible, lived, experiential sources of the civilizing spirit.*

Michael Novak, 1976

Will historians and anthropologists of the future refer to our times as the "era of sport"? When you look at all the data about sport—data on participation, spending, and so on—you may get that impression. If you look through a listing of television shows for any weekend, you may get that impression. If you go out for a leisurely drive in many areas, seeing the various indoor and outdoor sport spaces and facilities, you may get that impression.

There was a time, not too long ago, when sport was primarily for youths and young adults. Children played, but they did not *do* sport. Older adults watched, but they did not *do* sport. Children now can begin organized sport participation at a very early age. Young swimmers and gymnasts may undergo several years of intense training and competition before they reach puberty. In addition, many sports offer a large and growing number of masters-level or veterans competitions for people over age 40—competition graded in 5-year blocks all the way to age 70 and beyond. Most states now hold summer sport festivals that include competitors from young children to seniors.

In the past few years sports training for babies and toddlers has emerged through the development of private-sector sport training programs (*New York Times,* November 30, 2010). The Little Gym company now provides sport training classes for children beginning at 4 months old with children under 2 representing a quarter of their total enrollment. Another provider, My Gym, reported that 55 percent of children attending classes at 157 locations in the United States were 2.5 years and under. While there is substantial controversy about starting sport training at that early age, there is little evidence, one way or the other, to assess the positive or negative outcomes of such programs.

How big is sport in U.S. society? Very big! Is the United States the biggest sport culture in the world? We might be the largest in absolute size, but in relative importance of sport in a culture, you would get a real argument from an Australian, a Brazilian, or a German. Suffice it to say that in America and many developed countries sport have, in the second half of the twentieth century and the early part of the twenty-first, assumed unprecedented economic and cultural importance.

The purpose of this chapter is to describe what kinds of sport are done, who does them, what specialized roles have developed to support the sport culture, and what qualifications are necessary to work in those roles.

## CHILD AND YOUTH SPORT

There are many ways that children and youth participate in sport. The categories covered below are (1) informal game and activity participation, (2) out-of-school child and youth sport programs sponsored by local community agencies or recreation departments, (3) fee-for-service, sport-specialization instructional programs, (4) sport-specific, fee-for-service organizations that provide instruction and age-graded competition including "select" teams that travel widely, and (5) interscholastic sport sanctioned by state associations. Each of these will be considered individually.

The National Council on Youth Sports (NCYS) (www.ncys.org), a nonprofit organization representing 185 member organizations dedicated to advancing the values of participation and to developing and educating leaders, estimates that as many as 60 million American youths participate in at least one organized sport, which means that about 65 percent of American children and youths participate in organized sport. Estimates are that 58 percent of those participate in agency-sponsored programs, while community-sponsored programs

Some of the best sport is not formally organized.

account for 36 percent of the participants, with the remaining 6 percent in private clubs. These youth sport programs are administered and run by 7.34 million adults, including 2.4 million coaches, 909,333 officials, and 785,752 administrators.

The NCYS also reports that participation by girls has begun at an earlier age than previously and has increased significantly in the 16 to 18 age group. Organized sport programs for children and youth tend to rely heavily on school and community owned facilities, but there has been an increase in participation in privately owned indoor facilities.

There has been increasing concern that child and youth sport too often focuses on winning as the primary goal. To counter that concern, there has been substantial support for what are called "sports-based youth-development programs (Perkins & Noam, 2007). The focus within these programs is helping children and youths develop competence in sport skills through a motivational climate that focuses on gradual improvement and doing one's best with reduced focus on external rewards such as winning.

Child and youth sport programs should emphasize appropriate amounts physical activity during their practice sessions. A recent study (Leek, Carlson, Cain, Henrichon, Rosenberg, Patrick, & Sallis, 2010) examined the amount of physical activity by participants from 29 teams (soccer and baseball) using accelerometers worn during practice. While soccer players fared better than baseball players in this study, only 24 percent of participants met the 60-minute PA guideline during practice with only 10 percent of the 11 to 14 year olds meeting the guideline.

### Informal Participation

Many children and adolescents participate in sports that are organized and controlled by the players, in what have been traditionally called "pickup games," in backyards, parks, school playgrounds, driveways, and even on streets. Stickball, basketball shooting games, and in-line skating contests are typical of these activities. Coakley (2007) and his students have observed such activities over a number of years. What they have found is that children and youths who participate in these informal activities create games and competitions that emphasize four features: games that (1) have a lot of action, particularly scoring action; (2) optimize personal involvement; (3) are challenging and exciting, typically through close scores; and (4) allow participants to reaffirm their friendships with fellow competitors. The rules of these games and activities often resemble those of the "parent" game/activity but are modified to make these four features more likely. A primary goal is to keep the activity moving and to sanction actions that tend to disrupt the activity. Not all informal games and contests reflect these values. Sometimes equal participation is not tolerated as older or more skilled players dominate the action within the game/contest to the exclusion of less-skilled participants. There are no national data on the numbers of children and youth that participate in sport informally, although it is fair to speculate that the percentage of children/youth participating informally has gone down dramatically with the growing number of opportunities offered in community, private, and school sport programs.

Informal participation also includes the activity patterns of the Gen X generation and the current child/youth generation, referred to most often as the "millennial" generation (Gen Y). These activities are most frequently described as extreme sports and have been institutionalized in the X Games. Activities such as skateboarding, in-line skating, and snowboarding are activities that no doubt have widespread informal participation. Data on participation rates in these activities are more difficult to capture, but most experts agree that these activities represent a generational change in child/youth activity patterns (Lauer, 2006). Many communities are now trying to provide facilities for some of these, particularly skateboarding.

## After-School Sport and Physical Activity Programs

One of the major changes in the daily lives of children and youth is how they get to and from school. As late as the 1960s, most children and youth walked or biked to schools that were reasonably close to where they lived. By the late 1970s school districts had begun to consolidate schools and to build larger schools as towns, cities, and suburbs sought ways to provide education to the increasing child and youth populations. In many urban and suburban school districts there was also a growing concern about the safety of children and youths walking or biking to schools, with the result that most children were bussed to and from schools. A major negative effect of this change was the reduction of after-school sports and physical activity programs that served all the children and youths that wanted to participate.

Efforts to develop such programs using community facilities and local church facilities have been difficult to sustain due to funding and transportation issues. Team-Up for Youth, located in Oakland, California, is an organization that helps to "create after-school sports opportunities for girls and boys that build their confidence and skills, connect them to mentors and improve their prospects in school and in life" (www.teamupforyouth.org). In recent years this group has created 15,000 new after-school sport opportunities, trained 1,600 program leaders and 850 volunteer coaches, and awarded $5 million to fund and expand after-school sports programs.

Organized sport begins early for many children.

## Out-of-School, Nonprofit Public or Community Sport Programs

Child and youth sport includes all the organized sport activities that take place outside of school under the sponsorship of nonprofit public or community organizations. Many of these begin as neighborhood projects and develop over the years into larger, more organized operations (see Focus On Box 11.1). Other local sport programs are affiliated with national organizations, the largest of which is Little League Baseball. Participation in Pop Warner football has nearly doubled in the last 15 years, from about 130,000 to 380,000 (www.popwarner.com). Pop Warner football uses age-weight categories to ensure that injury rates are low. Still other programs are developed and sustained through local recreation departments. Boys still represent the largest participant group, but girls' participation has increased markedly over the past two decades and now represents about 40 percent of the participation. Many national service organizations, such as the Optimist and Kiwanis clubs, have traditionally sponsored teams at the local level.

Children are beginning to participate at younger ages. Age-group gymnastics and swimming programs now enroll 3-year-olds, and hockey, soccer, football, and T-ball, among others, enroll 4-year-olds. Many parents, however, prefer that their children not start at such an early age, preferring that girls and boys begin participation closer to age 10. Dropout rates for youths increase steadily from ages 11 to 18 years, with the percentage of dropouts higher for girls than for boys. A significant factor in understanding this dropout rate is the fact that middle-school and high-school interscholastic sport have "limits" for team membership; that is, only those girls and boys good enough to "make the team" are allowed to participate. This problem is made more complicated by the fact that the increase in the number of boys' teams and girls' teams in most middle and high schools has inadvertently led to the reduction of middle- and high-school intramural sports programs, due to budget and facility constraints.

## Fee-for-Service, Sport-Specialization Instructional Programs

Over the past 30 years, the cultural importance of sport has grown markedly. It can be seen in attendance, TV audiences, the predominance of

---

**FOCUS ON** — An Urban Community-Organized Sports Program for Children and Youths — **11.1**

The North Columbus Athletic Association (NCAC) was formed in 1966 to develop a softball program for children and youths in the neighborhoods of north Columbus, Ohio. In 1973 the NCAC purchased 25 acres of land to construct ball diamonds. In 1974 it added soccer, with 130 boys and girls participating. By the late 1970s, the programs had grown to serve over 2,000 participants. The original land was sold in order to buy a larger tract of 53 acres, which now includes soccer fields, ball diamonds, a concession stand, restrooms, a storage facility, and a shelter house.

The NCAC now has 1,500 children playing soccer on 66 recreational and 21 select teams each spring and fall. The program starts with the Soccer Academy for Sprouts, which serves children from 2.5 to 4 years old. Youth soccer leagues are organized for ages 5 to 12. Soccer leagues are also organized for 18+, 30+, and 40+ adults. About 1,200 youths participate in the summer softball and baseball program. They all play on 21 soccer fields of various sizes and on 17 permanent ball diamonds. As a service to member parents, adult soccer and softball leagues were started in 1997. Fees are kept minimal, and parent volunteers perform much of the upkeep and administration of the organization. Participation and instruction are emphasized in the bulk of the activities, the select teams having more intense involvement and travel. No public monies are involved, but local businesses have been very supportive of the organization.

interscholastic sports, and the number of sport opportunities for youngsters in most communities. This cultural change has led to an increasing commercialization of sport, that is, entrepreneurs have learned that there is money to be made by offering sport-specific training for young children. Specialized training for young children is one of the major trends to develop during this period. This is especially true for "individual" sports such as gymnastics, tennis, and figure skating (see www. olympiadgymnastics.org and www.topflightsports-center.com for two examples). Many of these centers market themselves as educational and developmental programs that promote physical development and socialization with an emphasis on fun. If, indeed, the programs are child friendly and do not expect year-round involvement, they can contribute to child development. If, however, they do involve year-round training in a single sport, they put children at risk.

Another aspect of this large and growing market for sport-specialization instructional programs is the summer sport-camp business. Mysummercamps.com lists 5,471 camps in 52 sports in 2010, ranging from 766 equestrian camps to 3 water polo camps. Key high-school sports—such as soccer (474), football (197), and basketball (463)—are among the most popular programs. Camps are either day camps serving boys and girls in a local community or residential camps where participants travel to and stay at the program site, typically for one week. Camps often offer other activities besides the primary focus on the sport.

In 2000 the American Academy of Pediatrics studied these issues from a number of different medical and developmental perspectives and published the following summary statement:

> Children involved in sports should be encouraged to participate in a variety of different activities and develop a wide range of skills. Young athletes who specialize in just one sport may be denied the benefits of varied activity while facing additional physical, physiologic, and psychologic demands from intense training and competition. (American Academy of Pediatrics, 2000)

Sport specialization has also become the norm for many high-school athletes. Football players are encouraged to use winter and spring for strength training instead of sport participation. Many parents and their high-school sons or daughters see the possibility of an athletic scholarship to a college or university, so they commit themselves to year-round participation, with travel to summer camps where their skills can be more fully developed. In Chapter 12, we will address the problems of overuse injuries that often accompany year-round participation.

## Sport-Specific, Fee-for-Service Organizations

Specialization in sports for children and youths is also available through local and national organizations. The sports where this is most fully developed are soccer and basketball. In soccer, it is now common for most metropolitan areas to have "clubs" that offer soccer instruction, age-group competition, and "select teams," which travel widely and often train and compete year-round.

Soccer clubs offer youngsters the opportunity to train year-round, coached by women and men with extensive playing and coaching experience in soccer, to participate in local competitions, and to travel widely as members of select teams. An example is the Lonestar Academy Soccer Club in Austin, Texas, that has more than 550 players forming 68 different teams to compete locally, regionally, and nationally. The club offers a youth-development program for U8–U10 boys and girls, as well as team membership for the U11–U18 age groups. The club has 40 staff members, and all coaches are nationally licensed, with coaching experience at state, regional, and national levels. The club offers "college showcases," where players are showcased to college and university coaches, and has an online system designed to support individual players making themselves available to college recruiters. The club also arranges college visits to "expose the players within the club to the overall experience of playing at the next level" (www.lonestar-sc.com).

Parents of club members often travel with their sons or daughters to local, regional, and national competitions. In this respect, the child's development in soccer becomes a focal point for the family and a considerable expense when one considers club fees, uniforms, and travel.

Another Austin, Texas, soccer club offers a somewhat different profile. The Austin United Capital Soccer Club serves nearly 3,000 students in three different programs and employs 15 professional staff members. The Club offers three programs. The Recreational program serves 2,040 boys and girls from 4 to 18 years of age who want to learn soccer and have fun, whatever their skill level. Teams practice twice weekly and play a game on Saturday. Coaches are volunteer adults who must first participate in a coaching course. The Academy program serves more than 100 boys and girls who qualify in the "preselect" U9 and U10 age groups. This program focuses on advanced technique training, tactical play, and fitness. The Select program offers local, regional, and national competition in Premiere, Division 1, Super 2, and Division 2 competitions for girls and boys from the U11 to U18 levels. Girls and boys are placed on teams through a tryout process. The club offers college-placement assistance for girls and boys who want to continue their soccer careers. The club also offers coed adult soccer.

Another example of sport-specific, fee-for-service programs is the girls' and boys' basketball programs sponsored by the Amateur Athletic Union (AAU). This program, built around local AAU clubs, offers basketball competition at the local, regional, and national levels. Competition for girls (www.aaugirlsbasketball.org) is offered for each grade level starting with second grade and going up to twelfth grade. Competitions for boys (www.aauboysbasketball.org) is based on grade level starting with first grade and going up to twelfth grade. A smaller basketball is used for all competitions in the early grade levels. Players are "attached" to AAU clubs when they participate in AAU-sanctioned competitions that involve two or more AAU clubs, which simply means that they are not allowed to change clubs. All players must be AAU members.

Funding for AAU basketball differs by club. Some clubs use a yearly or seasonal fee to cover basic costs. Others use separate fees for clinics, team membership, and the costs of participating in tournaments. A key marketing strategy for AAU basketball is "exposure," which means that players who make the teams are guaranteed to play in state and regional tournaments—and receive national exposure should teams be successful regionally. This exposure is meant to help players gain athletic scholarship to colleges and universities.

## Organizations That Support Child and Youth Sport

The Youth Sport Coalition of the National Association for Sport and Physical Education (NASPE) has developed a Parent's Checklist for Quality Youth Sports Programs (NASPE, 1995c). The document provides a series of statements to help parents evaluate the developmental and educational benefits likely to accrue from child and youth participation in sports programs. The checklist is organized into six areas: philosophy of the program, organization and administration of the program, coach qualifications, parental commitment to child participation, children's readiness to participate, and safety. Each area has 10 statements, which a parent can check off. The more statements checked off, the greater the possibility of a high-quality experience.

A welcome addition to resources for child and youth sport is the Center for Sport Parenting (www.centerforsportsparenting.org), a program developed by the Institute for International Sport. Their web-based initiative offers practical guidance for parents to help their children and youths handle the psychological and physical challenges involved in their sport experience. In March 2008, the center launched a new Web initiative, the Encyclopedia of Sports Parenting Social Network, that allows parents and others to interact online to discuss issues and solve problems. The Center's website offers advice from experts in sport psychology, health, nutrition, and sports medicine. The Center's main publication,

## FOCUS ON — NAYS Standards for Youth Sport — 11.2

The National Alliance for Youth Sports has developed a set of standards to guide organizations that sponsor sports programs for children and youth. Each standard has detailed implementation guidelines that together ensure a developmentally appropriate experience for participants.

1. *Proper sports environment.* Implementation guidelines include minimum play rules for all participants regardless of ability, programs organized in 2-year age group, no-cut rules, awards for participation only, and no league standings below age 9.

2. *Programs based on well-being of children.* Implementation guidelines include developmental programs for the 5–6 age group, sports introduction programs for the 7–8 age group, scores kept but standing de-emphasized for the 9–10 age group, and ability grouping for the 11–12 age group. There are weight and skill groupings in all age groups.

3. *Drug-, tobacco-, and alcohol-free environment.* Leagues prohibit use of drugs, tobacco, and alcohol by coaches, administrators, and game officials. Player and parent education programs are available.

4. *Part of a child's life.* Leagues adopt policies that encourage participation in a variety of youth activities, limit practices, and do not demand year-round involvement.

5. *Training.* Parents much insist that all coaches be trained and certified. The organization uses appropriate screening devices for selecting and assigning coaches.

6. *Parents' active role.* Parents are required to attend orientation meeting; teams have to have at least one team–parent meeting during the season; leagues encourage parent–child communication about the sport experience.

7. *Positive role models.* Leagues adopt a conduct code that includes unacceptable behaviors, and they communicate conduct expectations to parents, officials, and coaches.

8. *Parental commitment.* Parents must sign a parental code of ethics to have children participate.

9. *Safe playing situations.* Playing facilities and equipment chosen and inspected for safety, first-aid equipment and plans in place, no participation during unsafe conditions, and coaches required to take CPR and advanced first-aid training.

10. *Equal-play opportunity.* Implementation guidelines include nondiscrimination policy for all players, all youngsters able to play regardless of financial ability to pay fees, co-recreational programs through age 12, and affirmative action coaching-recruitment policy.

11. *Drug-, tobacco-, and alcohol-free adults.* Coaches, game officials, and league administrators refrain from use of these substances at youth sport events and encourage spectators to refrain. Enforcement plan in place for removing coaches, parents, and spectators who are under the influence of alcohol or illegal substances.

SOURCE: National Association for Youth Sports. www.NAYS.org.

*The Encyclopedia of Sports Parenting,* is sold in bookstores and online.

The nonprofit National Alliance for Youth Sport (NAYS) (www.nays.org) offers programs and services for organizations that sponsor youth sports, including administrators, parents, volunteer coaches, and volunteer officials. NAYS has also developed a comprehensive set of standards to guide child and youth sport programs (see Focus On Box 11.2). Each standard is defined by implementation guidelines. NAYS programs are offered through state park and recreation associations, national organizations such as YMCAs and Catholic Youth Organizations (CYOs), and community associations.

The NASPE Youth Sport Coalition has created a Bill of Rights for Young Athletes (NASPE, 1999), which are meant to apply to all sport and physical activity programs that involve children and youth. These include the right to

- Participate in sports.
- Participate at a level commensurate with each child's maturity and ability.
- Qualified adult leadership.
- Play as a child and not as an adult.
- Share in the leadership and decision making.
- Participate in safe and healthy environments.
- Proper preparation for participation in sports.
- Be treated with dignity.
- Have fun in sports.

The question that sport educators must ask of themselves is what kind of child or youth sport program reflects those characteristics? As you look back on your early sport experiences, how many of the proposed "rights" were represented in the programs in which you took part? Which of the rights were most likely to be violated?

## Coaching for Child and Youth Sport

There are as many as 7.5 million youth sport coaches in North America, the vast majority of whom have had no formal instruction in the educational, developmental, and health aspects of coaching children

Coaches are fundamental to success in all sports.

and youth (Eitzen & Sage, 2003). A half-million more can be described as paid or professional coaches, typically working in fee-for-service sport clubs focused primarily on the development of elite athletes. In some sports, there are now *sport academies* where youngsters can get top-level coaching and be with other young elite athletes as they live, train, compete, and go to school together. Many volunteer coaches played sports when they were younger, and many of them also watch a great deal of sport on television and in person, but that, of course, does not equip them with current knowledge from the fields of sport pedagogy, sport medicine, or sport psychology that would be useful in working with children and adolescents.

Child and youth sport programs are constantly changing, but as Coakley (2007) argues, the changes are too often functionalist in nature. Adults trying to "improve" child and youth sport programs typically focus on increasing the skill of the young athletes and making the organization more efficient. Although the typical changes that focus on training programs for coaches and regulating the behavior of parents and spectators are appropriate, these changes do not often enough include efforts to help coaches and parents make the experience more fun and meaningful for the youngsters.

Again, the situation for coaching is different in nations where the government has played a stronger role in developing and administering child and youth sport. Canada, Great Britain, New Zealand, Australia, and other nations have developed coach-education programs with different levels of training necessary for positions at different levels of competition—from a beginning level, necessary to work with local children's teams, to the highest level, necessary to coach a state or national team. The coach-education materials are often developed in conjunction with national sport organizations and delivered through local recreation agencies. For example, a national volleyball organization might develop beginning coaching materials for volleyball, and local recreation agencies would use those materials to prepare volunteer coaches for youth volleyball.

Coaching in specialized age-group sports is typically done with smaller classes and better equipment.

The nonprofit NAYS includes as one of its main programs the National Youth Sport Coaches Association (NYSCA), which has trained over 1.2 million coaches since its inception in 1981. Its program is offered through state offices and local/regional chapters. The program focuses on developmental and safety considerations, physiological and psychological concerns, and sport-coaching techniques. Participants must pass an exam on the materials they have covered and sign a pledge that they will uphold the association's code of ethics. Focus Box On 11.3 describes NAYS in more detail.

## INTERSCHOLASTIC SPORT

The U.S. Constitution specifically designates education as a *state* function. Therefore, interscholastic sport is organized and regulated at the state level. Although the organization of school sport differs somewhat from state to state, the similarities in governance and structure far outnumber the differences. Interscholastic sport occupies a place in the American sport culture that is unlike that in any other nation.

---

**FOCUS ON**    National Alliance for Youth Sports                    11.3

Founded in 1981, NAYS sponsors nine programs that educate volunteer coaches, parents, youth sport program administrators, and officials about their roles and responsibilities in youth sports. NAYS programs are provided at the local level through partnerships with community-based organizations.

- The National Youth Sport Coaches Association trains volunteer coaches.

- The National Youth Sports Officials Association trains volunteer youth sport officials.

- The Academy for Youth Sport Administrators offers a 20-hour program to earn the Certified Youth Sports Administrator credential.

- The National Clearinghouse for Youth Sports Information provides the public with access to a variety of materials pertaining to youth sports.

- Parents Association for Youth Sports provides materials and information to make parents aware of their roles and responsibilities in youth sports.

- Child Abuse and Youth Sports provides a comprehensive risk-management approach to building a protective shield around participants and programs.

- Hook a Kid on Golf™ helps communities develop comprehensive youth golf programs.

- Start Smart brings parents and children ages 3 years and over together in an instructional program that helps parents learn how to teach their children.

- Kids on Target is a team-oriented program for archery for youngsters ages 10–14.

SOURCE: www.nays.org.

The National Federation of State High School Associations (NFSHSA) is the national service and administrative organization for state high-school athletic associations. The mission of NFSHSA is to serve its 50 state associations members by providing leadership for and national coordination of the administration of high-school sport in ways that improve the educational experiences and reduce the risks associated with sport participation. NFSHSA publishes rules for 16 sports competed in high schools. Among its many service programs, NFSHSA regularly compiles data on participation in interscholastic sport throughout the nation (see Focus On Box 11.4).

During the 2009–10 school year, 4.46 million boys and 3.17 million girls competed in more than 46 different sports, compared to the first NFSHSA survey in 1971–72 when 3.67 million boys and 294,015 girls competed. It is fair to say that as a percentage of high-school enrollment, sport participation has increased steadily over the past 30 years, especially for girls. The initial survey showed that girls' participation was 7 percent of the overall participation, while the most recent survey showed that girls' participation had reached 41 percent of the overall participation. The change in girls' participation was rapid after Title IX became law in 1972. If one discounts the more than 1.1 million boys participating

## FOCUS ON   Most Popular Interscholastic Sports                    11.4

| Ten Most Popular Boys' Programs | Number of Schools Participating | Number of Participants |
|---|---|---|
| 1.  Basketball | 18,150 | 540,844 |
| 2.  Track and field (outdoor) | 15,954 | 579,302 |
| 3.  Baseball | 15,863 | 471,025 |
| 4.  Football (11 player) | 14,279 | 1,108,441 |
| 5.  Cross-country | 14,097 | 246,948 |
| 6.  Golf | 13,681 | 156,866 |
| 7.  Soccer | 11,503 | 398,351 |
| 8.  Wrestling | 10,407 | 273,732 |
| 9.  Tennis | 9,839 | 161,367 |
| 10. Swimming and diving | 6,899 | 133,900 |

| Ten Most Popular Girls' Programs | Number of Schools Participating | Number of Participants |
|---|---|---|
| 1.  Basketball | 17,767 | 438,933 |
| 2.  Track and field (outdoor) | 16,030 | 475,265 |
| 3.  Volleyball | 15,479 | 409,332 |
| 4.  Softball (fast pitch) | 15,338 | 373,535 |
| 5.  Cross-country | 13.839 | 204,653 |
| 6.  Soccer | 11,047 | 361,556 |
| 7.  Tennis | 10,181 | 182,074 |
| 8.  Golf | 9,609 | not in top ten |
| 9.  Swimming and diving | 7,164 | 160,881 |
| 10. Competitive spirit squads | 4,266 | 96,718 |

SOURCE: National Federation of State High School Associations, 2010–2011 "Athletics Participation Study" (www.nfhs.org).

Football grows in popularity at all levels.

in football, where team membership often includes 40 to 60 players, the participation of girls is nearly equal to that of boys. It should be noted that some students participated in more than one sport and are thus double- or triple-counted although the percentage of multisport athletes has likely subsided due to young athletes tending to specialize in one sport and training for that sport during the off-season.

The top 10 sports, in terms of number of participants, have remained stable over the past decade (see Focus On Box 11.4). Volleyball has increased steadily as a sport for girls but does not come close to making the top 10 for boys. Soccer continues to grow as a favored sport by both girls and boys. The number of boys participating in football is nearly twice that of any other sport.

## Organization of Interschool Sport

Most states have adopted a system of competition in which the number of students in a school determines the classification within which the school competes (AAA, AA, and A; A, B, C, and D; or V, IV, III, II, and I). **Interscholastic sport** is typically governed by a state organization, which in many states is *not* a government agency but, rather, a private corporation that schools join. For example, the Ohio High School Athletic Association (OHSAA) is a private organization to which Ohio high schools belong by virtue of paid membership. The OHSAA organizes and administers sports for the high schools that belong to the organization, including establishing rules for participation, length of season, starting times for practice and conducting regional, district, and state championships in a variety of sports.

The financing of interscholastic sport also differs from state to state. In some states, interscholastic sport is considered a regular part of the educational program and is funded directly from tax revenues through regular school budgets. In other states, however, laws limit the amount of regularly budgeted tax funds that may be spent on extracurricular activities. Interscholastic sport, as an extracurricular activity, then has to pay for itself through gate receipts and through fund-raising. It is in the latter area that high-school booster clubs have developed; such clubs often provide substantial financial support for athletic departments.

Many school districts suffering from budget shortfalls have recently instituted pay-to-play plans, which require a fee to be paid, typically by parents, for girls or boys to be on a sports team. Fees for varsity sports are typically more than for junior varsity or middle-school sports. This method of financing school sport has drawn national attention with the general concern that the impact will fall greatest on those least able to pay, therefore denying students the right to participate in a school-sponsored activity. This issue is described more specifically in the following paragraph and will be considered again in Chapter 12.

The Palo Alto, California, High School Boosters provides an example of the degree to which booster clubs have become important to interscholastic sport programs (www.palysports.com). This booster club had been supporting the Palo Alto High School teams for many years. But in recent years, as funding from the school district has withered, the boosters assumed a more central role in the funding of the high-school program. The club now pays for 100 percent of the noncoaching costs of the program, including transportation, officials, uniforms, equipment, janitorial expenses, tournament fees, and awards. Nearly 40 percent of the high-school students participate in the sports program.

Participation fees paid by parents, what are typically referred to as "pay-to-play fees," range from $150 to $200, covering about 80 percent of the program expenses. Although the fees are not mandatory, families must address the fee in some way—that is, through partial payment, during the season. The remainder of the budget is paid through fundraising of various kinds, including running the concessions at contests and selling clothing with school logos.

## School Coaches

The number of coaches required to staff the nearly 200,000 interscholastic sport teams in America each year is substantial (DeRenne, Morgan, Hetzler, & Taura, 2007). Since the enactment of Title IX, as girl participant numbers have increased each year, the

Coaching today relies heavily on technology.

need for coaches has increased significantly. In some sports, it is not unusual to have assistant coaches. Most high schools have varsity and reserve teams, but larger high schools might have separate freshman, reserve, and varsity teams. We have also seen a consistent increase in the number of sports offered in interscholastic programs, with the NFSHSA now tracking participation in 39 sports.

In the early 1960s, because there were fewer sports and girls' participation was severely limited, fewer coaches were needed. Nearly all of those coaches were certified teachers, and many of them were trained physical education teachers. Another confounding issue is that many certified teachers do not have the time to coach, the result of the strong national focus on the improvement of school performance, which began during the *Sputnik* era and continues today with the legislation known as No Child Left Behind. Thus, many high-school coaches are not certified teachers, and most of them have no specific preparation for coaching but draw from their own experience of participating in sports. As the number of sports and participants have increased, there has been a consistent effort to address the issues surrounding the qualifications of coaches. The increase, however, has been so steady that many states have found it difficult to pass legislation requiring qualifications for hiring coaches or coaching-education requirements once hired. Remember that our federal Constitution leaves the governance of education to the states, so the approach to establishing and applying standards or minimum requirements for coaching in school sport differs greatly from state to state.

In the early 1960s the lack of educational requirements for coaching began to generate concern nationally, particularly among educational associations. The National Association for Sport and Physical Education (NASPE) was among the early leaders in this movement, partnering with various national associations to address issues related to hiring qualifications and advocating for coaching-education programs. In the early 1970s, sport psychologist and physical education professor Rainer Martens, influenced by his research and the pioneering work of the Coaching Association of Canada, founded the American Coaching Effectiveness Program, which later expanded into the American Sport Education Program (ASEP) (www.asep.com). By 1981 the first ASEP courses in coaching philosophy and the basics of sport science were available through Human Kinetics. By 1986 ASEP had 1,400 certified instructors who had trained over 50,000 coaches. In 1990 the NFSHSA partnered with ASEP to offer Coaching Principles and Sport First Aid courses to high-school coaches. ASEP now works directly with more than 40 state high-school associations delivering the ASEP Professional Coaches Program to more than 28,000 coaches each year. Gradually, ASEP expanded its coaching curriculum and began to offer courses

online. ASEP now offers a Volunteer Education Program for beginning coaches of athletes 13 years of age and younger, plus courses for parents, officials, and sport administrators. ASEP's Professional Education Program consists of Bronze, Silver, and Gold levels. The Bronze level, for coaches of athletes 14 years of age and over, consists of a three-course program, which includes Coaching Principles, Sport First Aid, and Coaching (Sport) Technical and Tactical Skills. The Silver and Gold levels will cater to the more-specialized interests of coaches and are now in preparation.

A second coaching-education program that has made important contributions is the Program for Athletic Coaches Education (PACE), developed at the Institute for the Study of Youth Sports at Michigan State University (Seefeldt & Milligan, 1992). PACE is typically delivered without state organizations or universities, with materials that include a coachs' guide and DVDs that simulate situations related to coaching. The NFSHSA has recently severed its relationship with ASEP and launched its own program, which includes a Fundamentals of Coaching and First Aid for Coaches courses (www.nfhslearn.com, 2007). Twenty-four state athletic associations have so far adopted these courses. As with most coaching-education programs, these courses are offered online.

There is now a proliferation of coaching-education programs offered by a range of providers including universities and national sport-specific associations (see Focus On Box 11.5). It has been helpful to these organizations to have access to widely accepted standards that define broadly what the content of coaching-education programs should contain. The standards developed by the National Association for Youth Sports (see Focus On Box 11.2, page 242) focus primarily on age-group sports offered through community and agency programs while the NASPE's *National Standards for Sport Coaches* focuses primarily on interscholastic sports. These standards are helpful in defining the content that should be part of coaching-education programs.

## FOCUS ON · · · · Coaching Education Within National Governing Bodies · · · · 11.5

The national governing bodies (NGBs) of most Olympic sports have developed their own coaching-education programs. Many of them use ASEP or a similar entry-level program as the beginning program but then advance to levels of accreditation that are more specific to the sport sponsored by the NGB. The program below is for USA Volleyball.

### USA Volleyball Coaching Accreditation Program (CAP)

- Level 1: ASEP Coaching Principles, skills, games, drills, basic systems, and practice management. Candidate must pass test and sign coaching code of ethics statement.
- Level 2: Team systems, blocking and setting development, problem solving, and social issues.

Candidate must attend or instruct one non-CAP volleyball clinic.

- Level 3: Instruction from peer coaches, critical thinking, outreach project.
- Level 4: Mentor with Cadre or National Team for 1 week. Candidate must complete three experiences from four categories of higher-level coaching and develop a publishable manuscript.
- Level 5: All current and previous national team coaches are considered honorary Level 5.

Accreditation at most levels lasts for 4 years, during which time the candidate must advance to the next level or complete an accreditation-renewal course.

SOURCE: www.usavolleyball.org.

## FOCUS ON · · · · Maine's *Sports Done Right* Initiative · · · · 11.6

Funded by a federal Department of Education initiative and endorsed by Maine's governor and commissioner of education, the *Sports Done Right* initiative has provided a state model that has attracted the interest of more than thirty states.

As young athletes increasingly express concerns about unruly fans, overbearing coaches, and undue pressures to perform, the Maine initiative instills core principles and supporting practices to guide

youth sport and school sport experiences. The initiative aims to increase opportunities for positive learning through sports, promote fair play over a win-at-all-costs ethic, and hold parents and community members to higher standards and behavior.

The initiative's important report, "Sports Done Right: A Call to Action on Behalf of Maine's Student Athletes," is serving as a model for other states to develop similar programs.

SOURCE: *Education Week*, August 10, 2005.

Many state associations have either strongly suggested or made mandatory that coaches complete minimal coaching-education courses in order to be hired or to retain their roles in school sport programs. In some states, legislation has been passed to require coaching education. Typical is the recent Coaching Education and Steriod/Performance Enhancing Supplements bylaws passed by the California Interscholastic Federation (CIF), the governing body for interschool sport in that state. The

new bylaw requires that by December 31, 2008, all coaches will be certified in the CIF Coaching Education program or its equivalent. The CIF program requirements can be met by completing either the NFSHSA Fundamentals of Coaching course or the ASEP Coaching Principles course; both are offered online or can be completed locally by certified CIF coaching education instructors (for two other approaches see the Focus On Box 11.6 and Focus On Box 11.7).

| FOCUS ON   Montana's Innovative Coach Education Program | 11.7 |
| --- | --- |

Montana is a rural state with 190 school athletic programs divided into AA, A, B, and C classes. The A schools have a student enrollment of over 900; the C schools enroll fewer than 129 students. The Montana High School Athletic Association (MHSAA) faced a severe logistical problem with schools so widely dispersed across the large, thinly populated state. Its approach to coaching education had to address delivery of up-to-date information in an economical and user-friendly format.

Under the leadership of Craig Stewart of Montana State University, the staff of MHSAA developed an online coaching-education curriculum and assessment program. Using the coaching standards developed by NASPE as a starting point, MHSAA engaged athletic directors across the state to rank its program's priorities in the seven domains identified by NASPE. An additional domain, "coaching the female athlete," was added.

The curriculum materials and online assessments for the eight domains were developed and piloted. MHSAA made the coaching-education process mandatory by the end of the 2002 school year. Coach candidates get a password to access the materials and assessments involved. Coaches can register for university course credit as part of the process. About 2,000 to 3,000 coaches a year complete all eight exams.

Some universities offer coaching-education programs. West Virginia University offers an Athletic Coaching Education (ACE) in both bachelor's and master's degree programs. The ACE program is built on the eight domains of the NASPE's *National Standards for Sport Coaches*. The U.S. Sports Academy offers both certification programs and diploma programs in a variety of sports-related professions. Sport coaching is offered in continuing education, certification, and diploma programs.

The number of women coaching interscholastic sports teams has declined dramatically since its high-water mark just after Title IX was passed into law in 1972 (Pastore, 1994; Sisley & Capel, 1986). Several states have developed experimental programs to attract, train, and retain women in school coaching positions (Hasbrook, 1987; Schafer, 1987), but the shortage continues. A 1998 study in Ohio found that 33 percent of girls' teams had female head coaches and a 1994 Illinois study found that only 25 percent of girls' teams had female coaches (Pastore, 1994).

The National Council for Accreditation of Coaching Education (NCACE) was established in 2000 to ensure that coaching-education programs are of high quality and to encourage continuous improvement of coaching education. The NCACE uses NASPE's *National Standard for Sport Coaches* to review programs that seek accreditation, requiring that programs comply adequately with the standards defined in the eight domains of the NASPE standards.

In 1994 a national summit on coaching standards was convened by NASPE. LeRoy Walker, then president of the U.S. Olympic Committee, opened the summit by stating, "It is time to move the idea of national coaching standards 'off the back burner.' We need a framework that will guarantee us that there is at least a minimum level of competence among these coaches who are affecting the lives of our young people" (NASPE, 1994, p. 1).

These national standards now exist. In 1995 NASPE introduced the 37 standards grouped under eight domains. In 2006 NASPE gathered experts from various national governing bodies of sport (for example, U.S. Olympic Committee and NFSHSA) to review and revise the standards, which were published in 2007. The 40 new standards are grouped under eight domains:

- Philosophy and ethics
- Safety and injury prevention
- Physical conditioning
- Growth and development

- Teaching and communication
- Sports skills and tactics
- Organization and administration
- Evaluation

The standards are not meant to be a certification program but can be used by (1) coaching educators to develop targeted coaching-education programs and (2) sport administrators to develop evaluation protocols for the coaches in their programs.

The NCACE held its first meeting in the summer of 2000. The organization was formed by a variety of people interested in standardizing and improving coaching education at various levels. NCACE includes single-sport and multisport organizations, sport sciences and sport pedagogy organizations, and colleges and universities concerned about the availability of well-trained coaches at all levels of sport (NASPE, 2001). NCACE supports, facilitates the development of, and provides accreditation for coaching-education programs. It also offers workshops that address the eight domains of the National Standards for Athletic Coaches (NASPE, 2006b). The 2008 National Coaching Educators Conference was held in Park City, Utah. NCACE continues to provide accreditation services for college and university coaching-education programs as well as for coaching programs sponsored by national and state sport-specific organizations.

## COLLEGIATE SPORT PROGRAMS

### Intercollegiate Sport

In the post–World War II era, when America became a major sport culture in the world, a significant factor in the overall development of sport was the substantial growth in intercollegiate sport. To be sure, America had a significant history in intercollegiate sport dating to the late nineteenth century when student interest and pressure became so strong that universities began to incorporate sport into their programs (see Chapter 2). Major intercollegiate rivalries had for years captured the interest of the entire nation—the Army–Notre Dame football game, for example. Between 1945 and 1960, intercollegiate sport still grew enormously in importance. It became more important as entertainment, more important economically, and more important on campus. The United States is still the only country in the world where sport and college or university education have become so completely linked.

Most colleges and universities offer extensive sport programs to their students. The advent of Title IX provided the impetus for the phenomenal growth of intercollegiate sport for women in the 1970s. Many colleges and universities have joined with similar institutions in their region to form athletic conferences—the Big Ten, the Western Athletic Conference, and the Michigan Intercollegiate Athletic Association, for example. These athletic conferences govern issues such as eligibility and organize competition for the member institutions, including championships.

Nationally, college and university sport is governed by individual institutional membership in private organizations. The two organizations that dominate the governance of intercollegiate sport are the National Collegiate Athletic Association (NCAA) and the National Association of Intercollegiate Athletes (NAIA). As with child and youth sport, state and federal governments have not become involved in the administration of college and university sport in America.

The NCAA has three main divisions, based on level of competition and rules regarding financial aid to athletes. Focus On Box 11.8 shows the number of member institutions in each division and the participation rates for female and male athletes. Division I is subdivided into three divisions, again based on level of competition and rules for financial aid, but pertaining almost exclusively to football. Division I-A has 117 members, I-AA has 118 members, and I-AAA has 91 members. Division III is often referred to as the "college" division and is defined by not allowing athletic scholarships rather than by size of school. Indeed, some universities in Division III actually have larger enrollments than some in Division I.

**FOCUS ON** NCAA Sport Participation by Division, 2008–09 **11.8**

Division I—333 total members, 113 private
institutions, 220 public institutions
Division II—291 total members, 137 private
institutions, 154 public institutions
Division III—446 total members, 357 private
institutions, 89 public institutions

Average Number of Sports Offered
Division I—9 men's sports, 10 women's sports

Division II—7 men's sports, 8 women's sports
Division III—8 men's sports, 9 women's sports

Participation per Institution
Division I—327 men, 268 women
Division II—247 men, 141 women
Division III—303 men, 179 women

SOURCE: NCAA Membership Report 2008–09.

The NCAA conducts yearly championships in each division—19 in women's sports and 20 in men's sports. Nearly 100 athletic conferences are voting members of the NCAA, a major benefit of which is that conference champions automatically qualify for NCAA championship play.

In 1997 the NCAA completed a significant restructuring of its governance system. The restructuring gives each division greater autonomy and allows for more control over sport programs by the chief executive officers of the member schools, who are typically the presidents of the colleges and universities. An annual convention is held, at which all NCAA business is conducted. Each school and conference member has one vote on all issues before the convention.

In 2008 Title IX reached its 36th year. Female participation in high-school sports has increased by nearly 900 percent, but male athletes still receive 1.1 million more participation opportunities. Only 3 of the 51 directors of state high-school athletic associations are female. While women are 53 percent of the student body in Division I colleges, they represent only 41 percent of the athletes, 32 percent of the recruiting funds, and 36 percent of the overall operating budget (NAGWS, 2007). Women hold only 16.9 percent of the athletic director positions in higher education, only 12.3 percent of the sports information director positions, and 27.8 percent of the athletic trainer positions (Women's Sports Foundation, 2007). Nothing in Title IX requires colleges and universities to cut men's teams; indeed, a 2001

General Accounting Office study found that 72 percent of those colleges and universities that added women's teams did so without cutting any men's teams (NAGWS, 2007).

The NAIA, which was formed in 1940, has 300 institutional members that compete in 25 NAIA conferences. It organizes 25 championships for 13 sports in Divisions I and II. NAIA membership is divided into 14 regions serving North American colleges and universities. Thirty athletic conferences have official affiliation with the NAIA. NAIA institutions are typically smaller colleges and universities. Although they do not attract the national attention that the NCAA does, they do provide organized intercollegiate sports competition for a large number of women and men.

Many people work professionally within intercollegiate sport—coaches, assistant coaches, athletic directors, sport information directors, sport business managers, sport trainers, sport-medicine experts. Only in the medical area—trainers and physicians—are there any specific certification requirements that define entrance into those professional roles.

## College Recreational Intramural Programs

In addition to intercollegiate sport, college and university programs of recreation and intramural sports have grown tremendously in the recent past. Many institutions, seeking to attract and retain students, have built new recreation facilities that have all the amenities of upscale private health and fitness clubs. Programs include all the traditional sport competitions, yearly membership sport clubs, special events (weekend three-on-three basketball tournaments, for example), regularly scheduled fitness and aerobics classes, and drop-in activity for both sport and fitness. Weight-training rooms are typically crowded from early morning until late at night. Pools are filled with recreational and fitness-oriented swimmers.

Many of these programs offer additional opportunities for faculty and for the families of students, staff, and faculty. Recently, recreation and intramural departments have entered the lucrative business of offering summer-camp programs for youths. Recreation and intramural departments are typically staffed by trained professionals and have development programs for student employees. Programs are funded through some combination of subsidies from the university, direct student fees, user fees, and facility rentals (Noyes, 1996).

## PROFESSIONAL SPORT

A main purpose of professional sport is to make money—professional sport is a business. The number of players involved in professional sport is remarkably small. The number of players in the NBA is only 250 to 300, whereas the number of boys competing in high-school basketball in a given year is now 540,000. More than 400,000 girls participate in high-school volleyball, but only a few compete in the Women's Professional Volleyball League. Looking at the data from a different perspective, we can see that the odds for becoming a professional athlete are not good! There are about 3,000 professional athletes in the three major American professional sports for men—baseball, basketball, and football. Yet there are more than 110 million males in the country, which means that 1 out of every 42,000 makes it to the professional level. The number of players that can earn a good living from other sports is even less—the tennis player or golfer ranked as 250 is not getting rich from sport.

It seems as though, every day, we read on the sports page about an athlete who has signed a lucrative professional contract. We must remember, however, that the wealth in professional sport is distributed unevenly among the athletes. A few make the headline money; the more typical athlete makes considerably less. It is also important to understand that being a professional athlete seldom amounts to having a career. Although a few athletes remain in their sport for 10 to 20 years, the average length of stay is much shorter: 4.3 years for football, 4.2 years for basketball, 6.5 years for baseball, and 4.8 years for hockey. Although professional sport is not a realistic goal for most young men and women who compete in child, youth, interscholastic, and collegiate sport, the emergence of professional sport (and big-time intercollegiate sport) has been accompanied by the development of nonparticipant sport professions, many of which are reviewed in the final section of this chapter. Suffice it to say that an NBA team, with its 11 or 12 players, also has three coaches, at least one trainer, a general manager, and a publicity or promotion director, as well as assistant managerial and promotional staff. That is, the number of nonparticipant professionals is equal to or greater than the number of participants!

Professional sport is organized and regulated through its parent organizations: NBA, NFL, LPGA (Ladies Professional Golfers Association), National Hockey League (NHL), and so on. Most sports have commissioners who oversee the establishment and governance of standards and rules within the sport. Remember, however, that professional sport is a business. *Owners* exert the most influence on the governance of the sport, typically through an owners' council.

There are no formal qualifications for entrance into professional sport in most participant and nonparticipant roles. Concepts such as certification and training of personnel, which are so important to the future of youth and school sport, are not issues at the professional level.

In the early 1990s, in response to media criticism, many professional sports began to develop specific recruitment and development programs to increase the number of minority persons in coaching and managing roles and in administrative roles. It appears that some professional sports have had beginning success in attracting minority candidates to both positions. In the NBA, 59 percent of the head coaches are black, and 30 percent hold general manager positions. In Major League Baseball, 30 percent of the managers are black or Latino, but only 6 percent hold high-level management positions (Lapchick, 2005). It seems clear that development programs are needed at the interscholastic and collegiate level to encourage minority women and men, who might be interested in administrative roles, to pursue such roles and to assist them through support efforts that help them to succeed.

## ORGANIZED RECREATIONAL SPORT

The scope of organized recreational sport in the United States is enormous. By *organized*, we mean that a regular competition is organized and governed by a sponsoring agency, records are kept, and officials are provided to ensure appropriate play. Most organized recreational sport in the United States is sponsored by community recreation departments; businesses or industries; service clubs, such as the Kiwanis or Rotary; and private community organizations, typically started and maintained by interested parents.

The range of sport involvement at this level is as broad as sport itself—golf leagues, road races, fishing tournaments, baseball leagues, tennis tournaments, horseshoe leagues, and the like. We would also expect to find some major regional differences in organized recreational sport participation—curling in the Dakotas, surfing in southern California, cross-country skiing in New England. The major involvement in organized recreational sport, however, has been and continues to be in the dominant sports of basketball, touch football, volleyball, soccer, and, most of all, softball.

Here is a breakdown of the participation figures for the City of Columbus, Ohio, Parks and Recreation Department sports program in a recent year:

Softball: 195 leagues, 1,621 teams, 29,000 players

Basketball: 38 leagues, 308 teams, 4,600 players

Volleyball: 38 leagues, 376 teams, 4,500 players

Football: 7 leagues, 68 teams, 1,300 players

Soccer: 4 leagues, 32 teams, 500 players

In all 12,177 games were played in these various leagues, with 7,806 umpires, referees, and scorekeepers employed. There were, of course, similar kinds of programs in the many suburbs surrounding the city and active programs in the other cities, suburbs, and towns in the state—and all across the nation. This level of participation makes a mockery of accusations that we are a nation of spectators.

Different kinds of sporting interests are accommodated in organized recreation programs because the programs are most often sensitive to the needs and interests of those they serve. In the softball program in Columbus, Ohio, there are slow-pitch leagues for men, slow-pitch leagues for women, fast-pitch leagues for men, fast-pitch leagues for women, and *co-rec leagues*, where men and women compete together. These differentiations allow people to participate in a way that is most challenging and enjoyable to them. Some participate primarily as a *social* experience; others participate primarily as a *competitive* experience.

Similar kinds of organized recreational-sport programs are implemented in most colleges and universities. Students can participate in a wide variety of sport activities throughout the school year. As with community programs, college and university programs frequently offer men's, women's, and corecreational competition.

### Sport for People with Disabilities

One of the best features of recent sport history is the degree to which the benefits of sport participation have begun to be extended to people who historically have had difficulty finding ways to be involved in sport. I have mentioned many times the Title IX federal legislation, which opened the door to more

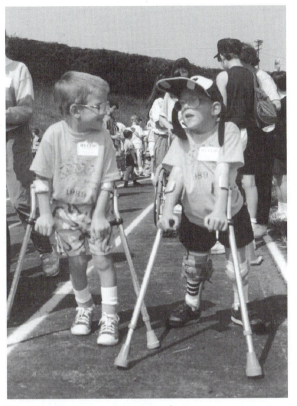

Meaningful sport is important for everyone.

equal opportunity in sport for girls and women. The next section considers the role of sport among older age groups. This section reviews sport opportunities for people with disabilities.

Should a physical or mental disability prohibit someone from participating in meaningful sport competition? No! Has it historically? Yes. Before World War II, there was virtually no opportunity for competitive sport participation for athletes with physical or mental disabilities (DePauw, 1984).

Since then, we have made major progress. That progress is associated with four specific pieces of federal legislation:

1. Public Law 93-112 (Rehabilitation Act—1973) specified that equal opportunity and access, including physical education, intramurals, and athletics, must be provided for people with disabilities.

2. Public Law 94-142 (Education for All Handicapped Children Act—1975) required a free and appropriate public education, including instruction in physical education, in the least restrictive environment possible, for children with disabilities.

3. Public Law 95-606 (Amateur Sports Act—1978) specifically included people with disabilities within the province of the law.

4. Public Law 105-117 (Individuals with Disabilities Education Act—1997) restructured the Individuals with Disabilities Education Act (IDEA) to become the primary law guiding the treatment of children and youth with disabilities in schools, including a requirement that they must have access to the general education curriculum.

Support for persons with disabilities (a term more appropriate than the term previously used, *handicapped*) has extended to concerns about their recreational and sport involvement. The more than 500 million persons with disabilities around the world represent approximately 10 percent of the human population (www.paralympic.org). More than 54 million of these individuals are Americans. Sport opportunities for persons with disabilities have broadened considerably over the past 20 years, from local recreation to adapted physical education in schools, to interscholastic sport, and to national and international competitions.

While adapted physical education is now a regular part of school programs that serve students with disabilities, participation by students with disabilities in interscholastic sports is developing only slowly. In 1992 Minnesota State Association became the first to sponsor adapted athletics for students with disabilities (Matter, Nash, & Frogley, 2002). Regular and postseason competitions are organized in adapted floor hockey, adapted soccer, and adapted softball. These students are eligible for athletic letters, letter jackets, and membership in school athletic clubs. Georgia has also been proactive in providing for adapted interschool sport competitions (American Association for Adapted Sports, 2008). Starting in 2001, the Georgia High School Association worked with the nonprofit

American Association of Adapted Sports Programs (AAASP) to better provide for the interscholastic sports experiences for students with disabilities. Hundreds of participants now compete in six sports—wheelchair soccer, wheelchair basketball, power hockey, wheelchair football, track and field, and beep baseball. There is a formal season in each sport, culminating with a state championship competition. The Alabama High School Athletic Association has recently partnered with AAASP to create and implement an inter-scholastic sports program for students with disabilities in their state. Legislation in New Jersey has recently required the New Jersey State Athletic Association to partner with AAASP to establish an interscholastic sports program for students with disabilities. The many organizations that support sport for persons with disabilities are shown in Focus On Box 11.9. The development and spread of sport for persons with disabilities not only have expanded the opportunities for a fuller life for the participants but also have served as a source of inspiration and motivation for countless others.

---

## FOCUS ON   Sport Organizations for People With Disabilities   11.9

| | |
|---|---|
| Alliance for Disability Sport and Recreation | National Disability Sports Alliance |
| American Athletic Association for the Deaf | National Foundation of Wheelchair Tennis |
| American Blind Bowling Association | National Wheelchair Basketball Association |
| American Wheelchair Bowling Association | National Wheelchair Marathon Association |
| American Wheelchair Pilots Association | National Wheelchair Racquetball Association |
| Amputee Sports Association | National Wheelchair Shooting Federation |
| Blind Outdoor Leisure Association | National Wheelchair Softball Association |
| Braille Sports Foundation | North American Riding for the Handicapped Association |
| Cerebral Palsy International Sports and Recreation Association | Paralyzed Veterans of America |
| Disabled Sportsmen of America | Skating Association for the Blind and Handicapped |
| Disabled Sports USA | Ski for Light, Inc. |
| Dwarf Athletic Association of America | Special Olympics International |
| Eastern Amputee Athletic Association | Tennis Association for the Mentally Retarded |
| 52 Association for the Handicapped | USA Deaf Sports Association |
| Goal Ball Championships | U.S. Amputee Athletic Association |
| Handicapped Scuba Association | U.S. Association for Blind Athletes |
| International Coordinating Committee of the World Sports Organization for the Disabled | U.S. Blind Golfer's Association |
| International Foundation of Wheelchair Tennis | U.S. Cerebral Palsy Athletic Association |
| International Paralympic Committee | U.S. Deaf Skiers Association |
| International Sports Organization for the Disabled | U.S. Olympic Committee, Sports for the Disabled |
| International Wheelchair Aviators | U.S. Organization for Disabled Athletes |
| International Wheelchair Road Racers Club | U.S. Quad Rugby Association |
| National Beep Baseball Association | Wheelchair Athletes of the USA |
| | Wheelchair Sports Federation |

SOURCE: DePauw, 1984.

---

**FOCUS ON** — The History of Special Olympics                    **11.10**

The Special Olympics is perhaps the most remarkable and successful sport programs in world history. Here is a brief chronology of key developments in that history.

- 1962: Eunice Kennedy Shriver invites thirty-five boys and girls with intellectual disabilities to a day camp, intended to explore their capabilities in a variety of sports and physical activities, at her home in Rockville, Maryland.
- 1963: The Kennedy Foundation, founded in 1946, supports eleven similar camps around the United States.
- 1963–1968: More than 300 camps based on the Camp Shriver model are started within the United States. W. Freeberg, Chair of Recreation and Outdoor Education at Southern Illinois University, develops 1-week workshops to train professionals to plan and provide the camp program. One of the students is a teacher, Anne Burke, from Chicago.

- Anne Burke works with the Chicago Park District to plan a citywide track-and-field meet, modeled after the Olympic Games, and submits a proposal to Shriver. The proposal is accepted after Shriver suggests that more athletes from across the country be included.
- July 20, 1968: Shriver opens the First International Special Olympic Games with 1,000 athletes with intellectual disabilities from twenty-six states and Canada, competing in track and field, floor hockey, and aquatics.
- December 1968: Special Olympics is established as a nonprofit charitable organization.
- February 1977: The First International Special Olympic Winter Games are held in Steamboat Springs, Colorado, with more than 500 athletes competing. Major television networks cover the events.
- October 2007: In the Special Olympics Summer Games in Shanghai, China, 7,500 athletes compete.

---

The sport organization for persons with intellectual disabilities that is most familiar to the general public is the **Special Olympics** (see Focus On Box 11.10). There are more than 200,000 community-oriented Special Olympic programs in the United States, operated primarily by an extensive organization of 450,000 volunteers who provide instruction and conduct competitions in 16 sports on a yearly basis. The Special Olympics movement has been so popular that it works with any person with intellectual disabilities above 8 years of age, including adults. The Special Olympics program has developed a number of instructional programs for use in training personnel to work in a sport environment with persons who have intellectual disabilities. More than 24,000 women and men have been trained as officials, instructors, coaches, and event directors.

Special Olympics now has more than 200 programs in 170 countries that serve 3.5 million children and youths with intellectual disabilities, with 1 million volunteer coaches. Children and adults who participate in Special Olympics show improved

fitness and motor skills as well as improved self-confidence. Special Olympics has transformed itself from a sports program to help children and youths improve their lives to an effective catalyst for social change throughout the world.

In 1989 the Special Olympics launched a new program called **unified sports** (www.specialolympics.org). The term *unified sports* refers to sporting events in which teams include athletes with and without intellectual disabilities. One of the many benefits of unified sports is that it allows Special Olympic athletes' families to participate on unified sports teams. Unified sports is a manifestation of the powerful movement toward inclusion so prevalent in American schools. Unified sports presently include basketball, bowling, cycling, distance running, soccer, softball, tennis, and volleyball. Unified sports have begun to spread at the local level through community recreation programs and through agency programs such as the Boys and Girls Clubs of America. Unified sports help schools meet the transition mandates imposed by IDEA.

A significant worldwide movement for athletes with disabilities is promoted and administered by the Paralympic Games organization (www.paralympic .org). Tracing its origins from the effort in 1948 to organize athletic competitions for World War II veterans with spinal cord injuries, the movement now has regular international competitions for summer and winter sport activities. The movement now accommodates athletes from six disability groups. The summer Paralympics first competed in 1960 after the Rome Olympic Games attracted 400 athletes from 24 countries. The most recent Paralympics, held in conjunction with the Athens Games, attracted 3,806 athletes from 136 countries. The International Olympic Committee and Paralympics have agreed that the games, both winter and summer, will be held together in the future. The 2012 Paralympics will be held in conjunction with the Olympic Games in London, England.

The U.S. Paralympics, a division of the U.S. Olympic Committee, works with 50 member organizations to provide programs and services to develop athletes and coaches to participate in national and international competitions. U.S. Paralympics provides sport clinics, competitions, training and discussion forums, and the Paralympic Academy in Colorado Springs, Colorado.

The key legislative provision supporting increased access to sport for people with disabilities is Section 504 of the 1973 Rehabilitation Act (French, Henderson, Kinnison, & Sherrill, 1998). The language of this key provision states:

> No otherwise qualified handicapped individual in the United States, shall solely by reason of his handicap be excluded from participation in, be denied the benefits of, or be subjected to discrimination under any program or activity receiving Federal financial assistance or under any program or activity conducted by an Executive agency. (U.S. Public Law 93-112, 1973)

The phrase *otherwise qualified* is legal terminology that means that the person has the skills or abilities to participate in the sport after reasonable accommodation has been made. As people with disabilities use Section 504 to challenge denial of access to participation in sport, more and more opportunities will open to them. A number of states are passing laws in this area that are even stricter than federal law. When state and federal law conflict, the more stringent requirement is used.

The major journal supporting sport, recreation, and physical education for persons with disabilities is *Palaestra* (www.Palaestra.com). For more than 20 years, *Palaestra* has provided a wide range of historical, topical, and informational articles on sport, recreation, and physical education for persons of all ages who have physical and intellectual disabilities. The journal has played a key leadership role in uniting the various dimensions of the *sports for the disabled movement* in the United States (Beaver, 2004).

## Masters or Veterans Sport

The historical approach to sport and aging was simple: Young people compete and older people watch. That too has changed. There is a growing movement for what, in the United States, is termed *masters sport* (in most of the world, the same movement is referred to as *veterans sport*). The general proposition underlying this movement is that men and women can continue to find meaningful competition in sport throughout their lifetimes.

Masters sport has become the major competitive outlet for people who want to devote more time to training or to test themselves in a wider arena of competition than is available through organized recreational sport. Masters competition typically begins at age 40 years and is graded in 5-year age groups. At regional and national competitions, it is no longer unusual to find spirited competition in the 70- to 74-year age group.

Masters programs are most well developed in track and field, road racing, swimming, and bowling. There are more than 42,000 registered swimmers in the United States Masters Swimming organization (www.usms.org), which holds an annual convention and has a regular calendar of regional and national events. The World Association of Veteran Athletes (WAVA) was renamed the World Masters Athletics

(WMA). WAVA held its first world championships event in Toronto, Canada, in 1971 with 1,408 competitors. In Brisbane, Australia, in 2001, more than 6,000 athletes from 79 countries competed in the WMA World Games. At the 2008 WMA Indoor World Championships held in Clermont Ferrand, France, nearly 3,500 athletes from 52 countries participated, organized in 5-year age groups starting with the 40–44 age group and going up to the 95–99 age group.

The World Masters Games is yet another age-group organization that holds regular national and international championship competitions. The first World Masters Games were held in Toronto in 1985 with 8,000 athletes from 61 countries competing in 22 sports. The 2005 Games were held in Edmonton with 21,600 athletes participating in 25 sports. The 2011 Games will be held in Sacramento, California.

Veterans and masters competitions in track and field use age-grading to adjust the athlete's performance according to age and gender. Age-grading tables, developed by the WMA, work by recording the world-record performance for each age at each distance, allowing older runners to compete on even terms with young runners. It also allows for athletes to compare their own performances over time and to identify their best-ever performance (www. runningforfitness.org).

The involvement of adults and senior citizens in sport has led to the creation of statewide sport festivals, the first of which was held in New York in 1978. A state sport festival typically involves competition in a large number of Olympic, national, and local sports across all age ranges but emphasizes adult and senior participation. Forty-four states have conducted state sport festivals over the past decade. These state games are good examples of the festive nature of sport competition, with goodwill and participation ranking as values equal to vigorous competition.

Like sport for people with disabilities, the growing availability of masters competition for older athletes not only enriches the lives of men and women who want to continue to train and compete in their sport but also serves as an important model for a healthy, active lifestyle, which has serious implications for fitness as well as for sport.

## NONPARTICIPANT SPORT INVOLVEMENT

There are many ways to be involved in sport besides playing or coaching. As a sport becomes more highly institutionalized, a variety of roles are created that require professional expertise to be applied to the interests of the sport. Thus, sport vocations develop as a sport becomes more highly institutionalized. Organized sport at the local level, typically in communities, often operates primarily with part-time and volunteer help. To the extent that sport is more highly organized and more institutionalized, there is a need for full-time, professional services.

The following list of vocational opportunities is evidence of the diverse professional roles in the field of sport. Each listed vocation is followed by typical places of employment.

*Athletic administration*—high schools, colleges, pro teams, clubs

*Sport administration*—corporations, pro clubs, colleges

*Sport leadership*—recreation centers, industry, camps, churches, resorts, commercial centers

*Sport broadcasting*—radio, television stations

*Sport journalism*—newspapers, magazines, self-employed

*Sport-facility design*—corporations, government, self-employed

*Sport camps*—established camps, self-employed

*Sport-facility management*—government, pro teams, industry, universities

*Sport medicine*—hospitals, sport-medicine centers, universities, pro teams

*Sport counseling*—high school, colleges and universities, private practice

*Athletic training*—schools, universities, pro teams, sport-medicine centers

*Sports officiating*—schools, universities, pro teams, recreational programs

*Sport psychologist*—universities, pro teams, national teams

*Sport scientist (physiology, biomechanics, and so on)*—universities

*Sport-equipment design*—self-employed, industry

*Sport studies (history, sociology, and so on)*—universities

*Sport fitness*—universities, pro teams, national teams

*Sport publicity*—universities, pro teams

*Sport promotion*—universities, pro teams

*Sport photography*—newspapers, magazines, self-employed

Athletic trainers have become commonplace in high-school and collegiate sports.

Although many men and women earn their living within these vocations, this does not mean that they have been *specifically prepared* for that vocation. There are a few universities where a person can study sport photography, sport journalism, or sport broadcasting. The more typical route to these vocations is through the broader field of study: photography, journalism, or broadcasting. The physician specializing in sport medicine is exactly that—a *physician* who, after completing medical training, specialized in the application of medical science to sport.

In some of these vocational areas, one can study the vocation directly and proceed to work in that vocation. That is the case for sport psychology, the sport sciences, sport studies, and sport management and administration. Direct training in these fields, however, is not the only way to enter the vocation. Many sport psychologists were trained as psychologists and have a deep interest in sport. Many sport administrators were trained in business administration and have a deep interest in sport. These are areas where direct training *is* available, but that training is not *necessary* to enter the vocation.

The vocation of athletic training is one of the few in the list where specific training is needed to enter the vocation—and it is difficult to enter the vocation without that training because of the certification required to practice as an athletic trainer. Athletic training major programs are now available in many colleges and universities.

Thus, preparation for a career in a nonparticipant sport vocation, at the current stage of sport development in America, presents a flexible set of options. As sport becomes more highly institutionalized, we can expect that more specific preparation for nonparticipant vocational roles will be made available and that certification or licensing programs will be developed to ensure that people entering the vocational roles have the requisite skills and knowledge. Two such areas—sport management and administration and athletic training—are reviewed in this chapter.

## Sport Management and Administration

One of the fastest-growing vocational specializations in sport, fitness, and physical education in recent years has been the area of **sport management** and administration. Sport-management programs currently attract large numbers of women and men who want a career in a sport-related field but have no interest in coaching or teaching. Many programs are now available. Some are undergraduate majors, providing a choice at that level for young men and women who traditionally might have majored in physical education. Undergraduate degrees in sport management are offered at 308 U.S colleges or universities, but only 51 of those programs have accreditation from the Commission on Sport Management Accreditation. Fifty-three universities offer a masters degree in sport management, typically for students who have majored in physical education, business administration, or some other non-sport-related undergraduate subject. Twenty-six universities offer a doctoral program in sport management, which typically leads to a career in teaching in university sport management programs.

The sport and activity industry can be divided into six segments (Miller, Stoldt, & Comfort, 2000). These are

- Professional sport entertainment (MLB, NFL, NASCAR, minor leagues)

- Amateur sport entertainment (college sport, high-school sport, Olympics-related events)

- Sport services (agents, event management, resorts, cruises)

- Sport and activity participation, for-profit (golf courses, bowling alleys, fitness centers, martial arts centers)

- Sport and activity goods (manufacturers, distributorships, retail)

- Sport and activity participation, nonprofit (parks and recreation, YMCA, hospital fitness)

The number of professional roles in these industry segments is quite varied and includes athletic directors, ticket agents, human resource managers, risk management, marketing, public relations, facility management, and financing/accounting. A facility manager, for example, might be employed by a university, a professional team, a community recreation department, or a resort hotel. Nearly all of these industry segments require marketing and publicity personnel. The nonprofit organizations almost always require professionals to direct and manage fund-raising.

The job opportunities are not evenly divided across the industry. Sporting goods and health and fitness management jobs appear to be most prevalent, with sports media and college athletics in the middle tier and professional sport and recreation administration in the lower tier (Miller et al., 2000).

In 1993 the National Association for Sport and Physical Education (NASPE) joined with the North American Society for Sport Management (NASSM) to develop competency standards for sport-management curricula at the undergraduate, master's, and doctoral levels. The core undergraduate curriculum for students in sport management includes 10 competency areas: sociocultural dimensions of sport, management and leadership in sport, ethics in sport management, sport marketing, sport communications, sport finance, legal aspects of sport, economics of sport, sport governance, and a field experience in sport management. Each of these 10 areas has required content that defines the minimum coverage to achieve the standard. The competency standards for the master's degree include nine areas, many of which are similar to the areas included in the undergraduate standards. Courses that fulfill these standards can be in the major department or in other departments, such as business, law, or economics.

Degree programs in sport management are widely available, especially as part of an undergraduate-degree program (www.nassm.org). Degree programs are also available at the master's and doctoral levels. NASSM has a program approval process for degree programs at all three levels. There are

240 college and universities offering a sport-management major at the undergraduate level, with 50 of them having successfully passed the NASSM review. There are 120 at the master's level, with 34 of them approved. There are 20 universities offering doctoral programs in sport management, with 5 of them approved.

Programs in sport management and administration often include an internship in which the student actually performs the skills necessary for the various roles. These may range from assisting an athletic director or working in a ticket office to helping in the promotions department of a professional team. Sport-management and administration programs are popular with young men and women who want a career in a sport-related vocation that is not directly in the coaching field.

## Athletic Training

The most highly developed sport vocation is that of athletic trainer. The National Athletic Trainers' Association is one of the strongest of all the sport, fitness, and physical education associations. Although athletic trainers are employed primarily by interscholastic, intercollegiate, and professional sport teams, they also find outlets for their professional services in sport-medicine centers. A more detailed presentation of the purposes of **athletic training** and the requirements for certification can be found in Chapter 8 under the section "Sport Medicine and the Rehabilitative Sciences."

## Nonparticipant Sport Vocations: By Whom?

Earlier in this chapter, we referred to the degree to which women were underrepresented in leadership roles in intercollegiate and professional sports. The same is true for African American men, especially in intercollegiate sports. Data shown in this chapter support the assertion that participation opportunities for girls/women and minorities have improved. The exception to that optimistic finding is for young boys and girls in urban poverty neighborhoods where participation opportunities are few due to poor facilities, inadequate programs, and concerns about safety.

In 2004, 44 percent of the coaches of women's intercollegiate teams (all divisions) were women, which is close to the lowest representation of female head coaches of women's teams since Title IX became the law of the land. In the same year, nearly 18 percent of all NCAA athletic programs did not have a woman in the administrative structure of the athletic department. Despite the fact that women account for 40–50 percent of our Olympic teams, they have only 11 of the 115 active members of the International Olympic Committee (Women's Sports Foundation, 2006).

Similar concerns have been expressed for women in officiating and in athletic administration at levels from interscholastic sport to professional sport. In response to media criticism, many of the organizations that control professional sports have developed specific recruitment and development programs to increase the number of women and minority persons in leadership and administrative positions.

When Title IX was passed in 1972, many women took coaching and administrative positions in newly expanded interscholastic and intercollegiate sport programs. In the 1980s, however, it became clear that the number of women in those roles had decreased substantially (Sisley & Capel, 1986).

A longitudinal study at the collegiate level conducted by Vivian Acosta and Linda Jean Carpenter (www.aahperd.org/nagws) shows both some promising results for athletes and some disturbing results for coaching.

- All three NCAA divisions show an increased number of sports offered to women.
- The average number of women's teams per school is 8.34.
- In the last several years, 885 new teams have been added.
- There are 8,132 head coaching jobs for NCAA women's teams.
- There is currently the lowest percentage of female head coaches in history (44 percent).

- Women filled only 10 percent of the 361 new positions in 2002.
- Division I programs are least likely to have female head administrators (8.4 percent).

Similar concerns have been expressed for women in officiating and in athletic administration at both collegiate and interscholastic levels.

The low incidence of minority personnel in coaching and administrative positions has received substantial national publicity since the early 1990s. In response to media criticism, many professional leagues have developed specific recruitment and development programs to increase the number of minority persons in coaching and administrative positions.

## Sport and Technology

Sport and technology have grown together since the early 1970s. Technology has been routinely used for years to improve athletic performance through computer simulations and comparison. The technology of strength development has changed the performance standards in most sports. Many elite athletes whose performance depends on optimum levels of strength and endurance are monitored daily through technology, and they adjust their workouts, sleep, and nutrition according to regular feedback, obtained through technology, from their bodily systems.

Newsgroups on the Internet and websites have created countless opportunities for gaining information about team and other sports. Professional basketball teams now typically have an assistant coach whose main role is to edit video clips of offensive and defensive play for immediate feedback during halftime at games and for scouting in preparation for future play. Data on coaching behaviors are collected from laptop computers that can produce instant profiles for coaches and their athletes (Partridge & Franks, 1996).

The largest bibliographic database on sport is available through SPORTDiscus, developed by the Sport Information Research Centre (SIRC) in Canada (www.sportdiscus.com). SPORTDiscus contains more than 500,000 references, 20,000 theses and dissertations, and 10,000 website addresses. Each month SIRC examines more than 1,200 magazines and journals, from practical to scholarly, to compile references related to sport, sport medicine, physical fitness, sport administration, coaching, physical education, sport law, physical therapy, and recreation. The system can be researched easily and quickly using keyword indicators to guide the search. SPORTDiscus is often available through university libraries or through a variety of fee-based services.

## SUMMARY

1. The sport culture of America is one of the most highly developed in the world. It extends from children's sport through age-group competition in masters-level sport.

2. All statistics—those on participation, attendance, money spent on leisure, coverage in the media, equipment, and cultural norms—indicate the growing size and importance of sport in American culture.

3. The idea that leisure abounds in contemporary American culture is a myth. Especially among the professional and business class—the group that is most involved in sport—much less leisure time is available than during most periods in history.

4. Sport participation can be classified as recreational, amateur, nonprofessional, and professional, with distinctions based on the degree of institutionalization of the sport involvement and the relationship of the involvement to monetary gain.

5. Participation in organized, nonschool sport for children and youths has grown substantially since the mid-1950s with even stronger growth patterns for girls more recently.

6. Organized sport for children begins as early as 2.5 years of age with an average early entry age of 5.8 years and an average entry age of 11 years.

7. Child and youth sport has developed in the United States almost entirely in the local government and private-community sectors with major organizational entities at the state and national levels.

8. Child and youth sport tends to be exclusionary in the sense that opportunity for participation decreases as young adolescents grow into their teens.

9. Coaching for child and youth sport is mostly volunteer with little control or certification of people who coach.

10. Countries that have a stronger federal involvement in child and youth sport tend to have coach-certification programs at various levels.

11. Interscholastic sport is regulated at the state level and occupies a place in the American sport culture unlike that in any other nation with more than 7.5 million boys and girls participating annually.

12. Most states have adopted a classification scheme that grades competition based on school enrollment. Financing differs from state to state, from full funding out of tax revenues to a model wherein most athletic funds have to be raised by boosters or earned in gate receipts.

13. Few states require any coaching certification beyond a valid teaching certificate; some states do not have any requirements; and only a few states require special certification in coaching.

14. Intercollegiate sport is primarily an American institution. Colleges and universities typically form leagues and affiliate voluntarily with a national governing organization such as the NCAA or the NAIA.

15. College and university competition is classified by size of school and by the degree of funding available to athletes.

16. Professional sport actually involves a relatively small number of athletes, who typically have short careers and whose pay scales within a given sport are uneven.

17. Professional sport is organized through parent organizations typically run by a commissioner but with the real power retained by owners.

18. Organized recreational sport is implemented through recreation departments, businesses, service clubs, and private community organizations. The range and amount of participation are extremely diversified.

19. The enactment of federal legislation in the 1970s greatly expanded the sport opportunities for people with disabilities. The scope of these people's sport involvement now rivals that of people without disabilities. The best-known example of these programs is the Special Olympics.

20. Masters sport is organized in 5-year age groups for people over age 40 years. It has recently experienced substantial growth, especially in road racing, track and field, and swimming.

21. With the institutionalization of sport in the twentieth century, a number of nonparticipant sport vocations developed, some of which require special preparation and certification.

22. Sport management and administration is the fastest-growing nonparticipant sport vocation. Many undergraduate and graduate programs are available throughout the country.

23. Athletic training is the most highly developed sport-related profession. Specific undergraduate and graduate programs lead to certification, which is typically necessary for entry into the vocation.

24. Nonparticipant sport vocations are dominated by white males; women and minorities continue to be underrepresented.

25. Technology has an impact on sport by providing more access to information and by offering highly sophisticated analysis of physiology, fitness, competitive strategy, and many other aspects of sport.

## DISCUSSION QUESTIONS

1. To what extent has your experience in sport been similar to or different from those described in this chapter?

2. What would be the benefits and liabilities of increasing local, state, and federal government involvement in child and youth sport?

3. What would school sport be like if it were based on an inclusionary, rather than an exclusionary, model?

4. If a program for coaching certification were to be required, what criteria would you want coaches to meet?

5. What opportunities are available for athletes between the ages of 18 and 23 years to continue to develop in their sport if they do not go to college and are not skilled enough to be hired as professional athletes?

6. How should school sport be financed? How should recreational sport be financed?

7. How does the sport experience differ for (a) the athlete with a disability, (b) the masters athlete, (c) the scholarship athlete, and (d) the child athlete?

8. In what ways will the quality of preparation for nonparticipant vocations in sport be related to the future development of sport?

9. What improvements could be made to ensure that high-school sports had positive developmental outcomes for athletes?

## CHAPTER 12

# Problems and Issues in Sport

*My high school coach forced me to run intervals until I vomited. I did both, exceedingly well, and after graduation turned my back on running for more than a decade. Not much has changed. Too many high school coaches still follow the same prescriptions.*

James C. McCullagh, editor, *Runner's World*

*My high school coach was short, white and out of shape—different than me. But he cared about me even though I wasn't the best player on our team. And it's a good thing too. Because nobody else was looking out for me then, and I needed his help more than once.*

Former athlete and current school coach,
from Coakley (1994, p. 189)

*Sports teach, it is their nature. They teach fairness or cheating, teamwork or selfishness, compassion or coldness.*

Wilfred Sheed, 1995

Chapter 10 explained the fundamental meanings of sport. It stressed the positive aspects of sport and the beauty that can be seen and the satisfaction that can be experienced through sport participation. It stressed that sport developed from play and was most meaningful when the sport experience was playful. Sport was described as a "natural religion" to which players and fans alike become committed.

Chapter 11 emphasized the degree to which sport has become central to American culture in the twentieth century and how it now extends from early-childhood sport opportunities to masters sport for women and men up to age 90. We also saw that sport has expanded not only in age range but also to previously underrepresented groups: women, minorities, and people with disabling conditions. The argument for the very positive potential of sport in the lives of all persons having been made, it is now time to examine the problems and issues that threaten sport, that have the potential to detract from and diminish sport's fundamental goodness. This task will not be difficult because the abundant problems within sport have been widely publicized.

While most experts and laypeople still recognize and support the positive benefits of sport participation, we have also become much more cognizant of the many problems that have developed, particularly in the last few decades. In newspapers, magazine articles, scholarly journals and on television, the problems in sports have been revealed and analyzed: parents misbehaving in youth sport, performance-enhancing drugs and supplements, abusive coaches, gender inequities, crippling injuries, illegal payments, and racism. If you are interested in a career in physical education, fitness, or sport, it is important that you understand these current issues and problems, are acquainted with the facts surrounding them, and are knowledgeable about current efforts to confront and solve those problems and issues. If sport is to play a central, positive role in the development of children and youths, it is the values, knowledge, and skills of the adults in charge that will determine whether positive outcomes will be realized.

All the contemporary scrutiny of sport—of sport's purposes, practices, and accomplishments—has shown two things clearly. First, sport has become vitally important in the culture for children, youths, and adults; unimportant issues do not attract the attention that sport generates in our daily lives. Second, to preserve and strengthen the sport culture for the next generation, there are problems in sport that we need to attend to. In this chapter, we review these problems with the primary goal of identifying practices that help improve sport for participants.

First, however, it is necessary to distinguish between what will be described as problems in sport from the many social problems in our society. Inevitably, some sport participants fall prey to those social problems. A basketball player dies from a drug overdose. A football player is arrested for participating in a robbery. A tennis player is arrested for driving while intoxicated. A baseball player is sentenced to jail for failing to pay child support. Many stories like these are reported on the sport pages of newspapers and on sport shows on television. The question is whether these are sport stories or stories about social problems that happen to involve sport participants. Most of the evidence suggests that children

Children need appropriate coaching and supervision as they learn sport.

and youths who participated in sport are *less likely* to be involved in such problems as adults than are their nonparticipating peers. In this chapter, the discussion is confined to problems that are specific to sport.

## CHILD AND YOUTH SPORT

If you plan to have a career in teaching or coaching, you need to be aware of issues in child and youth sport. Parents will ask you questions about local programs. It will certainly be within your professional role to work to ensure that children and youths who you serve also have good sport experiences in the community, to contribute to creating and sustaining positive child and youth sport programs in your local area.

Sport is an important part of the lives of many children and youths—and their parents. Estimates suggest that over 40 million girls and boys between the ages of 5 and 16 years participate in nonschool sports, coached mostly by 4 million volunteer coaches, 90 percent of whom are parents of the children playing (www.coachingschool.org). That is the good news. The bad news is that estimates suggest that up to 70 to 80 percent of the participants drop out of organized sport activities by their early teen years. Most children and youths who drop out are much less likely to engage in an appropriate amount of physical activity, while others may instead switch to forms of extreme or action sports such as skateboarding, BMX biking, and the like. Other youngsters quit out-of-school sport activities because they become involved in school sport, often in the middle-school years. Interscholastic sport, which will be considered in the following section, is an *exclusionary* model; that is, only those girls and boys who are good enough make the team. For those who try out and do not make the team, there are fewer out-of-school programs available to them as they advance through their teen years.

It is also clear that many youngsters drop out of youth sport programs because they are not having fun, most likely because there is an overemphasis on performance and winning. Others drop out due to excessive pressure from coaches or parents. Still others drop out because they find more interesting pastimes such as music, dance, or less-organized action sports such as in-line skating. Girls more than boys drop out to improve their grades in school.

In the past few years the starting age for sport training has become even younger. The Little Gym company begins classes for children at 4 months old. The My Gym company reported that 55 percent of children who attend classes in their 200 locations were 2.5 years old or younger (*New York Times*, November 30, 2010).

We should start by emphasizing the widespread agreement that sport participation, *properly conceptualized and properly delivered*, can be extremely valuable to the positive development of children and youths. Research has shown that substantial physical and psychosocial benefits are derived from child–youth sport involvement (Fraser-Thomas and Cote, 2007). Sport experiences enable children and youths to develop motor skills that serve as a foundation for lifetime involvement in physical activities. Sport participation provides physical activity that contributes to improved physical health, a particularly important outcome in an era when child and youth obesity has reached epidemic proportions. Sport participation also provides opportunities for children and youths to learn life skills such as cooperation, discipline, leadership, and self-control. Youth sport experiences correlate positively with adult career achievement (Larson & Verma, 1999) and correlate negatively with school dropout and delinquent behavior (Eccles & Barber, 1999). What we need to be aware of is that these positive outcomes do not occur automatically by enrolling children and youths in a local sport program; rather, they are achieved when the program is conceptualized and delivered in a way that is developmentally appropriate for the needs and capacities of the children and youths who participate. Sadly, The CDC reports that by age 13, 70 percent drop out of youth sports. The reasons most frequently cited were problems with adults, coaches, and parents.

In 2005 the Citizenship Through Sports Alliance (CTSA) convened a panel of youth sport experts to evaluate community-based youth sports in the United States. The panel reviewed evidence in five areas and gave each a grade (www.sportsmanship.org). The Child-Centered Philosophy area graded D, the Coaching area graded C, the Health and Safety area graded C, the Officiating area graded B, and the Parental Behavior/Involvement area graded D. The panel reported that many programs had lost a child-centered focus and replaced it with an emphasis on winning. They also reported that too many parents behaved in ways that did not support the development of the children and that too many programs focused on sport specialization leading to burnout. Furthermore, the panel suggested that too many programs failed to do background checks on coaches and did not invest in any coaching-education assistance for the volunteer coaches. It is clear that the parents of girls and boys playing in youth sport programs must play a proactive role in ensuring that the programs in which they enroll their children are quality programs. Each of these issues is discussed in this chapter.

Although requirements for volunteer coaches and for parents who come to watch their children play sport are few, a major effort in the past decade has been to provide educational materials and guidelines for coaches and parents. The National Youth Sport Coaches Association (NYSCA) provides 11 guidelines for parents to help them choose the right programs for their children and then ensure that the program is being administered appropriately (see Focus On Box 11.2). Research has consistently shown that positive, supportive parental involvement is related to a child's level of enjoyment and success in the sport he or she is playing (www.educated-sportsparent.com). Other research has shown that a moderate level of parental involvement is optimal because over-involved parents might create higher levels of pressure. Children mature physically and emotionally at different rates. Parents and coaches should work together to group young children according to skill level and size, rather than age (Seidman, 2009).

## Cooperation and Competition

A major criticism of child and youth sport is that it is often too competitive. The truth is that children learn to be appropriately or inappropriately competitive through their early experiences in sport. These early experiences should involve a variety of sport activities, each modified to be fun and exciting for the participants. These would include both organized sport activities modified to meet the beginning needs of the participants as well as infor-

mal activities organized by the children themselves.

Sport activities for younger children should be "small-sided" and intrinsically motivating, provide immediate gratification, and optimize enjoyment with their friends (Fraser-Thomas & Cote, 2007). All participants should get equal playing time. For these early activities to be successful, the participants must learn how to cooperate. The effects of winning or losing are momentary. Children especially do not like to be thrust into zero-sum situations where the only satisfaction comes from winning. The "fun quotient" is the more powerful motivator. See Focus On Box 12.1 for how the NYSCA's Coaches Code of Ethics reflects these goals.

The "fun" approach to sport for children stands in stark contrast to many youth sport programs that are driven by a *performance ethic*; that is, the quality of the performance, typically measured against a standard, becomes the primary way to measure program effectiveness. Even during late childhood (8–11 years), children tend to define their own competence by comparing it to their close peers (for

---

### FOCUS ON    Coaches Code of Ethics                    12.1

**I hereby pledge to live up to my certification as a NYSCA coach by following the NYSCA Coaches Code of Ethics:**

- I will place the emotional and physical well-being of my players ahead of a personal desire to win.

- I will treat each player as an individual, remembering the large range of emotional and physical development for the same age group.

- I will do my best to provide a safe playing situation for my players.

- I will promise to review and practice basic first-aid principles needed to treat injuries of my players.

- I will do my best to organize practices that are fun and challenging for all my players.

- I will lead by example in demonstrating fair play and sportsmanship to all my players.

- I will provide a sports environment for my team that is free of drugs, tobacco, and alcohol, and I will refrain from their use at all youth sports events.

- I will be knowledgeable in the rules of each sport I coach, and I will teach these rules to my players.

- I will use those coaching techniques appropriate for the all of the skills that I teach.

- I will remember that I am a youth sports coach and that the game is for the children and not for adults.

**Coach' Signature:** _____
**Date:** _____

SOURCE: National Youth Sports Coaches Association.

---

**FOCUS ON** — Children's Bill of Rights in Sport — **12.2**

Children in sport should have the right:

- To participate regardless of ability level
- To participate at a level commensurate with their development
- To have qualified adult leadership
- To participate in safe and healthy environments

- To share in leadership and decision making
- To play as a child and not as an adult
- To receive proper preparation for participation
- To have equal opportunity to strive for success
- To be trained with dignity
- To have fun

SOURCES: Adapted from *Youth Sports Guide*, by J. Thomas, 1977; American Alliance for Health, Physical Education, Recreation and Dance.

---

example, Billy knows that he can run faster than Michael) rather than in absolute terms (Billy can run 100 meters in 17.2 seconds). Young athletes in performance-oriented programs are encouraged to define *fun* in terms of improving their performance, often in ways that are measured by performance outcomes (for example, a lower time in swimming or executing a more difficult gymnastic skill) or by being moved from a "bronze" level to a "silver" level on a performance chart (Coakley, 2007).

## Developmentally Appropriate Sport

There is also substantial agreement among researchers that young children (grades 1–4) should be involved in a variety of physical activities, some of which can be organized and some in free playtime. Most scientific experts and pediatricians agree that children should not begin organized, competitive sport competition before the age of 8 years. At about 5 to 6 years, children develop the capacity to compare themselves to others in order to understand their own competence. They tend to learn competition as a social motivation around age 7 years. What this means is that community sport activities below 8 years of age should reduce the emphasis on competition. Programs for children should involve a lot of physical activity and help develop skills that involve large-muscle groups as well as help participants learn how to cooperate and play fairly. Activities should also be organized in ways that participants can experience success; that is, the complexity of the

activity and the skills needed to perform the activity are matched to the experience and skill levels of the participants. Program rules should ensure that all participants get equal playing time (see Focus On Box 12.2).

Green (1997) described a beginning program for young children, designed to help them learn soccer and to enjoy the experience. This coed program had no formal competition, no league standings, no trophies, and no statistics. Coaches led the coed play groups through a progression of soccer games over the course of a season. Each game emphasized one or more soccer techniques and tactics while maximizing the number of opportunities for players to touch the ball. There were no drills and no scrimmages, just games. In this sense, the well-designed games, following a clear progression to develop techniques and tactics, became the teachers. The age-appropriate games also had a high fun quotient.

All sports for children should be modified to fit the developmental status of the participants. Teams should be organized to make the modified-game competitions as close as possible—the most exciting and fun games are those where the score is close throughout the game and both teams have a chance to win. Modifications are especially important in games that, in their parent forms, involve complex tactics. Anybody who has watched young children trying to learn soccer in an 11 per side game on a regulation soccer pitch will see most participants "swarming" to the ball, with no offensive balance and no sense of tactics. To be played well, soccer,

Age-group sport training for youngsters is now commonplace.

like all invasion games, requires a fairly sophisticated understanding of offensive and defensive techniques and tactics. These are best learned through a series of small-sided, modified games through which techniques can be developed and tactics made gradually more complex.

If a child and youth sport program is defined primarily as a performance ethic rather than a "fun" ethic, many of the positive outcomes described previously will less likely be achieved. If children and youths are in programs where the main focus is on performance improvement and winning in competition, evidence suggests that the result for many will be decreased self-esteem and feelings of competence and increased levels of anxiety (Csikszentmihalyi, Rathunde, & Whalen, 1993). Inevitably, such negative outcomes lead to many participants dropping out of the programs.

## Specialization

Not too many years ago, children and youths often did not specialize in a sport until they reached the college level, and even at that level, it was not unusual to find two-sport athletes. In high schools, many boys played on a team in at least two of the three sport seasons of the school year (girls typically did not have the opportunity, or they would have done so also). That was then. Now it is rare to find a three-sport athlete in high school. What is more common is the *sport specialist,* the athlete who trains year-round for his or her sport, competes on the school team in that sport, and is likely a part of a sport club in that sport during the off-season.

Early specialization has also become more common. Gymnasts and swimmers start training at an early age and train year-round. Hockey and soccer players get early training in sport-specialization clubs; by the time they are in their teens, they are competing on select teams for their club in competition that is often of a higher grade than the local high-school competition. Ten-year-old hockey players play 90 games in a season. Young figure skaters train 30 hours per week. When soccer players finish their interscholastic season they often move immediately to their club team where they continue to compete in local, regional, and national competitions. There is no doubt that advances in exercise science have made year-round strength and endurance training another part of sport specialization.

Not only do young athletes specialize in a single sport, but in some cases they also specialize in a single position within that sport—that is, a quarterback in football, a pitcher in baseball or softball, a backstroke specialist in swimming, or a goalie in soccer. The more talented the young athlete, the more likely will be the pressure to specialize and train year-round. Some of the pressure to specialize comes from parents and others who see a college scholarship and eventually a professional career for the young athlete as the preferred future. Is specialization inappropriate? For those who survive, there is little doubt that the process breeds some talented elite athletes. Less is known about those who burn out during the process or suffer overuse injuries that derail their path to glory. There are few issues in child and youth sport about which there is more debate and less good evidence.

The National Association for Sport and Physical Education (2010c) has argued that year-round specialization in a single sport for boys and girls under age 15 is more often associated with developmental risks rather than rewards. NASPE believes that research shows that participating regularly in a variety of sports and physical activities has physical, psychological, and social benefits that contribute to both short- and long-term development and to continued participation in both recreational and competitive sports.

## Child and Youth Sport Injuries

Accurate and reliable data on the extent and nature of injuries in child or youth sport are difficult to obtain (whereas data on injuries in interscholastic sport are readily available as you will see in the next section). Acute injuries, referred to as *macrotrauma*—such as sprains of joint ligaments, strains of muscle tendon units, contusions involving muscle tendon units and their overlaying soft tissue, and fractures of the long bones and axial skeleton—are estimated to result in 4 million emergency-room visits every year

(Micheli, Glassman, & Klein, 2000). Children ages 5 to 14 account for nearly 40 percent of all sports-related injuries treated in hospitals each year, including 175,000 visits to hospital emergency rooms for treatment for concussions (Bakhos, Lockart, Myers, & Lanakis, 2010). What is clear is that the incidence of injuries is sufficient to cause some hospitals to open pediatric sport-medicine clinics. The more serious injuries are the overuse injuries that sometimes develop when children or youths specialize in a sport (Micheli et al., 2000). Overuse injuries are seen more often in younger children because of the softness of their bones and the relative tightness of their ligaments and tendons during growth spurts. What is known as "Little League elbow" is the result of damage to the growth cartilage of the elbow joint. Other common overuse injuries occur in the knee and ankle.

The current generation has seen a growing involvement of children and youths in various kinds of extreme or action sports such as skateboarding, BMX biking, and in-line skating—activities that are inherently risky. Indeed, risk is one of the attractions. Very little data exist on the nature or severity of injuries in these activities. Some, like handlebar injuries in BMX stunt-biking, are so serious that some government health units are beginning to release warnings to media to alert parents to the potential dangers. Handlebar injuries can result in ruptures of the spleen, liver, kidneys, and bowel, sometimes so severely that organs have to be removed.

Duquin (1988) suggests that what she called "sado-asceticism" has too frequently crept into child and youth sport. Too many adults, coaches, and parents, support a "no pain, no gain" ethic for practice, training, and competition. Duquin, however, argues that the wisdom of the body and the wisdom of childhood are to avoid pain, that "no pain is sane," and that children typically quit when they get hurt. The asceticism she describes as having crept into organized child and youth sport in recent years is to redefine pain as discomfort and to encourage young athletes to work through the discomfort. As she so eloquently states, "Adults may choose to sacrifice their bodies for their perceptions of truth. In youth sport, the 'truths' are those of adults, the sacrificial bodies are those of children" (Duquin, 1988, p. 35).

## Coaching Child and Youth Sport

A substantial percentage of the volunteer coaches for community child and youth sport are parents of participants. Typically, they coach for as long as their child or children are involved in the sport at that level, which is typically no longer than 3 years. Most community-based sport programs have difficulty attracting a sufficient number of coaches, so they have few requirements for those that volunteer to coach. Increasingly, however, programs are requiring background checks to ensure that volunteer coaches have no police record that would disqualify them from coaching children and youths. Many states and communities are encouraging volunteer coaches to take part in courses or workshops that provide at least a beginning understanding of coaching techniques that are appropriate for child and youth sport and, of course, those techniques that are inappropriate. The NYSCA has developed a code of ethics that describes the qualities and competencies that volunteer coaches should have or develop to optimize the potential of sport experiences for children and youths. The code of ethics is described in a "pledge" form that coaches sign before they begin their child or youth sport coaching assignment (see Focus On Box 12.1).

Research on volunteer coaches is sparse, but what has been done shows that they too often behave in ways that are not productive for young athletes—too much evaluation, too much criticism, too few supportive interactions (Eitzen & Sage, 2003). Research in the 1970s showed that volunteer coaches can change when they are helped through educational programs (Smith, Smoll, & Curtis, 1978). Out of that research grew a model for preparing volunteer coaches called "Coach Effectiveness Training" (Smoll, 1986), which has influenced many of the coaching-education programs now in use throughout the United States. The philosophy of that program was built on notions such as winning is an important goal but not the only goal, that losing does not imply failure, that success can be achieved in many ways including but not exclusive to winning, and that success is related as much to effort as it is to outcome. This approach stands in stark contrast to the "winning is the only thing" ethic that pervades so much of elite sport.

A risk for volunteer coaches is for them to adopt what Coakley (2007) describes as a "techno-science" approach that values improvement in techniques and tactics more than the developmental aspects of maturing children and youths. Many volunteer coaches have watched sport on television, with instant replay and with commentators making constant assessments on the technical and tactical decisions made by coaches. Although learning techniques and tactics is important, it must be done in a way that is gradual and is combined with at least equal focus on helping youngsters develop as competent, autonomous, and responsible people.

## Impact of Sport on Family Life

During the years in which their young children participate in sport, many families have to totally alter their lives (Harrington, 1998). That is particularly true for parents whose sons or daughters are skilled enough to make the "traveling" or "select" team. Participation costs can become substantial, especially for sports that require indoor facilities (for example, winter soccer and ice hockey). Summer camps have become the norm rather than the exception. Some parents put 40,000 miles on the family car taking sons or daughters to away competitions. There are early mornings and late nights. The family seldom is able to have a meal together. Parents can get very intense about the participation and performance of their sons or daughters and their team (see Focus On Boxes 12.3 and 12.4). Although most parents willingly support all those endeavors because they believe them to be

## FOCUS ON — What Kids Want to Tell Parents and Spectators 12.3

- Don't yell out instructions—then I can't concentrate on what the coach says.
- Don't put down the officials—that embarrasses me.
- Don't yell at me or the coach—that takes away from my fun.
- Don't put down my teammates—that hurts team spirit.
- Don't put down the other team—you're not being a good sport.
- Don't lose your temper—that embarrasses me too.
- Don't lecture me after the game—I've messed up, I already feel bad.
- Don't forget the things I did well—I'm proud of them.

- Don't forget it's just a game—I need to be reminded of that sometimes too.

***Resources for Positive Spectating and Parenting in Sport***

- Positive Coaching Alliance—www.positivecoach.org
- National Alliance for Youth Sports—www.nays.org
- Gatorade's "Playbook for Kids"—1-877-PLAYKIDS
- Character Counts Sports—www.charactercounts.org
- The Center for Sports Parenting—www.sportsparenting.org
- Citizenship Through Sports—www.sportsmanship.org

SOURCE: Gatorade's "Playbook for Kids: A Parent's Guide to Help Kids Get the Most Out of Sports."

## FOCUS ON — Problematic Parents 12.4

Most parents support their children/youths in their sport endeavors, whether in community sport or interschool sport. Still, there are parents who create problems for coaches. Shown below are the kinds of confrontation most commonly experienced by coaches.

- An angry parent confronts you immediately after a game.
- A parent blocks you from reaching your car in the parking lot after a game.
- A challenging parent schedules what you know will be a contentious meeting.
- A parent makes an unreasonable demand (such as taking away the MVP award just

presented and giving it instead to his/her son/daughter).
- A parent makes disparaging comments about you and your program behind your back.
- A parent challenges your decision about who you assign to the starting lineup.
- A parent angrily criticizes you about playing time of his/her son/daughter.

Coaches need to keep program directors or school athletic directors informed of such incidents. Using e-mail provides a time and date of the information.

SOURCE: Hoch, 2007.

beneficial to the development of their children, there is no doubt that severe dislocation of family life can occur. An increasingly significant motivation for parents to support this kind of traveling to support their son's or daughter's development in a particular sport is the hope that the son or daughter will receive an athletic scholarship to a college or university.

## Unequal Access Based on Socioeconomic Status

Opportunity to participate in child and youth sport in the United States is not offered on a level playing field. Opportunity is strongly tilted toward the daughters and sons of the middle and upper socioeconomic classes. The Carnegie Council on Adolescent Development (1992) found that boys and girls from lower-social-status communities were seriously underserved in all forms of childhood and youth services, including sport opportunities. They concluded that "young adolescents who live in low-income neighborhoods are most likely to benefit from supportive youth development services; yet they are the very youth who have least access to such programs and organizations" (p. 12). The Center for the Study of Sport in Society at Northeastern University (www.sportinsociety.org) estimates that 15 percent of urban children and youths participate in youth sport programs, as compared with 85 to 90 percent of their suburban counterparts. That makes a mockery of the concept of a "level playing field" in child and youth development.

If we believe that appropriately planned and conducted sport experiences for children and youths are developmentally and educationally valuable, and the evidence strongly supports that belief, then we must all work to see that such experiences are available to all youngsters, whether they are rich or poor. (See Focus On Box 12.4.)

## Trends in Child and Youth Sport

Sport for children and youths continues as an important part of the lives of many families in America, and there have been some positive recent improvements: the availability of coaching-education materials, the increasing requirement for background checks for volunteer coaches, a vast array of materials available for parents to better educate them about developmentally appropriate sport, and a better understanding of likely injuries that might occur through overtraining and sport specializa-

tion. At the same time, however, some developing trends are troublesome. Sport sociologist Jay Coakley (2007) has described five trends that are disturbing:

1. Decline in the number of publicly funded child and youth sport programs due to federal and state tax cuts that create local budget crises

2. Increased privatization of youth sports favoring families who can afford club and facility fees

3. Segregation of programs by socioeconomic status, race, and ethnicity

4. Decreasing opportunities for children in low-income families and communities

5. More children seeking alternatives to adult-controlled organized sports

Will these trends continue? If so, what will child and youth sports look like in another decade? It is important that all sport, fitness, and physical education professionals be aware of these issues and commit themselves to work toward a child and youth sport culture that is developmentally appropriate and equally available to children and youths throughout the nation.

## INTERSCHOLASTIC SPORT

Interscholastic sport for girls and boys plays a significant role in the American sport culture. The American model for interscholastic sport is unique in the world. Interscholastic sport often begins in the middle school, but its most robust presence is at the secondary-school level. In high schools that have adequate funding and a significant enrollment, it is common to find teams at the freshman, junior varsity, and varsity levels. Smaller schools or schools where funding is inadequate may have only junior varsity and varsity teams. Likewise, school size and school funding determine the number of sports that are offered.

Many people are rightfully proud of the interscholastic sports model in the United States, the

The high-school varsity model produces elite athletes but excludes most students from the opportunity to participate.

opportunities that it provides girls and boys to grow in their sports, and the cohesive force it creates in both the school and community (see Focus On Box 12.5). In many communities, high-school teams and their falling or rising fortunes provide a focal point around which the entire community coalesces. Like other parts of the sport culture, however, interscholastic sport is not without problems. In this section, we address the following problems and issues:

- Exclusion and the varsity model
- Youth and interscholastic sport injuries
- Eligibility and pass-to-play rules
- Specialization
- Performance-enhancing supplements
- Coaching issues
- Funding through pay-to-play plans and booster clubs

## Exclusion and the Varsity Model

If you examine participation in child and youth sport in America, you see a triangle with broad-based participation at the bottom (that is, child and youth sport) and less participation in interscholastic sport (ages 14 to 18). As we have noted, sport for children is programmed primarily through community sources and is widely available. Sport for high-school–aged youths is programmed mostly through the school and is *decreasingly* available as the youths get older. This tendency to make participation less available (or available only to the better players) is known as the **varsity model** of competition, and it is the dominant feature of American school sport.

Many children in communities across the nation play soccer or baseball when they are young, often continuing their competition until they are 12 or 13 years of age. Even small communities have a soccer league or a Little League Baseball competition involving many children. Each of these same

---

As we examine problems in interscholastic sport, it is important to show that there is good evidence that school sport has benefits for many participants and for the school:

- Better grades
- Better self-concept
- Higher educational aspirations
- Stronger sense of personal control
- More likely to eat healthy diet
- Less likely to used banned substances

There is also descriptive and anecdotal evidence that interschool sports can indeed create what we traditionally have called school spirit.

"Interschool sports competition, then, is a means of unifying the entire school. Different races, social classes, fraternities, teachers, school staff, and students unite in a common cause.... An athletic program sometimes keeps potentially hostile segments from fragmenting the school. The collective following of an athletic team can also lift morale, thereby serving to unify the school" (Eitzen & Sage, 2003, p. 93).

communities, however, has only *one* school team—or perhaps one reserve team and one varsity team. What happens to the further participation of all of those soccer and baseball players? The answer in most communities is *very little*!

The nature of an *exclusionary* model of sport development is that the entire system acts to identify and eventually cater to the more highly skilled player. Those players who are excluded have few opportunities to continue to develop in a sport, at least not until they are old enough to take part in more adult-oriented recreational sport. Adolescence is the time when boys and girls develop many, varied interests. Thus, we should not expect that they all will necessarily want to continue to develop within a certain sport or to try a new one. The issue here is *opportunity,* and unless a child is good enough for a varsity team, she or he has little opportunity to continue to develop in a sport in the current varsity model.

The varsity model used in the United States is quite different from school sport throughout the world. In most European countries, some school sport is available but is "low-key" compared to the United States. Instead, adolescents use the widely available *club system* for their continuing participation in sport. In sport clubs, which are community organizations not schools, boys and girls can compete at a level commensurate with their skills. If a soccer club or basketball club has enough interest among the 14- to 18-year-old group, they will organize a series of teams that compete against other clubs with similar groupings. In club sport, children join a club at a young age and can continue to compete for that club throughout their lifetime. The club system is *inclusionary*. The A team for each club would be analogous to an American varsity team in that it would have the best players, but in the club system, practice and competition would also be available for B, C, and D teams in the same age group if there was enough interest.

New Zealand has an inclusionary system that allows students to participate in high-school sports and club sports. Any high-school student who wants to compete in a sport can do so. Many more sports are offered than is typical in the United States. Students can compete both for their high school and their club. In New Zealand, it would be typical that 70 to 80 percent of students in a particular high school would be competing in school sport in a typical year. Teams typically practice 2 days a week and have one competition per week. For example, if girls' badminton is the sport, competitions typically involve two singles and a doubles team (four girls). If the high school has 48 girls on the badminton team, the competition would involve 12 four-girl teams that are organized by skill levels. No players are "cut" from the team. Focus On Box 12.6 provides a snapshot of the participation rates from girls and boys in one New Zealand high school.

## Youth and Interschool Sport Injuries

Despite the documented health benefits of participation in interscholastic sports (for example, weight management, improved self-esteem, and increased strength and endurance) there is continuing concern about injury prevention and treatment. Until recently, there was no way to document either the extent of sport-related injuries for high-school athletes or the seriousness of the injuries. The Centers for Disease Control sponsored a national study of sport injuries during the 2005–06 school year (Centers for Disease Control and Prevention, 2006). Nine high-school sports were studied with reports made by athletic trainers in the 425 participating schools. The data allowed researchers to conclude that high-school athletes account for an estimated 2 million injuries, 500,000 doctor visits, and 30,000 hospitalizations yearly.

Nearly 1.5 million injuries occurred for the nine sports studied in the sample schools. Football had the highest injury rate, followed by wrestling, boys' and girls' soccer, and girls' basketball. For all sports, injury rates were higher in competition than in practice. The most common injuries were sprains, contusions, fractures, and concussions. Eighty percent of the injuries reported were new injuries rather than recurrences of previous injuries. The severity

Tawa High School in New Zealand enrolls 1,389 students—638 girls and 751 boys—with 91 teachers. It competes primarily with other high schools in and around Wellington, which is New Zealand's second largest city. What follows is a snapshot of its interscholastic sports program for 2009–10:

- Seventy-nine percent of all students compete in at least one sport, and many participate in three to four sports.

- Ninety-one sports are offered.

- The most popular sports and number competing for girls were net ball (161), soccer (66), and badminton (56).

- The most popular sports for boys were soccer (123), rugby (109), and cricket (85).

- Other popular sports and number of boys and girls competing were basketball (90), field hockey (64), and track and field (51).

- Other sports offered included water polo, softball, tennis, road racing, indoor bowling, cross-country, field hockey, golf, squash, touch football, and rowing.

- Nearly 30 percent of the teachers coach teams.

- No athlete is "cut" from a team. Teams typically practice 2 days per week and compete once per week.

SOURCE: S. Smith, Personal Communication, (2010). Tawa High School, Wellington, NZ.

of injury, measured by days lost from play, varied by sport. Overall, about half of the injuries reported resulted in less than 7 days lost. Football, girls' basketball, and wrestling had higher proportions of injuries resulting in more than 7 days lost. Fortunately, surgery was required for only 2.4 percent of the cases in football, 2 percent in wrestling, and 1.4 percent in field hockey.

Dr. James Andrews, President of the American Orthopaedic Society for Sports Medicine says that adolescent athletes are at risk for injury due to improper techniques, ill-fitting equipment, errors in training, pressure from coaches or parents, failure of early injury recognition, and the shift to specialization in a single sport (www.pediatricsupersite.com). Over the past several decades, high-school students have tended to specialize in one sport rather than participate in different sports in the autumn, winter, and spring seasons. This has resulted in a major increase in overuse injuries, such as tendonitis (Quinn, 2009). Many players who suffer from overuse injuries eventually require surgery to repair the problem. Boys and girls who participate in different sports across the yearly seasons are much less likely to incur overuse injuries.

Data on youth sport injuries is considerably more difficult to gather. A study on youth football sheds some light on the issues (Dompier, Powell, Barron, & Moore, 2007). Their data suggest that 28 percent of the 5.5 million youths aged 5 to 14 years who participated in various forms of youth football are injured each year, with an estimated 187,000 emergency rooms visits. The study focused on 779 youth football players, ranging in age from grade 4 to grade 8. Injuries were categorized into time-loss injuries (TL) and non-time-lost injuries (NTL). Injury data collected by athletic trainers showed that 36.5 percent of the players sustained an injury during the season, with nearly 15 percent reporting more than one injury. Injury rates tend to increase by grade level. Cumulative NTL injury rate was 10.5 per 1,000 exposures, and TL injury rate was 7.4 per 1,000 exposures. What this suggests is the importance of coaches and officials having first-aid certification.

## Eligibility and Pass-to-Play Rules

In almost all high schools, students have to meet eligibility standards to be on a school team. Many athletic-eligibility standards go well beyond criteria a student is required to meet to stay in school. In recent years, many states have instituted new *pass-to-play* eligibility standards, producing even more stringent requirements for athletes to maintain their eligibility.

In some cases, these more stringent eligibility standards have been legislated because of abuses in school sport. The issue is not whether abuses should be tolerated. The issue is how abuses should be remedied. The more fundamental issue in eligibility rules, however, has little to do with abuses. Instead, it has to do with one's basic view of the educational importance of school sport.

If school sport is an extracurricular activity, a privilege to be earned, then eligibility rules are clearly appropriate. If, however, school sport has basic educational value, then why deny the experience to anybody who is legitimately a student at a school? If being on a team provides an important set of experiences for personal and social development, then why should that opportunity for development be denied to some students?

As you can see, this argument is also related to the exclusionary issue discussed previously. The same logic prevails. If school sport is such a strong developmental experience for adolescent boys and girls, why not make it more widely available so that more students can benefit? It is true that there are important economic issues here also. Could we afford—or, more accurately, would we be willing to pay for—a greatly expanded school sport program? Despite the economic overtones, however, some important philosophical issues are at stake in this debate.

## Specialization

The problem of specialization was discussed in the section on child and youth sport. The issue is similar for school sport, with one added dimension. Athletes in high schools do specialize much more today than they did even as recently as the mid-1980s. Many athletes compete in one sport only and train for that sport in the off-season, sometimes attending a specialized summer camp. Sport specialization at the high-school level seems to be related to two important developments in the American sport culture in recent years.

First, the value and importance of weight and endurance training have been widely recognized. For many school athletes, an off-season spent in the weight room is more important than training for and competing in another sport. Many coaches promote this view—some directly demanding it, others more tacitly encouraging it. Second, many high-school athletes have hopes for an athletic scholarship to a college or university. The number of scholarships available has increased dramatically since the mid-1980s. To be as competitive as possible in the scholarship area, many high-school athletes forgo multisport competition in favor of specialization. There is little doubt that sport specialization among adolescent athletes is likely to result in more overuse injuries.

Is specialization good or bad? There are few issues in sport about which there is more heated debate—and for which there is less solid evidence. At this time, at least, the debate is more philosophical than scientific.

## Performance-Enhancing Supplements

In 2004–2005, the performance-enhancing drug scandals in organized sport became front-page news. The accusations about steroid use among high-profile baseball players was the most prominent of those scandals, resulting in hearings in the U.S. Congress and new rules for steroid testing and stricter penalties for steroid use in baseball and other professional sports. Just several years earlier, the focus had been on the dietary supplement *creatine* and its alleged use by home-run slugger Mark McGwire.

For our purposes, however, the more disturbing problem is one that attracted national attention when the December 20, 2004, cover of *Newsweek* showed a high-school football player with the heading "Steroids and Kids: How Sports Doping Hits Home." Another article followed on March 7, 2005, describing admitted steroid use by nine football players at Heritage High School in Texas. Although this one high school was the main focus of the article, it was clear that steroid use among young athletes had spread nationwide and become a major problem.

The most common performance-enhancing drugs and supplements are creatine, anabolic steroids, and steroid precursors (www.mayclinic .com/heat/performance-enhancing-drugs). Creatine is produced naturally in the body and is also sold as an over-the-counter supplement. It is used primarily to enhance recovery after workouts and increase muscle mass and strength. Side effects include weight gain, nausea, muscle cramps, and kidney damage (Bowers, 1999). Anabolic steroids are synthetic versions of the hormone testosterone, used to build muscle and increase strength. Use of anabolic steroids can cause heart and liver damage, halt bone growth, and result in permanently short stature. Steroid precursors, such as androstenedione and dehyroepiandrosterone (DHEA), are substances that the body converts into anabolic steroids. DHEA is still available in over-the-counter preparations, even though the side effects are similar to those for steroids. Coaches and parents should recognize the warning signs of performance-enhancing drug use. They are behavioral and emotional changes, particularly increased aggressiveness, changes in body build, rapid weight gain, and development of the upper body, increased acne and facial bloating, needle marks in the buttocks or thighs, enlarged breasts in boys and smaller breast in girls.

Concerns about the growing incidence of high-school athletes using performance-enhancing drugs and supplements have caused states to consider legislation designed to reduce and eliminate such practices. State legislators often confront this issue as a result of new evidence of the use of performance-enhancing drugs in their own state. For example, in June 2006, the *Dallas Morning News* published a multipart series on steroid use among high-school athletes in Texas. The series focused particularly on the 13,700-student Grapevine–Colleyville School District, north of Dallas. Soon thereafter, that district's school board passed a requirement for random testing of students who participate in sports and other extracurricular activities (LaFee, 2006). In early 2007, the governing body of interschool

sports in Texas partnered with the Texas Association of School Administrators to develop a program to educate students about the dangers of using performance-enhancing supplements. By this time, 130 of the 1,300 high schools in Texas were already testing for steroid use. In 2007 the Texas House of Representatives voted 140 to 4 to support legislation requiring random drug testing of high-school athletes in Texas. When the governor signed the bill, Texas joined New Jersey and Florida as states requiring random testing. Other states have passed legislation allowing school districts to choose to do drug testing, while other states have passed legislation that allows for voluntary student drug testing.

In a sport environment where young athletes are striving to improve their performance, hoping to get an athletic scholarship to college, and are socialized into a view of sport that accepts the use of steroids and ergogenic aids in the form of nutritional supplements, it is no surprise that many young athletes use supplements. Coaches, athletic trainers, and parents need to play a stronger educational and supervisory role so that these young athletes do not use questionable substances that may prove harmful to them in the long run.

## The School Coach as Teacher-Coach

The tradition in America has been that sport coaches are certified teachers. As interscholastic sport programs grew by adding more sports and by having different grade levels in the same sport, it became necessary to have more coaches. Men and women who fill both teaching and coaching roles over a period of years sometimes spend more of their energies in coaching than they do in teaching. Traditionally, the United States has programmed the largest part of its sport culture for adolescents through the school.

The involvement of *teachers* in school sport is no mere convenience or coincidence. An important philosophical issue is represented in that arrangement—namely, that sport is educational and should be conducted in an educationally sound manner. Some states now require coaching certification and some states do

not require that school coaches have teaching credentials. Thus, the philosophical principle underlying the
system is not always followed.

In most school districts, coaching is compensated
on a supplemental contract, both for teachers and
for nonteachers. States and local school districts differ markedly in the amount of compensation paid to
coaches. In 2009–10, 12,732 school coaches in
North Carolina received an average coaching supplement of $1,978. The range of supplement for
coaching was from $600 to $7,190 (NC Department
of Public Instruction, 2010). Private schools often
spend considerably more on coaching contracts. For
example, Chaminade Prep, a private school in West
Hills, California, pays its head football coach nearly
$100,000 (*Los Angeles Times*, May 2010). Coaches
who do not have a teaching license typically have to
go through a background check and have completed
a first-aid course. A continuing issue is whether
school districts hire teachers first and foremost for
their potential as a classroom teacher or physical
education teacher, and then secondarily for their desire and qualifications to coach in the interscholastic
program. This is obviously the preferred approach,
but some coaches are hired first and foremost for
their record as a coach and then only secondarily
for their record as a teacher.

## Parental Pressures and Booster Clubs

Parents, coaches, and townspeople often care about
the sport performance of local school teams and athletes in ways that *differ* from the ways that athletes
care about them. Parents, coaches, and townspeople
are adults, spectators, fans, and enthusiasts. The
adolescent athletes are participants. The differences
in points of view can sometimes create pressures
that are counterproductive to the development of
the athlete and of school sport in general (Focus On
Box 12.7).

---

### FOCUS ON    Parents and Coaches Out of Control!    12.7

On July 5, 2000, a parent watching his son at a
youth hockey practice session assaulted the man
supervising the practice and beat him so severely
that he went into a coma and eventually died
(Nack & Munson, 2000). That tragic event
brought to the attention of the nation what appears to be widespread instances of parents and
even coaches out of control in youth sport.

- In an Illinois state soccer playoff game, a coach is
  accused of striking a referee.

- In Florida, a parent walks out of the stands and
  head-butts a referee.

- In Pennsylvania, police are called to quell a riot
  involving fifty parents after a football game for
  11- to 13-year-olds.

- In a California Little League Baseball game, a man
  coaching his son's team assaults and beats the
  manager of the opposing team.

- In Ohio, the father of a soccer player pleads no
  contest to the charge of assaulting a 14-year-old
  boy who had scuffled for the ball with the man's
  14-year-old son.

Community and agency sport groups are beginning to take a more proactive stance to prevent
such incidents. In Jupiter, Florida, for example, a
community sport organization now requires that

- Parents take a class that includes a video on the
  responsibilities of parenting a young athlete.

- Parents sign a code of ethics pledging to behave at
  youth sport contests—if they don't sign, their kids
  don't play.

- Parent behavior is monitored at games. For a first
  offense, they review the video and sign another
  pledge.

- The parent and child are sent home after a second
  offense and are not allowed to return.

SOURCES: Meadows, 2003; Nack & Munson, 2000; Sutton, 2000.

Dress an adolescent in a uniform, have him or her play in front of spectators that include peers, parents, and friends, under the gaze of a coach who looms as an important person in the athlete's immediate future in the sport, with the results written about in school and local newspapers and talked about among people in the town—and what do you have? Pressure! That kind of pressure is often important to the development of the adolescent, important in a positive way. The major point here, however, is that additional pressure can become detrimental.

When parents put undue pressure on their sons and daughters, when coaches put too much pressure on their athletes, and when the expectations of administrators and parents put too much pressure on coaches, then the conditions are such that the sport experience can rapidly become less enjoyable and rewarding than it should be. In states where support for school sport has to come from booster clubs and gate receipts, the conditions that might create undue pressures on coaches, athletes, and programs are even more likely to occur.

With the growing importance of sport generally and with the specific focus in local communities on the success of the high-school teams, there is enormous pressure on school coaches, especially those in the high-profile sports of football and basketball. The major sources of pressure for high-school coaches are parents, fans in the community, and boosters (Miller, Lutz, Shim, Fredenburg, & Miller, 2005). Principals report that the major reasons for dismissal of high-school coaches are poor player–coach relations, lack of coaching skill, and failure to win (Scantling & Lackey, 2005).

## Pay-to-Play Plans

School districts in many states have had problems raising monies through local tax initiatives to fund the continuing expenses of education. As a result, many districts have begun to charge user fees for many extracurricular activities offered by the schools. *User fees* are a form of direct taxation; that

is, those who use the services pay an additional tax for those privileges.

Pay-to-play plans have been declared illegal in California and New York on the basis of the discriminatory effects of such plans; that is, students who can't afford the fees should not be denied access to what is an approved school program (Swift, 1991). The National Federation of State High School Associations has also come out against such fees, arguing that interschool sport programs have documented educational value and that students should have access to them as part of the regular school program.

Still, pay-to-play plans are springing up all over the country. School districts in at least 43 states now charge a participation fee for students to be on a school sports team (King, 2010). Estimates suggest that the nation's high schools cut at least $2 billion in funding for athletics in 2008–09, while some experts suggest that cuts have grown perhaps as much as 10 times that amount. In some cases, the fees are charged by school districts, with additional financial sport from local boosters clubs.

It is spring as I write this, and the suburban school district in my immediate area is full into the spring sports schedule. The track teams in the three high schools in the district have a long tradition of successful competition in their league and at the state level. This year, however, it costs $425 for a student to participate in track and field at the three high schools. In one high school, 49 girls and boys participate under the new fee structure where last year, the track team had 125 members. Another of the high schools is down from 60 track-and-field athletes a year ago to 33 this year.

It is curious that pay-to-play programs have developed at the same time that state courts all over the United States have begun to force states to fund schools more equitably—that is, to ensure that schools in financially strained districts have per-pupil budgets that are similar to those in schools in wealthy districts. The basis for such decisions is always a clause in a state constitution that ensures an equal and appropriate education to all children and youths in public schools. If pay-to-play plans become the norm, then it is certain that youths in financially strained districts will have fewer sport opportunities than their counterparts in wealthy districts and that their equipment and training facilities will be inferior.

## INTERCOLLEGIATE SPORT

Intercollegiate sport in the United States has become big business for some schools, especially in Division I schools in the National College Athletic Association (NCAA). Yet big-time intercollegiate sport occupies an important niche in American sport culture. Events such as the Rose Bowl and the Final Four are truly national in scope. Intercollegiate sport provides a common ground of loyalty among alumni, students, and friends. Division I NCAA sports provide entertainment to millions via radio and television.

At the Division III level of the NCAA, thousands of student-athletes take part in competition that seems an appropriate extension of school sport. No scholarships are given for athletic prowess at this level. Athletes' commitments within and outside the boundaries of the season are more limited. There is less commercialism. Nobody expects the sports to pay for themselves.

Thus, when we talk about problems and issues in intercollegiate sport, we must keep in mind that there are major differences between big-time university sport and the kind of competition we might typically find at a local college. The major problems and issues in intercollegiate sport are the following:

1. Recruiting violations and pressures
2. Drugs used to enhance performance
3. Economic disparities among top powers
4. Economic pressure to win
5. Treatment of the student athlete

### Recruiting Violations and Pressures

Each year, the NCAA puts several university athletic programs on *sanctions* because of recruiting viola-

tions. The recruiting of athletes to play on university teams is governed by rules established by the NCAA. The rules are intended to protect the athlete and to ensure reasonably equal competition among schools trying to influence young athletes to attend their universities.

What is sad and alarming about many recruiting violations is that they are done with the help and (in some cases) at the insistence of influential alumni and friends of the universities, who are often in positions of prestige, trust, and power within the community. Recruiting violations occur because the pressures to attract the best athletes are so strong. Those pressures are so strong because pressures to have a winning program are immense. The pressures to have a winning program exist because of economic factors and because of the status that accrues to those associated with winning programs at universities—particularly alumni and friends of the university.

Coaches sometimes succumb to those pressures. In other situations, coaches sometimes initiate the cheating themselves because they want to win so badly or to advance their careers. Direct cash payments, cars, high-paying jobs that require little or no work, and sexual favors have all been used to recruit talented young athletes.

### Used to Enhance Performance

Drugs are a problem for many college-age youths. For athletes, however, there is a special set of problems that have to do with drugs taken to improve performance. The use of these drugs in certain sports, such as track and field and football, is thought to be widespread at elite levels of competition.

Most of the increased size of weight-event athletes in track and field and of linemen in football is the result of more scientific application of weight-training principles. There is widespread fear, however, that some of it is also due to the regular use of anabolic steroids. Drug testing has become a major issue in the NCAA. Student athletes at NCAA championship events are regularly tested for drugs that might affect performance. The issue of drug testing has caused a national debate that still persists. The debate hinges on the right to privacy of the athlete (or the worker, if in a business) and on whether such testing is constitutional under the prohibition of *unreasonable* search and seizure in the Fourth Amendment to the U.S. Constitution.

## Economic Disparities Among Top Powers

For a few universities, the sports of football and basketball generate most of the revenues that support all the rest of the sports in the program. The presence of 80,000 fans for every home football game or of 15,000 for every home basketball game means income for the athletic program. In addition, the monies earned from televised games or for bowl-game appearances can be even more important than the gate receipts. Nonetheless, the vast majority of NCAA Division I athletic programs do not even break even with their football and basketball programs, let alone provide support for other sports.

In big-time collegiate sport, the rich tend to get richer. For example, if you have a winning program and are consistently ranked in the top 20 in football or basketball, more fans come to your games, you are offered a large local television contract, you have more regional and national television appearances, and you play more postseason games. More people see your team play. More young athletes see your team play—and the better ones are easier to recruit as a result. Of course, some universities not in this inner circle would like to get in! The difficulties in doing so are enormous. Thus, the temptation is there to cheat in recruiting to overcome the natural advantage enjoyed by the established programs.

In professional football and basketball, there is a yearly player draft in which teams at the bottom of the yearly standings get to pick first, a system designed specifically to promote more even competition over time. No such system exists for university sport, so over time the same teams tend to dominate the top rankings. Remember, big-time sports are a losing proposition economically for most universities. Still, the temptations created by hoping to improve that situation are substantial.

## Economic Pressure to Win

The economic disparities that exist in big-time collegiate sport produce strong pressures to win simply because it is through winning over a period of years that university athletic programs either remain in the elite economic group or break into that group. The economic consequences of making it are substantial. Programs that do not make it still have to build stadiums, put Astroturf on their fields, erect fancy scoreboards, and pay for equipping and training 100 football players. Without the economic power that accrues to the elite programs from gate receipts and television, these other institutions are left with huge bills that they must pay from regular funds.

Of course, there are always the alumni and friends who would like the athletic program to be as good as those at the few universities with the largest gate receipts, television contracts, and visibility. The issue here is status. The combined pressures that result from the search for status and for economic gain through big-time collegiate sport are at the heart of most of the abuses within the system.

## Treatment of the Student Athlete

Many student athletes are in sport programs in American colleges and universities that do fit the best possible image of how sport and academic life can be combined, where each is enriched by the other for a better total college experience. There are others, however, for whom the term *student athlete* is badly misused. This is often not so much their fault as the fault of the institution that is misusing the young athlete.

What is the quality of life for an elite, scholarship athlete at a major university? Although there are surely as many answers to that question as there are individual athletes, there are some disturbing signs, to say the least. The NCAA

---

**FOCUS ON** — Do College Athletes Need a Bill of Rights?                    **12.8**

Many people close to Division I college athletics believe that too many athletes are exploited and that a bill of rights is needed to protect their interests. How do you react to the following possible provisions of a bill of rights?

- The right to transfer to a different college without having to lose eligibility
- The right to a 4-year scholarship rather than one renewable at the discretion of the institution
- For those who compete for 3 years, the right to scholarship support until they graduate

- The same rights to protection from physical and mental abuse and the right of free speech that other university students have
- The right to consult with agents concerning their future in sports
- The right to be compensated for endorsements, speeches, and appearances
- The right to adequate insurance to totally cover current injuries and problems that arise from them

What can you add? What would you delete?

SOURCE: Adapted from Eitzen & Sage, 2003.

---

commissioned a study of more than 4,000 athletes from 42 Division I schools (Wrisberg, 1996) (see Focus On Box 12.8). The major findings are as follows:

- Student athletes focus most of their attention on their sport. They miss more classes and participate in fewer other university activities than their student peers.

- Basketball and football players perform less well than student peers on every measure of academic performance, even though there are substantial academic support services provided for them.

- Many suffer from frequent or chronic injuries and, despite better access to good health care, feel pressure to practice and perform despite injuries.

- Many elite-scholarship athletes suffer from chronic fatigue.

- These athletes tend to attribute actions to external influences more than do nonathletes; that is, they report less of a feeling of personal control.

- These athletes report having little opportunity or time to participate in personal-development activities on campus.

The picture that emerges from this study "offers little evidence of a high level of life quality by any definition or measuring standard" (Wrisberg, 1996, p. 397). It should be noted that the NCAA has used the results of this study to foster changes in Division I athletic programs that are aimed at reversing these trends.

Some sport scholars have long argued that scholarship athletes are badly exploited by the system (Sack, 1977). Scholarship athletes can receive nothing more than tuition, room, board, fees, and books—at least not legally. The total cost of this package differs depending on the costs at the university, but even at the most expensive university, when one divides the number of hours of work that the athlete devotes to his or her sport by the total value of the scholarship, the pay per hour is low. Clearly, few athletes *feel* exploited. Most are happy to be where they are, and many feel extremely lucky to have been awarded the scholarship. The charge of exploitation comes from the huge financial rewards the institution can achieve, which are not shared in any way with the athlete.

## EQUITY ISSUES IN SPORT

Many issues in sport have a central theme—*equity*. Historically, much of organized sport has been the special province of wealthy, white males. When the first Olympic Games were held in ancient Greece, the competition was available only to male citizens of the Greek city-states. Citizens were males of privilege. The menial labor of the day was done by slaves. Not only were women disallowed from competition—they could not even watch!

When the Olympic Games were reborn in 1896, the tradition had not changed very much. The new games were much like the old games in that males dominated and wealth was assumed—the games were, after all, for *gentlemen* athletes. You were not a gentleman if you came from the working class or if you really trained hard for the competition. Much has changed since those days, particularly since the 1970s. Nonetheless, the traditions of inequity in sport still linger and need continually to be addressed. Women's issues and minority issues are two such areas.

### Women's Issues

Access to training and competition in sport has historically been denied to women. The nine-

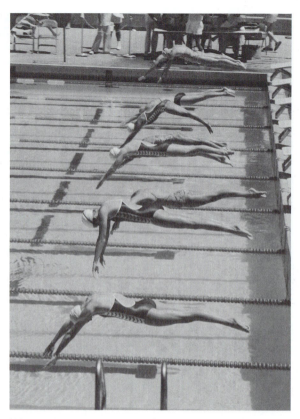

Women's competition in Olympic swimming is followed worldwide.

Learning to work together for a team goal is an important experience.

teenth-century "feminine virtues" of piety, purity, submissiveness, and domesticity were alien to sport competition. The philosophy of muscular Christianity from which twentieth-century sport and physical education emerged was, above all, a *masculine* philosophy. Clearly, those views have changed in recent years. The passage of Title IX of the Education Amendments Act of 1972 made equity for girls and women in sport the law of the land. Since then, girls have had access to more sports, their participation has increased dramatically, and scholarships for them have become more widely available. Moreover, there have been some notable successes by women in elite and professional sport. In 1984 women were finally allowed to compete in the marathon at the Olympic Games, and Joan

---

**FOCUS ON** — The Three Basic Parts for Title IX Compliance                    **12.9**

1. Participation: requires that women be provided with an opportunity equitable to men to participate in sports.
2. Scholarships: requires that female athletes receive athletic scholarship dollars proportional to their participation.
3. Other benefits: requires equal treatment in the provision of equipment and supplies, the scheduling of games and practice times, travel and daily allowance, access to tutoring, coaching, locker rooms, practice and competitive facilities and services, publicity and promotions, recruitment of student athletes, and support services.

Women's Sports Foundation, 2011, www.womenssportsfoundation.org.

---

Benoit showed extraordinary athletic prowess in winning the event. In the Barcelona Olympics in 1992, it became clear that Jackie Joyner Kersee was the greatest multi-event track-and-field athlete of all time, regardless of gender.

In sport, compliance with Title IX focuses particularly on equal provision of equipment and supplies, practice and game times, travel, compensation of coaches, publicity, tutoring and other such services, locker rooms, medical and training facilities, housing and dining facilities, and financial aid (Fox, 1992). (See Focus On Box 12.9.) These are easily identifiable factors, and discrimination against girls and women on the basis of these factors should be easily discernible. Yet problems related to these factors still exist in many schools and universities. The more subtle forms of discrimination—negative stereotyping, poor media coverage, underrepresentation in coaching and administration, and lack of female role models—will be more difficult to confront and correct (Fox, 1992).

Title IX became law in 1972. After a brief period of increased opportunity for women in coaching and administrative positions, the 1980s saw a decrease in the percentage of women in those roles. In 1984 Grove City College in Pennsylvania brought suit, charging that, because college athletic programs receive no direct federal support, Title IX did not apply to college athletics. The U.S. Supreme Court agreed. That decision led to a concerted lobbying effort in the U.S. Congress by advocates for women's sport and others interested in civil rights. Their efforts were rewarded when the Civil Rights Act of 1987 was passed with much stronger provisions for Title IX (Motley & Lavine, 2001). Thus, from the mid-1980s through the 1990s, we witnessed what might be called the first true "Title IX generation" of girl and woman athletes. All 50 states offered state championships for girls' sports, and the NCAA sanctioned 17 national championships for women.

Still, recent data show that the percentage of women in coaching, administrative, and training positions remains low and shows few signs of improving dramatically in the near future. Studies over the last decade have shown that 13 percent of interscholastic coaches were females and 10 percent of athletic director positions were held by women (Massengale & Lough, 2010). Women athletes receive only 30 percent of the scholarship dollars in intercollegiate sport, 23 percent of the athletic operating budgets, 17 percent of the recruiting dollars, and 35 percent of the participation opportunities (Motley & Lavine, 2001). Programs to attract, train, and place more female coaches have generally failed (Pastore, 1994), with the exception of a Colorado program that has increased the percentage of female coaches in school sport programs in that state. Male officials still dominate important women's sports such as basketball and softball (Casey, 1992). It is uncommon to see a woman as head athletic director at any level. In 2002 there were 3,210 administrative positions in NCAA women's athletic programs. Women held only 40 percent of those jobs. Acosta and Carpenter (1994) summarized the issues well:

> With the increase in women's participation in intercollegiate athletics has come a decrease in women's leadership opportunities at the administrative and coaching levels. If the women who currently enjoy collegiate athletics are to have the opportunity to remain in college athletics and exert leadership over the activities they enjoy, we must recognize the patterns of exclusion that presently exist in women's athletics and work to reverse this undesirable trend. (pp. 117–118)

The evidence strongly supports benefits of sport participation for girls and women. Research has shown the many ways in which sports participation benefits the development of girls and women (Strecker, 2010). Girls and women who participate in sports have better academic success and higher graduation rates, are at a lower risk of stroke and breast cancer, weigh less, have lower levels of blood sugar, cholesterol, and triglycerides, and lower blood pressure, have better bone health, have higher levels of self esteem and less depression, are at a lower risk for disordered eating, improve their cardiovascular fitness, muscle strength, and body composition, are less likely to use illicit drugs, and more likely to be physically active for life. Seldom has research produced such a positive outcome for participation in sports!

When interscholastic and intercollegiate sport budgets get tight, as they have in many places in recent years, it is now common to hear the requirements for gender equity in sports blamed for the reduced support for boys' and men's programs (Stourowsky, 1996). A men's volleyball program is eliminated at a university, and the reason given is the need to provide more support for the new women's tennis program—a zero-sum argument is forwarded suggesting that gains for women occur only at the expense of men. This is what Sage (1987) and Stourowsky (1996) refer to as "blaming the victim" strategy; that is, the fault is found in the group that has the least amount of power while the focus is deflected from the main issue, which is providing resources that are sufficient and equitable.

Another issue that girls and women are now contesting is the barrier to participation in contact and strength sports traditionally thought to be appropriate only for males. Participation for high-school girls in football, wrestling, ice hockey, and weight lifting has increased steadily over the past few years. For 2009–10, 1,249 girls participated in football, 6,134 in wrestling, 8,254 in ice hockey, and 7,416 in weight lifting. Athletic directors and coaches need to be sensitive to create conditions that are supportive of girls' participation, and their sensitivity can be increased through appropriate educational programs. The good news is that young girls and their support groups have continued to confront the stereotypes that have heretofore hindered their participation.

What seems clear is that the status of women in sport will not improve without vigorous advocacy by sport and physical education professionals. The National Association for Girls and Women in Sport (NAGWS) has adopted a strategic plan to remediate problems that exist for women because of unequal opportunity in sport and lack of compliance with Title IX (Hester & Dunaway, 1991). This plan includes advocacy for full participation both in athlete roles and in indirect roles in administration, training, officiating, and the like; recruitment, development, and promotion plans to help women assume leadership positions; and the initiation of new programs and enhancement of existing programs for females of all ages, races, economic levels, and ethnic origins.

Although the ideal of the athletic woman has become much more accepted today—even for substantial profit in advertising—the old conceptions linger in more subtle ways. We still hear male sports announcers describing a female athlete as "pretty, too" when prettiness or attractiveness has nothing to do with the competition. (When was the last time you heard a male announcer talk about a handsome baseball or football player?) Research indicates that adults frown on girls' participation in activities considered to be normal for boys and that signs of assertiveness typically reinforced in young boys are often not accepted in young girls (Elias, 1983). All of this indicates that the nineteenth-century views still linger in many ways—and that as long as they do, equity for girls and women in sport will not be complete.

## Minority Issues

If sport in America has been typically male dominated, it has also been "lily white." Blacks and other minorities have always participated in sport but were denied access to mainstream sport competition in schools, universities, and professional sport. The *color barrier* in major professional sport was not broken until Jackie Robinson played for the Brooklyn Dodgers in 1947. The integration of top-level collegiate sport did not come until much later, especially in the South. Although integrated schools were first mandated in 1954 (*Brown v. Board of Education*), school sport was not fully integrated until lawsuits were decided during the civil rights movements of the 1960s and 1970s.

Today, black and Hispanic players are abundant in some professional sports—particularly baseball, football, and basketball. Yet it is still rare to see a minority athlete on the tennis court or on the professional golf circuit. Minority athletes have been traditionally stereotyped by position in many sports (Loy & McElvogue, 1981), and they are seriously underrepresented in coaching and administrative positions in all sports (Coakley, 2007).

Many coaches and athletic administrators are former players. It has been more than 60 years since the color barrier was broken in professional baseball and more than a quarter-century since the implementation of Title IX, but gender and race inequalities are still prevalent in hiring and promotion practices in both intercollegiate and professional sport.

Recent studies show a small increase in the numbers of minority persons and women as head coaches, assistant coaches, and athletic directors in athletic programs at Division I and Division I-A universities (Lapchick, 2007). Still, the issues for minorities and women in high-level intercollegiate sport are substantial. In 2007,

- Eighty-two percent of athletic directors were white males.

- Sixty-five percent of faculty athletic representatives were white males.
- All Division I-A conference commissioners were white males.
- Ninety-three percent of head football coaches were white males.
- Eighty-seven percent of offensive and defensive coordinators were white males.
- Forty-five percent of student-athlete football players were white males.

Thus, at the top level of athletic management and coaching in collegiate football, minorities are substantially underrepresented. The 2008–09 NCAA Race and Gender Demographics Report showed that 18.9 percent of directors of athletics in all three divisions were female and only 4 percent of all athletic directors were black (Brown, 2010).

In our coverage of the various aspects of sport, it has been made clear that child and youth sport has enormous potential to contribute to the development of girls and boys. Yet, we have also seen that child and youth sport has problems, and one of them is the cost involved for families to keep their children involved in youth sport. For many minority families and others living in disadvantaged communities, the opportunities for quality youth sport experiences for children and youths are considerably less available. School physical education programs and community recreation programs in disadvantaged communities are typically underfunded and cannot provide comprehensive programs. These issues are most problematic for minority girls, who have been shown to be most at risk for physical inactivity and obesity.

Urban schools typically schedule less time in physical education, provide less opportunity for intramural sports, and offer fewer opportunities in interscholastic sports. Urban communities typically have fewer opportunities for child and youth sport participation. What is most disturbing is that there is good evidence that minority children and youths who do get the opportunity to participate in community and school sport are more resilient and more motivated to do well in school (Hawkins & Mulkey, 2005).

Problems of race in sport tend to interact with problems that are socioeconomic in nature. The idea of "sport for all," an ethic of access and participation, is being achieved much less in cities than in suburbs, much less among nonwhite children and youths than among white children and youths, much less for the poor than for the wealthy. Although these issues represent problems that institutionalized sport can help combat, we also need to recognize that the problems are manifestations of *structural* inequities in our society.

## SPORT SYSTEMS

The sport system of the United States is composed of diverse elements: child and youth sport, school sport, university sport, professional sport, and recreational sport. Some features of this system are distinct in the world sports community. Nowhere is school or university sport as important to a sport culture as in the United States. Nowhere is government support for and regulation of sport less than in the United States. The combination of youth, school, and university sport that serves youths and young adults as they develop in sport is primarily an *exclusionary* model, one in which a few skilled sportspersons get to continue in the system, whereas those who are less skilled have little access to continued training and competition in their sport.

In most of the rest of the world, the overall sport system of countries is guided and funded by government. The sport-club system is the primary vehicle of training and competition from youth sport through to elite sport. Coaching certification is more often required at all levels. Which system is better? The question is relevant only if we have previously agreed to the purposes and goals the systems should serve. Sport systems serve different goals and reflect different political and economic systems. The systems thus are most often not directly comparable.

## Alternative Goals and Structures For Sport Systems

Nationally, what goals should a sport system serve? In what order of priority should those goals be arranged? Can or should a country such as the United States balance its goals of accommodating the needs of those wish to compete at local levels well into their adulthood with the needs of elite athletes in their pursuits of medals and world championship? The former is a very common scene in countries that employ a more inclusionary system of sport delivery. The more exclusionary model of sport participation focuses on recruiting and supporting elite athletes with the goal of winning State, National, Olympic and world competitions. Interestingly, Tom Farrey's (2008) recent analysis of Olympic successes in terms of medal count showed that the United States typically has the highest total (and gold) medal counts in the Olympics. However, on a per capita basis, Australia actually outperforms every nation.

Potentially, sport is a central means of providing significant physical activity opportunities for all layers of the population. Thus, for the United States, the following questions are important to consider especially because there are real choices to be made given the limited resources are allocated in sport: To what extent should Olympic development programs dominate a sport system? Some countries keep national teams and athletes training year-round in a national training facility. Many countries have full-time national coaches. Should more resources be allocated to the continued training of elite athletes who are beyond their university years, especially in sports for which there is no way to earn a living in relation to those sports, or should resources be allocated more for increased participation at the recreational level?

Still another choice is whether to expand the opportunities for sport at the child and youth sport levels, providing better coaching and more developmentally appropriate sport forms and extending those opportunities to all children rather than just to sons and daughters of the middle and upper classes.

It would be nice if there were sufficient resources to do all the sport development implied in these questions. Finally, from the perspective of maintaining good health and quality of life, to what extent is it worth increasing investments, access and opportunity to active sport participation for people 40 and older? Resources are always limited, however, and choices must be made. What is interesting to consider is the means by which those choices are made in the United States. Do we need an overall national sport policy or a state-level policy? Instead, are we better off continuing to develop sport primarily through the private sector, with decisions made mostly on the basis of consumer demands?

## Sport in Perspective

In this chapter, we have focused on issues and problems in sport at all levels. To conclude the chapter, we need to reflect that in many instances sport is still just sport, an experience to be enjoyed and from which people derive substantial meaning for their lives. Sport does have problems. Sport can and often does provide substantial benefits to participants. In 1995 Nike (White & Sheets, 2001) developed a now famous television commercial featuring adolescent girls engaged in various sports. In each scene, a girl athlete began by speaking the same phrase, "If you let me play sports," which was followed by one of the following statements:

- I will like myself more.
- I will have more self-confidence.
- I will suffer less depression.
- I will be 60 percent less likely to develop breast cancer.
- I will be more likely to leave a man who beats me.
- I will be less likely to get pregnant before I want to.
- I will learn what it means to be strong.

All of these claims are backed by evidence, and the commercial was a powerful argument for increasing opportunities for girls in sport.

Compelling as the above argument is, we need to keep in mind that those are probably *not* the reasons why girls want to play sports. Robin Marantz Henig is a writer from the pre–Title IX generation. Her daughter, Sam, was an athlete, and watching Sam and her teammates compete caused Ms. Henig to argue that all those claims of benefits for girls are good and true (Henig, 1999). Because Ms. Henig was raised in a pre–Title IX era, she never came to view herself as an athlete, even though she was physically active. This is what she concluded as she watched her daughter compete:

> It is against this background that I find myself watching with great pleasure, as Sam plays basketball each winter—just as I love watching her play soccer in the fall and spring, and softball in the summer. I love the idea that she thinks of herself as an athlete and as a member of a team. When I join the other parents on those hard bleachers every Sunday afternoon of basketball season, we are all reveling in our daughters' freedom to dance a dance that was never really available to the mothers among us. Whether or not it keeps them out of harm's way, for these hours at least, basketball turns them into something quite remarkable: a group of graceful, agile, self-confident young women taking pride in their bodies, not for who or what they can attract, but for what they can accomplish.

The deepest meaning of sport is always in the moment. What the many moments do or do not do for any of us in other aspects of our lives is important, but it should never diminish our understanding or appreciation of sport as experience.

Do not be dismayed by the problems presented in this chapter. Take heart in the many organizations that are working diligently to make sport better for athletes at all levels. Some of these organizations were created by athletes for athletes. Among these are Athletes for a Better World, the Collegiate Athletes Coalition, the National Alliance of African American Athletes, the International Association of Athletes Against Drugs, and the National Student Athletes' Rights Movement. All of these organizations and others cited in this chapter work to make the sport experience more educational and more fun for all involved.

## SUMMARY

1. Traditionally, sport enthusiasts have ascribed almost mystical and miraculous qualities to sport participation; more recently, many of these myths have been questioned seriously.

2. Cooperation among athletes is essential to high-quality sport and is a fundamental aspect of the sport experience.

3. Appropriate competition—developmentally sound and psychologically suited to the participants—should be the goal, rather than less competition or noncompetitive activities.

4. Children lack the social and psychological abilities to benefit from organized sport before age 8 years.

5. Epiphyseal injury due to year-round specialization or weight training is the most dangerous, common injury in children's sport.

6. Sport for children and youths needs to be developmentally appropriate; equipment, space, and rules should be modified accordingly.

7. Early specialization increases the risk of physical injury and psychological burnout.

8. Children and youths from relatively low socioeconomic areas have much less opportunity to participate in appropriately conducted sport, compared with their wealthier peers.

9. Coaches in child and youth sport often behave in ways that are unproductive for player development, but evidence suggests that coaches can change easily once appropriate behaviors are made known to them, as is done in many coach-effectiveness training programs.

10. Children will play to win and then move on to the next interesting part of their daily life; inappropriate pressures to win are most often imposed by adults.

11. The large, diversified interscholastic sport program is unique to the American high school.

12. The interscholastic model is basically exclusionary in that opportunities are available to fewer and fewer athletes as they advance. This model differs markedly from the European sport-club approach.

13. Injury in school sport is not a major problem with the exception of injury in football. There, injury to the knee continues to be the biggest problem.

14. Eligibility for school sport continues to be a major issue. Legislation promoting pass-to-play practices is becoming more common.

15. Athletes tend to specialize more now than they did previously, with strength and endurance training occupying their off-season.

16. In most instances, school sport teams are coached by teachers; the problems associated with hiring teacher-coaches are substantial.

17. Pressure from parents and booster clubs is a potential source of problems for the adolescent athlete.

18. Pay-to-play plans are making access to interschool sport a socioeconomic issue.

19. Recruiting violations continue to be the major problem in intercollegiate sport, often resulting from economic pressures to win.

20. Performance-enhancing drugs have become a major problem in many sports.

21. Economic disparity among top powers and economic pressures to produce winning programs are responsible for many of the violations and abuses in intercollegiate sport.

22. Equity issues in sport are seen in the underrepresentation of women and minorities among athletes, coaches, and sport administrators. Furthermore, we are witnessing decreasing access to sport in low-income areas because of the shift of sport instruction and participation to the private sector.

23. Sport systems around the world differ markedly because they serve different goals, resulting in different resource allocation and different models for participation.

## ))) GET CONNECTED to Sport Web Sites

### Children and Youth Sport

| | |
|---|---|
| National Alliance for Youth Sports | www.nays.org |
| The NAYS Web site will also connect you to: | |
| National Youth Sport Coaches Association | |
| Parents Association for Youth Sports | |
| Academy for Youth Sports Administrators | |
| Start Smart Sports Development Program | |
| National Council on Youth Sports | www.ncys.org |
| National Youth Sports Safety Foundation | www.nyssf.org |
| Youth Sports Foundation | www.youthsportsfoundation.com |
| Center for Sports Parenting | www.sportsparenting.org |
| Institute for the Study of Youth Sports | http://ed-web3.educ.msu.edu/ysi/ |
| Positive Coaching Alliance | www.positivecoach.org |
| Sport for All | www.s4af.org |
| Character Counts Sports | www.charactercounts.org |
| Citizenship Through Sports | www.sportsmanship.org |
| American Sport Education Program | www.asep.com |
| Urban Youth Sports | www.sportinsociety.org/uys |
| Youth Sport Network | www.myteam.com |
| Mom's Team: Youth Sport Parenting Information | www.momsteam.com |
| North American Youth Sports Institute | www.naysi.com |
| Youth Sport Trust | www.youthsporttrust.org |
| Youth Sport Coalition | connect through www.aahperd.org/naspe |

### Interscholastic Sport

| | |
|---|---|
| National Federation of State High School Associations | www.nfhs.org |
| Through the NFHS Web site, you can also connect to: | |
| National Federation Coaches Association | |
| National Federation Officials Association | |
| National Federation Interscholastic Sport Association | |
| National Interscholastic Athletic Administrators Association | |
| NFHS Coaches Education Program | |

### Intercollegiate Sport

| | |
|---|---|
| National Collegiate Athletic Association | www.ncaa.org |
| National Association of Intercollegiate Athletics | www.naia.org |
| National Junior College Athletic Association | www.njcaa.org |
| Canadian Interuniversity Athletic Union | www.cisport.ca |
| National Association of Collegiate Directors of Athletics | www.nacda.com |
| National Association of College Women Athletic Administrators | www.nacwaa.org |

*(continued)*

Get Connected to Sport Web Sites (continued)

### Social Concerns for Athletes

| | |
|---|---|
| Athletes for a Better World | www.abw.org |
| Collegiate Athletes Coalition | www.cacnow.org |
| International Association of Athletes Against Drugs | www.adcd.org/iaad/eng/inicial.htm |
| National Alliance of African American Athletes | www.naaaa.com |
| National Student Athletes' Rights Movement | www.studentathletesrights.org |

### Sport for People with Disabilities

| | |
|---|---|
| American Association of Adapted Sports Programs | www.aaasp.org |
| Special Olympics | www.specialolympics.org |
| Athletes Helping Athletes | www.athleteshelpathletes.com |
| Paralympics | www.paralympic.org |
| Disability in Sport | www.sportinsociety.org/vpd/dis.php |
| National Disability Sports Alliance | www.ndsaonline.org |
| Disabled Sports USA | www.dsusa.org |
| National Beep Baseball Association | www.nbba.org |
| United States Quad Rugby Association | www.quadrugby.com |
| USA Deaf Sports Federation | www.usdeafsports.org |
| United States Association of Blind Athletes | www.usaba.org |
| Wheelchair Sports USA | www.wsusa.org |
| U.S. Paralympics | www.usparalympics.org |

### Masters Sports

| | |
|---|---|
| United States Masters Swimming | www.usms.org |
| International Masters Games Association | www.imga.ch |
| Masters Track and Field | www.masterstrack.com |
| World Masters Athletics | www.world-masters-athletics.org |

### State Games and Sport Festivals

| | |
|---|---|
| National Congress of State Games | www.stategames.org |
| Inner City Games | www.lainnercitygames.com |

### Women in Sport

| | |
|---|---|
| National Association for Girls and Women in Sport | www.aahperd.org/nagws |
| Women's Sports Foundation | www.womensportsfoundation.org |
| Women in Sports Careers Foundation | www.WiscFoundation.org |
| Empowering Women in Sports | www.feminist.org/research/sports2.html |
| Title IX—Equity Online | www.edc.org/womensEquity |
| Title IX—National Women's Law Center | www.nwlc.org |
| Title IX—Office of Civil Rights | www.ed.gov/offices/OCR |
| Women in Sports | www. Makeithappen.com/wis/ |

Get Connected to Sport Web Sites (continued)

*Other Relevant Sites*

| | |
|---|---|
| Amateur Athletic Union | www.aausports.org |
| International Amateur Athletics Federation | www.iaaf.org |
| United States Olympic Committee | www.usoc.org |
| National Association of Sports Officials | www.naso.org |
| North American Society for Sport Management | www.nassm.org |
| Active Americans | www.activeusa.com |
| North American Society for Sport Management | www.nassm.org |
| European Association for Sport Management | www.unb.ca/sportmanagement/easm |
| National Association of Police Athletic Leagues | www.nationalpal.org |

## DISCUSSION QUESTIONS

1. In what ways can poor cooperation destroy competition? In what ways can inappropriate competition destroy cooperation?

2. Do the ways in which child and youth sport are practiced in your area reflect developmentally appropriate forms of competition?

3. What kind of coaching-education program would you suggest for volunteer youth sport coaches in a local recreation department?

4. Do eligibility rules for sport participation in school discriminate against less talented students?

5. How early should athletes specialize? What are the benefits and the problems of specialization at the high-school level?

6. If you were making policy for the NCAA, what policies would you suggest for (a) drug abuse, (b) recruiting violations, and (c) academic progress of athletes?

7. How should youth and school sport be financed? What influences are exerted by differing approaches to financing sport?

8. What types of preparation should women and men have in order to coach at the middle or high-school levels?

9. Should America have a more developed national sport policy? Should it have a national sport system? How might such a system be structured?

# The Subdisciplines of Kinesiology That Support the Physical Education, Fitness, and Sport Professions

We all want children, youth, adults, and senior citizens to adopt lifestyles and participate in physical activity programs that not only help them to remain healthy throughout their lifespan but also to so thoroughly enjoy physical activity that it becomes a significant part of their lifestyle. We cannot achieve these goals with a thorough understanding of what makes a good physical activity program, what kinds of physical activity best serve specific health goals such as cardiovascular health, and how programs can be developed and sustained that make involvement pleasurable. These goals are achieved through research done by women and men who have chosen to specialize in the physical science or social science subdisciplines of Kinesiology. Chapter 13 describes the work done in these subdisciplines and how, working together, the research developed can help to improve our understanding of how to plan and deliver high-quality physical activity programs.

# The Kinesiology Subdisciplines Supporting the Professions

The field of Kinesiology has developed rapidly over the past four decades. In 2006, the National Research Council included Kinesiology in its taxonomy of graduate programs to be ranked, a recognition that showed clearly the degree to which Kinesiology had become a rigorous scholarly discipline (Clark, 2008). What follows in this chapter is a brief description of the subdisciplines that comprise the field of Kinesiology.

You will see that each of the subdisciplines approaches the study of human movement has its roots in broader areas of sciences. As the exercise science sub-disciplines mature, the questions studied increasingly require research at the cellular/molecular level. However, many studies also have a more clinical focus that are generally aimed at improving people's quality of life (See Focus On 13.1). The uniquely different focus in the questions studies across the various exercise sciences is reflected in the sample questions presented in Focus On 13.2.

## EXERCISE PHYSIOLOGY

Many of the great early leaders in our profession were trained as medical doctors. It is not surprising, therefore, that the early scientific endeavors in physical education focused on exercise and fitness. Indeed, our primary scientific tradition has been the measurement and promotion of physical fitness, a tradition that gradually developed into the field of exercise physiology.

Exercise physiology has been at the front of research on fitness and performance for over

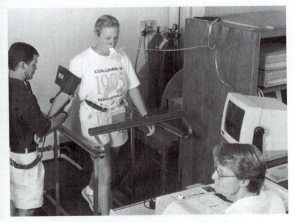

Exercise testing is an important step both in research and for prescriptive programs.

## FOCUS ON —— Areas of Study in Clinical-Exercise Science                13.1

| Area | Questions Typically Asked |
|------|---------------------------|
| Rehabilitation | What factors influence the exercise progression for patients who have had a heart attack? |
| | How can a muscle best be rehabilitated after trauma? |
| | What role does exercise play in treating depression? |
| Prevention | What level of fitness is needed to lower cardiovascular risk? |
| | How is exercise related to regulation of diseases such as diabetes? |
| | What level of fitness is needed to resist the onset of high blood pressure? |
| | How is children's fitness related to problems in their later years? |
| Age-related | At what age should children begin fitness training? |
| | How can exercise programs increase the quality of life for older people? |
| | What role does exercise play in changes that occur in adolescence? |
| | How can exercise deter traditional signs of aging? |

## FOCUS ON —— Areas of Study Within Kinesiology and Biomechanics      13.2

| Area | Questions Typically Asked |
|------|---------------------------|
| Kinesiology | How does the wrist joint move when baseball pitchers throw curve balls? |
| | How does muscle potential differ between middle- and long-distance running? |
| | What range of motion should be achieved in rehabilitation of the knee after surgery? |
| | How do kicking motions change as children develop? |
| Quantitative biomechanics | How do forces summate most efficiently to produce maximum performance in the discus throw? |
| | What variables influence human tolerance to externally imposed stress, such as is inflicted in football tackling? |
| | What are the performance patterns of world-class spikers in volleyball? |
| Qualitative biomechanics | What are the critical performance elements of various sport skills? |
| | What are the most common errors made at various developmental stages in acquiring a sport skill? |
| | How can these critical elements and common errors be taught to teachers and coaches? |
| Equipment analysis | What is the optimal design of a golf club? |
| | How can shoes better prevent overpronation in running? |
| | What materials can best absorb shock in contact sports where protective gear is worn? |

100 years now. Results from this research field dramatically changed some common practices that were based on erroneous understandings; for example, it was not too long ago that athletes were not allowed to drink water on hot days during practices, that girls were not allowed to compete in vigorous sports because of their supposedly weaker constitutions, that swimmers were cautioned not to train by weight lifting, and that children were discouraged from participating in vigorous exercise for fear of developing what was then called the "athlete's heart."

Exercise physiology is the "study of acute physiological responses to physical activity and changes in physiological responses to chronic physical activity" (Haymes, 2000, p. 383). There are two primary goals for exercise physiology (Brooks, 1994) and therefore two branches of the subdiscipline. One goal is to use exercise to further our understanding of human physiology, a goal typically guiding the work of basic scientists who focus on how oxygen is utilized in the cardiovascular system, and what the key metabolic responses are to exercise and training (Brooks, 1987). Exercise biochemistry has recently emerged as a specialization within the field. This new area was made possible by the development of the muscle-biopsy needle in Sweden in 1996 (Haymes, 2000), which enabled investigators to study energy sources, muscle mitochondria, and muscle-fiber types. There is no academic area in the field of Kinesiology where a popular literature (as opposed to a scientific literature) exists to the same extent as exercise and fitness. This popular literature has enabled teachers, coaches, and fitness instructors to develop programs that have a strong scientific base. A specialized field of exercise physiology, referred to as exercise epidemiology has emerged. Academics in this field study the relationships between activity patterns and mortality.

The other goal is to use physiology to understand human exercise. Those who focus on the second goal tend to be applied scientists. Applied-exercise physiologists use physiology to understand aerobic exercise, strength development, sport performance,

physical fitness, and the health benefits of physical activity. The field of **cardiac rehabilitation** is a more recent development from the applied side of exercise physiology. Cardiac rehabilitation involves the assessment of cardiovascular functioning and prescriptive work in preventing cardiovascular trauma or rehabilitating people who have experienced cardiac problems.

The increased cultural attention to health and fitness has further expanded and promoted the development of exercise physiology, both in the scientific study of exercise phenomena and the clinical applications of that knowledge. As exercise physiology developed it became the foundation science for a number of developing professional areas such as cardiac rehabilitation, adult fitness, strength training, and athletic training. These areas have developed sufficiently to have their own professional organizations, journals, textbooks, and training programs.

Exercise physiologists are involved in research, teaching, and clinical service, done mostly in colleges, universities, and laboratories, typically in departments of kinesiology, physical education, physiology, cardiology, general medicine, and veterinary medicine. The American College of Sports Medicine (ACSM) is the main professional and scientific association for this field.

## KINESIOLOGY AND BIOMECHANICS

The term *Kinesiology* has two distinct meanings. As the title of this chapter indicates, Kinesiology is the term used to identify the subdisciplines that have developed to better understand physical activity in its many forms. The subdisciplines of kinesiology and biomechanics have developed as research has become more specialized over the years. It is now common that universities offer courses in both kinesiology and biomechanics.

The study of kinesiology is often organized by joints or groups of joints in the same anatomical region of the body and subclassified by the type of movement at the joint. A primary grouping might

Display video images can precisely compare differences in performance.

include the foot and ankle, the knee, the hips and pelvic girdle, the spinal column, the elbow and wrist, and the shoulder girdle. The movements possible at each of these joints are determined by the nature of the joint and the positions of the muscles around the joint. Some of the movement possibilities at various joints are abduction and adduction (movement away from and toward the midline of the body), flexion and extention, pronation and supination, inversion and eversion, medial and lateral rotation, and elevation and depression. This approach is often referred to as anatomical kinesiology.

Biomechanics, often referred to as mechanical kinesiology, is the study of human motion from the standpoint of physics. Mechanics is the area of physics that studies how forces, both internal and external, affect the motion of objects, animate or inanimate (Brancazio, 1984). Biomechanical research is carried out using a number of methods, including high-speed photography and electromyography (EMG—a technique for recording the electrical impulses within muscles). For example, athletes have a certain rhythm to their performances that is detectable through EMG recordings. When they hit a slump, this is reflected in changes in their EMG patterns.

Technology has affected all of the sport sciences, but none more profoundly than biomechanics. Combinations of video, analog, and computer

Qualitative skill feedback depends on a teacher's knowledge of the skill.

technologies allow for viewing and analyzing the movement of athletes. Software programs are available to calculate kinematic measurements of linear and angular displacements, velocities, and accelerations that are necessary to analyze and improve techniques.

Coaches and teachers, on the other hand, have to rely on their knowledge of biomechanics to do qualitative analyses of their athletes and students as they learn and perform, what physical educator Shirl Hoffman (1977) described as a **pedagogical kinesiology;** that is, an approach to biomechanics that emphasizes recognition of the critical elements and common errors in sport-skill performance as it occurs in practical situations.

Biomechanics and kinesiology have a bright future because they not only have the ability to contribute to performance improvement in sport and physical education, but also a strong potential for contributing to areas such as medicine, rehabilitation, child development, and gerontology. In the field of sport equipment, too, we can expect continuing improvement of equipment based on research contributions made by sport biomechanists.

## MOTOR BEHAVIOR

Motor behavior is the subdiscipline of Kinesiology that focuses on how motor skills are acquired and improved across the lifespan (Thomas & Thomas,

2000). This subdiscipline includes three distinct but highly related fields, that each ask distinctly different questions (See Focus On 13.3). Motor learning focuses on how motor skills are learned and the conditions under which practice leads to improvement. Motor control focuses on the "neural and behavioral aspects of movement" (Schmidt, 1988, p. 17). Motor development focuses on how the acquisition, improvement, and control of motor skills change and vary across the lifespan.

Motor learning, motor control, and motor development have formed a family of scientific interests since the early 1970s. Researchers in motor learning seek to understand the processes through which motor skills are developed and the factors that facilitate or inhibit skill development (Shea, Shebilske, & Worchel, 1993). Researchers in motor control seek to understand how motor skills are actually executed and what factors lead to a

| FOCUS ON | Areas of Study Within Motor Behavior | 13.3 |
|---|---|---|

| Area | Questions Typically Asked |
|---|---|
| Motor learning | How do the frequency and timing of feedback influence skill acquisition and maintenance? |
| | How does skill performance change as it becomes more automatic? |
| | How does fatigue interfere with performance and learning? |
| | How does aging affect memory in motor-skill learning and performance? |
| Motor control | What series of cognitive steps does a beginner go through when acquiring a skill? |
| | How does the plan for executing a skill change from beginning to advanced levels of performance? |
| | What is the nature of the human information-processing system that stores and retrieves information for use in skill performance? |
| | How are verbal instructions for skill learning translated into images used by performers? |
| Motor development | At what age can a child safely benefit from cardiovascular training? |
| | What developmental stages do children go through as they learn to throw, catch, and strike objects? |
| | At what age or developmental status can young learners use mature motor forms? |
| | How is early motor stimulation related to the development of intelligence and thinking? |

breakdown of such skills. Motor development seeks to understand the hereditary basis of developing motor skills and the environmental factors that facilitate or inhibit such development. Motor development is often a key course in physical education teacher education programs because of the importance of the development of motor skills in the Pre-K to third-grade years.

Motor learning and motor control are fairly narrow fields of specialization conducted almost exclusively within departments of kinesiology, physical education, sport sciences, or psychology. In motor development, the link between research and practice is closer. Elementary classroom teachers, physical education teachers, preschool specialists, and infant-stimulation specialists all directly apply knowledge generated in the research field of motor development to the benefit

Good physical education presents challenges that lead to real accomplishments.

of young children during their key developmental stages.

To investigate aspects of motor control, researchers needed to extend their work beyond traditional boundaries of psychology. Fields such as neuropsychology, neurophysiology, cognitive psychology, biomechanics, and computer science all contributed to the development of the field of motor control (Christina, 1987). Gradually, the fields of motor learning and motor control became equal partners in the general area of perceptual-motor development.

The rapid increase of participation in early childhood fitness and sport programs and the rapid development of youth sport programs have captured the attention of motor development specialists. Even more recently, there have been efforts to develop skill and fitness programs for very young children, including infants. Motor development specialists are playing a critical role in investigating such efforts and providing evidence about inappropriate program features and recommending more age-appropriate features.

## SPORT SOCIOLOGY

Sociology, an accepted scholarly field for more than 100 years, is a discipline that focuses primarily on social organizations, social practices, and social behavior. Sport sociology focuses on "shared beliefs and social practices that constitute specific forms of physical activity (for example, sport, exercise)" (Harris, 2000, p. 207). Sport sociologists examine basic social units such as individuals, groups, societies, and cultures. Coakley (2007) stresses that sports and physical activity have to be examined as social constructions, that is, "aspects of the social world that are created by people as they interact with one another under the social, political, and economic conditions that exist in their society" (p. 12). Sport sociologists, therefore, study social processes such as socialization, social control, stratification, social conflict, and social changes (McPherson, 1981).

| FOCUS ON | Areas of Study Within Sport Sociology | 13.4 |
| --- | --- | --- |

| Area | Questions Typically Asked |
| --- | --- |
| Social class and sport involvement | How does social class affect sport participation? |
| | How does sport participation affect social mobility? |
| | How are social class and spectating related? |
| Team dynamics | How is team cohesiveness related to success? |
| | How are coach–player relationships related to player success and satisfaction? |
| | What are the characteristics of leadership on teams? |
| Sport and education | What role does sport play in school dynamics? |
| | Are school athletes better students than their peers? |
| | To what extent do athletes get preferential academic treatment? |
| Sport and social processes | How do integrated sport teams affect player relationships and team success? |
| | How is spectating affected by economic swings? |
| | How do different sports socialize children differently? |
| Sport and social problems | How is aggressiveness treated in different sports? |
| | To what extent can sport participation decrease delinquency? |
| | Do professional sports stack athletes in positions by race? |
| Gender relations and sport | How does sport influence our views of male and female bodies? |
| | How do the media portray female bodies in sport? |
| | How does sport socialize boys and girls differently? |
| Global/national relations | To what extent is a global sport culture emerging? |
| | How does sport change national identity? |

Sport sociologists conduct their research in the real worlds of sport and physical activity (See Focus On 13.4). They do so through surveys, interviews, thematic analysis of materials such as newspapers or the content of television coverage of sports, long-term observation of engagement in places where sport or exercise occur (called ethnography), theoretical analysis of trends in society, and historical analysis of changes in those trends (Harris, 2000). Sport is a social phenomenon that exists as part of a particular society. Thus, to understand high-school football in Texas, ice hockey in Minnesota, or ocean sports in Australia one has to understand them in the context of the particular culture.

Cultural differences in sport are topics for sport sociologists.

Although the term *sport* is used to label this subdiscipline, the scope of study within the subdiscipline is considerably broader than the label implies. Sport sociologists, along with sport philosophers, have been in the forefront of helping to clarify a group of related terms that, together, better define this area of interest as play, games, and sport.

The concept of play is of major importance in sport sociology. What is play? How is it related to games and sport? How does the play of children differ from the play of adolescents and adults? Games are structured, rule-governed forms of play, competitive games such as football and chess differ from games of chance, such as roulette and poker, and differ also from games that stress vertigo, such as skiing and children on a teeter-totter.

Since the early 1990s, a number of prominent sport sociologists have been influenced by the emergence of *critical theory,* a viewpoint that focuses on structural inequities in society and works to eliminate them through action-oriented programs. Sage (1991) argued that the enhancement of performance among elite athletes has largely ignored the athlete and his or her own life agendas. Harris (1991) offered a series of suggestions about how the sport-training fields can be made more sensitive to the social and ethical issues within which training and competition decisions are made.

## SPORT AND EXERCISE PSYCHOLOGY

Sport and exercise psychology are companion fields that examine psychological issues for those who engage in sport, fitness, and physical activity. Many national, international, professional, and collegiate sport programs employ full- or part-time sport psychologists. Sport and exercise psychologists use imagery, mental rehearsal, and behavior modification strategies to help their clients improve their performance (See Focus On 13.5). With physical activity and its relationship to health and longevity now fully established, exercise psychologists have found an increasing demand for their services.

Some sport and exercise psychologists have as their primary interest to better understand the issues that people deal with in various sport and exercise settings; that is, they are not involved in behavior change programs but rather in research that furthers our understanding of why people behave as they do in sport and physical activity settings. Other sport and exercise psychologists focus on helping persons behave more effectively in sport and exercise settings; that is, they develop behavior change programs to improve performance of their clients.

Consulting sport psychologists typically play two roles. One role is to use psychological strategies with athletes to improve performance directly—the performance-enhancement role. Athletes learn to relax during competition, cope with competitive stresses, and mentally rehearse positive performances. The second role is the counseling role that involves helping athletes to overcome problems, adjust to new situations, and deal with stresses in their lives.

In exercise psychology training programs, students focus on the relations between physical activity and public health, the sociological and psychological factors associated with adopting and maintaining physical activity programs, the role of physical activity related to body image and self-esteem, and the influence of various levels of fitness on psychological systems, using relaxation training, coping strategies, and the like.

Sport psychologist Dan Landers (1983) argued that research in sport psychology can be divided into three stages. The first stage (1950–1965) was dominated by research on how the personalities of athletes were related to performance. The second stage (1966–1976) was dominated by the borrowing of then current theories from mainstream psychology, to test them in sport settings, by the development of interactional psychology approaches, and by the emergence of behavior modification strategies.

Since the late 1980s, sport and exercise psychology, having established their field as an academic discipline, has moved into the third stage and toward more applied work. Because of the financial incentives working with professional golfers, Olympic-level teams, and professional sport teams, many sport

| FOCUS ON | Psychological Interventions Used With Athletes | 13.5 |
| --- | --- | --- |

| Intervention | Description and Examples of Use |
| --- | --- |
| Relaxation training | Teach athletes to feel tension in muscles and to learn how to control release of tension.<br><br>*Example*: Relax between events |
| Cue-controlled relaxation | Tie relaxation strategy to a word cue; allows the athlete to say the word to himself or herself to induce relaxation.<br><br>*Examples*: Preparation for diving, free-throw shooting, putting in golf |
| Desensitization | Gradually reduce anxiety caused in specific competitive situations by teaching athletes to relax while imaging a series of increasingly aversive competitive situations.<br><br>*Examples*: Fear of hitting head on platform in a back dive; fear associated with heights in climbing |
| Mental imaging | Teach athletes to rehearse successful performance mentally just before beginning the performance.<br><br>*Examples*: High jump, swim races, wrestling |
| Coping strategies | Predict what events might intrude in preperformance time and during performance, and help athletes to develop and rehearse behavioral strategies to cope with and overcome those incidents.<br><br>*Examples*: Rehearsing the specific procedures to follow when going to compete in a foreign land—how to cope with language, security, time, and food incidents; practicing what to do during an event if certain situations arise |
| Covert modeling | Teach athlete to imagine a model doing a particular performance as a means to help the athlete acquire that skill or ability.<br><br>*Example*: Helping an athlete become more competitive in tense situations |

American football is not the only popular form of football in the world.

psychologists, and subsequently the field itself, has tended to focus on elite performance.

## SPORT PEDAGOGY

In most school systems throughout the world, the physical education curriculum that includes sport and physical activity is considered to be of such importance that the teachers hired must be credentialed in physical education. The general field within which issues of sport and physical activity as part of the school curriculum are considered is sport pedagogy. Sport pedagogy, as it is defined internationally, encompasses both school programs of physical education and community-based club programs of sport and fitness.

The term *pedagogy* refers to teaching but should be taken in its broadest context; for example, it encompasses not just the act of teaching, but also the development of instructional programs, the plan for the implementation of those programs, and assessments of the outcomes of the program. The term *sport* should be considered to include not only competitive sports but also physical activity programs, fitness, and leisure-time activity. This is how the term *sport* is used throughout most of the world and it is the same broad meaning that underlies the Sport for All movement prevalent throughout the world.

Over the past 40 years, the research field of sport pedagogy has developed and provided much

needed guidance for the development of successful physical education and sport education programs. Areas of study include the analysis of teacher and student behaviors, teacher effectiveness, classroom management, curriculum development and implementation, and analyses of student achievement and the degree to which students come to adopt and value a physically active lifestyle (See Focus On 13.6).

Sport pedagogy research is now widely used in textbooks used by physical education teacher education faculty to prepare new teachers. For example, extensive research on classroom management has greatly influenced the inclusion of clear class management strategies such as developing managerial routines, keeping managerial time short, developing

---

## FOCUS ON    Areas of Study Within Sport Pedagogy                13.6

| Area | Questions Typically Asked |
|---|---|
| Teacher behavior | What kinds of feedback do teachers provide? |
| | Do elementary teachers behave differently than secondary teachers? |
| | How much time do teachers spend in various teaching activities? |
| | How does the behavior of teachers differ from that of coaches? |
| Student behavior | Do students enjoy and value physical education? |
| | How do students spend their time in classes? |
| | How many good learning opportunities do highly and poorly skilled students get during a class? |
| | How do children behave in youth sport? |
| Teacher effectiveness | What differentiates effective from ineffective teachers and coaches? |
| | What teaching methods are most effective? |
| | How do teachers cope with the problems encountered during their first year? |
| | What characteristics make a coach effective? |
| Teacher issues | To what extent is there role conflict in individuals who both teach and coach? |
| | How do teachers cope with burnout? |
| | What goals do teachers have for their students? |
| Curriculum | What is the ideal physical-education curriculum? |
| | How do teachers' values affect curriculum decisions? |
| | To what extent do teachers achieve their goals? |
| | How can fitness best be programmed? |
| | What outcomes occur in youth-sport programs? |

Plastic pipe javelins allow the learning of important track-and-field skills.

clear rules and consequences for violations, and using positive interactional strategies to support appropriate student behavior.

Within sport pedagogy there are those faculty whose main task is to do research on instructional strategies, student learning, student commitment to physically active lifestyles, and teacher effectiveness. Other sport pedagogy faculty spend most of their time working in the teacher education program that students must complete to gain a state license to teach physical education in public schools.

Sport pedagogy has grown rapidly over the past 25 years. It is regularly included as one of the sections at Olympic Scientific Congresses and is well represented by an International Committee of Sport Pedagogy, jointly sponsored by four major international organizations.

## THE SPORT HUMANITIES

When *Chariots of Fire* won the Academy Award for Best Picture in 1981 it became clear that the old argument that sport was not suitable for popular and serious literary consideration was no longer true. The fields of sport philosophy, sport literature, and sport history constitute the sport humanities (See Focus On 13.7). The development of the sport humanities accompanied the explosion of interest in sport in the 1970s within Western cultures in general and American culture in particular. Nearly 20 percent of newspaper space is devoted to sports reporting. Endless hours of television and radio coverage are widely available. International events such as the Olympics occupy the major share of television for extended periods of time. The sport and fitness magazine sections in bookstores are likely to be among the largest.

**History** not only chronicles the past, but also interprets the past, relates the past to the present, and provides guidelines to what might be expected or what courses might be taken in the future. Some *Sport History* books are written for popular consumption and may be read widely. One example is John Feingold's *A Season on the Brink*, a chronicle of one season of Indiana basketball and its former coach Bob Knight. Some are written for a much narrower audience and are more scholarly in nature. A classic example is H. A. Harris's *Greek Athletes and Athletics*, which is the most authoritative source of information about sport in ancient Greece and what purposes it served.

As sport came to be taken more seriously by the general public, books about sport that were more seriously written found acceptance in the general literary culture. Two shining examples of quality literature in sport history are Roger Kahn's poignant history of the fates of the 1958 Brooklyn Dodgers in *The Boys of Summer* and David Halberstam's chronicle of elite rowers preparing for the Olympic games in *The Amateurs*.

**Philosophy** is a formal field of study that includes four main areas. *Metaphysics* is the branch of philosophy that addresses questions about the nature of reality. *Axiology* is the study of values. How knowledge is acquired is the focus of *epistemology*, and how ideas are related composes the study of *logic*. Many people, however, are interested in what are popularly called "philosophical issues" although these differ from the concerns of formal philosophy.

| FOCUS ON | Areas of Study in the Sport Humanities | 13.7 |

| Area | Questions Typically Asked |
| --- | --- |
| Sport history | What causes certain sports to be more popular or less popular at certain times? |
| | How has sport been changed by television? |
| | How has Title IX changed participation by girls? |
| | How is sport changing as a social force in culture? |
| | How did the Olympics change in the twentieth century? |
| Sport philosophy | Does competition mean something different to spectator and competitor? |
| | How is the play element in sport changed as the sport competition becomes more highly organized? |
| | How does feminist philosophy interpret sport? |
| | What should "fair play" mean in elite sport? |
| | How do coach and athlete philosophies differ? |
| Sport literature | How are coaches portrayed in films emphasizing sport? |
| | How is the "sport hero past his or her prime" treated in sport fiction? |
| | How are failure and success treated in sport novels? |
| | What ideas and values are being expressed in sport poems? |
| | What role does sport play in fiction that focuses on adolescent development? |

Equipment should be modified to be developmentally appropriate for instruction and practice.

Harris (2000) suggests that the first goal of *philosophy of sport* is to clarify thinking about sport, play, games, and dance, including the relationship between body and mind. The second goal, she argues, is to encourage people to use their insights about sport and the relationship between body and mind to improve people's lives.

In the past 25 years, there has been a very strong literature in the philosophy of sport. Some books, such as Howard Slusher's *Man, Sport and Existence*, have been read mostly within the profession. Others, such as Paul Weiss's *Sport: A Philosophical Inquiry* and Michael Novak's *The Joy of Sports*, were written by people outside the field of sport philosophy and have been widely read both within the profession and by the general public. When famous and serious people take sport seriously and write about it, the public listens. Such was the case when A. Bartlett Giamatti, former president of Yale University and commissioner of Major League Baseball, wrote *Take Time for Paradise*, a philosophical and historical analysis of sport and play.

**Literature,** in the sense used here, refers to prose, poetry, and films that have a permanent value because of their excellence of form, their emotional effect, and their ability to provide insights about the human condition. Literature, in this sense, has literary value and is often contrasted with scientific writing, ordinary newswriting, and general nonfiction writing such as in textbooks. *Sport literature* is a recent and welcome addition to the sport humanities. It has arisen as a field because of the marked increase since the early 1970s in serious literary work that focuses specifically on sport or using sport themes as vehicles through which to examine basic human dilemmas and situations.

Sport literature is dominated by sport fiction with a lesser emphasis on sport poetry. Increasingly, films that are about sport or that use sport as a theme to examine important human questions have been included within sport literature. Some film scripts have been adapted from novels such as Bernard Malamud's *The Natural*, Mark Harris's *Bang the Drum Slowly*, and Pete Gent's *North Dallas Forty*. A few novels that have sport as a main theme or context have achieved critical acclaim and have become best-sellers—John Updike's *Rabbit Run* is perhaps the best example. Many more novels, although not achieving best-seller status, have received good critical reviews and have sold moderately well. Good examples are W. P. Kinsella's *Shoeless Joe*, Eric Rolfe Greenberg's *The Celebrant*, and Tom McNab's *Flannagan's Run*. Most recently, Tom Farrey, an investigative reporter for ESPN published perhaps the most well supported analysis and critique of efforts to create the next sport phenom. In *Game On: The All-American Race to Make Champions of Our Children*.

In recent years numerous books have been written about celebrities and sport teams (in most cases ghostwritten or written in collaboration with a local sportswriter). And although many of these books sell well, they are very seldom considered to have literary merit in the sense defined here. Yet, even though they constitute the fringe of sport literature, such books are nonetheless important vehicles through which sport is interpreted and made available to the public.

Sport films and documentaries are becoming more and more popular and are likely to increase in importance in the field of sport literature. In the past 25 years, sport films that have been very good entertainment have also made serious statements about sport. Primary examples are *Bull Durham*, *Field of Dreams*, and *A League of Their Own*, just to mention a few in which baseball was the sport focus. *Field of Dreams* had a strong philosophical focus, and *A League of Their Own* had more of a historical focus. Ken Burns' documentary Baseball, arguably offers the most in-depth visual history of our national pastime, weaving together this country's ethnic and racial struggles, along with changes in labor relations. *The Legend of Bagger Vance*, a philosophical treatise about golf and the game of life, found success both as a novel and as a popular film. And in 2005 *Million Dollar Baby*, a film about a female boxer, won the Academy Award for Best Picture.

))) **GET CONNECTED** to Physical-Sciences Subdiscipline Web Sites

*Exercise Physiology*

| | |
|---|---|
| American College of Sports Medicine | www.acsm.org |
| American Medical Society for Sports Medicine | www.amssm.org |
| American Orthopaedic Society for Sports Medicine | www.sportsmed.org |
| American Osteopathic Academy of Sports Medicine | www.aoasm.org |
| International Federation of Sports Medicine | www.fims.org |
| American Sports Medicine Institute | www.asmi.org |
| Gatorade Sports Science Institute | www.gssiweb.com |
| Institute for Preventive Sports Medicine | www.ipsm.org |
| SportsMedicine.com | www.sportsmedicine.com |
| The Physician and Sports Medicine Online | www.physsportsmed.com |
| American Society of Exercise Physiologists | www.asep.org |
| British Association of Sport and Exercise Sciences | www.bases.org.uk |
| Canadian Society of Exercise Physiologists | www.csep.ca |

*Kinesiology and Biomechanics*

| | |
|---|---|
| American Society of Biomechanics | www.asb-biomech.org |
| International Society of Biomechanics | www.isbweb.org |
| International Society of Biomechanics in Sports | www.uni-stuttgart.de/External/isbs |
| International Sports Engineering Association | www.sportsengineering.co.uk |
| Biomechanics Magazine | www.biomech.com |

*Motor Behavior*

| | |
|---|---|
| Canadian Society for Psychomotor Learning and Sport Psychology | www.scapps.org |

## SUMMARY

1. The physical science subdisciplines were the first to emerge in the last quarter of the twentieth century.

2. The social science subdisciplines emerged somewhat later than the physical science subdisciplines.

3. The physical science subdisciplines have a strong research focus but more recently a growing clinical focus.

4. From the beginning, the social science subdisciplines focused on investigating and improving practice in sport, physical activity, and physical education.

5. Beginning courses in the physical sciences subdisciplines are often required for students seeking professional degrees and teaching licenses in physical education.

6. Each of the physical science and social science subdisciplines now have their own organizations and scholarly journals that publish specialized research in their field.

## DISCUSSION QUESTIONS

1. If you are enrolled in a physical education teacher education program, which of the physical science subdisciplines would you consider as the most important for your professional roles as a teacher?

2. What have been your experiences in organized sports and to what extent did the

## ))) GET CONNECTED to Social-Science Subdisciplines Web Sites

*Motor Behavior*

| | |
|---|---|
| Canadian Society for Psychomotor Learning and Sport Psychology | www.scapps.org |

*Sport Sociology*

| | |
|---|---|
| American Sociological Association | www.asanet.org |
| North American Society for the Sociology of Sport | www.nasss.org |
| Center for the Study of Sport in Society | www.sportinsociety.org |
| Centre for Research on Sport and Society | www.le.ac.uk/crss |
| International Sociology of Sport Association | www.issa.otago.ac.nz |

*Sport and Exercise Psychology*

| | |
|---|---|
| Association for the Advancement of Applied Sport Psychology | www.appliedsportpsych.org |
| International Society for Sport Psychology | www.issponline.org |
| North American Society for Psychology of Sport and Physical Activity | www.naspspa.org |
| Athletic Insight | www.athleticinsight.com |
| Mental Skills | www.mentalskills.co.uk |

*Sport Pedagogy*

| | |
|---|---|
| National Association for Sport and Physical Education | www.aahperd.org/naspe |
| National Board for Professional Teaching Standards | www.nbpts.org |
| International Association of Physical Education in Higher Education (AIESEP) | www.aiesep.com |
| American Educational Research Association | www.aera.net |

*Sport Humanities*

| | |
|---|---|
| International Society for the History of Physical Education and Sport | www.ishpes.org |
| North American Society for Sport History | www.nassh.org |
| International Society for Comparative Physical Education and Sport | www.iscpes.org/ |
| British Society of Sport History | http://bssh.mcs-creations.com |
| International Society of Olympic Historians | www.olykamp.org.isoh |
| Sport Literature Association | www.isoh.org |
| Sport Literature | www.h-net.org/~arete |
| Canadian Center for Ethics in Sport | www.cces.ca |

coaches in your sports have adequate knowledge from the physical or social sciences subdisciplines?

3. How would you describe the quality of the physical education programs in your elementary-, middle-, and high-school experiences?

4. If you wanted to further your studies in one of the subdisciplines, which one would you choose?

5. How are sport, fitness, and physical education portrayed in books, films, and television shows you have read or seen?

6. How would you describe the "culture" of a fitness center?

7. How would you judge the quality of the sport programs in which you participated during your childhood and adolescence?

# Bibliography

AAALF Active Voice (2003). Fit versus fat: Can a person be both? 8(2), 8. American Association for Active Lifestyles and Fitness.

Acosta, R., & Carpenter, L. (1992). As the years go by: Coaching opportunities in the 1990s. *Journal of Physical Education, Recreation, and Dance,* 63(3), 36–41.

———. (1994). The status of women in intercollegiate athletics. In S. Birrell & C. Cole (Eds.), *Women, sport and culture* (pp. 111–118). Champaign, IL: Human Kinetics.

ACSM (American College of Sports Medicine) (1990). The recommended quantity and quality of exercise for developing and maintaining cardiorespiratory and muscular fitness in healthy adults. *Medicine and Science in Sports and Exercise,* 22, 265–274.

Active Education (2007). Physical education, physical activity, and academic performance. Active Living Research. Robert Wood Johnson Foundation.

Active Living Research (2009). *Active education: Physical Education, physical activity and academic performance-Research Brief.* San Diego, CA: Author.

Active Marketing Group. (2007). *Health club industry review.* San Diego: The Active Network.

Adelman, M. (1969). The role of the sports historian. *Quest,* 12, 61–65.

Adler, J. (2004, December 20). Toxic strength. *Newsweek,* 45–52.

Adrian, M. (1983). Biomechanics: Theory into practice. *Proceedings of the National Association for Physical Education in Higher Education,* 4, 37–50. Champaign, IL: Human Kinetics.

*Albany Times Union.* (1992, July 22). Empire State Games special section.

Alderman, R., & Wood, N. (1976). An analysis of incentive motivation in young Canadian athletes. *Canadian Journal of Sport Sciences,* 1, 169–176.

Alexander, K. (1994). Developing sport education in Western Australia. *Aussie Sport Action,* 5(1), 89.

Alexander, K., Taggart, A., & Luckman, J. (1998). Pilgrims progress: The sport education crusade down under. *Journal of Physical Education, Recreation, and Dance,* 69(4), 21–23.

Allen, B. (1988). Teaching training and discipline-based dance education. *Journal of Physical Education, Recreation, and Dance,* 59(9), 65–69.

Almond, L. (1983). Reflecting on themes: A games classification. *Bulletin of Physical Education,* 19(1), 33–36.

———. (1986). Primary and secondary rules in games. In R. Thorpe, D. Bunker, & L. Almond (Eds.), *Rethinking games teaching* (pp. 73–74). London: Esmonde.

Almond, L., Bunker, D., & Thorpe, R. (1983). Games teaching revisited. *Bulletin of Physical Education,* 19(3), 3–35.

American Academy of Pediatrics (2000). Intensive training and sports specialization in youth athletes. *Pediatrics,* 106, 154–157.

———. (2003). Prevention of pediatric overweight and obesity, committee on nutrition. *Pediatrics,* 112, 424–430.

American Association for Adapted Sports (2008). *Model state.* www.adaptedsports.org

American Association for Leisure and Recreation (2000). *Careers in recreation.* Reston, VA: AAHPERD.

American Sports Data (1999). *Tracking the fitness movement.* North Palm Beach, FL: Fitness Products Council.

Andersen, M., Williams, J., Aldridge, T., & Taylor, T. (1997). Tracking the training and careers of graduates of advanced degree programs in sport psychology, 1989–1994. *The Sport Psychologist,* 11, 326–344.

Anderson, P., & Butcher, K. (2006, Spring). Childhood Obesity: Trends and potential causes. *The Future of Children,* 16(1), 19–45.

Andrews, J. (2010). *Prevention and misconception are chief concerns in battling youth sport injuries.* www.pediatricsupersite.com

Antonelli, F. (1970). Opening address. In G. Kenyon (Ed.), *Contemporary psychology of sport* (p. 39). Chicago: The Athletic Institute.

*ARAPCS Newsletter* (1986). Our kids are out of shape, getting flabby. *ARAPCS Newsletter,* 3(1), 4.

A Report to the President (2000). Promoting better health for young people through physical activity and sports. *A Report to the President from the Secretary of*

*Health and Human Services and the Secretary of Education.*

Arnheim, D., & Prentice, W. (2000). *Principles of athletic training* (10th ed.). New York: McGraw-Hill.

Athletic Footwear Institute (1990). *American youth and sports participation.* North Palm Beach, FL: Athletic Footwear Institute.

Australian Sports Commission (1994). *National junior sport policy.* Canberra, Australia.

Bakhos, L., Lockart, G., Myers, R., & Lanakis, J. (2010). Emergency room visits for concussion in young child athletes. *Pediatrics,* 126(3), 550–556.

Bandura, A. (1994). Self-Efficacy. In V. S. Ramachaudran (Ed.), *Encyclopedia of human behavior* (vol. 4, pp. 71–81). New York: Academic Press.

Barrett, J. (2007). The price of childhood obesity. www.newsweek.com/id/73892

Basch, C. E. (2010). Healthier students are better learners: A missing link in school reforms to close the achievement gap. Equity Matters, *Research Review No. 6.* Campaign for Educational Equity, Teachers College, Columbia University.

Battagliola, M. (1993). Indian industries takes aim at employee health. *Business and Health,* 11, 12.

Baun, W. (1995). Culture change in worksite health promotion. In D. Dejoy & M. Wilson (Eds.), *Critical issues in worksite health promotion.* Boston: Allyn & Bacon.

Baun, W., & Bernacki, E. (1988). Who are corporate exercisers and what motivates them? In R. Dishman (Ed.), *Exercise adherence* (pp. 321–348). Champaign, IL: Human Kinetics.

Beaumont, C. E., & Pianca, E. G. (2002). *Why Johnny can't walk to school: Historic neighborhood schools in the age of sprawl.* Washington, DC: National Trust for Historic Preservation.

Beaver, D. (2004). Editor's corner, *Palaestra,* 20(1), 4, 15.

Becker, D. (1996, January 18). More women athletes head for Atlanta. *USA Today,* p. 12C.

Beighle, A., Pangrazi, R., & Vincent, S. (2001). Pedometers, physical activity and accountability. *Journal of Physical Education, Recreation, and Dance,* 72(9), 16–19, 36.

Bell, C. (1998). Sport education in the elementary school. *Journal of Physical Education, Recreation, and Dance,* 69(5), 36–39.

Bennett, W. (1986). *First lessons: A report on elementary education in America.* Washington, DC: U.S. Department of Education.

Bennett, R., & Hastie, P. (1997). A sport education curriculum model for a collegiate physical activity course. *Journal of Physical Education, Recreation, and Dance,* 68(1), 39–44.

Berg, K. (1988). A national curriculum in physical education. *Journal of Physical Education, Recreation, and Dance,* 59(8), 70–75.

Berger, B. (2004). Subjective well-being in obese individuals: The multiple roles of exercise. *Quest,* 56, 50–76.

Biddle, S. (1995). Exercise and psychosocial health. *Research Quarterly for Exercise and Sport,* 66, 292–297.

Biles, F. (1971). The physical education public information project. *Journal of Health, Physical Education, and Recreation,* 41(7), 53–55.

Blackledge, S. (1994, October 7). Pay-to-play takes toll at Big Walnut. *The Columbus Dispatch,* D-1.

Blair, S. (1992). Are American children and youth fit? The need for better data. *Research Quarterly for Exercise and Sport,* 63, 120–123.

Blair, S., & Connelly, J. (1996). How much physical activity should we do? The case for moderate amounts and intensities of physical activity. *Research Quarterly for Exercise and Sport,* 67, 193–205.

Blair, S., Kohl, H., III, Paffenbarger, R., Jr., Cooper, K., & Gibbons, L. (1989). Physical fitness and all-cause mortality: A prospective study of healthy men and women. *Journal of the American Medical Association,* 262, 2395–2401.

Blair, S., Kohl, H., & Powell, K. (1987). Physical activity, physical fitness, exercise, and the public's health. *The Academy Papers,* 20, 53–69.

Block, M. (1995). Americans with disabilities act: Its impact on youth sports. *Journal of Physical Education, Recreation, and Dance,* 66(5), 28–32.

Bond, L., Smith, T., Baker, W. K., & Hattie, J. A. (2000, September). *The certification system of the National Board for Professional Teaching Standards: A construct validity study.* Greensboro, NC: Center for Educational Research and Evaluation, The University of North Carolina at Greensboro.

Bookwalter, K., & Vander Zwaag, H. (1969). *Foundations and principles of physical education.* Philadelphia: W. B. Saunders.

Bouchard, C., & Rankinen, T. (2001). Individual differences in response to regular physical activity. *Medicine & Science in Sport & Exercise,* 33, S446–S451.

Bouchard, C., Shephard, R., & Stephens, T. (1993). *Physical activity, fitness and health: Consensus statement.* Champaign, IL: Human Kinetics.

Boucher, A. (1988). Good beginnings. *Journal of Physical Education, Recreation, and Dance,* 59(7), 42.

Bowerman, W., & Harris, W. (1967). *Jogging.* New York: Grosset & Dunlap.

Bowers, C. (1999). The creatine debate. *Strategies,* 12(6), 5–8.

Bowman, S., et al. (2004). Fast-food consumption of U.S. adults: Impact of energy and nutrient intakes and overweight status. *American College of Nutrition,* 23, 163–168.

Bradford-Krok, B. (1994). Citrus county fitness break: Funding and developing fitness videotapes. In R. Pate & D. Hohn (Eds.), *Health and fitness through physical education* (pp. 205–210). Champaign, IL: Human Kinetics.

Bradley, B. (1998). *Values of the game.* New York: Artisan.

Brady, E., & Glier, R. (2004, July 29). To play sports, many U.S. students must pay. *USA Today.* www.usatoday.com/sports/presps/2004-07-29-pay-to-play_x.htm

Brancazio, P. (1984). *Sport science: Physical laws and optimum performance.* New York: Simon & Schuster.

Bressan, E., & Pieter, W. (1985). Philosophic process and the study of human moving. *Quest,* 37, 1–15.

Brewer, J.D., Luebbers, P.E., & Shane, S.D. (2009). Increasing student physical activity during the school day: Opportunities for the physical educator. *Strategies,* 22(3), 20–23.

Brooks, G. (1987). The exercise physiology paradigm in contemporary biology: To molbiol or not to molbiol—that is the question. *Quest,* 39, 231–242.

———. (1994). 40 years of progress: Basic exercise physiology. In *40th Anniversary lectures.* Indianapolis, IN: American College of Sports Medicine.

Brooks, S. (2003, August 12). Virtual PE makes a splash. *USA Today,* 50.

Browder, K., & Darby, L. (1998). Individualizing exercise: Some biomechanical and physiological reminders. *Journal of Physical Education, Recreation, and Dance,* 69(4), 35–44.

Brown, G. (2010). NCAA study shows progress with women and minority hiring. The NCAA News.

Brusseau, T., Kulinna, P., Tudor-Locke, C., van der Mars, H., & Darst, P. (2011). Children's step counts on weekend, physical education, and non physical education days. *Journal of Human Kinetics,* 27, 116–134.

Bryant, C., & Peterson, J. (1999). Prescribing exercise for healthy adults. *Journal of Physical Education, Recreation, and Dance,* 70(6), 31.

Bucher, C. (1964). *Foundations of physical education* (4th ed.). St. Louis: Mosby.

Buckworth, J., & Dishman, R. (2001). Exercise psychology. In J. Williams (Ed.), *Applied sport psychology* (4th ed.) (pp. 497–518). Mountain View, CA: Mayfield.

Bulger, S., & Housner, L. (2009). Relocating from Easy Street: Strategies for moving physical education forward. *Quest,* 61, 442–469.

Bunker, L. (1998). Psycho-physiological contributions of physical activity and sports for girls. *President's Council on Physical Fitness and Sports Research Digest,* 3(1), 1–6.

Caillois, R. (1961). *Man, play and games.* New York: Free Press of Glencoe.

Caldwell, S. (1966). *Conceptions of physical education in twentieth century America: Rosalind Cassidy.* Doctoral dissertation, University of Southern California, Los Angeles.

California Department of Health and Human Services (2006). *Project Lean: Leaders encouraging activity and nutrition.* www.californiaprojectlean.org/

California Endowment. (2008). *Physical education matters: A full report.* Los Angeles: California Endowment.

Carlisle, R. (1974). Physical education and aesthetics. In H. Whiting & D. Masterson (Eds.), *Readings in the aesthetics of sport* (pp. 21–32). London: Lepus Books.

Carnegie Council on Adolescent Development (1992). *A matter of time: Risk and opportunity in the nonschool hours.* New York: Carnegie Corporation.

Casey, A. (1992). Title IX and women officials: How have they been affected? *Journal of Physical Education, Recreation, and Dance,* 63(3), 45–47.

Castelli, D., & Beighle, A. (2007). The Physical Education teacher as school activity director. *Journal of Physical Education, Recreation a Dance,* 78(5), 25–28.

Castelli, D., & Rink, J. (2003). A comparison of high and low performing secondary physical education programs. *Journal of Teaching in Physical Education,* 22, 512–532.

Cawley, J., Meyerhoefer, C, & Newhouse, D. (2007). The impact of state physical education requirements on youth physical activity and overweight. *Health Economics,* 16, 1287–1301.

Center on Education Policy (2007). *Choices, changes, and challenges: Curriculum and instruction in the NCLB era*. Washington, DC: Author.

Center on Education Policy (2008). *Instructional time in Elementary schools: A closer look at changes for specific subjects*. Washington, DC: Author.

Centers for Disease Control and Prevention (1991). *Healthy People 2000*. www.healthypeople.gov

———. (1997). Guidelines for school and community programs to promote lifelong physical activity among young people. U.S. Department of Health and Human Services, Centers for Disease Control and Prevention.

———. (2000). *Healthy People 2010*. www.healthypeople.gov

———. (2001). Increasing physical activity: A report on recommendations of the Task Force on Community Preventive Services. *Morbidity and Mortality Weekly Report, 50*, (No. RR-18) 1–14.

———. (2003). Physical activity levels among children aged 9–13 years—United States, 2002. *MMWR, 52*(33), 785–788.

———. (2006). Sports-related injuries among high school athletes—United States, 2005–06 school year. *MMWR, 55*(38), 1037–1040.

———. (2008). Defining overweight and obesity. www.cdc.gov/nccdphp/dnpa/obesity/defining.htm

———. (2010a). *The association between school based physical activity, including physical education, and academic performance*. Atlanta, GA: U.S. Department of Health and Human Services.

———. (2010b). *Strategies to improve the quality of Physical Education*. Atlanta, GA: U.S. Department of Health and Human Services. www.cdc.gov/HealthyYouth/physicalactivity/pdf/quality_pe.pdf

Christina, R. (1987). Motor learning: Future lines of research. *The Academy Papers, 20*, 26–41.

———. (1989). Whatever happened to applied research in motor learning? In J. Skinner et al. (Eds.), *Future directions for exercise science and sport research* (pp. 411–422). Champaign, IL: Human Kinetics.

Chu, D. (1981). Functional myths of educational organizations: College as career training and the relationship of formal title to actual duties on secondary school employment. In V. Crafts (Ed.), *Proceedings of the National Association for Physical Education in Higher Education* (pp. 36–46). Champaign, IL: Human Kinetics.

Cissell, W. (1992). Health educators as professionals in the year 2000: A prediction. *Journal of Physical Education, Recreation, and Dance, 63*(5), 27.

Civic Ventures (2011). *Fact sheet on older Americans*. www.civicventures.org

Clark, J. (2008). Kinesiology in the 21st century: A preface. *Quest, 60*, 1–2.

Clarke, D. (1986). Children and the research process. *The Academy Papers, 19*, 9–13.

Coakley, J. (1982). *Sport in society* (2nd ed.). St. Louis: Mosby.

———. (1994). *Sports and society: Issues and controversies* (5th ed.). St. Louis, MO: Mosby.

———. (2004). *Sports in society: Issues and controversies* (8th ed.). Boston: McGraw-Hill.

———. (2007). *Sports and society: Issues and Controversies* (9th ed.). New York: McGraw Hill.

Coffin, J. (2002, September 9). Football a focal point in the Title IX debate. *Golfweek*, 22.

Cohen, A. (1991). The children's crusade: In pursuit of youth fitness. *Athletic Business, 15*(10), 24–28.

———. (1995). Fitness equipment: The next generation. *Athletic Business, 19*(3), 26–36.

Colfer, G., Hamilton, K., Magill, R., & Hamilton, B. (1986). *Contemporary physical education*. Dubuque, IA: Brown.

*Columbus Dispatch*. (2005, March 17). Obesity threatens life expectancy, p. A-5.

Comstock, R., Nox, C., Yard, E., & Gilchrist, J. (2007). Sports-related injuries among high school athletes—United States, 2005–06 school year. *MMWR Weekly, 55*(38), 1037–1040.

Cooper, K. (1968). *Aerobics*. New York: Bantam Books.

Corbett, D., & Calloway, D. (2006, Winter). Physical activity challenges facing African-American girls and women. *President's Council on Physical Fitness and Sport Newsletter, 1*–5.

Corbin, C. (1981). First things first, but don't stop there. *Journal of Physical Education, Recreation, and Dance, 52*, 36–38.

———. (1987). Physical fitness in the K–12 curriculum: Some defensible solutions to perennial problems. *Journal of Physical Education, Recreation, and Dance, 58*(7), 49–54.

———. (2002). Physical activity for everyone: What every physical educator should know about promoting lifelong physical activity. *Journal of Teaching in Physical Education, 21*, 128.

Corbin, C., & Cardinal, B. (2008). Conceptual physical education: The anatomy of an innovation. *Quest, 60*, 467–487.

Corbin, C., Dowell, L., Lindsey, R., & Tolson, H. (1974). *Concepts in physical education* (2nd ed.). Dubuque, IA: Brown.

Corbin, C., Le Masurier, G., & Lambdin, D. (2007). *Fitness for life middle school.* Champaign, IL: Human Kinetics.

Corbin, C., Le Masurier, G., Lambdin, D., & Greiner, M. (2010). *Fitness for life elementary school program package.* Champaign, IL: Human Kinetics.

Corbin, C., & Lindsey, R. (2007). *Fitness for life* (5th ed.). Champaign, IL: Human Kinetics.

———. (1999). *Concepts of physical fitness* (10th ed.). New York: McGraw-Hill.

Corbin, C., & Pangrazi, R. (1992). Are American children and youth fit? *Research Quarterly for Exercise and Sport,* 63, 96–106.

———. (1996). How much PA is enough? *Journal of Physical Education, Recreation, and Dance,* 67(4), 33–37.

———. (1998). *Physical activity for children: A statement of guidelines.* Reston, VA: NASPE Publications.

Corbin, C., Pangrazi, R., & Franks, B. (2000). Definitions: Health, fitness, and physical activity. President's Council on Physical Fitness and Sport. *Research Digest,* 3(9), 1–8.

Corbin, C., Pangrazi, R., & LeMasurier, G. (2004). Physical activity for children: Current patterns and guidelines. *Research Digest,* 5(2), 1–8.

Corbin, C., Pangrazi, R., & Welk, G. (1994). Toward an understanding of appropriate physical activity levels for youth: Physical activity and fitness. *President's Council on Physical Fitness and Sport Research Digest,* 1, 1–8.

Corbin, C., Welk, G., Corbin, W., & Welk, K. (2008). *Concepts of physical fitness: Active lifestyles for wellness* (14th ed.). Boston: McGraw-Hill.

Cordes, K., & Ibrahim, H. (2003). *Applications in recreation and leisure* (3rd ed.). Boston: McGraw-Hill.

Costill, D. (1986). *Inside running: Basics of sport physiology.* Indianapolis: Benchmark Press.

Councilman, J. (1968). *The science of swimming.* Englewood Cliffs, NJ: Prentice Hall.

Cremin, L. (1961). *The transformation of the school: Progressivism in American education.* New York: Knopf.

Csikszentmihalyi, M., Rathunde, K., & Whalen, S. (1993). *Talented teenagers: The roots of success and failure.* Cambridge, MA: Cambridge University Press.

Cureton, K. (1994). Physical fitness and activity standards for youth. In R. Pate & D. Hohn (Eds.), *Health and fitness through physical education* (pp. 129–136). Champaign, IL: Human Kinetics.

Dale, D., & Corbin, C. (2000). Physical activity participation of high school graduates following exposure to conceptual or traditional Physical Education. *Research Quarterly for Exercise and Sport,* 71, 61–68.

Dale, D., Corbin, C., & Cuddihy, T. (1998). Can conceptual physical education promote physically active lifestyles? *Pediatric Exercise Science,* 10, 97–109.

Dale, D., Corbin, C., & Dale, K. (2000). Restricting opportunities to be active during school time: Do children compensate by increasing physical activity levels after school? *Research Quarterly for Exercise and Sport,* 71, 240–248.

Dalleck, L. & Kravitz, L. (2002). The history of fitness. http://www.unm.edu/~lkravitz/Article%20folder/history.html

Daniels, S. (2006). The consequences of childhood overweight and obesity. *The Future of Children,* 16(1), 47–67.

Darby, L., & Temple, I. (1992). A research project that combines research, teaching and service. *Journal of Physical Education, Recreation, and Dance,* 63(8), 65–67.

Darnell, J. (1994). Sport education in the elementary curriculum. In D. Siedentop (Ed.), *Sport education in physical education* (pp. 61–71). Champaign, IL: Human Kinetics.

Davis, K. (1999). Giving women a chance to learn: Gender equity principles for HPERD classes. *Journal of Physical Education, Recreation, and Dance,* 70(4), 13–14.

Davis, R. (2003). Running for life. *Journal of Physical Education, Recreation, and Dance,* 74(4), 11–13, 19.

De Grazia, S. (1962). *Of time, work and leisure.* New York: Twentieth Century Fund.

DePauw, K. (1984). Commitment and challenges. *Journal of Physical Education, Recreation, and Dance,* 55(2), 34–35.

———. (1996). Students with disabilities in physical education. In S. Silverman & C. Ennis (Eds.), *Student learning in physical education: Applying research to enhance instruction* (pp. 101–124). Champaign, IL: Human Kinetics.

DeRenne, C., Morgan, C., Hetzler, R., & Taura, B. (2007). A state analysis of high school certification requirements for head baseball coaches. *The Sports Journal,* 10(3). http://thesportjournal.org/article/

state-analysis-high-school-coaching-certification-requirements-head-baseball-coaches

Dietz, W. (2004). The effects of physical activity on obesity. *Quest, 56,* 1–11.

Dishman, R. (Ed.). (1988). *Exercise adherence.* Champaign, IL: Human Kinetics.

———. (1989). Determinants of physical activity and exercise for persons 65 years of age or older. *The Academy Papers, 22,* 140–162.

Dompier, T., Powell, J., Barron, M., & Moore, M. (2007). Time-loss and non-time-loss injuries in youth football players. *Journal of Athletic Training, 42,* 395–402.

Donnelly, J.E., Blair, S.N., Jakicic, J.M., Manore, M.M., Rankin, J.W., & Smith, B.K. (2009). Appropriate physical activity intervention strategies for weight loss and prevention of weight regain for adults. *Medicine & Science in Sports & Exercise, 41,* 459–471.

Duda, J. (1991). Motivating older adults for physical activity: It's never too late. *Journal of Physical Education, Recreation, and Dance, 62*(7), 44–48.

Dugas, D. (1994). Sport education in the secondary curriculum. In D. Siedentop, *Sport education: Quality PE through positive sport experiences* (pp. 105–112). Champaign, IL: Human Kinetics.

Dulles, F. R. (1940). *America learns to play.* New York: Appleton-Century.

Dunn, D. (1986a). An introduction. *Journal of Physical Education, Recreation, and Dance, 57*(8), 34–35.

———. (1986b). Professionalism and human resources. *Journal of Physical Education, Recreation, and Dance, 57*(8), 50–53.

Duquin, M. (1988). Gender and youth sport: Reflections on old and new fictions. In F. Smoll, R. Magill, & M. Ash (Eds.), *Children in sport* (pp. 31–41). Champaign, IL: Human Kinetics.

Dyson, G. (1964). *The mechanics of athletics.* London: University of London Press.

Earls, N. (1981). Distinctive teachers' personal qualities, perceptions of teacher education and the realities of teaching. *Journal of Teaching in Physical Education, 1*(1), 59–70.

Eccles, J., & Barber, B. (1999). Student council, volunteering, basketball, or marching band: What kind of extracurricular involvement matters? *Journal of Adolescent Research, 14,* 10–43.

Edlin, G., & Golanty, E. (1982). *Health and wellness.* Boston: Science Books International.

Eitzen, S., & Sage, G. (2003). *Sociology of North American sport* (7th ed.) Boston: McGraw Hill.

Elias, M. (1983, November 17). We frown on girls who play rough. *USA Today,* p. 1A.

Elliot, R. (1974). Aesthetics and sport. In H. Whiting & D. Masterson (Eds.), *Readings in the aesthetics of sport* (pp. 107–116). London: Lepus Books.

Ellis, M. (1988). *The business of physical education.* Champaign, IL: Human Kinetics.

Engbers L.H., van Poppel, M.N., Chin A Paw, M.J., & van Mechelen, W. (2005). Worksite health promotion programs with environmental changes: A systematic review. *American Journal of Preventive Medicine, 29,* 61–70.

Ennis, C., Ross, J., & Chen, A. (1992). The role of value orientations in curricular decision making: A rationale for teachers' goals and expectations. *Research Quarterly for Exercise and Sport, 63,* 38–47.

Ennis, C., Solmon, M., Satina, B., Loftus, S., Mensch, J., & McCauley, M. (1999). Creating a sense of family in urban schools using the "sport for peace" curriculum. *Research Quarterly for Exercise and Sport, 70,* 273–285.

Evans, J., & Roberts, G. (1987). Physical competence and the development of peer relations. *Quest, 39,* 23–35.

Everhart, B., & Turner, E. (1995). Computer feedback for improved teacher training. *Journal of Physical Education, Recreation, and Dance, 66*(9), 57–60.

Ewing, M., & Seefeldt, V. (1997). Youth sports in America: An overview. *President's Council on Physical Fitness and Sports Research Digest. 2*(11), 1–12.

Executive Summary. (1999). When school is out. *The Future of Children, 9*(2), 1–4.

Eyler, M. (1965). Sport historians. *Proceedings of the National College Physical Education Association for Men,* 57–60.

Fahey, T., Insel, P., & Roth, W. (2007). *Fit and well* (7th ed.). Mountain, View, CA: Mayfield.

———. (2008). *Fit and well* (8th ed.). New York: McGraw-Hill.

Faigenbaum, A. (2001). Strength training and children's health. *Journal of Physical Education, Recreation and Dance, 72*(3), 24–30.

Fain, G. (1983). Introduction. *Journal of Physical Education, Recreation, and Dance, 54*(8), 32–33.

Fanselow, J. (2004, March 21). With every mile they grow stronger. *Parade,* 5.

Farrey, T. (2008). *Game on: The all-American race to make champions of our children.* New York: ESPN Books.

Faucette, N., Nugent, P., Sallis, J., & McKenzie, T. (2002). "I'd rather chew on aluminum foil." Overcoming classroom teachers' resistance to teaching physical education. *Journal of Teaching in Physical Education, 21,* 287–308.

Feltz, D. (1987). The future of graduate education in sport and exercise science: A sport psychology perspective. *Quest, 39,* 217–222.

Finger, D. (2004). Before they were next. *ESPN the Magazine, 7*(12), 83–86.

Filardo, M., Vincent, J.M., Allen, M., & Franklin, J. (2010). *Joint use of public schools: A framework for a new social contract.* Washington, DC: 21st Century School Fund. Berkeley, CA: Center for Cities and Schools.

Finkelstein E.A., Trogdon, J.G., Cohen, J.W., & Dietz, W. (2009). Annual medical spending attributable to obesity: Payer- and service-specific estimates. *Health Affairs, 28*(5), w822–w831.

Flegal, K., Carroll, M., Ogden, C., & Johnson, C. (2002). Prevalence and trends in obesity among U.S. adults, 1999–2000. *Journal of the American Medical Association, 288,* 1723–1727.

Fletcher, J. & Banasik, J. (2001, May). Exercise self-efficacy. *Clinical Excellence for Nurse Practitioners, 5*(3), 134–143.

Foley, J., Tindall, D., Lieberman, L., & Kim, S. (2007). How to develop disability awareness using the Sport Education model. *Journal of Physical Education, Recreation and Dance, 78*(9), 32–36.

Fox, C. (1992). Title IX at twenty. *Journal of Physical Education, Recreation, and Dance, 63*(3), 33–35.

Fraleigh, W. (1985). Why the good foul is not good. In D. Vanderwerken & S. Wertz (Eds.), *Sport: Inside out* (pp. 462–466). Fort Worth: Texas Christian University Press.

Fraser-Thomas, J., & Cote, J. (2007). Youth sports: Implementing findings and moving forward with research. *Athletic Insight: The Online Journal of Sport Psychology, 3,* 1–12.

Freedson, P., & Rowland, T. (1992). Youth activity versus youth fitness: Let's redirect our efforts. *Research Quarterly for Exercise and Sport, 63*(2), 133–136.

Freeman, W. (1982). *Physical education and sport in a changing society* (2nd ed.). Minneapolis: Burgess.

French, R., Henderson, H., Kinnison, L., & Sherrill, C. (1998). Revisiting section 504, Physical Education and Sport. *Journal of Physical Education, Recreation, and Dance, 69*(7), 57–64.

Gabbei, R. (2004). Achieving balance: Secondary physical education gender-grouping options. *Journal of Physical Education, Recreation, and Dance, 75*(3), 33–39.

Gard, M. (2004). An elephant in the room and a bridge too far, or physical education and the "obesity epidemic." In J. Evans, B. Davies, & J. Wright (Eds.), *Body knowledge and control: Studies in the sociology of physical education and health* (pp. 68–82). London: Routledge.

Geadelmann, P. (1981). Co-educational physical education: For better or worse. *NASSP Bulletin, 65,* 91–95.

Gensemer, R. (1985). *Physical education: Perspectives, inquiry, applications.* Philadelphia: Saunders.

Gerber E., Felshin, J., Berlin, P., & Wyrick. Wyrick, W. (Eds.) (1974). *The American woman in sport.* Reading, MA: Addison-Wesley.

Giamatti, A. B. (1989). *Take time for paradise.* New York: Summit Books.

Gill, D. (1991). Social psychological contributions to performance enhancement. *The Academy Papers, 25,* 117–121.

Gober, B., & Franks, B. (1988). The physical and fitness education of young children. *Journal of Physical Education, Recreation, and Dance, 59*(7), 57–61.

Goetzel, R., Sepulveda, M., Knight, K., Eisen, M., Wade, B., Wong, C., & Fielding, N. (1994). Association of IBM's "A plan for life" health promotion program with changes in employees' health risk status. *American College of Occupational and Environmental Medicine, 36,* 1005–1009.

Goldhaber, D., & Anthony, E. (2004). Can teacher quality be effectively assessed? National Board Certification as a signal of effective teaching. *The Review of Economics and Statistics, 89,* 134–150.

Gorman, J., & Calhoun, K. (1994). *The name of the game: The business of sports.* New York: Wiley.

Gough, D. (1995). Specialization in youth sport. *Coaching Clinic, 34*(3), 5–6.

Government of South Australia (2007). Handlebar injuries causing life-threatening "mega trauma." *Children, Youth, and Women's Health Science.*

Graham, G. (1990). Physical education in U.S. schools, K–12. *Journal of Physical Education, Recreation, and Dance, 61*(2), 35–39.

Graham, G., Holt-Hale, S., & Parker, M. (2010). Children moving: A reflective approach to teaching physical education (8th ed.). Columbus, OH: McGraw-Hill.

Grant, B. (1992). Integrating sport into the physical education curriculum in New Zealand secondary schools. *Quest, 44,* 304–316.

Graves, M., & Townsend, J. (2000). Applying the sport education curriculum model to dance. *Journal of Physical Education, Recreation, and Dance, 71*(8), 50–54.

Green, J. (1997). Action research in youth soccer: Assessing the acceptability of an alternative program. *Journal of Sport Management, 11,* 29–44.

Griffey, D. (1987). Trouble for sure: A crisis perhaps. *Journal of Physical Education, Recreation, and Dance, 58*(2), 20–21.

Griffin, L., Mitchell, S., & Oslin, J. (1997). *Teaching sports concepts and skills: A tactical games approach.* Champaign, IL: Human Kinetics.

Gruneau, R. (1976). Sport as an area of sociological study: An introduction to major themes and perspectives. In R. Gruneau & J. Albinson (Eds.), *Canadian sport: Sociological perspectives* (pp. 3–7). Reading, MA: Addison-Wesley.

Gutin, B., Manos, T., & Strong, W. (1992). Defining health and fitness: First step toward establishing children's fitness standards. *Research Quarterly for Exercise and Sport, 63*(2), 128–132.

Hall, L., & Wilson, P. (1984). Industrial fitness, adult fitness, and cardiac rehabilitation graduate programs. *Journal of Physical Education, Recreation, and Dance, 55*(3), 40–44

Halstead. M., & Walter, K. (2010, September). Sport-related concussions in children and adolescents. *Pediatrics, 126*(3), 597–615.

Hannon, J., & Ratliffe, T. (2007). Opportunities to participate and teacher interactions in coed versus single-gender physical education settings. *Physical Educator, 64,* 11–20.

Harageones, M. (1987). Impact of educational reform: The quality of Florida's high school physical education programs. *Journal of Physical Education, Recreation, and Dance, 58*(6), 52–54.

Harrington, M. (1998, April 27). Families driven to keep competitive in sports. *USA Today,* 6D.

Harris, D. (1987). Frontiers in psychology of exercise and sport. *The Academy Papers, 20,* 42–52.

Harris, J. (1991). Modifying the performance enhancement ethos: Disciplinary and professional implications. *The Academy Papers, 25,* 96–103.

———. (1992, April). Using kinesiology: A comparison of applied veins in the subdisciplines. Amy Morris Homans Lecture, National Convention of the American Alliance for Health, Physical Education, Recreation, and Dance, Indianapolis.

———. (2000). Sociology of physical activity. In S. Hoffman & J. Harris (Eds.), *Introduction to kinesiology* (pp. 207–240). Champaign, IL: Human Kinetics.

Hasbrook, C. (1987). Interscholastic coaching and officiating: Programs designed to increase the number of women involved. *Journal of Physical Education, Recreation, and Dance, 58*(2), 35.

Hastie, P. (1998a). The participation and perception of girls during a unit of sport education. *Journal of Teaching in Physical Education, 18,* 157–171.

———. (1998b). Applied benefits of the sport education model. *Journal of Physical Education, Recreation, and Dance, 69*(4), 24–26.

Hastie, P., & Sharpe, T. (1999). Effects of a sport education curriculum on the positive social behaviors of at-risk rural adolescent boys. *Journal of Education for Students Placed at Risk, 4,* 417–430.

Hawkins, R., & Mulkey, L. (2005). Athletic investment and academic resilience in a national sample of African American females and males in middle grades. *Education and Urban Society, 38*(1), 62–88.

Hay, J. (1991). Reaction to performance feedback: Advances in biomechanics. *Quest, 25,* 33–37.

Hayes, E. (1980). History of dance in the Alliance. *Journal of Physical Education, Recreation, and Dance, 51*(5), 32.

Haymes, E. (2000). Physiology of physical activity. In S. Hoffman & J. Harris (Eds.) *Introduction to kinesiology* (pp. 381–412). Champaign, IL: Human Kinetics.

He, M., & Evans, A. (2007). Are parents aware that their children are overweight or obese? Do they care? *Canadian Family Physician, 53*(9), 1493–1499.

Hellison, D. (1973). *Humanistic physical education.* Englewood Cliffs, NJ: Prentice Hall.

———. (1978). *Beyond balls and bats: Alienated youth in the gym.* Washington, DC: AAHPERD.

———. (1983). Teaching self-responsibility (and more). *Journal of Physical Education, Recreation, and Dance, 54*(7), 23.

———. (1984). *Goals and strategies for teaching physical education.* Champaign, IL: Human Kinetics.

———. (1990). Teaching PE to at-risk youth in Chicago: A model. *Journal of Physical Education, Recreation, and Dance, 61*(6), 38–39.

———. (1995). *Teaching responsibility through physical activity.* Champaign, IL: Human Kinetics.

———. (1996). Teaching personal and social responsibility in physical education. In S. Silverman & C. Ennis (Eds.), *Student learning in physical education:*

*Applying research to enhance instruction* (pp. 269–286). Champaign, IL: Human Kinetics.

———. (2003). *Teaching responsibility through physical activity*, 2nd ed. Champaign, IL: Human Kinetics.

Henderson, K., & Bialeschki, M. (1991). Girls' and women's recreation programming: Constraints and opportunities. *Journal of Physical Education, Recreation, and Dance, 62*(1), 55–58.

Henig, R. (1999, January 21). Girls enjoy sports—isn't that enough? *USA Today*, 15A.

Henry, F. (1964). Physical education: An academic discipline. *Journal of Health, Physical Education, and Recreation, 37*(7), 32–33.

Herman, K., Craig, C., Gauvin, L., & Katzmarzyk, P. (2009). Tracking obesity and physical activity from childhood to adulthood: The Physical Activity Longitudinal Study. *International Journal of Pediatric Obesity, 4*, 281–288.

Hertzman, C. (1994). The lifelong impact of childhood experiences: A population health perspective. *Daedalus, 123*(4), 167–180.

Hester, D., & Dunaway, D. (1991). NAGWS: Paths to advocacy, recruitment, and enhancement. *Journal of Physical Education, Recreation, and Dance, 62*(3), 30–31.

Hetherington, C. (1910). Fundamental education. *American Physical Education Review, 15*, 629–635.

Hilgers, L. (2006, July 5). *Youth sports drawing more than ever.* CNN, Web article.

Hinson, C. (1994). Pulse power: A heart physiology program for children. *Journal of Physical Education, Recreation and Dance, 65*(1), 62–68.

Hirschhorn, D., & Loughead, T. (2000). Parental impact on youth participation in sport: The physical educator's role. *Journal of Physical Education, Recreation, and Dance, 72*, 41–46.

Hoch, D. (2007, Summer). Strategies for problematic parents. *Coaches' Quarterly*.

Hoffman, S. (1977). Toward a pedagogical kinesiology. *Quest, 28*, 38–48.

———. (1987). Dreaming the impossible dream: The decline and fall of physical education. In J. Massengale (Ed.), *Trends toward the future in physical education* (pp. 121–135). Champaign, IL: Human Kinetics.

Hoffman, S., & Harris, J. (2000). Discovering the field of physical activity. In S. Hoffman & J. Harris (Eds.), *Introduction to kinesiology* (pp. 1–33). Champaign, IL: Human Kinetics.

Houlihan, S., & DeBrock, L. (1991). Economics in sport. In B. Parkhouse (Ed.), *The management of sport* (pp. 198–209). St. Louis: Mosby.

Huizinga, J. (1962). *Homo ludens: A study of the play element in culture.* Boston: Beacon Press.

Hulstrand, B. (1990). Women in high school PE teaching positions: Diminishing in number. *Journal of Physical Education, Recreation, and Dance, 61*(9), 19–21.

Isaac, T., Baker, T., McCullick, B., Lux, K., & Tomporowski, P. (2011, March). *An Analysis of State Physical Education Policy Statutory Ambiguity.* Paper presented at the 2011 AAHPERD National Convention.

Isganaitis, E. & Lustig, L. (2005). Fast food, central nervous system, insulin resistance, and obesity. *Arteriosclerosis, Thrombosis, and Vascular Biology, 25*, 2451–2462.

Jack, H. (1985). Division of recreation. *Journal of Physical Education, Recreation, and Dance, 56*(4), 97–98.

Jacobson, S. & King, D. (2009). Measuring the potential for automobile fuel savings in the U.S.: The impact of obesity. *Transportation Research, 14*, 6–13.

James, M. (1995). Unified sports gains momentum at '95 World Games. *Exceptional Children, 25*(6), 56–57.

Jansma, P., & French, R. (1994). *Special physical education.* Englewood Cliffs, NJ: Prentice Hall.

Jago, R., & Baranowski, T. (2004). Non-curricular approaches for increasing physical activity in youth: A review. *Preventive Medicine, 39*, 157–163.

Jewett, A., & Bain, L. (1985). *The curriculum process in physical education.* Dubuque, IA: Wm. C. Brown.

Johns, E. (1985). Division of health education. *Journal of Physical Education, Recreation, and Dance, 56*(4), 105–106.

Johnson, D., & Harageones, E. (1994). A health fitness course in secondary physical education: The Florida experience. In R. Pate & D. Hohn (Eds.), *Health and fitness through physical education* (pp. 165–176). Champaign: IL: Human Kinetics.

Johnston, L., O'Malley, P., Bachman, J., & Schulenberg, J. (2010). *Youth, education, and society—Results on school policies and programs: Overview of Key Findings, 2009.* Ann Arbor, MI: Survey Research Center-Institute for Social Research. www.yesresearch.org/publications/reports/schoolreport2009.pdf

Jones, D., & Ward, P. (1998). Changing the face of secondary physical education through sport education. *Journal of Physical Education, Recreation, and Dance, 69*(5), 40–44.

Kahn, L., Collins, J., Pateman, B., Small, M., Ross, J., & Kolbe, L. (1995). The School Health Policies and Programs Study (SHPPS): Rationale for a nationwide status report on school health programs. *Journal of School Health, 65,* 291–302.

Kaman, R. (1995). Costs and benefits of corporate health promotion. *Fitness in Business, 5,* 39–44.

Kantrowitz, B., & Joseph, N. (1986, May 26). Building baby biceps. *Newsweek,* 79.

Karvonen, M. (1996). Physical activity for a healthy life. *Research Quarterly for Exercise and Sport, 67,* 209–212.

Kaufman, F. (2005). *Diabesity.* New York: Bantam Books.

Keating, J. (1973). The ethics of competition and its relation to some moral problems in athletics. In R. Osterhoudt (Ed.), *The philosophy of sport* (pp. 157–175). Springfield, IL: Thomas.

Kennedy, J. (1960, December). The soft American. *Sports Illustrated,* 15–23.

Kenyon, G., & Loy, J. (1965). Toward a sociology of sport. *Journal of Health, Physical Education, and Recreation, 36,* 24–25, 68–69.

Kerr, R. (1982). *Psychomotor learning.* Philadelphia: Saunders.

Kimm, S., Glynn, N., Kriska, A., Barton, B., Kronsberg, S., Daniels, S., Crawford, P., Sabry, Z., & Liu, K. (2002). Decline in physical activity in black girls and white girls during adolescence. *New England Journal of Medicine, 347,* 709–715.

Kinchin, G. (2006). Sport Education: A view of the research. In D. Kirk, D. Mcdonald & M. O'Sullivan (Eds.), *Handbook of Physical Education* (pp. 596–609). London: Sage.

King, B. (2010). High school sports running on empty. *Street & Smith's Sports Business Journal. www.sportsbusiness daily.com/Journal/Issues/2010/08/20100802/SBJ-In-Depth/High-School-Sports-Running-On-Empty.aspx*

Kirchner, G. (1970). *Introduction to human movement.* Dubuque, IA: Brown.

Kleinman, S. (1987). On the edge (of oblivion). *American Academy of Physical Education Papers, 20,* 109–114.

Knop, N. (1998). *Reconstructing physical education in an urban secondary school to create a more democratic environment. Teaching as praxis.* Unpublished doctoral dissertation, Ohio State University, Columbus.

Knop, N., Tannehill, D., & O'Sullivan, M. (2001). Making a difference for urban youth. *Journal of Physical Education, Recreation, and Dance, 72*(7), 38–44.

Knoppers, A. (1988). Equity for excellence in physical education. *Journal of Physical Education, Recreation, and Dance, 59*(6), 54–58.

Knudson, D., Magnusson, P., & McHugh, M. (2000). Current issues in flexibility fitness. *Research Digest* 3(10), 1–8. President's Council on Physical Fitness and Sport.

Konukman, F., Agbuga, B., Erdogan, S., Zorba, E., Demirhan, G, & Yilmaz, I. (2010). Teacher-coach role conflict in school-based physical education in USA: A literature review and suggestions for the future. *Biomedical Human Kinetics, 2,* 19–24.

Koplan, J., Liverman, C., Kraak, V., & Wisham, W. (Eds.). (2006). *Progress in preventing childhood obesity: How do we measure up?* Washington, DC: Institute of Medicine of the National Academies.

Kotulak, R., & Gorner, P. (1992, January 12). Diet, fitness proven keys to long life. *Columbus Dispatch,* p. 6F.

Kraus, H., & Hirschland, R. (1954). Minimum muscular fitness tests in school children. *Research Quarterly, 25,* 178–185.

Kraus, R. (1995). Play's new identity: Big business. *Journal of Physical Education, Recreation, and Dance, 66*(8), 36–40.

————. (2002). Careers in recreation: Expanding horizons. *Journal of Physical Education, Recreation, and Dance, 73*(5), 46–49, 54.

————. (1989). On beautiful games. *Journal of the Philosophy of Sport, 16*(1), 23–32.

Kretchmar, R. (2006). Life on Easy Street: The persistent need for embodied hopes and down-to-earth games. *Quest, 58,* 345–354.

————. (2008). The increasing utility of elementary school physical education: A mixed blessing and unique challenge. *The Elementary School Journal, 108,* 161–170.

LaFee, S. (2006). Steroids: To test or educate? *The School Administrator, 6*(63) 47.

LaMaster, K. (1996). Go on-line: Get new ideas from newsgroups. *Strategies, 9*(5), 18–20.

Landers, D. (1983). Whatever happened to theory testing in sport psychology? *Journal of Sport Psychology, 5,* 135–151.

————. (1997). The influence of exercise on mental health. *President's Council on Physical Fitness and Sport Research Digest, 2*(12), 1–8.

Lapchick, R. (2005). *2004 racial and gender scorecard.* Orlando: Institute for Diversity and Ethics in Sport, University of Central Florida.

————. (2006). *Division IA conference leadership study.* Orlando: Institute for Diversity and Ethics in Sport, University of Central Florida.

———. (2007). *The buck stops here: Assessing diversity among campus and conference leaders for Division IA school in 2008.* Orlando: Institute for Diversity and Ethics in Sport, University of Central Florida.

———. (2010). *The 2009 Racial and Gender Report Card: College Sport.* Orlando: Institute for Diversity and Ethics in Sport, University of Central Florida.

Larson, R., & Verma, S. (1999). How children and adolescents spend time across the world: Work, play, and developmental opportunities. *Psychological Bulletin, 125,* 701–736.

Lauer. H. (2006). *The new Americans: Defining ourselves through sports and fitness participation.* Fort Mill, SC: American Sports Data.

Launder, A. (2001) *Play practice: The games approach to teaching and coaching.* Champaign, IL: Human Kinetics.

Laurson, K., Brown, D., Cullen, R., & Dennis, K. (2008). Heart rates of high school physical education students during team sports, individual sports, and fitness activities. *Research Quarterly for Exercise and Sport, 79,* 85–91.

Lawson, H. (1994). Toward healthy learners, schools, and communities. *Journal of Teacher Education, 45*(1), 62–70.

Lawson, H., & Placek, J. (1981). *Physical education in the secondary schools: Curricular alternatives.* Boston: Allyn & Bacon.

Lee, I.-M., & Paffenbarger, R., Jr. (1996). How much physical activity is optimal for health? Methodological considerations. *Research Quarterly for Exercise and Sport, 67,* 206–208.

Lee, M., & Bennett, B. (1985a). 1885–1900: A time of gymnastics and measurement. *Journal of Physical Education, Recreation, and Dance, 56*(4), 19–26.

———. (1985b). 1930–1945: A time for affiliation and research. *Journal of Physical Education, Recreation, and Dance, 56*(4), 43–51.

Lee, S., Burgeson, C., Fulton, J., & Spain, C. (2007). Physical education and physical activity: Results from the School Health Policies and Programs Study 2006. *Journal of School Health, 77,* 435–463.

Leek, D., Carlson, J., Cain, K., Henrichon, S., Rosenberg, D., Patrick, K., & Sallis, J. (2010). Physical activity during youth sport practices. *Archives of Pediatric Adolescent Medicine, 165*(4), 294–299.

Leigh, D. (1994). Dance for social change. *Journal of Physical Education, Recreation, and Dance, 65*(5), 39–43.

Leonard, F., & Affleck, G. (1947). *A guide to the history of physical education.* Philadelphia: Lea & Febiger.

Leonard, G. (1974). *The ultimate athlete.* New York: Viking Press.

Levi, J., Segal, L., & Gadola, E. (2007). *F as in Fat: How obesity policies are failing in America.* Washington, DC: Trust for America's Health.

Levi, J., Segal, I., & Juliano, C. (2006). *F as in Fat: How obesity policies are failing in America.* Washington, DC: Trust for America's Health.

Levine, A., Wells, S., & Knopf, C. (1986, August 11). New rules of exercise. *U.S. News and World Report,* 52–56.

Lightwood, J., Bibbins-Domingo, K., et al. (2009, December). Forecasting the future economic burden of current adolescent overweight: An estimate of the coronary heart disease policy model. *American Journal of Public Health, 99,* 2230–2237.

Lister, V. (1993, December 9). More opportunities open, but roadblocks still there. *USA Today,* p. 9C.

Litchfield, R., Muldoon, J., Welk, G., Hallihan, J., & Lane, T. (2005). Lighten up Iowa: An interdisciplinary, collaborative health promotion campaign. *Journal of Extension, 43*(2), 1–13.

Locke, L. (1992). Changing secondary school physical education. *Quest, 44,* 361–372.

Locke, L., & Massengale, J. (1978). Role conflict in teacher/coaches. *Research Quarterly, 49,* 162–174.

Logsdon, B., Barrett, K., Broer, M., McKee, R., & Ammongs, M. (1977). *Physical education for children: A focus on the teaching process.* Philadelphia: Lea & Febiger.

Lopes, V., Vasques, C., Pereira, M., Maia, J., & Malina, R. (2006). Physical activity patterns during school recess: A study in children 6 to 10 years old. *The International Electronical Journal of Health Education, 9,* 192–201.

Lopez, M. (2006). Participation in sports and civic engagement. *Circle fact sheet.* College Park: The Center for Information and Research on Civic Learning and Engagement, School of Public Policy, University of Maryland.

Lounsbery, M., Gast, J., & Smith, N. (2005). The integrated curriculum of "Planned Approach to Healthier Schools." *Journal of Physical Education, Recreation, and Dance, 76*(3), 34–37.

Lowe, B. (1977). *The beauty of sport: A crossdisciplinary inquiry.* Englewood Cliffs, NJ: Prentice Hall.

Loy, J. (1969). The nature of sport: A definitional effort. In J. Loy & G. Kenyon (Eds.), *Sport, culture and society* (pp. 23–32). New York: Macmillan.

Loy, J., & McElvogue, J. (1981). Racial segregation in American sport. In J. Loy, G. Kenyon, & B. McPherson (Eds.), *Sport, culture and society: A reader on the sociology of sport* (pp. 103–116). Philadelphia: Lea & Febiger.

Lucas, J., & Smith, R. (1978). *Saga of American sport.* Philadelphia: Lea & Febiger.

Macdonald, D., & Leitch, S. (1994). Praxis in PE: The senior physical education syllabus on trial. *New Zealand Journal of Physical Education, 27*(2), 17–21.

Maeda, J., & Murata, N. (2004). Collaborating with classroom teachers to increase daily physical activity: The GEAR program. *Journal of Physical Education, Recreation, and Dance, 75*(5), 42–46.

Maloney, L. (1984, August 13). Sports crazy Americans. *U.S. News & World Report, 23.*

Marmot, M. (1994). Social differentials within and between populations. *Daedalus, 123*(4), 197–216.

Martens, R. (1986). Youth sport in the USA. In M. Weiss & D. Gould (Eds.), *Sport for children and youths* (pp. 27–33). Champaign, IL: Human Kinetics.

Martin, T. (2003). More kids paying to play sports. *Lansing State Journal.* www.lsj.com

Massengale, D., & Lough, N. (2010, April). Women leaders in sport: Where's the gender equity? *Journal of Physical Education, Recreation and Dance, 81,* 4.

Mathieu, M. (1999). The surgeon general's report on leisure services for older adults. *Journal of Physical Education, Recreation, and Dance, 70*(3), 28–31.

Matter, R., Nash, S., & Frogley, M. (2002). Interscholastic athletics for student-athletes with disabilities. *Palaestra, 18*(3), 32–38.

Matthews, D. (1969). A historical study of the aims, contents and methods of Swedish gymnastics. *Proceedings of the National College of Physical Education for Men.*

Mayo Foundation for Medical Education and Research (2010). *Performance-enhancing drugs and teen athletes.* www.mayoclinic.com/health/performance-enhancing-drugs/SM00045

McCloy, C. (1936). How about some muscle? *Journal of Health and Physical Education, 3*(4), 22–24.

McCubbin J., & Zittel, L. (1991). PL 99–457: What the law is all about. *Journal of Physical Education, Recreation, and Dance, 62*(6), 35–37, 47.

McGinnis, J., Kanner, L., & DeGraw, C. (1991). Physical education's role in achieving national health objectives. *Research Quarterly for Exercise and Sport, 62,* 138–142.

McKenzie, T. (2007). The preparation of physical educators: A public health perspective. *Quest, 59,* 345–357.

McKenzie, T., Cattelier, D., Conway, T., Lytle, L., Grieser, M., Webber, L., Pratt, C., & Elder, J. (2006). Girls' activity levels and lesson contexts in middle school PE: TAAG baseline. *Medicine and Science in Sports & Exercise, 38,* 1229–1235.

McKenzie, T., & Kahan, D. (2008). Physical activity, public health, and elementary schools. *The Elementary School Journal, 108,* 171–180.

McKenzie, T., & Lounsbery, M. (2009). School physical education: The pill not taken. *American Journal of Lifestyle Medicine, 3,* 219–225.

McKenzie, T., Prochaska, J., Sallis, J., & Lamaster, K. (2004). Coeducational and single-sex physical education in middle schools: Impact on physical activity. *Research Quarterly for Exercise and Sport, 75,* 446–449.

McKenzie, T., Nader, P., Strikmiller, P., Yang, M., Stone, E., Perry, C., Taylor, W., Epping, J., Feldman, H., Luepker, R., & Kelder, S. (1996). School physical education: Effect of the child and adolescent trial for cardiovascular health. *Preventive Medicine, 25,* 423–431.

McKenzie, T., & Sallis, J. (1996). Physical activity, fitness, and health-related physical education. In S. Silverman & C. Ennis (Eds.), *Student learning in physical education: Applying research to enhance learning* (pp. 223–246). Champaign: IL: Human Kinetics.

McKenzie, T., Sallis, J., Elder, J., Berry, C., Hoy, P., Nader, P., Zive, M., & Broyles, S. (1997). Physical activity levels and prompts in young children at recess: A two-year study of a bi-ethnic sample. *Research Quarterly for Exercise Sport, 68,* 195–202.

McKenzie, T., Sallis, J., & Rosengard, P. (2009). Beyond the stucco tower: Design, development, and dissemination of the SPARK physical education programs. *Quest, 61,* 114–127.

McLaughlin, J. (1988). A stepchild comes of age. *Journal of Physical Education, Recreation, and Dance, 59*(9), 58–60.

McLean, J., Peterson, J., & Martin, W. (1988). *Recreation and leisure: The changing scene* (4th ed.). New York: Macmillan.

McMillin C., & Reffner, C. (1998). *Directory of College and University Coaching Education Programs.* Morgantown, WV: Fitness Information Technology.

McPherson, B. (1981). Past, present and future perspectives for research in sport sociology. In J. Loy, G. Kenyon & B. McPherson (Eds.), *Sport, culture and society: A reader on the sociology of sport* (pp. 10–22). Philadelphia: Lea & Febiger.

Meadows, K. (2003, February 16). Parents have to play nice before kids can play sports. *Columbus Dispatch*, p. D1.

Mechikoff, R., & Estes, S. (2006). *A history and philosophy of sport and physical education: From ancient civilizations to the modern world* (5th ed.). Boston: McGraw-Hill.

Media Release (2007). Handlebar injuries causing life threatening 'mega trauma'. Children, Youths, and Womens Health, Government of South Australia. Downloaded from www.cywhs.sa.gov.au

Meeteer, W., Housner, L., Bulger, S., Hawkins, A., & Wiegand, R. (2012). Applying the Sport Education curriculum model in university basic instruction courses. In P. Hastie (Ed.) *Sport Education: International perspectives* (pp. 58–70). London: Routledge.

Meich, R., Kumanyika, S., Stettler, N., Link, B., Phelan, J., & Chang, V. (2006). Trends in the association of poverty with overweight among U.S. adolescents. *Journal of the American Medical Association*, 295(20), 24–31.

Metheny, E. (1954). The third dimension in physical education. *Journal of Health, Physical Education and Recreation*, 24(3), 27.

———. (1970). The excellence of Patroclus. In H. Slusher & A. Lockhart (Eds.), *Anthology of contemporary readings: An introduction to physical education* (pp. 63–66). Dubuque, IA: Brown.

Micheli, L., Glassman, R., & Klein, M. (2000). The prevention of sports injuries in children. *Clinics in Sports Medicine*, 19, 821–832.

Mihalich, J. (1982). *Sports and athletics: Philosophy in action*. Totowa, NJ: Littlefield, Adams.

Miller, G., Lutz, R., Shim, J., Fredenburg, K., & Miller, J. (2005). Dismissals and perceptions of pressure in coaching in Texas high schools. *Journal of Physical Education, Recreation, and Dance*, 76(1), 29–33.

Miller, L., Stoldt, G., & Comfort, G. (2000). Sport management professions. In S. Hoffman & J. Harris (Eds.), *Introduction to kinesiology* (pp. 525–552). Champaign, IL: Human Kinetics.

Mills, B. (1997). Opening the gymnasium to the World Wide Web. *Journal of Physical Education, Recreation, and Dance*, 68(8), 17–19.

Milverstedt, F. (1988). Are kids really so out of shape? *Athletic Business*, 12(1).

Mitchell, S., Oslin, J., & Griffin, L. (2006). *Teaching sports concepts and skills: A tactical games approach* (2nd ed.). Champaign, IL: Human Kinetics.

Mohr, D., Townsend, J., & Bulger, S. (2001). A pedagogical approach to sport education season planning. *Journal of Physical Education, Recreation, and Dance*, 72(9), 37–46.

Mokdad, A., Bowman, B., Ford, E., Vinicor, F., Marks, J., & Koplan, J. (2001). The continuing epidemics of obesity and diabetes in the United States. *JAMA*, 286(10), 1195–1120.

Molnar, A., Garcia, D., Boninger, E., & Merrill, B. (2006). *A national survey of the types and extent of the marketing of foods of minimal nutritional value in schools*. Tempe, AZ: Commercialism in Education Research Unit, Arizona State University.

Monroe, J. (1995). Developing cultural awareness through play. *Journal of Physical Education, Recreation, and Dance*, 66(8), 24–27.

Moore, G. (1986). Elementary physical education: Involving outdoor adventure activities. *Journal of Physical Education, Recreation, and Dance*, 57(5), 61–63.

Morgan, C., Beighle, A., & Pangrazi, R. (2007). What are the contributory and compensatory relationships between physical education and physical activity in children? *Research Quarterly for Exercise and Sport*, 78, 407–412.

Morgan, W. J. (2007). *Ethics in sports*. Champaign, IL: Human Kinetics.

Morrow, J., & Gill, D. (Eds.) (1995). The Academy Papers, No. 28 - The Role of Physical Activity in Fitness and Health - *James R. Morrow, Jr. and Diane L. Gill, Editors* - Physical Activity, Fitness, and Health: Introduction. *Quest*, 47, 261–262.

Motley, M., & Lavine, M. (2001). Century marathon: A race for equality in girls' and women's sports. *Journal of Physical Education, Recreation, and Dance*, 72(6), 56–59.

Mullan, M. (1986). Issues. *Journal of Physical Education, Recreation, and Dance*, 57(6), 18.

Nack, W., & Munson, L. (2000). Out of control. *Sports Illustrated*, 93(4), 86–95.

NAGWS (National Association for Girls and Women in Sports) (2007). Title IX quick facts. www.aahperd.org/nagws

Naisbitt, J. (1983). *Megatrends: Ten new directions transforming our lives*. New York: Warner Books.

NASPE (National Association for Sport and Physical Education) (1992). *Developmentally appropriate physical education practices for children*. Washington, DC: AAHPERD.

———. (1994). National summit on coaching standards. *NASPE News*, 39, 1, 9.

———. (1995a). *Moving into the future: National standards for physical education.* St. Louis: Mosby.

———. (1995b). *National standards for beginning physical education teachers.* Reston, VA: Author.

———. (1995c). *Parent's checklist for quality youth sport programs.* Reston, VA: Author.

———. (1995d). *National Standards for Athletic Coaches.* Reston, VA: Author.

———. (1998, Winter). Shape of the Nation Report, *NASPE News*, 50(1), 14.

———. (1999). *Bill of rights for young athletes.* Reston, VA: Author.

———. (2001, Spring). Quality sports begin with quality coaches. *NASPE News,* 56(6), 1.

———. (2002a). *2001 Shape of the Nation Report.* Reston, VA: Author

———. (2002b, Spring). Standards developed for strength and conditioning professionals. *NASPE News*, 60, 6.

———. (2004a). *Physical activity for children: A statement of guidelines for children ages 5–12* (2nd ed.). Reston, VA: Author.

———. (2004b). *Moving into the future: National standards for physical education* (2nd ed.). Reston, VA: Author.

———. (2004c). *Standards for initial programs in physical education teacher education.* Reston, VA: Author.

———. (2004d, Winter). Congratulations, national board certified teachers. *NASPE News,* 65, p. 8.

———. (2006a). *Shape of the nation report: State of physical education in the USA.* Reston, VA: Author.

———. (2006b). *Quality coaches, quality sports: National standards for sport coaches* (2nd ed.). Reston, VA: Author.

———. (2006c). *Position statement: Opposing substitution and waiver/exemptions for required physical education.* Reston, VA: Author.

———. (2009a). *National standards and guidelines for physical education teacher education* (3rd ed.). Reston, VA: Author.

———. (2009b). *Position statement: Physical activity used as punishment and/or behavior management.* Reston, VA: Author.

———. (2009c). *Appropriate instructional practice guidelines for elementary school Physical Education: A position statement from the National Association for Sport and Physical Education* (3rd ed.). Reston, VA: Author.

———. (2009d). *Appropriate instructional practice guidelines for middle school physical education: A position statement from the National Association for Sport and Physical Education* (3rd ed.). Reston, VA: Author.

———. (2009e). *Appropriate instructional practice guidelines for high school physical education: A position statement from the National Association for Sport and Physical Education* (3rd ed.). Reston, VA: Author.

———. (2010a). *2010 Shape of the nation report: Status of physical education in the USA.* Reston, VA: Author.

———. (2010b). *PE Metrics: Assessing National Standards 1–6 in Elementary School.* Reston VA: Author.

———. (2010c). Guidelines for participation in youth sports programs: specialization versus multiple-sport participation. Reston, VA: Author.

———. (2011). *PE Metrics: Assessing National Standards 1–6 in Secondary School.* Reston VA: Author.

National Blueprint on Physical Activity among Adults Age 50 and Older. (2000). Princeton, NJ: Robert Wood Johnson Foundation.

National Center for Health Statistics. (2004). www.cdc.gov/nchs/about/major/nhis/released 200212/

National Coalition for Promoting Physical Activity (2002). *A play for physical activity leadership*, (pp. 1–8). www.ncppa.org

National Federation of State High School Athletic Associations (2007). *2006–07 Athletics participation study.* www.nfhs.org

———. (2010). *2009–10 Athletics participation summary.* www.nfhs.org

NCPERID (National Consortium for Physical Education and Recreation for Individuals with Disabilities) (1995). *Adapted physical education national standards.* Champaign, IL: Human Kinetics.

NC Department of Public Instruction (2010). *2009–10 Local Salary Supplements.* Information and Reporting Section/School Business Division.

Nevins, A. (1962). *The gateway to history.* Garden City, NY: Anchor Books.

Newell, K. (1990a). Physical education in higher education: Chaos out of order. *Quest*, 42, 227–242.

———. (1990b). Kinesiology: The label for the study of physical activity in higher education. *Quest*, 42, 269–278.

News (2001). Active seniors less susceptible to depression. *Journal of Physical Education, Recreation, and Dance, 72*(1), 9–10.

———. (2002). Texas reinstates physical education. *Journal of Physical Education, Recreation, and Dance, 73*(5), 5.

Newsletter. (1996). *NIH panel links activity to improved cardiovascular health.* Washington, DC: President's Council on Physical Fitness and Sports, 96(1), 6.

NFSHSA (National Federation of High Schools). (2007). Available courses. www.nfhs.learn.com

Nieman, D. (1990). *Fitness and sports medicine: An Introduction.* Palo Alto, CA: Bull Publishing.

Novak, M. (1976). *The joy of sports.* New York: Basic Books.

Noyes, B. (1996). The program. *Athletic Business, 20*(4), 29–35.

NSRE (National Survey on Recreation and the Environment) (2000). *Summary report #1 from the National Survey on Recreation and the Environment: Outdoor recreation participation in the United States.* U.S.D.A. Forest Service & N.O.A.A., 1–9.

———. (2007). *National survey on recreation and the environment.* U.S. Department of Agriculture, Washington, D.C.

O'Connor, A., & Macdonald, D. (2002). Up close and personal on physical education teachers' identity: Is conflict an issue? *Sport, Education and Society, 7,* 37–54.

OECD. (2010). *OECD says governments must fight fat.* www.oecd.org/document/35/0-.3343/

Ogden, C., & Carroll, M. (2010). *Prevalence of obesity among children and adolescents: United States, Trends 1963–1965 through 2007–2008.* Washington DC: Center for Health Statistics.

Ogden, C., Flegal, K., Caroll, M., & Johnson, C. (2002). Prevalence and trends among overweight U.S. children and adolescents, 1999–2000. *Journal of the American Medical Association, 288,* 1728–1732.

Ohio Department of Health (2006). *A report on the body mass index of Ohio's third graders, 2004–2005.* Columbus: Division of Family and Community Health Services, School and Adolescent Health Section.

Ohio State University (2008). "Summer 2008 Fitness Class Descriptions." http://recsports.osu.edu/fitness_programs.asp.

Olafson, L. (2002). "I hate Phys. Ed.": Adolescent girls talk about physical education. *The Physical Educator, 59,* 67–74.

Olsen, E. (1986). Your number's up. *The Runner, 8*(8), 40–47.

Olson, J. (1995). Sports participation: Efforts to involve minorities, females prove fruitful in Madison schools. *Interscholastic Athletic Administration, 22*(2), 4–5.

Orlick, T. (1977). Cooperative games. *Journal of Physical Education, Recreation, and Dance, 48*(7), 33–36.

———. (1986). Evolution in children's sport. In M. Weiss & D. Gould (Eds.), *Sport for children and youths* (pp. 169–178). Champaign, IL: Human Kinetics.

O'Sullivan, M., Siedentop, D., & Tannehill, D. (1994). Breaking out: Codependency of high school physical education, *Journal of Teaching in Physical Education, 13,* 421–428.

Pacific Mutual Insurance Co. (1978). *Health maintenance* (Survey conducted by Louis Harris and Associates). San Francisco: Author.

Page, C. (1969). Reaction to Stone. In G. Kenyon (Ed.), *Aspects of contemporary sport sociology* (pp. 17–19). Chicago: Athletic Institute.

Pangrazi, R. (2010). Chasing unachievable outcomes. *Quest, 62,* 323–333.

———. (2003). Physical education K–12: "All for one and one for all." *Quest, 55*(2), 105–117.

Pangrazi, R., Corbin, C., & Welk, G. (1996). Physical activity for children and youth. *Journal of Physical Education, Recreation, and Dance, 67*(4), 38–43.

Papas, M., Alberg, A., Weing, R., Helzlsouer, K., Gary, T., & Klassen, A. (2007). The built environment and obesity. *Epidemiologic Reviews, 29*(1), 129–143.

Partlow, K. (1992). American Coaching Effectiveness Program (ACEP): Educating America's coaches. *Journal of Physical Education, Recreation, and Dance, 63*(7), 36–39.

Partridge, D., & Franks, I. (1996). Analyzing and modifying coaching behaviors by means of computer assisted observation. *The Physical Educator, 53*(1), 8–23.

Passer, M. (1986). A psychological perspective. In M. Weiss & D. Gould (Eds.), *Sport for children and youths* (pp. 55–58). Champaign, IL: Human Kinetics.

Pastore, D. (1994). Strategies for retaining female high school head coaches: A survey of administrators and coaches. *Journal of Sport and Social Issues, 17,* 169–182.

Pate, R. (1994). Fitness testing: Current approaches and purposes in physical education. In R. Pate & D. Hohn (Eds.), *Health and Fitness through Physical Education* (pp. 119–128). Champaign, IL: Human Kinetics.

————. (1995). Physical activity and health: Dose–response issues. *Research Quarterly for Exercise and Sport, 66*, 313–317.

Pate, R., Davis, M., Robinson, T., Stone, E., McKenzie, T., & Young, J. (2006). Promoting physical activity in children and youth—A leadership role for schools: A scientific statement from the American Heart Association Council on Nutrition, Physical Activity, and Metabolism (Physical Activity Committee) in Collaboration with the Councils on Cardiovascular Disease in the Young and Cardiovascular Nursing. *Circulation, 114*, 1214–1224.

Pate R., & Hohn D. (Eds.) (1994). *Health and fitness through physical education.* Champaign, IL: Human Kinetics.

Pate, R., Trost, S., Dowda, M., Ott. A., Ward, D., Saunders, R., & Felton, G. (1999). Tracking of physical activity, physical inactivity, and health related physical fitness in rural youth. *Pediatric Exercise Science,* 11, 364–376.

Pate, R., Trost, S., Levin, S., & Dowda, M. (2000). Sports participation and health-related behaviors. *Archives of Pediatric Adolescent Medicine,* 154, 904–911.

Paul, P., & Cartledge, G. (1996). Inclusive schools—the continuing debate. *Theory into Practice,* 35(1), 2–3.

*PCPFS Research Digests.* (1999). Physical activity and fitness for persons with disabilities: A paradigm shift.

Pellegrini, A., & Bohn, C.M. (2005). The role of recess in children's cognitive performance and school adjustment. *Educational Researcher,* 34, 13–19.

Perkins, D.F., & Noam, G.G. (2007). Characteristics of sports-based youth development programs. *New Directions for Youth Development,* 2007: 75–84. doi: 10.1002/yd.224

Piernas, C., & Popkin, B. (2010). Kids are moving to constant eating. Uncnews.unc.edu/content/view/3395/103.

Physical Activity Today. (1996). Exercise shown to lower breast cancer risk. *Physical Activity Today,* 2(1), 1.

————. (1999). Elderly walkers miles ahead of inactive peers. *Physical Activity Today,* 5(3), 1.

Pierce, P., & Herman, S. (2004). Obtaining, maintaining, and advancing your fitness certification. *Journal of Physical Education, Recreation, and Dance,* 75(7), 50–54.

Pifer, S. (1987). Secondary physical education: A new design. *Journal of Physical Education, Recreation, and Dance,* 58(6), 50–51.

Placek, J. (1983). Concepts of success in teaching: Busy, happy and good? In T. Templin & J. Olson (Eds.), *Teaching in physical education* (pp. 46–56). Champaign, IL: Human Kinetics.

————. (1996). Integration as a curriculum model in physical education: Possibilities and problems. In S. Silverman & C. Ennis (Eds.), *Student learning in physical education: Applying research to enhance learning* (pp. 287–312). Champaign, IL: Human Kinetics.

Policy Studies Associates. (2006). *Everyone plays!: A review of research on the integration of sports and physical activity into out-of-school time programs.* Washington, DC: Policy Study Associates.

Pollock, M., & Vincent, K. (1996). Resistance training for health. *President's Council on Physical Fitness and Sports Research Digest,* 1–6.

Portman, P. (1995). Who is having fun in physical education classes? Experiences of sixth grade students in elementary and middle schools. *Journal of Teaching in Physical Education,* 14, 445–453.

Posey, E. (1988). Discipline-based arts education: Developing a dance curriculum. *Journal of Physical Education, Recreation, and Dance,* 59(9), 61–64.

Powell, J., & Barber-Foss, K. (1999). Injury patterns in selected high school sports: A review of the 1995–1997 seasons. *Journal of Athletic Training,* 34, 277–284.

President's Council on Physical Fitness and Sport. (1973, May). National adult physical fitness survey. *Newsletter,* 1–27.

Pritchard, R., & Potter, G. (Eds.) (1990). *Fitness, Inc.: A guide to corporate health and wellness programs.* Homewood, IL: Dow-Jones-Irwin.

Prusak, K., Treasure, D., Darst, P., & Pangrazi, R. (2004). The effects of choice on the motivation of adolescent girls in physical education. *Journal of Teaching in Physical Education,* 23, 19–29.

Quain, R. (1990). Community based sport. In J. Parks & B. Zanger (Eds.), *Sport and fitness management* (pp. 57–62). Champaign, IL: Human Kinetics.

Quinn, E. (2009). Youth sport and overuse injuries. www.Sportsmedicine.bout.com

Rankin, J. (1989). Athletic trainer education: New directions. *Journal of Physical Education, Recreation, and Dance,* 60(6), 68–71.

Rankinen, T., & Bouchard, C. (2002). Dose–response issues concerning the relations between regular physical activity and health. *Research Digest,* 3(18), 1–6.

Rarick, L. (1967). The domain of physical education as a discipline. *Quest, 9,* 50–59.

Ratey, J. (2008). *Spark: The revolutionary new science of exercise and the brain.* New York: Little, Brown and Co.

Rauschenbach, J. (1992). Case studies of elementary physical education specialists. Unpublished doctoral dissertation, Ohio State University, Columbus.

Rice, E., Hutchinson, & Lee, M. (1958). *A brief history of physical education.* New York: The Ronald Press Co.

Richardson, M., & Oslin, J. (2003). Creating an authentic dance class using sport education. *Journal of Physical Education, Recreation and Dance, 74*(7), 49–55.

Richmond, J. (1979). *Healthy people: The surgeon general's report on health promotion and disease prevention* (DHEW Publication No. 79–55071). Washington, DC: U.S. Government Printing Office.

Rider, R., & Johnson, D. (1986). Effects of Florida's personal fitness course on cognitive, attitudinal, and physical fitness measures of secondary school students: A pilot study. *Perceptual and Motor Skills, 62,* 548–550.

Rimmer, J., Chen, M., McCubbin, J., Drum, C., & Peterson, J. (2010). Exercise intervention research on persons with disabilities: What we know and where we need to go. *American Journal of Physical Medicine and Rehabilitation, 89,* 249–263.

Rimmer, J., Yamaki, K., Davis, B., Wang, E., & Vogel, L., (2011). Obesity and overweight prevalence among adolescents with disabilities. *Preventing Chronic Disease, 8,* 1–6. http://www.cdc.gov/pcd/issues/2011/mar/10_0099.htm

Rink, J., & Mitchell, M. (2003). Introduction: State level assessment in physical education: The South Carolina experience. *Journal of Teaching in Physical Education, 22,* 471–472.

Rink, J., & Williams, J. (2003). Developing and implementing a state assessment program. *Journal of Teaching in Physical Education, 22,* 474–493.

Robert Wood Johnson Foundation. (2001). *National blueprint on physical activity among adults age 50 and older.* Princeton, NJ: Robert Wood Johnson Foundation.

———. (2009). F as in Fat: How obesity policies are failing in America, Executive Summary. www.rwjf.org

———. (2010a). F as in Fat: How obesity threatens America's Future. www.healthyamericans.org

———. (2010b). Increasing physical activity. The Robert Wood Johnson Foundation Center to Prevent Childhood Obesity.

Robinson, J., & Godbey, G. (1997). *Time for life: The surprising ways Americans use their time.* University Park, PA: Penn State Press.

Rosenbaum, M., & Leibel, R. (1989). Obesity in childhood. *Pediatric Review, 11*(2), 43–55.

Ross, J., Delpy, L., Christenson, G., Gold, R., & Damberg, C. (1987). Study procedures and quality control. *Journal of Physical Education, Recreation, and Dance, 58*(9), 57–62.

Ross, J., & Pate, R. (1987). A summary of findings. *Journal of Physical Education, Recreation, and Dance, 58*(9), 51–56.

Rowe, P., & Miller, L. (1991). Treating high school sports injuries: Are coaches/trainers competent? *Journal of Physical Education, Recreation, and Dance, 62*(1), 49–54.

Ryan, G., & Dzewaltowski, D. (2002). Comparing the relationships between different types of self-efficacy and physical activity in youth. *Health Education and Behavior, 29,* 491–504.

Sack, A. (1977). Big time college football: Whose free ride? *Quest, 27,* 87–96.

Sage, G. (1979). The current status and trends of sport sociology. In M. Krotee (Ed.), *The dimensions of sport sociology* (pp. 23–31). West Point, NY: Leisure Press.

———. (1984). *Motor learning and control: A neuropsychological approach.* Dubuque, IA: Brown.

———. (1987). Pursuit of knowledge in sociology of sport: Issues and prospects. *Quest, 39,* 255–281.

———. (1991). Beyond enhancing performance in sport: Toward empowerment and transformation. *The Academy Papers, 25,* 85–95.

Sallis, J.. (1994). Determinants of physical activity behavior in children. In R. Pate & D. Hohn (Eds.), *Health and fitness through physical education* (pp. 31–44). Champaign, IL: Human Kinetics.

———. (2011, March). *Increasing physical activity at school: Evidence-based approaches.* Presented at Primer Congreso de Educacion Fisica. Tijuana, Mexico.

Sallis, J., & Glanz, K. (2006). The role of built environments in physical activity, eating, and obesity in childhood. *The Future of Children, 16,* 89–108.

Sallis, J., & Kerr, J. (2006). Physical activity and the built environment. *Research Digest, 7*(4), 1–6.

Sallis, J., & McKenzie, T. (1991). Physical education's role in public health. *Research Quarterly for Exercise and Sport, 62,* 124–137.

Sallis, J., McKenzie, T., Kolody, B., Lewis, M., Marshall, S., & Rosengard, P. (1999). Effects of health-related physical education on academic achievement: Project SPARK. *Research Quarterly for Exercise and Sport, 70*, 127–134.

Samman, P. (1998). *Active youth: Ideas for implementing the CDC physical activity promotion guidelines.* Champaign: IL: Human Kinetics.

Sattelmair, J., & Ratey, J. (2009). Physically active play and cognition: An academic matter? *American Journal of Play, 1*, 365–374.

Scantling, E., & Lackey, D. (2005). Coaches under pressure: Four decades of studies. *Journal of Physical Education, Recreation, and Dance, 76*(1), 25–28.

Schafer, S. (1987). Sport needs you. The Colorado model. *Journal of Physical Education, Recreation, and Dance, 58*(2), 44–47.

Schiller, F. (1910). Letters upon the aesthetic education of man. In C. Eliot (Ed.), *The Harvard Classics* (Vol. 32). New York: P. F. Collier & Son.

Schmidt, R. (1988). *Motor control and learning: A behavioral emphasis* (2nd ed.). Champaign, IL: Human Kinetics.

Schmid, S. (1994a). Campus showpiece. *Athletic Business, 18*(1), 47–50.

———. (1994b). Community asset. *Athletic Business, 18*(3), 20.

Schor, J. (1991). *The overworked American: The unexpected decline of leisure.* New York: Basic Books.

Schwartz, M., & Brownell, K. (2007). Actions necessary to prevent childhood obesity: Creating the climate for change. *Journal of Law, Medicine & Ethics, 35*(1), 78–89.

Scott D. (2000). Tic, toc, the game is locked and nobody else can play. *Journal of Leisure Research, 32*, 133–137.

Scott, J. (1974). Sport and the radical chic. In G. McGlynn (Ed.), *Issues in physical education and sport* (pp. 155–162). Palo Alto, CA: National Press.

Scraton, S. (1990). *Shaping up to womanhood: Gender and girls' physical education.* Buckingham, England: Open University Press.

Seefeldt, V., & Milligan, M. (1992). Program for Athletic Coaches Education (PACE): Educating America's public and private school coaches. *Journal of Physical Education, Recreation, and Dance, 63*(7), 46–49.

Seidman, H. (2009). The rules of the game: What to consider when your child wants to play sports. My Optum Health. www.myoptUmhealth.com

Senate Report 108–345. (2006). *Wellness initiative.* Departments of Labor, Health and Human Services and Education, and Related Agencies, Appropriation Bill 2005.

Sepulveda, J., Tait, F., Zimmerman, E., & Edington, D. (2010). Impact of childhood obesity on employers. *Health Affairs, 29*, 513–521.

Serdula, M., Ivery, D., Coates, R., Freedman, D., Williamson, D., & Byers, T. (1993). Do obese children become obese adults? A review of the literature. *Preventive Medicine, 22*, 167–177.

Seymour, S. (2005, January 9). Schools sharing their exercise facilities. *Columbus Dispatch*, p. B6.

Shaping America's Youth. (2010). *The skyrocketing cost of obesity: It's everybody's business.* Academic Network.

Shea, C., Shebilske, W., & Worchel, S. (1993). *Motor learning and control.* Englewood Cliffs, NJ: Prentice Hall.

Sheed, W. (1995, Winter). Why sports matter. *Wilson Quarterly, 19*(1), 11–25.

Sheehan, G. (1982). Viewpoint. *Runner's World, 27*(7), 14.

Shephard, R. (1988). Exercise adherence in corporate settings: Personal traits and program barriers. In R. Dishman (Ed.), *Exercise adherence* (pp. 305–319). Champaign, IL: Human Kinetics.

———. (1995). Physical activity, health, and well-being at different life stages. *Research Quarterly for Exercise and Sport, 66*, 298–302.

———. (1996). Habitual physical activity and quality of life. *Quest, 48*, 354–365.

———. (1999, February). Do work-site exercise and health programs work? *The Physician and Sportsmedicine Online.*

Sherman, N. (2001). Tracking the long-term benefits of physical education. *Journal of Physical Education, Recreation, and Dance, 72*(3), 5.

Sherrill, C. (1993). *Adapted physical activity, recreation, and sport* (4th ed.), Dubuque, IA: Brown & Benchmark.

———. (2004). A celebration of the history of Adapted Physical Education. *Palaestra, 20*(1), 20–24, 45–47.

Siedentop, D. (1972). *Physical education: Introductory analysis.* Dubuque, IA: Brown.

———. (1976). *Physical education: Introductory analysis* (2nd ed.). Dubuque, IA: Brown.

———. (1980). *Physical education: Introductory analysis* (3rd ed.). Dubuque, IA: Brown.

———. (1981, August). Must competition be a zero-sum game? *The School Administrator, 38*, 11.

————. (1987). High school physical education: Still an endangered species. *Journal of Physical Education, Recreation, and Dance, 58*(2), 24–25.

————. (1989). The elementary specialist study. *Journal of Teaching in Physical Education,* 8, 187–270.

————. (1990). Commentary: The world according to Newell. *Quest,* 42, 315–322.

————. (1991). *Developing teaching skills in physical education* (3rd ed.). Mountain View, CA: Mayfield.

————. (1992). Thinking differently about secondary physical education. *Journal of Physical Education, Recreation, and Dance, 63*(7), 69–73.

————. (1994). *Sport education: Quality PE through positive sport experiences.* Champaign, IL: Human Kinetics.

————. (1996a). Physical education and education reform: The case for sport education. In S. Silverman & C. Ennis (Eds.), *Student learning in physical education: Applying research to enhance instruction* (pp. 247–268). Champaign, IL: Human Kinetics.

————. (1996b). Sport education: A curricular success story. *Teaching Secondary Physical Education, 2*(3), 8–9.

————. (1996c). Valuing the physically active life: Contemporary and future directions. *Quest,* 48, 266–274.

————. (1998). What is Sport Education and how does it work? *Journal of Physical Education, Recreation, and Dance, 69*(4), 18–20.

————. (2005). *The Ohio Project: Progress in Preventing Childhood/Youth Obesity. How do we measure up?* Columbus: The Ohio Collaborative: Research and Policy for Schools, Children, and Families, College of Education and Human Ecology, Ohio State University.

Siedentop, D., Hastie, P., & van der Mars, H. (2011). *Complete guide to Sport Education* (2nd ed.). Champaign, IL: Human Kinetics.

Siedentop, D. (2009). National plan for physical activity: Education sector. *Journal of Physical Activity and Health, 6*(Suppl 2), S168–S180.

Siedentop, D., Herkowitz, J., & Rink, J. (1984). *Elementary physical education methods.* Englewood Cliffs, NJ: Prentice Hall.

Siedentop, D., & Locke, L. (1997). Making a difference for physical education: What professors and practitioners must build together. *Journal of Physical Education, Recreation, and Dance.* 68(4), 25–33.

Siedentop, D., Mand, C., & Taggart, A. (1986). *Physical education: Teaching and curriculum strategies for grades 5–12.* Palo Alto, CA: Mayfield.

Siedentop, D., & O'Sullivan, M. (1992). Preface. *Quest,* 44(3), 285–286.

Siedentop, D., & Siedentop, B. (1985). Daily fitness in Australia. *Journal of Physical Education, Recreation, and Dance, 56*(2), 41–43.

Siedentop, D., & Tannehill, D. (2000). *Developing teaching skills in physical education* (4th ed.). Mountain View, CA: Mayfield.

Silverman, S., Keating, X.D., & Phillips, S.R. (2008). A lasting impression: A pedagogical perspective on youth fitness testing. *Measurement in Physical Education and Exercise Science,* 12, 146–166.

Simons-Morton, B. (1994). Implementing health-related physical education. In R. Pate & D. Hohn (Eds.). *Health and fitness through physical education* (pp. 137–146). Champaign, IL: Human Kinetics.

Simpson, K. (2000). Biomechanics of physical activity. In S. Hoffman & J. Harris (Eds.), *Introduction to kinesiology* (pp. 353–380). Champaign, IL: Human Kinetics.

Sinelnikov, O., Hastie, P., Cole, A., & Schneulle, D. (2005). Bicycle safety: Sport education style. *Journal of Physical Education, Recreation, and Dance, 76*(4), 24–29.

Singer, R. (Ed.) (1976). *Physical education: Foundations.* New York: Holt, Rinehart and Winston.

Singh, A., Mulder, C., Twisk, J., van Mechelen, W., & Chinapaw, M. (2008). Tracking of childhood overweight into adulthood: A systematic review of the literature. *Obesity Reviews,* 9, 474–488.

Sisley, B., & Capel, S. (1986). High school coaching: Filled with gender differences. *Journal of Physical Education, Recreation, and Dance, 57*(3), 39–44.

Sisley, B., & Weise, D. (1987). Current status: Requirements for interscholastic coaches. *Journal of Physical Education, Recreation, and Dance,* 58(7), 73–85.

Skidelsky, R. (1969). *English progressive schools.* Middlesex, England: Penguin Books.

Skinner, J. (1988). The fitness industry. *The Academy Papers,* 21, 67–72.

Slava, S., Laurie, D., & Corbin, C. (1984). The long-term effects of a conceptual physical education program. *Research Quarterly for Exercise and Sport,* 55, 161–165.

Sluder, J., Buchanan, A., & Sinelnikov, O. (2009). Using Sport Education to teach an autonomy-supportive fitness curriculum. *Journal of Physical Education, Recreation and Dance, 80*(5), 20–28.

Smith, C. (1992a, August 16). Equality's hurdles. *New York Times,* Sports Pages, p. 27.

———. (1992b, August 16). Too few changes since Campanis. *New York Times,* Sports Pages, pp. 27–28.

Smith, L. (Ed.). (1970). *Psychology of motor learning.* Chicago: Athletic Institute.

Smith, R., Smoll, F., & Curtis, B. (1978). Coaching behaviors in Little League baseball. In F. Smoll & R. Smith (Eds.), *Psychological perspectives in youth sports* (pp. 173–201). Washington, DC: Hemisphere.

Smoll, F. (1986). Stress reduction strategies in youth sport. In M. Weiss & D. Gould (Eds.), *Sport for children and youths* (pp. 127–136). Champaign, IL: Human Kinetics.

Sondheimer, E. (2010). As demand for high school football coaches rise, salaries soar. *Los Angeles Times.*

Spain, C., & Franks, D. (2001). Healthy people 2010: Physical activity and fitness. *President's Council on Physical Fitness and Sports. Research Digest,* 3(13), 1–12.

Sparkes, A. (1991). Alternative visions of health-related fitness: An exploration of problem- setting and its consequences. In N. Armstrong & A. Sparkes (Eds.), *Issues in physical education* (pp. 204–227). London: Caswell Educational Limited.

Spears, B., & Swanson, R. (1978). *History of sport and physical activity in the United States.* Dubuque, IA: Brown.

Sporting Goods Manufacturing Association. (2006). *Youth sport participation trends.* www.sgma.com

Stein, J. (2004). Adapted physical activity, the golden years. *Palaestra,* 20(1), 26–29, 56.

Steller, J. (1994). The physical education performance troupe: A skill and fitness approach. In R. Pate & D. Hohn (Eds.), *Health and fitness through physical education* (pp. 191–196). Champaign, IL: Human Kinetics.

Stevens, J. (1984). Special Olympics. *Journal of Physical Education, Recreation, and Dance,* 55(2), 42–43.

Stewart, C., & Sweet, L. (1992). Professional preparation of high school coaches: The problem continues. *Journal of Physical Education, Recreation, and Dance,* 63(6), 75–79.

Staurowsky, E. (1996). Blaming the victim: Resistance in the battle over gender equity in intercollegiate athletics. *Journal of Sport and Social Issues,* 20(2), 194–210.

Stratton, G., & Mullan, E. (2005). The effect of multicolor playground markings on children's physical activity level during recess. *Preventive Medicine,* 41, 828–833.

Strauss, R., & Pollock H. (2001). Epidemic increase in childhood overweight, 1986–1998. *JAMA,* 286(22), 2845–2848.

Strecker, C. (2010, July–August). Women in men's sports. *Update Plus,* 28–31.

Strecker, L., & Young, J. (2007, September–October). Today's coaching. *Update Plus,* 26–27.

Strong, W., Malina, R., Cameron, J., Bumkie, R., Daniels, S., Dishman, R., Gutin, B., Hergenroeder, A., Must, A., Nixon, P., Parvinik, J., Rowland, T., Trost, S., & Trudeau, F. (2005). Evidence based physical activity for school-age youth. *Journal of Pediatrics,* 146(6), 732–737.

Stroot, S., Carpenter, M., & Eisnaugle, K. (1991). Focus of physical education: Academic and physical excellence at Westgate Alternative School. *Journal of Physical Education, Recreation, and Dance,* 62(7), 49–53.

Stroot, S., Collier, C., O'Sullivan, M., & England, K. (1994). Hoops and hurdles: Workplace conditions in secondary physical education. *Journal of Teaching in Physical Education,* 13, 342–360.

Stroot, S., Faucette, N., & Schwager, S. (1993). In the beginning: The induction of physical educators, *Journal of Teaching Physical Education,* 12, 375–385.

Struna, N. (1991). Further reactions to Newell: Chaos is wonderful! *Quest,* 43, 230–235.

Sui, X., LaMonte, M., & Blair, S. (2007). Cardiorespiratory fitness as a predictor of nonfatal cardiovascular events in asymptomatic women and men. *American Journal of Epidemiology,* 165, 1413–1423.

Sui, X., LaMonte, M., Laditka, J., Hardin, J., Chase, N., Hooker, J., & Blair, G. (2008). Cardiorespiratory fitness and adiposity as mortality predictors in older adults. *JAMA,* 298(21) 2507–2516.

Suits, B. (1976). What is a game? *Philosophy of Science,* 34, 148–156.

Sutton, A. (2000, May 19). Parents out of control. *Chicago Tribune,* Internet edition. www.chicagosports.com

Sutton, W. (1984). Family involvement in youth sports: An examination of the YMCA Y-winners philosophy. *Journal of Physical Education, Recreation, and Dance,* 55(8), 59–60.

Sweeney, J., Tannehill, D., & Teeters, L. (1992). Team up for fitness. *Strategies,* 5(6), 20–23.

Swift, E. M. (1991). Why Johnny can't play. *Sports Illustrated,* 60–72.

Taggart, A., Taggart, J., & Siedentop, D. (1986). Effects of a home-based activity program. *Behavior Modification,* 10(4), 41–52.

Taylor, J., & Chiogioji, E. (1987). Implications of educational reform on high school programs. *Journal of Physical Education, Recreation, and Dance,* 58(2), 22–23.

Teague, M., & Mobily, K. (1983). Rust proofing people: Corporate recreation programs in perspective. *Journal of Physical Education, Recreation, and Dance,* 54(8), 42–44.

Templin, T., Sparkes, A., Grant, B., & Schempp, P. (1994). Matching the self: The paradoxical case and life history of a late career teacher/coach. *Journal of Teaching in Physical Education,* 13, 274–294.

Thomas, J. (1977). *Youth sports guide.* Reston, VA: AAHPERD.

Thomas, J., & Thomas, K. (2000). Motor behavior. In S. Hoffman & J. Harris (Eds.), *Introduction to kinesiology* (pp. 243–281). Champaign, IL: Human Kinetics.

Thomas, K. (2004). Riding to the rescue while holding on by a thread: Physical activity in the schools. *Quest,* 56, 150–170.

Thompson, D., Edelsberg, J., et al., (1998). Estimated costs of obesity to U.S. business. *American Journal of Health Promotion,* 13, 120–127.

Thorpe, R., Bunker, D., & Almond, L. (Eds.). (1986). *Rethinking games teaching.* London: Esmonde.

Timmermans, H., & Martin, M. (1987). Top ten potentially dangerous exercises. *Journal of Physical Education, Recreation, and Dance,* 58(6), 29–31.

Tinning, R. (1985). Physical education and the cult of slenderness. *ACHPER National Journal,* 1(7), 10–13.

———. (1990). *Ideology and physical education.* Geelong, Australia: Deaking University.

Title IX (2005). *I exercise my rights.* http://www.titleix .info

Toufexis, A. (1986, July 21). Putting on the Ritz at the Y. *Time,* 65.

Treanor, L., Graber, K., Housner, L., & Wiegand, R. (1998). Middle school students' perceptions of coeducational and same-sex physical education classes. *Journal of Teaching in Physical Education,* 18, 43–56.

Treasure, D. (2007). Interscholastic athletics, coach certification and professional development: Current status and next steps. *The State Education Standard,* 8(1), 32–34.

Trembal, M., Barnes, J., Copeland, J., & Esliger, D. (2005). Conquering childhood inactivity: Is the answer in the past? *Medicine & Science in Sports & Exercise.* http://www.acsm-msse.org

Trost, S., & van der Mars, H. (2009). Why we should not cut PE. *Educational Leadership,* 67(4), 60–65.

Trudeau, F., Laurencelle, L., Tremblay, J., Rajic, M., & Shephard, R. (1998). A long-term follow-up of participants in the Trois-Riviers semi-longitudinal study of growth and development. *Pediatric Exercise Science,* 10, 366–377.

Trudeau, F., & Shephard, R. (2010). Relationships of physical activity to brain health and the academic performance of schoolchildren. *American Journal of Lifestyle Medicine,* 4, 138–150.

Trust for America's Health (2004, October). Issue Report: *F as in Fat: How obesity policies are failing in America.* www.healthyamericans.org

Trust for America's Health (2010). Issue Report: *F as in Fat: How obesity threatens America's Future.* www.healthyamericans.org

Tucker Center for Research on Girls and Women in Sport. (2007). *Developing physically active girls: An evidence-based multidisciplinary approach.* University of Minnesota, Minneapolis, MN.

Tudor-Locke, C, Lee, S., Morgan, C., Beighle, A., & Pangrazi, R. (2004). Children's pedometer determined physical activity during the segmented school day. *Medicine & Science in Sports & Exercise,* 38, 1732–1738.

Turner, B. (1995). No more ifs, ands, or buts. *Teaching High School Physical Education,* 1(4), 11.

Turner, L. (2005, March 17). Obesity will cut U.S. life expectancy, researcher says. *Columbus Dispatch,* p. A5.

Ulrich, C. (1976). A ball of gold. In C. Ulrich (Ed.), *To seek and find* (pp. 150–160). Washington, DC: AAHPERD.

*Update.* (1995, July–September), AAHPERD, ACSM, AHA collaborate to launch national coalition for promoting physical activity. *American Alliance for Health, Physical Education, Recreation, and Dance,* 1.

*USA Today* (1988, November 11). Anabolic steroids. *USA Today,* p. 1C.

U.S. Census Bureau (2000). *Statistical abstract of the United States.* Washington, DC.

U.S. Congress (2004). *Child nutrition act* (42 U.S.C1751).

U.S. Congress Senate Report 108–345 (2006). *Wellness initiative.* Departments of Labor, Health and Human Services and Education, and Related Agencies, Appropriation Bill 2005.

U.S.D.H.H.S. (2008). *2008 Physical activity guidelines for Americans.* Washington DC: Author. www.health .gov/paguidelines/pdf/paguide.pdf

———. (2011). *Healthy People 2020 Summary of Objectives—Physical Activity.* Washington DC: Author.

http://www.healthypeople.gov/2020/topicsobjectives2020/overview.aspx?topicid=33

U.S. Department of Health and Human Services (1996). *Physical activity and health: A report of the surgeon general.* Atlanta: U.S. Department of Health and Human Services, Centers for Disease Control and Prevention, National Center for Chronic Disease Prevention and Health Promotion.

———. (2000a). *Healthy People 2010: Physical Activity and Fitness.* Washington, DC: Government Printing Office.

———. (2000b). *Promoting better health for young people through physical activity and sports,* Washington, DC: Government Printing Office.

U.S. Department of Health and Human Services (2001). *The surgeon general's call to action to prevent and decrease overweight and obesity.* Rockville, MC: Office of the Surgeon General.

———.(2002). *Physical activity fundamental to preventing disease.* Washington, DC: U.S. Department of Health and Human Services, Government Printing Office.

———. (2006). *Overweight and physical activity among children: A portrait of the states.* Health Resources and Services Administration.

U.S. Public Health Service (1991). *Healthy people 2000: National health promotion and disease objectives* (DHHSPublication No. [PHS] 91–50212). Washington, DC: Government Printing Office.

U.S. Public Law 93-112 (1973). *Rehabilitation Act.*

Vandevoort, L., Amrein-Beardsley, A., & Berliner, D. (2004). National board certified teachers and their students' achievement. *Education Policy Analysis Archives,* 12(46), http://epaa.asu.edu/epaa/v12n46/

Veal, M., Campbell, M., Johnson, D., & McKethan, R. (2002). The North Carolina PEPSE Project. *Journal of Physical Education, Recreation, and Dance,* 73(4), 19–23.

Vernon, J. (1980). Effects of vaulter and pole parameters on performance. In J. Cooper & B. Haven (Eds.), *Proceedings of the Biomechanics Symposium.* Indianapolis: Indiana State Board of Health.

Verstraete, S., Cardon, G., De Clercq, D., & De Bourdeaudhuij, I. (2006). Increasing children's physical activity levels during recess periods in elementary schools: The effects of providing game equipment. *European Journal of Public Health,* 16, 415–419.

Vertinsky, P. (1991). Science, social science, and the "hunger for wonders" in physical education: Moving toward a future healthy society. *The Academy Papers,* 24, 70–88.

———. (1992). Reclaiming space, revisioning the body: The quest for gender-sensitive physical education. *Quest,* 44, 373–397.

Vickers, J. (1992). While Rome burns: Meeting the challenge of the second wave of the reform movement in education. *Journal of Physical Education, Recreation, and Dance,* 63(7), 80–87.

Villeneuve, K., Weeks, D., & Schwied, M. (1983). Employee fitness: The bottom line. *Journal of Physical Education, Recreation, and Dance,* 54(8), 35–36.

Virgilio, S. (1996). A home, school, and community model for promoting healthy lifestyles. *Teaching Elementary Physical Education,* 7(1), 4–7.

Virgilio, S., & Berenson, G. (1988). SuperKids–SuperFit: A comprehensive fitness intervention model for elementary schools. *Journal of Physical Education, Recreation, and Dance,* 59(8), 19–25.

Walker, H. (1993). Youth sports: Parental concerns. *Physical Educator,* 50, 104–112.

Wallhead, T., & O'Sullivan, M. (2005). Sport Education: Physical education for the new millennium? *Physical Education and Sport Pedagogy,* 10(2), 181–210.

Wang, Y., & Beydoun, M. (2007). The obesity epidemic in the Unites States—gender, age, socioeconomic, racial/ethnic, and geographic characteristics: A systematic review and meta-regression analysis. *Epidemiologic Reviews,* 1(29), 6–28.

Wang, Y., & Lobstein, T. (2006). Worldwide trends in childhood overweight and obesity. *International Journal of Pediatric Obesity,* 1, 11–25.

Ward, D., Saunders, R., & Pate, R. (2007). *Physical activity interventions in children and adolescents.* Champaign, IL: Human Kinetics.

Weight-control Information Network. (2006). *Understanding adult obesity.* Washington, DC: U.S. Department of Health and Human Services, National Institutes of Health.

Weight-control Information Network (2007). *Statistics related to overweight and obesity.* Washington, DC: U.S. Department of Health and Human Services, National Institutes of Health.

———. (2007). *Do you know the health risks of being overweight?* Washington, DC: U.S. Department of Health and Human Services.

Weigle, S. (1994). A walking program in your school? Practice tips to make it work. In R. Pate & D. Hohn

(Eds.). *Health and fitness through physical education* (pp. 201–204). Champaign, IL: Human Kinetics.

Weinberg, R., & Williams, J. (2001). Integrating and implementing a psychological skills training program. In J. Williams (Ed.), *Applied sport psychology* (4th ed., pp. 347–377). Mountain View, CA: Mayfield.

Weiss, M. (2000). Motivating kids in physical activity. *President's Council on Physical Fitness and Sports. Research Digest,* 3(11), 1–8.

Weiss, P. (1969). *Sport: A philosophic inquiry.* Carbondale: Southern Illinois Press.

Wells, C. (1996). Physical activity and women's health. *President's Council on Physical Fitness and Sport Research Digest,* 2(5), 1–6.

Wessel, J., & Zittel, L. (1995). *Smart Start: A preschool movement curriculum for children of all abilities.* Austin, TX: PRO-ED.

Westcott, W. (1982). *Strength fitness.* Boston: Allyn & Bacon.

———. (1992). High school physical education: A fitness professional's perspective. *Quest,* 44, 342–351.

———. (1993). *Be strong: Strength training for muscular fitness for men and women.* Dubuque, IA: Brown & Benchmark.

Westcott, W., & Baechle, T. (1998). *Strength training past 50.* Champaign, IL: Human Kinetics.

Weston, A. (1962). *The making of American physical education.* New York: Appleton-Century-Crofts.

White, E., & Sheets, C. (2001). If you let them play, they will. *Journal of Physical Education, Recreation, and Dance,* 72(4), 27–28, 33.

Whitehead, J. (1994). Enhancing fitness and activity motivation in children. In R. Pate & D. Hohn (Eds.), *Health and fitness through physical education* (pp. 81–90). Champaign, IL: Human Kinetics.

Wier, T. (2004, December 16). New PE objective: Get kids in shape. *USA Today,* pp. 1, 4A.

Wilberg, R. (1975). The direction and definition of a field. In *Trabajos científicos* (Vol. 3). Madrid: Instituto Nacional de Education Fisica.

Wilkinson, C., Hillier, R., & Harrison, J. (1998). Improving the computer literacy of preservice teachers. *Journal of Physical Education, Recreation, and Dance,* 9(5), 10–13.

Wilkinson, R. (1994). The epidemiological transition: From material scarcity to social disadvantage? *Daedalus,* 23(4), 61–78.

Wilkinson, W., Eddy, N., MacFadden, G., & Burgess, B. (2002). *Increasing physical activity through community design: A guide for public health practitioners.* Washington, DC: National Center for Bicycling and Walking.

Williams, J. (1930). Education through the physical. *Journal of Higher Education,* 1, 279–282.

Williams, J., & Straub, W. (2001). Sport psychology: Past, present, future. In J. Williams (Ed.), *Applied sport psychology* (4th ed., pp. 1–12). Mountain View, CA: Mayfield.

Wilson, W. (1977). Social discontent and the growth of wilderness sport in America: 1965–1974. *Quest,* 27, 54–60.

Witt, P., & Baker, D. (1997). Developing after-school programs for youth in high-risk environments. *Journal of Physical Education, Recreation, and Dance,* 68(9), 18–20.

Women's Sports Foundation. (2006). *Report card on Olympic and Paralympic Winter Games.* www.womens sportsfoundation.org

———. (2007). Women in intercollegiate sport: A twenty-nine year update: 1977–2006. www.web pages.charter.net/womeninsport

Wrisberg, C. (1996). Quality of life for male and female athletes. *Quest,* 48, 392–408.

Wuest, D., & Bucher, C. (1995). *Foundations of physical education and sport.* (12th ed.). St. Louis, MO: Mosby.

Youth Sport Injuries (2010). *Youth sport injuries statistics.* www.stopsportsinjuries.org

Zeigler, E. (1962). A history of professional preparation for physical education (1861–1961). In *Professional preparation in health education, physical education, and recreation education* (pp. 116–133). Washington DC: AAHPERD.

———. (1979). *A history of physical education and sport.* Englewood Cliffs, NJ: Prentice Hall.

# Photo Credits

## Chapter 1
Page 13: © Digital Vision/Getty Images.

## Chapter 2
Page 19: © Ohio State University; p. 20: © Ohio State University; p. 20: © Ohio State University; p. 27: Photograph by Katherine Elizabeth McLellan, Smith College Archives; p. 28: © Ohio State University; p. 29: © Bettmann/CORBIS; p. 30: © Ohio State University.

## Chapter 3
Page 36: © Ohio State University; p. 39: Karl Weatherly/Getty Images; p. 43: Ryan McVay/Getty Images; p. 44: © Hans van der Mars; p. 45: © Hans van der Mars.

## Chapter 4
Page 50: © Lars Niki; p. 64: Royalty-Free/CORBIS; p. 68: © Palestra; p. 76: © Palestra; p. 76: © Lars Niki; p. 77: © Palestra.

## Chapter 5
Page 85: © Ohio State University; p. 86: Dave and Les Jacobs/Blend Images LLC; p. 88: © Hans van der Mars; p. 89: © Hans van der Mars; p. 93: © Ohio State University; p. 99: Digital Vision/Alamy; p. 111: Don Mason/Blend Images LLC.

## Chapter 7
Page 152: © Ohio State University; p. 152: PhotoLink/Getty Images; p. 163: © Daryl Siedentop; p. 166: © Daryl Siedentop; p. 167: © Daryl Siedentop.

## Chapter 8
Page 174: © Daryl Siedentop; p. 177: © Image Source/Punchstock; p. 180: © Ohio State University; p. 181: © Ohio State University; p. 182: Ingram Publishing; p. 189: © Ohio State University; p. 191: © SwimEx, Inc.

## Chapter 9
Page 205: © liquidlibrary/PictureQuest; p. 206: Radius Images/Getty Images; p. 210: © Ohio State University; p. 212: Corbis/Punchstock.

## Chapter 10
Page 210: © Royalty-Free/CORBIS; p. 219: Ingram Publishing; p. 222: Lawrence M. Sawyer/Getty; p. 226; Geoff Manasee/Getty Images; p. 230: PhotoLink/Getty Images; p. 231: Royalty-Free/CORBIS; p. 233: PhotoLink/Getty Images.

## Chapter 11
Page 237: © Ohio State University; p. 238: PhotoLink/Getty Images; p. 243: © Ohio State University; p. 244: © mylife photos/Alamy. p. 246: U.S. Air Force photo by John Van Winkle; p. 247: © Lars A. Niki; p. 255: © Palestra; p. 260: © William Prentice.

## Chapter 12
Page 267: © Ohio State University; p. 271: © BananaStock/Alamy; p. 276: PhotoLink/Getty Images; p. 286: © Ohio State University; p. 286: © Royalty-Free/CORBIS.

## Chapter 13
Page 298: © Ohio State University; p. 301: From Hamilton, Weimar, Luttgens: Kinesiology: Scientific Basis of Human Motion, 11th edition © 2008, McGraw-Hill; p. 301: © Daryl Siedentop; p. 303: © Image source/CORBIS; p. 304: © Ohio State University; p. 306: PhotoLink/Getty Images; p. 308: © Ohio State University; p. 309: © Daryl Siedentop.

# Subject Index